THE
CATHEDRAL PRAYER BOOK

BEING THE

Book of Common Prayer

WITH THE MUSIC NECESSARY FOR THE USE
OF CHOIRS

TOGETHER WITH THE

CANTICLES AND PSALTER

POINTED FOR CHANTING

EDITED BY

SIR JOHN STAINER, M.A., Mus. Doc., Ox
(PROFESSOR OF MUSIC IN THE UNIVERSITY OF OXFORD)

AND

WILLIAM RUSSELL, M.A., Mus. Bac.
(SUCCENTOR OF ST. PAUL'S CATHEDRAL).

LONDON & NEW YO

NOVELLO, EWER A
AND
HENRY FROWDE, OXFORD UNIVERSIT   IOUSE.
1891.

LONDON :
NOVELLO, EWER AND CO.,
PRINTERS.

CONTENTS.

* With the necessary Music.   † After Merbecke.

[Appendix.

CONTENTS.

APPENDIX.

EDITORS' PREFACE.

THE inconvenience and costliness of the number of separate Books usually requisite for the members of a Choir, in the performance of an ordinary Choral Service, have long pointed to the desirableness of a manual which should, as far as possible, unite under one cover all that is necessary for the choral rendering of, at least, those portions of the Church's Services which are less liable to variation.

The Music of the Versicles and Responses—Festal as well as Ferial—and a Psalter and Canticles pointed for chanting, are almost indispensable for the careful and accurate rendering of a Choral Service. And yet, hitherto, it has been scarcely possible to procure these, unless in separate numbers; involving not only much additional expense, but also the disadvantage arising from the continual shifting of books during Service time, which is such a hindrance to a devout participation in Divine Worship.

To remedy these evils, and to assist in promoting, as it is hoped, a more careful and reverent performance of the Divine Offices, the Cathedral Prayer Book has been compiled.

The Editors are fully aware that they are not the first to make an effort in this direction. But they believe that several circumstances have tended to favour their attempt, and ensure its success, which have been wanting in other instances. In the first place, they have been able to incorporate with their manual a system of pointing for the Psalms and Canticles which (as is shown by its wide and growing use, as well as the favour in which it is held wherever it has been introduced) appears to be considered more satisfactory than any other that has yet been tried. Secondly, they have been able to incorporate and utilise the results of the labour of many well-known musicians who have from time to time published valuable contributions to the various Offices of the Church in a more or less fragmentary form.

This manual provides not only for the daily Morning and Evening Prayer, and the choral celebration of the Holy Communion, in all its completeness, but also for the whole of the occasional Offices contained in the Book of Common

Prayer. A special feature of it, moreover, is that it includes an Appendix, in which are contained not only Tallis's Festival Responses and Litany, but a great deal of other additional and miscellaneous matter which it is conjectured will add greatly to its usefulness and value.

The text of the Book itself is mainly after that of the sealed copy of the Book of Common Prayer preserved in the Tower of London, and more especially after that reprint of it published by Mr. J. Masters, in 1853. But it has also in many instances been carefully compared with other good and standard Editions, and great care has been exercised throughout in the following of the authorised forms in respect of type, orthography, punctuation, &c. Where fresh rubrics or directions appertaining to the music are required, they are invariably distinguishable by being placed within brackets. Thus the directions relating to the *Gloria Tibi* before the Gospel, and the *Laus Tibi* after, are distinguished in this way. And so in other instances.

The Versicles and Responses throughout the Book (exclusive of the Appendix) and the Litany are from the arrangement used in St. Paul's Cathedral (Stainer and Martin, founded on Goss). They follow Merbecke, although with one or two slight variations which have become traditional in the Cathedral of the Metropolis, and, more recently, in many other Churches.

The Music to the Order for the Administration of the Holy Communion follows the Edition of Merbecke given in "A Choir Book of the Office of Holy Communion" (Stainer), and published some years since. The Order for the Burial of the Dead has also been arranged from Merbecke by the same Editor.

The *Veni Creator*, in the Ordination Service, is set to a well known Plain-Song Melody; the tune of the second, or alternative Hymn, is that known as Tallis's Ordinal.

The pointing of the Psalms and Canticles is that known as the Cathedral Psalter, edited by the Rev. S. Flood-Jones, the late Mr. James Turle, the Rev. J. Troutbeck, Sir John Stainer, and Mr. Joseph Barnby. An explanation of the pointing will be found immediately following this Preface.

For those having a special collection of Chants in use this Prayer Book is issued with the Canticles and Psalms pointed only; for those who prefer a complete musical manual an edition is issued containing the "Cathedral Psalter Chants."

The Appendix contains, besides the Festal Responses and Litany by Tallis as arranged in four parts by Mr. Joseph Barnby, the Ambrosian *Te Deum* arranged from Merbecke (Stainer), after that version given in his book by the late Dr. Rimbault; accompanying Harmonies to the Apostles' Creed (Bridge); the Creed of St. Athanasius, set to the Ancient Plain-Song Melody, with Organ Accompaniment (Stainer); the General Confession in the Communion Service, with Inflections, from an Ancient *Confiteor* given in

Guidetti's *Directorium Chori*, 1624, and harmonized (Stainer); the Comfortable Words and Proper Prefaces, with the addition of an organ accompaniment (Stainer); Rules for the Proper Inflections of the Collects, Epistles, and Gospels, from the Rev. H. A. Walker's Manual for the Holy Communion; the Psalms in the Burial Office, set to a Plain-Song Melody, from "The Psalter Noted," by the late Rev. Thomas Helmore; the 51st Psalm (*Miserere mei*), set to the Tonus Regalis, and as used at the Special Lenten Service in St. Paul's Cathedral (Stainer).

The Prayers, Versicles, Responses, &c., have, throughout this Book, been set in keys which experience has proved to be most convenient and suitable to the majority of Clergy and Choirs. But the pitch should, of course, be altered to suit special cases, and experienced Organists will find no difficulty in transposing the accompaniments as occasion may require, either "at sight" or by making a manuscript sketch. It will be noticed that in the Order for Morning and Evening Prayer no inflections are introduced until after the first reciting of the Lord's Prayer. This is partly for the reason that this portion of the service, not being derived, like the rest, from the ancient Offices of the Church, and not appearing in the First Prayer Book of Edward VI., is not provided for by Merbecke; and partly because this portion is introductory and penitential. It would seem advisable also to recite the Confession on a lower note than the Exhortation and Absolution, as suggested by the fact that the Minister bids the People to follow him with a "humble voice." But these details, with many others, must be left to the discretion of Precentors, Choirmasters, and Organists, as no manual, however carefully compiled, can be made absolutely applicable to the various conditions under which a choral service is maintained in our Churches.

The Editors cannot conclude without making their grateful acknowledgments to all those whose names are mentioned above, for the great advantages they have derived in being able to make use of their works. But especially they have to express their indebtedness to Mr. Henry King (Assistant Vicar-Choral of St. Paul's Cathedral) not only for many valuable suggestions respecting the arrangement, as well as the matter, of the book; but also for the painstaking care with which he has seen all the proof-sheets through the press, the accuracy of the whole work having depended, in no small degree, upon his diligent observation.

Doubtless, as time goes on (and especially if further editions of the book are called for), it will be possible to make good many defects which have as yet escaped notice, and to make many, as yet unthought of, improvements. But in the meanwhile, if this manual only serves the end in view, and is found in any degree to contribute to perfect the praise of Him in Whose service it is humbly offered, the Compilers will be more than satisfied.

April, 1891.

NOTES AND EXPLANATIONS

RESPECTING THE

POINTING OF THE CANTICLES AND PSALMS.

THE CHANTS in this Collection have been arranged with the following main principles in view :—

> (1) That single or double Chants should be used according to the character and construction of each Psalm.
>> *See* Psalms xv. (single); xxiv. (double).
>
> (2) That the construction of each Psalm should as far as possible govern the antiphonal arrangement; *e.g.*, if the parallel or antithesis occurs between the two halves of one verse, each half should be assigned to Decani and Cantoris respectively.
>> *See* Psalms xv. xix. l. xc.
>
> (3) That the variations of subject or sentiment in each Psalm should be marked by a change of Chant.
>> *See* Psalms xviii. lxxviii.

Should there be any difficulty in following the antiphonal marks (*Dec.* and *Can.*) as they stand, they can be simplified under the direction of the Choir-master without injury to the general arrangement of the Chants.

---

1. THE WORDS, from the commencement of each verse and half-verse up to the accented syllable, are called the Recitation.

2. On reaching the accented syllable, and beginning with it, the *music* of the chant commences, in strict time (*a tempo*), the upright strokes corresponding to the bars. The Recitation must therefore be considered as *outside* the chant, and may be of any length. The note on which the Recitation is made is called the Reciting note.

3. If there is no syllable after that which is accented, the accented syllable must be held for one whole bar or measure,* *e.g.*—

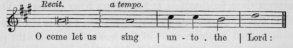

O come let us   sing | un - to . the | Lord :

If other syllables follow the one accented, the first measure or initial bar of the chant will have to be divided into *parts of a semibreve.*

---

* The melody of the following chant has been used throughout in the examples :—

Sir JOHN GOSS.

4. The following general rules will help to explain this, the accented syllable being called *the accent*. If one syllable follows the accent, the first bar is divided into a dotted minim and a crotchet, *e.g.*—

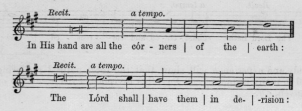

In His hand are all the cór - ners | of the | earth :

The Lórd shall | have them | in de- | -rision :

Sometimes, when only one syllable follows the accent, the first bar is divided into two minims, *e.g.*—

As for óur God, | He is . in | heaven :

And the flint - stone | in - to . a | spring - ing | well.

5. If two syllables follow the accent, the first bar is generally divided into a minim and two crotchets, *e.g.*—

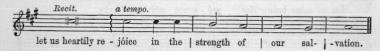

let us heartily re - jóice in the | strength of | our sal- | -vation.

or into two crotchets and one minim, *e.g.*—

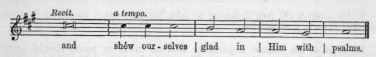

and shéw our - selves | glad in | Him with | psalms.

6. If three syllables follow the accent, the first bar is generally divided into four equal parts, or their equivalent value, *e.g.*—

Why do the heathen so fú - ri - ous - ly | rage to- | -gether :

O ye sons of men, how lóng will ye blas- | -pheme mine | honour :

B

7. In the rare cases in which four syllables follow the accent, the bar will be without difficulty divided into the equivalent of four crotchets, *e.g.*—

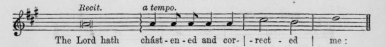

8. Study and experience will show that the most natural rendering of the words will in many instances call for other divisions of the bar, a few of which are here given, *e.g.*—

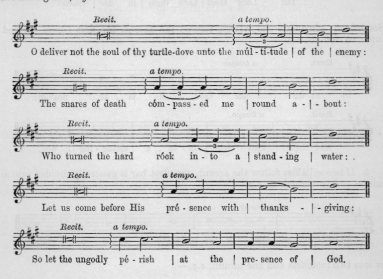

9. An asterisk (*) is a direction to take breath. Other stops (, ;) must be attended to as in good *reading*.

10. It is of the utmost importance that no break or pause should occur between the Recitation and Accent. The words should be deliberately recited; but the reciting note must not be held any longer than is absolutely necessary for this. Hence in some verses the reciting note will be only equal to a *very short* musical note, *e.g.*—

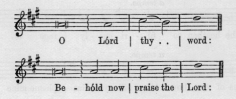

11. When a verse or half-verse commences with an accent, it is evident that there is *no recitation;* the rhythmical music therefore begins at once, *e.g.*—

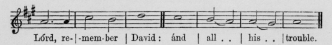

Lórd, re-|-mem-ber | David : ánd | all . . | his . . |trouble.

As the accent holds the position of the first beat of the first bar, it is unnecessary to sing it louder than any of the words recited ; its position, musically, will give it quite enough emphasis.

12. A dot is placed between words or syllables belonging to the second bar of the music, when their division would otherwise be doubtful, *e.g.*—

rai - ment . of   needlework :   *not*   rai - ment of

ab-sent . from | us   for | ever.   *not*   ab - sent from

13. Lines placed horizontally show that the preceding syllable must be continued for the space indicated, *e.g.*—

Práise | ‿   — | —   the | Lord.

14. *F.* signifies *Full*, that is, to be sung by both sides of the choir ; *f* signifies *forte*, loud ; *p, piano*, soft ; *mf, mezzo-forte*, moderately loud ; *2nd part*, directs the choir to repeat the second half of a double chant at the verse to which it is prefixed.

The thanks of the Editors are due to those professional and amateur musicians who have contributed original compositions to this work ; also to those who have granted permission for the insertion of such Chants as have appeared before, or of which they hold the copyright. The Editors likewise offer their apologies for any infringement of copyright of which they may have been unintentionally guilty.

THE PREFACE.

IT hath been the wisdom of the Church of *England*, ever since the first compiling of her Publick Liturgy, to keep the mean between the two extremes, of too much stiffness in refusing, and of too much easiness in admitting any variation from it. For, as on the one side common experience sheweth, that where a change hath been made of things advisedly established (no evident necessity so requiring) sundry inconveniences have thereupon ensued ; and those many times more and greater than the evils, that were intended to be remedied by such change : So on the other side, the particular Forms of Divine worship, and the Rites and Ceremonies appointed to be used therein, being things in their own nature indifferent, and alterable, and so acknowledged ; it is but reasonable, that upon weighty and important considerations, according to the various exigency of times and occasions, such changes and alterations should be made therein, as to those that are in place of Authority should from time to time seem either necessary or expedient. Accordingly we find, that in the Reigns of several Princes of blessed memory since the Reformation, the Church, upon just and weighty considerations her thereunto moving, hath yielded to make such alterations in some particulars, as in their respective times were thought convenient : Yet so, as that the main Body and Essentials of it (as well in the chiefest materials, as in the frame and order thereof) have still continued the same unto this day, and do yet stand firm and unshaken, notwithstanding all the vain attempts and impetuous assaults made against it, by such men as are given to change, and have always discovered a greater regard to their own private fancies and interests, than to that duty they owe to the publick.

By what undue means, and for what mischievous purposes the use of the Liturgy (though enjoined by the Laws of the Land, and those Laws never yet repealed) came, during the late unhappy confusions, to be discontinued, is too well known to the world, and we are not willing here to remember. But when, upon His Majesty's happy Restoration, it seemed probable, that, amongst other things, the use of the Liturgy would also return of course (the same having never been legally abolished) unless some timely means were used to prevent it ; those men who under the late usurped powers had made it a great part of their business to render the people disaffected thereunto, saw themselves in point of reputation and interest concerned (unless they would freely acknowledge themselves to have erred, which such men are very hardly brought to do) with their utmost endeavours to hinder the restitution thereof. In order whereunto divers Pamphlets were published against the Book of *Common Prayer*, the old objections mustered up, with the addition of some new ones, more than formerly had been made, to make the number swell. In fine, great importunities were used to His Sacred Majesty, that the said Book might be revised, and such Alterations therein, and Additions thereunto made, as should be thought requisite for the ease of tender Consciences : whereunto His Majesty, out of his pious inclination to give satisfaction (so far as could be reasonably expected) to all his subjects of what persuasion soever, did graciously condescend.

In which review we have endeavoured to observe the like moderation, as we find to have been used in the like case in former times. And therefore of the sundry alterations proposed unto us, we have rejected all such as were either of dangerous consequence (as secretly striking at some established Doctrine, or laudable Practice of the Church of *England*, or indeed of the whole Catholick Church of Christ) or else of no consequence at all, but utterly frivolous and vain. But such alterations as were tendered to us (by what persons, under what pretences, or to what purpose soever so tendered) as seemed to us in any degree requisite or expedient, we have willingly, and of our own accord assented unto : not enforced so to do by any strength of Argument, convincing us of the necessity of making the said Alterations : For we are fully persuaded in our judgements (and we here profess it to the world) that the Book, as it stood before established by Law, doth not contain in it any thing contrary to the Word of God, or to sound Doctrine, or which a godly man may not with a good

Conscience use and submit unto, or which is not fairly defensible against any that shall oppose the same ; if it shall be allowed such just and favourable construction as in common equity ought to be allowed to all human Writings, especially such as are set forth by Authority, and even to the very best translations of the holy Scripture itself.

Our general aim therefore in this undertaking was, not to gratify this or that party in any their unreasonable demands ; but to do that, which to our best understandings we conceived might most tend to the preservation of Peace and Unity in the Church ; the procuring of Reverence, and exciting of Piety and Devotion in the publick Worship of God ; and the cutting off occasion from them that seek occasion of cavil or quarrel against the Liturgy of the Church. And as to the several variations from the former Book, whether by Alteration, Addition, or otherwise, it shall suffice to give this general account, That most of the Alterations were made, either first, for the better direction of them that are to officiate in any part of Divine Service ; which is chiefly done in the Calendars and Rubricks : Or secondly, for the more proper expressing of some words or phrases of ancient usage in terms more suitable to the language of the present times, and the clearer explanation of some other words and phrases, that were either of doubtful signification, or otherwise liable to misconstruction : Or thirdly, for a more perfect rendering of such portions of holy Scripture, as are inserted into the Liturgy ; which, in the Epistles and Gospels especially, and in sundry other places, are

now ordered to be read according to the last Translation : and that it was thought convenient, that some Prayers and Thanksgivings, fitted to special occasions, should be added in their due places ; particularly for those at Sea, together with an Office for the Baptism of such as are of Riper Years : which, although not so necessary when the former Book was compiled, yet by the growth of Anabaptism, through the licentiousness of the late times crept in amongst us, is now become necessary, and may be always useful for the baptizing of Natives in our Plantations, and others converted to the Faith. If any man, who shall desire a more particular account of the several Alterations in any part of the Liturgy, shall take the pains to compare the present Book with the former ; we doubt not but the reason of the change may easily appear.

And having thus endeavoured to discharge our duties in this weighty affair, as in the sight of God, and to approve our sincerity therein (so far as lay in us) to the consciences of all men ; although we know it impossible (in such variety of apprehensions, humours and interests, as are in the world) to please all ; nor can expect that men of factious, peevish, and perverse spirits should be satisfied with any thing that can be done in this kind by any other than themselves : Yet we have good hope, that what is here presented, and hath been by the Convocations of both Provinces with great diligence examined and approved, will be also well accepted and approved by all sober, peaceable, and truly conscientious Sons of the Church of *England*.

CONCERNING THE SERVICE OF THE CHURCH.

THERE was never any thing by the wit of man so well devised, or so sure established, which in continuance of time hath not been corrupted : As, among other things, it may plainly appear by the Common Prayers in the Church, commonly called *Divine Service*. The first original and ground whereof if a man would search out by the ancient Fathers, he shall find, that the same was not ordained but of a good purpose, and for a great advancement of godliness. For they so ordered the matter, that all the whole Bible, (or the greatest part thereof) should be read over once every year ; intending thereby, that the Clergy, and especially such as were Ministers in the congregation, should (by often reading, and meditation in God's word) be stirred up to godliness themselves, and be more able to exhort others by wholesome Doctrine, and to confute them that were adversaries to the Truth ; and further, that the people (by daily hearing of holy Scripture

read in the Church) might continually profit more and more in the knowledge of God, and be the more inflamed with the love of his true Religion.

But these many years passed, this godly and decent order of the ancient Fathers hath been so altered, broken, and neglected, by planting in uncertain Stories, and Legends, with multitude of Responds, Verses, vain Repetitions, Commemorations, and Synodals ; that commonly when any Book of the Bible was begun, after three or four Chapters were read out, all the rest were unread. And in this sort the Book of *Isaiah* was begun in *Advent*, and the Book of *Genesis* in *Septuagesima ;* but they were only begun, and never read through : After like sort were other Books of holy Scripture used. And moreover, whereas St. *Paul* would have such language spoken to the people in the Church, as they might understand, and have profit by hearing the same ; The Service in this Church of *England* these many years hath been read in Latin to the people, which they understand not ; so that they have heard with their ears only, and their heart, spirit, and mind, have not been edified thereby. And furthermore, notwithstanding that the ancient Fathers have divided the *Psalms* into seven portions, whereof every one was called a *Nocturn :* Now of late time a few of them have been daily said, and the rest utterly omitted. Moreover, the number and hardness of the Rules called the *Pie*, and the manifold changings of the Service, was the cause, that to turn the Book only was so hard and intricate a matter, that many times there was more business to find out what should be read, than to read it when it was found out.

These inconveniences therefore considered, here is set forth such an Order, whereby the same shall be redressed. And for a readiness in this matter, here is drawn out a Calendar for that purpose, which is plain and easy to be understood ; wherein (so much as may be) the reading of holy Scripture is so set forth, that all things shall be done in order, without breaking one piece from another. For this cause be cut off Anthems, Responds, Invitatories, and such like things as did break the continual course of the reading of the Scripture.

Yet, because there is no remedy, but that of necessity there must be some Rules ; therefore certain Rules are here set forth ; which, as they are few in number, so they are plain and easy to be understood. So that here you have an Order for Prayer, and for the reading of the holy Scripture, much agreeable to the mind and purpose of the old Fathers, and a great deal more profitable and commodious, than that which of late was used. It is more profitable, because here are left out many things, whereof some are untrue, some uncertain, some vain and superstitious ; and nothing is ordained to be read, but the very pure Word of God, the holy Scriptures, or that which is agreeable to the same ; and that in such a Language and Order as is most easy and plain for the understanding both of the Readers and Hearers. It is also more com-

modious, both for the shortness thereof, and for the plainness of the Order, and for that the Rules be few and easy.

And whereas heretofore there hath been great diversity in saying and singing in Churches within this Realm ; some following *Salisbury* Use, some *Hereford* Use, and some the Use of *Bangor*, some of *York*, some of *Lincoln ;* now from henceforth all the whole Realm shall have but one Use.

And forasmuch as nothing can be so plainly set forth, but doubts may arise in the use and practice of the same ; to appease all such diversity (if any arise) and for the resolution of all doubts, concerning the manner how to understand, do, and execute, the things contained in this Book ; the parties that so doubt, or diversely take any thing, shall alway resort to the Bishop of the Diocese, who by his discretion shall take order for the quieting and appeasing of the same ; so that the same order be not contrary to any thing contained in this Book. And if the Bishop of the Diocese be in doubt, then he may send for the resolution thereof to the Archbishop.

THOUGH it be appointed, That all things shall be read and sung in the Church in the *English* Tongue, to the end that the congregation may be thereby edified ; yet it is not meant, but that when men say Morning and Evening Prayer privately, they may say the same in any language that they themselves do understand.

And all Priests and Deacons are to say daily the Morning and Evening Prayer either privately or openly, not being let by sickness, or some other urgent cause.

And the Curate that ministereth in every Parish-Church or Chapel, being at home, and not being otherwise reasonably hindered, shall say the same in the Parish-Church or Chapel where he ministereth, and shall cause a Bell to be tolled thereunto a convenient time before he begin, that the people may come to hear God's Word, and to pray with him.

OF CEREMONIES,

Why some be abolished, and some retained.

OF such Ceremonies as be used in the Church, and have had their beginning by the institution of man, some at the first were of godly intent and purpose devised, and yet at length turned to vanity and superstition ; some entered into the Church

by undiscreet devotion, and such a zeal as was without knowledge ; and for because they were winked at in the beginning, they grew daily to more and more abuses, which not only for their unprofitableness, but also because they have much blinded the people, and obscured the glory of God, are worthy to be cut away, and clean rejected : other there be, which although they have been devised by man, yet it is thought good to reserve them still, as well for a decent order in the Church, (for the which they were first devised) as because they pertain to edification, whereunto all things done in the Church (as the Apostle teacheth) ought to be referred.

And although the keeping or omitting of a Ceremony, in itself considered, is but a small thing ; yet the wilful and contemptuous transgression and breaking of a common order and discipline is no small offence before God, *Let all things be done among you,* saith St. *Paul, in a seemly and due order :* The appointment of the which order pertaineth not to private men ; therefore no man ought to take in hand, nor presume to appoint or alter any publick or common Order in Christ's Church, except he be lawfully called and authorized thereunto.

And whereas in this our time, the minds of men are so diverse, that some think it a great matter of conscience to depart from a piece of the least of their Ceremonies, they be so addicted to their old customs ; and again on the other side, some be so new-fangled, that they would innovate all things, and so despise the old, that nothing can like them, but that is new : It was thought expedient, not so much to have respect how to please and satisfy either of these parties, as how to please God, and profit them both. And yet lest any man should be offended, whom good reason might satisfy, here be certain causes rendered, why some of the accustomed Ceremonies be put away, and some retained and kept still.

Some are put away, because the great excess and multitude of them hath so increased in these latter days, that the burden of them was intolerable ; whereof St. *Augustine* in his time complained, that they were grown to such a number, that the estate of Christian people was in worse case concerning that matter, than were the Jews. And he counselled that such yoke and burden should be taken away, as time would serve quietly to do it. But what would St. *Augustine* have said, if he had seen the Ceremonies of late days used among us ; whereunto the multitude used in his time was not to be compared ? This our excessive multitude of Ceremonies was so great, and many of them so dark, that they did more confound and darken, than declare and set forth Christ's benefits unto us. And besides this, Christ's Gospel is not a Ceremonial Law (as much of *Moses'* Law was), but it is a Religion to serve God, not

in bondage of the figure or shadow, but in the freedom of the Spirit ; being content only with those Ceremonies which do serve to a decent Order and godly Discipline, and such as be apt to stir up the dull mind of man to the remembrance of his duty to God, by some notable and special signification, whereby he might be edified. Furthermore, the most weighty cause of the abolishment of certain Ceremonies was, That they were so far abused, partly by the superstitious blindness of the rude and unlearned, and partly by the unsatiable avarice of such as sought more their own lucre, than the glory of God, that the abuses could not well be taken away, the thing remaining still.

But now as concerning those persons, which peradventure will be offended, for that some of the old Ceremonies are retained still : If they consider that without some Ceremonies it is not possible to keep any Order, or quiet Discipline in the Church, they shall easily perceive just cause to reform their judgements. And if they think much, that any of the old do remain, and would rather have all devised anew : then such men granting some Ceremonies convenient to be had, surely where the old may be well used, there they cannot reasonably reprove the old only for their age, without bewraying of their own folly. For in such a case they ought rather to have reverence unto them for their antiquity, if they will declare themselves to be more studious of unity and concord, than of innovations and new-fangleness, which (as much as may be with true setting forth of Christ's Religion) is always to be eschewed. Furthermore, such shall have no just cause with the Ceremonies reserved to be offended. For as those be taken away which were most abused, and did burden men's consciences without any cause ; so the other that remain, are retained for a discipline and order, which (upon just causes) may be altered and changed, and therefore are not to be esteemed equal with God's Law. And moreover, they be neither dark nor dumb Ceremonies, but are so set forth, that every man may understand what they do mean, and to what use they do serve. So that it is not like that they in time to come should be abused as other have been. And in these our doings we condemn no other Nations, nor prescribe any thing but to our own people only : For we think it convenient that every Country should use such Ceremonies as they shall think best to the setting forth of God's honour and glory, and to the reducing of the people to a most perfect and godly living, without error or superstition ; and that they should put away other things, which from time to time they perceive to be most abused, as in men's ordinances it often chanceth diversely in divers countries.

¶ THE ORDER HOW THE PSALTER IS APPOINTED TO BE READ.

THE Psalter shall be read through once every Month, as it is there appointed, both for Morning and Evening Prayer. But in *February* it shall be read only to the twenty-eighth, or twenty-ninth Day of the Month.

And, whereas *January, March, May, July, August, October,* and *December* have One-and-thirty days apiece ; It is ordered, that the same Psalms shall be read the last day of the said months, which were read the day before : So that the Psalter may begin again the first day of the next month ensuing.

And, whereas the 119th Psalm is divided into twenty-two portions, and is over-long to be read at one time ; It is so ordered, that at one time shall not be read above four or five of the said portions.

And at the end of every Psalm, and of every such part of the 119th Psalm, shall be repeated this Hymn,

Glory be to the Father, and to the Son : and to the Holy Ghost ;
As it was in the beginning, is now, and ever shall be : world without end. Amen.

NOTE, That the Psalter followeth the division of the Hebrews, and the Translation of the great English Bible, set forth and used in the time of King *Henry* the Eighth, and *Edward* the Sixth.

¶ THE ORDER HOW THE REST OF HOLY SCRIPTURE IS APPOINTED TO BE READ.

THE Old Testament is appointed for the First Lessons at Morning and Evening Prayer, so as the most part thereof will be read every year once, as in the Calendar is appointed.

The New Testament is appointed for the Second Lessons at Morning and Evening Prayer, and shall be read over orderly every year twice, once in the Morning and once in the Evening, besides the Epistles and Gospels, except the Apocalypse, out of which there are only certain Lessons appointed at the end of the year, and certain Proper Lessons appointed upon divers Feasts.

And to know what Lessons shall be read every day, look for the day of the Month in the Calendar following, and there ye shall find the Chapters and portions of Chapters that shall be read for the Lessons, both at Morning and Evening Prayer, except only the Moveable Feasts, which are not in the Calendar, and the Immoveable, where there is a blank left in the Column of Lessons, the Proper Lessons for all which days are to be found in the Table of Proper Lessons.

If Evening Prayer is said at two different times in the same place of worship on any Sunday (except a Sunday for which Alternative Second Lessons are specially appointed in the Table,) the Second Lesson at the second time may, at the discretion of the minister, be any Chapter from the four Gospels, or any Lesson appointed in the Table of Lessons from the four Gospels.

Upon occasions, to be approved by the Ordinary, other Lessons may, with his consent, be substituted for those which are appointed in the Calendar.

And note, that whensoever Proper Psalms or Lessons are appointed, then the Psalms and Lessons of ordinary course appointed in the Psalter and Calendar (if they be different) shall be omitted for that time.

Note also, that upon occasions to be appointed by the Ordinary, other Psalms may, with his consent, be substituted for those appointed in the Psalter.

If any of the Holy-days for which Proper Lessons are appointed in the Table fall upon a Sunday which is the first Sunday in Advent, Easter Day, Whitsunday, or Trinity Sunday, the Lessons appointed for such Sunday shall be read, but if it fall upon any other Sunday, the Lessons appointed either for the Sunday or for the Holy-day may be read at the discretion of the minister.

Note also, that the Collect, Epistle, and Gospel appointed for the Sunday shall serve all the week after where it is not in this Book otherwise ordered.

¶ PROPER LESSONS

¶ LESSONS PROPER FOR SUNDAYS.

	MATTINS.	EVENSONG.	
Sundays of Advent.			
The 1st	Isaiah 1	Isaiah 2	or Isaiah 4, *v.* 2
2nd	—— 5	—— 11, to *v.* 11	,, —— 24
3rd	—— 25	—— 26	,, —— 28, *v.* 5 to *v.* 19
4th	—— 30 to *v.* 27	—— 32	,, —— 33, *v.* 2 to *v.* 23
Sundays after Christmas.			
The 1st	—— 35	—— 38	,, —— 40
2nd	—— 42	—— 43	,, —— 44
Sundays after Epiphany.			
The 1st	—— 51	—— 52, *v.* 13 & 53	,, —— 54
2nd	—— 55	—— 57	,, —— 61
3rd	—— 62	—— 65	,, —— 66
4th	Job 27	Job 28	,, Job 29
5th	Prov. 1	Prov. 3	,, Prov. 8
6th	—— 9	—— 11	,, —— 15
Septuagesima	Gen. 1 & 2, to *v.* 4	Gen. 2, *v.* 4	,, Job 38
2nd Lesson	Rev. 21, to *v.* 9	Rev. 21, *v.* 9 to 22, *v.* 6	
Sexagesima	Gen. 3	Gen. 6	,, Gen. 8
Quinquagesima	—— 9, to *v.* 20	—— 12	,, —— 13
Sundays in Lent.			
The 1st	—— 19, *v.* 12 to *v.* 30	—— 22, to *v.* 20	,, —— 23
2nd	—— 27, to *v.* 41	—— 28	,, —— 32
3rd	—— 37	—— 39	,, —— 40
4th	—— 42	—— 43	,, —— 45
5th	Exod. 3	Exod. 5	,, Exod. 6, to *v.* 14
6th	—— 9	—— 10	,, —— 11
2nd Lesson	Matt. 26	Luke 19, *v.* 28	,, Luke 20, *v.* 9 to *v.* 21
Easter Day	Exod. 12, to *v.* 29	Exod. 12, *v.* 29	,, Exod. 14.
2nd Lesson	Rev. 1, *v.* 10 to *v.* 19	John 20, *v.* 11 to *v.* 19,	,, Rev. 5
Sundays after Easter.			
The 1st	Numb. 16, to *v.* 36	Numb. 16, *v.* 36	,, Numb. 17, to *v.* 12
2nd Lesson	1 Cor. 15, to *v.* 29	John 20, *v.* 24 to *v.* 30	
2nd	Numb. 20, to *v.* 14	Numb. 20, *v.* 14 to 21 , *v.* 10	,, —— 21, *v.* 10
3rd	—— 22	—— 23	,, —— 24
4th	Deut. 4, to *v.* 23	Deut. 4, *v.* 23 to *v.* 41,	,, Deut. 5
5th	—— 6	—— 9	,, —— 10
Sunday aft. Ascen. Day.	—— 30	—— 34	,, Joshua 1
Whitsunday	—— 16 to *v.* 18	Isaiah 11	,, Ezek. 36, *v.* 25
2nd Lesson	Rom. 8, to *v.* 18	Gal. 5, *v.* 16	,, Acts 18, *v.* 24 to 19, *v.* 21
Trinity Sunday	Isaiah 6, to *v.* 11	Gen. 18	,, Gen. 1 & 2, to *v.* 4
2nd Lesson	Rev. 1, to *v.* 9	Eph. 4, to *v.* 17	,, Matt. 3
Sundays after Trinity.			
The 1st	Josh. 3, *v.* 7 to 4, v. 15	Josh. 5, *v.* 13 to 6, *v.* 21,	,, Joshua 24
2nd	Judges 4	Judges 5	,, Judges 6, *v.* 11
3rd	1 Sam. 2, to *v.* 27	1 Sam. 3	,, 1 Sam. 4, to *v.* 19
4th	—— 12	—— 13	,, Ruth 1
5th	—— 15, to *v.* 24	—— 16	,, 1 Sam. 17
6th	2 Sam. 1	2 Sam. 12, to *v.* 24	,, 2 Sam. 18
7th	1 Chron. 21	1 Chron. 22	,, 1 Chron. 28, to *v.* 21
8th	—— 29, *v.* 9 to *v.* 29	2 Chron. 1	,, 1 Kings 3
9th	1 Kings 10, to *v.* 25	1 Kings 11, to *v.* 15	,, —— 11, *v.* 26
10th	—— 12	—— 13	,, —— 17
11th	—— 18	—— 19	,, —— 21
12th	—— 22, to *v.* 41	2 Kings 2, to *v.* 16	,, 2 Kings 4, *v.* 8 to *v.* 38
13th	2 Kings 5	—— 6, to *v.* 24	,, —— 7

	MATTINS.	EVENSONG.
Sundays after Trinity.		
14th	2 Kings 9	2 Kings 10, to v. 32 or 2 Kings 13
15th	—— 18	—— 19 ,, —— 23, to v. 31.
16th	2 Chron. 36	Nehem. 1 & 2, to v. 9,, Nehem. 8
17th	Jerem. 5	Jerem. 22 ,, Jerem. 35
18th	—— 36	Ezek. 2 ,, Ezek. 13, to v. 17
19th	Ezek. 14	—— 18 ,, —— 24, v. 15
20th	—— 34	—— 37 ,, Daniel 1
21st	Daniel 3	Daniel 4 ,, —— 5
22nd	—— 6	—— 7, v. 9 ,, —— 12
23rd	Hosea 14	Joel 2, v. 21 ,, Joel 3, v. 9
24th	Amos 3	Amos 5 ,, Amos 9
25th	Micah 4 & 5, to v. 8	Micah 6 ,, Micah 7
26th	Habak. 2	Habak. 3 ,, Zephaniah 3
27th	Eccles. 11 & 12	Haggai, 2 to v. 10 ,, Malachi 3 & 4

NOTE.—That the Lessons appointed in the above Table for the Twenty-seventh Sunday after Trinity shall always be read on the Sunday next before Advent.

¶ LESSONS PROPER FOR HOLY-DAYS.

	MATTINS.	EVENSONG.
St. Andrew.		
1st Lesson	Isaiah 54	Isaiah 65 to v. 17
2nd Lesson	John 1 v. 35 to v. 43	John 12 v. 20 to v. 42
St. Thomas.		
1st Lesson	Job 42 to v. 7	Isaiah 35
2nd Lesson	John 20 v. 19 to v. 24	John 14 to v. 8
Nativity of Christ.		
1st Lesson	Isaiah 9 to v. 8	Isaiah 7 v. 10 to v. 17
2nd Lesson	Luke 2 to v. 15	Titus 3 v. 4 to v. 9
St. Stephen.		
1st Lesson	Gen. 4 to v. 11	2 Chron. 24 v. 15 to v. 23
2nd Lesson	Acts 6	Acts 8 to v. 9
St. John Evangelist.		
1st Lesson	Exod. 33 v. 9	Isaiah 6
2nd Lesson	John 13 v. 23 to v. 36	Rev. 1
Innocents' Day.		
1st Lesson	Jer. 31 to v. 18	Baruch 4, v. 21 to v. 31
Circumcision.		
1st Lesson	Gen. 17 v. 9	Deut. 10 v. 12
2nd Lesson	Rom. 2 v. 17	Col. 2 v. 8 to v. 18
Epiphany.		
1st Lesson	Isaiah 60	Isaiah 49 v. 13 to v. 24
2nd Lesson	Luke 3 v. 15 to v. 23	John 2 to v. 12
Conversion of St. Paul.		
1st Lesson	Isaiah 49 to v. 13.	Jer. 1 to v. 11
2nd Lesson	Gal. 1 v. 11	Acts 26 to v. 21
Purification of the Virgin Mary.		
1st Lesson	Exod. 13 to v. 17	Haggai 2 to v. 10
St. Matthias.		
1st Lesson	1 Sam. 2 v. 27 to v. 36	Isaiah 22 v. 15
Annunciation of our Lady.		
1st Lesson	Gen. 3 to v. 16	Isaiah 52 v. 7 to v. 13
Ash Wednesday.		
1st Lesson	Isaiah 58 to v. 13	Jonah 3
2nd Lesson	Mark 2 v. 13 to v. 23	Heb. 12 v. 3 to v. 18
Monday before Easter.		
1st Lesson	Lament. 1 to v. 15	Lament. 2 v. 13
2nd Lesson	John 14 to v. 15	John 14 v. 15
Tuesday before Easter.		
1st Lesson	Lament. 3 to v. 34	Lament. 3 v. 34
2nd Lesson	John 15 to v. 14	John 15 v. 14
Wednesday before Easter.		
1st Lesson	Lament. 4 to v. 21	Daniel 9 v. 20
2nd Lesson	John 16 to v. 16	John 16 v. 16

	MATTINS.	EVENSONG.
Thursday before Easter.		
1st Lesson	Hosea 13 to *v.* 15	Hosea 14
2nd Lesson	John 17	John 13 to *v.* 36
Good Friday.		
1st Lesson	Gen. 22 to *v.* 20	Isaiah 52 *v.* 13 & 53
2nd Lesson	John 18	1 Peter 2
Easter Even.		
1st Lesson	Zech. 9	Hosea 5 *v.* 8 to 6 *v.* 4
2nd Lesson	Luke 23 *v.* 50	Rom. 6 to *v.* 14
Monday in Easter Week.		
1st Lesson	Exod. 15 to *v.* 22	Cant. 2 *v.* 10
2nd Lesson	Luke 24 to *v.* 13	Matt. 28 to *v.* 10
Tuesday in Easter Week.		
1st Lesson	2 Kings 13 *v.* 14 to *v.* 22...	Ezek. 37 to *v.* 15
2nd Lesson	John 21 to *v.* 15	John 21 *v.* 15
St. Mark.		
1st Lesson	Isaiah 62 *v.* 6	Ezek. 1 to *v.* 15
St. Philip and St. James.		
1st Lesson	Isaiah 61	Zechariah 4
2nd Lesson	John 1 *v.* 43	
Ascension Day.		
1st Lesson	Dan. 7 *v.* 9 to *v.* 15	2 Kings 2 to *v.* 16
2nd Lesson	Luke 24 *v.* 44	Hebrews 4
Monday in Whitsun Week.		
1st Lesson	Gen. 11 to *v.* 10	Num. 11 *v.* 16 to *v.* 31
2nd Lesson	1 Cor. 12 to *v.* 14	1 Cor. 12 *v.* 27 & 13
Tuesday in Whitsun Week.		
1st Lesson	Joel 2 *v.* 21	Micah 4 to *v.* 8
2nd Lesson	1 Thess. 5 *v.* 12 to *v.* 24 ...	1 John 4 to *v.* 14
St. Barnabas.		
1st Lesson	Deut. 33 to *v.* 12	Nahum 1
2nd Lesson	Acts 4 *v.* 31	Acts 14 *v.* 8
St. John Baptist.		
1st Lesson	Malachi 3 to *v.* 7	Malachi 4
2nd Lesson	Matt. 3	Matt. 14 to *v.* 13
St. Peter.		
1st Lesson	Ezek. 3 *v.* 4 to *v.* 15	Zechariah 3
2nd Lesson	John 21 *v.* 15 to *v.* 23	Acts 4 *v.* 8 to *v.* 23
St. James.		
1st Lesson	2 Kings 1 to *v.* 16	Jer. 26 *v.* 8 to *v.* 16
2nd Lesson	Luke 9 *v.* 51 to *v.* 57	
St. Bartholomew.		
1st Lesson	Gen. 28 *v.* 10 to *v.* 18	Deut. 18 *v.* 15
St. Matthew.		
1st Lesson	1 Kings 19 *v.* 15	1 Chron. 29 to *v.* 20
St. Michael.		
1st Lesson	Gen. 32	Dan. 10 *v.* 4
2nd Lesson	Acts 12 *v.* 5 to *v.* 18	Rev. 14 *v.* 14
St. Luke.		
1st Lesson	Isaiah 55	Ecclus. 38 to *v.* 15
St. Simon and St. Jude.		
1st Lesson	Isaiah 28 *v.* 9 to *v.* 17	Jer. 3 *v.* 12 to *v.* 19
All Saints.		
1st Lesson	Wisd. 3 to *v.* 10	Wisd. 5 to *v.* 17
2nd Lesson	Heb. 11 *v.* 33 & 12 to *v.* 7	Rev. 19 to *v.* 17

¶ PROPER PSALMS ON CERTAIN DAYS.

	MATTINS.			EVENSONG.		
CHRISTMAS DAY	19,	45,	85	89,	110,	132
ASH WEDNESDAY	6,	32,	38	102,	130,	143
GOOD FRIDAY	22,	40,	54	69,	88	
EASTER DAY	2,	57,	111	113,	114,	118
ASCENSION DAY	8,	15,	21	24,	47,	108
WHITSUNDAY	48,	68		104,	145	

THE CALENDAR,

WITH

THE TABLE OF LESSONS.

JANUARY HATH XXXI DAYS.			MORNING PRAYER.		EVENING PRAYER.	
			FIRST LESSON.	SECOND LESSON.	FIRST LESSON.	SECOND LESSON.
1	A	*Circumcis. of our Lord.*	....	....	....	....
2	b	....	Gen. 1, to v. 20	Matt. 1, v. 18	Gen. 1, v. 20 to 2, v. 4	Acts 1
3	c	....	—— 2, v. 4	—— 2	—— 3, to v. 20	—— 2, to v. 22
4	d	....	—— 3, v. 20 to 4, v. 16	—— 3	—— 4, v. 16	—— 2, v. 22
5	e	....	—— 5, to v. 28	—— 4, to v. 23	—— 5, v. 28 to 6, v. 9	—— 3
6	f	*Epiphany of our Lord.*	....	....	....	....
7	g	....	—— 6, v. 9	—— 4, v. 23 to 5, v. 13	—— 7	—— 4, to v. 32
8	A	Lucian, Priest & Mart.	—— 8	—— 5, v. 13 to v. 33	—— 9, to v. 20	—— 4, v. 32 to 5, v. 17
9	b	....	—— 11, to v. 10	—— 5, v. 33	—— 12	—— 5, v. 17
10	c	....	—— 13	—— 6, to v. 19	—— 14	—— 6
11	d	....	—— 15	—— 6, v. 19 to 7, v. 7	—— 16	—— 7, to v. 35
12	e	....	—— 17, to v. 23	—— 7, v. 7	—— 18, to v. 17	—— 7, v. 35 to 8, v. 5
13	f	Hilary, Bishop & Conf.	—— 18, v. 17	—— 8, to v. 18	—— 19, v. 12 to v. 30	—— 8, v. 5, to v. 26
14	g	....	—— 20	—— 8, v. 18	—— 21, to v. 22	—— 8, v. 26
15	A	....	—— 21, v. 33 to 22, v. 20	—— 9, to v. 18	—— 23	—— 9, to v. 23
16	b	....	—— 24, to v. 29	—— 9, v 18	—— 24, v. 29 to v. 52	—— 9, v. 23
17	c	....	—— 24, v. 52	—— 10, to v. 24	—— 25, v. 5 to v. 19	—— 10, to v. 24
18	d	Prisca, Virgin & Mart.	—— 25, v. 19	—— 10, v. 24	—— 26, to v. 18	—— 10, v. 24
19	e	....	—— 26, v. 18	—— 11	—— 27, to v. 30	—— 11
20	f	Fabian, Bishop & Mart.	—— 27, v. 30	—— 12, to v. 22	—— 28	—— 12
21	g	Agnes, Virgin & Martyr	—— 29, to v. 21	—— 12, v. 22	—— 31, to v. 25	—— 13, to v. 26
22	A	Vincent, Deac. & Mart.	—— 31, v. 36	—— 13, to v. 24	—— 32, to v. 22	—— 13, v. 26
23	b	....	—— 32, v. 22	—— 13, v. 24 to v. 53	—— 33	—— 14
24	c	....	—— 35, to v. 21	—— 13, v. 53 to 14, v. 13	—— 37, to v. 12	—— 15, to v. 30
25	d	*Conversion of St. Paul.*	....	....	....	....
26	e	....	—— 37, v. 12	—— 14, v. 13	—— 39	—— 15, v. 30 to 16, v. 16
27	f	....	—— 40	—— 15, to v. 21	—— 41, to v. 17	—— 16, v. 16
28	g	....	—— 41, v. 17 to v. 53	—— 15, v. 21	—— 41, v. 53 to 42, v. 25	—— 17, to v. 16
29	A	....	—— 42, v. 25	—— 16, to v. 24	—— 43, to v. 25	—— 17, v. 16
30	b	....	—— 43, v. 25 to 44, v. 14	—— 16, v. 24 to 17, v. 14	—— 44, v. 14	—— 18, to v. 24
31	c	....	—— 45, to v. 25	—— 17, v. 14	—— 45, v. 25 to 46, v. 8	—— 18, v. 24 to 19, v. 21

THE CALENDAR,

WITH

THE TABLE OF LESSONS.

FEBRUARY HATH XXVIII DAYS, In every Leap Year 29 Days.		MORNING PRAYER.		EVENING PRAYER.	
		FIRST LESSON.	SECOND LESSON.	FIRST LESSON.	SECOND LESSON.
1	d	.... *Fast*	Gen. 46, *v.* 26 to 47, *v.* 13	Matt. 18, to *v.* 21	Gen. 47, *v.* 13	Acts 19, *v.* 21
2	e	*Purification of V. Mary*	....	—— 18, *v.* 21 to 19, *v.* 3	....	—— 20, to *v.* 17
3	f	Blasius, Bp. & Martyr .	—— 48	—— 19, *v.* 3 to *v.* 27	—— 49	—— 20, *v.* 17
4	g	....	—— 50	—— 19, *v.* 27 to 20 *v* 17	Exod. 1	—— 21, to *v.* 17
5	A	Agatha, Virg. & Martyr	Exod. 2	—— 20, *v.* 17	—— 3	—— 21, *v.* 17 to *v.* 37
6	b	....	—— 4, to *v.* 24	—— 21, to *v.* 23	—— 4, *v.* 27 to 5, *v.* 15	—— 21, *v.* 37 to 22, *v.* 23
7	c	....	—— 5, *v.* 15 to 6, *v.* 14	—— 21, *v.* 23	—— 6, *v.* 28 to 7, *v.* 14	—— 22, *v.* 23 to 23, *v.* 12
8	d	....	—— 7, *v.* 14	—— 22, to *v.* 15	—— 8, to *v.* 20	—— 23, *v.* 12
9	e	....	—— 8, *v.* 20 to 9, *v.* 13	—— 22, *v.* 15 to *v.* 41	—— 9, *v.* 13	—— 24
10	f	....	—— 10, to *v.* 21	—— 22, *v.* 41 to 23, *v.* 13	—— 10, *v.* 21 & 11	—— 25
11	g	....	—— 12, to *v.* 21	—— 23, *v.* 13	—— 12, *v.* 21 to *v.* 43	—— 26
12	A	....	—— 12, *v.* 43 to 13, *v.* 17	—— 24, to *v.* 29	—— 13, *v.* 17 to 14, *v.* 10	—— 27, to *v.* 18
13	b	....	—— 14, *v.* 10	—— 24, *v.* 29	—— 15, to *v.* 22	—— 27, *v.* 18
14	c	Valentine, Bp. & Mar. .	—— 15, *v.* 22 to 16, *v.* 11	—— 25 to *v.* 31	—— 16, *v.* 11	—— 28, to *v.* 17
15	d	....	—— 17	—— 25, *v.* 31	—— 18	—— 28, *v.* 17
16	e	....	—— 19	—— 26, to *v.* 31	—— 20, to *v.* 22	Rom. 1
17	f	....	—— 21, to *v.* 18	—— 26, *v.* 31 to *v.* 57	—— 22, *v.* 21 to 23, *v.* 10	—— 2, to *v.* 17
18	g	....	—— 23, *v.* 14	—— 26, *v.* 57	—— 24	—— 2, *v.* 17
19	A	....	—— 25, to *v.* 23	—— 27, to *v.* 27	—— 28, to *v.* 13	—— 3
20	b	....	—— 28, *v.* 29 to *v.* 42	—— 27, *v.* 27 to *v.* 57	—— 29, *v.* 35 to 30, *v.* 11	—— 4
21	c	....	—— 31	—— 27, *v.* 57	—— 32, to *v.* 15	—— 5
22	d	....	—— 32, *v.* 15	—— 28	—— 33, to *v.* 12	—— 6
23	e	.... *Fast*	—— 33, *v.* 12 to 34, *v.* 10	Mark 1, to *v.* 21	—— 34, *v.* 10 to *v.* 27	—— 7
24	f	*St. Matthias*, Apostle .	....	—— 1, *v.* 21	....	—— 8, to *v.* 18
25	g	....	—— 34, *v.* 27	—— 2, to *v.* 23	—— 35, *v.* 29 to 36, *v.* 8	—— 8, *v.* 18
26	A	....	—— 39, *v.* 30	—— 2, *v.* 23 to 3, *v.* 13	—— 40, to *v.* 17	—— 9, to *v.* 19
27	b	....	—— 40, *v.* 17	—— 3, *v.* 13	Levit. 9, *v.* 22 to 10, *v.* 12	—— 9, *v.* 19
28	c	....	Levit. 14, to *v.* 23	—— 4, to *v.* 35	—— 16, to *v.* 23	—— 10
29	..	....	—— 19, to *v.* 19	Matt. 7	—— 19, *v.* 30 to 20, *v.* 9	—— 12
..	..	....	....	....	....	....
..	..	....	....	....	....	....

THE CALENDAR,

WITH

THE TABLE OF LESSONS.

		MARCH HATH XXXI DAYS.	MORNING PRAYER.		EVENING PRAYER.	
			FIRST LESSON.	SECOND LESSON.	FIRST LESSON.	SECOND LESSON.
	1	d	David, Archbishop ..	Levit. 25, to v. 18	Mark 4, v. 35 to 5, v. 21	Levit. 25, v. 18 to v. 44	Rom. 11, to v. 25
	2	e	Chad, Bishop........	—— 26, to v. 21	—— 5, v. 21	—— 26, v. 21	—— 11, v. 25
	3	f	....	Num. 6	—— 6, to v. 14	Num. 9, v. 15 to 10, v. 11	—— 12
	4	g	....	—— 10, v. 11	—— 6, v. 14 to v. 30	—— 11, to v. 24	—— 13
	5	A	....	—— 11, v. 24	—— 6, v. 30	—— 12	—— 14 & 15, to v. 8
	6	b	....	—— 13, v. 17	—— 7, to v. 24	—— 14, to v. 26	—— 15, v. 8
	7	c	Perpetua, Martyr....	—— 14, v. 26	—— 7, v. 24 to 8, v. 10	—— 16, to v. 23	—— 16
	8	d	....	—— 16, v. 23	—— 8, v. 10 to 9, v. 2	—— 17	1 Cor. 1, to v. 26
	9	e	....	—— 20, to v. 14	—— 9, v. 2 to v. 30	—— 20, v. 14	—— 1, v. 26 & 2
	10	f	....	—— 21, to v. 10	—— 9, v. 30	—— 21, v. 10 to v. 32	—— 3
	11	g	....	—— 22, to v. 22	—— 10, to v. 32	—— 22, v. 22	—— 4, to v. 18
	12	A	Gregory, Bishop	—— 23	—— 10, v. 32	—— 24	—— 4, v. 18 & 5
	13	b	....	—— 25	—— 11, to v. 27	—— 27, v. 12	—— 6
	14	c	....	Deut. 1, to v. 19	—— 11, v. 27 to 12, v. 13	Deut. 1, v. 19	—— 7, to v. 25
	15	d	....	—— 2, to v. 26	—— 12, v. 13 to v. 35	—— 2, v. 26 to 3, v. 18	—— 7, v. 25
	16	e	....	—— 3, v. 18	—— 12, v. 35 to 13, v. 14	—— 4, to v. 25	—— 8
	17	f	....	—— 4, v. 25 to v. 41	—— 13, v. 14	—— 5, to v. 22	—— 9
	18	g	Edward, King of W. [Saxons	—— 5, v. 22	—— 14, to v. 27	—— 6	—— 10 & 11, v. 1
	19	A	....	—— 7, to v. 12	—— 14, v. 27 to v. 53	—— 7, v. 12	—— 11, v. 2 to v. 17
	20	b	....	—— 8	—— 14, v. 53	—— 10, v. 8	—— 11, v. 17
14	21	c	Benedict, Abbot	—— 11, to v. 18	—— 15, to v. 42	—— 11, v. 18	—— 12, to v. 28
3	22	d	....	—— 15, to v. 16	—— 15, v. 42 & 16	—— 17, v. 8	—— 12, v. 28 & 13
	23	e	....	—— 18, v. 9	Luke 1, to v. 26	—— 24, v. 5	—— 14, to v. 20
11	24	f	.... *Fast*	—— 26	—— 1, v. 26 to v. 46	—— 27	—— 14, v. 20
	25	g	*Annunc. of V. Mary*	....	—— 1, v. 46	....	—— 15, to v. 35
19	26	A	....	—— 28, to v. 15	—— 2, to v. 21	—— 28, v. 15 to v. 47	—— 15, v. 35
8	27	b	....	—— 28, v. 47	—— 2, v. 21	—— 29, v. 9	—— 16
	28	c	....	—— 30	—— 3, to v. 23	—— 31, to v. 14	2 Cor. 1, to v. 23
16	29	d	....	—— 31, v. 14 to v. 30	—— 4, to v. 16	—— 31, v. 30 to 32, v. 44	—— 1, v. 23 to 2, v. 14
5	30	e	....	—— 32, v. 44	—— 4, v. 16	—— 33	—— 2, v. 14 & 3
	31	f	....	—— 34	—— 5, to v. 17	Joshua 1	—— 4

THE CALENDAR,

THE TABLE OF LESSONS.

	APRIL HATH XXX DAYS.		MORNING PRAYER.		EVENING PRAYER.	
			FIRST LESSON.	SECOND LESSON.	FIRST LESSON.	SECOND LESSON.
13	1	g	....	Joshua 2	Luke 5, v. 17	Joshua 3	2 Cor. 5
2	2	A	....	—— 4	—— 6, to v. 20	—— 5	—— 6 & 7, v. 1
	3	b	Richard, Bishop	—— 6	—— 6, v. 20	—— 7	—— 7, v. 2
10	4	c	St. Ambrose, Bishop	—— 9, v. 3	—— 7, to v. 24	—— 10, to v. 16	—— 8
	5	d	....	—— 21, v. 43 to 22, v. 11	—— 7, v. 24	—— 22, v. 11	—— 9
18	6	e	....	—— 23	—— 8, to v. 26	—— 24	—— 10
7	7	f	....	Judges 2	—— 8, v. 26	Judges 4	—— 11, to v. 30
	8	g	....	—— 5	—— 9, to v. 28	—— 6, to v. 24	—— 11, v. 30 to 12, v. 14
15	9	A	....	—— 6, v. 24	—— 9, v. 28 to v. 51	—— 7	—— 12, v. 14 & 13
4	10	b	....	—— 8, v. 32 to 9, v. 25	—— 9, v. 51 to 10, v. 17	—— 10	Gal. 1
	11	c	....	—— 11, to v. 29	—— 10, v. 17	—— 11, v. 29	—— 2
12	12	d	....	—— 13	—— 11, to v. 29	—— 14	—— 3
1	13	e	....	—— 15	—— 11, v. 29	—— 16	—— 4, to v. 21
	14	f	....	Ruth 1	—— 12, to v. 35	Ruth 2	—— 4, v. 21 to 5, v. 13
9	15	g	....	—— 3	—— 12, v. 35	—— 4	—— 5, v. 13
	16	A	....	1 Sam. 1	—— 13, to v. 18	1 Sam. 2, to v. 21	—— 6
17	17	b	....	—— 2, v. 21	—— 13, v. 18	—— 3	Eph. 1
6	18	c	....	—— 4	—— 14, to v. 25	—— 5	—— 2
	19	d	Alphege, Archbishop.	—— 6	—— 14, v. 25 to 15, v. 11	—— 7	—— 3
	20	e	....	—— 8	—— 15, v. 11	—— 9	—— 4, to v. 25
	21	f	....	—— 10	—— 16	—— 11	—— 4, v. 25 to 5, v. 22
	22	g	....	—— 12	—— 17, to v. 20	—— 13	—— 5, v. 22 to 6, v. 10
	23	A	St. George, Martyr ..	—— 14, to v. 24	—— 17, v. 20	—— 14, v. 24 to v. 47	—— 6, v. 10
	24	b	....	—— 15	—— 18, to v. 31	—— 16	Phil. 1
	25	c	*St. Mark*, Evang.	....	—— 18, v. 31 to 19, v. 11	....	—— 2
	26	d	....	—— 17, to v. 31	—— 19, v. 11 to v. 28	—— 17, v. 31 to v. 55	—— 3
	27	e	....	—— 17, v. 55 to 18, v. 17	—— 19, v. 28	—— 19	—— 4
	28	f	....	—— 20, to v. 18	—— 20, to v. 27	—— 20, v. 18	Col. 1, to v. 21
	29	g	....	—— 21	—— 20, v. 27 to 21, v. 5	—— 22	—— 1, v. 21 to 2, v. 8
	30	A	....	—— 23	—— 21, v. 5	—— 24 & 25, v. 1	—— 2, v. 8
..	..		....	....	....	....	....

THE CALENDAR,

WITH

THE TABLE OF LESSONS.

MAY HATH XXXI DAYS.		MORNING PRAYER.		EVENING PRAYER.	
		FIRST LESSON.	SECOND LESSON.	FIRST LESSON.	SECOND LESSON.
1	b	*St. Philip & St. James*	....	....	....	Colos. 3, to *v.* 18
2	c	....	1 Sam. 26	Luke 22, to *v.* 31	1 Sam. 28, *v.* 3	—— 3, *v.* 18 to 4, *v.* 7
3	d	Invention of the Cross.	—— 31	—— 22, *v.* 31, to *v.* 54	2 Sam. 1	—— 4, *v.* 7
4	e	....	2 Sam. 3, *v.* 17	—— 22, *v.* 54	—— 4	1 Thess. 1
5	f	....	—— 6	—— 23, to *v.* 26	—— 7, to *v.* 18	—— 2
6	g	St. John Port. Lat.....	—— 7, *v.* 18	—— 23, *v.* 26 to *v.* 50	—— 9	—— 3
7	A	....	—— 11	—— 23, *v.* 50 to 24, *v.* 13	—— 12, to *v.* 24	—— 4
8	b	....	—— 13, *v.* 38 to 14, *v.* 26	—— 24, *v.* 13	—— 15, to *v.* 16	—— 5
9	c	....	—— 15, *v.* 16	John 1, to *v.* 29	—— 16, to *v.* 15	2 Thess. 1
10	d	....	—— 16, *v.* 15 to 17, *v.* 24	—— 1, *v.* 29	—— 17, *v.* 24 to 18, *v.* 18	—— 2
11	e	....	—— 18, *v.* 18	—— 2	—— 19, to *v.* 24	—— 3
12	f	....	—— 19, *v.* 24	—— 3, to *v.* 22	—— 21, to *v.* 15	1 Tim. 1, to *v.* 18
13	g	....	—— 23, to *v.* 24	—— 3, *v.* 22	—— 24	—— 1, *v.* 18 & 2
14	A	....	1 Kings 1, to *v.* 28	—— 4, to *v.* 31	1 Kings 1, *v.* 28 to *v.* 49	—— 3
15	b	....	1 Chron. 29, *v.* 10	—— 4, *v.* 31	—— 3	—— 4
16	c	....	1 Kings 4, *v.* 20	—— 5, to *v.* 24	—— 5	—— 5
17	d	....	—— 6, to *v.* 15	—— 5, *v.* 24	—— 8, to *v.* 22	—— 6
18	e	....	—— 8, *v.* 22 to *v.* 54	—— 6, to *v.* 22	—— 8, *v.* 54 to 9, *v.* 10	2 Tim. 1
19	f	Dunstan, Archbishop..	—— 10	—— 6, *v.* 22 to *v.* 41	—— 11, to *v.* 26	—— 2
20	g	....	—— 11, *v.* 26	—— 6, *v.* 41	—— 12, to *v.* 25	—— 3
21	A	....	—— 12, *v.* 25 to 13, *v.* 11	—— 7, to *v.* 25	—— 13, *v.* 11	—— 4
22	b	....	—— 14, to *v.* 21	—— 7, *v.* 25	—— 15, *v.* 25 to 16, *v.* 8	Titus 1
23	c	....	—— 16, *v.* 8	—— 8, to *v.* 31	—— 17	—— 2
24	d	....	—— 18, to *v.* 17	—— 8, *v.* 31	—— 18, *v.* 17	—— 3
25	e	....	—— 19	—— 9, to *v.* 39	—— 21	Philemon
26	f	Augustine, Archbishop	—— 22, to *v.* 41	—— 9, *v.* 39 to 10, *v.* 22	2 Kings 1	Heb. 1
27	g	Ven. Bede, Presbyter..	2 Kings 2	—— 10, *v.* 22	—— 4, *v.* 8	—— 2 & 3, to *v.* 7
28	A	....	—— 5	—— 11, to *v.* 17	—— 6, to *v.* 24	—— 3, *v.* 7 to 4, *v.* 14
29	b	....	—— 6, *v.* 24	—— 11, *v.* 17 to *v.* 47	—— 7	—— 4, *v.* 14 & 5
30	c	....	—— 8, to *v.* 16	—— 11, *v.* 47 to 12, *v.* 20	—— 9	—— 6
31	d	....	—— 10, to *v.* 18	—— 12, *v.* 20	—— 10, *v.* 18	—— 7

C

THE CALENDAR,

WITH

THE TABLE OF LESSONS.

JUNE HATH XXX DAYS.		MORNING PRAYER.		EVENING PRAYER.	
		FIRST LESSON.	SECOND LESSON.	FIRST LESSON.	SECOND LESSON.
1	e	Nicomede, Martyr	2 Kings 13	John 13, to v. 21	2 Kings 17, to v. 24	Heb. 8
2	f	....	—— 17, v. 24	—— 13, v. 21	2 Chron. 12	—— 9
3	g	....	2 Chron. 13	—— 14	—— 14	—— 10, to v. 19
4	A	....	—— 15	—— 15	—— 16 & 17, to v. 14	—— 10, v. 19
5	b	Boniface, Bp. & Martyr	—— 19	—— 16, to v. 16	—— 20, to v. 31	—— 11, to v. 17
6	c	....	—— 20, v. 31 & 21	—— 16, v. 16	—— 22	—— 11, v. 17
7	d	....	—— 23,	—— 17	—— 24	—— 12
8	e	....	—— 25	—— 18, to v. 28	—— 26 & 27	—— 13
9	f	....	—— 28	—— 18, v. 28	2 Kings 18, to v. 9	James 1
10	g	....	—— 29, v. 3 to v. 21	—— 19, to v. 25	2 Chron. 30 & 31, v. 1	—— 2
11	A	St. Barnabas, Apostle [and Martyr.	....	....	....	....
12	b	....	2 Kings 18, v. 13	—— 19, v. 25	2 Kings 19, to v. 20	—— 3
13	c	....	—— 19, v. 20	—— 20, to v. 19	—— 20	—— 4
14	d	....	Isaiah 38, v. 9 to v. 21	—— 20, v. 19	2 Chron. 33	—— 5
15	e	....	2 Kings 22	—— 21	2 Kings 23, to v. 21	1 Peter 1, to v. 22
16	f	....	—— 23, v. 21 to 24, v. 8	Acts 1	—— 24, v. 8 to 25, v. 8	—— 1, v. 22 to 2, v. 11
17	g	St. Alban, Martyr	—— 25, v. 8	—— 2, to v. 22	Ezra 1 & 3	—— 2, v. 11 to 3, v. 8
18	A	....	Ezra 4	—— 2, v. 22	—— 5	—— 3, v. 8 to 4 v. 7
19	b	....	—— 7	—— 3	—— 8, v. 15	—— 4, v. 7
20	c	Trans. of Edw. King of [W. Sax.	—— 9	—— 4, to v. 32	—— 10, to v. 20	—— 5
21	d	....	Nehem. 1	—— 4, v. 32 to 5, v. 17	Nehem. 2	2 Peter 1
22	e	....	—— 4	—— 5, v. 17	—— 5	—— 2
23	f	.... Fast	—— 6 & 7, to v. 5	—— 6	—— 7, v. 73 & 8	—— 3
24	g	St. John Baptist	....	....	....	....
25	A	....	—— 13, to v. 15	—— 7, to v. 35	—— 13, v. 15	1 John 1
26	b	....	Esther 1	—— 7, v. 35 to 8, v. 5	Esther 2, v. 15 & 3	—— 2, to v. 15
27	c	....	—— 4	—— 8, v. 5 to v. 26	—— 5	—— 2, v. 15
28	d	.... Fast	—— 6	—— 8, v. 26	—— 7	—— 3, to v. 16
29	e	St. Peter, Apost. & Mar.	....	....	....	....
30	f	....	Job 1	—— 9, to v. 23	Job. 2	—— 3, v. 16 to 4, v. 7
..	..		....	....	....	....

THE CALENDAR,

WITH

THE TABLE OF LESSONS.

JULY HATH XXXI DAYS.		MORNING PRAYER.		EVENING PRAYER.	
		FIRST LESSON.	SECOND LESSON.	FIRST LESSON.	SECOND LESSON.
1	g	Job 3	Acts 9, *v.* 23	Job 4	1 John 4, *v.* 7
2	A	Visit. of Bl. Virg. Mary	—— 5	—— 10, to *v.* 24	—— 6	—— 5
3	b	—— 7	—— 10, *v.* 24	—— 9	2 John
4	c	Tran. of St. Martin, Bp.	—— 10	—— 11	—— 11	3 John
5	d	—— 12	—— 12	—— 13	Jude
6	e	—— 14	—— 13, to *v.* 26	—— 16	Matt. 1, *v.* 18
7	f	—— 17	—— 13, *v.* 26	—— 19	—— 2
8	g	—— 21	—— 14	—— 22, *v.* 12 to *v.* 29	—— 3
9	A	—— 23	—— 15, to *v.* 30	—— 24	—— 4, to *v.* 23
10	b	—— 25 & 26	—— 15, *v.* 30 to 16, *v.* 16	—— 27	—— 4, *v.* 23 to 5, *v.* 13
11	c	—— 28	—— 16, *v.* 16	—— 29 & 30, *v.* 1	—— 5, *v.* 13 to 5, *v.* 33
12	d	—— 30, *v.* 12 to *v.* 27	—— 17, to *v.* 16	—— 31, *v.* 13	—— 5, *v.* 33
13	e	—— 32	—— 17, *v.* 16	—— 38, to *v.* 39	—— 6, to *v.* 19
14	f	—— 38, *v.* 39 & 39	—— 18, to *v.* 24	—— 40	—— 6, *v.* 19 to 7, *v.* 7
15	g	Swithun, Bishop, Tran.	—— 41	—— 18, *v.* 24 to 19, *v.* 21	—— 42	—— 7, *v.* 7
16	A	Prov. 1, to *v.* 20	—— 19, *v.* 21	Prov. 1, *v.* 20	—— 8, to *v.* 18
17	b	—— 2	—— 20, to *v.* 17	—— 3, to *v.* 27	—— 8, *v.* 18
18	c	—— 3, *v.* 27 to 4, *v.* 20	—— 20, *v.* 17	—— 4, *v.* 20 to 5, *v.* 15	—— 9, to *v.* 18
19	d	—— 5, *v.* 15	—— 21, to *v.* 17	—— 6, to *v.* 20	—— 9, *v.* 18
20	e	Margaret, Virg. & Mart.	—— 7	—— 21, *v.* 17 to *v.* 37	—— 8	—— 10, to *v.* 24
21	f	—— 9	—— 21, *v.* 37 to 22, *v.* 23	—— 10, *v.* 16	—— 10, *v.* 24
22	g	St. Mary Magdalene....	—— 11, to *v.* 15	—— 22, *v.* 23 to 23, *v.* 12	—— 11, *v.* 15	—— 11
23	A	—— 12, *v.* 10	—— 23, *v.* 12	—— 13	—— 12, to *v.* 22
24	b	*Fast.*	—— 14, *v.* 9 to *v.* 28	—— 24	—— 14, *v.* 28 to 15, *v.* 18	—— 12, *v.* 22
25	c	*St. James*, Ap. & Mart.	....	....	....	—— 13, to *v.* 24
26	d	St. Anne	—— 15, *v.* 18	—— 25	—— 16, to *v.* 20	—— 13, *v.* 24 to *v.* 53
27	e	—— 16, *v.* 31 to 17, *v.* 18	—— 26	—— 18, *v.* 10	—— 13, *v.* 53 to 14, *v.* 13
28	f	—— 19, *v.* 13	—— 27	—— 20, to *v.* 23	—— 14, *v.* 13
29	g	—— 21, to *v.* 17	—— 28, to *v.* 17	—— 22, to *v.* 17	—— 15, to *v.* 21
30	A	—— 23, *v.* 10	—— 28, *v.* 17	—— 24, *v.* 21	—— 15, *v.* 21
31	b	—— 25	Rom. 1	—— 26, to *v.* 21	—— 16, to *v.* 24

AUGUST HATH XXXI DAYS.			MORNING PRAYER.		EVENING PRAYER.	
			FIRST LESSON.	SECOND LESSON.	FIRST LESSON.	SECOND LESSON.
1	c	Lammas Day.........	Prov. 27, to v. 23	Rom. 2, to v. 17	Prov. 28, to v. 15	Matt. 16, v. 24 to 17, v. 14
2	d	....	—— 30, to v. 18	—— 2, v. 17	—— 31, v. 10	—— 17, v. 14
3	e	....	Eccles. 1	—— 3	Eccles. 2, to v. 12	—— 18, to v. 21
4	f	....	—— 3	—— 4	—— 4	—— 18, v. 21 to 19, v. 3
5	g	....	—— 5	—— 5	—— 6	—— 19, v. 3 to v. 27
6	A	Transfig. of our Lord..	—— 7	—— 6	—— 8	—— 19, v. 27 to 20, v. 17
7	b	Name of Jesus	—— 9	—— 7	—— 11	—— 20, v. 17
8	c	....	—— 12	—— 8, to v. 18	Jeremiah 1	—— 21, to v. 23
9	d	....	Jeremiah 2, to v. 14	—— 8, v. 18	—— 5, to v. 19	—— 21, v. 23
10	e	St. Laurence, Martyr..	—— 5, v. 19	—— 9, to v. 19	—— 6, to v. 22	—— 22, to v. 15
11	f	....	—— 7, to v. 17	—— 9, v. 19	—— 8, v. 4	—— 22, v. 15, to v. 41
12	g	....	—— 9, to v. 17	—— 10	—— 13, v. 8 to v. 24	—— 22, v. 41 to 23, v. 13
13	A	....	—— 15	—— 11, to v. 25	—— 17, to v. 19	—— 23, v. 13
14	b	....	—— 18, to v. 18	—— 11, v. 25	—— 19	—— 24, to v. 29
15	c	....	—— 21	—— 12	—— 22, to v. 13	—— 24, v. 29
16	d	....	—— 22, v. 13	—— 13	—— 23, to v. 16	—— 25, to v. 31
17	e	....	—— 24	—— 14 & 15, to v. 8	—— 25, to v. 15	—— 25, v. 31
18	f	....	—— 26	—— 15, v. 8	—— 28	—— 26, to v. 31
19	g	....	—— 29, v. 4 to v. 20	—— 16	—— 30	—— 26, v. 31 to v. 57
20	A	....	—— 31, to v. 15	1 Cor. 1, to v. 26	—— 31, v. 15 to v. 38	—— 26, v. 57
21	b	....	—— 33, to v. 14	—— 1, v. 26 & 2	—— 33, v. 14	—— 27, to v. 27
22	c	....	—— 35	—— 3	—— 36, to v. 14	—— 27, v. 27 to v. 57
23	d	*Fast*	—— 36, v. 14	—— 4, to v. 18	—— 38, to v. 14	—— 27, v. 57
24	e	*St. Bartholomew*, Apos.	....	—— 4, v. 18 & 5	....	—— 28
25	f	....	—— 38, v. 14	—— 6	—— 39	Mark 1, to v. 21
26	g	....	—— 50, to v. 21	—— 7, to v. 25	—— 51, v. 54	—— 1, v. 21
27	A	....	Ezek. 1, to v. 15	—— 7, v. 25	Ezek. 1, v. 15	—— 2, to v. 23
28	b	St. Augustine, Bishop..	—— 2	—— 8	—— 3, to v. 15	—— 2, v. 23 to 3, v. 13
29	c	St. John Bapt. beheaded	—— 3, v. 15	—— 9	—— 8	—— 3, v. 13
30	d	....	—— 9	—— 10 & 11, v. 1	—— 11, v. 14	—— 4, to v. 35
31	e	....	—— 12, v. 17	—— 11, v. 2 to v. 17	—— 13, to v. 17	—— 4, v. 35 to 5, v. 21

THE CALENDAR,

WITH

THE TABLE OF LESSONS.

		SEPTEMBER HATH XXX DAYS.	MORNING PRAYER.		EVENING PRAYER.	
			FIRST LESSON.	SECOND LESSON.	FIRST LESSON.	SECOND LESSON.
1	f	Giles, Abbot & Confes.	Ezek. 13, v. 17	1 Cor. 11, v. 17	Ezek.14, to v.12	Mark 5, v. 21
2	g	....	— 14, v. 12	— 12, to v. 28	— 16, v. 44	— 6, to v. 14
3	A	....	— 18, to v. 19	— 12, v. 28 & 13	— 18, v. 19	— 6, v. 14 to v. 30
4	b	....	— 20, to v. 18	— 14, to v. 20	— 20, v. 18 to v. 33	— 6, v. 30
5	c	....	— 20, v. 33 to v. 44	— 14, v. 20	— 22, v. 23	— 7, to v. 24
6	d	....	— 24, v. 15	— 15, to v. 35	— 26	— 7, v. 24 to 8, v. 10
7	e	Enurchus, Bishop	— 27, to v. 26	— 15, v.35	— 27, v. 26	— 8, v. 10 to 9, v. 2
8	f	Nativity of Bl. V. Mary	— 28, to v. 20	— 16	— 31	— 9, v. 2 to v. 30
9	g	....	— 32, to v. 17	2 Cor. 1, to v. 23	— 33, to v. 21	— 9, v. 30
10	A	....	— 33, v. 21	— 1, v. 23 to 2, v. 14	— 34, to v 17	— 10, to v. 32
11	b	....	— 34, v. 17	— 2, v. 14 & 3	— 36, v. 16 to v. 33	— 10, v. 32
12	c	....	— 37, to v. 15	— 4	— 37, v. 15	— 11, to v. 27
13	d	....	— 47, to v. 13	— 5	Dan. 1	— 11, v. 27 to 12, v. 13
14	e	Holy Cross Day	Dan. 2, to v. 24	— 6 & 7, v. 1	— 2, v. 24	— 12, v. 13 to v. 35
15	f	....	— 3	— 7, v. 2	— 4, to v. 19	— 12, v. 35 to 13, v. 14
16	g	....	— 4, v. 19	— 8	— 5, to v. 17	— 13, v. 14
17	A	Lambert, Bp. & Martyr	— 5, v. 17	— 9	— 6	— 14, to v. 27
18	b	....	— 7, to v. 15	— 10	— 7, v. 15	— 14, v. 27 to v. 53
19	c	....	— 9, to v. 20	— 11, to v. 30	— 9, v. 20	— 14, v. 53
20	d	.... *Fast*	— 10, to v. 20	— 11, v. 30 to 12, v. 14	— 12	— 15, to v. 42
21	e	*St. Matthew,* Apostle..	....	— 12, v. 14 & 13	....	— 15, v. 42 & 16
22	f	....	Hosea 2, v. 14	Gal. 1	Hosea 4, to v.13	Luke 1, to v. 26
23	g	....	— 5, v. 8 to 6, v. 7	— 2	— 7, v. 8	— 1, v. 26 to v. 57
24	A	....	— 8	— 3	— 9	— 1, v. 57
25	b	....	— 10	— 4, to v. 21	— 11 & 12, to v. 7	— 2, to v. 21
26	c	St. Cyprian, Archbp. ...	— 13, to v. 15	— 4, v. 21 to 5, v. 13	— 14	— 2, v. 21
27	d	....	Joel 1	— 5, v. 13	Joel 2, to v.15	— 3, to v. 23
28	e	....	— 2, v. 15 to v. 28	— 6	— 2, v. 28 to 3, v. 9	— 4, to v. 16
29	f	*St. Michael & all Angels*	....	....	....	....
30	g	St. Jerom, Pr. & Conf.	— 3, v. 9	Eph. 1	Amos 1 & 2, to v. 4	— 4, v. 16
..	..	....	....	....	....	....

THE CALENDAR,

WITH

THE TABLE OF LESSONS.

OCTOBER HATH XXXI DAYS.			MORNING PRAYER.		EVENING PRAYER.	
			FIRST LESSON.	SECOND LESSON.	FIRST LESSON.	SECOND LESSON.
1	A	Remigius, Bishop......	Amos 2, *v.* 4 to 3, *v.* 9	Eph. 2	Amos 4, *v.* 4	Luke 5, to *v.* 17
2	b	....	—— 5, to *v.* 18	—— 3	—— 5, *v.* 18 to 6, *v.* 9	—— 5, *v.* 17
3	c	....	—— 7	—— 4, to *v.* 25	—— 8	—— 6, to *v.* 20
4	d	....	—— 9	—— 4, *v.* 25 to 5, *v.* 22	Obadiah	—— 6, *v.* 20
5	e	....	Jonah 1	—— 5, *v.* 22 to 6, *v.* 10	Jonah 2	—— 7, to *v.* 24
6	f	Faith, Virgin & Martyr	—— 3	—— 6, *v.* 10	—— 4	—— 7, *v.* 24
7	g	....	Micah 1, to *v.* 10	Phil. 1	Micah 2	—— 8, to *v.* 26
8	A	....	—— 3	—— 2	—— 4	—— 8, *v.* 26
9	b	St. Denys, Bp. & Mart.	—— 5	—— 3	—— 6	—— 9, to *v.* 28
10	c	....	—— 7	—— 4	Nahum 1	—— 9, *v.* 28 to *v.* 51
11	d	....	Nahum 2	Col. 1, to *v.* 21	—— 3	—— 9, *v.* 51 to 10, *v.* 17
12	e	....	Habak. 1	—— 1, *v.* 21, to 2, *v.* 8	Habak. 2	—— 10, *v.* 17
13	f	Trans. of K. Edw., Conf.	—— 3	—— 2, *v.* 8	Zeph. 1, to *v.* 14	—— 11, to *v.* 29
14	g	....	Zeph. 1, *v.* 14 to 2, *v.* 4	—— 3, to *v.* 18	—— 2, *v.* 4	—— 11, *v.* 29
15	A	....	—— 3	—— 3, *v.* 18 & 4	Haggai 1	—— 12, to *v.* 35
16	b	....	Haggai 2, to *v.* 10	1 Thess. 1	—— 2, *v.* 10	—— 12, *v.* 35
17	c	Etheldreda, Virgin	Zech. 1, to *v.* 18	—— 2	Zech. 1, *v.* 18 & 2	—— 13, to *v.* 18
18	d	*St. Luke*, Evangelist ..	....	—— 3	....	—— 13, *v.* 18
19	e	....	—— 3	—— 4	—— 4	—— 14, to *v.* 25
20	f	....	—— 5	—— 5	—— 6	—— 14, *v.* 25 to 15, *v.* 11
21	g	....	—— 7	2 Thess. 1	—— 8, to *v.* 14	—— 15, *v.* 11
22	A	....	—— 8, *v.* 14	—— 2	—— 9, *v.* 9	—— 16
23	b	....	—— 10	—— 3	—— 11	—— 17, to *v.* 20
24	c	....	—— 12	1 Tim. 1, to *v.* 18	—— 13	—— 17, *v.* 20
25	d	Crispin, Martyr........	—— 14	—— 1, *v.* 18 & 2	Mal. 1	—— 18, to *v.* 31
26	e	....	Mal. 2	—— 3	—— 3, to *v.* 13	—— 18, *v.* 31 to 19, *v.* 11
27	f	.... *Fast*	—— 3, *v.* 13 & 4	—— 4	Wisdom 1	—— 19, *v.* 11 to *v.* 28
28	g	*St. Simon & St. Jude* ..	....	—— 5	....	—— 19, *v.* 28
29	A	....	Wisdom 2	—— 6	—— 4, *v.* 7	—— 20, to *v.* 27
30	b	....	—— 6, to *v.* 22	2 Tim. 1	—— 6, *v.* 22 to 7, *v.* 15	—— 20, *v.* 27 to 21, *v.* 5
31	c	.... *Fast*	—— 7, *v.* 15	—— 2	—— 8, to *v.* 19	—— 21, *v.* 5

THE CALENDAR,

WITH

THE TABLE OF LESSONS.

NOVEMBER HATH XXX DAYS.		MORNING PRAYER.		EVENING PRAYER.	
		FIRST LESSON.	SECOND LESSON.	FIRST LESSON.	SECOND LESSON.
1	d	*All Saints' Day*........	....	....	....
2	e	....	Wisdom 9	2 Tim. 3	Wisdom 11, to v. 15	Luke 22, to v. 31
3	f	....	—— 11, v. 15 to 12, v. 3	—— 4	—— 17	—— 22, v. 31 to v. 54
4	g	....	Ecclus 1, to v. 14	Titus 1	Ecclus, 2	—— 22, v. 54
5	A	....	—— 3, v. 17 to v. 30	—— 2	—— 4, v. 10	—— 23, to v. 26
6	b	Leonard, Confessor....	—— 5	—— 3	—— 7, v. 27	—— 23, v. 23 to v. 50
7	c	....	—— 10, v. 18	Philemon	—— 14, to v. 20	—— 23, v. 50 to 24, v. 13
8	d	....	—— 15, v. 9	Heb. 1	—— 16, v. 17	—— 24, v. 13
9	e	....	—— 18, to v. 15	—— 2 & 3, to v. 7	—— 18, v. 15	John 1, to v. 29
10	f	....	—— 19, v. 13	—— 3, v. 7 to 4, v. 14	—— 22, v. 6 to v. 24	—— 1, v. 29
11	g	St. Martin, Bp. & Conf.	—— 24, to v. 24	—— 4, v. 14 & 5	—— 24, v. 24	—— 2
12	A	....	—— 33, v. 7 to v. 23	—— 6	—— 34, v. 15	—— 3, to v. 22
13	b	Britius, Bishop........	—— 35	—— 7	—— 37, v. 8 to v. 19	—— 3, v. 22
14	c	....	—— 39, to v. 13	—— 8	—— 39, v. 13	—— 4, to v. 31
15	d	Machutus, Bishop	—— 41, to v. 14	—— 9	—— 42, v. 15	—— 4, v. 31
16	e	....	—— 44, to v. 16	—— 10, to v. 19	—— 50, to v. 25	—— 5, to v. 24
17	f	Hugh, Bp. of Lincoln..	—— 51, v. 10	—— 10, v. 19	Baruch 4, to v. 21	—— 5, v. 24
18	g	....	Baruch 4, v. 36 & 5	—— 11, to v. 17	Isaiah 1, to v. 21	—— 6, to v. 22
19	A	....	Isaiah 1, v. 21	—— 11, v. 17	—— 2	—— 6, v. 22 to v. 41
20	b	Edmund, King & Mart.	—— 3, to v. 16	—— 12	—— 4, v. 2	—— 6, v. 41
21	c	....	—— 5, to v. 18	—— 13	—— 5, v. 18	—— 7, to v. 25
22	d	Cecilia, Virg. & Martyr	—— 6	James 1	—— 7, to v. 17	—— 7, v. 25
23	e	St. Clement, Bishop ..	—— 8, v. 5 to v. 18	—— 2	—— 8, v. 18 to 9, v. 8	—— 8, to v. 31
24	f	....	—— 9, v. 8 to 10, v. 5	—— 3	—— 10, v. 5 to v. 20	—— 8, v. 31
25	g	Catherine, Vir. & Mart.	—— 10, v. 20	—— 4	—— 11, to v. 10	—— 9, to v. 39
26	A	....	—— 11, v. 10	—— 5	—— 12	—— 9, v. 39 to 10, v. 22
27	b	....	—— 13	1 Pet. 1, to v. 22	—— 14, to v. 24	—— 10, v. 22
28	c	....	—— 17	—— 1, v. 22 to 2, v. 11	—— 18	—— 11, to v. 17
29	d	.... *Fast*	—— 19, to v. 16	—— 2, v. 11 to 3, v. 8	—— 19, v. 16	—— 11, v. 17 to v. 47
30	e	*St. Andrew*, Apostle ..	....	....	....	....
..	..	....	....	....	....	....

THE CALENDAR,

THE TABLE OF LESSONS.

DECEMBER HATH XXXI DAYS.		MORNING PRAYER.		EVENING PRAYER.	
		FIRST LESSON.	SECOND LESSON.	FIRST LESSON.	SECOND LESSON.
1	f	.... Isaiah 21 to v. 13	1 Pet. 3, v. 8 to 4, v. 7	Isaiah 22, to v. 15	John 11, v. 47 to 12, v. 20
2	g	.... —— 22, v. 15	—— 4, v. 7	—— 23	—— 12, v. 20
3	A	.... —— 24	—— 5	—— 25	—— 13, to v. 21
4	b	.... —— 26, to v. 20	2 Pet. 1	—— 26, v. 20 & 27	—— 13, v. 21
5	c	.... —— 28, to v. 14	—— 2	—— 28, v. 14	—— 14
6	d	Nicolas, Bishop........ —— 29, to v. 9	—— 3	—— 29, v. 9	—— 15
7	e	.... —— 30, to v. 18	1 John 1	—— 30, v. 18	—— 16, to v. 16
8	f	Concep. of Virg. Mary . —— 31	—— 2, to v. 15	—— 32	—— 16, v. 16
9	g	.... —— 33	—— 2, v. 15	—— 34	—— 17
10	A	.... —— 35	—— 3, to v. 16	—— 40, to v. 12	—— 18, to v. 28
11	b	.... —— 40, v. 12	—— 3, v. 16 to 4, v. 7	—— 41, to v. 17	—— 18, v. 28
12	c	.... —— 41, v. 17	—— 4, v. 7	—— 42, to v. 18	—— 19, to v. 25
13	d	Lucy, Virg. & Martyr.. —— 42, v. 18 to 43, v. 8	—— 5	—— 43, v. 8	—— 19, v. 25
14	e	.... —— 44, to v. 21	2 John	—— 44, v. 21 to 45, v. 8	—— 20, to v. 19
15	f	.... —— 45, v. 8	3 John	—— 46	—— 20, v. 19
16	g	O Sapientia............ —— 47	Jude	—— 48	—— 21
17	A	.... —— 49, to v. 13	Rev. 1	—— 49, v. 13	Rev. 2, to v. 18
18	b	.... —— 50	—— 2, v. 18 to 3, v. 7	—— 51, to v. 9	—— 3, v. 7
19	c	.... —— 51, v. 9	—— 4	—— 52, to v. 13	—— 5
20	d	.... Fast —— 52, v. 13 & 53	—— 6	—— 54	—— 7
21	e	St. Thomas, Ap. & Mart.	....	....	....
22	f	.... —— 55	—— 8	—— 56	—— 10
23	g	.... —— 57	—— 11	—— 58	—— 12
24	A	.... Fast —— 59	—— 14	—— 60	—— 15
25	b	Christmas Day........	....	....	....
26	c	St. Stephen, Martyr....	....	....	....
27	d	St. John, Ap. & Evang.	....	....	....
28	e	Innocents' Day	—— 16	....	—— 18
29	f	.... —— 61	—— 19, to v. 11	—— 62	—— 19, v. 11
30	g	.... —— 63	—— 20	—— 64 & 65, to v. 8	—— 21, to v. 15
31	A	Silvester, Bishop ...... —— 65, v. 8	—— 21, v. 15 to 22, v. 6	—— 66	—— 22, v. 6

TABLES AND RULES

FOR THE MOVEABLE AND IMMOVEABLE FEASTS ; TOGETHER WITH THE DAYS OF
FASTING AND ABSTINENCE, THROUGH THE WHOLE YEAR.

RULES to know when the Moveable Feasts and Holy-days begin.

*E*ASTER-DAY (on which the rest depend) is always the First *Sunday* after the Full
Moon which happens upon, or next after the Twenty-first day of *March ;* and if the
Full Moon happens upon a *Sunday, Easter Day* is the *Sunday* after.

Advent Sunday is always the nearest *Sunday* to the Feast of *St. Andrew,* whether before
or after.

Septuagesima			Nine	
Sexagesima	*Sunday* is		Eight	Weeks before *Easter.*
Quinquagesima			Seven	
Quadragesima			Six	

Rogation Sunday		Five Weeks	
Ascension Day	is	Forty Days	after *Easter.*
Whitsunday		Seven Weeks	
Trinity Sunday		Eight Weeks	

A TABLE OF ALL THE FEASTS THAT ARE TO BE OBSERVED IN THE CHURCH OF ENGLAND THROUGHOUT THE YEAR.

All Sundays in the Year.

The Days of the Feasts of		The Days of the Feasts of
The Circumcision of our Lord JESUS CHRIST.		The Nativity of *St. John* Baptist.
The Epiphany.		*St. Peter* the Apostle.
The Conversion of *St. Paul.*		*St. James* the Apostle.
The Purification of the Blessed Virgin.		*St. Bartholomew* the Apostle.
St. Matthias the Apostle.		*St. Matthew* the Apostle.
The Annunciation of the Blessed Virgin.		*St. Michael* and all Angels.
St. Mark the Evangelist.		*St. Luke* the Evangelist.
St. Philip and *St. James* the Apostles.		*St. Simon* and *St. Jude,* Apostles.
The Ascension of our Lord JESUS CHRIST.		All Saints.
St. Barnabas.		*St. Andrew* the Apostle.
		St. Thomas the Apostle.
		The Nativity of our Lord.
		St. Stephen the Martyr.
		St. John the Evangelist.
		The Holy Innocents.

Monday and *Tuesday* in *Easter Week. Monday* and *Tuesday* in *Whitsun Week.*

A TABLE OF THE VIGILS, FASTS, AND DAYS OF ABSTINENCE, TO BE OBSERVED IN THE YEAR.

The Evens or Vigils before		The Evens or Vigils before
The Nativity of our Lord.		*St. John* Baptist.
The Purification of the Blessed Virgin *Mary.*		*St. Peter.— St. James.*
The Annunciation of the Blessed Virgin.		*St. Bartholomew.*
Easter Day.—Ascension Day.		*St. Matthew.*
Pentecost.—*St. Matthias.*		*St. Simon* and *St. Jude.*
		St. Andrew.—St. Thomas.
		All Saints.

Note, that if any of these Feast-Days fall upon a *Monday,* then the Vigil or Fast-Day shall
be kept upon the *Saturday,* and not upon the *Sunday* next before it.

Days of Fasting, or Abstinence.

I. The Forty Days of Lent.

II. The Ember Days at the Four Seasons, being the
Wednesday, Friday, and *Saturday* after ....
{
1. The First *Sunday* in Lent.
2. The Feast of *Pentecost.*
3. *September* 14.
4. *December* 13.
}

III. The Three *Rogation Days,* being the *Monday, Tuesday,* and *Wednesday,* before *Holy
Thursday,* or the *Ascension* of our LORD.

IV. All the *Fridays* in the Year, except CHRISTMAS DAY.

A Solemn Day, for which a particular Service is appointed.

The Twentieth Day of *June,* being the Day on which her Majesty began her happy Reign.

A TABLE TO FIND EASTER DAY,

Golden Number.	Days of the Month.	Sunday Letter.
XIV.	March 21	C
III.	—— 22	D
	—— 23	E
XI.	—— 24	F
	—— 25	G
XIX.	—— 26	A
VIII.	—— 27	B
	—— 28	C
XVI.	—— 29	D
V.	—— 30	E
	—— 31	F
XIII.	April 1	G
II.	—— 2	A
	—— 3	B
X.	—— 4	C
	—— 5	D
XVIII.	—— 6	E
VII.	—— 7	F
	—— 8	G
XV.	—— 9	A
IV.	—— 10	B
	—— 11	C
XII.	—— 12	D
I.	—— 13	E
	—— 14	F
IX.	—— 15	G
	—— 16	A
XVII.	—— 17	B
VI.	—— 18	C
	—— 19	D
	—— 20	E
	—— 21	F
	—— 22	G
	—— 23	A
	—— 24	B
	—— 25	C

THIS Table contains so much of the Calendar as is necessary for the determining of *Easter*; to find which, look for the Golden Number of the Year in the First Column of the Table, against which stands the Day of the Paschal Full Moon; then look in the Third Column for the Sunday Letter, next after the Day of the Full Moon, and the Day of the Month standing against that Sunday Letter is *Easter Day.* If the Full Moon happens upon a Sunday, then (according to the First Rule) the next Sunday after is *Easter Day.*

To find the Golden Number, or Prime, add one to the Year of Our Lord, and then divide by 19; the Remainder, if any, is the Golden Number; but if nothing remaineth, then 19 is the Golden Number.

To find the Dominical or Sunday Letter, according to the Calendar, until the Year 1799 inclusive, add to the Year of Our Lord its fourth part, omitting fractions; and also the number 1; Divide the sum by 7; and if there is no remainder, then A is the Sunday Letter: But if any number remaineth, then the Letter standing against that number in the small annexed Table is the Sunday Letter.

0	A
1	G
2	F
3	E
4	D
5	C
6	B

For the next Century, that is, from the Year 1800 till the Year 1899 inclusive, add to the current Year only its Fourth Part, and then divide by 7, and proceed as in the last Rule.

Note, that in all Bissextile or Leap-Years, the Letter found as above will be the Sunday Letter, from the intercalated Day exclusive to the end of the year.

Another TABLE to find EASTER till the Year 1899 inclusive.

SUNDAY LETTERS.

Golden Numb.	A	B	C	D	E	F	G
I.	April 16	—— 17	—— 18	19	—— 20	—— 14	—— 15
II.	April 9	—— 3	—— 4	5	—— 6	—— 7	—— 8
III.	Mar. 26	—— 27	—— 28	29	—— 23	—— 24	—— 25
IV.	April 16	—— 17	—— 11	12	—— 13	—— 14	—— 15
V.	April 2	—— 3	—— 4	5	—— 6	Mar. 31	April 1
VI.	April 23	—— 24	—— 25	19	—— 20	—— 21	—— 22
VII.	April 9	—— 10	—— 11	12	—— 13	—— 14	—— 8
VIII.	April 2	—— 3	Mar. 28	29	—— 30	—— 31	April 1
IX.	April 16	—— 17	—— 18	19	—— 20	—— 21	—— 22
X.	April 9	—— 10	—— 11	5	—— 6	—— 7	—— 8
XI.	Mar. 26	—— 27	—— 28	29	—— 30	—— 31	—— 25
XII.	April 16	—— 17	—— 18	19	—— 13	—— 14	—— 15
XIII.	April 2	—— 3	—— 4	5	—— 6	—— 7	—— 8
XIV.	Mar. 26	—— 27	—— 28	22	—— 23	—— 24	—— 25
XV.	April 16	—— 10	—— 11	12	—— 18	—— 14	—— 15
XVI.	April 2	—— 3	—— 4	5	Mar. 30	—— 31	April 1
XVII.	April 23	—— 24	—— 18	19	—— 20	—— 21	—— 22
XVIII.	April 9	—— 10	—— 11	12	—— 13	—— 7	—— 8
XIX.	April 2	Mar. 27	—— 28	29	—— 30	—— 31	April 1

TO make use of the preceding Table, find the Sunday Letter for the Year in the uppermost Line, and the Golden Number, or Prime, in the Column of Golden Numbers, and against the Prime, in the same Line under the Sunday Letter, you have the Day of the Month on which *Easter* falleth that Year. But note, that the Name of the Month is set on the Left Hand, or just with the Figure, and followeth not, as in other Tables, by Descent, but Collateral.

A TABLE OF THE MOVEABLE FEASTS

FOR FIFTY-ONE YEARS,

ACCORDING TO THE FOREGOING CALENDAR.

Year of our Lord.	The Golden Number.	The Epact.	Sunday Letter.	Sundays after Epiphany.	Septuagesima Sunday.	The First Day of Lent.	Easter Day.	Rogation Sunday.	Ascension Day.	Whitsunday.	Sundays after Trinity.	Advent Sunday.
1880	19	18	DC	2	Jan. 25	Feb. 11	Mar. 28	May 2	May 6	May 16	26	Nov. 28
1881	1	0	B	5	Feb. 13	Mar. 2	Apr. 17	— 22	— 26	June 5	23	— 27
1882	2	11	A	4	— 5	Feb. 22	— 9	— 14	May 18	May 28	25	Dec. 3
1883	3	22	G	2	Jan. 21	— 7	Mar. 25	Apr. 29	— 3	— 13	27	— 2
1884	4	3	FE	4	Feb. 10	— 27	Apr. 13	May 18	— 22	June 1	24	Nov. 30
1885	5	14	D	3	— 1	— 18	— 5	— 10	— 14	May 24	25	— 29
1886	6	25	C	6	— 21	Mar. 10	— 25	— 30	June 3	June 13	22	— 28
1887	7	6	B	4	— 6	Feb. 23	— 10	— 15	May 19	May 29	24	— 27
1888	8	17	AG	3	Jan. 29	— 15	— 1	— 6	— 10	— 20	26	Dec. 2
1889	9	28	F	5	Feb. 17	Mar. 6	— 21	— 26	— 30	June 9	23	— 1
1890	10	9	E	3	— 2	Feb. 19	— 6	— 11	— 15	May 25	25	Nov. 30
1891	11	20	D	2	Jan. 25	— 11	Mar. 29	— 3	— 7	— 17	26	— 29
1892	12	1	CB	5	Feb. 14	Mar. 2	Apr. 17	— 22	— 26	June 5	23	— 27
1893	13	12	A	3	Jan. 29	Feb. 15	— 2	— 7	— 11	May 21	26	Dec. 3
1894	14	23	G	2	— 21	— 7	Mar. 25	Apr. 29	— 3	— 13	27	— 2
1895	15	4	F	4	Feb. 10	— 27	Apr. 14	May 19	— 23	June 2	24	— 1
1896	16	15	ED	3	— 2	— 19	— 5	— 10	— 14	May 24	25	Nov. 29
1897	17	26	C	5	— 14	Mar. 3	— 18	— 23	— 27	June 6	23	— 28
1898	18	7	B	4	— 6	Feb. 23	— 10	— 15	— 19	May 29	24	— 27
1899	19	18	A	3	Jan. 29	— 15	— 2	— 7	— 11	— 21	26	Dec. 3
1900	1	29	G	5	Feb. 11	— 28	— 15	— 20	— 24	June 3	24	— 2
1901	2	10	F	3	— 3	— 20	— 7	— 12	— 16	May 26	25	— 1
1902	3	21	E	2	Jan. 26	— 12	Mar. 30	— 4	— 8	— 18	26	Nov. 30
1903	4	2	D	4	Feb. 8	— 25	Apr. 12	— 17	— 21	— 31	24	— 29
1904	5	13	CB	3	Jan. 31	— 17	— 3	— 8	— 12	— 22	25	— 27
1905	6	24	A	6	Feb. 19	Mar. 8	— 23	— 28	June 1	June 11	23	Dec. 3
1906	7	5	G	5	— 11	Feb. 28	— 15	— 20	May 24	— 3	24	— 2
1907	8	16	F	2	Jan. 27	— 13	Mar. 31	— 5	— 9	May 19	26	— 1
1908	9	27	ED	5	Feb. 16	Mar. 4	Apr. 19	— 24	— 28	June 7	23	Nov. 29
1909	10	8	C	4	— 7	Feb. 24	— 11	— 16	— 20	May 30	24	— 28
1910	11	19	B	2	Jan. 23	— 9	Mar. 27	— 1	— 5	— 15	26	— 27
1911	12	30	A	5	Feb. 12	Mar. 1	Apr. 16	— 21	— 25	June 4	24	Dec. 3
1912	13	11	GF	4	— 4	Feb. 21	— 7	— 12	— 16	May 26	25	— 1
1913	14	22	E	1	Jan. 19	— 5	Mar. 23	Apr. 27	— 1	— 11	27	Nov. 30
1914	15	3	D	4	Feb. 8	— 25	Apr. 12	May 17	— 21	— 31	24	— 29
1915	16	14	C	3	Jan. 31	— 17	— 4	— 9	— 13	— 23	25	— 28
1916	17	26	BA	6	Feb. 20	Mar. 8	— 23	— 28	June 1	June 11	23	Dec. 3
1917	18	6	G	4	— 4	Feb. 21	— 8	— 13	May 17	— 27	25	— 2
1918	19	17	F	2	Jan. 27	— 13	Mar. 31	— 5	— 9	May 19	26	— 1
1919	1	29	E	5	Feb. 16	Mar. 4	Apr. 20	— 25	— 29	June 8	23	Nov. 30
1920	2	10	DC	3	— 1	Feb. 18	— 4	— 9	— 13	May 23	25	— 28
1921	3	21	B	2	Jan. 23	— 9	Mar. 27	— 1	— 5	— 15	26	— 27
1922	4	2	A	5	Feb. 12	Mar. 1	Apr. 16	— 21	— 25	June 4	24	Dec. 3
1923	5	13	G	3	Jan. 28	Feb. 14	— 1	— 6	— 10	May 20	26	— 2
1924	6	24	FE	5	Feb. 17	Mar. 5	— 20	— 25	— 29	June 8	23	Nov. 30
1925	7	5	D	4	— 8	Feb. 25	— 12	— 17	— 21	May 31	24	— 29
1926	8	16	C	3	Jan. 31	— 17	— 4	— 9	— 13	— 23	25	— 28
1927	9	27	B	5	Feb. 13	Mar. 2	— 17	— 22	— 26	June 5	23	— 27
1928	10	8	AG	4	— 5	Feb. 22	— 8	— 13	— 17	May 27	25	Dec. 2
1929	11	19	F	2	Jan. 27	— 13	Mar. 31	— 5	— 9	— 19	26	— 1
1930	12	30	E	5	Feb. 16	Mar. 5	Apr. 20	— 25	— 29	June 8	23	Nov. 30

A

TABLE OF THE MOVEABLE FEASTS,

ACCORDING TO THE SEVERAL DAYS THAT EASTER CAN POSSIBLY FALL UPON.

Easter Day.	Sundays after Epiphany.	Septuagesima Sunday.	The First Day of Lent.	Rogation Sunday.	Ascension Day.	Whitsunday.	Sundays after Trinity.	Advent Sunday.
Mar. 22	1	Jan. 18	Feb. 4	April 26	April 30	May 10	27	Nov. 29
— 23	1	— 19	— 5	— 27	May 1	— 11	27	— 30
— 24	1	— 20	— 6	— 28	— 2	— 12	27	Dec. 1
— 25	2	— 21	— 7	— 29	— 3	— 13	27	— 2
— 26	2	— 22	— 8	— 30	— 4	— 14	27	— 3
— 27	2	— 23	— 9	May 1	— 5	— 15	26	Nov. 27
— 28	2	— 24	— 10	— 2	— 6	— 16	26	— 28
— 29	2	— 25	— 11	— 3	— 7	— 17	26	— 29
— 30	2	— 26	— 12	— 4	— 8	— 18	26	— 30
— 31	2	— 27	— 13	— 5	— 9	— 19	26	Dec. 1
April 1	3	— 28	— 14	— 6	— 10	— 20	26	— 2
— 2	3	— 29	— 15	— 7	— 11	— 21	26	— 3
— 3	3	— 30	— 16	— 8	— 12	— 22	25	Nov. 27
— 4	3	— 31	— 17	— 9	— 13	— 23	25	— 28
— 5	3	Feb. 1	— 18	— 10	— 14	— 24	25	— 29
— 6	3	— 2	— 19	— 11	— 15	— 25	25	— 30
— 7	3	— 3	— 20	— 12	— 16	— 26	25	Dec. 1
— 8	4	— 4	— 21	— 13	— 17	— 27	25	— 2
— 9	4	— 5	— 22	— 14	— 18	— 28	25	— 3
— 10	4	— 6	— 23	— 15	— 19	— 29	24	Nov. 27
— 11	4	— 7	— 24	— 16	— 20	— 30	24	— 28
— 12	4	— 8	— 25	— 17	— 21	— 31	24	— 29
— 13	4	— 9	— 26	— 18	— 22	June 1	24	— 30
— 14	4	— 10	— 27	— 19	— 23	— 2	24	Dec. 1
— 15	5	— 11	— 28	— 20	— 24	— 3	24	— 2
— 16	5	— 12	Mar. 1	— 21	— 25	— 4	24	— 3
— 17	5	— 13	— 2	— 22	— 26	— 5	23	Nov. 27
— 18	5	— 14	— 3	— 23	— 27	— 6	23	— 28
— 19	5	— 15	— 4	— 24	— 28	— 7	23	— 29
— 20	5	— 16	— 5	— 25	— 29	— 8	23	— 30
— 21	5	— 17	— 6	— 26	— 30	— 9	23	Dec. 1
— 22	6	— 18	— 7	— 27	— 31	— 10	23	— 2
— 23	6	— 19	— 8	— 28	June 1	— 11	23	— 3
— 24	6	— 20	— 9	— 29	— 2	— 12	22	Nov. 27
— 25	6	— 21	— 10	— 30	— 3	— 13	22	— 28

Note, That in a Bissextile or Leap-Year, the Number of *Sundays* after Epiphany will be the same, as if *Easter Day* had fallen One Day later than it really does. And for the same reason, One Day must, in every Leap-Year, be added to the Day of the Month given by the Table for *Septuagesima* Sunday: And the like must be done for the First Day of *Lent* (commonly called *Ash Wednesday*) unless the Table gives some Day in the Month of *March* for it; for in that case, the Day given by the Table is the right Day.

A TABLE TO FIND EASTER,

THE YEAR 1900 TO THE YEAR 2199 INCLUSIVE.

GOLDEN NUMBER.	DAY OF THE MONTH.		SUNDAY LETTER.
XIV.	March	22	D
III.	——	23	E
	——	24	F
XI.	——	25	G
	——	26	A
XIX.	——	27	B
VIII.	——	28	C
	——	29	D
XVI.	——	30	E
V.	——	31	F
	April	1	G
XIII.	——	2	A
II.	——	3	B
	——	4	C
X.	——	5	D
	——	6	E
XVIII.	——	7	F
VII.	——	8	G
	——	9	A
XV.	——	10	B
IV.	——	11	C
	——	12	D
XII.	——	13	E
I.	——	14	F
	——	15	G
IX.	——	16	A
XVII.	——	17	B
VI.	——	18	C
	——	19	D
	——	20	E
	——	21	F
	——	22	G
	——	23	A
	——	24	B
	——	25	C

THE Golden Numbers in the foregoing Calendar will point out the Days of the Paschal Full Moons, till the Year of our Lord 1900 ; at which time, in order that the Ecclesiastical Full Moons may fall nearly on the same days with the real Full Moons, the Golden Numbers must be removed to different Days of the Calendar, as is done in the annexed Table, which contains so much of the Calendar then to be used, as is necessary for finding the Paschal Full Moons, and the Feast of *Easter*, from the Year 1900, to the Year 2199 inclusive. This Table is to be made use of, in all respects, as the First Table before inserted, for finding *Easter* till the Year 1899.

GENERAL TABLES

FINDING THE DOMINICAL OR SUNDAY LETTER.

AND THE

PLACES OF THE GOLDEN NUMBERS IN THE CALENDAR.

TABLE I.

6	5	4	3	2	1	0
B	C	D	E	F	G	A
				1600	1700	1800
1900 2000	2100	2200	2300 2400	2500	2600	2700 2800
2900	3000	3100 3200	3300	3400	3500 3600	3700
3800	3900 4000	4100	4200	4300 4400	4500	4600
4700 4800	4900	5000	5100 5200	5300	5400	5500 5600
5700	5800	5900 6000	6100	6200	6300 6400	6500
6600	6700 6800	6900	7000	7100 7200	7300	7400
7500 7600	7700	7800	7900 8000	8100	8200	8300 8400
8500	&c.					

TO find the Dominical or Sunday Letter for any given Year of our Lord, add to the Year its fourth part, omitting fractions, and also the number, which in Table I. standeth at the top of the column, wherein the number of hundreds contained in that given year is found : Divide the sum by 7, and if there is no remainder, then A is the Sunday Letter ; but if any number remaineth, then the Letter, which standeth under that number at the top of the Table, is the Sunday Letter.

TABLE II.

I.	II.	III.	I.	II.	III.
	YEARS OF OUR LORD.			YEARS OF OUR LORD.	
B	1600	0	B	5200	15
	1700	1		5300	16
	1800	1		5400	17
	1900	2		5500	17
B	2000	2	B	5600	17
	2100	2		5700	18
	2200	3		5800	18
	2300	4		5900	19
B	2400	3	B	6000	19
	2500	4		6100	19
	2600	5		6200	20
	2700	5		6300	21
B	2800	5	B	6400	20
	2900	6		6500	21
	3000	6		6600	22
	3100	7		6700	23
B	3200	7	B	6800	22
	3300	7		6900	23
	3400	8		7000	24
	3500	9		7100	24
B	3600	8	B	7200	24
	3700	9		7300	25
	3800	10		7400	25
	3900	10		7500	26
B	4000	10	B	7600	26
	4100	11		7700	26
	4200	12		7800	27
	4300	12		7900	28
B	4400	12	B	8000	27
	4500	13		8100	28
	4600	13		8200	29
	4700	14		8300	29
B	4800	14	B	8400	29
	4900	14		8500	30
	5000	15		&c.	
	5100	16			

TO find the Month and Days of the Month to which the Golden Numbers ought to be prefixed in the Calendar, in any given Year of Our Lord, consisting of entire hundred years, and in all the intermediate years betwixt that and the next hundredth Year following, look in the second column of Table II. for the given Year consisting of entire hundreds, and Note the Number or Cypher which stands against it in the third column; then, in Table III. look for the same number in the Column under any given Golden Number, which when you have found, guide your eye side-ways to the left hand, and in the First Column you will find the Month and Day to which that Golden Number ought to be prefixed in the Calendar, during that period of one hundred years.

The Letter B prefixed to certain hundredth years in Table II. denotes those years which are still to be accounted Bissextile or Leap Years in the New Calendar; whereas all the other hundredth years are to be accounted only common years.

TABLE III.

PASCHAL FULL MOON	SUNDAY LETTER	\	THE GOLDEN NUMBERS.																
		1	2	3	4	5	6	7	8	9	10	11	12	13	14	15	16	17	18	19
March 21	C	8	19	0	11	22	3	14	25	6	17	28	9	20	1	12	23	4	15	26
March 22	D	9	20	1	12	23	4	15	26	7	18	29	10	21	2	13	24	5	16	27
March 23	E	10	21	2	13	24	5	16	27	8	19	0	11	22	3	14	25	6	17	28
March 24	F	11	22	3	14	25	6	17	28	9	20	1	12	23	4	15	26	7	18	29
March 25	G	12	23	4	15	26	7	18	29	10	21	2	13	24	5	16	27	8	19	0
March 26	A	13	24	5	16	27	8	19	0	11	22	3	14	25	6	17	28	9	20	1
March 27	B	14	25	6	17	28	9	20	1	12	23	4	15	26	7	18	29	10	21	2
March 28	C	15	26	7	18	29	10	21	2	13	24	5	16	27	8	19	0	11	22	3
March 29	D	16	27	8	19	0	11	22	3	14	25	6	17	28	9	20	1	12	23	4
March 30	E	17	28	9	20	1	12	23	4	15	26	7	18	29	10	21	2	13	24	5
March 31	F	18	29	10	21	2	13	24	5	16	27	8	19	0	11	22	3	14	25	6
April 1	G	19	0	11	22	3	14	25	6	17	28	9	20	1	12	23	4	15	26	7
April 2	A	20	1	12	23	4	15	26	7	18	29	10	21	2	13	24	5	16	27	8
April 3	B	21	2	13	24	5	16	27	8	19	0	11	22	3	14	25	6	17	28	9
April 4	C	22	3	14	25	6	17	28	9	20	1	12	23	4	15	26	7	18	29	10
April 5	D	23	4	15	26	7	18	29	10	21	2	13	24	5	16	27	8	19	0	11
April 6	E	24	5	16	27	8	19	0	11	22	3	14	25	6	17	28	9	20	1	12
April 7	F	25	6	17	28	9	20	1	12	23	4	15	26	7	18	29	10	21	2	13
April 8	G	26	7	18	29	10	21	2	13	24	5	16	27	8	19	0	11	22	3	14
April 9	A	27	8	19	0	11	22	3	14	25	6	17	28	9	20	1	12	23	4	15
April 10	B	28	9	20	1	12	23	4	15	26	7	18	29	10	21	2	13	24	5	16
April 11	C	29	10	21	2	13	24	5	16	27	8	19	0	11	22	3	14	25	6	17
April 12	D	0	11	22	3	14	25	6	17	28	9	20	1	12	23	4	15	26	7	18
April 13	E	1	12	23	4	15	26	7	18	29	10	21	2	13	24	5	16	27	8	19
April 14	F	2	13	24	5	16	27	8	19	0	11	22	3	14	25	6	17	28	9	20
April 15	G	3	14	25	6	17	28	9	20	1	12	23	4	15	26	7	18	29	10	21
April 16	A	4	15	26	7	18	29	10	21	2	13	24	5	16	27	8	19	0	11	22
April 17	B	5	16	27	8	19	0	11	22	3	14	25	6	17	28	9	20	1	12	23
April 17	B												7	18	29	10	21	2	13	24
April 18	C	6	17	28	9	20	1	12	23	4	15	26								
April 18	C	7	18	29	10	21	2	13	24	5	16	27	8	19	0	11	22	3	14	25

¶ THE ORDER FOR

MORNING AND EVENING PRAYER

DAILY TO BE SAID AND USED THROUGHOUT THE YEAR.

THE Morning and Evening Prayer shall be used in the accustomed Place of the Church, Chapel, or Chancel ; except it shall be otherwise determined by the Ordinary of the Place. And the Chancels shall remain as they have done in times past.

And here is to be noted, that such Ornaments of the Church, and of the Ministers thereof, at all Times of their Ministrations, shall be retained, and be in use, as were in this Church of *England*, by the Authority of Parliament, in the Second Year of the reign of King *Edward* the Sixth.

THE ORDER FOR

MORNING PRAYER

DAILY THROUGHOUT THE YEAR.

¶ *At the beginning of Morning Prayer the Minister shall read with a loud voice some one or more of these Sentences of the Scriptures that follow. And then he shall say that which is written after the said Sentences.*

WHEN the wicked man turneth away from his wickedness that he hath committed, and doeth that which is lawful and right, he shall save his soul alive. *Ezek.* xviii. 27.

I acknowledge my transgressions, and my sin is ever before me. *Psalm* li. 3.

Hide thy face from my sins, and blot out all mine iniquities. *Psalm* li. 9.

The sacrifices of God are a broken spirit: a broken and a contrite heart, O God, thou wilt not despise. *Psalm* li. 17.

Rend your heart, and not your garments, and turn unto the Lord your God: for he is gracious and merciful, slow to anger, and of great kindness, and repenteth him of the evil. *Joel* ii. 13.

To the Lord our God belong mercies and forgivenesses, though we have rebelled against him: neither have we obeyed the voice of the Lord our God, to walk in his laws which he set before us. *Dan.* ix. 9, 10.

O Lord, correct me, but with judgement; not in thine anger, lest thou bring me to nothing. *Jer.* x. 24. *Psalm* vi. 1.

Repent ye; for the Kingdom of heaven is at hand. *St. Matth.* iii. 2.

I will arise, and go to my father, and will say unto him, Father, I have sinned against heaven, and before thee, and am no more worthy to be called thy son. *St. Luke* xv. 18, 19.

Enter not into judgement with thy servant, O Lord; for in thy sight shall no man living be justified. *Psalm* cxliii. 2.

If we say that we have no sin, we deceive ourselves, and the truth is not in us: but, if we confess our sins, he is faithful and just to forgive us our sins, and to cleanse us from all unrighteousness. 1 *St. John* i. 8, 9.

D

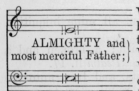 DEARLY beloved brethren, the Scripture moveth us in sundry places to acknowledge and confess our manifold sins and wickedness; and that we should not dissemble nor cloke them before the face of Almighty God our heavenly Father; but confess them with an humble, lowly, penitent, and obedient heart; to the end that we may obtain forgiveness of the same, by his infinite goodness and mercy. And although we ought at all times humbly to acknowledge our sins before God; yet ought we most chiefly so to do, when we assemble and meet together to render thanks for the great benefits that we have received at his hands, to set forth his most worthy praise, to hear his most holy Word, and to ask those things which are requisite and necessary, as well for the body as the soul. Wherefore I pray and beseech you, as many as are here present, to accompany me with a pure heart, and humble voice, unto the throne of the heavenly grace, saying after me;

¶ *A general Confession to be said of the whole Congregation after the Minister, all kneeling.*

ALMIGHTY and most merciful Father; We have erred, and strayed from thy ways like lost sheep. We have followed too much the devices and desires of our own hearts. We have offended against thy holy laws. We have left undone those things which we ought to have done; And we have done those things which we ought not to have done; And there is no health in us. But thou, O Lord, have mercy upon us, miserable offenders. Spare thou them, O God, which confess their faults. Restore thou them that are penitent; According to thy promises declared unto mankind in Christ Jesu our Lord. And grant, O most merciful Father, for his sake; That we may hereafter live a godly, righteous, and sober life, To the glory of thy holy Name.

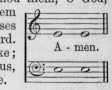

A - men.

¶ *The Absolution, or Remission of sins, to be pronounced by the Priest alone, standing; the people still kneeling.*

 ALMIGHTY God, the Father of our Lord Jesus Christ, who desireth not the death of a sinner, but rather that he may turn from his wickedness, and live; and hath given power, and commandment, to his Ministers, to declare and pronounce to his people, being penitent, the Absolution and Remission of their sins: He pardoneth and absolveth all them that truly repent, and unfeignedly believe his holy Gospel. Wherefore let us beseech him to grant us true repentance, and his Holy Spirit, that those things may please him, which we do at this present; and that the rest of our life hereafter may be pure, and holy; so that at the last we may come to his eternal joy; through Jesus Christ our Lord.

¶ *The people shall answer here, and at the end of all other prayers,*

A - men.

¶ *Then the Minister shall kneel, and say the Lord's Prayer with an audible voice; the people also kneeling, and repeating it with him, both here, and wheresoever else it is used in Divine Service.*

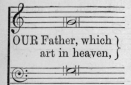

OUR Father, which art in heaven,

Hallowed be thy Name. Thy kingdom come. Thy will be done in earth, As it is in heaven. Give us this day our daily bread. And forgive us our trespasses, As we forgive them that trespass against us. And lead us not into temptation; But deliver us from evil: For thine is the kingdom, The power, and the glory, For ever and ever.

A - men.

¶ *Then likewise he shall say,* *

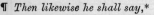

O Lord, o - pen thou our lips.

Answer.

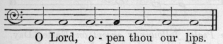

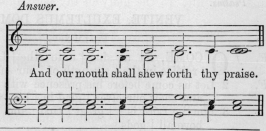

And our mouth shall shew forth thy praise.

* Tallis's Festal Responses will be found on p. 2 of the Appendix.

D 2

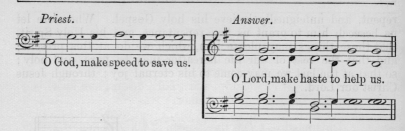

Priest.
O God, make speed to save us.

Answer.
O Lord, make haste to help us.

¶ *Here all standing up, the Priest shall say,*

Glory be to the Father, and to the Son : and to the Holy Ghost ;

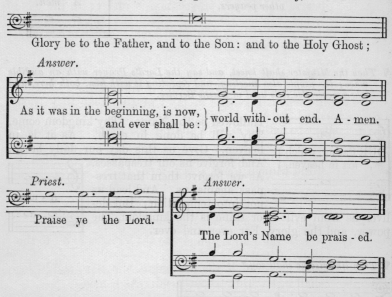

Answer.
As it was in the beginning, is now, and ever shall be : world with-out end. A - men.

Priest.
Praise ye the Lord.

Answer.
The Lord's Name be prais - ed.

¶ *Then shall be said or sung this Psalm following : except on* Easter Day, *upon which another Anthem is appointed ; and on the Nineteenth Day of every Month it is not to be read here, but in the ordinary course of the Psalms.*

VENITE, EXULTEMUS DOMINO.

Psalm xcv.

F. *f* O COME, let us síng | unto . the | Lord : let us heartily rejóice in the | strength of | our sal- | -vation.

F. 2 Let us come before his présence with | thanks- | -giving : and shéw ourselves | glad in | him with | Psalms.

3 For the Lórd is a | great | God : and a gréat | King a- | bove all | gods.

4 In his hand are all the córners | of the | earth : and the
strength of the | hills is | his | also.

2nd part. 5 The séa is his, | and he | made it : and his hánds pre- |
pared . the | dry | land.

mf 6 O come, let us wórship, and | fall | down : and knéel be- |
fore the | Lord our | Maker.

7 For hé is the | Lord our | God : and we are the people of
his pasture * ánd the | sheep of | his | hand.

8 To-day if ye will hear his voice * hárden | not your |
hearts : as in the provocation * and as in the dáy of
tempt- | -ation | in the | wilderness ;

9 When your fáthers .| tempted | me : próved | me and |
saw my | works.

10 Forty years long was I grieved with thís gener- | -ation .
and | said : It is a people that do err in their hearts *
fór they | have not | known my | ways.

11 Unto whom I swáre | in my | wrath : that they shóuld
not | enter | into . my | rest.

F. f Glory be to the Fáther, | and . to the | Son : ánd | to the |
Holy | Ghost ;

F. As it was in the beginning * is nów, and | ever | shall be :
wórld without | end. | A- | -men.

¶ *Then shall follow the Psalms in order as they are appointed. And at the
end of every Psalm throughout the Year, and likewise at the end of* Bene-
dicite, Benedictus, Magnificat, *and* Nunc dimittis, *shall be repeated,*

Glory be to the Fáther, | and . to the | Son : ánd | to the |
Holy | Ghost ;
Answer. As it was in the beginning * is nów, and | ever |
shall be : wórld without | end. | A- | -men.

¶ *Then shall be read distinctly with an audible voice the First Lesson, taken
out of the Old Testament, as is appointed in the Calendar, except there be
proper Lessons assigned for that day : He that readeth so standing and
turning himself, as he may best be heard of all such as are present. And
after that, shall be said or sung, in* English, *the Hymn called* Te Deum
Laudamus, *daily throughout the Year.*

¶ NOTE. *That before every Lesson the Minister shall say,* Here beginneth such
a Chapter, *or* Verse of such a Chapter, of such a Book : *And after every
Lesson,* Here endeth the First, *or* the Second Lesson.

*TE DEUM LAUDAMUS.

F. f **W**E práise | thee O | God : we acknówledge | thee to | be
the | Lord.

F. 2 All the éarth doth | worship | thee : thé | Father | ever- |
lasting.

---

* The Ambrosian Te Deum (harmonized), after Merbecke, will be found on p. 9 of
the Appendix.

3 To thee all A'ngels | cry a- | -loud : the Héavens, and | all the | Powers there- | -in.

4 To thee Chérubin, and | Seraph- | -in : cón- | -tinual- | -ly do | cry,

5 Hóly, | Holy | Holy : Lórd | God of | Saba- | -oth ;

6 Heaven and earth are fúll of the | Majes- | -ty : óf | thy | Glo- | -ry.

7 The glorious cómpany | of . the A- | -postles : práise | — | — | thee.

8 The goodly féllowship | of the | Prophets : práise | — | — | thee.

2nd part. 9 The nóble | army . of | Martyrs : práise | — | — | thee.

10 The holy Chúrch throughout | all the | world : dóth ac- | know- | -ledge | thee ;

11 Thé | Fa- | -ther : óf an | infinite | Majes- | -ty ;

12 Thine hónour- | -able | true : ánd | on- | — -ly | Son ;

13 A'lso the | Holy | Ghost : thé | Com- | -fort- | -er.

14 Thóu art the | King of | Glory : O' | — | — | Christ.

15 Thou art the éver- | -lasting | Son : óf | the | Fa- | -ther.

mf 16 When thou tookest upón thee to de- | -liver | man : thou dídst not ab- | -hor the | Virgin's | womb.

17 When thou hadst overcóme the ' sharpness . of | death : thou didst open the Kíngdom of | Heaven to | all be- | -lievers.

18 Thou sittest at the ríght | hand of | God : ín the | Glory | of the | Father.

19 We belíeve that | thou shalt | come : tó | be | our | Judge.

20 We therefore práy thee, | help thy | servants : whom thou hast redéemed | with thy | precious | blood.

21 Make them to be númbered | with thy | Saints : ín | glory | ever- | -lasting.

22 O Lórd, | save thy | people : ánd | bless thine | herit- | -age.

23 Góv- | — -ern | them : ánd | lift them | up for | ever.

F. f 24 Dáy | by | day : wé | magni- | -fy | thee ;

F. 25 A'nd we | worship . thy | Name : éver | world with- | out | end.

mf 26 Vóuch- | -safe O | Lord : to kéep us this | day with- | out | sin.

27 O Lórd, have | mercy . up- | -on us : háve | mer- | -cy up- | on us.

28 O Lord, let thy mércy | lighten . up- | -on us : ás our | trust | is in | thee.

29 O Lord, in thée | have I | trusted : lét me | never | be con- | -founded.

¶ *Or this Canticle.*

BENEDICITE, OMNIA OPERA.

mf **O** ALL ye Works of the Lórd, | bless . ye the | Lord :
F. *f* práise him, and | magnify | him for | ever.

F. 2 O ye Angels of the Lórd, | bless . ye the | Lord : práise
him, and | magnify | him for | ever.

3 O ye Héavens, | bless . ye the | Lord : práise him, and |
magnify | him for | ever.

4 O ye Waters that be above the Fírmament, | bless . ye the |
Lord : práise him, and | magnify | him for | ever.

5 O all ye Powers of the Lórd, | bless . ye the | Lord : práise
him, and | magnify | him for | ever.

6 O ye Sun and Móon, | bless . ye the | Lord : práise him,
and | magnify | him for | ever.

7 O ye Stars of Héaven, | bless . ye the | Lord : práise him,
and | magnify | him for | ever.

8 O ye Showers and Déw, | bless . ye the | Lord : práise him,
and | magnify | him for | ever.

9 O ye Winds of Gód, | bless . ye the | Lord : práise him,
and | magnify | him for | ever.

10 O ye Fire and Héat, | bless . ye the | Lord : práise him,
and | magnify | him for | ever.

11 O ye Winter and Súmmer, | bless . ye the | Lord : práise
him, and | magnify | him for | ever.

12 O ye Dews and Frósts, | bless . ye the | Lord : práise him,
and | magnify | him for | ever.

13 O ye Frost and Cóld, | bless . ye the | Lord : práise him,
and | magnify | him for | ever.

14 O ye Ice and Snów, | bless . ye the | Lord : práise him,
and | magnify | him for | ever.

15 O ye Nights and Dáys, | bless . ye the | Lord : práise him,
and | magnify | him for | ever.

16 O ye Light and Dárkness, | bless . ye the | Lord : práise
him, and | magnify | him for | ever.

17 O ye Lightnings and Clóuds, | bless . ye the | Lord : práise
him, and | magnify | him for | ever.

18 O let the Eárth | bless the | Lord : yea, let it práise him,
and | magnify | him for | ever.

19 O ye Mountains and Hílls, | bless . ye the | Lord : práise
him, and | magnify | him for | ever.

20 O all ye Green Things upon the Eárth, | bless . ye the |
Lord : práise him, and | magnify | him for | ever.

21 O ye Wélls, | bless . ye the | Lord : práise him, and |
magnify | him for | ever

22 O ye Seas and Flóods, | bless . ye the | Lord : práise him, and | magnify | him for | ever.

23 O ye Whales, and all that move in the Wáters, | bless . ye the | Lord : práise him, and | magnify | him for | ever.

24 O all ye Fowls of the Aír, | bless . ye the | Lord : práise him, and | magnify | him for | ever.

25 O all ye Beasts and Cáttle, | bless . ye the | Lord : práise him, and | magnify | him for | ever.

26 O ye Children of Mén, | bless . ye the | Lord : práise him, and | magnify | him for | ever.

27 O let I'srael | bless the | Lord : práise him, and | magnify | him for | ever.

28 O ye Priests of the Lórd, | bless . ye the | Lord : práise him, and | magnify | him for | ever.

29 O ye Servants of the Lórd, | bless . ye the | Lord : práise him, and | magnify | him for | ever.

30 O ye Spirits and Souls of the Ríghteous, | bless . ye the | Lord : práise him, and | magnify | him for | ever.

31 O ye holy and humble Men of héart, | bless . ye the | Lord : práise him, and | magnify | him for | ever.

32 O Ananias, Azarias, and Mísael, | bless . ye the | Lord : práise him, and | magnify | him for | ever.

F. *f*   Glory be to the Fáther, | and . to the | Son : ánd | to the | Holy | Ghost ;

F.   As it was in the beginning * is nów, and | ever | shall be : wórld without | end. | A- | -men.

¶ *Then shall be read in like manner the Second Lesson, taken out of the New Testament. And after that, the Hymn following ; except when that shall happen to be read in the Chapter for the Day, or for the Gospel on* St. John Baptist's *Day.*

BENEDICTUS.

St. Luke i. 68.

F. mf   BLESSED be the Lórd | God of | Israel : for he hath vísited, | and re- | -deemed . his | people ;

F.   2 And hath raised up a míghty sal- | -vation | for us : in the hóuse | of his | servant | David ;

3 As he spake by the móuth of his | holy | Prophets : which have béen | since the | world be- | -gan ;

4 That we should be sáved | from our | enemies : and fróm the | hands of | all that | hate us ;

5 To perform the mercy prómised | to our | forefathers : ánd to re- | -member . his | holy | Covenant ;

6 To perform the oath which he sware to our | forefather |
Abraham : that | he would | give | us ;

7 That we being delivered out of the hand | of our | enemies :
might serve | him with- | -out | fear ;

8 In holiness and righteous- | -ness be- | -fore him : all
the | days | of our | life.

9 And thou Child, shalt be called the Prophet | of the |
Highest : for thou shalt go before the face of the Lord |
to pre- | -pare his | ways ;

10 To give knowledge of salvation | unto . his | people : for
the re- | -mission | of their | sins,

11 Through the tender mercy | of our | God : whereby the
day-spring from on | high hath | visited | us ;

12 To give light to them that sit in darkness * and in the |
shadow . of | death : and to guide our feet | into . the |
way of | peace.

F. *f*   Glory be to the Father, | and . to the | Son : and | to the |
Holy | Ghost ;

F.   As it was in the beginning * is now, and | ever | shall be :
world without | end. | A- | -men.

¶ *Or this Psalm.*

JUBILATE DEO.

Psalm c.

F. *f* O BE joyful in the Lord, | all ye | lands : serve the Lord
with gladness * and come before his | presence | with
a | song.

F.   2 Be ye sure that the Lord | he is | God : it is he that hath
made us, and not we ourselves * we are his people, and
the | sheep of | his | pasture.

3 O go your way into his gates with thanksgiving * and
into his | courts with | praise : be thankful unto him,
and | speak good | of his | Name.

mf 4 For the Lord is gracious * his mercy is | ever- | -lasting :
and his truth endureth from gener- | -ation . to | gener- |
ation.

F. *f*   Glory be to the Father, | and . to the | Son : and | to the |
Holy | Ghost ;

F.   As it was in the beginning * is now, and | ever | shall be :
world without | end. | A- | -men.

¶ Then shall be sung or said the Apostles' Creed by the Minister and the people, standing : except only such days as the Creed of St. Athanasius is appointed to be read.

I BELIEVE in God the Father Almighty, Maker of heaven and earth : And in Jesus Christ his only Son our Lord, Who was conceived by the Holy Ghost, Born of the Virgin Mary, Suffered under Pontius Pilate, Was crucified, dead, and buried, He descended into hell ; The third day he rose again from the dead, He ascended into heaven, And sitteth on the right hand of God the Father Almighty ; From thence he shall come to judge the quick and the dead. I believe in the Holy Ghost ; The holy Catholick Church ; The Communion of Saints ; The Forgiveness of sins ; The Resurrection of the body, And the life everlasting.

A - men.

¶ And after that, these Prayers following, all devoutly kneeling ; the Minister first pronouncing with a loud voice,

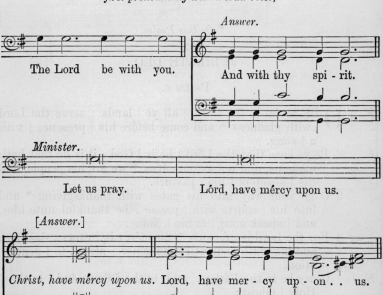

The Lord be with you.

Answer.

And with thy spi - rit.

Minister.

Let us pray. Lórd, have mércy upon us.

[Answer.]

Christ, have mércy upon us. Lord, have mer - cy up - on . . us.

¶ *Then the Minister, Clerks, and people, shall say the Lord's Prayer with a loud voice.*

OUR Father, which art in heaven, Hallowed be thy Name. Thy kingdom come. Thy will be done in earth, As it is in heaven. Give us this day our daily bread. And forgive us our trespasses, As we forgive them that trespass against us. And lead us not into temptation; But deliver us from evil.

A - men.

¶ *Then the Priest standing up shall say,*

O Lord, shew thy mer - cy up - on us.

Answer.

And grant us thy sal - va - tion.

Priest.

O Lord, save the Queen.

Answer.

And mercifully hear us when we call up - on . . thee.

Priest.

Endue thy Ministers with right - eous - ness.

Answer.

And make thy chosen peo - ple joy - ful.

Priest. O Lord, save thy peo-ple.

Answer. And bless thine in-her-it-ance.

Priest. Give peace in our time, O Lord.

Answer. Because there is none other that fighteth for us, but on-ly thou, O . . God.

Priest. O God, make clean our hearts with-in us.

Answer. [*Soft and slow.*] And take not thy Ho-ly Spir-it from us.

¶ *Then shall follow three Collects; the first of the Day, which shall be the same that is appointed at the Communion; the second for Peace; the third for Grace to live well. And the two last Collects shall never alter, but daily be said at Morning Prayer throughout all the Year, as followeth; all kneeling.*

[*After each Collect, or Prayer.*]

A - men.

THE SECOND COLLECT, FOR PEACE.

O GOD, who art the author of peace and lover of concord, in knowledge of whom standeth our eternal life, whose service is perfect freedom; Defend us thy humble servants in all assaults of our enemies; that we, surely trusting in thy defence, may not fear the power of any adversaries; through the might of Jesus Christ our Lord. *Amen.*

THE THIRD COLLECT, FOR GRACE.

O LORD, our heavenly Father, Almighty and everlasting God, who hast safely brought us to the beginning of this day; Defend us in the same with thy mighty power; and grant that this day we fall into no sin, neither run into any kind of danger; but that all our doings may be ordered by thy governance, to do always that is righteous in thy sight; through Jesus Christ our Lord. *Amen.*

¶ *In Quires and Places where they sing, here followeth the Anthem.*

¶ *Then these five Prayers following are to be read here, except when the Litany is read; and then only the two last are to be read, as they are there placed.*

A PRAYER FOR THE QUEEN'S MAJESTY.

O LORD our heavenly Father, high and mighty, King of kings, Lord of lords, the only Ruler of princes, who dost from thy throne behold all the dwellers upon earth; Most heartily we beseech thee with thy favour to behold our most gracious Sovereign Lady, Queen *VICTORIA;* and so replenish her with the grace of thy Holy Spirit, that she may alway incline to thy will, and walk in thy way: Endue her plenteously with heavenly gifts; grant her in health and wealth long to live; strengthen her that she may vanquish and overcome all her enemies; and finally, after this life, she may attain everlasting joy and felicity; through Jesus Christ our Lord. *Amen.*

A PRAYER FOR THE ROYAL FAMILY.

A LMIGHTY God, the fountain of all goodness, we humbly beseech thee to bless *Albert Edward* Prince of *Wales,* the Princess of *Wales,* and all the Royal Family: Endue them with thy Holy Spirit ; enrich them with thy heavenly grace ; prosper them with all happiness ; and bring them to thine everlasting kingdom ; through Jesus Christ our Lord. *Amen.*

A PRAYER FOR THE CLERGY AND PEOPLE.

A LMIGHTY and everlasting God, who alone workest great marvels ; Send down upon our Bishops, and Curates, and all Congregations committed to their charge, the healthful Spirit of thy grace ; and that they may truly please thee, pour upon them the continual dew of thy blessing. Grant this, O Lord, for the honour of our Advocate and Mediator, Jesus Christ. *Amen.*

A PRAYER OF ST. CHRYSOSTOM.

A LMIGHTY God, who hast given us grace at this time with one accord to make our common supplications unto thee ; and dost promise, that when two or three are gathered together in Thy Name thou wilt grant their requests : Fulfil now, O Lord, the desires and petitions of thy servants, as may be most expedient for them ; granting us in this world knowledge of thy truth, and in the world to come life everlasting. *Amen.*

2 *Cor.* xiii.

T HE grace of our Lord Jesus Christ, and the love of God, and the fellowship of the Holy Ghost, be with us all evermore. *Amen.*

Here endeth the Order of Morning Prayer throughout the Year.

THE ORDER FOR
EVENING PRAYER
DAILY THROUGHOUT THE YEAR.

¶ *At the beginning of Evening Prayer the Minister shall read with a loud voice some one or more of these Sentences of the Scriptures that follow. And then he shall say that which is written after the said Sentences.*

WHEN the wicked man turneth away from his wickedness that he hath committed, and doeth that which is lawful and right, he shall save his soul alive. *Ezek.* xviii. 27.

I acknowledge my transgressions, and my sin is ever before me. *Psalm* li. 3.

Hide thy face from my sins, and blot out all mine iniquities. *Psalm* li. 9.

The sacrifices of God are a broken spirit : a broken and a contrite heart, O God, thou wilt not despise. *Psalm* li. 17.

Rend your heart, and not your garments, and turn unto the Lord your God : for he is gracious and merciful, slow to anger, and of great kindness, and repenteth him of the evil. *Joel* ii. 13.

To the Lord our God belong mercies and forgivenesses, though we have rebelled against him : neither have we obeyed the voice of the Lord our God, to walk in his laws which he set before us. *Dan.* ix. 9, 10.

O Lord, correct me, but with judgement ; not in thine anger, lest thou bring me to nothing. *Jer.* x. 24. *Psalm* vi. 1.

Repent ye ; for the Kingdom of heaven is at hand. *St. Matth.* iii. 2.

I will arise, and go to my father, and will say unto him, Father, I have sinned against heaven, and before thee, and am no more worthy to be called thy son. *St. Luke* xv. 18, 19.

Enter not into judgement with thy servant, O Lord ; for in thy sight shall no man living be justified. *Psalm* cxliii. 2.

If we say that we have no sin, we deceive ourselves, and the truth is not in us : but, if we confess our sins, he is faithful and just to forgive us our sins, and to cleanse us from all unrighteousness. 1 *St. John* i. 8, 9.

DEARLY beloved brethren, the Scripture moveth us in sundry places to acknowledge and confess our manifold sins and wickedness ; and that we should not dissemble nor cloke them before the face of Almighty God our heavenly

Father; but confess them with an humble, lowly, penitent, and obedient heart; to the end that we may obtain forgiveness of the same, by his infinite goodness and mercy. And although we ought at all times humbly to acknowledge our sins before God; yet ought we most chiefly so to do, when we assemble and meet together to render thanks for the great benefits that we have received at his hands, to set forth his most worthy praise, to hear his most holy Word, and to ask those things which are requisite and necessary, as well for the body as the soul. Wherefore I pray and beseech you, as many as are here present, to accompany me with a pure heart, and humble voice, unto the throne of the heavenly grace, saying after me;

¶ *A General Confession to be said of the whole Congregation after the Minister, all kneeling.*

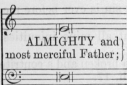

ALMIGHTY and most merciful Father; We have erred, and strayed from thy ways like lost sheep. We have followed too much the devices and desires of our own hearts. We have offended against thy holy laws. We have left undone those things which we ought to have done; And we have done those things which we ought not to have done; And there is no health in us. But thou, O Lord, have mercy upon us, miserable offenders. Spare thou them, O God, which confess their faults. Restore thou them that are penitent; According to thy promises declared unto mankind in Christ Jesu our Lord. And grant, O most merciful Father, for his sake; That we may hereafter live a godly, righteous, and sober life, to the glory of thy holy Name.

A - men.

¶ *The Absolution, or Remission of sins, to be pronounced by the Priest alone, standing; the people still kneeling.*

ALMIGHTY God, the Father of our Lord Jesus Christ, who desireth not the death of a sinner, but rather that he may turn from his wickedness, and live; and hath given power, and commandment, to his Ministers, to declare and pronounce to his people, being penitent, the Absolution and Remission of their sins: He pardoneth and absolveth all them that truly repent, and unfeignedly believe his holy Gospel. Wherefore let us beseech him to grant us true repentance, and his Holy Spirit, that those things may please him, which we do at this present; and that the rest of our life hereafter may be pure, and holy; so that at the last we may come to his eternal joy; through Jesus Christ our Lord.

A - men.

¶ *Then the Minister shall kneel, and say the Lord's Prayer; the people also kneeling, and repeating it with him.*

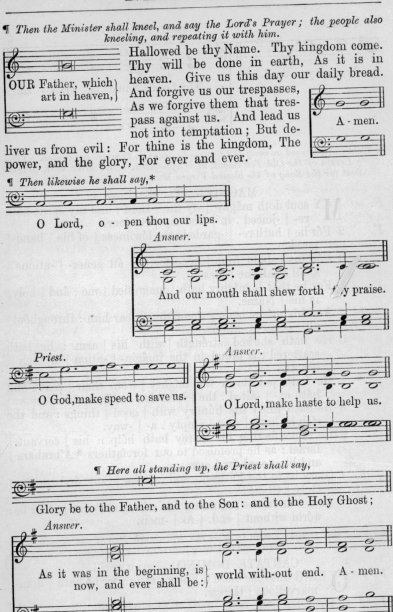

OUR Father, which art in heaven, Hallowed be thy Name. Thy kingdom come. Thy will be done in earth, As it is in heaven. Give us this day our daily bread. And forgive us our trespasses, As we forgive them that trespass against us. And lead us not into temptation; But deliver us from evil: For thine is the kingdom, The power, and the glory, For ever and ever. A-men.

¶ *Then likewise he shall say,**

O Lord, o - pen thou our lips.

Answer.

And our mouth shall shew forth thy praise.

Priest.

O God, make speed to save us.

Answer.

O Lord, make haste to help us.

¶ *Here all standing up, the Priest shall say,*

Glory be to the Father, and to the Son: and to the Holy Ghost;

Answer.

As it was in the beginning, is now, and ever shall be: world with-out end. A-men.

* Tallis's Festal Responses will be found on p. 2 of the Appendix.

E

Priest.

Praise ye the Lord.

Answer.

The Lord's Name be prais - ed.

¶ *Then shall be said or sung the Psalms in order as they are appointed. Then a Lesson of the Old Testament, as is appointed. And after that, Magnificat (or the Song of the blessed Virgin* Mary) *in English, as followeth.*

MAGNIFICAT. St. Luke i.

F. mf MY soul doth magni- | -fy the | Lord : and my spirit hath re- | -joiced . in | God my | Saviour.

F. 2 For he | hath re- | -garded : the lowliness | of his | hand- | maiden.

3 For be- | -hold from | henceforth : all gener- | -ations . shall | call me | blessed.

4 For he that is mighty hath | magnified | me : and | holy | is his | Name.

2nd part. 5 And his mercy is on | them that | fear him : throughout | all | gener- | -ations.

6 He hath shewed strength | with his | arm : he hath scattered the proud in the imagin- | -ation | of their | hearts.

7 He hath put down the mighty | from their | seat : and hath ex- | -alted . the | humble . and | meek.

8 He hath filled the hungry with | good | things : and the rich he hath | sent | empty . a- | -way.

9 He remembering his mercy hath holpen his | servant. | Israel : as he promised to our forefathers * A'braham | and his | seed for | ever.

F. f Glory be to the Father, | and . to the | Son : and | to the | Holy | Ghost ;

F. As it was in the beginning * is now, and | ever | shall be : world without | end. | A- | -men.

¶ *Or else this Psalm; except it be on the Nineteenth Day of the Month, when it is read in the ordinary course of the Psalms.*

CANTATE DOMINO. Psalm xcviii.

F. f O SING unto the Lord a | new | song : for he hath | done | marvellous | things.

F. 2 With his own right hand * and with his | holy | arm : hath he | gotten . him- | -self the | victory.

3 The Lord declåred | his sal- | -vation : his righteousness
   hath he openly shéwed in the | sight | of the | heathen.

4 He hath remembered his mercy and truth tóward the |
   house of | Israel : and all the ends of the world have
   séen the sal- | -vation | of our | God.

5 Shew yourselves joyful unto the Lórd, | all ye | lands :
   síng, re- | -joice and | give | thanks.

6 Praise the Lórd up- | -on the | harp : sing to the hárp
   with a | psalm of | thanks- | -giving.

7 With trúmpets | also and | shawms : O shew yourselves
   jóyful be- | -fore the | Lord the | King.

8 Let the sea make a noise * and åll that | therein | is : the
   round wórld, and | they that | dwell there- | -in.

9 Let the floods clap their hands * and let the hills be joyful
   togéther be- | -fore the | Lord : fór he | cometh . to |
   judge the | earth.

10 With righteousness shåll he | judge the | world : ånd the |
   people | with | equity.

F. *f*   Glory be to the Fáther, | and . to the | Son : ånd | to the |
         Holy | Ghost;

F.   As it was in the beginning * is nów, and | ever | shall be :
         wórld without | end. | A- | -men.

¶ *Then a Lesson of the New Testament, as it is appointed. And after that,*
Nunc dimittis (*or the Song of* Simeon) *in English, as followeth.*

NUNC DIMITTIS. St. Luke ii. 29.

F. *mp* L ORD, now lettest thou thy sérvant de- | -part in | peace :
        åc- | -cording | to thy | word,

2 Fór mine | eyes have | seen : thý | — sal- | -va- | -tion,

3 Whích thou | hast pre- | -pared : befóre the | face of |
   all | people;

4 To be a líght to | lighten . the | Gentiles : and to be the
   glóry | of thy | people | Israel.

F. *f*   Glory be to the Fáther, | and . to the | Son : ånd | to the |
         Holy | Ghost;

F.   As it was in the beginning * is nów, and | ever | shall be :
         wórld without | end. | A- | -men.

¶ *Or else this Psalm ; except it be on the Twelfth Day of the Month.*

DEUS MISEREATUR. Psalm lxvii.

F. *mf* G OD be merciful únto | us and | bless us : and shew us the
        light of his countenance * ånd be | merciful | unto | us :

F.   2 That thy way may be knówn up- | -on | earth : thy
         såving | health a- | -mong all | nations.

E 2

F. 3 Let the people práise | thee O | God : yéa, let | all the | people | praise thee.

4 O let the nations rejóice | and be | glad : for thou shalt judge the folk righteously * and góvern the | nations . up- | -on | earth.

F. 5 Let the people práise | thee O | God : yéa, let | all the | people | praise thee.

6 Then shall the éarth bring | forth her | increase : and God, even our own Gód, shall | give | us his | blessing.

2nd part. 7 Gód | shall | bless us : and all the énds of the | world shall | fear | him.

F. f Glory be to the Fáther, | and . to the | Son : ánd | to the | Holy | Ghost ;

F. As it was in the beginning * is nów, and | ever | shall be : wórld without | end. | A- | -men.

¶ *Then shall be said or sung the Apostles' Creed by the Minister and the people, standing.*

I BELIEVE in God) the Father Almighty,) Maker of heaven and earth : And in Jesus Christ his only Son our Lord, Who was conceived by the Holy Ghost, Born of the Virgin Mary, Suffered under Pontius Pilate, Was crucified, dead, and buried. He descended into hell; The third day he rose again from the dead, He ascended into heaven, And sitteth on the right hand of God the Father Almighty ; From thence he shall come to judge the quick and the dead.

I believe in the Holy Ghost ; The holy Catholick Church ; The Communion of Saints ; The Forgiveness of sins ; The Resurrection of the body, And the life everlasting.

A - men.

¶ *And after that, these Prayers following, all devoutly kneeling ; the Minister first pronouncing with a loud voice,*

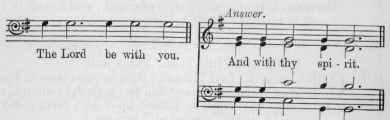

The Lord be with you.

Answer.

And with thy spi - rit.

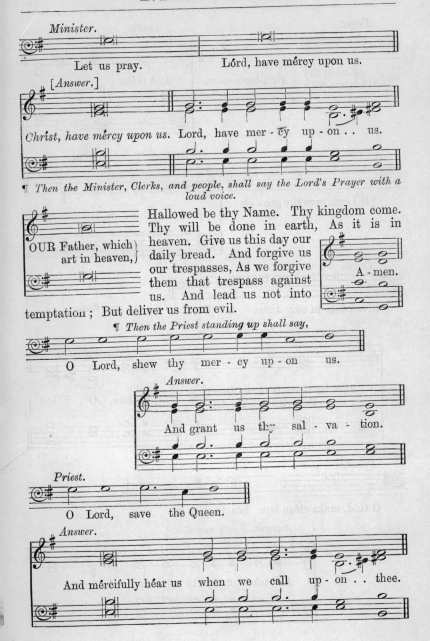

Minister.

Let us pray. Lord, have mercy upon us.

[Answer.]

Christ, have mercy upon us. Lord, have mer - cy up - on . . us.

¶ *Then the Minister, Clerks, and people, shall say the Lord's Prayer with a loud voice.*

OUR Father, which art in heaven, Hallowed be thy Name. Thy kingdom come. Thy will be done in earth, As it is in heaven. Give us this day our daily bread. And forgive us our trespasses, As we forgive them that trespass against us. And lead us not into temptation ; But deliver us from evil.

A - men.

¶ *Then the Priest standing up shall say,*

O Lord, shew thy mer - cy up - on us.

Answer.

And grant us thy sal - va - tion.

Priest.

O Lord, save the Queen.

Answer.

And mercifully hear us when we call up - on . . thee.

¶ *Then shall follow three Collects; the first of the Day; the second for Peace; the third for Aid against all Perils, as hereafter followeth : which two last Collects shall be daily said at Evening Prayer without alteration.*

[*After each Collect, or Prayer.*]

A - men.

THE SECOND COLLECT AT EVENING PRAYER.

O GOD, from whom all holy desires, all good counsels, and all just works do proceed; Give unto thy servants that peace which the world cannot give; that both our hearts may be set to obey thy commandments, and also that by thee we being defended from the fear of our enemies may pass our time in rest and quietness; through the merits of Jesus Christ our Saviour. *Amen.*

THE THIRD COLLECT, FOR AID AGAINST ALL PERILS.

L IGHTEN our darkness, we beseech thee, O Lord; and by thy great mercy defend us from all perils and dangers of this night; for the love of thy only Son, our Saviour, Jesus Christ. 'men.

¶ *In Quires and Places where they sing, here followeth the Anthem.*

A PRAYER FOR THE QUEEN'S MAJESTY.

O LORD our heavenly Father, high and mighty, King of kings, Lord of lords, the only Ruler of princes, who dost from thy throne behold all the dwellers upon earth; Most heartily we beseech thee with thy favour to behold our most gracious Sovereign Lady, Queen *VICTORIA ;* and so replenish her with the grace of thy Holy Spirit, that she may alway incline to thy will, and walk in thy way: Endue her plenteously with heavenly gifts; grant her in health and wealth long to live; strengthen her that she may vanquish and overcome all her enemies; and finally, after this life, she may attain everlasting joy and felicity; through Jesus Christ our Lord. *Amen.*

A PRAYER FOR THE ROYAL FAMILY.

ALMIGHTY God, the fountain of all goodness, we humbly beseech thee to bless *Albert Edward* Prince of *Wales*, the Princess of *Wales*, and all the Royal Family : Endue them with thy Holy Spirit ; enrich them with thy heavenly grace ; prosper them with all happiness ; and bring them to thine everlasting kingdom ; through Jesus Christ our Lord. *Amen.*

A PRAYER FOR THE CLERGY AND PEOPLE.

ALMIGHTY and everlasting God, who alone workest great marvels ; Send down upon our Bishops, and Curates, and all Congregations committed to their charge, the healthful Spirit of thy grace ; and that they may truly please thee, pour upon them the continual dew of thy blessing. Grant this, O Lord, for the honour of our Advocate and Mediator, Jesus Christ. *Amen.*

A PRAYER OF ST. CHRYSOSTOM.

ALMIGHTY God, who hast given us grace at this time with one accord to make our common supplications unto thee ; and dost promise, that when two or three are gathered together in thy Name thou wilt grant their requests : Fulfil now, O Lord, the desires and petitions of thy servants, as may be most expedient for them ; granting us in this world knowledge of thy truth, and in the world to come life everlasting. *Amen.*

2 *Cor.* xiii.

THE grace of our Lord Jesus Christ, and the love of God, and the fellowship of the Holy Ghost, be with us all evermore. *Amen.*

Here endeth the Order of Evening Prayer throughout the Year.

AT MORNING PRAYER.

¶ *Upon these Feasts;* Christmas Day, *the* Epiphany, *Saint* Matthias, Easter Day, Ascension Day, Whitsunday, *Saint* John Baptist, *Saint* James, *Saint* Bartholomew, *Saint* Matthew, *Saint* Simon *and Saint* Jude, *Saint* Andrew, *and upon* Trinity Sunday, *shall be sung or said at Morning Prayer, instead of the Apostles' Creed, this Confession of our Christian Faith, commonly called the Creed of Saint* ATHANASIUS, *by the Minister and people standing.*

QUICUNQUE VULT. *

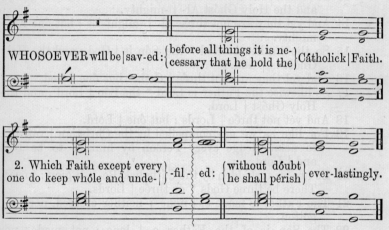

WHOSOEVER will be | sav-ed : {before all things it is ne-} {cessary that he hold the} Cátholick | Faith.

2. Which Faith except every | one do keep whóle and unde- | } -fil - { ed : {without dóubt} {he shall pérish} ever-lastingly.

[N.B.—The notes between the wavy line and the first double bar are to be sung only when the last word of the first division of the verse has more than one syllable.]

3 And the Catholick Fáith is | this : That we worship one God in Trinity * and Trínity in | Unity ;

4 Neither confóunding the | Per-sons : nor divíding the | Substance.

5 For there is one Person of the Father * anóther of the | Son : and another of the Hóly | Ghost.

6 But the Godhead of the Father, of the Son, and of the Holy Ghost * is áll | one : the Glory equal * the Majesty có-e- | -ternal.

7 Such as the Father is * súch is the | Son : and such is the Hóly | Ghost.

---

* An Organ Accompaniment will be found on p. 16 of the Appendix.

F

8 The Father uncreate * the Són uncre- | -ate : and the Holy Ghóst uncre- | -ate.

9 The Father incomprehensible * the Són incompre- | -hensible : and the Holy Ghóst incompre- | -hensible.

10 The Father eternal * the Són e- | -ter-nal : and the Holy Ghóst e- | -ternal.

11 And yet they are not thrée e- | -ter-nals : but óne e- | ternal.

12 As also there are not three incomprehensibles * nor thrée uncre- | -a-ted : but one uncreated * and óne incompre- | hensible.

13 So likewise the Father is Almighty * the Són Al-|-might-y : and the Holy Ghóst Al- | -mighty.

14 And yet they are not thrée Al- | -might-ies : but óne Al- | mighty.

15 So the Father is God * the Són is | God : and the Holy Ghóst is | God.

16 And yet they are not thrée | Gods : but óne | God.

17 So likewise the Father is Lord * the Són | Lord : and the Holy Ghóst | Lord.

18 And yet not thrée | Lords : but óne | Lord.

19 For like as we are compelled by the Chrístian | veri-ty : to acknowledge every Person by himself to be Gód and | Lord ;

20 So are we forbidden by the Cátholick Re- | -li-gion : to say, There be three Gods * or thrée | Lords.

21 The Father is máde of | none : neither created, nór be- | gotten.

22 The Son is of the Fáther a- | -lone : not made, nor created * bút be- | -gotten.

23 The Holy Ghost is of the Father and óf the | Son : neither made, nor created, nor begotten * bút pro- | ceeding.

24 So there is one Father, not three Fathers * one Son, not thrée | Sons : one Holy Ghost, not thrée Holy | Ghosts.

25 And in this Trinity none is afore, or áfter | o-ther : none is greater, or léss than an- | -other ;

26 But the whole three Persons are co-etérnal to- | -geth-er : ánd co- | -equal.

27 So that in all things, ás is a- | -fore-said : the Unity in Trinity * and the Trinity in Unity ís to be | worshipped.

28 He therefore that wíll be | sav-ed : must thus thínk of the | Trinity.

29 Furthermore, it is necessary to everlásting sal- | -va-tion :
that he also believe rightly the Incarnation of our Lord
Jésus | Christ.

30 For the right Faith is, that we beliéve and con- | -fess :
that our Lord Jesus Christ, the Son of God * is Gód
and | Man ;

31 God, of the Substance of the Father * begotten befóre
the | worlds : and Man, of the Substance of his Mother *
bórn in the | world.

32 Perfect God, and pérfect | Man : of a reasonable soul and
human flésh sub- | -sisting.

33 Equal to the Father, as tóuching his | God-head : and
inferior to the Father, as tóuching his | Manhood.

34 Who although he be Gód and | Man : yet he is not two *
but óne | Christ ;

35 One ; not by conversion of the Gódhead into | flesh : but
by taking of the Mánhood into | God ;

36 One altogether * not by confúsion of | Sub-stance : but by
únity of | Person.

37 For as the reasonable soul and flesh is óne | man : so God
and Man is óne | Christ ;

38 Who suffered for óur sal- | -va-tion : descended into hell *
rose again the third dáy from the | dead.

39 He ascended into heaven * he sitteth on the right hand of
the Father, Gód Al- | -might-y : from whence he shall
come to judge the qúick and the | dead.

40 At whose coming áll men shall rise agáin with their |
bod-ies : and shall give account for their ówn | works.

41 And they that have done good shall go into lífe ever- |
last-ing : and they that have done evil into everlásting |
fire.

42 This is the Cátholick | Faith : which except a man believe
faithfully * he cánnot be | saved.

F. f   Glory be to the Father * ánd . to the | Son : and to the
Hóly | Ghost ;

F.   As it was in the beginning * is now, and éver | shall be :
world without end. * A´- | -men.

THE LITANY.*

¶ *Here followeth the LITANY, or General Supplication, to be sung or said after Morning Prayer upon* Sundays, Wednesdays, *and* Fridays, *and at other times when it shall be commanded by the Ordinary.*

O God the Father, of heaven: have mercy upon us * mis- er- a - ble sinners.

*O God the Father, of heaven: have mercy upon us * mis- er- a - ble sin-ners.*

O God the Son,
Redeemer of the } world: have mercy upon us * mis -er-a - ble sinners.

*O God the Son,
Redeemer of the } world: have mercy upon us * mis - er- a - ble sin-ners.*

O God the Holy Ghost,
proceeding from the
Father and the . . } Son: have mercy upon us * mis- er-a-ble sinners.

*O God the Holy Ghost,
proceeding from the
Father and the . . } Son: have mercy upon us * mis - er-a-ble sinners.*

* Tallis's Litany will be found on p. 29 of the Appendix.

O holy, blessed, and glorious Trinity, three Persons and one . . } God : have mércy upon us * mis-er-a-ble sinners.

O holy, blessed, and glorious Trinity, three Persons and one . . . } *God : have mércy upon * us mis-er-a-ble sinners.*

Remember not, Lord, our offences, nor the offences of our forefathers ; neither take thou vengeance of our sins : spare us, good Lord, spare thy people, whom thou hast redeemed with thy most precious blood, and be not . . . } an - gry with us for ever.

[*Soft.*]

Spare us, good Lord.

From all evil and mischief; from sin, from the crafts and assaults of the devil ; from thy wrath, and from ever- - -. } last - ing dam-nation,

mp

Good Lord, de - liv - er us.

mp

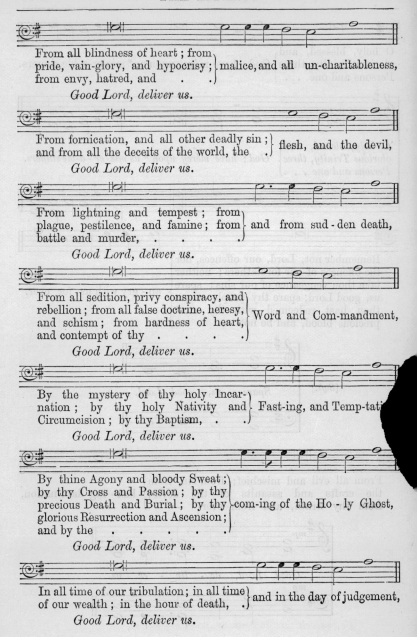

From all blindness of heart ; from pride, vain-glory, and hypocrisy ; from envy, hatred, and . . } malice, and all un-charitableness,

Good Lord, deliver us.

From fornication, and all other deadly sin ; and from all the deceits of the world, the . } flesh, and the devil,

Good Lord, deliver us.

From lightning and tempest ; from plague, pestilence, and famine ; from battle and murder, ... } and from sud - den death,

Good Lord, deliver us.

From all sedition, privy conspiracy, and rebellion ; from all false doctrine, heresy, and schism ; from hardness of heart, and contempt of thy . . . . } Word and Com-mandment,

Good Lord, deliver us.

By the mystery of thy holy Incarnation ; by thy holy Nativity and Circumcision ; by thy Baptism, . . } Fast-ing, and Temp-tati

Good Lord, deliver us.

By thine Agony and bloody Sweat ; by thy Cross and Passion ; by thy precious Death and Burial ; by thy glorious Resurrection and Ascension ; and by the . . . . . } com-ing of the Ho - ly Ghost,

Good Lord, deliver us.

In all time of our tribulation ; in all time of our wealth ; in the hour of death, . } and in the day of judgement,

Good Lord, deliver us.

We sinners do beseech thee to hear us, O Lord
God ; and that it may please thee to rule and ⎱ in the right way.
govern thy holy Church universal . . ⎰

We be - seech thee to hear us, good Lord.

That it may please thee to keep ⎫
and strengthen in the true wor- ⎮
shipping of thee, in righteousness ⎬ gracious Queen and Governour ;
and holiness of life, thy Servant ⎮
VICTORIA, our most . . . ⎭

We beseech thee to hear us, good Lord.

That it may please thee to rule her ⎫
heart in thy faith, fear, and love, and ⎮ ho - nour a
that she may evermore have affiance ⎬
in thee, and ever seek thy . . ⎭

We beseech thee to hear us, good Lord.

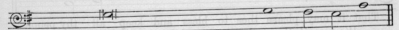

That it may please thee to be her defender ⎫ o - ver all her enemies ;
and keeper, giving her the victory . . ⎭

We beseech thee to hear us, good Lord.

That it may please thee to bless and ⎫
preserve *Albert Edward* Prince of *Wales,* ⎬ all the Roy - al Family ;
the Princess of *Wales,* and . . . ⎭

We beseech thee to hear us, good Lord.

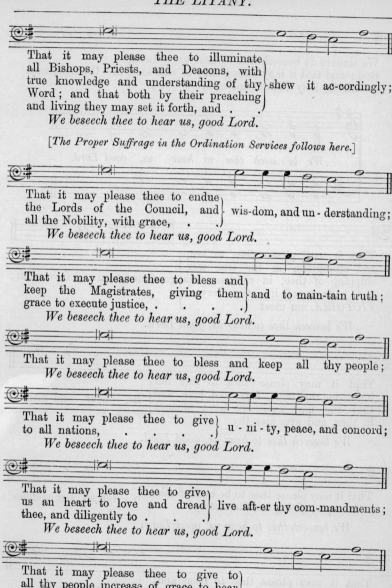

That it may please thee to illuminate all Bishops, Priests, and Deacons, with true knowledge and understanding of thy Word; and that both by their preaching and living they may set it forth, and . . -shew it ac-cordingly;

We beseech thee to hear us, good Lord.

[*The Proper Suffrage in the Ordination Services follows here.*]

That it may please thee to endue the Lords of the Council, and all the Nobility, with grace, . . -wis-dom, and un - derstanding;

We beseech thee to hear us, good Lord.

That it may please thee to bless and keep the Magistrates, giving them grace to execute justice, ... -and to main-tain truth;

We beseech thee to hear us, good Lord.

That it may please thee to bless and keep all thy people;

We beseech thee to hear us, good Lord.

That it may please thee to give to all nations, ... -u - ni - ty, peace, and concord;

We beseech thee to hear us, good Lord.

That it may please thee to give us an heart to love and dread thee, and diligently to . . . -live aft-er thy com-mandments;

We beseech thee to hear us, good Lord.

That it may please thee to give to all thy people increase of grace to hear meekly thy Word, and to receive it with pure affection, and to bring forth the . . -fruits of the Spirit;

We beseech thee to hear us, good Lord.

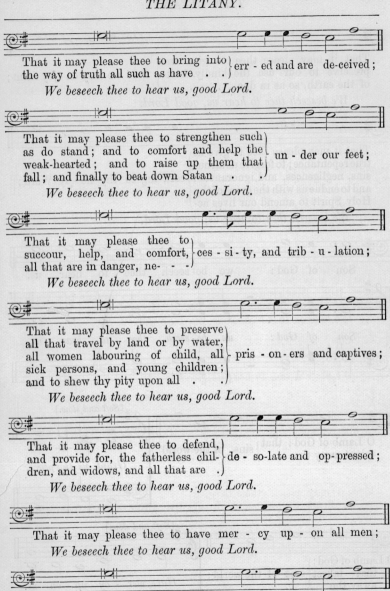

That it may please thee to bring into the way of truth all such as have . . err - ed and are de-ceived;

We beseech thee to hear us, good Lord.

That it may please thee to strengthen such as do stand; and to comfort and help the weak-hearted; and to raise up them that fall; and finally to beat down Satan . . un - der our feet;

We beseech thee to hear us, good Lord.

That it may please thee to succour, help, and comfort, all that are in danger, ne- - - ces - si - ty, and trib - u - lation;

We beseech thee to hear us, good Lord.

That it may please thee to preserve all that travel by land or by water, all women labouring of child, all sick persons, and young children; and to shew thy pity upon all . . pris - on - ers and captives;

We beseech thee to hear us, good Lord.

That it may please thee to defend, and provide for, the fatherless children, and widows, and all that are . de - so-late and op-pressed;

We beseech thee to hear us, good Lord.

That it may please thee to have mer - cy up - on all men;

We beseech thee to hear us, good Lord.

That it may please thee to forgive our enemies, persecutors, and slanderers, and to turn their hearts;

We beseech thee to hear us, good Lord.

That it may please thee to give and preserve to our use the kindly fruits of the earth, so as in due . . . time we may en-joy them;

We beseech thee to hear us, good Lord.

That it may please thee to give us true repentance; to forgive us all our sins, negligences, and ignorances; and to endue us with the grace of thy Holy Spirit to amend our lives ac-cord-ing to thy ho-ly Word;

We beseech thee to hear us, good Lord.

Son of God: we be-seech thee to hear us.

Son of God: we be-seech thee to hear us.

O Lamb of God: that takest away the . . sins of the world;

[*Soft and slow.*]

Grant us thy peace.

O Lamb of God: that takest away the . . sins of the world;

[*Soft and slow.*]

Have mer - cy up-on us.

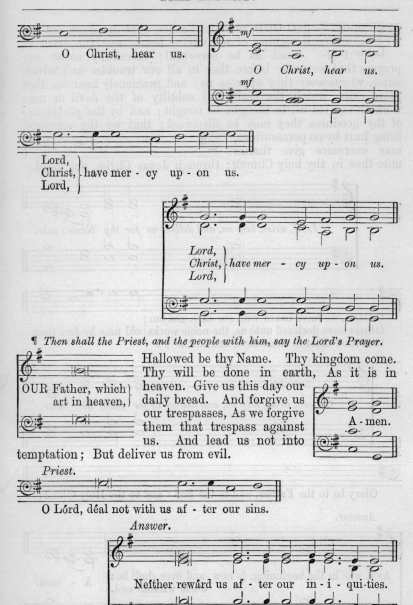

O Christ, hear us.

mf

O Christ, hear us.

Lord,
Christ, } have mer - cy up - on us.
Lord,

Lord,
Christ, } have mer - cy up - on us.
Lord,

¶ *Then shall the Priest, and the people with him, say the Lord's Prayer.*

OUR Father, which art in heaven, } Hallowed be thy Name. Thy kingdom come. Thy will be done in earth, As it is in heaven. Give us this day our daily bread. And forgive us our trespasses, As we forgive them that trespass against us. And lead us not into temptation; But deliver us from evil.

A - men.

Priest.

O Lórd, déal not with us af - ter our sins.

Answer.

Neíther rewárd us af - ter our in - i - qui - ties.

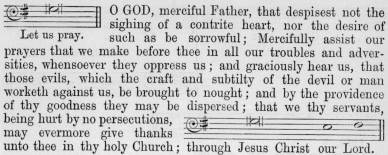

Let us pray. O GOD, merciful Father, that despisest not the sighing of a contrite heart, nor the desire of such as be sorrowful; Mercifully assist our prayers that we make before thee in all our troubles and adversities, whensoever they oppress us; and graciously hear us, that those evils, which the craft and subtilty of the devil or man worketh against us, be brought to nought; and by the providence of thy goodness they may be dispersed; that we thy servants, being hurt by no persecutions, may evermore give thanks unto thee in thy holy Church; through Jesus Christ our Lord.

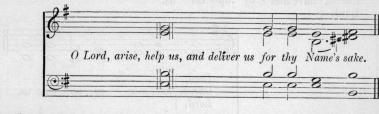

O Lord, arise, help us, and deliver us for thy Name's sake.

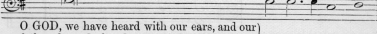

O GOD, we have heard with our ears, and our fathers have declared unto us, the noble works that thou didst in their days, and in the . . } old time be-fore them.

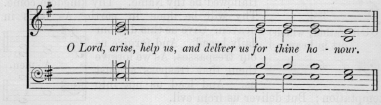

O Lord, arise, help us, and deliver us for thine ho - nour.

Glory be to the Father, and to the Son : and to the Holy Ghost;

Answer.

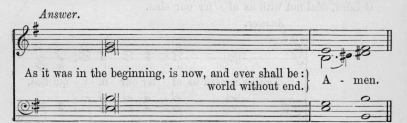

As it was in the beginning, is now, and ever shall be :} world without end.} A - men.

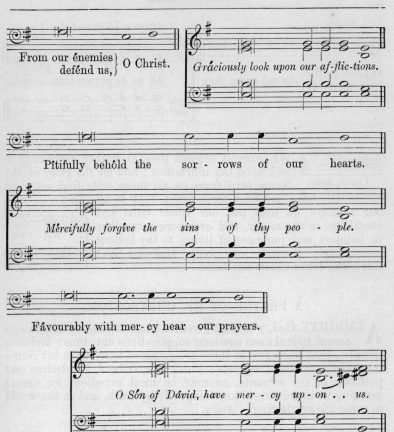

From our énemies defénd us, } O Christ.

Gráciously look upon our af-flíc-tions.

Pítifully behóld the sor - rows of our hearts.

Mércifully forgive the sins of thy peo - ple.

Fávourably with mer- cy hear our prayers.

O Són of Dávid, have mer - cy up-on . . us.

Both nów and éver vouchsáfe to hear us, O Christ.

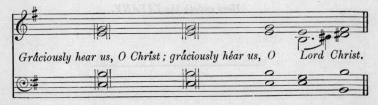

Gráciously hear us, O Christ; gráciously héar us, O Lord Christ.

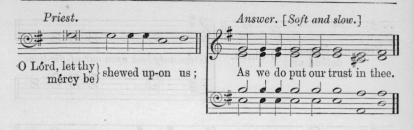

Priest.

O Lórd, let thy mércy be shewed up-on us ;

Answer. [*Soft and slow.*]

As we do put our trust in thee.

Let us pray. WE humbly beseech thee, O Father, mercifully to look upon our infirmities ; and for the glory of thy Name turn from us all those evils that we most righteously have deserved; and grant, that in all our troubles we may put our whole trust and confidence in thy mercy, and evermore serve thee in holiness and pureness of living, to thy honour and glory ; through our only Mediator and Advocate, Jesus Christ our Lord.

A - men.

A PRAYER OF ST. CHRYSOSTOM.

ALMIGHTY God, who hast given us grace at this time with one accord to make our common supplications unto thee ; and dost promise, that when two or three are gathered together in thy Name thou wilt grant their requests ; Fulfil now, O Lord, the desires and petitions of thy servants, as may be most expedient for them ; granting us in this world knowledge of thy truth, and in the world to come life everlasting. *Amen.*

2 *Cor.* xiii.

THE grace of our Lord Jesus Christ, and the love of God, and the fellowship of the Holy Ghost, be with us all evermore. *Amen.*

Here endeth the LITANY.

PRAYERS AND THANKSGIVINGS,

UPON SEVERAL OCCASIONS,

¶ *To be used before the two final Prayers of the Litany, or of Morning and Evening Prayer.*

Prayers.

For Rain.

O GOD, heavenly Father, who by thy Son Jesus Christ hast promised to all them that seek thy kingdom, and the righteousness thereof, all things necessary to their bodily sustenance ; Send us, we beseech thee, in this our necessity, such moderate rain and showers, that we may receive the fruits of the earth to our comfort, and to thy honour ; through Jesus Christ our Lord. *Amen.*

For fair Weather.

O ALMIGHTY Lord God, who for the sin of man didst once drown all the world, except eight persons, and afterward of thy great mercy didst promise never to destroy it so again ; We humbly beseech thee, that although we for our iniquities have worthily deserved a plague of rain and waters, yet upon our true repentance thou wilt send us such weather, as that we may receive the fruits of the earth in due season ; and learn both by thy punishment to amend our lives, and for thy clemency to give thee praise and glory ; through Jesus Christ our Lord. *Amen.*

In the time of Dearth and Famine.

O GOD, heavenly Father, whose gift it is, that the rain doth fall, the earth is fruitful, beasts increase, and fishes do multiply ; Behold, we beseech thee, the afflictions of thy people ; and grant that the scarcity and dearth, which we do now most justly suffer for our iniquity, may through thy goodness be mercifully turned into cheapness and plenty ; for the love of Jesus Christ our Lord, to whom with thee and the Holy Ghost be all honour and glory, now and for ever. *Amen.*

Or this.

O GOD, merciful Father, who, in the time of Elisha the prophet, didst suddenly in Samaria turn great scarcity and dearth into plenty and cheapness ; Have mercy upon us, that we, who are now for our sins punished with like adversity, may likewise find a seasonable relief : Increase the fruits of the earth by thy heavenly benediction ; and grant that we, receiving thy bountiful liberality, may use the same to thy glory, the relief of those that are needy, and our own comfort ; through Jesus Christ our Lord. *Amen.*

In the time of War and Tumults.

O ALMIGHTY God, King of all kings, and Governour of all things, whose power no creature is able to resist, to whom it belongeth justly to punish sinners, and to be merciful to them that truly repent; Save and deliver us, we humbly beseech thee, from the hands of our enemies ; abate their pride, assuage their malice, and confound their devices ; that we, being armed with thy defence, may be preserved evermore from all perils, to glorify thee, who art the only giver of all victory ; through the merits of thy only Son, Jesus Christ our Lord. *Amen.*

In the time of any common Plague or Sickness.

O ALMIGHTY God, who in thy wrath didst send a plague upon thine own people in the wilderness, for their obstinate rebellion against Moses and Aaron ; and also, in the time of king David, didst slay with the plague of Pestilence threescore and ten thousand, and yet remembering thy mercy didst save the rest ; Have pity upon us miserable sinners, who now are visited with great sickness and mortality ; that like as thou didst then accept of an atonement, and didst command the destroying Angel to cease from punishing, so it may now please thee to withdraw from us this plague and grievous sickness ; through Jesus Christ our Lord. *Amen.*

¶ *In the Ember Weeks, to be said every day, for those that are to be admitted into Holy Orders.*

A LMIGHTY God, our heavenly Father, who hast purchased to thyself an universal Church by the precious blood of thy dear Son ; Mercifully look upon the same, and at this time so guide and govern the minds of thy servants the Bishops and Pastors of thy flock, that they may lay hands suddenly on no man, but faithfully and wisely make choice of fit persons to serve in the sacred Ministry of thy Church. And to those which shall be ordained to any holy function give thy grace and heavenly benediction ; that both by their life and doctrine they may set forth thy glory, and set forward the salvation of all men ; through Jesus Christ our Lord. *Amen.*

Or this.

A LMIGHTY God, the giver of all good gifts, who of thy divine providence hast appointed divers Orders in thy Church ; Give thy grace, we humbly beseech thee, to all those who are to be called to any office and administration in the same; and so replenish them with the truth of thy doctrine, and endue them with innocency of life, that they may faithfully serve before thee, to the glory of thy great Name, and the benefit of thy holy Church; through Jesus Christ our Lord. *Amen.*

¶ *A Prayer that may be said after any of the former.*

O GOD, whose nature and property is ever to have mercy and to forgive, receive our humble petitions; and though we be tied and bound with the chain of our sins, yet let the pitifulness of thy great mercy loose us; for the honour of Jesus Christ, our Mediator and Advocate. *Amen.*

¶ *A Prayer for the High Court of Parliament, to be read during their Session.*

M OST gracious God, we humbly beseech thee, as for this Kingdom in general, so especially for the High Court of Parliament, under our most religious and gracious Queen at this time assembled: That thou wouldest be pleased to direct and prosper all their consultations to the advancement of thy glory, the good of thy Church, the safety, honour, and welfare of our Sovereign, and her Dominions; that all things may be so ordered and settled by their endeavours, upon the best and surest foundations, that peace and happiness, truth and justice, religion and piety, may be established among us for all generations. These and all other necessaries, for them, for us, and thy whole Church, we humbly beg in the Name and Mediation of Jesus Christ our most blessed Lord and Saviour. *Amen.*

¶ *A Collect or Prayer for all conditions of men, to be used at such times when the Litany is not appointed to be said.*

O GOD, the Creator and Preserver of all mankind, we humbly beseech thee for all sorts and conditions of men; that thou wouldest be pleased to make thy ways known unto them, thy saving health unto all nations. More especially, we pray for the good estate of the Catholick Church; that it may be so guided and governed by thy good Spirit, that all who profess and call themselves Christians may be led into the way of truth, and hold the faith in unity of spirit, in the bond of peace, and in righteousness of life. Finally, we commend to thy fatherly goodness all those, * This to be who are any ways afflicted, or distressed, in mind, said when any de-body, or estate; [*especially those for whom our sire the Prayers of the Congrega-prayers are desired,*] that it may please thee to com-tion. fort and relieve them, according to their several necessities, giving them patience under their sufferings, and a happy issue out of all their afflictions. And this we beg for Jesus Christ his sake. *Amen.*

G

Thanksgivings.

¶ *A General Thanksgiving.*

ALMIGHTY God, Father of all mercies, we thine unworthy servants do give thee most humble and hearty thanks for all *This to be* thy goodness and loving-kindness to us, and to all *said when any* men; [*particularly to those who desire now to offer up* *that have been* *prayed for desire* *their praises and thanksgivings for thy late mercies* *to return praise.* *vouchsafed unto them.*] We bless thee for our creation, preservation, and all the blessings of this life; but above all, for thine inestimable love in the redemption of the world by our Lord Jesus Christ; for the means of grace, and for the hope of glory. And, we beseech thee, give us that due sense of all thy mercies, that our hearts may be unfeignedly thankful, and that we shew forth thy praise, not only with our lips, but in our lives; by giving up ourselves to thy service, and by walking before thee in holiness and righteousness all our days; through Jesus Christ our Lord, to whom with thee and the Holy Ghost be all honour and glory, world without end. *Amen.*

For Rain.

O GOD our heavenly Father, who by thy gracious providence dost cause the former and the latter rain to descend upon the earth, that it may bring forth fruit for the use of man; We give thee humble thanks that it hath pleased thee, in our great necessity, to send us at the last a joyful rain upon thine inheritance, and to refresh it when it was dry, to the great comfort of us thy unworthy servants, and to the glory of thy holy Name; through thy mercies in Jesus Christ our Lord. *Amen.*

For Fair Weather.

O LORD God, who hast justly humbled us by thy late plague of immoderate rain and waters, and in thy mercy hast relieved and comforted our souls by this seasonable and blessed change of weather; We praise and glorify thy holy Name for this thy mercy, and will always declare thy loving-kindness from generation to generation; through Jesus Christ our Lord. *Amen.*

For Plenty.

O MOST merciful Father, who of thy gracious goodness hast heard the devout prayers of thy Church, and turned our dearth and scarcity into cheapness and plenty; We give thee humble thanks for this thy special bounty; beseeching thee to continue thy loving-kindness unto us, that our land may yield us her fruits of increase, to thy glory and our comfort; through Jesus Christ our Lord. *Amen.*

For Peace and Deliverance from our Enemies.

O ALMIGHTY God, who art a strong tower of defence unto thy servants against the face of their enemies; We yield thee praise and thanksgiving for our deliverance from those great and apparent dangers wherewith we were compassed: We acknowledge it thy goodness that we were not delivered over as a prey unto them; beseeching thee still to continue such thy mercies towards us, that all the world may know that thou art our Saviour and mighty Deliverer; through Jesus Christ our Lord. *Amen.*

For restoring Publick Peace at Home.

O ETERNAL God, our heavenly Father, who alone makest men to be of one mind in a house, and stillest the outrage of a violent and unruly people; We bless thy holy Name, that it hath pleased thee to appease the seditious tumults which have been lately raised up amongst us; most humbly beseeching thee to grant to all of us grace, that we may henceforth obediently walk in thy holy commandments; and, leading a quiet and peaceable life in all godliness and honesty, may continually offer unto thee our sacrifice of praise and thanksgiving for these thy mercies towards us; through Jesus Christ our Lord. *Amen.*

For Deliverance from the Plague, or other common Sickness.

O LORD God, who hast wounded us for our sins, and consumed us for our transgressions, by thy late heavy and dreadful visitation; and now, in the midst of judgement remembering mercy, hast redeemed our souls from the jaws of death; We offer unto thy fatherly goodness ourselves, our souls and bodies which thou hast delivered, to be a living sacrifice unto thee, always praising and magnifying thy mercies in the midst of thy Church; through Jesus Christ our Lord. *Amen.*

Or this.

WE humbly acknowledge before thee, O most merciful Father, that all the punishments which are threatened in thy law might justly have fallen upon us, by reason of our manifold transgressions and hardness of heart: Yet seeing it hath pleased thee of thy tender mercy, upon our weak and unworthy humiliation, to assuage the contagious sickness wherewith we lately have been sore afflicted, and to restore the voice of joy and health into our dwellings; We offer unto thy Divine Majesty the sacrifice of praise and thanksgiving, lauding and magnifying thy glorious Name for such thy preservation and providence over us; through Jesus Christ our Lord. *Amen.*

THE
COLLECTS, EPISTLES, AND GOSPELS,
TO BE USED THROUGHOUT THE YEAR.

¶ Note, *That the Collect appointed for every Sunday, or for any Holy-day that hath a Vigil or Eve, shall be said at the Evening Service next before.*

The First Sunday in Advent.

THE COLLECT.

ALMIGHTY God, give us grace that we may cast away the works of darkness, and put upon us the armour of light, now in the time of this mortal life, in which thy Son Jesus Christ came to visit us in great humility; that in the last day, when he shall come again in his glorious Majesty to judge both the quick and dead, we may rise to the life immortal, through him who liveth and reigneth with thee and the Holy Ghost, now and ever. *Amen.*

¶ *This Collect is to be repeated every day, with the other Collects in Advent, until Christmas Eve.*

THE EPISTLE. Rom. xiii. 8.

OWE no man any thing, but to love one another: for he that loveth another hath fulfilled the law. For this, Thou shalt not commit adultery, Thou shalt not kill, Thou shalt not steal, Thou shalt not bear false witness, Thou shalt not covet; and if there be any other commandment, it is briefly comprehended in this saying, namely, Thou shalt love thy neighbour as thyself. Love worketh no ill to his neighbour; therefore love is the fulfilling of the law. And that, knowing the time, that now it is high time to awake out of sleep: for now is our salvation nearer than when we believed. The night is far spent, the day is at hand; let us therefore cast off the works of darkness, and let us put on the armour of light. Let us walk honestly as in the day; not in rioting and drunkenness, not in chambering and wantonness, not in strife and envying. But put ye on the Lord Jesus Christ, and make not provision for the flesh, to fulfil the lusts thereof.

THE GOSPEL. St. Matth. xxi. 1.

WHEN they drew nigh unto Jerusalem, and were come to Bethphage, unto the mount of Olives, then sent Jesus two disciples, saying unto them, Go into the village over against you, and straightway ye shall find an ass tied, and a colt with her : loose them, and bring them unto me. And if any man say ought unto you, ye shall say, The Lord hath need of them ; and straight- way he will send them. All this was done, that it might be fulfilled which was spoken by the Prophet, saying, Tell ye the daughter of Sion, Behold, thy King cometh unto thee, meek, and sitting upon an ass, and a colt the foal of an ass. And the disciples went, and did as Jesus commanded them ; and brought the ass, and the colt, and put on them their clothes, and they set him thereon. And a very great multitude spread their garments in the way ; others cut down branches from the trees, and strawed them in the way. And the multitudes that went before, and that followed, cried, saying, Hosanna to the Son of David ; Blessed is he that cometh in the Name of the Lord ; Hosanna in the highest. And when he was come into Jerusalem all the city was moved, saying, Who is this ? And the multitude said, This is Jesus the Prophet of Nazareth of Galilee. And Jesus went into the temple of God, and cast out all them that sold and bought in the temple ; and overthrew the tables of the money-changers, and the seats of them that sold doves ; and said unto them, It is written, My house shall be called the house of prayer ; but ye have made it a den of thieves.

The Second Sunday in Advent.

THE COLLECT.

BLESSED Lord, who hast caused all holy Scriptures to be written for our learning; Grant that we may in such wise hear them, read, mark, learn, and inwardly digest them, that by patience, and comfort of thy holy Word, we may embrace, and ever hold fast the blessed hope of everlasting life, which thou hast given us in our Saviour Jesus Christ. *Amen.*

THE EPISTLE. Rom. xv. 4.

WHATSOEVER things were written aforetime, were written for our learning ; that we through patience, and comfort of the Scriptures, might have hope. Now the God of patience and con- solation grant you to be like-minded one towards another, according to Christ Jesus : that ye may with one mind, and one mouth, glorify God, even the Father of our Lord Jesus Christ. Wherefore receive ye one another, as Christ also received us, to the glory of

God. Now I say, that Jesus Christ was a minister of the circumcision for the truth of God, to confirm the promises made unto the fathers : And that the Gentiles might glorify God for his mercy ; as it is written, For this cause I will confess to thee among the Gentiles, and sing unto thy Name. And again he saith, Rejoice, ye Gentiles, with his people. And again, Praise the Lord, all ye Gentiles, and laud him, all ye people. And again, Esaias saith, There shall be a root of Jesse, and he that shall rise to reign over the Gentiles, in him shall the Gentiles trust. Now the God of hope fill you with all joy and peace in believing, that ye may abound in hope, through the power of the Holy Ghost.

THE GOSPEL. St. Luke xxi. 25.

A ND there shall be signs in the sun, and in the moon, and in the stars ; and upon the earth distress of nations, with perplexity, the sea and the waves roaring ; men's hearts failing them for fear, and for looking after those things which are coming on the earth : for the powers of heaven shall be shaken. And then shall they see the Son of Man coming in a cloud with power and great glory. And when these things begin to come to pass, then look up, and lift up your heads ; for your redemption draweth nigh. And he spake to them a parable, Behold the fig-tree, and all the trees ; when they now shoot forth, ye see and know of your own selves that summer is now nigh at hand. So likewise ye, when ye see these things come to pass, know ye that the Kingdom of God is nigh at hand. Verily I say unto you, This generation shall not pass away, till all be fulfilled : heaven and earth shall pass away ; but my words shall not pass away.

The Third Sunday in Advent.
THE COLLECT.

O LORD Jesu Christ, who at thy first coming didst send thy messenger to prepare thy way before thee ; Grant that the ministers and stewards of thy mysteries may likewise so prepare and make ready thy way, by turning the hearts of the disobedient to the wisdom of the just, that at thy second coming to judge the world we may be found an acceptable people in thy sight, who livest and reignest with the Father and the Holy Spirit, ever one God, world without end. *Amen.*

THE EPISTLE. 1 Cor. iv. 1.

L ET a man so account of us, as of the ministers of Christ, and stewards of the mysteries of God. Moreover, it is required in stewards, that a man be found faithful. But with me it is a very small thing that I should be judged of you, or of man's judgement : yea, I judge not mine own self. For I know nothing by myself, yet am I not hereby justified ; but he that judgeth me is the Lord. Therefore judge nothing before the time, until the Lord come, who both will bring to light the hidden things of darkness, and will make manifest the counsels of the hearts ; and then shall every man have praise of God.

THE GOSPEL. St. Matth. xi. 2.

NOW when John had heard in the prison the works of Christ, he sent two of his disciples, and said unto him, Art thou he that should come, or do we look for another ? Jesus answered and said unto them, Go and shew John again those things which ye do hear and see : The blind receive their sight, and the lame walk, the lepers are cleansed, and the deaf hear, the dead are raised up, and the poor have the Gospel preached to them : And blessed is he whosoever shall not be offended in me. And as they departed, Jesus began to say unto the multitudes concerning John, What went ye out into the wilderness to see ? a reed shaken with the wind ? But what went ye out for to see ? a man clothed in soft raiment ? behold, they that wear soft clothing are in kings' houses. But what went ye out for to see ? a prophet ? yea, I say unto you, and more than a prophet. For this is he of whom it is written, Behold, I send my messenger before thy face, which shall prepare thy way before thee.

The Fourth Sunday in Advent.

THE COLLECT.

O LORD, raise up (we pray thee) thy power, and come among us, and with great might succour us ; that whereas, through our sins and wickedness, we are sore let and hindered in running the race that is set before us, thy bountiful grace and mercy may speedily help and deliver us ; through the satisfaction of thy Son our Lord, to whom with thee and the Holy Ghost be honour and glory, world without end. *Amen.*

THE EPISTLE. Philip. iv. 4.

REJOICE in the Lord alway, and again I say, Rejoice. Let your moderation be known unto all men. The Lord is at hand. Be careful for nothing : but in every thing, by prayer and supplication with thanksgiving, let your requests be made known unto God. And the peace of God, which passeth all understanding, shall keep your hearts and minds through Christ Jesus.

THE GOSPEL. St. John i. 19.

THIS is the record of John, when the Jews sent Priests and Levites from Jerusalem to ask him, Who art thou? And he confessed, and denied not; but confessed, I am not the Christ. And they asked him, What then? Art thou Elias? And he saith, I am not. Art thou that Prophet? And he answered, No. Then said they unto him, Who art thou? that we may give an answer to them that sent us. What sayest thou of thyself? He said, I am the voice of one crying in the wilderness, Make straight the way of the Lord, as said the prophet Esaias. And they which were sent were of the Pharisees. And they asked him, and said unto him, Why baptizest thou then, if thou be not that Christ, nor Elias, neither that Prophet? John answered them, saying, I baptize with water: but there standeth one among you, whom ye know not: He it is who coming after me is preferred before me, whose shoe's latchet I am not worthy to unloose. These things were done in Bethabara beyond Jordan, where John was baptizing.

THE NATIVITY OF OUR LORD, OR THE BIRTHDAY OF CHRIST, COMMONLY CALLED

Christmas Day.

THE COLLECT.

ALMIGHTY God, who hast given us thy only begotten Son to take our nature upon him, and as at this time to be born of a pure Virgin; Grant that we being regenerate, and made thy children by adoption and grace, may daily be renewed by thy Holy Spirit; through the same our Lord Jesus Christ, who liveth and reigneth with thee and the same Spirit, ever one God, world without end. *Amen.*

THE EPISTLE. Hebr. i. 1.

GOD, who at sundry times and in divers manners spake in time past unto the fathers by the prophets, hath in these last days spoken unto us by his Son, whom he hath appointed heir of all things, by whom also he made the worlds; who being the brightness of his glory, and the express image of his person, and upholding all things by the word of his power, when he had by himself purged our sins, sat down on the right hand of the Majesty on high; being made so much better than the angels, as he hath by inheritance obtained a more excellent name than they. For unto which of the angels said he at any time, Thou art my Son, this day have I begotten thee? And again, I will be to him a Father, and he shall be to me a Son? And again, when he bringeth in the first-begotten into the world, he saith, And let all the angels of God worship him. And of the angels he saith, Who maketh his angels spirits, and his ministers a flame of fire. But unto the Son he saith, Thy throne, O God, is for ever and ever; a sceptre of righteousness is the sceptre of thy kingdom: Thou hast loved righteousness, and hated iniquity; therefore God, even thy God, hath anointed thee with the oil of gladness above thy fellows. And, Thou, Lord, in the beginning hast laid the foundation of the earth; and the heavens are the works of thine hands: they shall perish, but thou remainest; and they all shall wax old as doth a garment; and as a vesture shalt thou fold them up, and they shall be changed; but thou art the same, and thy years shall not fail.

THE GOSPEL. St. John i. 1.

IN the beginning was the Word, and the Word was with God, and the Word was God. The same was in the beginning with God. All things were made by him; and without him was not any thing made that was made. In him was life, and the life was the light of men. And the light shineth in darkness, and the darkness comprehended it not. There was a man sent from God, whose name was John. The same came for a witness, to bear witness of the light, that all men through him might believe. He was not that light, but was sent to bear witness of that light. That was the true light, which lighteth every man that cometh into the world. He was in the world, and the world was made by him, and the world knew him not. He came unto his own, and his own received him not. But as many as received him, to them gave he power to become the sons of God, even to them that believe on his Name: which were born, not of blood, nor of the will of the flesh, nor of the will of man, but of God. And the Word was made flesh, and dwelt among us (and we beheld his glory, the glory as of the only-begotten of the Father) full of grace and truth.

Saint Stephen's Day.
THE COLLECT.

GRANT, O Lord, that, in all our sufferings here upon earth for the testimony of thy truth, we may stedfastly look up to heaven, and by faith behold the glory that shall be revealed; and, being filled with the Holy Ghost, may learn to love and bless our persecutors by the example of thy first Martyr Saint Stephen, who prayed for his murderers to thee, O blessed Jesus, who standest at the right hand of God to succour all those that suffer for thee, our only Mediator and Advocate. *Amen.*

¶ *Then shall follow the Collect of the Nativity, which shall be said continually unto New-Year's Eve.*

FOR THE EPISTLE. Acts vii. 55.

STEPHEN, being full of the Holy Ghost, looked up stedfastly into heaven, and saw the glory of God, and Jesus standing on the right hand of God, and said, Behold, I see the heavens opened, and the Son of Man standing on the right hand of God. Then they cried out with a loud voice, and stopped their ears, and ran upon him with one accord, and cast him out of the city, and stoned him : and the witnesses laid down their clothes at a young man's feet, whose name was Saul. And they stoned Stephen, calling upon God, and saying, Lord Jesus, receive my spirit. And he kneeled down, and cried with a loud voice, Lord, lay not this sin to their charge. And when he had said this, he fell asleep.

THE GOSPEL. St. Matth. xxiii. 34.

BEHOLD, I send unto you prophets, and wise men, and scribes; and some of them ye shall kill and crucify ; and some of them shall ye scourge in your synagogues, and persecute them from city to city ; that upon you may come all the righteous blood shed upon the earth, from the blood of righteous Abel unto the blood of Zacharias, son of Barachias, whom ye slew between the temple and the altar. Verily I say unto you, All these things shall come upon this generation. O Jerusalem, Jerusalem, thou that killest the prophets, and stonest them which are sent unto thee ; how often would I have gathered thy children together, even as a hen gathereth her chickens under her wings, and ye would not ! Behold, your house is left unto you desolate. For I say unto you, Ye shall not see me henceforth, till ye shall say, Blessed is he that cometh in the Name of the Lord.

Saint John the Evangelist's Day.

THE COLLECT.

MERCIFUL Lord, we beseech thee to cast thy bright beams of light upon thy Church, that it being enlightened by the doctrine of thy blessed Apostle and Evangelist Saint John, may so walk in the light of thy truth, that it may at length attain to the light of everlasting life ; through Jesus Christ our Lord. *Amen*

THE EPISTLE. 1 St. John i. 1.

THAT which was from the beginning, which we have heard, which we have seen with our eyes, which we have looked upon, and our hands have handled of the word of life ; (for the life was manifested, and we have seen it, and bear witness, and shew unto you that eternal life, which was with the Father, and was manifested unto us ;) That which we have seen and heard declare we unto you, that ye also may have fellowship with us ; and truly our fellowship is with the Father, and with his Son Jesus Christ. And these things write we unto you, that your joy may be full. This then is the message which we have heard of him, and declare unto you, That God is light, and in him is no darkness at all. If we say that we have fellowship with him, and walk in darkness, we lie, and do not the truth : but if we walk in the light, as he is in the light, we have fellowship one with another, and the blood of Jesus Christ his Son cleanseth us from all sin. If we say that we have no sin, we deceive ourselves, and the truth is not in us. If we confess our sins, he is faithful and just to forgive us our sins, and to cleanse us from all unrighteousness. If we say that we have not sinned, we make him a liar, and his word is not in us.

THE GOSPEL. St. John xxi. 19.

JESUS said unto Peter, Follow me. Then Peter, turning about, seeth the disciple whom Jesus loved following; which also leaned on his breast at supper, and said, Lord, which is he that betrayeth thee ? Peter seeing him saith to Jesus, Lord, and what shall this man do ? Jesus saith unto him, If I will that he tarry till I come, what is that to thee ? Follow thou me. Then went this saying abroad among the brethren, That that disciple should not die : yet Jesus said not unto him, He shall not die ; but, If I will that he tarry till I come, what is that to thee ? This is the disciple which testifieth of these things, and wrote these things, and we know that his testimony is true. And there are also many other things which Jesus did, the which if they should be written every one, I suppose, that even the world itself could not contain the books that should be written.

The Innocents' Day.

THE COLLECT.

O ALMIGHTY God, who out of the mouths of babes and sucklings hast ordained strength, and madest infants to glorify thee by their deaths; Mortify and kill all vices in us, and so strengthen us by thy grace, that by the innocency of our lives, and constancy of our faith even unto death, we may glorify thy holy Name ; through Jesus Christ our Lord. *Amen.*

FOR THE EPISTLE. Rev. xiv. 1.

I LOOKED, and lo, a Lamb stood on the mount Sion, and with him an hundred forty and four thousand, having his Father's Name written in their foreheads. And I heard a voice from heaven, as the voice of many waters, and as the voice of a great thunder : and I heard the voice of harpers harping with their harps : and they sung as it were a new song before the throne, and before the four beasts, and the elders ; and no man could learn that song, but the hundred and forty and four thousand, which were redeemed from the earth. These are they which were not defiled with women, for they are virgins : these are they which follow the Lamb whithersoever he goeth : these were redeemed from among men, being the first-fruits unto God, and to the Lamb. And in their mouth was found no guile ; for they are without fault before the throne of God.

THE GOSPEL. St. Matth. ii. 13.

THE Angel of the Lord appeareth to Joseph in a dream, saying, Arise, and take the young child, and his mother, and flee into Egypt, and be thou there until I bring thee word ; for Herod will seek the young child to destroy him. When he arose he took the young child and his mother by night, and departed into Egypt, and was there until the death of Herod ; that it might be fulfilled which was spoken of the Lord by the prophet, saying, Out of Egypt have I called my Son. Then Herod, when he saw that he was mocked of the wise men, was exceeding wroth ; and sent forth, and slew all the children that were in Bethlehem, and in all the coasts thereof, from two years old and under, according to the time which he had diligently inquired of the wise men. Then was fulfilled that which was spoken by Jeremy the prophet, saying, In Rama was there a voice heard, lamentation, and weeping, and great mourning, Rachel weeping for her children, and would not be comforted because they are not.

The Sunday after Christmas Day.

THE COLLECT.

ALMIGHTY God, who hast given us thy only begotten Son to take our nature upon him, and as at this time to be born of a pure Virgin ; Grant that we being regenerate, and made thy children by adoption and grace, may daily be renewed by thy Holy Spirit ; through the same our Lord Jesus Christ, who liveth and reigneth with thee and the same Spirit, ever one God, world without end. *Amen.*

THE EPISTLE. Gal. iv. 1.

NOW I say, that the heir, as long as he is a child, differeth nothing from a servant, though he be lord of all; but is under tutors and governours, until the time appointed of the father. Even so we, when we were children, were in bondage under the elements of the world: but when the fulness of the time was come, God sent forth his Son, made of a woman, made under the law, to redeem them that were under the law, that we might receive the adoption of sons. And because ye are sons, God hath sent forth the Spirit of his Son into your hearts, crying, Abba, Father. Wherefore thou art no more a servant, but a son; and if a son, then an heir of God through Christ.

THE GOSPEL. St. Matth. i. 18.

THE birth of Jesus Christ was on this wise: When as his mother Mary was espoused to Joseph, before they came together she was found with child of the Holy Ghost. Then Joseph her husband, being a just man, and not willing to make her a publick example, was minded to put her away privily. But while he thought on these things, behold, the angel of the Lord appeared unto him in a dream, saying, Joseph thou son of David, fear not to take unto thee Mary thy wife; for that which is conceived in her is of the Holy Ghost: And she shall bring forth a Son, and thou shalt call his name Jesus; for he shall save his people from their sins. (Now all this was done, that it might be fulfilled which was spoken of the Lord by the prophet, saying, Behold, a Virgin shall be with child, and shall bring forth a Son, and they shall call his name Immanuel, which being interpreted is, God with us.) Then Joseph, being raised from sleep, did as the angel of the Lord had bidden him, and took unto him his wife; and knew her not till she had brought forth her first-born son: and he called his name Jesus.

The Circumcision of Christ.

THE COLLECT.

ALMIGHTY God, who madest thy blessed Son to be circumcised, and obedient to the law for man; Grant us the true circumcision of the Spirit; that, our hearts, and all our members, being mortified from all worldly and carnal lusts, we may in all things obey thy blessed will; through the same thy Son Jesus Christ our Lord. *Amen.*

THE EPISTLE. Rom. iv. 8.

BLESSED is the man to whom the Lord will not impute sin. Cometh this blessedness then upon the circumcision only, or upon the uncircumcision also ? For we say, that faith was reckoned to Abraham for righteousness. How was it then reckoned ? when he was in circumcision, or in uncircumcision? Not in circumcision, but in uncircumcision. And he received the sign of circumcision, a seal of the righteousness of the faith which he had yet being uncircumcised ; that he might be the father of all them that believe, though they be not circumcised ; that righteousness might be imputed unto them also ; And the father of circumcision to them who are not of the circumcision only, but also walk in the steps of that faith of our father Abraham, which he had being yet uncircumcised. For the promise, that he should be the heir of the world, was not to Abraham, or to his seed, through the law, but through the righteousness of faith. For if they which are of the law be heirs, faith is made void, and the promise made of none effect.

THE GOSPEL. St. Luke ii. 15.

AND it came to pass, as the angels were gone away from them into heaven, the shepherds said one to another, Let us now go even unto Bethlehem, and see this thing which is come to pass, which the Lord hath made known unto us. And they came with haste, and found Mary and Joseph, and the babe lying in a manger. And when they had seen it, they made known abroad the saying which was told them concerning this child. And all they that heard it wondered at those things which were told them by the shepherds. But Mary kept all these things, and pondered them in her heart. And the shepherds returned, glorifying and praising God for all the things that they had heard and seen, as it was told unto them. And when eight days were accomplished for the circumcising of the child, his name was called Jesus, which was so named of the angel before he was conceived in the womb.

¶ *The same Collect, Epistle, and Gospel shall serve for every day after unto the Epiphany.*

The Epiphany,

OR

THE MANIFESTATION OF CHRIST TO THE GENTILES.

THE COLLECT.

O GOD, who by the leading of a star didst manifest thy only begotten Son to the Gentiles ; Mercifully grant, that we, which know thee now by faith, may after this life have the fruition of thy glorious Godhead ; through Jesus Christ our Lord. *Amen.*

THE EPISTLE. Ephes. iii. 1.

FOR this cause, I Paul, the prisoner of Jesus Christ for you Gentiles; if ye have heard of the dispensation of the grace of God, which is given me to you-ward: How that by revelation he made known unto me the mystery (as I wrote afore in few words, whereby, when ye read, ye may understand my knowledge in the mystery of Christ) which in other ages was not made known unto the sons of men, as it is now revealed unto his holy Apostles and Prophets by the Spirit; That the Gentiles should be fellow-heirs, and of the same body, and partakers of his promise in Christ, by the Gospel: whereof I was made a minister, according to the gift of the grace of God given unto me by the effectual working of his power. Unto me, who am less than the least of all saints, is this grace given, that I should preach among the Gentiles the unsearchable riches of Christ; and to make all men see what is the fellowship of the mystery, which from the beginning of the world hath been hid in God, who created all things by Jesus Christ: to the intent, that now unto the principalities and powers in heavenly places might be known by the Church the manifold wisdom of God, according to the eternal purpose which he purposed in Christ Jesus our Lord: In whom we have boldness and access with confidence by the faith of him.

THE GOSPEL. St. Matth. ii. 1.

WHEN Jesus was born in Bethlehem of Judæa, in the days of Herod the king, behold, there came wise men from the east to Jerusalem, saying, Where is he that is born King of the Jews? for we have seen his star in the east, and are come to worship him. When Herod the king had heard these things, he was troubled, and all Jerusalem with him. And when he had gathered all the chief priests and scribes of the people together, he demanded of them, where Christ should be born. And they said unto him, In Bethlehem of Judæa: for thus it is written by the prophet, And thou, Bethlehem, in the land of Juda, art not the least among the princes of Juda: for out of thee shall come a Governour that shall rule my people Israel. Then Herod, when he had privily called the wise men, inquired of them diligently what time the star appeared. And he sent them to Bethlehem, and said, Go, and search diligently for the young child, and when ye have found him, bring me word again, that I may come and worship him also. When they had heard the king, they departed; and lo, the star which they saw in the east went before them, till it came and stood over where the young child was. When they saw the star, they rejoiced with exceeding great joy. And when they were come into the house, they saw the young child with Mary his mother, and fell down and worshipped him : and when they had opened their treasures, they presented unto him gifts ; gold, and frankincense, and myrrh. And being warned of God in a dream that they should not return to Herod, they departed into their own country another way.

The First Sunday after the Epiphany.
THE COLLECT.

O LORD, we beseech thee mercifully to receive the prayers of thy people which call upon thee ; and grant that they may both perceive and know what things they ought to do, and also may have grace and power faithfully to fulfil the same ; through Jesus Christ our Lord. *Amen.*

THE EPISTLE. Rom. xii. 1.

I BESEECH you therefore, brethren, by the mercies of God, that ye present your bodies a living sacrifice, holy, acceptable unto God, which is your reasonable service. And be not conformed to this world ; but be ye transformed by the renewing of your mind, that ye may prove what is that good, and acceptable, and perfect will of God. For I say, through the grace given unto me, to every man that is among you, not to think of himself more highly than he ought to think, but to think soberly, according as God hath dealt to every man the measure of faith. For as we have many members in one body, and all members have not the same office ; so we being many, are one body in Christ, and every one members one of another.

THE GOSPEL. St. Luke ii. 41.

NOW his parents went to Jerusalem every year at the feast of the Passover. And when he was twelve years old, they went up to Jerusalem, after the custom of the feast. And when they had fulfilled the days, as they returned, the child Jesus tarried behind in Jerusalem ; and Joseph and his mother knew not of it. But they, supposing him to have been in the company, went a day's journey, and they sought him among their kinsfolk and acquaintance. And when they found him not, they turned back again to Jerusalem, seeking him. And it came to pass, that after three days they found him in the temple, sitting in the midst of the doctors, both hearing them, and asking them questions. And all that heard him were astonished at his understanding and answers. And when they saw him, they were amazed : and his mother said unto him, Son, why hast thou thus dealt with us ? behold, thy father and I have sought thee sorrowing. And he said unto them, How is it that ye sought me ? wist ye not that I must be about my Father's business ? And they understood not the saying which he spake unto them. And he went down with them, and came to Nazareth, and was subject unto them : but his mother kept all these sayings in her heart. And Jesus increased in wisdom, and stature, and in favour with God and man.

The Second Sunday after the Epiphany.

THE COLLECT.

A LMIGHTY and everlasting God, who dost govern all things in heaven and earth ; Mercifully hear the supplications of thy people, and grant us thy peace all the days of our life ; through Jesus Christ our Lord. *Amen.*

THE EPISTLE. Rom. xii. 6.

H AVING then gifts differing according to the grace that is given to us, whether prophecy, let us prophesy according to the proportion of faith ; or ministry, let us wait on our ministering ; or he that teacheth, on teaching ; or he that exhorteth, on exhortation : he that giveth, let him do it with simplicity ; he that ruleth, with diligence ; he that sheweth mercy, with cheerfulness. Let love be without dissimulation. Abhor that which is evil, cleave to that which is good. Be kindly affectioned one to another with brotherly love, in honour preferring one another : not slothful in business ; fervent in spirit ; serving the Lord ; rejoicing in hope ; patient in tribulation ; continuing instant in prayer ; distributing to the necessity of saints : given to hospitality. Bless them which persecute you ; bless, and curse not. Rejoice with them that do rejoice, and weep with them that weep. Be of the same mind one towards another. Mind not high things, but condescend to men of low estate.

THE GOSPEL. St. John ii. 1.

A ND the third day there was a marriage in Cana of Galilee, and the mother of Jesus was there. And both Jesus was called, and his disciples, to the marriage. And when they wanted wine, the mother of Jesus saith unto him, They have no wine. Jesus saith unto her, Woman, what have I to do with thee ? mine hour is not yet come. His mother saith unto the servants, Whatsoever he saith unto you, do it. And there were set there six water-pots of stone, after the manner of the purifying of the Jews, containing two or three firkins apiece. Jesus saith unto them, Fill the water-pots with water. And they filled them up to the brim. And he saith unto them, Draw out now, and bear unto the governour of the feast.

And they bare it. When the ruler of the feast had tasted the water that was made wine, and knew not whence it was, (but the servants which drew the water knew,) the governour of the feast called the bridegroom, and saith unto him, Every man at the beginning doth set forth good wine, and when men have well drunk, then that which is worse : but thou hast kept the good wine until now. This beginning of miracles did Jesus in Cana of Galilee, and manifested forth his glory, and his disciples believed on him.

The Third Sunday after the Epiphany.

THE COLLECT.

ALMIGHTY and everlasting God, mercifully look upon our infirmities, and in all our dangers and necessities stretch forth thy right hand to help and defend us; through Jesus Christ our Lord. *Amen.*

THE EPISTLE. Rom. xii. 16.

BE not wise in your own conceits. Recompense to no man evil for evil. Provide things honest in the sight of all men. If it be possible, as much as lieth in you, live peaceably with all men. Dearly beloved, avenge not yourselves, but rather give place unto wrath ; for it is written, Vengeance is mine ; I will repay, saith the Lord. Therefore, if thine enemy hunger, feed him ; if he thirst, give him drink : for in so doing thou shalt heap coals of fire on his head. Be not overcome of evil, but overcome evil with good.

THE GOSPEL. St. Matth. viii. 1.

WHEN he was come down from the mountain, great multitudes followed him. And behold, there came a leper and worshipped him, saying, Lord, if thou wilt, thou canst make me clean. And Jesus put forth his hand, and touched him, saying, I will ; be thou clean. And immediately his leprosy was cleansed. And Jesus saith unto him, See thou tell no man, but go thy way, shew thyself to the priest, and offer the gift that Moses commanded, for a testimony unto them. And when Jesus was entered into Capernaum, there came unto him a centurion beseeching him, and saying, Lord, my servant lieth at home sick of the palsy, grievously tormented. And Jesus saith unto him, I will come and heal him. The centurion answered and said, Lord, I am not worthy that thou shouldest come under my roof ; but speak the word only, and my servant shall be healed. For I am a man under authority, having soldiers under me : and I say unto this man, Go, and he goeth ;

and to another, Come, and he cometh ; and to my servant, Do this, and he doeth it. When Jesus heard it, he marvelled, and said to them that followed, Verily I say unto you, I have not found so great faith, no not in Israel. And I say unto you, That many shall come from the east and west, and shall sit down with Abraham, and Isaac, and Jacob, in the kingdom of heaven. But the children of the kingdom shall be cast out into outer darkness : there shall be weeping and gnashing of teeth. And Jesus said unto the centurion, Go thy way, and as thou hast believed, so be it done unto thee. And his servant was healed in the self-same hour.

The Fourth Sunday after the Epiphany.

THE COLLECT.

O GOD, who knowest us to be set in the midst of so many and great dangers, that by reason of the frailty of our nature we cannot always stand upright ; Grant to us such strength and protection, as may support us in all dangers, and carry us through all temptations ; through Jesus Christ our Lord. *Amen.*

THE EPISTLE. Rom. xiii. 1.

L ET every soul be subject unto the higher powers ; for there is no power but of God : the powers that be are ordained of God. Whosoever therefore resisteth the power resisteth the ordinance of od : and they that resist shall receive to themselves damnation. 'or rulers are not a terror to good works, but to the evil. Wilt hou then not be afraid of the power ? do that which is good, and thou shalt have praise of the same : for he is the minister of God to thee for good. But if thou do that which is evil, be afraid ; for he beareth not the sword in vain : for he is the minister of God, a revenger to execute wrath upon him that doeth evil. Wherefore ye must needs be subject, not only for wrath, but also for conscience sake. For for this cause pay ye tribute also ; for they are God's ministers, attending continually upon this very thing. Render therefore to all their dues ; tribute to whom tribute is due, custom to whom custom, fear to whom fear, honour to whom honour.

THE GOSPEL. St. Matth. viii. 23.

A ND when he was entered into a ship, his disciples followed him. And behold, there arose a great tempest in the sea, insomuch that the ship was covered with the waves : but he was asleep. And his disciples came to him, and awoke him, saying, Lord, save us, we perish. And he saith unto them, Why are ye fearful, O ye of little faith ? Then he arose, and rebuked the winds and the sea, and there was a great calm. But the men marvelled, saying, What manner of man is this, that even the winds and the sea obey him! And when he was come to the other side into the country of the Gergesenes, there met him two possessed with devils, coming out of the tombs, exceeding fierce, so that no man might pass by that way. And behold, they cried out, saying, What have we to do with thee, Jesus, thou Son of God? art thou come hither to torment us before the time? And there was a good way off from them an herd of many swine, feeding. So the devils besought him, saying, If thou cast us out, suffer us to go away into the herd of swine. And he said unto them, Go. And when they were come out, they went into the herd of swine: and behold, the whole herd of swine ran violently down a steep place into the sea, and perished in the waters. And they that kept them fled, and went their ways into the city, and told every thing, and what was befallen to the possessed of the devils. And behold, the whole city came out to meet Jesus: and when they saw him, they besought him, that he would depart out of their coasts.

The Fifth Sunday after the Epiphany.

THE COLLECT.

O LORD, we beseech thee to keep thy Church and household continually in thy true religion; that they who do lean only upon the hope of thy heavenly grace may evermore be defended b thy mighty power; through Jesus Christ our Lord. *Amen.*

THE EPISTLE. Coloss. iii. 12.

PUT on therefore, as the elect of God, holy and beloved, bowels of mercies, kindness, humbleness of mind, meekness, long-suffering; forbearing one another, and forgiving one another, if any man have a quarrel against any; even as Christ forgave you, so also do ye. And above all these things put on charity, which is the bond of perfectness. And let the peace of God rule in your hearts, to the which also ye are called in one body; and be ye thankful. Let the word of Christ dwell in you richly in all wisdom, teaching and admonishing one another in psalms, and hymns, and spiritual songs, singing with grace in your hearts to the Lord. And whatsoever ye do, in word or deed, do all in the Name of the Lord Jesus, giving thanks to God and the Father by him.

THE GOSPEL. St. Matth. xiii. 24.

THE kingdom of heaven is likened unto a man which sowed good seed in his field. But while men slept, his enemy came and sowed tares among the wheat, and went his way. But when the blade was sprung up, and brought forth fruit, then appeared the tares also. So the servants of the householder came, and said unto him, Sir, didst not thou sow good seed in thy field? from whence then hath it tares? He said unto them, An enemy hath done this. The servants said unto him, Wilt thou then that we go and gather them up? But he said, Nay; lest while ye gather up the tares, ye root up also the wheat with them. Let both grow together until the harvest; and in the time of harvest I will say to the reapers, Gather ye together first the tares, and bind them in bundles to burn them: but gather the wheat into my barn.

The Sixth Sunday after the Epiphany.
THE COLLECT.

O GOD, whose blessed Son was manifested that he might destroy the works of the devil, and make us the sons of God, and heirs of eternal life; Grant us, we beseech thee, that, having this hope, we may purify ourselves, even as he is pure; that, when he shall appear again with power and great glory, we may be made like unto him in his eternal and glorious kingdom; where with thee, O Father, and thee, O Holy Ghost, he liveth and reigneth, ever one God, world without end. *Amen.*

THE EPISTLE. 1 St. John iii. 1.

BEHOLD, what manner of love the Father hath bestowed upon us, that we should be called the sons of God: therefore the world knoweth us not, because it knew him not. Beloved, now are we the sons of God, and it doth not yet appear what we shall be: but we know, that, when he shall appear, we shall be like him; for we shall see him as he is. And every man that hath this hope in him purifieth himself, even as he is pure. Whosoever committeth sin transgresseth also the law: for sin is the transgression of the law. And ye know that he was manifested to take away our sins; and in him is no sin. Whosoever abideth in him sinneth not: whosoever sinneth hath not seen him, neither known him. Little children, let no man deceive you: he that doeth righteousness is righteous, even as he is righteous. He that committeth sin is of the devil: for the devil sinneth from the beginning. For this purpose the Son of God was manifested, that he might destroy the works of the devil.

THE GOSPEL. St. Matth. xxiv. 23.

THEN if any man shall say unto you, Lo, here is Christ, or there; believe it not. For there shall arise false Christs, and false prophets, and shall shew great signs and wonders; insomuch that (if it were possible) they shall deceive the very elect. Behold, I have told you before. Wherefore, if they shall say unto you, Behold, he is in the desert; go not forth: behold, he is in the secret chambers; believe it not. For as the lightning cometh out of the east, and shineth even unto the west; so shall also the coming of the Son of Man be. For wheresoever the carcase is, there will the eagles be gathered together. Immediately after the tribulation of those days shall the sun be darkened, and the moon shall not give her light, and the stars shall fall from heaven, and the powers of the heavens shall be shaken. And then shall appear the sign of the Son of Man in heaven: and then shall all the tribes of the earth mourn, and they shall see the Son of Man coming in the clouds of heaven, with power and great glory. And he shall send his angels with a great sound of a trumpet, and they shall gather together his elect from the four winds, from one end of heaven to the other.

The Sunday called Septuagesima,

OR

THE THIRD SUNDAY BEFORE LENT.

THE COLLECT.

O LORD, we beseech thee favourably to hear the prayers of thy people; that we, who are justly punished for our offences, may be mercifully delivered by thy goodness, for the glory of thy Name, through Jesus Christ our Saviour, who liveth and reigneth with thee and the Holy Ghost, ever one God, world without end. Amen.

THE EPISTLE. 1 Cor. ix. 24.

KNOW ye not, that they which run in a race run all, but one receiveth the prize? So run that ye may obtain. And every man that striveth for the mastery is temperate in all things: now they do it to obtain a corruptible crown, but we an incorruptible. I therefore so run, not as uncertainly; so fight I, not as one that beateth the air: but I keep under my body, and bring it into subjection, lest that by any means, when I have preached to others, I myself should be a cast-away.

THE GOSPEL. St. Matth. xx. 1.

THE kingdom of heaven is like unto a man that is an householder, which went out early in the morning to hire labourers into his vineyard. And when he had agreed with the labourers for a penny a day, he sent them into his vineyard. And he went out about the third hour, and saw others standing idle in the market-place, and said unto them, Go ye also into the vineyard, and whatsoever is right I will give you. And they went their way. Again he went out about the sixth and ninth hour, and did likewise. And about the eleventh hour he went out, and found others standing idle, and saith unto them, Why stand ye here all the day idle? They say unto him, Because no man hath hired us. He saith unto them, Go ye also into the vineyard, and whatsoever is right, that shall ye receive. So when even was come, the lord of the vineyard saith unto his steward, Call the labourers, and give them their hire, beginning from the last unto the first. And when they came that were hired about the eleventh hour, they received every man a penny. But when the first came, they supposed that they should have received more; and they likewise received every man a penny. And when they had received it, they murmured against the good-man of the house, saying, These last have wrought but one hour, and thou hast made them equal unto us, which have borne the burden and heat of the day. But he answered one of them, and said, Friend, I do thee no wrong; didst not thou agree with me for a penny? Take that thine is, and go thy way; I will give unto this last even as unto thee. Is it not lawful for me to do what I will with mine own? Is thine eye evil, because I am good? So the last shall be first, and the first last: for many be called, but few chosen.

The Sunday called Sexagesima,

OR

THE SECOND SUNDAY BEFORE LENT.

THE COLLECT.

O LORD God, who seest that we put not our trust in anything that we do; Mercifully grant that by thy power we may be defended against all adversity; through Jesus Christ our Lord. *Amen.*

THE EPISTLE. 2 COR. xi. 19.

YE suffer fools gladly, seeing ye yourselves are wise. For ye suffer if a man bring you into bondage, if a man devour you, if a man take of you, if a man exalt himself, if a man smite you on the face. I speak as concerning reproach, as though we had been weak: howbeit, whereinsoever any is bold, (I speak foolishly,) I am bold also. Are they Hebrews? so am I. Are they Israelites? so am I. Are they the seed of Abraham? so am I. Are they ministers of Christ? (I speak as a fool,) I am more: in labours more abundant; in stripes above measure; in prisons more frequent; in deaths oft. Of the Jews five times received I forty stripes save one; thrice was I beaten with rods; once was I stoned; thrice I suffered shipwreck; a night and a day I have been in the deep; in journeyings often; in perils of waters; in perils of robbers; in perils by mine own countrymen; in perils by the heathen; in perils in the city; in perils in the wilderness; in perils in the sea; in perils among false brethren; in weariness and painfulness; in watchings often; in hunger and thirst; in fastings often; in cold and nakedness; besides those things that are without, that which cometh upon me daily, the care of all the churches. Who is weak, and I am not weak? who is offended, and I burn not? If I must needs glory, I will glory of the things which concern mine infirmities. The God and Father of our Lord Jesus Christ, which is blessed for evermore, knoweth that I lie not.

THE GOSPEL. St. Luke viii. 4.

WHEN much people were gathered together, and were come to him out of every city, he spake by a parable: A sower went out to sow his seed; and as he sowed, some fell by the way-side, and it was trodden down, and the fowls of the air devoured it. And some fell upon a rock, and as soon as it was sprung up, it withered away, because it lacked moisture. And some fell among thorns, and the thorns sprang up with it, and choked it. And other fell on good ground, and sprang up, and bare fruit an hundred-fold. And when he had said these things, he cried, He that hath ears to hear, let him hear. And his disciples asked him, saying, What might this parable be? And he said, Unto you it is given to know the mysteries of the kingdom of God: but to others in parables; that seeing they might not see, and hearing they might not understand. Now the parable is this: The seed is the Word of God. Those by the way-side are they that hear; then cometh the devil, and taketh away the word out of their hearts, lest they should believe, and be saved. They on the rock are they, which, when they hear, receive the word with joy; and these have no root, which for a while believe, and in time of temptation fall away. And that which fell among thorns, are they, which, when they have heard, go forth, and are choked with cares, and riches, and pleasures of this life, and bring no fruit to perfection. But that on the good ground, are they, which in an honest and good heart, having heard the word, keep it, and bring forth fruit with patience.

The Sunday called Quinquagesima,

OR

THE NEXT SUNDAY BEFORE LENT.

THE COLLECT.

O LORD, who hast taught us that all our doings without charity are nothing worth; Send thy Holy Ghost, and pour into our hearts that most excellent gift of charity, the very bond of peace and of all virtues, without which whosoever liveth is counted dead before thee : Grant this for thine only Son Jesus Christ's sake. *Amen.*

THE EPISTLE. 1 Cor. xiii. 1.

THOUGH I speak with the tongues of men and of angels, and have not charity, I am become as sounding brass, or a tinkling cymbal. And though I have the gift of prophecy, and understand all mysteries, and all knowledge ; and though I have all faith, so that I could remove mountains, and have not charity, I am nothing. And though I bestow all my goods to feed the poor, and though I give my body to be burned, and have not charity, it profiteth me nothing. Charity suffereth long, and is kind ; charity envieth not ; charity vaunteth not itself, is not puffed up, doth not behave itself unseemly, seeketh not her own, is not easily provoked, thinketh no evil, rejoiceth not in iniquity, but rejoiceth in the truth ; beareth all things, believeth all things, hopeth all things, endureth all things. Charity never faileth : but whether there be prophecies, they shall fail ; whether there be tongues, they shall cease ; whether there be knowledge, it shall vanish away. For we know in part, and we prophesy in part. But when that which is perfect is come, then that which is in part shall be done away. When I was a child, I spake as a child, I understood as a child, I thought as a child ; but when I became a man, I put away childish things. For now we see through a glass darkly ; but then face to face : now I know in part ; but then shall I know even as also I am known. And now abideth faith, hope, charity, these three ; but the greatest of these is charity.

THE GOSPEL. St. Luke xviii. 31.

THEN Jesus took unto him the twelve, and said unto them, Behold, we go up to Jerusalem, and all things that are written by the prophets concerning the Son of Man shall be accomplished. For he shall be delivered unto the Gentiles, and shall be mocked, and spitefully entreated, and spitted on : and they shall scourge him, and put him to death ; and the third day he shall rise again.

And they understood none of these things : and this saying was hid from them, neither knew they the things which were spoken. And it came to pass, that as he was come nigh unto Jericho, a certain blind man sat by the way-side begging : and hearing the multitude pass by, he asked what it meant. And they told him, that Jesus of Nazareth passeth by. And he cried, saying, Jesus, thou Son of David, have mercy on me. And they which went before rebuked him, that he should hold his peace : but he cried so much the more, Thou Son of David, have mercy on me. And Jesus stood, and commanded him to be brought unto him : and when he was come near, he asked him, saying, What wilt thou that I should do unto thee ? And he said, Lord, that I may receive my sight. And Jesus said unto him, Receive thy sight ; thy faith hath saved thee. And immediately he received his sight, and followed him, glorifying God : and all the people, when they saw it, gave praise unto God.

THE FIRST DAY OF LENT,

COMMONLY CALLED

Ash Wednesday.

THE COLLECT.

ALMIGHTY and everlasting God, who hatest nothing that thou hast made, and dost forgive the sins of all them that are penitent ; Create and make in us new and contrite hearts, that we worthily lamenting our sins, and acknowledging our wretchedness, may obtain of thee, the God of all mercy, perfect remission and forgiveness ; through Jesus Christ our Lord. *Amen.*

¶ *This Collect is to be read every day in Lent after the Collect appointed for the Day.*

FOR THE EPISTLE. Joel ii. 12.

TURN ye even to me, saith the Lord, with all your heart, and with fasting, and with weeping, and with mourning. And rend your heart, and not your garments, and turn unto the Lord your God : for he is gracious and merciful, slow to anger, and of great kindness, and repenteth him of the evil. Who knoweth if he will return, and repent, and leave a blessing behind him, even a meat-offering and a drink-offering unto the Lord your God ? Blow the trumpet in Zion, sanctify a fast, call a solemn assembly, gather the people, sanctify the congregation, assemble the elders, gather the children, and those that suck the breasts ; let the bridegroom go forth of his chamber, and the bride out of her closet ; let the priests, the ministers of the Lord, weep between the porch and the altar, and let them say, Spare thy people, O Lord, and give not thine heritage to reproach, that the heathen should rule over them : wherefore should they say among the people, Where is their God?

THE GOSPEL. St. Matth. vi. 16.

WHEN ye fast, be not as the hypocrites, of a sad countenance : for they disfigure their faces, that they may appear unto men to fast. Verily I say unto you, They have their reward. But thou, when thou fastest, anoint thine head, and wash thy face, that thou appear not unto men to fast, but unto thy Father which is in secret ; and thy Father, which seeth in secret, shall reward thee openly. Lay not up for yourselves treasures upon earth, where moth and rust doth corrupt, and where thieves break through and steal : but lay up for yourselves treasures in heaven, where neither moth nor rust doth corrupt, and where thieves do not break through nor steal : for where your treasure is, there will your heart be also.

The First Sunday in Lent.

THE COLLECT.

O LORD, who for our sake didst fa. 'orty days and forty nights ; Give us grace to use such abst.... ?, that, our flesh being subdued to the Spirit, we may ever ob..., thy godly motions in righteousness, and true holiness, to thy honour and glory, who livest and reignest with the Father and the Holy Ghost, one God, world without end. *Amen.*

THE EPISTLE. 2 Cor. vi. 1.

WE then, as workers together with him, beseech you also, that ye receive not the grace of God in vain ; (for he saith, I have heard thee in a time accepted, and in the day of salvation have I succoured thee : behold, now is the accepted time ; behold, now is the day of salvation ;) giving no offence in any thing, that the ministry be not blamed ; but in all things approving ourselves as the ministers of God, in much patience, in afflictions, in necessities, in distresses, in stripes, in imprisonments, in tumults, in labours, in watchings, in fastings ; by pureness, by knowledge, by long-suffering, by kindness, by the Holy Ghost, by love unfeigned, by the word of truth, by the power of God, by the armour of righteousness on the right hand and on the left, by honour and dishonour, by evil report and good report ; as deceivers, and yet true ; as unknown, and yet well known ; as dying, and behold, we live ; as chastened, and not killed ; as sorrowful, yet alway rejoicing ; as poor, yet making many rich ; as having nothing, and yet possessing all things.

THE GOSPEL. St. Matth. iv. 1.

THEN was Jesus led up of the Spirit into the wilderness, to be tempted of the devil. And when he had fasted forty days and forty nights, he was afterward an hungred. And when the tempter came to him, he said, If thou be the Son of God, command that these stones be made bread. But he answered and said, It is written, Man shall not live by bread alone, but by every word that proceedeth out of the mouth of God. Then the devil taketh him up into the holy city, and setteth him on a pinnacle of the temple, and saith unto him, If thou be the Son of God, cast thyself down ; for it is written, He shall give his angels charge concerning thee, and in their hands they shall bear thee up, lest at any time thou dash thy foot against a stone. Jesus said unto him, It is written again, Thou shalt not tempt the Lord thy God. Again, the devil taketh him up into an exceeding high mountain, and sheweth him all the kingdoms of the world, and the glory of them ; and saith unto him, All these things will I give thee, if thou wilt fall down and worship me. Then saith Jesus unto him, Get thee hence, Satan ; for it is written, Thou shalt worship the Lord thy God, and him only shalt thou serve. Then the devil leaveth him, and behold, angels came and ministered unto him.

The Second Sunday in Lent.
THE COLLECT.

ALMIGHTY God, who seest that we have no power of ourselves to help ourselves ; Keep us both outwardly in our bodies, and inwardly in our souls ; that we may be defended from all adversities which may happen to the body, and from all evil thoughts which may assault and hurt the soul ; through Jesus Christ our Lord. *Amen.*

THE EPISTLE. 1 Thess. iv. 1.

WE beseech you, brethren, and exhort you by the Lord Jesus, that as ye have received of us how ye ought to walk, and to please God, so ye would abound more and more. For ye know what commandments we gave you by the Lord Jesus. For this is the will of God, even your sanctification, that ye should abstain from fornication ; that every one of you should know how to possess his vessel in sanctification and honour ; not in the lust of concupiscence, even as the Gentiles which know not God ; that no man go beyond and defraud his brother in any matter ; because that the Lord is the avenger of all such, as we also have forewarned you, and testified. For God hath not called us unto uncleanness, but unto holiness. He therefore that despiseth despiseth not man, but God, who hath also given unto us his Holy Spirit.

THE GOSPEL. St. Matth. xv. 21.

JESUS went thence and departed into the coasts of Tyre and Sidon. And behold, a woman of Canaan came out of the same coasts, and cried unto him, saying, Have mercy on me, O Lord, thou Son of David; my daughter is grievously vexed with a devil. But he answered her not a word. And his disciples came and besought him, saying, Send her away; for she crieth after us. But he answered and said, I am not sent, but unto the lost sheep of the house of Israel. Then came she and worshipped him, saying, Lord, help me. But he answered and said, It is not meet to take the children's bread, and to cast it to dogs. And she said, Truth, Lord; yet the dogs eat of the crumbs which fall from their masters' table. Then Jesus answered and said unto her, O woman, great is thy faith: be it unto thee even as thou wilt. And her daughter was made whole from that very hour.

The Third Sunday in Lent.

THE COLLECT.

WE beseech thee, Almighty God, look upon the hearty desires of thy humble servants, and stretch forth the right hand of thy Majesty, to be our defence against all our enemies; through Jesus Christ our Lord. *Amen.*

THE EPISTLE. Ephes. v. 1.

BE ye therefore followers of God, as dear children; and walk in love, as Christ also hath loved us, and hath given himself for us, an offering and a sacrifice to God for a sweet-smelling savour. But fornication, and all uncleanness, or covetousness, let it not be once named amongst you, as becometh saints; neither filthiness, nor foolish-talking, nor jesting, which are not convenient; but rather giving of thanks: for this ye know, that no whoremonger, nor unclean person, nor covetous man, who is an idolater, hath any inheritance in the kingdom of Christ, and of God. Let no man deceive you with vain words: for because of these things cometh the wrath of God upon the children of disobedience. Be not ye therefore partakers with them: for ye were sometimes darkness, but now are ye light in the Lord: walk as children of light; (for the fruit of the Spirit is in all goodness, and righteousness, and truth;) proving what is acceptable unto the Lord. And have no fellowship with the unfruitful works of darkness, but rather reprove them: for it is a shame even to speak of those things which are done of them in secret. But all things that are reproved are made manifest by the light : for whatsoever doth make manifest is light. Wherefore he saith, Awake, thou that sleepest, and arise from the dead, and Christ shall give thee light.

THE GOSPEL. St. Luke xi. 14.

JESUS was casting out a devil, and it was dumb. And it came to pass, when the devil was gone out, the dumb spake; and the people wondered. But some of them said, He casteth out devils through Beelzebub, the chief of the devils. And others, tempting him, sought of him a sign from heaven. But he, knowing their thoughts, said unto them, Every kingdom divided against itself is brought to desolation; and a house divided against a house falleth. If Satan also be divided against himself, how shall his kingdom stand? because ye say, that I cast out devils through Beelzebub. And if I by Beelzebub cast out devils, by whom do your sons cast them out? therefore shall they be your judges. But if I with the finger of God cast out devils, no doubt the kingdom of God is come upon you. When a strong man armed keepeth his palace, his goods are in peace; but when a stronger than he shall come upon him, and overcome him, he taketh from him all his armour wherein he trusted, and divideth his spoils. He that is not with me is against me : and he that gathereth not with me scattereth. When the unclean spirit is gone out of a man, he walketh through dry places, seeking rest; and finding none, he saith, I will return unto my house whence I came out. And when he cometh, he findeth it swept and garnished. Then goeth he and taketh to him seven other spirits more wicked than himself, and they enter in, and dwell there; and the last state of that man is worse than the first. And it came to pass, as he spake these things, a certain woman of the company lift up her voice, and said unto him, Blessed is the womb that bare thee, and the paps which thou hast sucked. But he said, Yea rather, blessed are they that hear the Word of God, and keep it.

The Fourth Sunday in Lent.
THE COLLECT.

GRANT, we beseech thee, Almighty God, that we, who for our evil deeds do worthily deserve to be punished, by the comfort of thy grace may mercifully be relieved; through our Lord and Saviour Jesus Christ. *Amen.*

THE EPISTLE. Gal. iv. 21.

TELL me, ye that desire to be under the law, do ye not hear the law? For it is written, that Abraham had two sons, the one by a bond-maid, the other by a free-woman. But he who was of the bond-woman was born after the flesh; but he of the free-woman was by promise. Which things are an allegory: for these are the two covenants; the one from the mount Sinai, which gendereth to bondage, which is Agar. For this Agar is mount Sinai in Arabia, and answereth to Jerusalem which now is, and is in bondage with her children. But Jerusalem which is above is free; which is the mother of us all. For it is written, Rejoice, thou barren that bearest not; break forth and cry, thou that travailest not: for the desolate hath many more children than she which hath an husband. Now we, brethren, as Isaac was, are the children of promise. But as then he that was born after the flesh persecuted him that was born after the Spirit; even so it is now. Nevertheless, what saith the Scripture? Cast out the bond-woman and her son; for the son of the bond-woman shall not be heir with the son of the free-woman. So then, brethren, we are not children of the bond-woman, but of the free.

THE GOSPEL. St. John vi. 1.

JESUS went over the sea of Galilee, which is the sea of Tiberias. And a great multitude followed him, because they saw his miracles which he did on them that were diseased. And Jesus went up into a mountain, and there he sat with his disciples. And the Passover, a feast of the Jews, was nigh. When Jesus then lift up his eyes, and saw a great company come unto him, he saith unto Philip, Whence shall we buy bread, that these may eat? (And this he said to prove him; for he himself knew what he would do.) Philip answered him, Two hundred penny-worth of bread is not sufficient for them, that every one of them may take a little. One of his disciples, Andrew, Simon Peter's brother, saith unto him, There is a lad here, which hath five barley-loaves, and two small fishes: but what are they among so many? And Jesus said, Make the men sit down. Now there was much grass in the place. So the men sat down, in number about five thousand. And Jesus took the loaves, and when he had given thanks he distributed to the disciples, and the disciples to them that were set down; and likewise of the fishes as much as they would. When they were filled, he said unto his disciples, Gather up the fragments that remain, that nothing be lost. Therefore they gathered them together, and filled twelve baskets with the fragments of the five barley-loaves, which remained over and above unto them that had eaten. Then those men, when they had seen the miracle that Jesus did, said, This is of a truth that Prophet that should come into the world.

The Fifth Sunday in Lent.

THE COLLECT.

WE beseech thee, Almighty God, mercifully to look upon thy people; that by thy great goodness they may be governed and preserved evermore, both in body and soul; through Jesus Christ our Lord. *Amen.*

THE EPISTLE. Hebr. ix. 11.

CHRIST being come an High Priest of good things to come, by a greater and more perfect tabernacle, not made with hands; that is to say, not of this building; neither by the blood of goats and calves; but by his own blood he entered in once into the holy place, having obtained eternal redemption for us. For if the blood of bulls and of goats, and the ashes of an heifer sprinkling the unclean, sanctifieth to the purifying of the flesh; how much more shall the blood of Christ, who, through the eternal Spirit, offered himself without spot to God, purge your conscience from dead works to serve the living God? And for this cause he is the Mediator of the new testament, that by means of death, for the redemption of the transgressions that were under the first testament, they which are called might receive the promise of eternal inheritance.

THE GOSPEL. St. John viii. 46.

JESUS said, Which of you convinceth me of sin? and if I say the truth, why do ye not believe me? He that is of God heareth God's words; ye therefore hear them not, because ye are not of God. Then answered the Jews, and said unto him, Say we not well, that thou art a Samaritan, and hast a devil? Jesus answered, I have not a devil; but I honour my Father, and ye do dishonour me. And I seek not mine own glory; there is one that seeketh and judgeth. Verily, verily, I say unto you, If a man keep my saying, he shall never see death. Then said the Jews unto him, Now we know that thou hast a devil: Abraham is dead, and the prophets; and thou sayest, If a man keep my saying, he shall never taste of death. Art thou greater than our father Abraham, which is dead? and the prophets are dead: whom makest thou thyself? Jesus answered, If I honour myself, my honour is nothing; it is my Father that honoureth me, of whom ye say, that he is your God: yet ye have not known him; but I know him: and if I should say, I know him not, I shall be a liar like unto you; but I know him, and keep his saying. Your father Abraham rejoiced to see my day, and he saw it, and was glad. Then said the Jews unto him, Thou art not yet fifty years old, and hast thou seen Abraham? Jesus said unto them, Verily, verily, I say unto you, Before Abraham was, I am. Then took they up stones to cast at him: but Jesus hid himself, and went out of the temple.

The Sunday next before Easter.

THE COLLECT.

ALMIGHTY and everlasting God, who, of thy tender love towards mankind, hast sent thy Son, our Saviour Jesus Christ, to take upon him our flesh, and to suffer death upon the cross, that all mankind should follow the example of his great humility; Mercifully grant, that we may both follow the example of his patience, and also be made partakers of his resurrection; through the same Jesus Christ our Lord. *Amen.*

THE EPISTLE. Philip. ii. 5.

LET this mind be in you, which was also in Christ Jesus: who, being in the form of God, thought it not robbery to be equal with God; but made himself of no reputation, and took upon him the form of a servant, and was made in the likeness of men: and being found in fashion as a man he humbled himself, and became obedient unto death, even the death of the cross. Wherefore God also hath highly exalted him, and given him a Name which is above every name; that at the Name of Jesus every knee should bow, of things in heaven, and things in earth, and things under the earth; and that every tongue should confess that Jesus Christ is Lord, to the glory of God the Father.

THE GOSPEL. St. Matth. xxvii. 1.

WHEN the morning was come, all the chief priests and elders of the people took counsel against Jesus, to put him to death. And when they had bound him, they led him away, and delivered him to Pontius Pilate the governour. Then Judas who had betrayed him, when he saw that he was condemned, repented himself, and brought again the thirty pieces of silver to the chief priests and elders, saying, I have sinned, in that I have betrayed the innocent blood. And they said, What is that to us? see thou to that. And he cast down the pieces of silver in the temple, and departed, and went and hanged himself. And the chief priests took the silver pieces, and said, It is not lawful for to put them into the treasury, because it is the price of blood. And they took counsel, and bought with them the potter's field, to bury strangers in. Wherefore that field was called, The field of blood, unto this

I

day. (Then was fulfilled that which was spoken by Jeremy the prophet, saying, And they took the thirty pieces of silver, the price of him that was valued, whom they of the children of Israel did value, and gave them for the potter's field, as the Lord appointed me.) And Jesus stood before the governour; and the governour asked him, saying, Art thou the King of the Jews? And Jesus said unto him, Thou sayest. And when he was accused of the chief priests and elders, he answered nothing. Then saith Pilate unto him, Hearest thou not how many things they witness against thee? And he answered him to never a word, insomuch that the governour marvelled greatly. Now at that feast the governour was wont to release unto the people a prisoner, whom they would. And they had then a notable prisoner, called Barabbas. Therefore when they were gathered together, Pilate said unto them, Whom will ye that I release unto you? Barabbas, or Jesus which is called Christ? For he knew that for envy they had delivered him. When he was set down on the judgement-seat, his wife sent unto him, saying, Have thou nothing to do with that just man: for I have suffered many things this day in a dream because of him. But the chief priests and elders persuaded the multitude that they should ask Barabbas, and destroy Jesus. The governour answered and said unto them, Whether of the twain will ye that I release unto you? They said, Barabbas. Pilate saith unto them, What shall I do then with Jesus, which is called Christ? They all say unto him, Let him be crucified. And the governour said, Why, what evil hath he done? But they cried out the more, saying, Let him be crucified. When Pilate saw that he could prevail nothing, but that rather a tumult was made, he took water, and washed his hands before the multitude, saying, I am innocent of the blood of this just person: see ye to it. Then answered all the people, and said, His blood be on us, and on our children. Then released he Barabbas unto them: and when he had scourged Jesus he delivered him to be crucified. Then the soldiers of the governour took Jesus into the common hall, and gathered unto him the whole band of soldiers. And they stripped him, and put on him a scarlet robe. And when they had platted a crown of thorns they put it upon his head, and a reed in his right hand: and they bowed the knee before him, and mocked him, saying, Hail, King of the Jews. And they spit upon him, and took the reed, and smote him on the head. And after that they had mocked him they took the robe off from him, and put his own raiment on him, and led him away to crucify him. And as they came out they found a man of Cyrene, Simon by name; him they compelled to bear his cross. And when they were come unto a place called Golgotha, that is to say, a place of a skull, they gave him vinegar to drink mingled with gall : and when he had tasted thereof, he would not drink. And they crucified him, and parted his garments, casting lots : that it might be fulfilled, which was spoken by the prophet, They parted my garments among them, and upon my vesture did they cast lots. And sitting down they watched him there ; and set up over his head his accusation written, THIS IS JESUS THE KING OF THE JEWS. Then were there two thieves crucified with him ; one on the right hand, and another on the left. And they that passed by reviled him, wagging their heads, and saying, Thou that destroyest the temple, and buildest it in three days, save thyself : if thou be the Son of God, come down from the cross. Likewise also the chief priests mocking him, with the scribes and elders, said, He saved others, himself he cannot save : if he be the King of Israel, let him now come down from the cross, and we will believe him. He trusted in God ; let him deliver him now, if he will have him : for he said, I am the Son of God. The thieves also, which were crucified with him, cast the same in his teeth. Now from the sixth hour there was darkness over all the land unto the ninth hour. And about the ninth hour Jesus cried with a loud voice, saying, *Eli, Eli, lama sabachthani?* that is to say, My God, my God, why hast thou forsaken me ? Some of them that stood there, when they heard that, said, This man calleth for Elias. And straightway one of them ran, and took a sponge, and filled it with vinegar, and put it on a reed, and gave him to drink. The rest said, Let be, let us see whether Elias will come to save him. Jesus, when he had cried again with a loud voice, yielded up the ghost. And behold the vail of the temple was rent in twain from the top to the bottom, and the earth did quake, and the rocks rent, and the graves were opened, and many bodies of saints which slept arose, and came out of the graves after his resurrection, and went into the holy city, and appeared unto many. Now when the centurion, and they that were with him, watching Jesus, saw the earthquake, and those things that were done, they feared greatly, saying, Truly this was the Son of God.

Monday before Easter.

FOR THE EPISTLE. Isai. lxiii. 1.

WHO is this that cometh from Edom, with dyed garments from Bozrah ? this that is glorious in his apparel, travelling in the greatness of his strength ? I that speak in righteousness, mighty to save. Wherefore art thou red in thine apparel, and thy garments like him that treadeth in the wine-fat ? I have trodden the wine-press alone, and of the people there was none with me :

for I will tread them in mine anger, and trample them in my fury, and their blood shall be sprinkled upon my garments, and I will stain all my raiment. For the day of vengeance is in mine heart, and the year of my redeemed is come. And I looked, and there was none to help; and I wondered that there was none to uphold: therefore mine own arm brought salvation unto me, and my fury it upheld me. And I will tread down the people in mine anger, and make them drunk in my fury, and I will bring down their strength to the earth. I will mention the loving-kindnesses of the Lord, and the praises of the Lord, according to all that the Lord hath bestowed on us, and the great goodness towards the house of Israel, which he hath bestowed on them, according to his mercies, and according to the multitude of his loving-kindnesses. For he said, Surely they are my people, children that will not lie: so he was their Saviour. In all their affliction he was afflicted, and the angel of his presence saved them: in his love, and in his pity, he redeemed them, and he bare them, and carried them all the days of old. But they rebelled, and vexed his Holy Spirit; therefore he was turned to be their enemy, and he fought against them. Then he remembered the days of old, Moses and his people, saying, Where is he that brought them up out of the sea with the shepherd of his flock? where is he that put his Holy Spirit within him? that led them by the right hand of Moses, with his glorious arm, dividing the water before them, to make himself an everlasting Name? that led them through the deep as an horse in the wilderness, that they should not stumble? As a beast goeth down into the valley, the Spirit of the Lord caused him to rest: so didst thou lead thy people, to make thyself a glorious Name. Look down from heaven, and behold from the habitation of thy holiness, and of thy glory: where is thy zeal, and thy strength, the sounding of thy bowels, and of thy mercies towards me? Are they restrained? Doubtless thou art our Father, though Abraham be ignorant of us, and Israel acknowledge us not: Thou, O Lord, art our Father, our Redeemer, thy Name is from everlasting. O Lord, why hast thou made us to err from thy ways? and hardened our heart from thy fear? Return for thy servants' sake, the tribes of thine inheritance. The people of thy holiness have possessed it but a little while: our adversaries have trodden down thy sanctuary. We are thine: thou never barest rule over them; they were not called by thy Name.

THE GOSPEL. St. Mark xiv. 1.

AFTER two days was the feast of the Passover, and of unleavened bread: and the chief priests and the scribes sought how they might take him by craft, and put him to death. But they said,

Not on the feast-day, lest there be an uproar of the people. And being in Bethany, in the house of Simon the leper, as he sat at meat, there came a woman having an alabaster box of ointment of spikenard, very precious; and she brake the box, and poured it on his head. And there were some that had indignation within themselves, and said, Why was this waste of the ointment made? for it might have been sold for more than three hundred pence, and have been given to the poor: and they murmured against her. And Jesus said, Let her alone; why trouble ye her? she hath wrought a good work on me: for ye have the poor with you always, and whensoever ye will ye may do them good; but me ye have not always. She hath done what she could; she is come aforehand to anoint my body to the burying. Verily I say unto you, Wheresoever this Gospel shall be preached throughout the whole world, this also that she hath done shall be spoken of for a memorial of her. And Judas Iscariot, one of the twelve, went unto the chief priests to betray him unto them. And when they heard it they were glad, and promised to give him money. And he sought how he might conveniently betray him. And the first day of unleavened bread, when they killed the passover, his disciples said unto him, Where wilt thou that we go and prepare, that thou mayest eat the passover? And he sendeth forth two of his disciples, and saith unto them, Go ye into the city, and there shall meet you a man bearing a pitcher of water; follow him: And wheresoever he shall go in, say ye to the good-man of the house, The Master saith, Where is the guest-chamber, where I shall eat the passover with my disciples? And he will shew you a large upper-room furnished, and prepared: there make ready for us. And his disciples went forth, and came into the city, and found as he had said unto them: and they made ready the passover. And in the evening he cometh with the twelve. And as they sat, and did eat, Jesus said, Verily I say unto you, One of you which eateth with me shall betray me. And they began to be sorrowful, and to say unto him one by one, Is it I? and another said, Is it I? And he answered and said unto them, It is one of the twelve that dippeth with me in the dish. The Son of Man indeed goeth, as it is written of him: but woe to that man by whom the Son of Man is betrayed: good were it for that man if he had never been born. And as they did eat, Jesus took bread, and blessed, and brake it, and gave to them, and said, Take, eat: this is my body. And he took the cup, and when he had given thanks he gave it to them: and they all drank of it. And he said unto them, This is my blood of the new testament, which is shed for many. Verily I say unto you, I will drink no more of the fruit of the vine, until that day that I drink it new in the Kingdom of God.

And when they had sung an hymn they went out into the mount of Olives. And Jesus saith unto them, All ye shall be offended because of me this night : for it is written, I will smite the shepherd, and the sheep shall be scattered. But, after that I am risen, I will go before you into Galilee. But Peter said unto him, Although all shall be offended, yet will not I. And Jesus saith unto him, Verily I say unto thee, That this day, even in this night, before the cock crow twice, thou shalt deny me thrice. But he spake the more vehemently, If I should die with thee, I will not deny thee in any wise. Likewise also said they all. And they came to a place which was named Gethsemane : and he saith to his disciples, Sit ye here, while I shall pray. And he taketh with him Peter, and James, and John, and began to be sore amazed, and to be very heavy, and saith unto them, My soul is exceeding sorrowful unto death ; tarry ye here, and watch. And he went forward a little, and fell on the ground, and prayed, that, if it were possible, the hour might pass from him. And he said, Abba, Father, all things are possible unto thee; take away this cup from me ; nevertheless, not what I will, but what thou wilt. And he cometh and findeth them sleeping, and saith unto Peter, Simon, sleepest thou ? couldest not thou watch one hour ? Watch ye and pray, lest ye enter into temptation : the spirit truly is ready, but the flesh is weak. And again he went away, and prayed, and spake the same words. And when he returned he found them asleep again, (for their eyes were heavy,) neither wist they what to answer him. And he cometh the third time, and saith unto them, Sleep on now, and take your rest : it is enough, the hour is come ; behold, the Son of Man is betrayed into the hands of sinners. Rise up, let us go ; lo, he that betrayeth me is at hand. And immediately, while he yet spake, cometh Judas, one of the twelve, and with him a great multitude with swords and staves, from the chief priests, and the scribes, and the elders. And he that betrayed him had given them a token, saying, Whomsoever I shall kiss, that same is he ; take him, and lead him away safely. And as soon as he was come he goeth straightway to him, and saith, Master, master ; and kissed him. And they laid their hands on him, and took him. And one of them that stood by drew a sword, and smote a servant of the high priest, and cut off his ear. And Jesus answered, and said unto them, Are ye come out as against a thief, with swords and with staves, to take me ? I was daily with you in the temple teaching, and ye took me not : but the Scriptures must be fulfilled. And they all forsook him, and fled. And there followed him a certain young man, having a linen cloth cast about his naked body ; and the young men laid hold on him : and he left the linen cloth, and fled from them naked. And they led Jesus away to the high priest: and with him were assembled all the chief priests, and the elders, and the scribes. And Peter followed him afar off, even into the palace of the high priest; and he sat with the servants, and warmed himself at the fire. And the chief priests and all the council sought for witness against Jesus to put him to death; and found none. For many bare false witness against him, but their witness agreed not together. And there arose certain, and bare false witness against him, saying, We heard him say, I will destroy this temple that is made with hands, and within three days I will build another made without hands. But neither so did their witness agree together. And the high priest stood up in the midst, and asked Jesus, saying, Answerest thou nothing? what is it which these witness against thee? But he held his peace, and answered nothing. Again the high priest asked him, and said unto him, Art thou the Christ, the Son of the Blessed? And Jesus said, I am; and ye shall see the Son of Man sitting on the right hand of power, and coming in the clouds of heaven. Then the high priest rent his clothes, and saith, What need we any further witnesses? ye have heard the blasphemy: what think ye? And they all condemned him to be guilty of death. And some began to spit on him, and to cover his face, and to buffet him, and to say unto him, Prophesy: and the servants did strike him with the palms of their hands. And as Peter was beneath in the palace there cometh one of the maids of the high priest; and when she saw Peter warming himself she looked upon him, and said, And thou also wast with Jesus of Nazareth. But he denied, saying, I know not, neither understand I what thou sayest. And he went out into the porch; and the cock crew. And a maid saw him again, and began to say to them that stood by, This is one of them. And he denied it again. And a little after, they that stood by said again to Peter, Surely thou art one of them; for thou art a Galilean, and thy speech agreeth thereto. But he began to curse and to swear, saying, I know not this man of whom ye speak. And the second time the cock crew. And Peter called to mind the word that Jesus said unto him, Before the cock crow twice, thou shalt deny me thrice. And when he thought thereon, he wept.

Tuesday before Easter.

FOR THE EPISTLE. Isai. l. 5.

THE Lord God hath opened mine ear, and I was not rebellious, neither turned away back. I gave my back to the smiters, and my cheeks to them that plucked off the hair: I hid not my face from shame and spitting. For the Lord God will help me, therefore shall I not be confounded : therefore have I set my face like a flint, and I know that I shall not be ashamed. He is near that justifieth me ; who will contend with me ? Let us stand together ; who is mine adversary? let him come near to me. Behold, the Lord God will help me ; who is he that shall condemn me ? Lo, they all shall wax old as a garment : the moth shall eat them up. Who is among you that feareth the Lord, that obeyeth the voice of his servant, that walketh in darkness, and hath no light ? let him trust in the Name of the Lord, and stay upon his God. Behold, all ye that kindle a fire, that compass yourselves about with sparks ; walk in the light of your fire, and in the sparks that ye have kindled. This shall ye have of mine hand, ye shall lie down in sorrow.

THE GOSPEL. St. Mark xv. 1.

AND straightway in the morning the chief priests held a consultation with the elders, and scribes, and the whole council, and bound Jesus, and carried him away, and delivered him to Pilate. And Pilate asked him, Art thou the King of the Jews ? And he answering said unto him, Thou sayest it. And the chief priests accused him of many things : but he answered nothing. And Pilate asked him again, saying, Answerest thou nothing ? behold how many things they witness against thee. But Jesus yet answered nothing : so that Pilate marvelled. Now at that feast he released unto them one prisoner, whomsoever they desired. And there was one named Barabbas, which lay bound with them that had made insurrection with him, who had committed murder in the insurrection. And the multitude, crying aloud, began to desire him to do as he had ever done unto them. But Pilate answered them, saying, Will ye that I release unto you the King of the Jews ? For he knew that the chief priests had delivered him for envy. But the chief priests moved the people, that he should rather release Barabbas unto them. And Pilate answered, and said again unto them, What will ye then that I shall do unto him whom ye call the King of the Jews ? And they cried out again, Crucify him. Then Pilate said unto them, Why, what evil hath he done ? And they cried out the more exceedingly, Crucify him. And so Pilate, willing to content the people, released Barabbas unto them, and delivered Jesus, when he had scourged him, to be crucified. And the soldiers led him away into the hall, called Prætorium ; and they called together the whole band. And they clothed him with purple, and platted a crown of thorns, and put it about his head : and began to salute him, Hail, King of the Jews. And they smote him on the head with a reed, and did spit upon him, and bowing their knees worshipped him. And when they had mocked him, they took off the purple from him, and put his own clothes on him, and led him out to crucify him. And they compel one Simon a Cyrenian, who passed by, coming out of the country, the father of Alexander and Rufus, to bear his cross. And they bring him unto the place Golgotha, which is, being interpreted, The place of a skull. And they gave him to drink wine mingled with myrrh; but he received it not. And when they had crucified him they parted his garments, casting lots upon them, what every man should take. And it was the third hour, and they crucified him. And the superscription of his accusation was written over, THE KING OF THE JEWS. And with him they crucify two thieves, the one on his right hand, and the other on his left. And the scripture was fulfilled, which saith, And he was numbered with the transgressors. And they that passed by railed on him, wagging their heads, and saying, Ah, thou that destroyest the temple, and buildest it in three days, save thyself, and come down from the cross. Likewise also the chief priests mocking said among themselves, with the scribes, He saved others; himself he cannot save. Let Christ the King of Israel descend now from the cross, that we may see and believe. And they that were crucified with him reviled him. And when the sixth hour was come, there was darkness over the whole land until the ninth hour. And at the ninth hour, Jesus cried with a loud voice, saying, *Eloi, Eloi, lama sabachthani?* which is, being interpreted, My God, my God, why hast thou forsaken me? And some of them that stood by, when they heard it, said, Behold, he calleth Elias. And one ran and filled a sponge full of vinegar, and put it on a reed, and gave him to drink, saying, Let alone; let us see whether Elias will come to take him down. And Jesus cried with a loud voice, and gave up the ghost. And the vail of the temple was rent in twain from the top to the bottom. And when the centurion, which stood over against him, saw that he so cried out, and gave up the ghost, he said, Truly this man was the Son of God.

Wednesday before Easter.

THE EPISTLE. Hebr. ix. 16.

WHERE a testament is, there must also of necessity be the death of the testator : for a testament is of force after men are dead; otherwise it is of no strength at all whilst the testator liveth. Whereupon, neither the first testament was dedicated without blood: for when Moses had spoken every precept to all the people, according to the law, he took the blood of calves and of goats, with water, and scarlet wool, and hyssop, and sprinkled both the book, and all the people, saying, This is the blood of the testament, which God hath enjoined unto you. Moreover, he sprinkled with blood both the tabernacle, and all the vessels of the ministry. And almost all things are by the law purged with blood ; and without shedding of blood is no remission. It was therefore necessary that the patterns of things in the heavens should be purified with these ; but the heavenly things themselves with better sacrifices than these. For Christ is not entered into the holy places made with hands, which are the figures of the true, but into heaven itself, now to appear in the presence of God for us ; nor yet that he should offer himself often, as the high priest entereth into the holy place every year with blood of others : for then must he often have suffered since the foundation of the world ; but now once in the end of the world hath he appeared to put away sin by the sacrifice of himself. And as it is appointed unto men once to die, but after this the judgement : so Christ was once offered to bear the sins of many ; and unto them that look for him shall he appear the second time without sin unto salvation.

THE GOSPEL. St. Luke xxii. 1.

NOW the feast of unleavened bread drew nigh, which is called the Passover. And the chief priests and scribes sought how they might kill him ; for they feared the people. Then entered Satan into Judas surnamed Iscariot, being of the number of the twelve. And he went his way, and communed with the chief priests and captains, how he might betray him unto them. And they were glad, and covenanted to give him money. And he promised, and sought opportunity to betray him unto them in the absence of the multitude. Then came the day of unleavened bread, when the passover must be killed. And he sent Peter and John, saying, Go and prepare us the passover, that we may eat. And they said unto him, Where wilt thou that we prepare ? And he said unto them, Behold, when ye are entered into the city, there shall a man meet you, bearing a pitcher of water ; follow him into the house where he entereth in. And ye shall say unto the good-man of the house, The Master saith unto thee, Where is the guest-chamber, where I shall eat the passover with my disciples ? And he shall shew you a large upper-room furnished ; there make ready. And they went, and found as he had said unto them : and they made ready the passover. And when the hour was come he sat down, and the twelve Apostles with him. And he said unto them, With desire I have desired to eat this passover with you before I suffer : for I say unto you, I will not any more eat thereof, until it be fulfilled in the Kingdom of God. And he took the cup, and gave thanks, and said, Take this, and divide it among yourselves. For I say unto you, I will not drink of the fruit of the vine, until the Kingdom of God shall come. And he took bread, and gave thanks, and brake it, and gave unto them, saying, This is my body, which is given for you : this do in remembrance of me. Likewise also the cup after supper, saying, This cup is the new testament in my blood, which is shed for you. But behold, the hand of him that betrayeth me is with me on the table. And truly the Son of Man goeth as it was determined ; but woe unto that man by whom he is betrayed. And they began to inquire among themselves, which of them it was that should do this thing. And there was also a strife among them, which of them should be accounted the greatest. And he said unto them, The kings of the Gentiles exercise lordship over them, and they that exercise authority upon them are called benefactors. But ye shall not be so : but he that is greatest among you, let him be as the younger ; and he that is chief, as he that doth serve. For whether is greater, he that sitteth at meat, or he that serveth ? is not he that sitteth at meat ? but I am among you as he that serveth. Ye are they which have continued with me in my temptations. And I appoint unto you a kingdom, as my Father hath appointed unto me ; that ye may eat and drink at my table in my kingdom, and sit on thrones, judging the twelve tribes of Israel. And the Lord said, Simon, Simon, behold, Satan hath desired to have you, that he may sift you as wheat : but I have prayed for thee, that thy faith fail not ; and when thou art converted, strengthen thy brethren. And he said unto him, Lord, I am ready to go with thee both into prison and to death. And he said, I tell thee, Peter, the cock shall not crow this day, before that thou shalt thrice deny that thou knowest me. And he said unto them, When I sent you without purse, and scrip, and shoes, lacked ye any thing ? And they said, Nothing. Then said he unto them, But now, he that hath a purse, let him take it, and likewise his scrip : and he that hath no sword, let him sell his garment, and buy one. For I say unto you, That this that is written must yet be accomplished in me, And he was reckoned among the transgressors : for the things concerning me have an end. And they said, Lord, behold, here are two swords. And he said unto them, It is enough. And he came out, and went, as he was wont, to the mount of Olives, and his disciples also followed him. And when he was at the place, he said unto them, Pray, that ye enter not into temptation. And he was withdrawn from them about a stone's cast, and kneeled down and prayed, saying, Father, if thou be willing, remove this cup from me : nevertheless, not my will, but thine be done. And there appeared an angel unto him from heaven, strengthening him. And being in an agony, he prayed more earnestly ; and his sweat was as it were great drops of blood falling down to the ground. And when he rose up from prayer, and was come to his disciples, he found them sleeping for sorrow, and said unto them, Why sleep ye? rise and pray, lest ye enter into temptation. And while he yet spake, behold, a multitude, and he that was called Judas, one of the twelve, went before them, and drew near unto Jesus to kiss him. But Jesus said unto him, Judas, betrayest thou the Son of Man with a kiss? When they who were about him saw what would follow, they said unto him, Lord, shall we smite with the sword? And one of them smote the servant of the high priest, and cut off his right ear. And Jesus answered and said, Suffer ye thus far. And he touched his ear, and healed him. Then Jesus said unto the chief priests, and captains of the temple, and the elders who were come to him, Be ye come out as against a thief, with swords and staves? When I was daily with you in the temple, ye stretched forth no hands against me: but this is your hour, and the power of darkness. Then took they him, and led him, and brought him into the high priest's house: and Peter followed afar off. And when they had kindled a fire in the midst of the hall, and were set down together, Peter sat down among them. But a certain maid beheld him, as he sat by the fire, and earnestly looked upon him, and said, This man was also with him. And he denied him, saying, Woman, I know him not. And after a little while another saw him, and said, Thou art also of them. And Peter said, Man, I am not. And about the space of one hour after, another confidently affirmed, saying, Of a truth this fellow also was with him; for he is a Galilean. And Peter said, Man, I know not what thou sayest. And immediately, while he yet spake, the cock crew. And the Lord turned, and looked upon Peter; and Peter remembered the word of the Lord, how he had said unto him, Before the cock crow, thou shalt deny me thrice. And Peter went out, and wept bitterly. And the men that held Jesus mocked him, and smote him. And when they had blindfolded him, they struck him on the face, and asked him, saying, Prophesy, who is it that smote thee? And many other things blasphemously spake they against him. And as soon as it was day, the elders of the people, and the chief priests, and the scribes, came together, and led him into their council, saying, Art thou the Christ? tell us. And he said unto them, If I tell you, ye will not believe: and if I also ask you, ye will not answer me, nor let me go. Hereafter shall the Son of Man sit on the right hand of the power of God. Then said they all, Art thou then the Son of God? And he said unto them, Ye say that I am. And they said, What need we any further witness? for we ourselves have heard of his own mouth.

Thursday before Easter.

THE EPISTLE. 1 Cor. xi. 17.

IN this that I declare unto you, I praise you not; that ye come together not for the better, but for the worse. For first of all, when ye come together in the church, I hear that there be divisions among you, and I partly believe it. For there must be also heresies among you, that they who are approved may be made manifest among you. When ye come together therefore into one place, this is not to eat the Lord's supper : for in eating every one taketh before other his own supper ; and one is hungry, and another is drunken. What, have ye not houses to eat and to drink in ? or despise ye the church of God, and shame them that have not ? What shall I say to you ? shall I praise you in this ? I praise you not. For I have received of the Lord that which also I delivered unto you, That the Lord Jesus, the same night in which he was betrayed, took bread; and when he had given thanks, he brake it, and said, Take, eat ; this is my body, which is broken for you : this do in remembrance of me. After the same manner also he took the cup, when he had supped, saying, This cup is the new testament in my blood : this do ye, as oft as ye drink it, in remembrance of me. For as often as ye eat this bread, and drink this cup, ye do shew the Lord's death till he come. Wherefore, whosoever shall eat this bread, and drink this cup of the Lord, unworthily, shall be guilty of the body and blood of the Lord. But let a man examine himself, and so let him eat of that bread, and drink of that cup. For he that eateth and drinketh unworthily eateth and drinketh damnation to himself, not discerning the Lord's body. For this cause many are weak and sickly among you, and many sleep. For if we would judge ourselves, we should not be judged. But when we are judged, we are chastened of the Lord, that we should not be condemned with the world. Wherefore, my brethren, when ye come together to eat, tarry one for another. And if any man hunger, let him eat at home ; that ye come not together unto condemnation. And the rest will I set in order when I come.

THE GOSPEL. St. Luke xxiii. 1.

THE whole multitude of them arose, and led him unto Pilate. And they began to accuse him, saying, We found this fellow perverting the nation, and forbidding to give tribute to Cæsar, saying, That he himself is Christ a King. And Pilate asked him, saying, Art thou the King of the Jews ? And he answered him, and said, Thou sayest it. Then said Pilate to the chief priests, and to the people, I find no fault in this man. And they were the more fierce, saying, He stirreth up the people, teaching throughout all Jewry, beginning from Galilee to this place. When Pilate heard of Galilee, he asked whether the man were a Galilean. And as soon as he knew that he belonged unto Herod's jurisdiction, he sent him to Herod, who himself was also at Jerusalem at that time. And when Herod saw Jesus he was exceeding glad; for he was desirous to see him of a long season, because he had heard many things of him; and he hoped to have seen some miracle done by him. Then he questioned with him in many words; but he answered him nothing. And the chief priests and scribes stood and vehemently accused him. And Herod with his men of war set him at nought, and mocked him, and arrayed him in a gorgeous robe, and sent him again to Pilate. And the same day Pilate and Herod were made friends together ; for before they were at enmity between themselves. And Pilate, when he had called together the chief priests, and the rulers, and the people, said unto them, Ye have brought this man unto me, as one that perverteth the people: and behold, I, having examined him before you, have found no fault in this man touching those things whereof ye accuse him : No, nor yet Herod : for I sent you to him ; and lo, nothing worthy of death is done unto him. I will therefore chastise him, and release him. For of necessity he must release one unto them at the feast. And they cried out all at once, saying, Away with this man, and release unto us Barabbas: (who for a certain sedition, made in the city, and for murder, was cast into prison.) Pilate therefore, willing to release Jesus, spake again to them. But they cried, saying, Crucify him, crucify him. And he said unto them the third time, Why, what evil hath he done ? I have found no cause of death in him : I will therefore chastise him, and let him go. And they were instant with loud voices, requiring that he might be crucified: and the voices of them and of the chief priests prevailed. And Pilate gave sentence that it should be as they required. And he released unto them him that for sedition and murder was cast into prison, whom they had desired ; but he delivered Jesus to their will. And as they led him away, they laid hold upon one Simon a Cyrenian, coming out of the country, and on him they laid the cross, that he might bear it after Jesus. And there followed him a great company of people, and of women, which also bewailed and lamented him. But Jesus, turning unto them, said, Daughters of Jerusalem, weep not for me, but weep for yourselves, and for your children. For behold, the days are coming, in the which they shall say, Blessed are the barren, and the wombs that never bare, and the paps which never gave suck. Then shall they begin to say to the mountains, Fall on us; and to the hills, Cover us. For if they do these things in a green tree, what shall be done in the dry? And there were also two other, malefactors, led with him to be put to death. And when they were come to the place which is called Calvary, there they crucified him; and the malefactors, one on the right hand, and the other on the left. Then said Jesus, Father, forgive them, for they know not what they do. And they parted his raiment, and cast lots. And the people stood beholding; and the rulers also with them derided him, saying, He saved others; let him save himself, if he be Christ, the chosen of God. And the soldiers also mocked him, coming to him, and offering him vinegar, and saying, If thou be the King of the Jews, save thyself. And a superscription also was written over him in letters of Greek, and Latin, and Hebrew, THIS IS THE KING OF THE JEWS. And one of the malefactors, which were hanged, railed on him, saying, If thou be Christ, save thyself, and us. But the other answering rebuked him, saying, Dost not thou fear God, seeing thou art in the same condemnation? And we indeed justly; for we receive the due reward of our deeds, but this man hath done nothing amiss. And he said unto Jesus, Lord, remember me when thou comest into thy kingdom. And Jesus said unto him, Verily I say unto thee, To-day shalt thou be with me in paradise. And it was about the sixth hour: and there was a darkness over all the earth until the ninth hour. And the sun was darkened, and the vail of the temple was rent in the midst. And when Jesus had cried with a loud voice, he said, Father, into thy hands I commend my spirit: and having said thus, he gave up the ghost. Now when the centurion saw what was done, he glorified God, saying, Certainly this was a righteous man. And all the people that came together to that sight, beholding the things that were done, smote their breasts, and returned. And all his acquaintance, and the women that followed him from Galilee, stood afar off, beholding these things.

Good Friday.

THE COLLECTS.

ALMIGHTY God, we beseech thee graciously to behold this thy family, for which our Lord Jesus Christ was contented to be betrayed, and given up into the hands of wicked men, and to suffer death upon the cross, who now liveth and reigneth with thee and the Holy Ghost, ever one God, world without end. *Amen.*

ALMIGHTY and everlasting God, by whose Spirit the whole body of the Church is governed and sanctified; Receive our supplications and prayers, which we offer before thee for all estates of men in thy holy Church, that every member of the same, in his vocation and ministry, may truly and godly serve thee; through our Lord and Saviour Jesus Christ. *Amen.*

O MERCIFUL God, who hast made all men, and hatest nothing that thou hast made, nor wouldest the death of a sinner, but rather that he should be converted and live; Have mercy upon all Jews, Turks, Infidels, and Hereticks, and take from them all ignorance, hardness of heart, and contempt of thy Word; and so fetch them home, blessed Lord, to thy flock, that they may be saved among the remnant of the true Israelites, and be made one fold under one shepherd, Jesus Christ our Lord, who liveth and reigneth with thee and the Holy Spirit, one God, world without end. *Amen.*

THE EPISTLE. Hebr. x. 1.

THE law having a shadow of good things to come, and not the very image of the things, can never with those sacrifices, which they offered year by year continually, make the comers thereunto perfect: for then would they not have ceased to be offered? because that the worshippers once purged should have had no more conscience of sins. But in those sacrifices there is a remembrance again made of sins every year. For it is not possible that the blood of bulls and of goats should take away sins. Wherefore, when he cometh into the world, he saith, Sacrifice and offering thou wouldest not, but a body hast thou prepared me: In burnt-offerings and sacrifices for sin thou hast had no pleasure: Then said I, Lo, I come (in the volume of the book it is written of me) to do thy will, O God. Above, when he said, Sacrifice and offering, and burnt-offerings, and offering for sin, thou wouldest not, neither hadst pleasure therein, which are offered by the Law: then said he, Lo, I come to do thy will, O God. He taketh away the first, that he may establish the second. By the which will we are sanctified, through the offering of the body of Jesus Christ once for all. And every priest standeth daily ministering, and offering oftentimes the same sacrifices, which can never take away sins. But this man, after he had offered one sacrifice for sins for ever, sat down on the right hand of God; from henceforth expecting till his enemies be made his foot-stool. For by one offering he hath perfected for ever them that are sanctified: Whereof the Holy Ghost also is a witness to us: for after that he had said before, This is the covenant that I will make with them after those days, saith the Lord, I will put my laws into their hearts, and in their minds will I write them; and their sins and iniquities will I remember no more. Now where remission of these is, there is no more offering for sin. Having therefore, brethren, boldness to enter into the holiest by the blood of Jesus, by a new and living way, which he hath consecrated for us, through the vail, that is to say, his flesh ; and having an High Priest over the house of God ; let us draw near with a true heart, in full assurance of faith, having our hearts sprinkled from an evil conscience, and our bodies washed with pure water. Let us hold fast the profession of our faith without wavering ; (for he is faithful that promised ;) and let us consider one another to provoke unto love, and to good works ; not forsaking the assembling of ourselves together, as the manner of some is ; but exhorting one another : and so much the more, as ye see the day approaching.

THE GOSPEL. St. John xix. 1.

PILATE therefore took Jesus, and scourged him. And the soldiers platted a crown of thorns, and put it on his head, and they put on him a purple robe, and said, Hail, King of the Jews : and they smote him with their hands. Pilate therefore went forth again, and saith unto them, Behold, I bring him forth to you, that ye may know that I find no fault in him. Then came Jesus forth, wearing the crown of thorns, and the purple robe. And Pilate saith unto them, Behold the man ! When the chief priests therefore and officers saw him, they cried out, saying, Crucify him, crucify him. Pilate saith unto them, Take ye him, and crucify him : for I find no fault in him. The Jews answered him, We have a law, and by our law he ought to die, because he made himself the Son of God. When Pilate therefore heard that saying, he was the more afraid ; and went again into the judgement-hall, and saith unto Jesus, Whence art thou ? But Jesus gave him no answer. Then saith Pilate unto him, Speakest thou not unto me ? knowest thou not that I have power to crucify thee, and have power to release thee ? Jesus answered, Thou couldest have no power at all against me, except it were given thee from above : therefore he that delivered me unto thee hath the greater sin. And from thenceforth Pilate sought to release him : but the Jews cried out, saying, If thou let this man go, thou art not Cæsar's friend : whosoever maketh himself a king speaketh against Cæsar. When Pilate therefore heard that saying, he brought Jesus forth, and sat down in the judgement-seat, in a place that is called the Pavement, but in the Hebrew, Gabbatha. And it was the preparation of the passover, and about the sixth hour : and he saith unto the Jews, Behold your King ! But they cried out, Away with him, away with him, crucify him. Pilate saith unto them, Shall I crucify your

K

King ? The chief priests answered, We have no king but Cæsar. Then delivered he him therefore unto them to be crucified : and they took Jesus, and led him away. And he, bearing his cross, went forth into a place called the place of a skull, which is called in the Hebrew, Golgotha : where they crucified him, and two other with him, on either side one, and Jesus in the midst. And Pilate wrote a title, and put it on the cross ; and the writing was, JESUS OF NAZARETH THE KING OF THE JEWS. This title then read many of the Jews : for the place where Jesus was crucified was nigh to the city : and it was written in Hebrew, and Greek, and Latin. Then said the chief priests of the Jews to Pilate, Write not, The King of the Jews ; but that he said, I am the King of the Jews. Pilate answered, What I have written, I have written. Then the soldiers, when they had crucified Jesus, took his garments, and made four parts, to every soldier a part ; and also his coat : now the coat was without seam, woven from the top throughout. They said therefore among themselves, Let us not rend it, but cast lots for it, whose it shall be : that the Scripture might be fulfilled, which saith, They parted my raiment among them, and for my vesture they did cast lots. These things therefore the soldiers did. Now there stood by the cross of Jesus, his mother, and his mother's sister, Mary the wife of Cleophas, and Mary Magdalene. When Jesus therefore saw his mother, and the disciple standing by, whom he loved, he saith unto his mother, Woman, behold thy son. Then saith he to the disciple, Behold thy mother. And from that hour that disciple took her unto his own home. After this, Jesus, knowing that all things were now accomplished, that the Scripture might be fulfilled, saith, I thirst. Now there was set a vessel full of vinegar : and they filled a sponge with vinegar, and put it upon hyssop, and put it to his mouth. When Jesus therefore had received the vinegar, he said, It is finished : and he bowed his head, and gave up the ghost. The Jews therefore, because it was the preparation, that the bodies should not remain upon the cross on the sabbath-day, (for that sabbath-day was an high day,) besought Pilate that their legs might be broken, and that they might be taken away. Then came the soldiers, and brake the legs of the first, and of the other which was crucified with him. But when they came to Jesus, and saw that he was dead already, they brake not his legs. But one of the soldiers with a spear pierced his side, and forthwith came there out blood and water. And he that saw it bare record, and his record is true : and he knoweth that he saith true, that ye might believe. For these things were done that the Scripture should be fulfilled, A bone of him shall not be broken. And again, another Scripture saith, They shall look on him whom they pierced.

Easter Even.

THE COLLECT.

GRANT, O Lord, that as we are baptized into the death of thy blessed Son our Saviour Jesus Christ, so by continual mortifying our corrupt affections we may be buried with him; and that through the grave, and gate of death, we may pass to our joyful resurrection; for his merits, who died, and was buried, and rose again for us, thy Son Jesus Christ our Lord. *Amen.*

THE EPISTLE. 1 St. Peter iii. 17.

IT is better, if the will of God be so, that ye suffer for well-doing, than for evil-doing. For Christ also hath once suffered for sins, the just for the unjust, that he might bring us to God, being put to death in the flesh, but quickened by the Spirit. By which also he went and preached unto the spirits in prison; which sometime were disobedient, when once the long-suffering of God waited in the days of Noah, while the ark was a preparing; wherein few, that is, eight souls, were saved by water. The like figure whereunto, even baptism, doth also now save us, (not the putting away the filth of the flesh, but the answer of a good conscience towards God,) by the resurrection of Jesus Christ: who is gone into heaven, and is on the right hand of God, angels and authorities and powers being made subject unto him.

THE GOSPEL. St. Matth. xxvii. 57.

WHEN the even was come, there came a rich man of Arimathæa, named Joseph, who also himself was Jesus' disciple. He went to Pilate, and begged the body of Jesus. Then Pilate commanded the body to be delivered. And when Joseph had taken the body, he wrapped it in a clean linen cloth, and laid it in his own new tomb, which he had hewn out in the rock; and he rolled a great stone to the door of the sepulchre, and departed. And there was Mary Magdalene, and the other Mary, sitting over against the sepulchre. Now the next day that followed the day of the preparation, the chief priests and Pharisees came together unto Pilate, saying, Sir, we remember that that deceiver said, while he was yet alive, After three days I will rise again. Command therefore that the sepulchre be made sure until the third day, lest his disciples come by night and steal him away, and say unto the people, He is risen from the dead: so the last error shall be worse than the first. Pilate said unto them, Ye have a watch; go your way, make it as sure as you can. So they went and made the sepulchre sure, sealing the stone, and setting a watch.

K 2

Easter Day.

¶ *At Morning Prayer, instead of the Psalm,* O come, let us sing, *&c., the* Anthems, Christ our Passover, *&c., shall be sung or said* [*see Proper Psalms*].

THE COLLECT.

ALMIGHTY God, who through thine only begotten Son Jesus Christ hast overcome death, and opened unto us the gate of everlasting life; We humbly beseech thee, that, as by thy special grace preventing us thou dost put into our minds good desires, so by thy continual help we may bring the same to good effect; through Jesus Christ our Lord, who liveth and reigneth with thee and the Holy Ghost, ever one God, world without end. *Amen.*

THE EPISTLE. Coloss. iii. 1.

IF ye then be risen with Christ, seek those things which are above, where Christ sitteth on the right hand of God. Set your affections on things above, not on things on the earth : For ye are dead, and your life is hid with Christ in God. When Christ, who is our life, shall appear, then shall ye also appear with him in glory. Mortify therefore your members which are upon the earth; fornication, uncleanness, inordinate affection, evil concupiscence, and covetousness, which is idolatry : For which things' sake the wrath of God cometh on the children of disobedience. In the which ye also walked some time, when ye lived in them.

THE GOSPEL. St. John xx. 1.

THE first day of the week cometh Mary Magdalene early, when it was yet dark, unto the sepulchre, and seeth the stone taken away from the sepulchre. Then she runneth and cometh to Simon Peter, and to the other disciple whom Jesus loved, and saith unto them, They have taken away the Lord out of the sepulchre, and we know not where they have laid him. Peter therefore went forth, and that other disciple, and came to the sepulchre. So they ran both together; and the other disciple did outrun Peter, and came first to the sepulchre; and he, stooping down and looking in, saw the linen clothes lying; yet went he not in. Then cometh Simon Peter following him, and went into the sepulchre, and seeth the linen clothes lie; and the napkin that was about his head, not lying with the linen clothes, but wrapped together in a place by itself. Then went in also that other disciple which came first to the sepulchre, and he saw, and believed. For as yet they knew not the Scripture, that he must rise again from the dead. Then the disciples went away again unto their own home.

Monday in Easter Week.

THE COLLECT.

A LMIGHTY God, who through thy only-begotten Son Jesus Christ hast overcome death, and opened unto us the gate of everlasting life; We humbly beseech thee, that, as by thy special grace preventing us thou dost put into our minds good desires, so by thy continual help we may bring the same to good effect; through Jesus Christ our Lord, who liveth and reigneth with thee and the Holy Ghost, ever one God, world without end. *Amen.*

FOR THE EPISTLE. Acts x. 34.

P ETER opened his mouth, and said, Of a truth I perceive that God is no respecter of persons; but in every nation he that feareth him, and worketh righteousness, is accepted with him. The word which God sent unto the children of Israel, preaching peace by Jesus Christ; (he is Lord of all;) that word (I say) ye know, which was published throughout all Judæa, and began from Galilee, after the baptism which John preached: how God anointed Jesus of Nazareth with the Holy Ghost, and with power; who went about doing good, and healing all that were oppressed of the devil: for God was with him. And we are witnesses of all things which he did, both in the land of the Jews, and in Jerusalem; whom they slew, and hanged on a tree: Him God raised up the third day, and shewed him openly; not to all the people, but unto witnesses chosen before of God, even to us, who did eat and drink with him after he rose from the dead. And he commanded us to preach unto the people, and to testify that it is he who was ordained of God to be the Judge of quick and dead. To him give all the prophets witness, that through his Name whosoever believeth in him shall receive remission of sins.

THE GOSPEL. St. Luke xxiv. 13.

B EHOLD, two of his disciples went that same day to a village called Emmaus, which was from Jerusalem about three-score furlongs. And they talked together of all these things which had happened. And it came to pass, that while they communed together, and reasoned, Jesus himself drew near, and went with them. But their eyes were holden, that they should not know him. And he said unto them, What manner of communications are these that ye have one to another, as ye walk, and are sad? And the one of them, whose name was Cleopas, answering, said unto him, Art thou only a stranger in Jerusalem, and hast not known the things which are come to pass there in these days? And he said unto them, What things? And they said unto him, Concerning Jesus of Nazareth, who was a prophet mighty in deed and word, before God and all the people: and how the chief priests and our rulers delivered him to be condemned to death, and have crucified him. But we trusted that it had been he which should have redeemed Israel: and beside all this, to-day is the third day since these things were done. Yea, and certain women also of our company made us astonished, which were early at the sepulchre: and when they found not his body, they came, saying, that they had also seen a vision of angels, which said that he was alive. And certain of them which were with us went to the sepulchre, and found it even so as the women had said: but him they saw not. Then he said unto them, O fools, and slow of heart to believe all that the prophets have spoken: ought not Christ to have suffered these things, and to enter into his glory? And beginning at Moses, and all the prophets, he expounded unto them in all the Scriptures the things concerning himself. And they drew nigh unto the village whither they went; and he made as though he would have gone further: but they constrained him, saying, Abide with us, for it is towards evening, and the day is far spent. And he went in to tarry with them. And it came to pass, as he sat at meat with them, he took bread, and blessed it, and brake, and gave to them. And their eyes were opened, and they knew him, and he vanished out of their sight. And they said one to another, Did not our heart burn within us, while he talked with us by the way, and while he opened to us the Scriptures? And they rose up the same hour, and returned to Jerusalem, and found the eleven gathered together, and them that were with them, saying, The Lord is risen indeed, and hath appeared to Simon. And they told what things were done in the way, and how he was known of them in breaking of bread.

Tuesday in Easter Week.

THE COLLECT.

ALMIGHTY God, who through thy only-begotten Son Jesus Christ hast overcome death, and opened unto us the gate of everlasting life; We humbly beseech thee, that, as by thy special grace preventing us thou dost put into our minds good desires, so by thy continual help we may bring the same good effect; through Jesus Christ our Lord, who liveth and reigneth with thee and the Holy Ghost, ever one God, world without end. *Amen.*

FOR THE EPISTLE. Acts xiii. 26.

MEN and brethren, children of the stock of Abraham, and who-soever among you feareth God, to you is the word of this salvation sent. For they that dwell at Jerusalem, and their rulers, because they knew him not, nor yet the voices of the prophets which are read every sabbath-day, they have fulfilled them in condemning him. And though they found no cause of death in him, yet desired they Pilate that he should be slain. And when they had fulfilled all that was written of him, they took him down from the tree, and laid him in a sepulchre. But God raised him from the dead : and he was seen many days of them which came up with him from Galilee to Jerusalem, who are his witnesses unto the people. And we declare unto you glad tidings, how that the promise which was made unto the fathers, God hath fulfilled the same unto us their children, in that he hath raised up Jesus again; as it is also written in the second Psalm, Thou art my Son, this day have I begotten thee. And as concerning that he raised him up from the dead, now no more to return to corruption, he said on this wise, I will give you the sure mercies of David. Wherefore he saith also in another Psalm, Thou shalt not suffer thine Holy One to see corruption. For David, after he had served his own generation by the will of God, fell on sleep, and was laid unto his fathers, and saw corruption : but he whom God raised again saw no corruption. Be it known unto you therefore, men and brethren, that through this man is preached unto you the forgiveness of sins : and by him all that believe are justified from all things, from which ye could not be justified by the law of Moses. Beware therefore, lest that come upon you which is spoken of in the prophets; Behold, ye despisers, and wonder, and perish : for I work a work in your days, a work which ye shall in no wise believe, though a man declare it unto you.

THE GOSPEL. St. Luke xxiv. 36.

JESUS himself stood in the midst of them, and saith unto them, Peace be unto you. But they were terrified and affrighted, and supposed that they had seen a spirit. And he said unto them, Why are ye troubled, and why do thoughts arise in your hearts ? Behold my hands and my feet, that it is I myself : handle me, and see ; for a spirit hath not flesh and bones, as ye see me have. And when he had thus spoken, he shewed them his hands and his feet. And while they yet believed not for joy, and wondered, he said unto them, Have ye here any meat ? And they gave him a piece of a broiled fish, and of an honey-comb. And he took it, and did eat before them. And he said unto them, These are the words which

I spake unto you, while I was yet with you, that all things must be fulfilled which were written in the law of Moses, and in the Prophets, and in the Psalms concerning me. Then opened he their understanding, that they might understand the Scriptures, and said unto them, Thus it is written, and thus it behoved Christ to suffer, and to rise from the dead the third day; and that repentance and remission of sins should be preached in his Name among all nations, beginning at Jerusalem. And ye are witnesses of these things.

The First Sunday after Easter.

THE COLLECT.

ALMIGHTY Father, who hast given thine only Son to die for our sins, and to rise again for our justification; Grant us so to put away the leaven of malice and wickedness, that we may alway serve thee in pureness of living and truth; through the merits of the same thy Son Jesus Christ our Lord. *Amen.*

THE EPISTLE. 1 St. John v. 4.

WHATSOEVER is born of God overcometh the world; and this is the victory that overcometh the world, even our faith. Who is he that overcometh the world, but he that believeth that Jesus is the Son of God? This is he that came by water and blood, even Jesus Christ; not by water only, but by water and blood: and it is the Spirit that beareth witness, because the Spirit is truth. For there are three that bear record in heaven, the Father, the Word, and the Holy Ghost: and these three are one. And there are three that bear witness in earth, the spirit, and the water, and the blood: and these three agree in one. If we receive the witness of men, the witness of God is greater: for this is the witness of God, which he hath testified of his Son. He that believeth on the Son of God hath the witness in himself: he that believeth not God hath made him a liar, because he believeth not the record that God gave of his Son. And this is the record, that God hath given to us eternal life; and this life is in his Son. He that hath the Son hath life; and he that hath not the Son hath not life.

THE GOSPEL. St. John xx. 19.

THE same day at evening, being the first day of the week, when the doors were shut, where the disciples were assembled for fear of the Jews, came Jesus and stood in the midst, and saith unto them, Peace be unto you. And when he had so said, he shewed unto them his hands and his side. Then were the disciples glad when they saw the Lord. Then said Jesus to them again, Peace be unto you : As my Father hath sent me, even so send I you. And when he had said this, he breathed on them, and saith unto them, Receive ye the Holy Ghost. Whosesoever sins ye remit, they are remitted unto them ; and whosesoever sins ye retain, they are retained.

The Second Sunday after Easter.

THE COLLECT.

ALMIGHTY God, who hast given thine only Son to be unto us both a sacrifice for sin, and also an ensample of godly life ; Give us grace that we may always most thankfully receive that his inestimable benefit, and also daily endeavour ourselves to follow the blessed steps of his most holy life ; through the same Jesus Christ our Lord. *Amen.*

THE EPISTLE. 1 St. Peter ii. 19.

THIS is thank-worthy, if a man for conscience toward God endure grief, suffering wrongfully. For what glory is it, if, when ye be buffeted for your faults, ye shall take it patiently ? But if, when ye do well, and suffer for it, ye take it patiently ; this is acceptable with God. For even hereunto were ye called ; because Christ also suffered for us, leaving us an example, that ye should follow his steps : who did no sin, neither was guile found in his mouth : who, when he was reviled, reviled not again ; when he suffered, he threatened not ; but committed himself to him that judgeth right-eously : who his own self bare our sins in his own body on the tree, that we, being dead to sins, should live unto righteousness : by whose stripes ye were healed. For ye were as sheep going astray ; but are now returned unto the Shepherd and Bishop of your souls.

THE GOSPEL. St. John x. 11.

JESUS said, I am the good shepherd : the good shepherd giveth his life for the sheep. But he that is an hireling, and not the shepherd, whose own the sheep are not, seeth the wolf coming, and leaveth the sheep, and fleeth ; and the wolf catcheth them, and scattereth the sheep. The hireling fleeth, because he is an hireling, and careth not for the sheep. I am the good shepherd, and know my sheep, and am known of mine. As the Father knoweth me, even so know I the Father : and I lay down my life for the sheep. And other sheep I have, which are not of this fold ; them also I must bring, and they shall hear my voice ; and there shall be one fold, and one shepherd.

The Third Sunday after Easter.

THE COLLECT.

ALMIGHTY God, who shewest to them that be in error the light of thy truth, to the intent that they may return into the way of righteousness; Grant unto all them that are admitted into the fellowship of Christ's Religion, that they may eschew those things that are contrary to their profession, and follow all such things as are agreeable to the same; through our Lord Jesus Christ. *Amen.*

THE EPISTLE. 1 St. Peter ii. 11.

DEARLY beloved, I beseech you as strangers and pilgrims, abstain from fleshly lusts, which war against the soul; having your conversation honest among the Gentiles; that, whereas they speak against you as evil-doers, they may, by your good works which they shall behold, glorify God in the day of visitation. Submit yourselves to every ordinance of man for the Lord's sake; whether it be to the King, as supreme; or unto governours, as unto them that are sent by him, for the punishment of evil-doers, and for the praise of them that do well. For so is the will of God, that with well-doing ye may put to silence the ignorance of foolish men: as free, and not using your liberty for a cloke of maliciousness; but as the servants of God. Honour all men. Love the brotherhood. Fear God. Honour the King.

THE GOSPEL. St. John xvi. 16.

JESUS said to his disciples, A little while and ye shall not see me; and again, a little while and ye shall see me; because I go to the Father. Then said some of his disciples among themselves, What is this that he saith unto us, A little while and ye shall not see me; and again, a little while and ye shall see me; and, Because I go to the Father? They said therefore, What is this that he saith, A little while? we cannot tell what he saith. Now Jesus knew that they were desirous to ask him, and said unto them, Do ye enquire among yourselves of that I said, A little while and ye shall not see me; and again, a little while and ye shall see me? Verily, verily I say unto you, That ye shall weep and lament, but the world shall rejoice: and ye shall be sorrowful, but your sorrow shall be turned into joy. A woman, when she is in travail, hath sorrow, because her hour is come: but as soon as she is delivered of the child, she remembereth no more the anguish, for joy that a man is born into the world. And ye now therefore have sorrow; but I will see you again, and your heart shall rejoice, and your joy no man taketh from you.

The Fourth Sunday after Easter.

THE COLLECT.

O ALMIGHTY God, who alone canst order the unruly wills and affections of sinful men; Grant unto thy people, that they may love the thing which thou commandest, and desire that which thou dost promise; that so, among the sundry and manifold changes of the world, our hearts may surely there be fixed, where true joys are to be found; through Jesus Christ our Lord. *Amen.*

THE EPISTLE. St. James i. 17.

EVERY good gift, and every perfect gift is from above, and cometh down from the Father of lights, with whom is no variableness, neither shadow of turning. Of his own will begat he us with the Word of truth, that we should be a kind of first-fruits of his creatures. Wherefore, my beloved brethren, let every man be swift to hear, slow to speak, slow to wrath; for the wrath of man worketh not the righteousness of God. Wherefore lay apart all filthiness and superfluity of naughtiness, and receive with meekness the engrafted word, which is able to save your souls.

THE GOSPEL. St. John xvi. 5.

JESUS said unto his disciples, Now I go my way to him that sent me, and none of you asketh me, Whither goest thou? But, because I have said these things unto you, sorrow hath filled your heart. Nevertheless, I tell you the truth; it is expedient for you that I go away: for if I go not away, the Comforter will not come unto you; but if I depart, I will send him unto you. And when he is come, he will reprove the world of sin, and of righteousness, and of judgement: of sin, because they believe not on me; of righteousness, because I go to my Father, and ye see me no more; of judgement, because the prince of this world is judged. I have yet many things to say unto you, but ye cannot bear them now. Howbeit, when he, the Spirit of truth, is come, he will guide you into all truth: for he shall not speak of himself; but whatsoever he shall hear, that shall he speak: and he will shew you things to come. He shall glorify me: for he shall receive of mine, and shall shew it unto you. All things that the Father hath are mine: therefore said I, that he shall take of mine, and shall shew it unto you.

The Fifth Sunday after Easter.

THE COLLECT.

O LORD, from whom all good things do come; Grant to us thy humble servants, that by thy holy inspiration we may think those things that be good, and by thy merciful guiding may perform the same; through our Lord Jesus Christ. *Amen.*

THE EPISTLE. St. James i. 22.

BE ye doers of the Word, and not hearers only, deceiving your own selves. For if any be a hearer of the Word, and not a doer, he is like unto a man beholding his natural face in a glass. For he beholdeth himself, and goeth his way, and straightway forgetteth what manner of man he was. But whoso looketh into the perfect law of liberty, and continueth therein, he being not a forgetful hearer, but a doer of the work, this man shall be blessed in his deed. If any man among you seem to be religious, and bridleth not his tongue, but deceiveth his own heart, this man's religion is vain. Pure religion, and undefiled before God and the Father, is this, To visit the fatherless and widows in their affliction, and to keep himself unspotted from the world.

THE GOSPEL. St. John xvi. 23.

VERILY, verily I say unto you, Whatsoever ye shall ask the Father in my Name, he will give it you. Hitherto have ye asked nothing in my name: ask, and ye shall receive, that your joy may be full. These things have I spoken unto you in proverbs: the time cometh when I shall no more speak unto you in proverbs, but I shall shew you plainly of the Father. At that day ye shall ask in my Name: and I say not unto you, that I will pray the Father for you; for the Father himself loveth you, because ye have loved me, and have believed that I came out from God. I came forth from the Father, and am come into the world: again, I leave the world, and go to the Father. His disciples said unto him, Lo, now speakest thou plainly, and speakest no proverb. Now are we sure that thou knowest all things, and needest not that any man should ask thee: by this we believe that thou camest forth from God. Jesus answered them, Do ye now believe? Behold, the hour cometh, yea, is now come, that ye shall be scattered every man to his own, and shall leave me alone: and yet I am not alone, because the Father is with me. These things I have spoken unto you, that in me ye might have peace. In the world ye shall have tribulation; but be of good cheer, I have overcome the world.

The Ascension Day.

THE COLLECT.

GRANT, we beseech thee, Almighty God, that like as we do believe thy only begotten Son our Lord Jesus Christ to have ascended into the heavens; so we may also in heart and mind thither ascend, and with him continually dwell, who liveth and reigneth with thee and the Holy Ghost, one God, world without end. *Amen.*

FOR THE EPISTLE. Acts i. 1.

THE former treatise have I made, O Theophilus, of all that Jesus began both to do and teach, until the day in which he was taken up, after that he through the Holy Ghost had given commandments unto the Apostles whom he had chosen: to whom also he shewed himself alive after his passion, by many infallible proofs; being seen of them forty days, and speaking of the things pertaining to the Kingdom of God: and, being assembled together with them, commanded them that they should not depart from Jerusalem, but wait for the promise of the Father, which, saith he, ye have heard of me. For John truly baptized with water, but ye shall be baptized with the Holy Ghost not many days hence. When they therefore were come together, they asked of him, saying, Lord, wilt thou at this time restore again the kingdom to Israel? And he said unto them, It is not for you to know the times or the seasons, which the Father hath put in his own power. But ye shall receive power after that the Holy Ghost is come upon you; and ye shall be witnesses unto me, both in Jerusalem, and in all Judæa, and in Samaria, and unto the uttermost part of the earth. And when he had spoken these things, while they beheld, he was taken up, and a cloud received him out of their sight. And while they looked stedfastly toward heaven, as he went up, behold, two men stood by them in white apparel; which also said, Ye men of Galilee, why stand ye gazing up into heaven? This same Jesus, which is taken up from you into heaven, shall so come, in like manner as ye have seen him go into heaven.

THE GOSPEL. St. Mark xvi. 14.

JESUS appeared unto the eleven as they sat at meat, and upbraided them with their unbelief and hardness of heart, because they believed not them which had seen him after he was risen. And he said unto them, Go ye into all the world, and preach the Gospel to every creature. He that believeth and is baptized shall be saved; but he that believeth not shall be damned.

And these signs shall follow them that believe : In my Name shall they cast out devils; they shall speak with new tongues; they shall take up serpents; and if they drink any deadly thing, it shall not hurt them; they shall lay hands on the sick, and they shall recover. So then after the Lord had spoken unto them, he was received up into heaven, and sat on the right hand of God. And they went forth and preached every where, the Lord working with them, and confirming the Word with signs following.

Sunday after Ascension Day.

THE COLLECT.

O GOD the King of glory, who hast exalted thine only Son Jesus Christ with great triumph unto thy kingdom in heaven; We beseech thee, leave us not comfortless; but send to us thine Holy Ghost to comfort us, and exalt us unto the same place whither our Saviour Christ is gone before, who liveth and reigneth with thee and the Holy Ghost, one God, world without end. *Amen.*

THE EPISTLE. 1 St. Peter iv. 7.

THE end of all things is at hand; be ye therefore sober, and watch unto prayer. And above all things have fervent charity among yourselves : for charity shall cover the multitude of sins. Use hospitality one to another without grudging. As every man hath received the gift, even so minister the same one to another, as good stewards of the manifold grace of God. If any man speak, let him speak as the oracles of God : if any man minister, let him do it as of the ability which God giveth; that God in all things may be glorified through Jesus Christ, to whom be praise and dominion for ever and ever. Amen.

THE GOSPEL. St. John xv. 26, *and part of* Chapter xvi.

WHEN the Comforter is come, whom I will send unto you from the Father, even the Spirit of truth, which proceedeth from the Father, he shall testify of me. And ye also shall bear witness, because ye have been with me from the beginning. These things have I spoken unto you, that ye should not be offended. They shall put you out of the synagogues : yea, the time cometh, that whosoever killeth you will think that he doeth God service. And these things will they do unto you, because they have not known the Father, nor me. But these things have I told you, that, when the time shall come, ye may remember that I told you of them.

Whitsunday.

THE COLLECT.

GOD, who as at this time didst teach the hearts of thy faithful
people, by the sending to them the light of thy Holy Spirit;
Grant us by the same Spirit to have a right judgement in all things,
and evermore to rejoice in his holy comfort; through the merits of
Christ Jesus our Saviour, who liveth and reigneth with thee, in the
unity of the same Spirit, one God, world without end. *Amen.*

FOR THE EPISTLE. Acts ii. 1.

WHEN the day of Pentecost was fully come, they were all with
one accord in one place. And suddenly there came a sound
from heaven, as of a rushing mighty wind, and it filled all the
house where they were sitting. And there appeared unto them
cloven tongues, like as of fire, and it sat upon each of them : and
they were all filled with the Holy Ghost, and began to speak with
other tongues, as the Spirit gave them utterance. And there were
dwelling at Jerusalem Jews, devout men, out of every nation under
heaven. Now when this was noised abroad, the multitude came
together, and were confounded, because that every man heard
them speak in his own language. And they were all amazed, and
marvelled, saying one to another, Behold, are not all these which
speak Galileans ? And how hear we every man in our own tongue
wherein we were born ? Parthians, and Medes, and Elamites, and
the dwellers in Mesopotamia, and in Judæa, and Cappadocia, in
Pontus, and Asia, Phrygia, and Pamphylia, in Egypt, and in the
parts of Libya about Cyrene, and strangers of Rome, Jews, and
Proselytes, Cretes, and Arabians, we do hear them speak in our
tongues the wonderful works of God.

THE GOSPEL. St. John xiv. 15.

JESUS said unto his disciples, If ye love me, keep my commandments. And I will pray the Father, and he shall give you
another Comforter, that he may abide with you for ever ; even the
Spirit of truth, whom the world cannot receive, because it seeth him
not, neither knoweth him : but ye know him ; for he dwelleth with
you, and shall be in you. I will not leave you comfortless ; I will
come to you. Yet a little while, and the world seeth me no more ;
but ye see me : because I live, ye shall live also. At that day ye
shall know, that I am in my Father, and ye in me, and I in
you. He that hath my commandments, and keepeth them,
he it is that loveth me ; and he that loveth me shall be loved

of my Father, and I will love him, and will manifest myself to him. Judas saith unto him, (not Iscariot,) Lord, how is it that thou wilt manifest thyself unto us, and not unto the world? Jesus answered and said unto him, If a man love me, he will keep my words, and my Father will love him, and we will come unto him, and make our abode with him. He that loveth me not keepeth not my sayings: and the word which ye hear is not mine, but the Father's which sent me. These things have I spoken unto you, being yet present with you. But the Comforter, which is the Holy Ghost, whom the Father will send in my Name, he shall teach you all things, and bring all things to your remembrance, whatsoever I have said unto you. Peace I leave with you, my peace I give unto you: not as the world giveth, give I unto you. Let not your heart be troubled, neither let it be afraid. Ye have heard how I said unto you, I go away, and come again unto you. If ye loved me, ye would rejoice, because I said, I go unto the Father: for my Father is greater than I. And now I have told you before it come to pass, that, when it is come to pass, ye might believe. Hereafter I will not talk much with you: for the prince of this world cometh, and hath nothing in me. But that the world may know that I love the Father; and as the Father gave me commandment, even so I do.

Monday in Whitsun Week.

THE COLLECT.

GOD, who as at this time didst teach the hearts of thy faithful people, by the sending to them the light of thy Holy Spirit; Grant us by the same Spirit to have a right judgement in all things, and evermore to rejoice in his holy comfort; through the merits of Christ Jesus our Saviour, who liveth and reigneth with thee, in the unity of the same Spirit, one God, world without end. *Amen.*

FOR THE EPISTLE. ACTS x. 34.

THEN Peter opened his mouth, and said, Of a truth I perceive that God is no respecter of persons; but in every nation he that feareth him, and worketh righteousness, is accepted with him. The Word which God sent unto the children of Israel, preaching peace by Jesus Christ; (he is Lord of all;) that Word, I say, ye know, which was published throughout all Judæa, and began from Galilee, after the baptism which John preached: how God anointed Jesus of Nazareth with the Holy Ghost, and with power; who went about doing good, and healing all that were oppressed of the devil:

for God was with him. And we are witnesses of all things which he did, both in the land of the Jews, and in Jerusalem; whom they slew, and hanged on a tree: Him God raised up the third day, and shewed him openly; not to all the people, but unto witnesses chosen before of God; even to us who did eat and drink with him after he rose from the dead. And he commanded us to preach unto the people, and to testify that it is he which was ordained of God to be the Judge of quick and dead. To him give all the prophets witness, that through his Name whosoever believeth in him shall receive remission of sins. While Peter yet spake these words, the Holy Ghost fell on all them which heard the word. And they of the circumcision, which believed, were astonished, as many as came with Peter, because that on the Gentiles also was poured out the gift of the Holy Ghost. For they heard them speak with tongues, and magnify God. Then answered Peter, Can any man forbid water, that these should not be baptized, which have received the Holy Ghost as well as we? And he commanded them to be baptized in the Name of the Lord. Then prayed they him to tarry certain days.

THE GOSPEL. St. John iii. 16.

GOD so loved the world, that he gave his only begotten Son, that whosoever believeth in him should not perish, but have everlasting life. For God sent not his Son into the world to condemn the world, but that the world through him might be saved. He that believeth on him is not condemned: but he that believeth not is condemned already; because he hath not believed in the Name of the only begotten Son of God. And this is the condemnation, that light is come into the world, and men loved darkness rather than light, because their deeds were evil. For every one that doeth evil hateth the light, neither cometh to the light, lest his deeds should be reproved. But he that doeth truth cometh to the light, that his deeds may be made manifest, that they are wrought in God.

Tuesday in Whitsun Week.

THE COLLECT.

GOD, who as at this time didst teach the hearts of thy faithful people, by the sending to them the light of thy Holy Spirit; Grant us by the same Spirit to have a right judgement in all things, and evermore to rejoice in his holy comfort; through the merits of Christ Jesus our Saviour, who liveth and reigneth with thee, in the unity of the same Spirit, one God, world without end. *Amen.*

L

FOR THE EPISTLE. Acts viii. 14.

WHEN the Apostles, which were at Jerusalem, heard that Samaria had received the word of God, they sent unto them Peter and John; who, when they were come down, prayed for them, that they might receive the Holy Ghost: (for as yet he was fallen upon none of them; only they were baptized in the Name of the Lord Jesus.) Then laid they their hands on them, and they received the Holy Ghost.

THE GOSPEL. St. John x. 1.

VERILY, verily I say unto you, He that entereth not by the door into the sheepfold, but climbeth up some other way, the same is a thief and a robber. But he that entereth in by the door is the shepherd of the sheep: to him the porter openeth; and the sheep hear his voice, and he calleth his own sheep by name, and leadeth them out. And, when he putteth forth his own sheep, he goeth before them, and the sheep follow him; for they know his voice. And a stranger will they not follow; but will flee from him; for they know not the voice of strangers. This parable spake Jesus unto them: but they understood not what things they were which he spake unto them. Then said Jesus unto them again; Verily, verily I say unto you, I am the door of the sheep. All that ever came before me are thieves and robbers; but the sheep did not hear them. I am the door; by me if any man enter in, he shall be saved, and shall go in and out, and find pasture. The thief cometh not but for to steal, and to kill, and to destroy: I am come that they might have life, and that they might have it more abundantly.

Trinity Sunday.

THE COLLECT.

ALMIGHTY and everlasting God, who hast given unto us thy servants grace by the confession of a true faith to acknowledge the glory of the eternal Trinity, and in the power of the Divine Majesty to worship the Unity; We beseech thee, that thou wouldest keep us stedfast in this faith, and evermore defend us from all adversities, who livest and reignest one God, world without end. *Amen.*

FOR THE EPISTLE. Rev. iv. 1.

AFTER this I looked, and behold, a door was opened in heaven: and the first voice which I heard was as it were of a trumpet talking with me; which said, Come up hither, and I will shew thee things which must be hereafter. And immediately I was in the Spirit; and behold, a throne was set in heaven, and one sat on the throne : and he that sat was to look upon like a jasper and a sardine stone : and there was a rainbow round about the throne, in sight like unto an emerald. And round about the throne were four and twenty seats; and upon the seats I saw four and twenty elders sitting, clothed in white raiment; and they had on their heads crowns of gold : and out of the throne proceeded lightnings, and thunderings, and voices. And there were seven lamps of fire burning before the throne, which are the seven spirits of God. And before the throne there was a sea of glass like unto crystal : and in the midst of the throne, and round about the throne, were four beasts full of eyes before and behind. And the first beast was like a lion, and the second beast like a calf, and the third beast had a face as a man, and the fourth beast was like a flying eagle. And the four beasts had each of them six wings about him; and they were full of eyes within : and they rest not day and night, saying, Holy, holy, holy, Lord God Almighty, which was, and is, and is to come. And when those beasts give glory, and honour, and thanks, to him that sat on the throne, who liveth for ever and ever, the four and twenty elders fall down before him that sat on the throne, and worship him that liveth for ever and ever, and cast their crowns before the throne, saying, Thou art worthy, O Lord, to receive glory, and honour, and power; for thou hast created all things, and for thy pleasure they are and were created.

THE GOSPEL. St. John iii. 1.

THERE was a man of the Pharisees, named Nicodemus, a ruler of the Jews : the same came to Jesus by night, and said unto him, Rabbi, we know that thou art a teacher come from God : for no man can do these miracles that thou doest, except God be with him. Jesus answered and said unto him, Verily, verily I say unto thee, Except a man be born again, he cannot see the Kingdom of God. Nicodemus saith unto him, How can a man be born when he is old? can he enter the second time into his mother's womb, and be born? Jesus answered, Verily, verily I say unto thee, Except a man be born of water, and of the Spirit, he cannot enter into the Kingdom of God. That which is born of the flesh is flesh; and that which is born of the Spirit is spirit. Marvel not that I said unto thee, Ye must be born again. The wind bloweth where it listeth, and thou hearest the sound thereof, but canst not tell whence it cometh, and whither it goeth; so is every one that is born of the Spirit. Nicodemus answered and said unto him, How can these things be? Jesus answered and said unto him, Art thou a master of Israel, and knowest not these things? Verily, verily I say unto thee, We speak that we do know, and testify that we have seen; and ye receive not our witness. If I have told you earthly things, and ye believe not; how shall ye believe, if I tell you of heavenly things? And no man hath ascended up to heaven, but he that came down from heaven, even the Son of man, who is in heaven. And as Moses lifted up the serpent in the wilderness, even so must the Son of man be lifted up: that whosoever believeth in him should not perish, but have eternal life.

The First Sunday after Trinity.

THE COLLECT.

O GOD, the strength of all them that put their trust in thee, mercifully accept our prayers; and because through the weakness of our mortal nature we can do no good thing without thee, grant us the help of thy grace, that in keeping of thy commandments we may please thee, both in will and deed; through Jesus Christ our Lord. *Amen.*

THE EPISTLE. 1 St. John iv. 7.

BELOVED, let us love one another: for love is of God, and every one that loveth is born of God, and knoweth God. He that loveth not knoweth not God; for God is love. In this was manifested the love of God towards us, because that God sent his only-begotten Son into the world, that we might live through him. Herein is love, not that we loved God, but that he loved us, and sent his Son to be the propitiation for our sins. Beloved, if God so loved us, we ought also to love one another. No man hath seen God at any time. If we love one another, God dwelleth in us, and his love is perfected in us. Hereby know we that we dwell in him, and he in us; because he hath given us of his Spirit. And we have seen, and do testify, that the Father sent the Son to be the Saviour of the world. Whosoever shall confess that Jesus is the Son of God, God dwelleth in him, and he in God. And we have known and believed the love that God hath to us. God is love; and he that dwelleth in love dwelleth in God, and God in him. Herein is our love made perfect, that we may have boldness in the day of judgement; because as he is, so are we in this world. There is no fear in love; but perfect love casteth out fear; because fear hath torment: He that feareth is not made perfect in love. We love him, because he first loved us. If a man say, I love God, and hateth his brother, he is a liar: for he that loveth not his brother, whom he hath seen, how can he love God, whom he hath not seen? And this commandment have we from him, That he who loveth God love his brother also.

THE GOSPEL. St. Luke xvi. 19.

THERE was a certain rich man, which was clothed in purple, and fine linen, and fared sumptuously every day. And there was a certain beggar named Lazarus, which was laid at his gate full of sores, and desiring to be fed with the crumbs which fell from the rich man's table; moreover, the dogs came and licked his sores. And it came to pass, that the beggar died, and was carried by the angels into Abraham's bosom. The rich man also died, and was buried : and in hell he lift up his eyes being in torments, and seeth Abraham afar off, and Lazarus in his bosom. And he cried and said, Father Abraham, have mercy on me, and send Lazarus, that he may dip the tip of his finger in water, and cool my tongue ; for I am tormented in this flame. But Abraham said, Son, remember that thou in thy life-time receivedst thy good things, and likewise Lazarus evil things ; but now he is comforted, and thou art tormented. And besides all this, between us and you there is a great gulf fixed : so that they who would pass from hence to you cannot ; neither can they pass to us, that would come from thence. Then he said, I pray thee therefore, father, that thou wouldest send him to my father's house : for I have five brethren ; that he may testify unto them, lest they also come into this place of torment. Abraham saith unto him, They have Moses and the prophets ; let them hear them. And he said, Nay, father Abraham ; but if one went unto them from the dead, they will repent. And he said unto him, If they hear not Moses and the prophets, neither will they be persuaded, though one rose from the dead.

The Second Sunday after Trinity.

THE COLLECT.

O LORD, who never failest to help and govern them whom thou dost bring up in thy stedfast fear and love ; Keep us, we beseech thee, under the protection of thy good providence, and make us to have a perpetual fear and love of thy holy Name ; through Jesus Christ our Lord. *Amen.*

THE EPISTLE. 1 St. John iii. 13.

MARVEL not, my brethren, if the world hate you. We know that we have passed from death unto life, because we love the brethren. He that loveth not his brother abideth in death. Whosoever hateth his brother is a murderer : and ye know that no murderer hath eternal life abiding in him. Hereby perceive we the love of God, because he laid down his life for us : and we ought to lay down our lives for the brethren. But whoso hath this world's good, and seeth his brother have need, and shutteth up his bowels of compassion from him; how dwelleth the love of God in him? My little children, let us not love in word, neither in tongue; but in deed, and in truth. And hereby we know that we are of the truth, and shall assure our hearts before him. For if our heart condemn us, God is greater than our heart, and knoweth all things. Beloved, if our heart condemn us not, then have we confidence towards God. And whatsoever we ask, we receive of him, because we keep his commandments, and do those things that are pleasing in his sight. And this is his commandment, That we should believe on the Name of his Son Jesus Christ, and love one another, as he gave us commandment. And he that keepeth his commandments dwelleth in him, and he in him : and hereby we know that he abideth in us, by the Spirit which he hath given us.

THE GOSPEL. St. Luke xiv. 16.

A CERTAIN man made a great supper, and bade many ; and sent his servant at supper-time to say to them that were bidden, Come, for all things are now ready. And they all with one consent began to make excuse. The first said unto him, I have bought a piece of ground, and I must needs go and see it ; I pray thee have me excused. And another said, I have bought five yoke of oxen, and I go to prove them ; I pray thee have me excused. And another said, I have married a wife, and therefore I cannot come. So that servant came, and shewed his lord these things. Then the master of the house being angry said to his servant, Go out quickly into the streets and lanes of the city, and bring in hither the poor, and the maimed, and the halt, and the blind. And the servant said, Lord, it is done as thou hast commanded, and yet there is room. And the lord said unto the servant, Go out into the high-ways and hedges, and compel them to come in, that my house may be filled. For I say unto you, That none of those men which were bidden shall taste of my supper.

The Third Sunday after Trinity.

THE COLLECT.

O LORD, we beseech thee mercifully to hear us ; and grant that we, to whom thou hast given an hearty desire to pray, may by thy mighty aid be defended and comforted in all dangers and adversities ; through Jesus Christ our Lord. *Amen.*

THE EPISTLE. 1 St. Peter v. 5.

ALL of you be subject one to another, and be clothed with humility : for God resisteth the proud, and giveth grace to the humble. Humble yourselves therefore under the mighty hand of God, that he may exalt you in due time ; casting all your care upon him, for he careth for you. Be sober, be vigilant ; because your adversary the devil, as a roaring lion, walketh about seeking whom he may devour : whom resist stedfast in the faith, knowing that the same afflictions are accomplished in your brethren that are in the world. But the God of all grace, who hath called us into his eternal glory by Christ Jesus, after that ye have suffered a while, make you perfect, stablish, strengthen, settle you. To him be glory and dominion for ever and ever. Amen.

THE GOSPEL. St. Luke xv. 1.

THEN drew near unto him all the Publicans and sinners for to hear him. And the Pharisees and Scribes murmured, saying, This man receiveth sinners, and eateth with them. And he spake this parable unto them saying, What man of you having an hundred sheep, if he lose one of them, doth not leave the ninety and nine in the wilderness, and go after that which is lost, until he find it ? And when he hath found it, he layeth it on his shoulders, rejoicing. And when he cometh home, he calleth together his friends and neighbours, saying unto them, Rejoice with me, for I have found my sheep which was lost. I say unto you, That likewise joy shall be in heaven over one sinner that repenteth, more than over ninety and nine just persons, which need no repentance. Either what woman having ten pieces of silver, if she lose one piece, doth not light a candle, and sweep the house, and seek diligently till she find it ? And when she hath found it, she calleth her friends and her neighbours together, saying, Rejoice with me, for I have found the piece which I had lost. Likewise, I say unto you, There is joy in the presence of the angels of God over one sinner that repenteth.

The Fourth Sunday after Trinity.

THE COLLECT.

O GOD, the protector of all that trust in thee, without whom nothing is strong, nothing is holy ; Increase and multiply upon us thy mercy ; that, thou being our ruler and guide, we may so pass through things temporal, that we finally lose not the things eternal : Grant this, O heavenly Father, for Jesus Christ's sake our Lord. *Amen.*

THE EPISTLE. Rom. viii. 18.

I RECKON that the sufferings of this present time are not worthy to be compared with the glory which shall be revealed in us. For the earnest expectation of the creature waiteth for the manifestation of the sons of God. For the creature was made subject to vanity, not willingly, but by reason of him who hath subjected the same in hope: because the creature itself also shall be delivered from the bondage of corruption, into the glorious liberty of the children of God. For we know that the whole creation groaneth, and travaileth in pain together until now. And not only they, but ourselves also, which have the first-fruits of the Spirit, even we ourselves groan within ourselves, waiting for the adoption, to wit, the redemption of our body.

THE GOSPEL. St. Luke vi. 36.

B E ye therefore merciful, as your Father also is merciful. Judge not, and ye shall not be judged: condemn not, and ye shall not be condemned: forgive, and ye shall be forgiven: give, and it shall be given unto you; good measure, pressed down, and shaken together, and running over, shall men give into your bosom. For with the same measure that ye mete withal, it shall be measured to you again. And he spake a parable unto them, Can the blind lead the blind? shall they not both fall into the ditch? The disciple is not above his master; but every one that is perfect shall be as his master. And why beholdest thou the mote that is in thy brother's eye, but perceivest not the beam that is in thine own eye? Either how canst thou say to thy brother, Brother, let me pull out the mote that is in thine eye, when thou thyself beholdest not the beam that is in thine own eye? Thou hypocrite, cast out first the beam out of thine own eye, and then shalt thou see clearly to pull out the mote that is in thy brother's eye.

The Fifth Sunday after Trinity.

THE COLLECT.

G RANT, O Lord, we beseech thee, that the course of this world may be so peaceably ordered by thy governance, that thy Church may joyfully serve thee in all godly quietness; through Jesus Christ our Lord. *Amen.*

THE EPISTLE. 1 St. Peter iii. 8.

B E ye all of one mind, having compassion one of another, love as brethren, be pitiful, be courteous; not rendering evil for evil, or railing for railing; but contrariwise blessing; knowing that ye are thereunto called, that ye should inherit a blessing. For he that will love life, and see good days, let him refrain his tongue from evil, and his lips that they speak no guile : let him eschew evil, and do good ; let him seek peace, and ensue it. For the eyes of the Lord are over the righteous, and his ears are open unto their prayers : but the face of the Lord is against them that do evil. And who is he that will harm you, if ye be followers of that which is good ? But and if ye suffer for righteousness' sake, happy are ye : and be not afraid of their terror, neither be troubled ; but sanctify the Lord God in your hearts.

THE GOSPEL. St. Luke v. 1.

IT came to pass, that as the people pressed upon him to hear the Word of God, he stood by the lake of Gennesareth, and saw two ships standing by the lake ; but the fishermen were gone out of them, and were washing their nets. And he entered into one of the ships, which was Simon's, and prayed him that he would thrust out a little from the land : and he sat down, and taught the people out of the ship. Now when he had left speaking, he said unto Simon, Launch out into the deep, and let down your nets for a draught. And Simon answering said unto him, Master, we have toiled all the night, and have taken nothing ; nevertheless, at thy word I will let down the net. And when they had this done, they inclosed a great multitude of fishes, and their net brake. And they beckoned unto their partners which were in the other ship, that they should come and help them. And they came, and filled both the ships, so that they began to sink. When Simon Peter saw it, he fell down at Jesus' knees, saying, Depart from me, for I am a sinful man, O Lord. For he was astonished, and all that were with him, at the draught of the fishes which they had taken ; and so was also James, and John, the sons of Zebedee, which were partners with Simon. And Jesus said unto Simon, Fear not, from henceforth thou shalt catch men. And when they had brought their ships to land, they forsook all, and followed him.

The Sixth Sunday after Trinity.

THE COLLECT.

O GOD, who hast prepared for them that love thee such good things as pass man's understanding ; Pour into our hearts such love toward thee, that we, loving thee above all things, may obtain thy promises, which exceed all that we can desire ; through Jesus Christ our Lord. *Amen.*

THE EPISTLE. Rom. vi. 3.

KNOW ye not, that so many of us as were baptized into Jesus Christ were baptized into his death? Therefore we are buried with him by baptism into death; that like as Christ was raised up from the dead by the glory of the Father, even so we also should walk in newness of life. For if we have been planted together in the likeness of his death, we shall be also in the likeness of his resurrection: knowing this, that our old man is crucified with him, that the body of sin might be destroyed, that henceforth we should not serve sin. For he that is dead is freed from sin. Now if we be dead with Christ, we believe that we shall also live with him; knowing that Christ being raised from the dead dieth no more; death hath no more dominion over him. For in that he died, he died unto sin once; but in that he liveth, he liveth unto God. Likewise reckon ye also yourselves to be dead indeed unto sin, but alive unto God through Jesus Christ our Lord.

THE GOSPEL. St. Matth. v. 20.

JESUS said unto his disciples, Except your righteousness shall exceed the righteousness of the Scribes and Pharisees, ye shall in no case enter into the Kingdom of heaven. Ye have heard that it was said by them of old time, Thou shalt not kill: and whosoever shall kill, shall be in danger of the judgement. But I say unto you, that whosoever is angry with his brother without a cause shall be in danger of the judgement: and whosoever shall say to his brother, Raca, shall be in danger of the council: but whosoever shall say, Thou fool, shall be in danger of hell-fire. Therefore if thou bring thy gift to the altar, and there rememberest that thy brother hath ought against thee; leave there thy gift before the altar, and go thy way, first be reconciled to thy brother, and then come and offer thy gift. Agree with thine adversary quickly, whiles thou art in the way with him; lest at any time the adversary deliver thee to the judge, and the judge deliver thee to the officer, and thou be cast into prison. Verily I say unto thee, Thou shalt by no means come out thence, till thou hast paid the uttermost farthing.

The Seventh Sunday after Trinity.

THE COLLECT.

LORD of all power and might, who art the author and giver of all good things; Graft in our hearts the love of thy Name, increase in us true religion, nourish us with all goodness, and of thy great mercy keep us in the same; through Jesus Christ our Lord. *Amen.*

THE EPISTLE. Rom. vi. 19.

I SPEAK after the manner of men, because of the infirmity of your flesh : for as ye have yielded your members servants to uncleanness, and to iniquity, unto iniquity ; even so now yield your members servants to righteousness, unto holiness. For when ye were the servants of sin, ye were free from righteousness. What fruit had ye then in those things whereof ye are now ashamed ? for the end of those things is death. But now being made free from sin, and become servants to God, ye have your fruit unto holiness, and the end everlasting life. For the wages of sin is death : but the gift of God is eternal life, through Jesus Christ our Lord.

THE GOSPEL. St. Mark viii. 1.

IN those days the multitude being very great, and having nothing to eat, Jesus called his disciples unto him, and saith unto them, I have compassion on the multitude, because they have now been with me three days, and have nothing to eat : and if I send them away fasting to their own houses, they will faint by the way ; for divers of them came from far. And his disciples answered him, From whence can a man satisfy these men with bread here in the wilderness ? And he asked them, How many loaves have ye ? And they said, Seven. And he commanded the people to sit down on the ground. And he took the seven loaves, and gave thanks, and brake, and gave to his disciples to set before them ; and they did set them before the people. And they had a few small fishes ; and he blessed, and commanded to set them also before them. So they did eat, and were filled : and they took up of the broken meat that was left seven baskets. And they that had eaten were about four thousand. And he sent them away.

The Eighth Sunday after Trinity.

THE COLLECT.

O GOD, whose never-failing providence ordereth all things both in heaven and earth ; We humbly beseech thee to put away from us all hurtful things, and to give us those things which be profitable for us ; through Jesus Christ our Lord. *Amen.*

THE EPISTLE. Rom. viii. 12.

BRETHREN, we are debtors, not to the flesh, to live after the flesh. For if ye live after the flesh, ye shall die ; but if ye through the Spirit do mortify the deeds of the body, ye shall live. For as many as are led by the Spirit of God, they are the sons of

God. For ye have not received the spirit of bondage again to fear; but ye have received the spirit of adoption, whereby we cry, Abba, Father. The Spirit itself beareth witness with our spirit, that we are the children of God : and if children, then heirs ; heirs of God, and joint-heirs with Christ : if so be that we suffer with him, that we may be also glorified together.

THE GOSPEL. St. Matth. vii. 15.

BEWARE of false prophets, which come to you in sheep's clothing, but inwardly they are ravening wolves. Ye shall know them by their fruits. Do men gather grapes of thorns, or figs of thistles ? Even so every good tree bringeth forth good fruit; but a corrupt tree bringeth forth evil fruit. A good tree cannot bring forth evil fruit ; neither can a corrupt tree bring forth good fruit. Every tree that bringeth not forth good fruit is hewn down, and cast into the fire. Wherefore by their fruits ye shall know them. Not every one that saith unto me, Lord, Lord, shall enter into the Kingdom of heaven ; but he that doeth the will of my Father which is in heaven.

The Ninth Sunday after Trinity.

THE COLLECT.

GRANT to us, Lord, we beseech thee, the spirit to think and do always such things as be rightful ; that we, who cannot do any thing that is good without thee, may by thee be enabled to live according to thy will ; through Jesus Christ our Lord. *Amen.*

THE EPISTLE. 1 Cor. x. 1.

BRETHREN, I would not that ye should be ignorant, how that all our fathers were under the cloud, and all passed through the sea ; and were all baptized unto Moses in the cloud, and in the sea ; and did all eat the same spiritual meat, and did all drink the same spiritual drink : (for they drank of that spiritual Rock that followed them ; and that Rock was Christ.) But with many of them God was not well pleased ; for they were overthrown in the wilderness. Now these things were our examples, to the intent we should not lust after evil things, as they also lusted. Neither be ye idolaters, as were some of them ; as it is written, The people sat down to eat and drink, and rose up to play. Neither let us commit fornication, as some of them committed, and fell in one day three and twenty thousand. Neither let us tempt Christ, as some of them also tempted, and were destroyed of serpents. Neither murmur ye, as some of them also murmured, and were destroyed of the destroyer. Now all these things happened unto them for ensamples : and they are written for our admonition, upon whom the ends of the world are come. Wherefore let him that thinketh he standeth take heed lest he fall. There hath no temptation taken you, but such as is common to man : but God is faithful, who will not suffer you to be tempted above that ye are able ; but will with the temptation also make a way to escape, that ye may be able to bear it.

THE GOSPEL. St. Luke xvi. 1.

JESUS said unto his disciples, There was a certain rich man which had a steward ; and the same was accused unto him that he had wasted his goods. And he called him, and said unto him, How is it that I hear this of thee ? Give an account of thy stewardship ; for thou mayest be no longer steward. Then the steward said within himself, What shall I do ? for my lord taketh away from me the stewardship : I cannot dig, to beg I am ashamed. I am resolved what to do, that, when I am put out of the steward-ship, they may receive me into their houses. So he called every one of his lord's debtors unto him, and said unto the first, How much owest thou unto my lord ? And he said, An hundred measures of oil. And he said unto him, Take thy bill, and sit down quickly, and write fifty. Then said he to another, And how much owest thou ? And he said, An hundred measures of wheat. And he said unto him, Take thy bill, and write fourscore. And the lord commended the unjust steward, because he had done wisely : for the children of this world are in their generation wiser than the children of light. And I say unto you, Make to yourselves friends of the mammon of unrighteousness ; that when ye fail, they may receive you into everlasting habitations.

The Tenth Sunday after Trinity.

THE COLLECT.

LET thy merciful ears, O Lord, be open to the prayers of thy humble servants ; and that they may obtain their petitions make them to ask such things as shall please thee ; through Jesus Christ our Lord. *Amen.*

THE EPISTLE. 1 Cor. xii. 1.

CONCERNING spiritual gifts, brethren, I would not have you ignorant. Ye know that ye were Gentiles, carried away unto these dumb idols, even as ye were led. Wherefore I give you to understand, that no man speaking by the Spirit of God calleth Jesus accursed ; and that no man can say that Jesus is the Lord, but by the Holy Ghost. Now there are diversities of gifts, but the same Spirit. And there are differences of administrations, but the same Lord. And there are diversities of operations, but it is the same God, who worketh all in all. But the manifestation of the Spirit is given to every man to profit withal. For to one is given by the Spirit the word of wisdom ; to another the word of knowledge by the same Spirit ; to another faith by the same Spirit ; to another the gifts of healing by the same Spirit ; to another the working of miracles ; to another prophecy ; to another discerning of spirits ; to another divers kinds of tongues ; to another the interpretation of tongues. But all these worketh that one and the self-same Spirit, dividing to every man severally as he will.

THE GOSPEL. St. Luke xix. 41.

AND when he was come near, he beheld the city, and wept over it, saying, If thou hadst known, even thou, at least in this thy day, the things which belong unto thy peace ! but now they are hid from thine eyes. For the days shall come upon thee, that thine enemies shall cast a trench about thee, and compass thee round, and keep thee in on every side, and shall lay thee even with the ground, and thy children within thee ; and they shall not leave in thee one stone upon another ; because thou knewest not the time of thy visitation. And he went into the temple, and began to cast out them that sold therein, and them that bought, saying unto them, It is written, My house is the house of prayer : but ye have made it a den of thieves. And he taught daily in the temple.

The Eleventh Sunday after Trinity.

THE COLLECT.

O GOD, who declarest thy almighty power most chiefly in shewing mercy and pity ; Mercifully grant unto us such a measure of thy grace, that we, running the way of thy commandments, may obtain thy gracious promises, and be made partakers of thy heavenly treasure ; through Jesus Christ our Lord. *Amen.*

THE EPISTLE. 1 Cor. xv. 1.

BRETHREN, I declare unto you the Gospel which I preached unto you, which also ye have received, and wherein ye stand : by which also ye are saved, if ye keep in memory what I preached unto you, unless ye have believed in vain. For I delivered unto you first of all, that which I also received, how that Christ died for our sins, according to the Scriptures ; and that he was buried ; and that he rose again the third day, according to the Scriptures ;

and that he was seen of Cephas, then of the twelve : after that, he was seen of above five hundred brethren at once ; of whom the greater part remain unto this present; but some are fallen asleep : after that, he was seen of James; then of all the Apostles : and last of all, he was seen of me also, as of one born out of due time. For I am the least of the Apostles, that am not meet to be called an Apostle, because I persecuted the Church of God. But by the grace of God I am what I am : and his grace which was bestowed upon me was not in vain ; but I laboured more abundantly than they all ; yet not I, but the grace of God which was with me. Therefore whether it were I or they, so we preach, and so ye believed.

THE GOSPEL. St. Luke xviii. 9.

JESUS spake this parable unto certain which trusted in themselves that they were righteous, and despised others : Two men went up into the temple to pray ; the one a Pharisee, and the other a Publican. The Pharisee stood and prayed thus with himself, God, I thank thee, that I am not as other men are, extortioners, unjust, adulterers, or even as this Publican : I fast twice in the week, I give tithes of all that I possess. And the Publican, standing afar off, would not lift up so much as his eyes unto heaven, but smote upon his breast, saying, God be merciful to me a sinner. I tell you, this man went down to his house justified rather than the other : for every one that exalteth himself shall be abased ; and he that humbleth himself shall be exalted.

The Twelfth Sunday after Trinity.

THE COLLECT.

ALMIGHTY and everlasting God, who art always more ready to hear than we to pray, and art wont to give more than either we desire, or deserve ; Pour down upon us the abundance of thy mercy ; forgiving us those things whereof our conscience is afraid, and giving us those good things which we are not worthy to ask, but through the merits and mediation of Jesus Christ, thy Son, our Lord. *Amen.*

THE EPISTLE. 2 Cor. iii. 4.

SUCH trust have we through Christ to God-ward : not that we are sufficient of ourselves to think anything as of ourselves ; but our sufficiency is of God. Who also hath made us able ministers of the New Testament ; not of the letter, but of the Spirit : for the letter killeth, but the Spirit giveth life. But if the ministration of death written and engraven in stones was glorious, so that the children of Israel could not stedfastly behold the face of Moses for the glory of his countenance, which glory was to be done away; how shall not the ministration of the Spirit be rather glorious? For if the ministration of condemnation be glory, much more doth the ministration of righteousness exceed in glory.

THE GOSPEL. St. Mark vii. 31.

JESUS, departing from the coasts of Tyre and Sidon, came unto the sea of Galilee, through the midst of the coasts of Decapolis. And they bring unto him one that was deaf, and had an impediment in his speech; and they beseech him to put his hand upon him. And he took him aside from the multitude, and put his fingers into his ears, and he spit, and touched his tongue; and looking up to heaven, he sighed, and saith unto him, *Ephphatha*, that is, Be opened. And straightway his ears were opened, and the string of his tongue was loosed, and he spake plain. . And he charged them that they should tell no man : but the more he charged them, so much the more a great deal they published it; and were beyond measure astonished, saying, He hath done all things well; he maketh both the deaf to hear, and the dumb to speak.

The Thirteenth Sunday after Trinity.

THE COLLECT.

ALMIGHTY and merciful God, of whose only gift it cometh that thy faithful people do unto thee true and laudable service; Grant, we beseech thee, that we may so faithfully serve thee in this life, that we fail not finally to attain thy heavenly promises; through the merits of Jesus Christ our Lord. *Amen.*

THE EPISTLE. Gal. iii. 16.

TO Abraham and his seed were the promises made. He saith not, And to seeds, as of many; but as of one; And to thy seed, which is Christ. And this I say, That the covenant that was confirmed before of God in Christ, the Law, which was four hundred and thirty years after, cannot disannul, that it should make the promise of none effect. For if the inheritance be of the Law, it is no more of promise; but God gave it to Abraham by promise. Wherefore then serveth the Law? It was added because of transgressions, till the seed should come, to whom the promise was made; and it was ordained by angels in the hand of a mediator. Now a mediator is not a mediator of one; but God is one. Is the Law then against the promises of God? God forbid: for if there had been a law given which could have given life, verily righteousness should have been by the Law. But the Scripture hath concluded all under sin, that the promise by faith of Jesus Christ might be given to them that believe.

THE GOSPEL. St. Luke x. 23.

BLESSED are the eyes which see the things that ye see. For I tell you, That many prophets and kings have desired to see those things which ye see, and have not seen them; and to hear those things which ye hear, and have not heard them. And behold, a certain Lawyer stood up, and tempted him, saying, Master, what shall I do to inherit eternal life? He said unto him, What is written in the Law? how readest thou? And he answering said, Thou shalt love the Lord thy God with all thy heart, and with all thy soul, and with all thy strength, and with all thy mind; and thy neighbour as thyself. And he said unto him, Thou hast answered right; this do, and thou shalt live. But he, willing to justify himself, said unto Jesus, And who is my neighbour? And Jesus answering said, A certain man went down from Jerusalem to Jericho, and fell among thieves, which stripped him of his raiment, and wounded him, and departed, leaving him half dead. And by chance there came down a certain Priest that way, and, when he saw him, he passed by on the other side. And likewise a Levite, when he was at the place, came and looked on him, and passed by on the other side. But a certain Samaritan, as he journeyed, came where he was; and, when he saw him, he had compassion on him, and went to him, and bound up his wounds, pouring in oil and wine, and set him on his own beast, and brought him to an inn, and took care of him. And on the morrow, when he departed, he took out two pence, and gave them to the host, and said unto him, Take care of him; and whatsoever thou spendest more, when I come again, I will repay thee. Which now of these three, thinkest thou, was neighbour unto him that fell among the thieves? And he said, He that shewed mercy on him. Then said Jesus unto him, Go, and do thou likewise.

The Fourteenth Sunday after Trinity.

THE COLLECT.

ALMIGHTY and everlasting God, give unto us the increase of faith, hope, and charity; and, that we may obtain that which thou dost promise, make us to love that which thou dost command; through Jesus Christ our Lord. *Amen.*

M

THE EPISTLE. GAL. v. 16.

I SAY then, Walk in the Spirit, and ye shall not fulfil the lust of the flesh. For the flesh lusteth against the Spirit, and the Spirit against the flesh; and these are contrary the one to the other; so that ye cannot do the things that ye would. But if ye be led by the Spirit, ye are not under the law. Now the works of the flesh are manifest, which are these, adultery, fornication, uncleanness, lasciviousness, idolatry, witchcraft, hatred, variance, emulations, wrath, strife, seditions, heresies, envyings, murders, drunkenness, revellings, and such like: of the which I tell you before, as I have also told you in time past, That they who do such things shall not inherit the kingdom of God. But the fruit of the Spirit is love, joy, peace, long-suffering, gentleness, goodness, faith, meekness, temperance: against such there is no law. And they that are Christ's have crucified the flesh, with the affections and lusts.

THE GOSPEL. St. Luke xvii. 11.

A ND it came to pass, as Jesus went to Jerusalem, that he passed through the midst of Samaria, and Galilee. And as he entered into a certain village, there met him ten men that were lepers, which stood afar off. And they lifted up their voices, and said, Jesus, Master, have mercy on us. And when he saw them, he said unto them, Go, shew yourselves unto the priests. And it came to pass, that, as they went, they were cleansed. And one of them, when he saw that he was healed, turned back, and with a loud voice glorified God, and fell down on his face at his feet, giving him thanks; and he was a Samaritan. And Jesus answering said, Were there not ten cleansed? but where are the nine? There are not found that returned to give glory to God, save this stranger. And he said unto him, Arise, go thy way, thy faith hath made thee whole.

The Fifteenth Sunday after Trinity.

THE COLLECT.

K EEP, we beseech thee, O Lord, thy Church with thy perpetual mercy: and, because the frailty of man without thee cannot but fall, keep us ever by thy help from all things hurtful, and lead us to all things profitable to our salvation; through Jesus Christ our Lord. *Amen.*

THE EPISTLE. GAL. vi. 11.

Y E see how large a letter I have written unto you with mine own hand. As many as desire to make a fair shew in the flesh, they constrain you to be circumcised; only lest they should suffer persecution for the cross of Christ. For neither they themselves who are circumcised keep the law; but desire to have you circumcised, that they may glory in your flesh. But God forbid that I should glory, save in the cross of our Lord Jesus Christ, by whom the world is crucified unto me, and I unto the world. For in Christ Jesus neither circumcision availeth any thing, nor uncircumcision, but a new creature. And as many as walk according to this rule, peace be on them, and mercy, and upon the Israel of God. From henceforth let no man trouble me; for I bear in my body the marks of the Lord Jesus. Brethren, the grace of our Lord Jesus Christ be with your spirit. Amen.

THE GOSPEL. St. Matth. vi. 24.

NO man can serve two masters : for either he will hate the one, and love the other ; or else he will hold to the one, and despise the other. Ye cannot serve God and Mammon. Therefore I say unto you, Take no thought for your life, what ye shall eat, or what ye shall drink; nor yet for your body, what ye shall put on : Is not the life more than meat, and the body than raiment? Behold the fowls of the air ; for they sow not, neither do they reap, nor gather into barns ; yet your heavenly Father feedeth them. Are ye not much better than they? Which of you by taking thought can add one cubit unto his stature ? And why take ye thought for raiment ? Consider the lilies of the field how they grow : they toil not, neither do they spin : and yet I say unto you, That even Solomon in all his glory was not arrayed like one of these. Wherefore, if God so clothe the grass of the field, which to-day is, and to-morrow is cast into the oven ; shall he not much more clothe you, O ye of little faith ? Therefore take no thought, saying, What shall we eat ? or what shall we drink? or wherewithal shall we be clothed? (for after all these things do the Gentiles seek :) for your heavenly Father knoweth that ye have need of all these things. But seek ye first the kingdom of God, and his righteousness, and all these things shall be added unto you. Take therefore no thought for the morrow ; for the morrow shall take thought for the things of itself : sufficient unto the day is the evil thereof.

The Sixteenth Sunday after Trinity.

THE COLLECT.

O LORD, we beseech thee, let thy continual pity cleanse and defend thy Church ; and, because it cannot continue in safety without thy succour, preserve it evermore by thy help and goodness; through Jesus Christ our Lord. *Amen.*

THE EPISTLE. Ephes. iii. 13.

I DESIRE that ye faint not at my tribulations for you, which is your glory. For this cause I bow my knees unto the Father of our Lord Jesus Christ, of whom the whole family in heaven and earth is named, that he would giant you, according to the riches of his glory, to be strengthened with might by his Spirit in the inner man; that Christ may dwell in your hearts by faith; that ye, being rooted and grounded in love, may be able to comprehend with all saints, what is the breadth, and length, and depth, and height; and to know the love of Christ, which passeth knowledge, that ye might be filled with all the fulness of God. Now unto him that is able to do exceeding abundantly above all that we ask or think, according to the power that worketh in us, unto him be glory in the Church by Christ Jesus, throughout all ages, world without end. Amen.

THE GOSPEL. St. Luke vii. 11.

AND it came to pass the day after, that Jesus went into a city called Nain; and many of his disciples went with him, and much people. Now when he came nigh to the gate of the city, behold, there was a dead man carried out, the only son of his mother, and she was a widow; and much people of the city was with her. And when the Lord saw her, he had compassion on her, and said unto her, Weep not. And he came and touched the bier, (and they that bare him stood still,) and he said, Young man, I say unto thee, Arise. And he that was dead sat up, and began to speak: and he delivered him to his mother. And there came a fear on all, and they glorified God, saying, That a great Prophet is risen up among us, and that God hath visited his people. And this rumour of him went forth throughout all Judæa, and throughout all the region round about.

The Seventeenth Sunday after Trinity.

THE COLLECT.

LORD, we pray thee that thy grace may always prevent and follow us, and make us continually to be given to all good works; through Jesus Christ our Lord. *Amen.*

THE EPISTLE. Ephes. iv. 1.

I THEREFORE the prisoner of the Lord beseech you, that ye walk worthy of the vocation wherewith ye are called, with all lowliness and meekness, with long-suffering, forbearing one another in love; endeavouring to keep the unity of the spirit in the bond of peace. There is one body, and one Spirit, even as ye are called in one hope of your calling; one Lord, one faith, one baptism, one God and Father of all, who is above all, and through all, and in you all.

THE GOSPEL. St. Luke xiv. 1.

IT came to pass, as Jesus went into the house of one of the chief Pharisees to eat bread on the sabbath-day, that they watched him. And behold, there was a certain man before him which had the dropsy. And Jesus answering spake unto the Lawyers and Pharisees, saying, Is it lawful to heal on the sabbath-day? And they held their peace. And he took him, and healed him, and let him go; and answered them, saying, Which of you shall have an ass, or an ox, fallen into a pit, and will not straightway pull him out on the sabbath-day? And they could not answer him again to these things. And he put forth a parable to those which were bidden, when he marked how they chose out the chief rooms, saying unto them, When thou art bidden of any man to a wedding, sit not down in the highest room; lest a more honourable man than thou be bidden of him; and he that bade thee and him come and say to thee, Give this man place; and thou begin with shame to take the lowest room. But when thou art bidden, go and sit down in the lowest room; that, when he that bade thee cometh, he may say unto thee, Friend, go up higher: then shalt thou have worship in the presence of them that sit at meat with thee. For whosoever exalteth himself shall be abased; and he that humbleth himself shall be exalted.

The Eighteenth Sunday after Trinity.

THE COLLECT.

LORD, we beseech thee, grant thy people grace to withstand the temptations of the world, the flesh, and the devil, and with pure hearts and minds to follow thee the only God; through Jesus Christ our Lord. *Amen.*

THE EPISTLE. 1 Cor. i. 4.

I THANK my God always on your behalf, for the grace of God which is given you by Jesus Christ; that in every thing ye are enriched by him, in all utterance, and in all knowledge; even as the testimony of Christ was confirmed in you; so that ye come behind in no gift; waiting for the coming of our Lord Jesus Christ, who shall also confirm you unto the end, that ye may be blameless in the day of our Lord Jesus Christ.

THE GOSPEL. St. Matth. xxii. 34.

WHEN the Pharisees had heard that Jesus had put the Sadducees to silence, they were gathered together. Then one of them, who was a Lawyer, asked him a question, tempting him, and saying, Master, which is the great commandment in the Law? Jesus said unto him, Thou shalt love the Lord thy God with all thy heart, and with all thy soul, and with all thy mind. This is the first and great commandment. And the second is like unto it, Thou shalt love thy neighbour as thyself. On these two commandments hang all the Law and the Prophets. While the Pharisees were gathered together, Jesus asked them, saying, What think ye of Christ? whose son is he? They say unto him, The Son of David. He saith unto them, How then doth David in spirit call him Lord, saying, The Lord said unto my Lord, Sit thou on my right hand, till I make thine enemies thy foot-stool? If David then call him Lord, how is he his Son? And no man was able to answer him a word; neither durst any man from that day forth ask him any more questions.

The Nineteenth Sunday after Trinity.
THE COLLECT.

O GOD, forasmuch as without thee we are not able to please thee; Mercifully grant, that thy Holy Spirit may in all things direct and rule our hearts; through Jesus Christ our Lord. *Amen.*

THE EPISTLE. Ephes. iv. 17.

THIS I say therefore, and testify in the Lord, that ye henceforth walk not as other Gentiles walk, in the vanity of their mind; having the understanding darkened, being alienated from the life of God through the ignorance that is in them, because of the blindness of their heart: who, being past feeling, have given themselves over unto lasciviousness, to work all uncleanness with greediness. But ye have not so learned Christ; if so be that ye have heard him, and have been taught by him, as the truth is in Jesus: that ye put off, concerning the former conversation, the old man, which is corrupt according to the deceitful lusts; and be renewed in the spirit of your mind; and that ye put on the new man, which after God is created in righteousness and true holiness. Wherefore, putting away lying, speak every man truth with his neighbour: for we are members one of another. Be ye angry and sin not: let not the sun go down upon your wrath: neither give place to the devil. Let him that stole steal no more; but rather let him labour, working with his hands the thing which is good, that he may have to give to him that needeth. Let no corrupt communication proceed out of your mouth, but that which is good to the use of edifying, that it may minister grace unto the hearers. And grieve not the Holy Spirit of God, whereby ye are sealed unto the day of redemption. Let all bitterness, and wrath, and anger, and clamour, and evil-speaking, be put away from you, with all malice. And be ye kind one to another, tender-hearted, forgiving one another, even as God for Christ's sake hath forgiven you.

THE GOSPEL. St. Matth. ix. 1.

JESUS entered into a ship, and passed over, and came into his own city. And behold, they brought to him a man sick of the palsy, lying on a bed. And Jesus, seeing their faith, said unto the sick of the palsy, Son, be of good cheer, thy sins be forgiven thee. And behold, certain of the Scribes said within themselves, This man blasphemeth. And Jesus, knowing their thoughts, said, Wherefore think ye evil in your hearts? For whether is easier to say, Thy sins be forgiven thee? or to say, Arise, and walk? But that ye may know that the Son of man hath power on earth to forgive sins, (then saith he to the sick of the palsy,) Arise, take up thy bed, and go unto thine house. And he arose, and departed to his house. But when the multitude saw it, they marvelled, and glorified God, who had given such power unto men.

The Twentieth Sunday after Trinity.

THE COLLECT.

O ALMIGHTY and most merciful God, of thy bountiful goodness keep us, we beseech thee, from all things that may hurt us; that we, being ready both in body and soul, may cheerfully accomplish those things that thou wouldest have done; through Jesus Christ our Lord. *Amen.*

THE EPISTLE. Ephes. v. 15.

SEE then that ye walk circumspectly, not as fools, but as wise, redeeming the time, because the days are evil. Wherefore be ye not unwise, but understanding what the will of the Lord is. And be not drunk with wine, wherein is excess; but be filled with the Spirit; speaking to yourselves in psalms, and hymns, and spiritual songs; singing and making melody in your heart to the Lord; giving thanks always for all things unto God and the Father, in the Name of our Lord Jesus Christ; submitting yourselves one to another in the fear of God.

THE GOSPEL. St. Matth. xxii. 1.

JESUS said, The Kingdom of heaven is like unto a certain king, who made a marriage for his son ; and sent forth his servants to call them that were bidden to the wedding; and they would not come. Again, he sent forth other servants, saying, Tell them which are bidden, Behold, I have prepared my dinner ; my oxen and my fatlings are killed, and all things are ready; come unto the marriage. But they made light of it, and went their ways, one to his farm, another to his merchandise : and the remnant took his servants, and entreated them spitefully, and slew them. But when the king heard thereof, he was wroth ; and he sent forth his armies, and destroyed those murderers, and burnt up their city. Then saith he to his servants, The wedding is ready, but they who were bidden were not worthy. Go ye therefore into the high-ways, and as many as ye shall find bid to the marriage. So those servants went out into the high-ways, and gathered together all, as many as they found, both bad and good; and the wedding was furnished with guests. And when the king came in to see the guests, he saw there a man which had not on a wedding-garment. And he saith unto him, Friend, how camest thou in hither, not having a wedding-garment ? And he was speechless. Then said the king to the servants, Bind him hand and foot, and take him away, and cast him into outer darkness : there shall be weeping and gnashing of teeth. For many are called, but few are chosen.

The Twenty=first Sunday after Trinity.

THE COLLECT.

GRANT, we beseech thee, merciful Lord, to thy faithful people pardon and peace, that they may be cleansed from all their sins, and serve thee with a quiet mind; through Jesus Christ our Lord. *Amen.*

THE EPISTLE. Ephes. vi. 10.

MY brethren, be strong in the Lord, and in the power of his might. Put on the whole armour of God, that ye may be able to stand against the wiles of the devil. For we wrestle not against flesh and blood, but against principalities, against powers, against the rulers of the darkness of this world, against spiritual wickedness in high places. Wherefore take unto you the whole armour of God, that ye may be able to withstand in the evil day, and, having done all, to stand. Stand therefore, having your loins girt about with truth ; and having on the breast-plate of righteousness ; and your feet shod with the preparation of the Gospel of peace; above all, taking the shield of faith, wherewith ye shall be able to quench all the fiery darts of the wicked; and take the helmet of salvation, and the sword of the Spirit, which is the Word of God: praying always with all prayer and supplication in the Spirit, and watching thereunto with all perseverance, and supplication for all saints; and for me, that utterance may be given unto me, that I may open my mouth boldly, to make known the mystery of the Gospel, for which I am an ambassador in bonds; that therein I may speak boldly, as I ought to speak.

THE GOSPEL. St. John iv. 46.

THERE was a certain nobleman, whose son was sick at Capernaum. When he heard that Jesus was come out of Judæa into Galilee, he went unto him, and besought him that he would come down and heal his son; for he was at the point of death. Then said Jesus unto him, Except ye see signs and wonders, ye will not believe. The nobleman saith unto him, Sir, come down ere my child die. Jesus saith unto him, Go thy way, thy son liveth. And the man believed the word that Jesus had spoken unto him, and he went his way. And, as he was now going down, his servants met him, and told him, saying, Thy son liveth. Then enquired he of them the hour when he began to amend: and they said unto him, Yesterday at the seventh hour the fever left him. So the father knew that it was at the same hour, in the which Jesus said unto him, Thy son liveth; and himself believed, and his whole house. This is again the second miracle that Jesus did, when he was come out of Judæa into Galilee.

The Twenty=Second Sunday after Trinity.

THE COLLECT.

LORD, we beseech thee to keep thy household the Church in continual godliness; that through thy protection it may be free from all adversities, and devoutly given to serve thee in good works, to the glory of thy Name; through Jesus Christ our Lord. *Amen.*

THE EPISTLE. Philip. i. 3.

I THANK my God upon every remembrance of you, (always in every prayer of mine for you all making request with joy,) for your fellowship in the Gospel from the first day until now; being confident of this very thing, that he who hath begun a good work in you will perform it until the day of Jesus Christ; even as it is meet for me to think this of you all, because I have you in my heart, inasmuch as both in my bonds, and in the defence and confirmation of the Gospel, ye all are partakers of my grace. For God is my record, how greatly I long after you all in the bowels of Jesus Christ. And this I pray, that your love may abound yet more and more in knowledge, and in all judgement: that ye may approve things that are excellent, that ye may be sincere, and without offence, till the day of Christ: being filled with the fruits of righteousness, which are by Jesus Christ, unto the glory and praise of God.

THE GOSPEL. St. Matth. xviii. 21.

PETER said unto Jesus, Lord, how oft shall my brother sin against me, and I forgive him? till seven times? Jesus saith unto him, I say not unto thee, until seven times; but until seventy times seven. Therefore is the Kingdom of heaven likened unto a certain king, which would take account of his servants. And when he had begun to reckon, one was brought unto him, which owed him ten thousand talents. But forasmuch as he had not to pay, his lord commanded him to be sold, and his wife and children, and all that he had, and payment to be made. The servant therefore fell down and worshipped him, saying, Lord, have patience with me, and I will pay thee all. Then the lord of that servant was moved with compassion, and loosed him, and forgave him the debt. But the same servant went out, and found one of his fellow-servants, which owed him an hundred pence; and he laid hands on him, and took him by the throat, saying, Pay me that thou owest. And his fellow-servant fell down at his feet, and besought him, saying, Have patience with me, and I will pay thee all. And he would not; but went and cast him into prison, till he should pay the debt. So when his fellow-servants saw what was done, they were very sorry, and came and told unto their lord all that was done. Then his lord, after that he had called him, said unto him, O thou wicked servant, I forgave thee all that debt, because thou desiredst me: shouldst not thou also have had compassion on thy fellow-servant, even as I had pity on thee? And his lord was wroth, and delivered him to the tormentors, till he should pay all that was due unto him. So likewise shall my heavenly Father do also unto you, if ye from your hearts forgive not every one his brother their trespasses.

The Twenty-third Sunday after Trinity.
THE COLLECT.

O GOD, our refuge and strength, who art the author of all godliness; Be ready, we beseech thee, to hear the devout prayers of thy Church; and grant that those things which we ask faithfully we may obtain effectually; through Jesus Christ our Lord. *Amen.*

THE EPISTLE. Philip. iii. 17.

BRETHREN, be followers together of me, and mark them which walk so as ye have us for an ensample. (For many walk, of whom I have told you often, and now tell you even weeping, that they are the enemies of the cross of Christ; whose end is destruction, whose god is their belly, and whose glory is in their shame, who mind earthly things.) For our conversation is in heaven; from whence also we look for the Saviour, the Lord Jesus Christ; who shall change our vile body, that it may be fashioned like unto his glorious body, according to the working whereby he is able even to subdue all things unto himself.

THE GOSPEL. St. Matth. xxii. 15.

THEN went the Pharisees and took counsel how they might entangle him in his talk. And they sent out unto him their disciples, with the Herodians, saying, Master, we know that thou art true, and teachest the way of God in truth, neither carest thou for any man: for thou regardest not the person of men. Tell us therefore, what thinkest thou? Is it lawful to give tribute unto Cæsar, or not? But Jesus perceived their wickedness, and said, Why tempt ye me, ye hypocrites? shew me the tribute-money. And they brought unto him a penny. And he saith unto them, Whose is this image and superscription? They say unto him, Cæsar's. Then saith he unto them, Render therefore unto Cæsar the things which are Cæsar's; and unto God the things that are God's. When they had heard these words they marvelled, and left him, and went their way.

The Twenty-fourth Sunday after Trinity.
THE COLLECT.

O LORD, we beseech thee, absolve thy people from their offences; that through thy bountiful goodness we may all be delivered from the bands of those sins, which by our frailty we have committed: Grant this, O heavenly Father, for Jesus Christ's sake, our blessed Lord and Saviour. *Amen.*

THE EPISTLE. Coloss. i. 3.

WE give thanks to God and the Father of our Lord Jesus Christ, praying always for you, since we heard of your faith in Jesus Christ, and of the love which ye have to all the saints; for the hope which is laid up for you in heaven, whereof ye heard before in the word of the truth of the Gospel; which is come unto you, as it is in all the world, and bringeth forth fruit, as it doth also in you, since the day ye heard of it, and knew the grace of God in truth. As ye also learned of Epaphras, our dear fellow-servant, who is for you a faithful minister of Christ; who also declared unto us your love in the Spirit. For this cause we also, since the day we heard it, do not cease to pray for you, and to desire that ye might be filled with the knowledge of his will in all wisdom and spiritual understanding : that ye might walk worthy of the Lord unto all pleasing, being fruitful in every good work, and increasing in the knowledge of God; strengthened with all might, according to his glorious power, unto all patience and long-suffering with joyfulness; giving thanks unto the Father, which hath made us meet to be partakers of the inheritance of the saints in light.

THE GOSPEL. St. Matth. ix. 18.

WHILE Jesus spake these things unto John's disciples, behold, there came a certain ruler, and worshipped him, saying, My daughter is even now dead; but come and lay thy hand upon her, and she shall live. And Jesus arose, and followed him, and so did his disciples. (And behold, a woman, which was diseased with an issue of blood twelve years, came behind him, and touched the hem of his garment ; for she said within herself, If I may but touch his garment, I shall be whole. But Jesus turned him about, and, when he saw her, he said, Daughter, be of good comfort, thy faith hath made thee whole. And the woman was made whole from that hour.) And when Jesus came into the ruler's house, and saw the minstrels and the people making a noise, he said unto them, Give place ; for the maid is not dead, but sleepeth. And they laughed him to scorn. But when the people were put forth, he went in, and took her by the hand, and the maid arose. And the fame hereof went abroad into all that land.

The Twenty-fifth Sunday after Trinity.
THE COLLECT.

STIR up, we beseech thee, O Lord, the wills of thy faithful people; that they, plenteously bringing forth the fruit of good works, may of thee be plenteously rewarded ; through Jesus Christ our Lord. *Amen.*

FOR THE EPISTLE. Jer. xxiii. 5.

BEHOLD, the days come, saith the Lord, that I will raise unto David a righteous Branch, and a King shall reign, and prosper, and shall execute judgement and justice in the earth. In his days

Judah shall be saved, and Israel shall dwell safely : and this is his Name whereby he shall be called, THE LORD OUR RIGHTEOUS- NESS. Therefore behold, the days come, saith the Lord, that they shall no more say, The Lord liveth, which brought up the children of Israel out of the land of Egypt ; but, The Lord liveth, which brought up, and which led the seed of the house of Israel out of the north-country, and from all countries whither I had driven them ; and they shall dwell in their own land.

THE GOSPEL. St. John vi. 5.

WHEN Jesus then lift up his eyes, and saw a great company come unto him, he saith unto Philip, Whence shall we buy bread that these may eat ? (And this he said to prove him ; for he himself knew what he would do.) Philip answered him, Two hundred penny-worth of bread is not sufficient for them, that every one of them may take a little. One of his disciples, Andrew, Simon Peter's brother, saith unto him, There is a lad here, which hath five barley-loaves, and two small fishes ; but what are they among so many ? And Jesus said, Make the men sit down. Now there was much grass in the place. So the men sat down, in number about five thousand. And Jesus took the loaves, and, when he had given thanks, he distributed to the disciples, and the disciples to them that were set down, and likewise of the fishes, as much as they would. When they were filled, he said unto his disciples, Gather up the fragments that remain, that nothing be lost. Therefore they gathered them together, and filled twelve baskets with the fragments of the five barley-loaves, which remained over and above unto them that had eaten. Then those men, when they had seen the miracle that Jesus did, said, This is of a truth that Prophet that should come into the world.

¶ *If there be any more Sundays before Advent Sunday, the Service of some of those Sundays that were omitted after the Epiphany shall be taken in to supply so many as are here wanting. And if there be fewer, the overplus may be omitted : Provided that this last Collect, Epistle, and Gospel shall always be used upon the Sunday next before Advent.*

Saint Andrew's Day.

THE COLLECT.

ALMIGHTY God, who didst give such grace unto thy holy Apostle Saint Andrew, that he readily obeyed the calling of thy Son Jesus Christ, and followed him without delay ; Grant unto us all, that we, being called by thy holy Word, may forthwith give up ourselves obediently to fulfil thy holy commandments ; through the same Jesus Christ our Lord. *Amen.*

THE EPISTLE. Rom. x. 9.

IF thou shalt confess with thy mouth the Lord Jesus, and shalt believe in thine heart that God hath raised him from the dead, thou shalt be saved. For with the heart man believeth unto righteousness, and with the mouth confession is made unto salvation. For the Scripture saith, Whosoever believeth on him shall not be ashamed. For there is no difference between the Jew and the Greek: for the same Lord over all is rich unto all that call upon him. For whosoever shall call upon the Name of the Lord shall be saved. How then shall they call on him, in whom they have not believed? And how shall they believe in him, of whom they have not heard? And how shall they hear without a preacher? And how shall they preach, except they be sent? As it is written, How beautiful are the feet of them that preach the Gospel of peace, and bring glad tidings of good things! But they have not all obeyed the Gospel. For Esaias saith, Lord, who hath believed our report? So then faith cometh by hearing, and hearing by the Word of God. But I say, Have they not heard? Yes verily, their sound went into all the earth, and their words unto the ends of the world. But I say, Did not Israel know? First Moses saith, I will provoke you to jealousy by them that are no people, and by a foolish nation I will anger you. But Esaias is very bold, and saith, I was found of them that sought me not; I was made manifest unto them that asked not after me. But to Israel he saith, all day long I have stretched forth my hands unto a disobedient and gainsaying people.

THE GOSPEL. St. Matth. iv. 18.

JESUS, walking by the sea of Galilee, saw two brethren, Simon called Peter, and Andrew his brother, casting a net into the sea, (for they were fishers;) and he saith unto them, Follow me; and I will make you fishers of men. And they straightway left their nets, and followed him. And going on from thence he saw other two brethren, James the son of Zebedee, and John his brother, in a ship with Zebedee their father, mending their nets; and he called them. And they immediately left the ship and their father, and followed him.

Saint Thomas the Apostle.
THE COLLECT.

ALMIGHTY and everliving God, who for the more confirmation of the faith didst suffer thy holy Apostle Thomas to be doubtful in thy Son's resurrection; Grant us so perfectly, and without all doubt, to believe in thy Son Jesus Christ, that our faith in thy sight may never be reproved. Hear us, O Lord, through the same Jesus Christ, to whom, with thee and the Holy Ghost, be all honour and glory, now and for evermore. *Amen.*

THE EPISTLE. Ephes. ii. 19.

NOW therefore ye are no more strangers and foreigners, but fellow-citizens with the saints, and of the household of God; and are built upon the foundation of the Apostles and Prophets, Jesus Christ himself being the chief corner-stone; in whom all the building, fitly framed together, groweth unto an holy temple in the Lord; in whom ye also are builded together for an habitation of God, through the Spirit.

THE GOSPEL. St. John xx. 24.

THOMAS, one of the twelve, called Didymus, was not with them when Jesus came. The other disciples therefore said unto him, We have seen the Lord. But he said unto them, Except I shall see in his hands the print of the nails, and put my finger into the print of the nails, and thrust my hand into his side, I will not believe. And after eight days again his disciples were within, and Thomas with them: then came Jesus, the doors being shut, and stood in the midst, and said, Peace be unto you. Then saith he to Thomas, Reach hither thy finger, and behold my hands; and reach hither thy hand, and thrust it into my side; and be not faithless, but believing. And Thomas answered and said unto him, My Lord, and my God. Jesus saith unto him, Thomas, because thou hast seen me, thou hast believed; blessed are they that have not seen, and yet have believed. And many other signs truly did Jesus in the presence of his disciples, which are not written in this book. But these are written, that ye might believe that Jesus is the Christ, the Son of God; and that believing ye might have life through his Name.

The Conversion of Saint Paul.
THE COLLECT.

O GOD, who, through the preaching of the blessed Apostle Saint Paul, hast caused the light of the Gospel to shine throughout the world; Grant, we beseech thee, that we, having his wonderful conversion in remembrance, may shew forth our thankfulness unto thee for the same, by following the holy doctrine which he taught; through Jesus Christ our Lord. *Amen.*

FOR THE EPISTLE. Acts ix. 1.

AND Saul, yet breathing out threatenings and slaughter against the disciples of the Lord, went unto the high priest, and desired of him letters to Damascus to the synagogues, that, if he found any of this way, whether they were men or women, he might bring them bound unto Jerusalem. And, as he journeyed, he came near Damascus, and suddenly there shined round about him a light from heaven. And he fell to the earth, and heard a voice saying unto him, Saul, Saul, why persecutest thou me? And he said, Who art thou, Lord? And the Lord said, I am Jesus whom thou persecutest: it is hard for thee to kick against the pricks. And he, trembling and astonished, said, Lord, what wilt thou have me to do? And the Lord said unto him, Arise, and go into the city, and it shall be told thee what thou must do. And the men which journeyed with him stood speechless, hearing a voice, but seeing no man. And Saul arose from the earth, and when his eyes were opened he saw no man; but they led him by the hand, and brought him into Damascus. And he was three days without sight, and neither did eat nor drink. And there was a certain disciple at Damascus, named Ananias, and to him said the Lord in a vision, Ananias. And he said, Behold, I am here, Lord. And the Lord said unto him, Arise, and go into the street which is called Straight, and enquire in the house of Judas for one called Saul, of Tarsus: for behold, he prayeth, and hath seen in a vision a man named Ananias, coming in, and putting his hand on him, that he might receive his sight. Then Ananias answered, Lord, I have heard by many of this man, how much evil he hath done to thy saints at Jerusalem; and here he hath authority from the chief priests to bind all that call on thy Name. But the Lord said unto him, Go thy way; for he is a chosen vessel unto me, to bear my Name before the Gentiles, and kings, and the children of Israel: for I will shew him how great things he must suffer for my Name's sake. And Ananias went his way, and entered into the house; and, putting his hands on him, said, Brother Saul, the Lord, (even Jesus that appeared unto thee in the way as thou camest,) hath sent me, that thou mightest receive thy sight, and be filled with the Holy Ghost. And immediately there fell from his eyes as it had been scales; and he received sight forthwith, and arose, and was baptized. And when he had received meat, he was strengthened. Then was Saul certain days with the disciples which were at Damascus. And straightway he preached Christ in the synagogues, that he is the Son of God. But all that heard him were amazed, and said, Is not this he that destroyed them which called on this Name in Jerusalem, and came hither for that intent, that he might bring them bound unto the chief priests? But Saul increased the more in strength, and confounded the Jews which dwelt at Damascus, proving that this is very Christ.

THE GOSPEL. St. Matth. xix. 27.

PETER answered and said unto Jesus, Behold, we have forsaken all, and followed thee; what shall we have therefore? And Jesus said unto them, Verily I say unto you, That ye which have followed me, in the regeneration when the Son of man shall sit in the throne of his glory, ye also shall sit upon twelve thrones, judging the twelve tribes of Israel. And every one that hath forsaken houses, or brethren, or sisters, or father, or mother, or wife, or children, or lands, for my Name's sake, shall receive an hundred-fold, and shall inherit everlasting life. But many that are first shall be last, and the last shall be first.

THE PRESENTATION OF CHRIST IN THE TEMPLE,

COMMONLY CALLED

The Purification of Saint Mary the Virgin.

THE COLLECT.

ALMIGHTY and everliving God, we humbly beseech thy Majesty, that, as thy only begotten Son was this day presented in the temple in substance of our flesh, so we may be presented unto thee with pure and clean hearts, by the same thy Son Jesus Christ our Lord. *Amen.*

FOR THE EPISTLE. Mal. iii. 1.

BEHOLD, I will send my messenger, and he shall prepare the way before me: and the Lord, whom ye seek, shall suddenly come to his temple; even the messenger of the covenant, whom ye delight in; behold, he shall come, saith the Lord of hosts. But who may abide the day of his coming? and who shall stand when he appeareth? for he is like a refiner's fire, and like fullers' soap. And he shall sit as a refiner and purifier of silver; and he shall purify the sons of Levi, and purge them as gold and silver, that they may offer unto the Lord an offering in righteousness. Then shall the offerings of Judah and Jerusalem be pleasant unto the Lord, as in the days of old, and as in former years. And I will come near to you to judgement, and I will be a swift witness against the sorcerers, and against the adulterers, and against false-swearers, and against those that oppress the hireling in his wages, the widow, and the fatherless, and that turn aside the stranger from his right, and fear not me, saith the Lord of hosts.

N

THE GOSPEL. St. Luke ii. 22.

AND when the days of her purification, according to the Law of Moses, were accomplished, they brought him to Jerusalem, to present him to the Lord; (as it is written in the Law of the Lord, Every male that openeth the womb shall be called holy to the Lord;) and to offer a sacrifice, according to that which is said in the Law of the Lord, A pair of turtle-doves, or two young pigeons. And behold, there was a man in Jerusalem, whose name was Simeon; and the same man was just and devout, waiting for the consolation of Israel: and the Holy Ghost was upon him. And it was revealed unto him by the Holy Ghost, that he should not see death, before he had seen the Lord's Christ. And he came by the Spirit into the temple; and when the parents brought in the child Jesus, to do for him after the custom of the Law, then took he him up in his arms, and blessed God, and said, Lord, now lettest thou thy servant depart in peace, according to thy word : for mine eyes have seen thy salvation, which thou hast prepared before the face of all people; a light to lighten the Gentiles, and the glory of thy people Israel. And Joseph and his mother marvelled at those things which were spoken of him. And Simeon blessed them, and said unto Mary his mother, Behold, this child is set for the fall and rising again of many in Israel; and for a sign which shall be spoken against; (yea, a sword shall pierce through thy own soul also;) that the thoughts of many hearts may be revealed. And there was one Anna a prophetess, the daughter of Phanuel, of the tribe of Aser; she was of a great age, and had lived with an husband seven years from her virginity : and she was a widow of about fourscore and four years; which departed not from the temple, but served God with fastings and prayers night and day. And she coming in that instant gave thanks likewise unto the Lord, and spake of him to all them that looked for redemption in Jerusalem. And when they had performed all things according to the law of the Lord, they returned into Galilee to their own city Nazareth. And the child grew, and waxed strong in spirit, filled with wisdom; and the grace of God was upon him.

Saint Matthias's Day.

THE COLLECT.

O ALMIGHTY God, who into the place of the traitor Judas didst choose thy faithful servant Matthias to be of the number of the twelve Apostles; Grant that thy Church, being alway preserved from false Apostles, may be ordered and guided by faithful and true pastors; through Jesus Christ our Lord. *Amen.*

FOR THE EPISTLE. Acts i. 15.

IN those days Peter stood up in the midst of the disciples, and said, (the number of the names together were about an hundred and twenty,) Men and brethren, this Scripture must needs have been fulfilled, which the Holy Ghost by the mouth of David spake before concerning Judas, which was guide to them that took Jesus : for he was numbered with us, and had obtained part of this ministry. Now this man purchased a field with the reward of iniquity; and falling headlong he burst asunder in the midst, and all his bowels gushed out. And it was known unto all the dwellers at Jerusalem, insomuch as that field is called in their proper tongue, Aceldama, that is to say, The field of blood. For it is written in the book of Psalms, Let his habitation be desolate, and let no man dwell therein; and, His bishoprick let another take. Wherefore, of these men which have companied with us all the time that the Lord Jesus went in and out among us, beginning from the baptism of John, unto that same day that he was taken up from us, must one be ordained to be a witness with us of his resurrection. And they appointed two, Joseph called Barsabas, who was surnamed Justus, and Matthias. And they prayed, and said, Thou, Lord, which knowest the hearts of all men, shew whether of these two thou hast chosen; that he may take part of this ministry and apostleship, from which Judas by transgression fell, that he might go to his own place. And they gave forth their lots; and the lot fell upon Matthias, and he was numbered with the eleven Apostles.

THE GOSPEL. St. Matth. xi. 25.

AT that time Jesus answered and said, I thank thee, O Father, Lord of heaven and earth, because thou hast hid these things from the wise and prudent, and hast revealed them unto babes. Even so, Father, for so it seemed good in thy sight. All things are delivered unto me of my Father : and no man knoweth the Son, but the Father; neither knoweth any man the Father, save the Son, and he to whomsóever the Son will reveal him. Come unto me, all ye that labour and are heavy laden, and I will give you rest. Take my yoke upon you, and learn of me; for I am meek and lowly in heart : and ye shall find rest unto your souls. For my yoke is easy, and my burden is light.

The Annunciation of the Blessed Virgin Mary.

THE COLLECT.

WE beseech thee, O Lord, pour thy grace into our hearts; that, as we have known the incarnation of thy Son Jesus Christ by the message of an angel, so by his cross and passion we may be brought unto the glory of his resurrection; through the same Jesus Christ our Lord. *Amen.*

FOR THE EPISTLE. Isai. vii. 10.

MOREOVER, the Lord spake again unto Ahaz, saying, Ask thee a sign of the Lord thy God; ask it either in the depth, or in the height above. But Ahaz said, I will not ask, neither will I tempt the Lord. And he said, Hear ye now, O house of David; Is it a small thing for you to weary men, but will ye weary my God also? Therefore the Lord himself shall give you a sign; Behold, a virgin shall conceive, and bear a son, and shall call his name Immanuel. Butter and honey shall he eat, that he may know to refuse the evil, and choose the good.

THE GOSPEL. St. Luke i. 26.

AND in the sixth month the angel Gabriel was sent from God unto a city of Galilee named Nazareth, to a Virgin espoused to a man whose name was Joseph, of the house of David; and the Virgin's name was Mary. And the angel came in unto her, and said, Hail, thou that art highly favoured, the Lord is with thee; blessed art thou among women. And when she saw him she was troubled at his saying, and cast in her mind what manner of salutation this should be. And the angel said unto her, Fear not, Mary; for thou hast found favour with God. And behold, thou shalt conceive in thy womb, and bring forth a Son, and shalt call his name JESUS. He shall be great, and shall be called the Son of the Highest; and the Lord God shall give unto him the throne of his father David. And he shall reign over the house of Jacob for ever; and of his kingdom there shall be no end. Then said Mary unto the angel, How shall this be, seeing I know not a man? And the angel answered and said unto her, The Holy Ghost shall come upon thee, and the power of the Highest shall overshadow thee: therefore also that holy thing which shall be born of thee shall be called the Son of God. And behold, thy cousin Elizabeth, she hath also conceived a son in her old age; and this is the sixth month with her who was called barren: for with God nothing shall be impossible. And Mary said, Behold the handmaid of the Lord; be it unto me according to thy word. And the angel departed from her.

Saint Mark's Day.

THE COLLECT.

O ALMIGHTY God, who hast instructed thy holy Church with the heavenly doctrine of thy Evangelist Saint Mark; Give us grace, that, being not like children carried away with every blast of vain doctrine, we may be established in the truth of thy holy Gospel; through Jesus Christ our Lord. *Amen.*

THE EPISTLE. Ephes. iv. 7.

UNTO every one of us is given grace, according to the measure of the gift of Christ. Wherefore he saith, When he ascended up on high, he led captivity captive, and gave gifts unto men. (Now that he ascended, what is it but that he also descended first into the lower parts of the earth? He that descended is the same also that ascended up far above all heavens, that he might fill all things.) And he gave some Apostles, and some Prophets, and some Evangelists, and some Pastors and Teachers; for the perfecting of the saints, for the work of the ministry, for the edifying of the body of Christ; till we all come in the unity of the faith, and of the knowledge of the Son of God, unto a perfect man, unto the measure of the stature of the fulness of Christ; that we henceforth be no more children, tossed to and fro, and carried about with every wind of doctrine, by the sleight of men, and cunning craftiness, whereby they lie in wait to deceive; but speaking the truth in love, may grow up into him in all things, which is the head, even Christ: from whom the whole body fitly joined together, and compacted by that which every joint supplieth, according to the effectual working in the measure of every part, maketh increase of the body, unto the edifying of itself in love.

THE GOSPEL. St. John xv. 1.

I AM the true vine, and my Father is the husbandman. Every branch in me that beareth not fruit he taketh away; and every branch that beareth fruit, he purgeth it, that it may bring forth more fruit. Now ye are clean through the word which I have spoken unto you. Abide in me, and I in you. As the branch cannot bear fruit of itself, except it abide in the vine; no more can ye, except ye abide in me. I am the vine, ye are the branches. He that abideth in me, and I in him, the same bringeth forth much fruit; for without me ye can do nothing. If a man abide not in me, he is cast forth as a branch, and is withered; and men gather them, and cast them into the fire, and they are burned. If ye abide in me, and my words abide in you, ye shall ask what ye will, and it shall be done unto you. Herein is my Father glorified, that ye bear much fruit; so shall ye be my disciples. As the Father hath loved me, so have I loved you: continue ye in my love. If ye keep my commandments, ye shall abide in my love; even as I have kept my Father's commandments, and abide in his love. These things have I spoken unto you, that my joy might remain in you, and that your joy might be full.

Saint Philip and Saint James's Day.

THE COLLECT.

O ALMIGHTY God, whom truly to know is everlasting life; Grant us perfectly to know thy Son Jesus Christ to be the way, the truth, and the life; that, following the steps of thy holy Apostles, Saint Philip and Saint James, we may steadfastly walk in the way that leadeth to eternal life; through the same thy Son Jesus Christ our Lord. *Amen.*

THE EPISTLE. St. James i. 1.

JAMES, a servant of God and of the Lord Jesus Christ, to the twelve tribes which are scattered abroad, greeting. My brethren, count it all joy when ye fall into divers temptations; knowing this, that the trying of your faith worketh patience. But let patience have her perfect work, that ye may be perfect and entire, wanting nothing. If any of you lack wisdom, let him ask of God, that giveth to all men liberally, and upbraideth not, and it shall be given him. But let him ask in faith, nothing wavering; for he that wavereth is like a wave of the sea, driven with the wind, and tossed. For let not that man think that he shall receive any thing of the Lord. A double-minded man is unstable in all his ways. Let the brother of low degree rejoice in that he is exalted; but the rich in that he is made low; because as the flower of the grass he shall pass away. For the sun is no sooner risen with a burning heat, but it withereth the grass, and the flower thereof falleth, and the grace of the fashion of it perisheth: so also shall the rich man fade away in his ways. Blessed is the man that endureth temptation; for when he is tried, he shall receive the crown of life, which the Lord hath promised to them that love him.

THE GOSPEL. St. John xiv. 1.

AND Jesus said unto his disciples, Let not your heart be troubled; ye believe in God, believe also in me. In my Father's house are many mansions; if it were not so, I would have told you. I go to prepare a place for you: and if I go and prepare a place for you, I will come again, and receive you unto myself, that where I am, there ye may be also. And whither I go ye know, and the way ye know. Thomas saith unto him, Lord, we know not whither thou goest, and how can we know the way? Jesus saith unto him, I am the way, the truth, and the life: no man cometh unto the Father but by me. If ye had known me, ye should have known my Father also: and from henceforth ye know him, and have seen him. Philip saith unto him, Lord, shew us the Father, and it sufficeth us. Jesus saith unto him, Have I been so long time with you, and yet hast thou not known me, Philip? He that hath seen me hath seen the Father; and how sayest thou then, Shew us the Father? Believest thou not that I am in the Father, and the Father in me? The words that I speak unto you I speak not of myself; but the Father that dwelleth in me, he doeth the works. Believe me, that I am in the Father, and the Father in me; or else believe me for the very works' sake. Verily, verily I say unto you, He that believeth on me, the works that I do shall he do also; and greater works than these shall he do; because I go unto my Father. And whatsoever ye shall ask in my Name, that will I do, that the Father may be glorified in the Son. If ye shall ask any thing in my Name, I will do it.

Saint Barnabas the Apostle.

THE COLLECT.

O LORD God Almighty, who didst endue thy holy Apostle Barnabas with singular gifts of the Holy Ghost; Leave us not, we beseech thee, destitute of thy manifold gifts, nor yet of grace to use them alway to thy honour and glory; through Jesus Christ our Lord. *Amen.*

FOR THE EPISTLE. Acts xi. 22.

TIDINGS of these things came unto the ears of the Church which was in Jerusalem; and they sent forth Barnabas, that he should go as far as Antioch. Who, when he came, and had seen the grace of God, was glad; and exhorted them all, that with purpose of heart they would cleave unto the Lord. For he was a good man, and full of the Holy Ghost, and of faith: and much people was added unto the Lord. Then departed Barnabas to Tarsus, for to seek Saul. And when he had found him, he brought him unto Antioch. And it came to pass, that a whole year they assembled themselves with the Church, and taught much people: and the disciples were called Christians first in Antioch. And in these days came prophets from Jerusalem unto Antioch. And there stood up one of them named Agabus, and signified by the Spirit, that there should be great dearth throughout all the world:

which came to pass in the days of Claudius Cæsar. Then the disciples, every man according to his ability, determined to send relief unto the brethren which dwelt in Judæa. Which also they did, and sent it to the elders by the hands of Barnabas and Saul.

THE GOSPEL. St. John xv. 12.

THIS is my commandment, That ye love one another, as I have loved you. Greater love hath no man than this, that a man lay down his life for his friends. Ye are my friends, if ye do whatsoever I command you. Henceforth I call you not servants; for the servant knoweth not what his Lord doeth: but I have called you friends; for all things that I have heard of my Father I have made known unto you. Ye have not chosen me, but I have chosen you, and ordained you, that ye should go and bring forth fruit, and that your fruit should remain: that whatsoever ye shall ask of the Father in my Name, he may give it you.

Saint John Baptist's Day.
THE COLLECT.

ALMIGHTY God, by whose providence thy servant John Baptist was wonderfully born, and sent to prepare the way of thy Son our Saviour, by preaching of repentance; Make us so to follow his doctrine and holy life, that we may truly repent according to his preaching; and after his example constantly speak the truth, boldly rebuke vice, and patiently suffer for the truth's sake; through Jesus Christ our Lord. *Amen.*

FOR THE EPISTLE. Isai. xl. 1.

COMFORT ye, comfort ye my people, saith your God. Speak ye comfortably to Jerusalem, and cry unto her, That her warfare is accomplished; that her iniquity is pardoned: for she hath received of the Lord's hand double for all her sins. The voice of him that crieth in the wilderness, Prepare ye the way of the Lord, make straight in the desert a high-way for our God. Every valley shall be exalted, and every mountain and hill shall be made low, and the crooked shall be made straight, and the rough places plain. And the glory of the Lord shall be revealed, and all flesh shall see it together: for the mouth of the Lord hath spoken it. The voice said, Cry. And he said, What shall I cry? All flesh is grass, and all the goodliness thereof is as the flower of the field. The grass withereth, the flower fadeth, because the Spirit of the Lord bloweth upon it: surely the people is grass. The grass withereth, the flower fadeth; but the word of our God shall stand for ever. O Zion, that bringest good tidings, get thee up into the high mountain: O Jerusalem, that bringest good tidings, lift up thy voice with strength ; lift it up, be not afraid : say unto the cities of Judah, Behold your God. Behold, the Lord God will come with strong hand, and his arm shall rule for him : behold, his reward is with him, and his work before him. He shall feed his flock like a shepherd; he shall gather the lambs with his arm, and carry them in his bosom, and shall gently lead those that are with young.

THE GOSPEL. St. Luke i. 57.

ELIZABETH'S full time came that she should be delivered ; and she brought forth a son. And her neighbours and her cousins heard how the Lord had shewed great mercy upon her ; and they rejoiced with her. And it came to pass, that on the eighth day they came to circumcise the child ; and they called him Zacharias, after the name of his father. And his mother answered and said, Not so ; but he shall be called John. And they said unto her, There is none of thy kindred that is called by this name. And they made signs to his father, how he would have him called. And he asked for a writing-table, and wrote, saying, His name is John. And they marvelled all. And his mouth was opened immediately, and his tongue loosed, and he spake, and praised God. And fear came on all that dwelt round about them ; and all these sayings were noised abroad throughout all the hill-country of Judæa. And all they that had heard them laid them up in their hearts, saying, What manner of child shall this be ? And the hand of the Lord was with him. And his father Zacharias was filled with the Holy Ghost, and prophesied, saying, Blessed be the Lord God of Israel : for he hath visited and redeemed his people, and hath raised up an horn of salvation for us in the house of his servant David ; as he spake by the mouth of his holy prophets, which have been since the world began ; that we should be saved from our enemies, and from the hand of all that hate us ; to perform the mercy promised to our forefathers, and to remember his holy covenant ; the oath which he sware to our father Abraham, that he would grant unto us, that we, being delivered out of the hands of our enemies, might serve him without fear, in holiness and righteousness before him all the days of our life. And thou, Child, shalt be called the Prophet of the Highest : for thou shalt go before the face of the Lord to prepare his ways; to give knowledge of salvation unto his people, by the remission of their sins, through the tender mercy of our God, whereby the day-spring from on high hath visited us ; to give light to them that sit in darkness and in the shadow of death, to guide our feet into the way of peace. And the child grew, and waxed strong in spirit ; and was in the deserts till the day of his shewing unto Israel.

Saint Peter's Day.

THE COLLECT.

O ALMIGHTY God, who by thy Son Jesus Christ didst give to thy Apostle Saint Peter many excellent gifts, and commandedst him earnestly to feed thy flock; Make, we beseech thee, all Bishops and Pastors diligently to preach thy holy Word, and the people obediently to follow the same, that they may receive the crown of everlasting glory; through Jesus Christ our Lord. *Amen.*

FOR THE EPISTLE. Acts xii. 1.

A BOUT that time Herod the king stretched forth his hands to vex certain of the Church. And he killed James the brother of John with the sword. And, because he saw it pleased the Jews, he proceeded further to take Peter also. (Then were the days of unleavened bread.) And when he had apprehended him, he put him in prison, and delivered him to four quaternions of soldiers to keep him, intending after Easter to bring him forth to the people. Peter therefore was kept in prison; but prayer was made without ceasing of the Church unto God for him. And when Herod would have brought him forth, the same night Peter was sleeping between two soldiers, bound with two chains; and the keepers before the door kept the prison. And behold, the angel of the Lord came upon him, and a light shined in the prison; and he smote Peter on the side, and raised him up, saying, Arise up quickly. And his chains fell off from his hands. And the angel said unto him, Gird thyself, and bind on thy sandals : and so he did. And he saith unto him, Cast thy garment about thee, and follow me. And he went out and followed him; and wist not that it was true which was done by the angel; but thought he saw a vision. When they were past the first and second ward, they came unto the iron gate that leadeth unto the city, which opened to them of his own accord; and they went out, and passed on through one street, and forthwith the angel departed from him. And when Peter was come to himself, he said, Now I know of a surety, that the Lord hath sent his angel, and hath delivered me out of the hand of Herod, and from all the expectation of the people of the Jews.

THE GOSPEL. St. Matth. xvi. 13.

W HEN Jesus came into the coasts of Cæsarea Philippi, he asked his disciples, saying, Whom do men say that I, the Son of man, am? And they said, Some say that thou art John the Baptist, some Elias, and others Jeremias, or one of the prophets. He saith unto them, But whom say ye that I am? And Simon

Peter answered and said, Thou art Christ, the Son of the living God. And Jesus answered and said unto him, Blessed art thou, Simon Bar-jona : for flesh and blood hath not revealed it unto thee, but my Father which is in heaven. And I say also unto thee, That thou art Peter, and upon this rock I will build my Church ; and the gates of hell shall not prevail against it. And I will give unto thee the keys of the kingdom of heaven : and whatsoever thou shalt bind on earth shall be bound in heaven ; and whatsoever thou shalt loose on earth shall be loosed in heaven.

Saint James the Apostle.

THE COLLECT.

GRANT, O merciful God, that as thine holy Apostle Saint James, leaving his father and all that he had, without delay was obedient unto the calling of thy Son Jesus Christ, and followed him ; so we, forsaking all worldly and carnal affections, may be evermore ready to follow thy holy commandments ; through Jesus Christ our Lord. *Amen.*

FOR THE EPISTLE. ACTS xi. 27, *ana part of* Chapter xii.

IN those days came prophets from Jerusalem unto Antioch. And there stood up one of them named Agabus, and signified by the Spirit, that there should be great dearth throughout all the world ; which came to pass in the days of Claudius Cæsar. Then the disciples, every man according to his ability, determined to send relief unto the brethren which dwelt in Judæa. Which also they did, and sent it to the elders by the hands of Barnabas and Saul. Now about that time Herod the king stretched forth his hands to vex certain of the Church. And he killed James the brother of John with the sword. And, because he saw it pleased the Jews, he proceeded further to take Peter also.

THE GOSPEL. ST. MATTH. xx. 20.

THEN came to him the mother of Zebedee's children with her sons, worshipping him, and desiring a certain thing of him. And he said unto her, What wilt thou ? She saith unto him, Grant that these my two sons may sit, the one on thy right hand, and the other on the left, in thy kingdom. But Jesus answered and said, Ye know not what ye ask. Are ye able to drink of the cup that I shall drink of, and to be baptized with the baptism that I am baptized with ? They say unto him, We are able. And he saith unto them, Ye shall drink indeed of my cup, and be baptized with the baptism that I am baptized with : but to sit on my right hand, and on my left, is not mine to give ; but it shall be given to them for whom it is prepared of my Father. And when the ten heard it, they were moved with indignation against the two brethren. But Jesus called them unto him, and said, Ye know that the princes of the Gentiles exercise dominion over them, and they that are great exercise authority upon them. But it shall not be so among you: but whosoever will be great among you, let him be your minister; and whosoever will be chief among you, let him be your servant: even as the Son of man came not to be ministered unto, but to minister, and to give his life a ransom for many.

Saint Bartholomew the Apostle.
THE COLLECT.

O ALMIGHTY and everlasting God, who didst give to thine Apostle Bartholomew grace truly to believe and to preach thy Word; Grant, we beseech thee, unto thy Church, to love that Word which he believed, and both to preach and receive the same; through Jesus Christ our Lord. *Amen.*

FOR THE EPISTLE. Acts v. 12.

BY the hands of the Apostles were many signs and wonders wrought among the people: (and they were all with one accord in Solomon's porch: and of the rest durst no man join himself to them: but the people magnified them: and believers were the more added to the Lord, multitudes both of men and women:) insomuch that they brought forth the sick into the streets, and laid them on beds and couches, that at the least the shadow of Peter passing by might overshadow some of them. There came also a multitude out of the cities round about unto Jerusalem, bringing sick folks, and them which were vexed with unclean spirits; and they were healed every one.

THE GOSPEL. St. Luke xxii. 24.

AND there was also a strife among them, which of them should be accounted the greatest. And he said unto them, The kings of the Gentiles exercise lordship over them; and they that exercise authority upon them are called benefactors. But ye shall not be so: but he that is greatest among you, let him be as the younger; and he that is chief, as he that doth serve. For whether is greater, he that sitteth at meat, or he that serveth? is not he that sitteth at meat? but I am among you as he that serveth. Ye are they which have continued with me in my temptations. And I appoint unto you a kingdom, as my Father hath appointed unto me; that ye may eat and drink at my table in my kingdom, and sit on thrones judging the twelve tribes of Israel.

Saint Matthew the Apostle.

THE COLLECT.

O ALMIGHTY God, who by thy blessed Son didst call Matthew from the receipt of custom to be an Apostle and Evangelist; Grant us grace to forsake all covetous desires, and inordinate love of riches, and to follow the same thy Son Jesus Christ, who liveth and reigneth with thee and the Holy Ghost, one God, world without end. *Amen.*

THE EPISTLE. 2 Cor. iv. 1.

THEREFORE seeing we have this ministry, as we have received mercy, we faint not; but have renounced the hidden things of dishonesty, not walking in craftiness, nor handling the Word of God deceitfully, but by manifestation of the truth commending ourselves to every man's conscience in the sight of God. But if our Gospel be hid, it is hid to them that are lost: in whom the God of this world hath blinded the minds of them which believe not, lest the light of the glorious Gospel of Christ, who is the image of God, should shine unto them. For we preach not ourselves, but Christ Jesus the Lord; and ourselves your servants for Jesus' sake. For God, who commanded the light to shine out of darkness, hath shined in our hearts, to give the light of the knowledge of the glory of God, in the face of Jesus Christ.

THE GOSPEL. St. Matth. ix. 9.

AND as Jesus passed forth from thence, he saw a man named Matthew, sitting at the receipt of custom; and he saith unto him, Follow me. And he arose, and followed him. And it came to pass, as Jesus sat at meat in the house, behold, many Publicans and sinners came, and sat down with him and his disciples. And when the Pharisees saw it, they said unto his disciples, Why eateth your Master with Publicans and sinners? But when Jesus heard that, he said unto them, They that be whole need not a physician, but they that are sick. But go ye and learn what that meaneth, I will have mercy, and not sacrifice; for I am not come to call the righteous, but sinners to repentance.

Saint Michael and all Angels.

THE COLLECT.

O EVERLASTING God, who hast ordained and constituted the services of Angels and men in a wonderful order; Mercifully grant, that as thy holy Angels alway do thee service in heaven, so by thy appointment they may succour and defend us on earth; through Jesus Christ our Lord. *Amen.*

FOR THE EPISTLE. Rev. xii. 7.

THERE was war in heaven. Michael and his angels fought against the dragon, and the dragon fought and his angels; and prevailed not, neither was their place found any more in heaven. And the great dragon was cast out, that old serpent, called the devil and Satan, which deceiveth the whole world; he was cast out into the earth, and his angels were cast out with him. And I heard a loud voice saying in heaven, Now is come salvation, and strength, and the kingdom of our God, and the power of his Christ: for the accuser of our brethren is cast down, which accused them before our God, day and night. And they overcame him by the blood of the Lamb, and by the word of their testimony; and they loved not their lives unto the death. Therefore rejoice, ye heavens, and ye that dwell in them. Woe to the inhabiters of the earth, and of the sea: for the devil is come down unto you, having great wrath, because he knoweth that he hath but a short time.

THE GOSPEL. St. Matth. xviii. 1.

AT the same time came the disciples unto Jesus, saying, Who is the greatest in the Kingdom of heaven? And Jesus called a little child unto him, and set him in the midst of them, and said, Verily I say unto you, Except ye be converted, and become as little children, ye shall not enter into the Kingdom of heaven. Whosoever therefore shall humble himself as this little child, the same is greatest in the Kingdom of heaven. And whoso shall receive one such little child in my Name, receiveth me. But whoso shall offend one of these little ones which believe in me, it were better for him that a millstone were hanged about his neck, and that he were drowned in the depth of the sea. Woe unto the world because of offences: for it must needs be that offences come: but woe to that man by whom the offence cometh. Wherefore if thy hand or thy foot offend thee, cut them off, and cast them from thee: it is better for thee to enter into life halt or maimed, rather than having two hands or two feet to be cast into everlasting fire. And if thine eye offend thee, pluck it out, and cast it from thee: it is better for thee to enter into life with one eye, rather than having two eyes to be cast into hell-fire. Take heed that ye despise not one of these little ones; for I say unto you, That in heaven their angels do always behold the face of my Father which is in heaven.

Saint Luke the Evangelist.

THE COLLECT.

ALMIGHTY God, who calledst Luke the Physician, whose praise is in the Gospel, to be an Evangelist, and Physician of the soul; May it please thee, that, by the wholesome medicines of the doctrine delivered by him, all the diseases of our souls may be healed; through the merits of thy Son Jesus Christ our Lord. *Amen.*

THE EPISTLE. 2 Tim. iv. 5.

WATCH thou in all things, endure afflictions, do the work of an Evangelist, make full proof of thy ministry. For I am now ready to be offered, and the time of my departure is at hand. I have fought a good fight, I have finished my course, I have kept the faith. Henceforth there is laid up for me a crown of righteousness, which the Lord, the righteous Judge, shall give me at that day: and not to me only, but unto all them also that love his appearing. Do thy diligence to come shortly unto me: for Demas hath forsaken me, having loved this present world, and is departed unto Thessalonica; Crescens to Galatia, Titus unto Dalmatia. Only Luke is with me. Take Mark and bring him with thee: for he is profitable to me for the ministry. And Tychicus have I sent to Ephesus. The cloke that I left at Troas with Carpus, when thou comest, bring with thee; and the books, but especially the parchments. Alexander the copper-smith did me much evil: the Lord reward him according to his works. Of whom be thou ware also, for he hath greatly withstood our words.

THE GOSPEL. St. Luke x. 1.

THE Lord appointed other seventy also, and sent them two and two before his face into every city and place whither he himself would come. Therefore said he unto them, The harvest truly is great, but the labourers are few; pray ye therefore the Lord of the harvest, that he would send forth labourers into his harvest. Go your ways; behold, I send you forth as lambs among wolves. Carry neither purse, nor scrip, nor shoes, and salute no man by the way. And into whatsoever house ye enter, first say, Peace be to this house. And if the son of peace be there, your peace shall rest upon it: if not, it shall turn to you again. And in the same house remain, eating and drinking such things as they give: for the labourer is worthy of his hire.

Saint Simon and Saint Jude, Apostles.

THE COLLECT.

O ALMIGHTY God, who hast built thy Church upon the foundation of the Apostles and Prophets, Jesus Christ himself being the head corner-stone; Grant us so to be joined together in unity of spirit by their doctrine, that we may be made an holy temple acceptable unto thee; through Jesus Christ our Lord. *Amen.*

THE EPISTLE. St. Jude 1.

JUDE, the servant of Jesus Christ, and brother of James, to them that are sanctified by God the Father, and preserved in Jesus Christ, and called: Mercy unto you, and peace, and love be multiplied. Beloved, when I gave all diligence to write unto you of the common salvation, it was needful for me to write unto you, and exhort you, that ye should earnestly contend for the faith which was once delivered unto the saints. For there are certain men crept in unawares, who were before of old ordained to this condemnation; ungodly men, turning the grace of our God into lasciviousness, and denying the only Lord God, and our Lord Jesus Christ. I will therefore put you in remembrance, though ye once knew this, how that the Lord, having saved the people out of the land of Egypt, afterward destroyed them that believed not. And the angels which kept not their first estate, but left their own habitation, he hath reserved in everlasting chains under darkness unto the judgement of the great day. Even as Sodom and Gomorrha, and the cities about them in like manner giving themselves over to fornication, and going after strange flesh, are set forth for an example, suffering the vengeance of eternal fire. Likewise also these filthy dreamers defile the flesh, despise dominion, and speak evil of dignities.

THE GOSPEL. St. John xv. 17.

THESE things I command you, that ye love one another. If the world hate you, ye know that it hated me before it hated you. If ye were of the world, the world would love his own: but because ye are not of the world, but I have chosen you out of the world, therefore the world hateth you. Remember the word that I said unto you, The servant is not greater than the Lord: if they have persecuted me, they will also persecute you; if they have kept my saying, they will keep yours also. But all these things will they do unto you for my Name's sake, because they know not him that sent me. If I had not come and spoken unto them, they had not had sin : but now they have no cloke for their sin. He that hateth me hateth my Father also. If I had not done among them the works which none other man did, they had not had sin ; but now have they both seen, and hated both me and my Father. But this cometh to pass, that the word might be fulfilled that is written in their law, They hated me without a cause. But when the Comforter is come, whom I will send unto you from the Father, even the Spirit of truth, which proceedeth from the Father, he shall testify of me. And ye also shall bear witness, because ye have been with me from the beginning.

All Saints' Day.

THE COLLECT.

O ALMIGHTY God, who hast knit together thine elect in one communion and fellowship, in the mystical body of thy Son Christ our Lord; Grant us grace so to follow thy blessed Saints in all virtuous and godly living, that we may come to those unspeakable joys, which thou hast prepared for them that unfeignedly love thee; through Jesus Christ our Lord. *Amen.*

FOR THE EPISTLE. Rev. vii. 2.

A ND I saw another angel ascending from the east, having the seal of the living God ; and he cried with a loud voice to the four angels, to whom it was given to hurt the earth, and the sea, saying, Hurt not the earth, neither the sea, nor the trees, till we have sealed the servants of our God in their foreheads. And I heard the number of them which were sealed ; and there were sealed an hundred and forty and four thousand, of all the tribes of the children of Israel.

Of the tribe of Juda were sealed twelve thousand.
Of the tribe of Reuben were sealed twelve thousand.
Of the tribe of Gad were sealed twelve thousand.
Of the tribe of Aser were sealed twelve thousand.
Of the tribe of Nephthali were sealed twelve thousand.
Of the tribe of Manasses were sealed twelve thousand.
Of the tribe of Simeon were sealed twelve thousand.
Of the tribe of Levi were sealed twelve thousand.
Of the tribe of Issachar were sealed twelve thousand.
Of the tribe of Zabulon were sealed twelve thousand.
Of the tribe of Joseph were sealed twelve thousand.
Of the tribe of Benjamin were sealed twelve thousand.

After this I beheld, and lo, a great multitude, which no man could number, of all nations, and kindreds, and people, and tongues, stood before the throne, and before the Lamb, clothed with white robes, and palms in their hands; and cried with a loud voice, saying, Salvation to our God which sitteth upon the throne, and unto the Lamb. And all the angels stood round about the throne, and about the elders, and the four beasts, and fell before the throne on their faces, and worshipped God, saying, Amen; Blessing, and glory, and wisdom, and thanksgiving, and honour, and power, and might, be unto our God for ever and ever. Amen.

THE GOSPEL. St. Matth. v. 1.

JESUS, seeing the multitudes, went up into a mountain; and when he was set, his disciples came unto him. And he opened his mouth, and taught them, saying, Blessed are the poor in spirit: for theirs is the kingdom of heaven. Blessed are they that mourn: for they shall be comforted. Blessed are the meek: for they shall inherit the earth. Blessed are they which do hunger and thirst after righteousness: for they shall be filled. Blessed are the merciful: for they shall obtain mercy. Blessed are the pure in heart: for they shall see God. Blessed are the peace-makers: for they shall be called the children of God. Blessed are they which are persecuted for righteousness' sake: for theirs is the kingdom of heaven. Blessed are ye, when men shall revile you, and persecute you, and shall say all manner of evil against you falsely for my sake. Rejoice, and be exceeding glad; for great is your reward in heaven: for so persecuted they the prophets which were before you.

THE ORDER FOR THE

ADMINISTRATION OF THE LORD'S SUPPER,

OR

HOLY COMMUNION.

¶ *So many as intend to be partakers of the holy Communion shall signify their names to the Curate, at least some time the day before.*

¶ *And if any of those be an open and notorious evil liver, or have done any wrong to his neighbours by w--d or deed, so that the Congregation be thereby offended ; the Cura'----aving knowledge thereof, shall call him and advertise him, that in any wise he presume not to come to the Lord's Table, until he hath openly declared himself to have truly repented and amended his former naughty life, that the Congregation may thereby be satisfied, which before were offended ; and that he hath recompensed the parties, to whom he hath done wrong ; or at least declare himself to be in full purpose so to do, as soon as he conveniently may.*

¶ *The same order shall the Curate use with those betwixt whom he perceiveth malice and hatred to reign ; not suffering them to be partakers of the Lord's Table, until he know them to be reconciled. And if one of the parties so at variance be content to forgive from the bottom of his heart all that the other hath trespassed against him, and to make amends for that he himself hath offended ; and the other party will not be persuaded to a godly unity, but remain still in his frowardness and malice : the Minister in that case ought to admit the penitent person to the holy Communion, and not him that is obstinate. Provided that every Minister so repelling any, as is specified in this, or the next precedent Paragraph of this Rubrick, shall be obliged to give an account of the same to the Ordinary within fourteen days after at the farthest. And the Ordinary shall proceed against the offending person according to the Canon.*

¶ *The Table, at the Communion-time having a fair white linen cloth upon it, shall stand in the Body of the Church, or in the Chancel, where Morning and Evening Prayer are appointed to be said. And the Priest standing at the North-side of the Table shall say the Lord's Prayer, with the Collect following, the people kneeling.*

OUR Father, which art in Heaven, Hallowed be thy Name. Thy kingdom come. Thy will be done in earth, As it is in heaven. Give us this day our daily bread. And forgive us our trespasses, As we forgive them that trespass against us. And lead us not into temptation ; But deliver us from evil. Amen.

o 2

THE COLLECT.

ALMIGHTY God, unto whom all hearts be open, all desires known, and from whom no secrets are hid ; Cleanse the thoughts of our hearts by the inspiration of thy Holy Spirit, that we may perfectly love thee, and worthily magnify thy Holy Name ; through Christ our Lord.

A - men.

¶ *Then shall the Priest, turning to the people, rehearse distinctly all the TEN COMMANDMENTS; and the people still kneeling shall, after every Commandment, ask God mercy for their transgression thereof for the time past, and grace to keep the same for the time to come, as followeth.*

Minister.

GOD spake these words, and said ; I am the Lord thy God : Thou shalt have none other Gods but me.

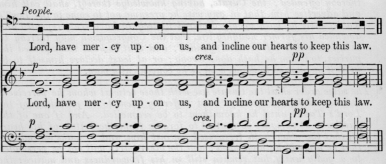

Lord, have mer - cy up - on us, and incline our hearts to keep this law.

Minister. Thou shalt not make to thyself any graven image, nor the likeness of any thing that is in heaven above, or in the earth beneath, or in the water under the earth. Thou shalt not bow down to them, nor worship them : for I the Lord thy God am a jealous God, and visit the sins of the fathers upon the children, unto the third and fourth generation of them that hate me, and shew mercy unto thousands in them that love me, and keep my commandments.

People. Lord, have mercy upon us, and incline our hearts to keep this law.

Minister. Thou shalt not take the Name of the Lord thy God in vain: for the Lord will not hold him guiltless, that taketh his Name in vain.

People. Lord, have mercy upon us, and incline our hearts to keep this law.

Minister. Remember that thou keep holy the Sabbath-day. Six days shalt thou labour, and do all that thou hast to do; but the seventh day is the Sabbath of the Lord thy God. In it thou shalt do no manner of work, thou, and thy son, and thy daughter, thy man-servant, and thy maid-servant, thy cattle, and the stranger that is within thy gates. For in six days the Lord made heaven and earth, the sea, and all that in them is, and rested the seventh day: wherefore the Lord blessed the seventh day, and hallowed it.

People. Lord, have mercy upon us, and incline our hearts to keep this law.

Minister. Honour thy father and thy mother; that thy days may be long in the land, which the Lord thy God giveth thee.

People. Lord, have mercy upon us, and incline our hearts to keep this law.

Minister. Thou shalt do no murder.

People. Lord, have mercy upon us, and incline our hearts to keep this law.

Minister. Thou shalt not commit adultery.

People. Lord, have mercy upon us, and incline our hearts to keep this law.

Minister. Thou shalt not steal.

People. Lord, have mercy upon us, and incline our hearts to keep this law.

Minister. Thou shalt not bear false witness against thy neighbour.

People. Lord, have mercy upon us, and incline our hearts to keep this law.

Minister. Thou shalt not covet thy neighbour's house, thou shalt not covet thy neighbour's wife, nor his servant, nor his maid, nor his ox, nor his ass, nor any thing that is his.

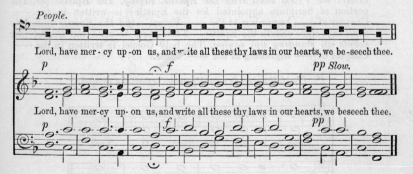

Lord, have mer-cy up-on us, and write all these thy laws in our hearts, we be-seech thee.

Lord, have mer-cy up-on us, and write all these thy laws in our hearts, we beseech thee.

¶ Then shall follow one of these two Collects for the Queen, the Priest standing as before, and saying,

Let us pray.

ALMIGHTY God, whose kingdom is everlasting, and power infinite ; Have mercy upon the whole Church ; and so rule the heart of thy chosen Servant *VICTORIA,* our Queen and Governour, that she (knowing whose minister she is) may above all things seek thy honour and glory : and that we, and all her subjects (duly considering whose authority she hath) may faithfully serve, honour, and humbly obey her, in thee, and for thee, according to thy blessed Word and ordinance ; through Jesus Christ our Lord, who with thee and the Holy Ghost liveth and reigneth, ever one God, world without end.

A - men.

Or,

ALMIGHTY and everlasting God, we are taught by thy holy Word, that the hearts of Kings are in thy rule and governance, and that thou dost dispose and turn them as it seemeth best to thy godly wisdom : We humbly beseech thee so to dispose and govern the heart of *VICTORIA* thy Servant, our Queen and Governour, that, in all her thoughts, words, and works, she may ever seek thy honour and glory, and study to preserve thy people committed to her charge, in wealth, peace, and godliness : Grant this, O merciful Father, for thy dear Son's sake, Jesus Christ our Lord. *Amen.*

¶ Then shall be said the Collect of the Day.* And immediately after the Collect the Priest shall read the Epistle, saying, The Epistle [or, The portion of Scripture appointed for the Epistle] is written in the —— Chapter of —— beginning at the —— Verse. *And the Epistle ended, he shall say,* Here endeth the Epistle. *Then shall he read the Gospel (the people all standing up) saying,* The holy Gospel is written in the —— Chapter of —— beginning at the —— Verse.

[*¶ The following is usually sung before the Gospel.*]

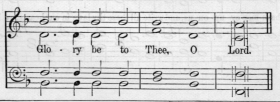
Glo - ry be to Thee, O Lord.

* For the proper Inflections of the Collect, Epistle, and Gospel, see p. 60 of the Appendix

[*After the Gospel.*]

Thanks be to Thee, O Lord.

¶ *And the Gospel ended, shall be sung or said the Creed following, the people still standing, as before.*

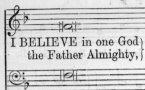

I BELIEVE in one God the Father Almighty, Maker of heaven and earth, And of all things visible and invisible :

And in one Lord Jesus Christ, the only begotten Son of God, Begotten of his Father before all worlds, God of God, Light of Light, Very God of very God, Begotten, not made, Being of one substance with the Father, By whom all things were made : Who for us men, and for our salvation came down from heaven, And was incarnate by the Holy Ghost of the Virgin Mary, And was made man, And was crucified also for us under Pontius Pilate. He suffered and was buried, And the third day he rose again according to the Scriptures, And ascended into heaven, And sitteth on the right hand of the Father. And he shall come again with glory to judge both the quick and the dead : Whose kingdom shall have no end.

And I believe in the Holy Ghost, The Lord and Giver of life, Who proceedeth from the Father and the Son, Who with the Father and the Son together is worshipped and glorified, Who spake by the Prophets. And I believe one Catholick and Apostolick Church. I acknowledge one Baptism for the remission of sins, And I look for the Resurrection of the dead, And the life of the world to come.

A - men.

[*Or this.*]

Priest. FULL.

I BELIEVE in one God the Fa - ther Al - migh - ty,
Voices in Unison.

Org.

Ma-ker of heav'n and earth, And of all things vi-si-ble and in-vi-si-ble:

And in one Lord Je-sus Christ, the on-ly be-got-ten Son of God, Be-

-got-ten of his Fa-ther be-fore all worlds, God of God,

Light of Light, Ve-ry God of ve-ry God, Be-got-ten, not made,

Be - ing of one sub-stance with the Fa - ther; By whom all things were

Faster. *Slow.*

made, Who for us men, and for our sal - va - tion came down from heaven,

p

Very soft and slow.

And was in - car - nate by the Ho - ly Ghost of the Vir - gin

Voices in Harmony, soft and slow.

And was in - car - nate by the Ho - ly Ghost of the Vir - gin

Ma - ry, And was made man, And was cru - ci - fi - ed al - so for us

Ma - ry, And was made man, And was cru - ci - fi - ed al - so for us

dead: Whose king-dom shall have no end. And I be-lieve in the

Ho-ly Ghost, The Lord and Gi-ver of life, Who pro-ceed-eth from the

Fa-ther and the Son, Who with the Fa-ther and the Son to-gether is

wor-ship-ped and glo-ri-fied, Who spake by the Pro-phets. And

I be-lieve one Ca-tho-lick and A-pos-tolick Church. I ac-knowledge

one Bap-tism for the re-mis-sion of sins, And I look for the

Re-sur-rection of the dead, And the life of the world to come. A-men.

¶ *Then the Curate shall declare unto the people what Holy-days, or Fasting-days, are in the Week following to be observed. And then also (if occasion be) shall notice be given of the Communion ; and the Banns of Matrimony published ; and Briefs, Citations, and Excommunications read. And nothing shall be proclaimed or published in the Church, during the time of Divine Service, but by the Minister : nor by him any thing, but what is prescribed in the Rules of this Book, or enjoined by the Queen, or by the Ordinary of the place.*

¶ *Then shall follow the Sermon, or one of the Homilies already set forth, or hereafter to be set forth, by authority.*

¶ *Then shall the Priest return to the Lord's Table, and begin the Offertory, saying one or more of these Sentences following, as he thinketh most con-venient in his discretion.*

LET your light so shine before men, that they may see your good works, and glorify your Father which is in heaven. *St. Matth.* v.

Lay not up for yourselves treasure upon the earth; where the rust and moth doth corrupt, and where thieves break through and steal: but lay up for yourselves treasures in heaven; where neither rust nor moth doth corrupt, and where thieves do not break through and steal. *St. Matth.* vi.

Whatsoever ye would that men should do unto you, even so do unto them; for this is the Law and the Prophets. *St. Matth.* vii.

Not every one that saith unto me, Lord, Lord, shall enter into the Kingdom of heaven; but he that doeth the will of my Father which is in heaven. *St. Matth.* vii.

Zacchæus stood forth, and said unto the Lord, Behold, Lord, the half of my goods I give to the poor; and if I have done any wrong to any man, I restore four-fold. *St. Luke* xix.

Who goeth a warfare at any time of his own cost? Who planteth a vineyard, and eateth not of the fruit thereof? Or who feedeth a flock, and eateth not of the milk of the flock? 1 *Cor.* ix.

If we have sown unto you spiritual things, is it a great matter if we shall reap your worldly things? 1 *Cor.* ix.

Do ye not know, that they who minister about holy things live of the sacrifice; and they who wait at the altar are partakers with the altar? Even so hath the Lord also ordained, that they who preach the Gospel should live of the Gospel. 1 *Cor.* ix.

He that soweth little shall reap little; and he that soweth plenteously shall reap plenteously. Let every man do according as he is disposed in his heart, not grudgingly, or of necessity; for God loveth a cheerful giver. 2 *Cor.* ix.

Let him that is taught in the Word minister unto him that teacheth in all good things. Be not deceived, God is not mocked: for whatsoever a man soweth that shall he reap. *Gal.* vi.

While we have time, let us do good unto all men; and specially unto them that are of the household of faith. *Gal.* vi.

Godliness is great riches, if a man be content with that he hath: for we brought nothing into the world, neither may we carry any thing out. 1 *Tim.* vi.

Charge them who are rich in this world, that they be ready to give, and glad to distribute; laying up in store for themselves a good foundation against the time to come, that they may attain eternal life. 1 *Tim.* vi.

God is not unrighteous, that he will forget your works, and labour that proceedeth of love; which love ye have shewed for his Name's sake, who have ministered unto the saints, and yet do minister. *Hebr.* vi.

To do good, and to distribute, forget not; for with such sacrifices God is well pleased. *Hebr.* xiii.

Whoso hath this world's good, and seeth his brother have need, and shutteth up his compassion from him, how dwelleth the love of God in him? 1 *St. John* iii.

Give alms of thy goods, and never turn thy face from any poor man; and then the face of the Lord shall not be turned away from thee. *Tobit* iv.

Be merciful after thy power. If thou hast much, give plenteously: if thou hast little, do thy diligence gladly to give of that little: for so gatherest thou thyself a good reward in the day of necessity. *Tobit* iv.

He that hath pity upon the poor lendeth unto the Lord: and look, what he layeth out, it shall be paid him again. *Prov.* xix.

Blessed be the man that provideth for the sick and needy: the Lord shall deliver him in the time of trouble. *Psal.* xli.

¶ *Whilst these Sentences are in reading, the Deacons, Churchwardens, or other fit person appointed for that purpose, shall receive the Alms for the Poor, and other devotions of the people, in a decent basin to be provided by the Parish for that purpose; and reverently bring it to the Priest, who shall humbly present and place it upon the holy Table.*

¶ *And when there is a Communion, the Priest shall then place upon the Table so much Bread and Wine, as he shall think sufficient.*

After which done, the Priest shall say,

Org.

LET us pray for the whole state of Christ's Church militant here in earth.

ALMIGHTY and everliving God, who by thy holy Apostle hast taught us to make prayers, and supplications, and to give thanks, for all men; We humbly beseech thee most mercifully [*to accept our alms and oblations, and*] to receive these our prayers, which we offer unto thy Divine Majesty; beseeching thee to inspire continually the universal Church with the spirit of truth, unity, and concord: And grant, that all they that do confess thy holy Name may agree in the truth of thy holy Word, and live in unity, and godly love. We beseech thee also to save and defend all Christian Kings, Princes, and Governours; and specially thy Servant *VICTORIA* our Queen; that under her we may be godly and quietly governed: And grant unto her whole Council, and to all that are put in authority under her, that they may truly and indifferently minister justice, to the punishment of wickedness and vice, and to the maintenance of thy true religion and virtue. Give grace, O heavenly Father, to all Bishops and Curates, that they may both by their life and doctrine set forth thy true and lively Word, and rightly and duly administer thy holy Sacraments: And to all thy people give thy heavenly grace; and

* If there be no alms or oblations, then shall the words [of accepting our alms and oblations] be left out unsaid.

especially to this congregation here present; that, with meek heart and due reverence, they may hear, and receive thy holy Word; truly serving thee in holiness and righteousness all the days of their life. And we most humbly beseech thee of thy goodness, O Lord, to comfort and succour all them, who in this transitory life are in trouble, sorrow, need, sickness, or any other adversity. And we also bless thy holy Name for all thy servants departed this life in thy faith and fear; beseeching thee to give us grace so to follow their good examples, that with them we may be partakers of thy heavenly kingdom: Grant this, O Father, for Jesus Christ's sake, our only Mediator and Advocate.

A - men.

¶ *When the Minister giveth warning for the celebration of the holy Communion, (which he shall always do upon the Sunday, or some Holy-day, immediately preceding,) after the Sermon or Homily ended, he shall read this Exhortation following.*

DEARLY beloved, on —— day next I purpose, through God's assistance, to administer to all such as shall be religiously and devoutly disposed the most comfortable Sacrament of the Body and Blood of Christ; to be by them received in remembrance of his meritorious Cross and Passion; whereby alone we obtain remission of our sins, and are made partakers of the Kingdom of heaven. Wherefore it is our duty to render most humble and hearty thanks to Almighty God our heavenly Father, for that he hath given his Son our Saviour Jesus Christ, not only to die for us, but also to be our spiritual food and sustenance in that holy sacrament. Which being so divine and comfortable a thing to them who receive it worthily, and so dangerous to them that will presume to receive it unworthily; my duty is to exhort you in the mean season to consider the dignity of that holy mystery, and the great peril of the unworthy receiving thereof; and so to search and examine your own consciences, (and that not lightly, and after the manner of dissemblers with God; but so) that ye may come holy and clean to such a heavenly Feast, in the marriage-garment required by God in holy Scripture, and be received as worthy partakers of that holy Table.

The way and means thereto is; First, to examine your lives and conversations by the rule of God's commandments; and wheresoever ye shall perceive yourselves to have offended, either by will, word, or deed, there to bewail your own sinfulness, and to confess yourselves to Almighty God, with full purpose of amendment of life. And if ye shall perceive your offences to be such as are not only against God, but also against your neighbours; then ye shall reconcile yourselves unto them; being ready to make restitution and satisfaction, according to the uttermost of your powers, for all injuries and wrongs done by you to any other; and being likewise ready to forgive others that have offended you, as ye would have forgiveness of your offences at God's hand: for otherwise the receiving of the holy Communion doth nothing else but increase your damnation. Therefore if any of you be a blasphemer of God, an hinderer or slanderer of his Word, an adulterer, or be in malice, or envy, or in any other grievous crime, repent you of your sins, or else come not to that holy Table; lest, after the taking of that holy Sacrament, the devil enter into you, as he entered into Judas, and fill you full of all iniquities, and bring you to destruction both of body and soul.

And because it is requisite, that no man should come to the holy Communion, but with a full trust in God's mercy, and with a quiet conscience; therefore if there be any of you, who by this means cannot quiet his own conscience herein, but requireth further comfort or counsel, let him come to me, or to some other discreet and learned Minister of God's Word, and open his grief; that by the ministry of God's holy Word he may receive the benefit of absolution, together with ghostly counsel and advice, to the quieting of his conscience, and avoiding of all scruple and doubtfulness.

¶ *Or, in case he shall see the people negligent to come to the holy Communion, instead of the former, he shall use this Exhortation.*

DEARLY beloved brethren, on —— I intend, by God's grace, to celebrate the Lord's Supper: unto which, in God's behalf, I bid you all that are here present; and beseech you, for the Lord Jesus Christ's sake, that ye will not refuse to come thereto, being so lovingly called and bidden by God himself. Ye know how grievous and unkind a thing it is, when a man hath prepared a rich feast, decked his table with all kind of provision, so that there lacketh nothing but the guests to sit down; and yet they who are called (without any cause) most unthankfully refuse to come. Which of you in such a case would not be moved? Who would not think a great injury and wrong done unto him? Wherefore, most dearly beloved in Christ, take ye good heed, lest ye, withdrawing yourselves from this holy Supper, provoke God's indignation against you. It is an easy matter for a man to say, I will not communicate, because I am otherwise hindered with worldly business. But such excuses are not so easily accepted and allowed before God. If any man say, I am a grievous sinner, and therefore am afraid to come: wherefore then do ye not repent and amend? When God calleth you, are ye not ashamed to say ye will not come? When ye should return to God, will ye excuse yourselves, and say ye are not ready? Consider earnestly with yourselves how little such feigned excuses will avail before God. They that refused the feast in the Gospel, because they had bought a farm, or would try their yokes of oxen, or because they were married, were not so excused, but counted unworthy of the heavenly feast. I, for my part, shall be ready; and, according to mine Office, I bid you in the Name of God, I call you in Christ's behalf, I exhort you, as ye love your own salvation, that ye will be partakers of this holy Communion. And as the Son of God did vouchsafe to yield up his soul by death upon the Cross for your salvation; so it is your duty to receive the Communion in remembrance of the sacrifice of his death, as he himself hath commanded: which if ye shall neglect to do, consider with yourselves how great injury ye do unto God, and how sore punishment hangeth over your heads for the same; when ye wilfully abstain from the Lord's Table, and separate from your brethren, who come to feed on the banquet of that most heavenly food. These things if ye earnestly consider, ye will by God's grace return to a better mind: for the obtaining whereof we shall not cease to make our humble petitions unto Almighty God our heavenly Father.

¶ *At the time of the celebration of the Communion, the Communicants being conveniently placed for the receiving of the holy Sacrament, the Priest shall say this Exhortation.*

DEARLY beloved in the Lord, ye that mind to come to the holy Communion of the Body and Blood of our Saviour Christ, must consider how Saint Paul exhorteth all persons diligently to try and examine themselves, before they presume to eat of that Bread, and drink of that Cup. For as the benefit is great, if with a true penitent heart and lively faith we receive that holy Sacrament; (for then we spiritually eat the flesh of Christ, and drink his blood; then we dwell in Christ, and Christ in us; we are one with Christ, and Christ with us;) so is the danger great, if we receive the same unworthily. For then we are guilty of the Body and Blood of Christ our Saviour; we eat and drink our own damnation, not considering the Lord's Body; we kindle God's wrath against us; we provoke him to plague us with divers diseases, and sundry kinds of death. Judge therefore yourselves, brethren, that ye be not judged of the Lord; repent you truly for your sins past; have a lively and steadfast faith in Christ our Saviour; amend your lives, and be in perfect charity with all men; so shall ye be meet partakers of those holy mysteries. And above all things ye must give most humble and hearty thanks to God the Father, the Son, and the Holy Ghost, for the redemption of the world by the death and passion of our Saviour Christ, both God and man; who did humble himself, even to the death upon the

P

Cross, for us, miserable sinners, who lay in darkness and the shadow of death; that he might make us the children of God, and exalt us to everlasting life. And to the end that we should alway remember the exceeding great love of our Master, and only Saviour, Jesus Christ, thus dying for us, and the innumerable benefits which by his precious blood-shedding he hath obtained to us; he hath instituted and ordained holy mysteries, as pledges of his love, and for a continual remembrance of his death, to our great and endless comfort. To him therefore, with the Father and the Holy Ghost, let us give (as we are most bounden) continual thanks; submitting ourselves wholly to his holy will and pleasure, and studying to serve him in true holiness and righteousness all the days of our life.

A - men.

¶ *Then shall the Priest say to them that come to receive the holy Communion,*

YE that do truly and earnestly repent you of your sins, and are in love and charity with your neighbours, and intend to lead a new life, following the commandments of God, and walking from henceforth in his holy ways; Draw near with faith, and take this holy Sacrament to your comfort; and make your humble confession to Almighty God, meekly kneeling upon your knees.

¶ *Then shall this general Confession be made, in the name of all those that are minded to receive the holy Communion, by one of the Ministers; both he and all the people kneeling humbly upon their knees, and saying,*

ALMIGHTY God, Father of our Lord Jesus Christ, Maker of all things, Judge of all men; We acknowledge and bewail our manifold sins and wickedness, Which we, from time to time, most grievously have committed, By thought, word, and deed, Against thy Divine Majesty, Provoking most justly thy wrath and indignation against us. We do earnestly repent, And are heartily sorry for these our misdoings; The remembrance of them is grievous unto us; The burden of them is intolerable, Have mercy upon us, Have mercy upon us, most merciful Father; For thy Son our Lord Jesus Christ's sake, Forgive us all that is past; And grant that we may ever hereafter Serve and please thee In newness of life, To the honour and glory of thy Name; Through Jesus Christ our Lord.

A-men.

* A Harmonized Version of this Confession will be found on p. 42 of the Appendix.

THE COMMUNION.

¶ *Then shall the Priest (or the Bishop, being present,) stand up, and turning himself to the people, pronounce this Absolution.*

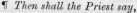

Org.

ALMIGHTY God, our heavenly Father, who of his great mercy hath promised forgiveness of sins to all them that with hearty repentance and true faith turn unto him; Have mercy upon you; pardon and deliver you from all your sins; confirm and strengthen you in all goodness; and bring you to everlasting life; through Jesus Christ our Lord.

A - men.

¶ *Then shall the Priest say,*

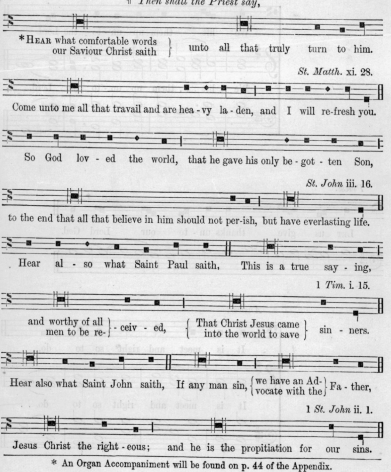

HEAR what comfortable words our Saviour Christ saith } unto all that truly turn to him.

St. Matth. xi. 28.

Come unto me all that travail and are hea - vy la - den, and I will re-fresh you.

So God lov - ed the world, that he gave his only be - got - ten Son,

St. John iii. 16.

to the end that all that believe in him should not per-ish, but have everlasting life.

Hear al - so what Saint Paul saith, This is a true say - ing,

1 Tim. i. 15.

and worthy of all men to be re- } - ceiv - ed, { That Christ Jesus came into the world to save } sin - ners.

Hear also what Saint John saith, If any man sin, { we have an Ad-vocate with the } Fa - ther,

1 St. John ii. 1.

Jesus Christ the right - eous; and he is the propitiation for our sins.

* An Organ Accompaniment will be found on p. 44 of the Appendix.

P 2

¶ *After which the Priest shall proceed, saying,*

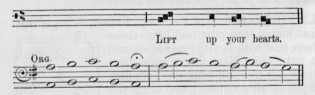

LIFT up your hearts.

ORG.

Answer.

We lift them up un-to the Lord.

We lift . . . them up un-to the Lord.

Priest.

LET us give thanks un-to our Lord God.

Answer.

It is meet and right so to do.

It is meet and right so to do. . .

¶ *Then shall the Priest turn to the Lord's Table, and say,*

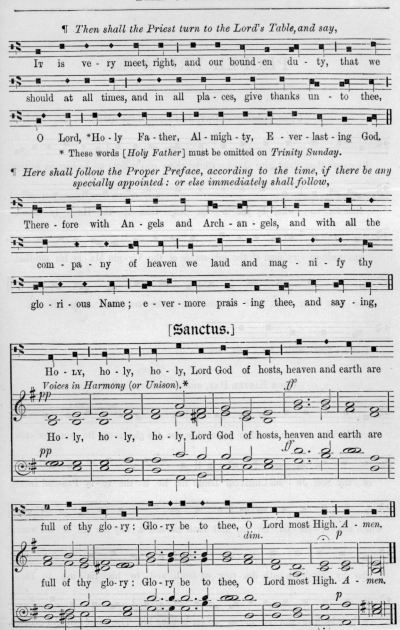

It is ve - ry meet, right, and our bound - en du - ty, that we

should at all times, and in all pla - ces, give thanks un - to thee,

O Lord, *Ho - ly Fa - ther, Al - migh - ty, E - ver - last - ing God.

* These words [*Holy Father*] must be omitted on *Trinity Sunday.*

¶ *Here shall follow the Proper Preface, according to the time, if there be any specially appointed: or else immediately shall follow,*

There - fore with An - gels and Arch - an - gels, and with all the

com - pa - ny of heaven we laud and mag - ni - fy thy

glo - ri - ous Name; e - ver - more prais - ing thee, and say - ing,

[Sanctus.]

Ho - LY, ho - ly, ho - ly, Lord God of hosts, heaven and earth are

*Voices in Harmony (or Unison).**

pp *ff*

Ho - ly, ho - ly, ho - ly, Lord God of hosts, heaven and earth are

pp *ff*

full of thy glo - ry: Glo - ry be to thee, O Lord most High. *A* - *men.*

dim. *p*

full of thy glo - ry: Glo - ry be to thee, O Lord most High. *A* - *men.*

p

* This must be sung in Unison, if in B flat. [*See* Note, Appendix, p. 48.]

PROPER PREFACES.

Upon CHRISTMAS DAY, *and seven days after.*

BE-CAUSE thou didst give Je - sus Christ thine on - ly Son to be born as at this

time for us; who, by the o - pe - ra - tion of the Ho - ly Ghost,

was made ve - ry man of the sub -stance of the Vir - gin Ma - ry his mo-ther,

and that with - out spot of sin, to make us clean from all sin.

There - fore with An - gels, &c.

Upon EASTER DAY, *and seven days after.*

BUT chief- ly are we bound to praise thee for the glo - ri-ous Re - sur - rec - tion

of thy Son Je - sus Christ our Lord : for he is the ve - ry Pas-chal Lamb,

which was of - fer - ed for us, and hath ta - ken a - way the sin of the world ;

who by his death hath des - troy - ed death, and by his ris - ing to life

a - gain hath re - stor - ed to us e - ver-last-ing life. There-fore with An-gels, &c.

Upon ASCENSION DAY, *and seven days after.*

THROUGH thy most dear -ly be - lov - ed Son Je - sus Christ our Lord; who af - ter his most glo - ri - ous re - sur -rec- tion man - i - fest - ly ap-pear - ed to all his A - pos -tles, and in their sight as - cend - ed up in - to heaven to pre- pare a place for us; that where he is, thi - ther we might al - so as - cend, and reign with him in glo - ry. There - fore with An - gels, &c.

Upon WHITSUNDAY, *and six days after.*

THROUGH Je - sus Christ our Lord; ac-cord-ing to whose most true pro- mise, the Ho - ly Ghost came down as at this time from hea-ven with a sud-den great sound, as it had been a migh - ty wind, in the like - ness of fi - e - ry tongues, light -ing up - on the A - pos-tles, to teach them, and to lead them to all truth; giv- ing them both the gift of di -vers lan-gua-ges, and al-so boldness with fervent zeal con-stant-ly to preach the Gos - pel un -.to all na - tions; where-by we have been brought out of dark-ness and er - ror in - to the clear light and true knowledge of thee, and of thy Son Je - sus Christ. There-fore with An - gels, &c.

Upon the Feast of TRINITY *only.*

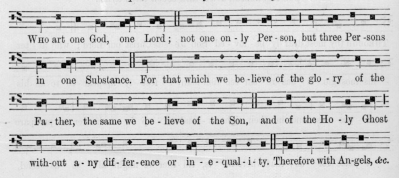

WHO art one God, one Lord; not one on - ly Per - son, but three Per -sons

in one Substance. For that which we be -lieve of the glo - ry of the

Fa - ther, the same we be - lieve of the Son, and of the Ho - ly Ghost

with-out a - ny dif - fer - ence or in - e - qual - i - ty. Therefore with An-gels, &c.

¶ *After each of which Prefaces shall immediately be sung or said,*

THEREFORE with Angels and Archangels, and with all the company of heaven, we laud and magnify thy glorious Name; evermore praising thee, and saying, Holy, holy, holy, Lord God of hosts, heaven and earth are full of thy glory: Glory be to thee, O Lord most High. *Amen.*

¶ *Then shall the Priest, kneeling down at the Lord's Table, say in the name of all them that shall receive the Communion this Prayer following.*

Org.

WE do not presume to come to this thy Table, O merciful Lord, trusting in our own righteousness, but in thy manifold and great mercies. We are not worthy so much as to gather up the crumbs under thy Table. But thou art the same Lord, whose property is always to have mercy: Grant us therefore, gracious Lord, so to eat the flesh of thy dear Son Jesus Christ, and to drink his blood, that our sinful bodies may be made clean by his body, and our souls washed through his most precious blood, and that we may ever-more dwell in him, and he in us.

A - men.

¶ *When the Priest, standing before the Table, hath so ordered the Bread and Wine, that he may with the more readiness and decency break the Bread before the people, and take the Cup into his hands, he shall say the Prayer of Consecration, as followeth.*

ALMIGHTY God, our heavenly Father, who of thy tender mercy didst give thine only Son Jesus Christ to suffer death upon the cross for our redemption; who made there (by his one oblation of himself once offered) a full, perfect, and sufficient sacrifice, oblation, and satisfaction, for the sins of the whole world ; and did institute, and in his holy Gospel command us to continue, a perpetual memory of that his precious death, until his coming again ; Hear us, O merciful Father, we most humbly beseech thee ; and grant that we receiving these thy creatures of bread and wine, according to thy Son our Saviour Jesus Christ's holy institution, in remembrance of his death and passion, may be partakers of his most blessed Body and Blood : who, in the same night that he was betrayed, *took Bread ; and when he had given thanks, †he brake it, and gave it to his disciples, saying, Take, eat, ‡this is my Body which is given for you : Do this in remembrance of me. Like-wise after supper he ‖took the Cup ; and, when he had given thanks, he gave it to them, saying, Drink ye all of this ; for this §is my Blood of the New Testament, which is shed for you and for many for the remission of sins : Do this, as oft as ye shall drink it, in remembrance of me.

* Here the Priest is to take the Paten into his hands :

† And here to break the Bread :

‡ And here to lay his hand upon all the Bread.

‖ Here he is to take the Cup into his hand :

§ And here to lay his hand upon every vessel (be it Chalice or Flagon) in which there is any Wine to be consecrated.

A - men.

[Or this.]

¶ *Then shall the Minister first receive the Communion in both kinds himself, and then proceed to deliver the same to the Bishops, Priests, and Deacons, in like manner, (if any be present,) and after that to the people also in order, into their hands, all meekly kneeling. And, when he delivereth the Bread to any one, he shall say,*

THE Body of our Lord Jesus Christ, which was given for thee, preserve thy body and soul unto everlasting life. Take and eat this in remembrance that Christ died for thee, and feed on him in thy heart by faith with thanksgiving.

¶ *And the Minister that delivereth the Cup to any one shall say,*

THE Blood of our Lord Jesus Christ, which was shed for thee, preserve thy body and soul unto everlasting life. Drink this in remembrance that Christ's Blood was shed for thee, and be thankful.

[A Hymn may be sung, or the Organ may be played softly while the Clergy and People receive the Communion.]

¶ *If the consecrated Bread or Wine be all spent before all have communicated, the Priest is to consecrate more according to the Form before prescribed; beginning at* [Our Saviour Christ in the same night, &c.] *for the blessing of the Bread; and at* [Likewise after Supper, &c.] *for the blessing of the Cup.*

¶ *When all have communicated, the Minister shall return to the Lord's Table, and reverently place upon it what remaineth of the consecrated Elements, covering the same with a fair linen cloth.*

¶ *Then shall the Priest say the Lord's Prayer, the people repeating after him every Petition.*

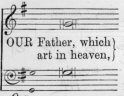

OUR Father, which art in heaven, Hallowed be thy Name. Thy kingdom come. Thy will be done in earth, As it is in heaven. Give us this day our daily bread. And forgive us our trespasses, As we forgive them that trespass against us. And lead us not into temptation: But deliver us from evil: For thine is the kingdom, The power, and the glory, For ever and ever.

A - men.

THE COMMUNION.

in - to temp-ta - tion; But de - li - ver us from e vil: For thine is

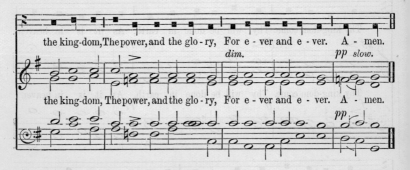

the king-dom, The power, and the glo - ry, For e - ver and e - ver. A - men.

¶ After shall be said as followeth.

O LORD and heavenly Father, we thy humble servants entirely desire thy fatherly goodness mercifully to accept this our sacrifice of praise and thanksgiving; most humbly beseeching thee to grant, that by the merits and death of thy Son Jesus Christ, and through faith in his blood, we and all thy whole Church may obtain remission of our sins, and all other benefits of his passion. And here we offer and present unto thee, O Lord, ourselves, our souls and bodies, to be a reasonable, holy, and lively sacrifice unto thee; humbly beseeching thee, that all we, who are partakers of this holy Communion, may be fulfilled with thy grace and heavenly benediction. And although we be unworthy, through our manifold sins, to offer unto thee any sacrifice, yet we beseech thee to accept this our bounden duty and service; not weighing our merits, but pardoning our offences, through Jesus Christ our Lord; by whom, and with whom, in the unity of the Holy Ghost, all honour and glory be unto thee, O Father Almighty, world without end.

A - men.

Or this.

ALMIGHTY and everliving God, we most heartily thank thee, for that thou dost vouchsafe to feed us, who have duly received these holy mysteries, with the spiritual food of the most precious Body and Blood of thy Son our Saviour Jesus Christ; and dost assure us thereby of thy favour and goodness towards us; and that we are very members incorporate in the mystical body of thy Son, which is the blessed company of all faithful people; and are also heirs through hope of thy everlasting kingdom, by the merits of the most precious death and passion of thy dear Son. And we most humbly beseech thee, O heavenly Father, so to assist us with thy grace, that we may continue in that holy fellowship, and do all such good works as thou hast prepared for us to walk in; through Jesus Christ our Lord, to whom, with thee and the Holy Ghost, be all honour and glory, world without end.

A - men.

¶ *Then shall be said or sung,*

GLORY be to God on high,

and in earth peace, good will towards men. We praise thee, we bless thee, we worship thee, we glorify thee, we give thanks to thee for thy great glory, O Lord God, heavenly King, God the Father Almighty.

O Lord, the only begotten Son Jesu Christ; O Lord God, Lamb of God, Son of the Father, that takest away the sins of the world, have mercy upon us. Thou that takest away the sins of the world, have mercy upon us. Thou that takest away the sins of the world, receive our prayer. Thou that sittest at the right hand of God the Father, have mercy upon us.

For thou only art holy; thou only art the Lord; thou only, O Christ, with the Holy Ghost, art most high in the glory of God the Father.

A - men.

[*Or this.*]

Priest.

peace, good will towards men. We praise thee, we bless thee, we

peace, good will towards men. We praise thee, we bless thee, we

wor - ship thee, we glo - ri - fy thee, we give thanks to thee for thy great

wor - ship thee, we glo - ri - fy thee, we give thanks to thee for thy great

glo - ry, O Lord God, heaven - ly King, God the Fa - ther Al-

glo - ry, O Lord God, heaven - ly King, God the Fa - ther Al-

- migh - ty. O Lord, the on - ly be - got - ten Son Je - su Christ;

- migh - ty. O Lord, the on - ly be - got - ten Son Je - su Christ;

¶ *Then the Priest (or Bishop if he be present) shall let them depart with this Blessing.*

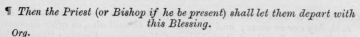

THE peace of God, which passeth all understanding, keep your hearts and minds in the knowledge and love of God, and of his Son Jesus Christ our Lord: and the blessing of God Almighty, the Father, the Son, and the Holy Ghost, be amongst you and remain with you always.

[*Or this.*]

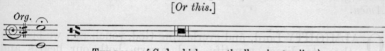

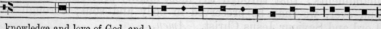

Q

¶ *Collects to be said after the Offertory, when there is no Communion, every such day one or more; and the same may be said also, as often as occasion shall serve, after the Collects either of Morning or Evening Prayer, Communion, or Litany, by the discretion of the Minister.*

ASSIST us mercifully, O Lord, in these our supplications and prayers, and dispose the way of thy servants towards the attainment of everlasting salvation; that, among all the changes and chances of this mortal life, they may ever be defended by thy most gracious and ready help; through Jesus Christ our Lord. *Amen.*

O ALMIGHTY Lord, and everlasting God, vouchsafe, we beseech thee, to direct, sanctify, and govern, both our hearts and bodies, in the ways of thy laws, and in the works of thy commandments; that through thy most mighty protection, both here and ever, we may be preserved in body and soul; through our Lord and Saviour Jesus Christ. *Amen.*

GRANT, we beseech thee, Almighty God, that the words, which we have heard this day with our outward ears, may through thy grace be so grafted inwardly in our hearts, that they may bring forth in us the fruit of good living, to the honour and praise of thy Name; through Jesus Christ our Lord. *Amen.*

PREVENT us, O Lord, in all our doings with thy most gracious favour, and further us with thy continual help; that in all our works begun, continued, and ended in thee, we may glorify thy holy Name, and finally by thy mercy obtain everlasting life; through Jesus Christ our Lord. *Amen.*

ALMIGHTY God, the fountain of all wisdom, who knowest our necessities before we ask, and our ignorance in asking; We beseech thee to have compassion upon our infirmities; and those things, which for our unworthiness we dare not, and for our blindness we cannot ask, vouchsafe to give us, for the worthiness of thy Son Jesus Christ our Lord. *Amen.*

ALMIGHTY God, who hast promised to hear the petitions of them that ask in thy Son's Name; We beseech thee mercifully to incline thine ears to us that have made now our prayers and supplications unto thee; and grant, that those things, which we have faithfully asked according to thy will, may effectually be obtained, to the relief of our necessity, and to the setting forth of thy glory; through Jesus Christ our Lord. *Amen.*

¶ *Upon the Sundays and other Holy-days (if there be no Communion) shall be said all that is appointed at the Communion, until the end of the general Prayer* [For the whole state of Christ's Church militant here in earth] *together with one or more of these Collects last before rehearsed, concluding with the Blessing.*

¶ *And there shall be no celebration of the Lord's Supper, except there be a convenient number to communicate with the Priest, according to his discretion.*

¶ *And if there be not above twenty persons in the Parish of discretion to receive the Communion; yet there shall be no Communion, except four (or three at the least) communicate with the Priest.*

¶ *And in Cathedral and Collegiate Churches, and Colleges, where there are many Priests and Deacons, they shall all receive the Communion with the Priest every Sunday at the least, except they have a reasonable cause to the contrary.*

¶ *And to take away all occasion of dissension, and superstition, which any person hath or might have concerning the Bread and Wine, it shall suffice that the Bread be such as is usual to be eaten; but the best and purest Wheat Bread that conveniently may be gotten.*

¶ *And if any of the Bread and Wine remain unconsecrated, the Curate shall have it to his own use: but if any remain of that which was consecrated, it shall not be carried out of the Church, but the Priest and such other of the Communicants as he shall then call unto him, shall, immediately after the Blessing, reverently eat and drink the same.*

¶ *The Bread and Wine for the Communion shall be provided by the Curate and the Church-wardens at the charges of the Parish.*

¶ *And note, that every Parishioner shall communicate at the least three times in the year, of which Easter to be one. And yearly at Easter every Parishioner shall reckon with the Parson, Vicar, or Curate, or his or their Deputy or Deputies; and pay to them or him all Ecclesiastical Duties, accustomably due, then and at that time to be paid.*

¶ *After the Divine Service ended, the money given at the Offertory shall be disposed of to such pious and charitable uses, as the Minister and Church-wardens shall think fit. Wherein if they disagree, it shall be disposed of as the Ordinary shall appoint.*

" WHEREAS it is ordained in this Office for the Administration of the
" Lord's Supper, that the Communicants should receive the same
" kneeling; (which order is well meant, for a signification of our humble and
" grateful acknowledgement of the benefits of Christ therein given to all worthy
" Receivers, and for the avoiding of such profanation and disorder in the holy
" Communion, as might otherwise ensue ;) yet, lest the same kneeling should
" by any persons, either out of ignorance and infirmity, or out of malice and
" obstinacy, be misconstrued and depraved ; It is hereby declared, That
" thereby no adoration is intended, or ought to be done, either unto the Sacra-
" mental Bread or Wine there bodily received, or unto any Corporal Presence
" of Christ's natural Flesh and Blood. For the Sacramental Bread and Wine
" remain still in their very natural substances, and therefore may not be adored ;
" (for that were Idolatry, to be abhorred of all faithful Christians ;) and the
" natural Body and Blood of our Saviour Christ are in Heaven, and not here ;
" it being against the truth of Christ's natural Body to be at one time in more
" places than one."

THE MINISTRATION OF

PUBLICK BAPTISM OF INFANTS,

TO BE USED IN THE CHURCH.

¶ *The people are to be admonished, that it is most convenient that Baptism should not be administered but upon Sundays, and other Holy-days, when the most number of people come together; as well for that the Congregation there present may testify the receiving of them that be newly baptized into the number of Christ's Church; as also because in the Baptism of Infants every Man present may be put in remembrance of his own profession made to God in his Baptism. For which cause also it is expedient that Baptism be ministered in the vulgar tongue. Nevertheless, (if necessity so require,) Children may be baptized upon any other day.*

¶ *And note that there shall be for every Male-child to be baptized two Godfathers and one Godmother; and for every Female, one Godfather and two Godmothers.*

¶ *When there are Children to be baptized, the Parents shall give knowledge thereof overnight, or in the morning before the beginning of Morning Prayer, to the Curate. And then the Godfathers and Godmothers, and the people with the Children, must be ready at the Font, either immediately after the last Lesson at Morning Prayer, or else immediately after the last Lesson at Evening Prayer, as the Curate by his discretion shall appoint. And the Priest coming to the Font, (which is then to be filled with pure Water,) and standing there, shall say,*

HATH this child been already baptized, or no?

¶ *If they answer, No: Then shall the Priest proceed as followeth.*

DEARLY beloved, forasmuch as all men are conceived and born in sin; and that our Saviour Christ saith, None can enter into the kingdom of God, except he be regenerate and born anew of Water and of the Holy Ghost; I beseech you to call upon God the Father, through our Lord Jesus Christ, that of his bounteous mercy he will grant to *this Child* that thing which by nature *he* cannot have; that *he* may be baptized with Water and the Holy Ghost, and received into Christ's holy Church, and be made *a lively member* of the same.

¶ *Then shall the Priest say,*

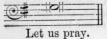

Let us pray.

ALMIGHTY and everlasting God, who of thy great mercy didst save Noah and his family in the ark from perishing by water; and also didst safely lead the children of Israel thy people through the Red Sea, figuring thereby thy holy Baptism : and by the Baptism of thy well-beloved Son Jesus Christ, in the river Jordan, didst sanctify Water to the mystical washing away of sin ; We beseech thee, for thine infinite mercies, that thou wilt mercifully look upon *this Child;* wash *him* and sanctify *him* with the Holy Ghost ; that *he,* being delivered from thy wrath, may be received into the ark of Christ's Church ; and being stedfast in faith, joyful through hope, and rooted in charity, may so pass the waves of this troublesome world, that finally *he* may come to the land of everlasting life, there to reign with thee world without end ; through Jesus Christ our Lord.

A - men.

ALMIGHTY and immortal God, the aid of all that need, the helper of all that flee to thee for succour, the life of them that believe, and the resurrection of the dead ; We call upon thee for *this Infant,* that *he,* coming to thy holy Baptism, may receive remission of *his* sins by spiritual regeneration. Receive *him,* O Lord, as thou hast promised by thy well-beloved Son, saying, Ask, and ye shall have ; seek, and ye shall find ; knock, and it shall be opened unto you : So give now unto us that ask ; let us that seek find ; open the gate unto us that knock ; that *this Infant* may enjoy the everlasting benediction of thy heavenly washing, and may come to the eternal kingdom which thou hast promised by Christ our Lord. *Amen.*

¶ *Then shall the people stand up, and the Priest shall say,*

HEAR the words of the Gospel, written by Saint *Mark,* in the tenth Chapter, at the thirteenth Verse.

THEY brought young children to Christ, that he should touch them ; and his disciples rebuked those that brought them. But when Jesus saw it, he was much displeased, and said unto them, Suffer the little children to come unto me, and forbid them not ; for of such is the kingdom of God. Verily I say unto you, Whosoever shall not receive the kingdom of God as a little child, he shall not enter therein. And he took them up in his arms, put his hands upon them, and blessed them.

¶ *After the Gospel is read, the Minister shall make this brief Exhortation upon the words of the Gospel.*

BELOVED, ye hear in this Gospel the words of our Saviour Christ, that he commanded the children to be brought unto him ; how he blamed those that would have kept them from him ;

how he exhorteth all men to follow their innocency. Ye perceive how by his outward gesture and deed he declared his good will toward them; for he embraced them in his arms, he laid his hands upon them, and blessed them. Doubt ye not therefore, but earnestly believe, that he will likewise favourably receive *this* present *Infant;* that he will embrace *him* with the arms of his mercy; that he will give unto *him* the blessing of eternal life, and make *him partaker* of his everlasting kingdom. Wherefore we being thus persuaded of the good will of our heavenly Father toward *this Infant,* declared by his Son Jesus Christ; and nothing doubting but that he favourably alloweth this charitable work of ours in bringing *this Infant* to his holy Baptism; let us faithfully and devoutly give thanks unto him and say,

ALMIGHTY and everlasting God, heavenly Father, we give thee humble thanks, for that thou hast vouchsafed to call us to the knowledge of thy grace, and faith in thee: Increase this knowledge, and confirm this faith in us evermore. Give thy Holy Spirit to *this Infant,* that *he* may be born again, and be made *an heir* of everlasting salvation; through our Lord Jesus Christ, who liveth and reigneth with thee and the Holy Spirit, now and for ever.

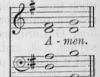

¶ *Then shall the Priest speak unto the Godfathers and Godmothers on this wise.*

DEARLY beloved, ye have brought *this Child* here to be baptized, ye have prayed that our Lord Jesus Christ would vouchsafe to receive *him,* to release *him* of *his* sins, to sanctify *him* with the Holy Ghost, to give *him* the kingdom of heaven, and everlasting life. Ye have heard also that our Lord Jesus Christ hath promised in his Gospel to grant all these things that ye have prayed for: which promise he, for his part, will most surely keep and perform. Wherefore, after this promise made by Christ, *this Infant* must also faithfully, for *his* part, promise by you that are *his* sureties, (until *he* come of age to take it upon *himself,*) that *he* will renounce the devil and all his works, and constantly believe God's holy Word, and obediently keep his commandments.

I demand therefore,

DOST thou, in the name of this Child, renounce the devil and all his works, the vain pomp and glory of the world, with all covetous desires of the same, and the carnal desires of the flesh, so that thou wilt not follow, nor be led by them?

Answer. I renounce them all.

Minister.

DOST thou believe in God the Father Almighty, Maker of heaven and earth?

And in Jesus Christ his only-begotten Son our Lord? And that he was conceived by the Holy Ghost; born of the Virgin Mary; that he suffered under Pontius Pilate, was crucified, dead, and buried; that he went down into hell, and also did rise again the third day; that he ascended into heaven, and sitteth at the right hand of God the Father Almighty; and from thence shall come again at the end of the world, to judge the quick and the dead?

And dost thou believe in the Holy Ghost; the holy Catholick Church; the Communion of Saints; the Remission of sins; the Resurrection of the flesh; and everlasting life after death?

Answer. All this I stedfastly believe.

Minister.

WILT thou be baptized in this faith?
Answer. That is my desire.

Minister.

WILT thou then obediently keep God's holy will and commandments, and walk in the same all the days of thy life?
Answer. I will.

¶ *Then shall the Priest say,*

A - men.

O MERCIFUL God, Grant that the old Adam in *this Child* may be so buried, that the new man may be raised up in *him.*

Grant that all carnal affections may die in *him*, and that all things belonging to the Spirit may live and grow in *him*. *Amen.*

Grant that *he* may have power and strength to have victory, and to triumph, against the devil, the world, and the flesh. *Amen.*

Grant that whosoever is here dedicated to thee by our office and ministry may also be endued with heavenly virtues, and everlastingly rewarded, through thy mercy, O blessed Lord God, who dost live and govern all things, world without end. *Amen.*

ALMIGHTY, everliving God, whose most dearly beloved Son Jesus Christ, for the forgiveness of our sins, did shed out of his most precious side both water and blood; and gave commandment to his disciples, that they should go teach all nations, and baptize them In the Name of the Father, and of the Son, and of the Holy Ghost; Regard, we beseech thee, the supplications of thy congregation; sanctify this Water to the mystical washing away of sin; and grant that *this Child,* now to be baptized therein, may receive the fulness of thy grace, and ever remain in the number of thy faithful and elect children; through Jesus Christ our Lord. *Amen.*

¶ *Then the Priest shall take the Child into his hands, and shall say to the Godfathers and Godmothers,*

Name this Child.

¶ *And then naming it after them (if they shall certify him that the Child may well endure it) he shall dip it in the Water discreetly and warily, saying,*

N. I baptize thee In the Name of the Father, and of the Son, and of the Holy Ghost. Amen.

¶ *But if they certify that the Child is weak, it shall suffice to pour Water upon it, saying the foresaid words,*

N. I baptize thee In the Name of the Father, and of the Son, and of the Holy Ghost. Amen.

¶ *Then the Priest shall say,*

WE receive this Child into the congregation of Christ's flock, *and do sign *him* with the sign of the Cross, in token that hereafter *he* shall not be ashamed to confess the faith of Christ crucified, and manfully to fight under his banner, against sin, the world, and the devil; and to continue Christ's faithful soldier and servant unto *his* life's end. Amen.

*Here the Priest shall make a Cross upon the Child's forehead.

¶ *Then shall the Priest say,*

SEEING now, dearly beloved brethren, that *this Child is* regenerate, and grafted into the body of Christ's Church, let us give thanks unto Almighty God for these benefits; and with one accord make our prayers unto him, that *this Child* may lead the rest of *his* life according to this beginning.

¶ *Then shall be said, all kneeling;*

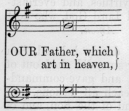
OUR Father, which art in heaven,

Hallowed be thy Name. Thy kingdom come. Thy will be done in earth, As it is in heaven. Give us this day our daily bread. And forgive us our trespasses, As we forgive them that trespass against us. And lead us not into temptation; But deliver us from evil.

A - men.

¶ Then shall the Priest say,

WE yield thee hearty thanks, most merciful Father, that it hath pleased thee to regenerate *this Infant* with thy Holy Spirit, to receive *him* for thine own *Child* by adoption, and to incorporate *him* into thy holy Church. And humbly we beseech thee to grant, that *he*, being dead unto sin, and living unto righteousness, and being buried with Christ in his death, may crucify the old man, and utterly abolish the whole body of sin; and that, as *he is* made *partaker* of the death of thy Son, *he* may also be *partaker* of his resurrection; so that finally, with the residue of thy holy Church, *he* may be *an inheritor* of thine everlasting kingdom; through Christ our Lord. *A - men.*

¶ Then, all standing up, the Priest shall say to the Godfathers and Godmothers this Exhortation following.

FORASMUCH as *this Child hath* promised by you *his* sureties to renounce the devil and all his works, to believe in God, and to serve him; ye must remember, that it is your parts and duties to see that *this Infant* be taught, so soon as *he* shall be able to learn, what a solemn vow, promise, and profession, *he hath* here made by you. And that *he* may know these things the better, ye shall call upon *him* to hear Sermons; and chiefly ye shall provide, that *he* may learn the Creed, the Lord's Prayer, and the Ten Commandments, in the vulgar tongue, and all other things which a Christian ought to know and believe to his soul's health; and that *this Child* may be virtuously brought up to lead a godly and a christian life; remembering always, that Baptism doth represent unto us our profession; which is, to follow the example of our Saviour Christ, and to be made like unto him; that, as he died, and rose again for us, so should we, who are baptized, die from sin, and rise again unto righteousness; continually mortifying all our evil and corrupt affections, and daily proceeding in all virtue and godliness of living.

¶ Then shall he add and say,

YE are to take care that *this Child* be brought to the Bishop to be confirmed by him, so soon as *he* can say the Creed, the Lord's Prayer, and the Ten Commandments, in the vulgar tongue, and be further instructed in the Church-Catechism set forth for that purpose.

IT is certain by God's Word, that Children which are baptized, dying before they commit actual sin, are undoubtedly saved.

To take away all scruple concerning the use of the sign of the Cross in Baptism; the true explication thereof, and the just reasons for the retaining of it, may be seen in the xxxth Canon, first published in the Year MDCIV.

THE MINISTRATION OF

PRIVATE BAPTISM OF CHILDREN

IN HOUSES.

¶ *The Curates of every Parish shall often admonish the people, that they defer not the Baptism of their Children longer than the first or second Sunday next after their birth, or other Holy-day falling between, unless upon a great and reasonable cause, to be approved by the Curate.*

¶ *And also they shall warn them, that without like great cause and necessity they procure not their Children to be baptized at home in their houses. But when need shall compel them so to do, then Baptism shall be administered on this fashion:*

¶ *First, let the Minister of the Parish (or, in his absence, any other lawful Minister that can be procured) with them that are present call upon God, and say the Lord's Prayer, and so many of the Collects appointed to be said before in the Form of Publick Baptism, as the time and present exigence will suffer. And then, the Child being named by some one that is present, the Minister shall pour Water upon it, saying these words;*

N. I baptize thee In the Name of the Father, and of the Son, and of the Holy Ghost. Amen.

¶ *Then, all kneeling down, the Minister shall give thanks unto God, and say,*

WE yield thee hearty thanks, most merciful Father, that it hath pleased thee to regenerate this Infant with thy Holy Spirit, to receive *him* for thine own Child by adoption, and to incorporate *him* into thy holy Church. And we humbly beseech thee to grant, that as *he* is now made partaker of the death of thy Son, so *he* may be also of his resurrection; and that finally, with the residue of thy Saints, *he* may inherit thine everlasting kingdom; through the same thy Son Jesus Christ our Lord. *Amen.*

¶ *And let them not doubt, but that the Child so baptized is lawfully and sufficiently baptized, and ought not to be baptized again. Yet nevertheless, if the Child, which is after this sort baptized, do afterward live, it is expedient that it be brought into the Church, to the intent that, if the Minister of the same Parish did himself baptize that Child, the Congregation may be certified of the true Form of Baptism, by him privately before used: In which case he shall say thus,*

I CERTIFY you, that according to the due and prescribed Order of the Church, *at such a time*, and *at such a place*, before divers witnesses I baptized this Child.

¶ *But if the Child were baptized by any other lawful Minister, then the Minister of the Parish, where the Child was born or christened, shall examine and try whether the Child be lawfully baptized, or no. In which case, if those that bring any Child to the Church do answer, that the same Child is already baptized, then shall the Minister examine them further, saying,*

BY whom was this Child baptized?
Who was present when this Child was baptized?
Because some things essential to this Sacrament may happen to be omitted through fear or haste, in such times of extremity; therefore I demand further of you,
With what matter was this Child baptized?
With what words was this Child baptized?

¶ *And if the Minister shall find by the answers of such as bring the Child, that all things were done as they ought to be; then shall not he christen the Child again, but shall receive him as one of the flock of true Christian people, saying thus,*

I CERTIFY you, that in this case all is well done, and according unto due order, concerning the baptizing of this Child; who being born in original sin, and in the wrath of God, is now, by the laver of Regeneration in Baptism, received into the number of the children of God, and heirs of everlasting life: for our Lord Jesus Christ doth not deny his grace and mercy unto such Infants, but most lovingly doth call them unto him, as the holy Gospel doth witness to our comfort on this wise.

St. Mark x. 13.

THEY brought young children to Christ, that he should touch them; and his disciples rebuked those that brought them. But when Jesus saw it, he was much displeased, and said unto them, Suffer the little children to come unto me, and forbid them not; for of such is the kingdom of God. Verily I say unto you, Whosoever shall not receive the kingdom of God as a little child, he shall not enter therein. And he took them up in his arms, put his hands upon them, and blessed them.

¶ *After the Gospel is read, the Minister shall make this brief Exhortation upon the words of the Gospel.*

BELOVED, ye hear in this Gospel the words of our Saviour Christ, that he commanded the children to be brought unto him; how he blamed those that would have kept them from him; how he exhorted all men to follow their innocency. Ye perceive how by his outward gesture and deed he declared his good will toward them ; for he embraced them in his arms, he laid his hands upon them, and blessed them. Doubt ye not therefore, but earnestly believe, that he hath likewise favourably received this present Infant; that he hath embraced *him* with the arms of his mercy ; and (as he hath promised in his holy Word) will give unto *him* the blessing of eternal life, and make *him* partaker of his everlasting kingdom. Wherefore, we being thus persuaded of the good will of our heavenly Father, declared by his Son Jesus Christ, towards this Infant, let us faithfully and devoutly give thanks unto him, and say the Prayer which the Lord himself taught us :

OUR Father, which art in heaven, Hallowed be thy Name. Thy kingdom come. Thy will be done in earth, As it is in heaven. Give us this day our daily bread. And forgive us our trespasses, As we forgive them that trespass against us. And lead us not into temptation ; But deliver us from evil. Amen.

ALMIGHTY and everlasting God, heavenly Father, we give thee humble thanks, that thou hast vouchsafed to call us to the knowledge of thy grace, and faith in thee ; Increase this knowledge, and confirm this faith in us evermore. Give thy Holy Spirit to this Infant, that *he*, being born again, and being made an heir of everlasting salvation, through our Lord Jesus Christ, may continue thy servant, and attain thy promise ; through the same our Lord Jesus Christ thy Son, who liveth and reigneth with thee and the Holy Spirit, now and for ever. *Amen.*

¶ *Then shall the Priest demand the Name of the Child ; which being by the Godfathers and Godmothers pronounced, the Minister shall say,*

DOST thou, in the name of this Child, renounce the devil and all his works, the vain pomp and glory of this world, with all covetous desires of the same, and the carnal desires of the flesh, so that thou wilt not follow, nor be led by them ?
Answer. I renounce them all.

Minister.

DOST thou believe in God the Father Almighty, Maker of heaven and earth ?
And in Jesus Christ his only begotten Son our Lord ? And that he was conceived by the Holy Ghost ; born of the Virgin Mary ; that he suffered under Pontius Pilate, was crucified, dead, and buried ; that he went down into hell, and also did rise again the third day ; that he ascended into heaven, and sitteth at the right

hand of God the Father Almighty; and from thence shall come again at the end of the world, to judge the quick and the dead?

And dost thou believe in the Holy Ghost; the holy Catholick Church; the Communion of Saints; the Remission of sins; the Resurrection of the flesh; and everlasting life after death?

Answer. All this I stedfastly believe.

Minister.

WILT thou then obediently keep God's holy will and commandments, and walk in the same all the days of thy life?

Answer. I will.

¶ *Then the Priest shall say,*

WE receive this Child into the congregation of Christ's flock, *and do sign *him* with the sign of the Cross, *Here the Priest* in token that hereafter *he* shall not be ashamed to *shall make a Cross* confess the faith of Christ crucified, and manfully to *upon the Child's* fight under his banner, against sin, the world, and *forehead.* the devil; and to continue Christ's faithful soldier and servant unto *his* life's end. Amen.

¶ *Then shall the Priest say,*

SEEING now, dearly beloved brethren, that this Child is by Baptism regenerate, and grafted into the body of Christ's Church, let us give thanks unto Almighty God for these benefits; and with one accord make our prayers unto him, that *he* may lead the rest of *his* life according to this beginning.

¶ *Then shall the Priest say,*

WE yield thee most hearty thanks, most merciful Father, that it hath pleased thee to regenerate this Infant with thy Holy Spirit, to receive *him* for thine own Child by adoption, and to incorporate *him* into thy holy Church. And humbly we beseech thee to grant, that *he* being dead unto sin, and living unto righteousness, and being buried with Christ in his death, may crucify the old man, and utterly abolish the whole body of sin; and that, as *he* is made partaker of the death of thy Son, *he* may also be partaker of his resurrection; so that finally, with the residue of thy holy Church, *he* may be an inheritor of thine everlasting kingdom; through Jesus Christ our Lord. *Amen.*

¶ *Then, all standing up, the Minister shall make this Exhortation to the Godfathers and Godmothers.*

FORASMUCH as this Child hath promised by you *his* sureties to renounce the devil and all his works, to believe in God, and to serve him; ye must remember, that it is your parts and duties to see that this Infant be taught, so soon as *he* shall be able to learn, what a solemn vow, promise, and profession *he* hath made by you. And that *he* may know these things the better, ye shall call upon *him* to hear Sermons; and chiefly ye shall provide, that *he* may learn the Creed, the Lord's Prayer, and the Ten Commandments, in the vulgar tongue, and all other things which a Christian ought to know and believe to his soul's health; and that this Child may be virtuously brought up to lead a godly and a christian life; remembering alway, that Baptism doth represent unto us our profession; which is, to follow the example of our Saviour Christ, and to be made like unto him; that, as he died, and rose again for us, so should we, who are baptized, die from sin, and rise again unto righteousness; continually mortifying all our evil and corrupt affections, and daily proceeding in all virtue and godliness of living.

¶ *But if they which bring the Infant to the Church do make such uncertain answers to the Priest's questions, as that it cannot appear that the Child was baptized with* Water, In the Name of the Father, and of the Son, and of the Holy Ghost, *(which are essential parts of Baptism,) then let the Priest baptize it in the form before appointed for Publick Baptism of Infants; saving that at the dipping of the Child in the Font, he shall use this form of words.*

IF thou art not already baptized, *N.* I baptize thee In the Name of the Father, and of the Son, and of the Holy Ghost. Amen.

THE MINISTRATION OF

BAPTISM TO SUCH AS ARE OF RIPER YEARS,

AND ABLE TO ANSWER FOR THEMSELVES.

¶ *When any such persons, as are of riper years, are to be baptized, timely notice shall be given to the Bishop, or whom he shall appoint for that purpose, a week before at the least, by the Parents, or some other discreet persons; that so due care may be taken for their Examination, whether they be sufficiently instructed in the Principles of the Christian Religion; and that they may be exhorted to prepare themselves with Prayers and Fasting for the receiving of this holy Sacrament.*

¶ *And if they shall be found fit, then the Godfathers and Godmothers (the people being assembled upon the Sunday or Holy-day appointed) shall be ready to present them at the Font immediately after the second Lesson, either at Morning or Evening Prayer, as the Curate in his discretion shall think fit.*

¶ *And standing there, the Priest shall ask, whether any of the persons here presented be baptized, or no: If they shall answer, No; then shall the Priest say thus,*

DEARLY beloved, forasmuch as all men are conceived and born in sin, (and that which is born of the flesh is flesh,) and they that are in the flesh cannot please God, but live in sin, committing many actual transgressions; and that our Saviour Christ saith, None can enter into the kingdom of God, except he be regenerate and born anew of Water and of the Holy Ghost; I beseech you to call upon God the Father, through our Lord Jesus Christ, that of his bounteous goodness he will grant to *these persons* that which by nature *they* cannot have; that *they* may be baptized with Water and the Holy Ghost, and received into Christ's holy Church, and be made lively *members* of the same.

¶ *Then shall the Priest say,*

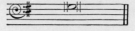

Let us pray.

(¶ *And here all the Congregation shall kneel.*)

ALMIGHTY and everlasting God, who of thy great mercy didst save Noah and his family in the ark from perishing by water; and also didst safely lead the children of Israel thy people through the Red Sea, figuring thereby thy holy Baptism; and by the Baptism of thy well-beloved Son Jesus Christ, in the river Jordan, didst sanctify the element of water to the mystical washing away of sin; We beseech thee, for thine infinite mercies, that thou wilt mercifully look upon *these* thy *servants;* wash *them* and sanctify *them* with the Holy Ghost, that *they*, being delivered from thy wrath, may be received into the ark of Christ's Church; and being stedfast in faith, joyful through hope, and rooted in charity, may so pass the waves of this troublesome world, that finally *they* may come to the land of everlasting life, there to reign with thee world without end; through Jesus Christ our Lord.

A - men.

ALMIGHTY and immortal God, the aid of all that need, the helper of all that flee to thee for succour, the life of them that believe, and the resurrection of the dead; We call upon thee for *these persons*, that *they*, coming to thy holy Baptism, may receive remission of *their* sins by spiritual regeneration. Receive *them*, O Lord, as thou hast promised by thy well-beloved Son, saying, Ask, and ye shall receive; seek, and ye shall find; knock, and it shall be opened unto you: So give now unto us that ask; let us that seek find; open the gate unto us that knock; that *these persons* may enjoy the everlasting benediction of thy heavenly washing, and may come to the eternal kingdom which thou hast promised by Christ our Lord. *Amen.*

¶ *Then shall the people stand up, and the Priest shall say,*

Hear the words of the Gospel, written by Saint *John,* in the third Chapter, beginning at the first Verse.

THERE was a man of the Pharisees, named Nicodemus, a ruler of the Jews. The same came to Jesus by night, and said unto him, Rabbi, we know that thou art a teacher come from God; for no man can do these miracles that thou doest, except God be with him. Jesus answered and said unto him, Verily, verily I say unto thee, Except a man be born again, he cannot see the kingdom of God. Nicodemus saith unto him, How can a man be born when he is old? Can he enter the second time into his mother's womb, and be born? Jesus answered, Verily, verily I say unto thee, Except a man be born of water and of the Spirit, he cannot enter into the kingdom of God. That which is born of the flesh is flesh; and that which is born of the Spirit is spirit. Marvel not that I said unto thee, Ye must be born again. The wind bloweth where it listeth, and thou hearest the sound thereof; but canst not tell whence it cometh, and whither it goeth: so is every one that is born of the Spirit.

¶ *After which he shall say this Exhortation following.*

BELOVED, ye hear in this Gospel the express words of our Saviour Christ, that except a man be born of water and of the Spirit, he cannot enter into the kingdom of God. Whereby ye may perceive the great necessity of this Sacrament, where it may be had. Likewise, immediately before his ascension into heaven, (as we read in the last Chapter of Saint Mark's Gospel,) he gave command to his disciples, saying, Go ye into all the world, and preach the Gospel to every creature. He that believeth and is baptized shall be saved; but he that believeth not shall be damned. Which also sheweth unto us the great benefit we reap thereby. For which cause Saint Peter the Apostle, when upon his first preaching of the Gospel many were pricked at the heart, and said to him and the rest of the Apostles, Men and brethren, what shall we do? replied and said unto them, Repent, and be baptized every one of you for the remission of sins, and ye shall receive the gift of the Holy Ghost. For the promise is to you and your children, and to all that are afar off, even as many as the Lord our God shall call. And with many other words exhorted he them, saying, Save yourselves from this untoward generation. For (as the same Apostle testifieth in another place) even Baptism doth also now save us, (not the putting away of the filth of the flesh, but the answer of a good conscience towards God,) by the resurrection of Jesus Christ. Doubt ye not therefore, but earnestly believe, that he will favourably receive *these* present *persons*, truly repenting, and coming unto him by faith; that he will grant *them* remission of *their* sins, and bestow upon *them* the Holy Ghost; that he will give *them* the blessing of eternal life, and make *them partakers* of his everlasting kingdom.

Wherefore we being thus persuaded of the good will of our heavenly Father towards *these persons*, declared by his Son Jesus Christ; let us faithfully and devoutly give thanks to him, and say,

R

ALMIGHTY and everlasting God, heavenly Father, we give thee humble thanks, for that thou hast vouchsafed to call us to the knowledge of thy grace, and faith in thee: Increase this knowledge, and confirm this faith in us evermore. Give thy Holy Spirit to *these persons*, that *they* may be born again, and be made *heirs* of everlasting salvation; through our Lord Jesus Christ, who liveth and reigneth with thee and the Holy Spirit, now and for ever.

¶ *Then the Priest shall speak to the* persons *to be baptized on this wise :*

WELL-BELOVED, who are come hither desiring to receive holy Baptism, *ye* have heard how the congregation hath prayed, that our Lord Jesus Christ would vouchsafe to receive you and bless you, to release you of your sins, to give you the kingdom of heaven, and everlasting life. *Ye* have heard also, that our Lord Jesus Christ hath promised in his holy Word to grant all those things that we have prayed for; which promise he, for his part, will most surely keep and perform.

Wherefore, after this promise made by Christ, *ye* must also faithfully, for your part, promise in the presence of these your Witnesses, and this whole congregation, that *ye* will renounce the devil and all his works, and constantly believe God's holy Word and obediently keep his commandments.

¶ *Then shall the Priest demand of each of the persons to be baptized, severally, these Questions following :*

Question.

DOST thou renounce the devil and all his works, the vain pomp and glory of the world, with all covetous desires of the same, and the carnal desires of the flesh, so that thou wilt not follow, nor be led by them ?

Answer. I renounce them all.

Question.

DOST thou believe in God the Father Almighty, Maker of heaven and earth ?

And in Jesus Christ his only begotten Son our Lord ? And that he was conceived by the Holy Ghost; born of the Virgin Mary; that he suffered under Pontius Pilate, was crucified, dead, and buried; that he went down into hell, and also did rise again the third day; that he ascended into heaven, and sitteth at the right hand of God the Father Almighty; and from thence shall come again at the end of the world, to judge the quick and the dead ?

And dost thou believe in the Holy Ghost; the holy Catholick Church; the Communion of Saints; the Remission of sins; the Resurrection of the flesh; and everlasting life after death?

Answer. All this I stedfastly believe.

Question.

WILT thou be baptized in this faith?
Answer. That is my desire.

Question.

WILT thou then obediently keep God's holy will and commandments, and walk in the same all the days of thy life?

Answer. I will endeavour so to do, God being my helper.

¶ *Then shall the Priest say,*

O MERCIFUL God, grant that the old Adam in *these persons* may be so buried, that the new man may be raised up in *them.*

Grant that all carnal affections may die in *them*, and that all things belonging to the Spirit may live and grow in *them*. *Amen.*

Grant that *they* may have power and strength to have victory, and to triumph, against the devil, the world, and the flesh. *Amen.*

Grant that *they*, being here dedicated to thee by our office and ministry, may also be endued with heavenly virtues, and everlastingly rewarded, through thy mercy, O blessed Lord God, who dost live, and govern all things, world without end. *Amen.*

ALMIGHTY, everliving God, whose most dearly beloved Son Jesus Christ, for the forgiveness of our sins, did shed out of his most precious side both water and blood, and gave commandment to his disciples, that they should go teach all nations, and baptize them In the Name of the Father, the Son, and the Holy Ghost; Regard, we beseech thee, the supplications of this congregation; sanctify this Water to the mystical washing away of sin; and grant that the *persons* now to be baptized therein may receive the fulness of thy grace, and ever remain in the number of thy faithful and elect children, through Jesus Christ our Lord. *Amen.*

¶ *Then shall the Priest take each person to be baptized by the right hand, and placing him conveniently by the Font, according to his discretion, shall ask the Godfathers and Godmothers the Name; and then shall dip him in the water, or pour water upon him, saying,*

N. I baptize thee In the Name of the Father, and of the Son, and of the Holy Ghost. Amen.

¶ *Then shall the Priest say,*

WE receive this person into the congregation of Christ's flock; *and do sign *him* with the sign of the Cross, *Here the Priest* in token that hereafter *he* shall not be ashamed to *shall make a Cross* confess the faith of Christ crucified, and manfully to *upon the person's* fight under his banner, against sin, the world, and *forehead.* the devil; and to continue Christ's faithful soldier and servant unto *his* life's end. Amen.

¶ *Then shall the Priest say,*

SEEING now, dearly beloved brethren, that *these persons are* regenerate, and grafted into the body of Christ's Church, let us give thanks unto Almighty God for these benefits, and with one accord make our prayers unto him, that *they* may lead the rest of *their* life according to this beginning.

¶ *Then shall be said the Lord's Prayer, all kneeling.*

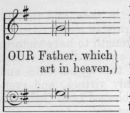 Hallowed be thy Name. Thy kingdom come. Thy will be done in earth, As it is in heaven. Give us this day our daily bread. And forgive us our trespasses, As we forgive them that trespass against us. And lead us not into temptation; But deliver us from evil.

A - men.

WE yield thee humble thanks, O heavenly Father, that thou hast vouchsafed to call us to the knowledge of thy grace, and faith in thee; Increase this knowledge, and confirm this faith in us evermore. Give thy Holy Spirit to *these persons;* that, being now born again, and made *heirs* of everlasting salvation, through our Lord Jesus Christ, *they* may continue thy *servants,* and attain thy promises; through the same Lord Jesus Christ thy Son, who liveth and reigneth with thee, in the unity of the same Holy Spirit, everlastingly.

A - men.

¶ *Then, all standing up, the Priest shall use this Exhortation following ; speaking to the Godfathers and Godmothers first.*

FORASMUCH as *these persons have* promised in your presence to renounce the devil and all his works, to believe in God, and to serve him ; ye must remember that it is your part and duty to put *them* in mind, what a solemn vow, promise, and profession *they have* now made before this congregation, and especially before you *their* chosen witnesses. And ye are also to call upon *them* to use all diligence to be rightly instructed in God's holy Word ; that so *they* may grow in grace, and in the knowledge of our Lord Jesus Christ, and live godly, righteously, and soberly in this present world.

(¶ *And then, speaking to the new baptized* persons, *he shall proceed, and say,*)

AND as for you, who have now by Baptism put on Christ, it is your part and duty also, being made the *children* of God and of the light, by faith in Jesus Christ, to walk answerably to your Christian calling, and as becometh the children of light ; remembering always that Baptism representeth unto us our profession ; which is, to follow the example of our Saviour Christ, and to be made like unto him ; that as he died, and rose again for us ; so should we, who are baptized, die from sin, and rise again unto righteousness ; continually mortifying all our evil and corrupt affections, and daily proceeding in all virtue and godliness of living.

¶ *It is expedient that every person, thus baptized, should be confirmed by the Bishop so soon after his Baptism as conveniently may be ; that so he may be admitted to the holy Communion.*

¶ *If any persons not baptized in their infancy shall be brought to be baptized before they come to years of discretion to answer for themselves ; it may suffice to use the Office for Publick Baptism of Infants, or (in case of extreme danger) the Office for Private Baptism ; only changing the word* [Infant] *for* [Child *or* Person] *as occasion requireth.*

A CATECHISM,

THAT IS TO SAY,

AN INSTRUCTION TO BE LEARNED OF EVERY PERSON BEFORE HE BE BROUGHT TO BE CONFIRMED BY THE BISHOP.

———

Question.

WHAT is your Name?
　Answer. N. or M.
Question. Who gave you this Name?
Answer. My Godfathers and Godmothers in my Baptism; wherein I was made a member of Christ, the child of God, and an inheritor of the kingdom of heaven.
Question. What did your Godfathers and Godmothers then for you?
Answer. They did promise and vow three things in my name. First, that I should renounce the devil and all his works, the pomps and vanity of this wicked world, and all the sinful lusts of the flesh. Secondly, that I should believe all the Articles of the Christian Faith. And thirdly, that I should keep God's holy will and commandments, and walk in the same all the days of my life.
Question. Dost thou not think that thou art bound to believe, and to do, as they have promised for thee?
Answer. Yes verily; and by God's help so I will. And I heartily thank our heavenly Father, that he hath called me to this state of salvation, through Jesus Christ our Saviour. And I pray unto God to give me his grace, that I may continue in the same unto my life's end.

Catechist.

Rehearse the Articles of thy Belief.

Answer.

I BELIEVE in God the Father Almighty, Maker of heaven and earth:
　And in Jesus Christ his only Son our Lord, Who was conceived by the Holy Ghost, Born of the Virgin Mary, Suffered under Pontius Pilate, Was crucified, dead, and buried, He descended into hell; The third day he rose again from the dead, He ascended into

heaven, And sitteth at the right hand of God the Father Almighty; From thence he shall come to judge the quick and the dead.

I believe in the Holy Ghost; The holy Catholick Church; The Communion of Saints; The Forgiveness of sins; The Resurrection of the body; And the Life everlasting. Amen.

Question. What dost thou chiefly learn in these Articles of thy Belief?

Answer. First, I learn to believe in God the Father, who hath made me, and all the world.

Secondly, in God the Son, who hath redeemed me, and all mankind.

Thirdly, in God the Holy Ghost, who sanctifieth me, and all the elect people of God.

Question.

You said, that your Godfathers and Godmothers did promise for you, that you should keep God's commandments. Tell me how many there be?

Answer. Ten.

Question. Which be they?

Answer.

THE same which God spake in the twentieth Chapter of Exodus, saying, I am the Lord thy God, who brought thee out of the land of Egypt, out of the house of bondage.

I. Thou shalt have none other gods but me.

II. Thou shalt not make to thyself any graven image, nor the likeness of any thing that is in heaven above, or in the earth beneath, or in the water under the earth. Thou shalt not bow down to them, nor worship them: for I the Lord thy God am a jealous God, and visit the sins of the fathers upon the children unto the third and fourth generation of them that hate me, and shew mercy unto thousands in them that love me, and keep my commandments.

III. Thou shalt not take the Name of the Lord thy God in vain: for the Lord will not hold him guiltless that taketh his Name in vain.

IV. Remember that thou keep holy the Sabbath-day. Six days shalt thou labour, and do all that thou hast to do; but the seventh day is the Sabbath of the Lord thy God. In it thou shalt do no manner of work, thou, and thy son, and thy daughter, thy manservant, and thy maid-servant, thy cattle, and the stranger that is within thy gates. For in six days the Lord made heaven and earth, the sea, and all that in them is, and rested the seventh day; wherefore the Lord blessed the seventh day, and hallowed it.

V.   Honour thy father and thy mother, that thy days may be long in the land which the Lord thy God giveth thee.

VI.   Thou shalt do no murder.

VII.   Thou shalt not commit adultery.

VIII.   Thou shalt not steal.

IX.   Thou shalt not bear false witness against thy neighbour.

X.   Thou shalt not covet thy neighbour's house, thou shalt not covet thy neighbour's wife, nor his servant, nor his maid, nor his ox, nor his ass, nor any thing that is his.

Question.

What dost thou chiefly learn by these Commandments?

Answer.   I learn two things : my duty towards God, and my duty towards my Neighbour.

Question.   What is thy duty towards God?

Answer.   My duty towards God, is to believe in him, to fear him, and to love him with all my heart, with all my mind, with all my soul, and with all my strength; to worship him, to give him thanks, to put my whole trust in him, to call upon him, to honour his holy Name and his Word, and to serve him truly all the days of my life.

Question.   What is thy duty towards thy Neighbour?

Answer.   My duty towards my Neighbour, is to love him as myself, and to do to all men, as I would they should do unto me : To love, honour, and succour my father and mother : To honour and obey the Queen, and all that are put in authority under her : To submit myself to all my governours, teachers, spiritual pastors and masters : To order myself lowly and reverently to all my betters : To hurt nobody by word nor deed : To be true and just in all my dealing : To bear no malice nor hatred in my heart : To keep my hands from picking and stealing, and my tongue from evil speaking, lying, and slandering : To keep my body in temperance, soberness, and chastity : Not to covet nor desire other men's goods; but to learn and labour truly to get mine own living, and to do my duty in that state of life, unto which it shall please God to call me.

Catechist.

My good Child, know this, that thou art not able to do these things of thyself, nor to walk in the Commandments of God, and to serve him, without his special grace; which thou must learn at all times to call for by diligent prayer. Let me hear, therefore, if thou canst say the Lord's Prayer.

Answer.

OUR Father, which art in heaven, Hallowed be thy Name. Thy kingdom come. Thy will be done in earth, As it is in heaven. Give us this day our daily bread. And forgive us our trespasses, As we forgive them that trespass against us. And lead us not into temptation; But deliver us from evil. Amen.

Question. What desirest thou of God in this Prayer?

Answer. I desire my Lord God our heavenly Father, who is the giver of all goodness, to send his grace unto me, and to all people; that we may worship him, serve him, and obey him, as we ought to do. And I pray unto God, that he will send us all things that be needful both for our souls and bodies; and that he will be merciful unto us, and forgive us our sins; and that it will please him to save and defend us in all dangers ghostly and bodily; and that he will keep us from all sin and wickedness, and from our ghostly enemy, and from everlasting death. And this I trust he will do of his mercy and goodness, through our Lord Jesus Christ. And therefore I say, Amen, So be it.

Question.

HOW many Sacraments hath Christ ordained in his Church?
   Answer. Two only, as generally necessary to salvation, that is to say, Baptism, and the Supper of the Lord.

Question. What meanest thou by this word *Sacrament?*

Answer. I mean an outward and visible sign of an inward and spiritual grace given unto us, ordained by Christ himself, as a means whereby we receive the same, and a pledge to assure us thereof.

Question. How many parts are there in a Sacrament?

Answer. Two; the outward visible sign, and the inward spiritual grace.

Question. What is the outward visible sign or form in Baptism?

Answer. Water; wherein the person is baptized *In the Name of the Father, and of the Son, and of the Holy Ghost.*

Question. What is the inward and spiritual grace?

Answer. A death unto sin, and a new birth unto righteousness: for being by nature born in sin, and the children of wrath, we are hereby made the children of grace.

Question. What is required of persons to be baptized?

Answer. Repentance, whereby they forsake sin; and Faith, whereby they stedfastly believe the promises of God made to them in that Sacrament.

Question. Why then are Infants baptized, when by reason of their tender age they cannot perform them?

Answer. Because they promise them both by their Sureties; which promise, when they come to age, themselves are bound to perform.

Question. Why was the Sacrament of the Lord's Supper ordained?

Answer. For the continual remembrance of the sacrifice of the death of Christ, and of the benefits which we receive thereby.

Question. What is the outward part or sign of the Lord's Supper?

Answer. Bread and Wine, which the Lord hath commanded to be received.

Question. What is the inward part, or thing signified?

Answer. The Body and Blood of Christ, which are verily and indeed taken and received by the faithful in the Lord's Supper.

Question. What are the benefits whereof we are partakers thereby?

Answer. The strengthening and refreshing of our souls by the Body and Blood of Christ, as our bodies are by the Bread and Wine.

Question. What is required of them who come to the Lord's Supper?

Answer. To examine themselves, whether they repent them truly of their former sins, stedfastly purposing to lead a new life; have a lively faith in God's mercy through Christ, with a thankful remembrance of his death; and be in charity with all men.

¶ *The Curate of every Parish shall diligently upon Sundays and Holy-days, after the second Lesson at Evening Prayer, openly in the Church instruct and examine so many Children of his Parish sent unto him, as he shall think convenient, in some part of this Catechism.*

¶ *And all Fathers, Mothers, Masters, and Dames, shall cause their Children, Servants, and Apprentices, (which have not learned their Catechism,) to come to the Church at the time appointed, and obediently to hear, and be ordered by the Curate, until such time as they have learned all that is here appointed for them to learn.*

¶ *So soon as Children are come to a competent age, and can say, in their Mother Tongue, the Creed, the Lord's Prayer, and the Ten Commandments; and also can answer to the other Questions of this short Catechism; they shall be brought to the Bishop. And every one shall have a God-father, or a Godmother, as a Witness of their Confirmation.*

¶ *And whensoever the Bishop shall give knowledge for Children to be brought unto him for their Confirmation, the Curate of every Parish shall either bring, or send in writing, with his hand subscribed thereunto, the names of all such Persons within his Parish, as he shall think fit to be presented to the Bishop to be confirmed. And, if the Bishop approve of them, he shall confirm them in manner following.*

THE ORDER OF CONFIRMATION,

OR LAYING ON OF HANDS UPON THOSE THAT ARE BAPTIZED AND COME TO YEARS OF DISCRETION.

¶ *Upon the day appointed, all that are to be then confirmed, being placed, and standing in order, before the Bishop; he (or some other Minister appointed by him) shall read this Preface following.*

TO the end that Confirmation may be ministered to the more edifying of such as shall receive it, the Church hath thought good to order, That none hereafter shall be confirmed, but such as can say the Creed, the Lord's Prayer, and the Ten Commandments; and can also answer to such other Questions, as in the short Catechism are contained : which order is very convenient to be observed ; to the end, that children, being now come to the years of discretion, and having learned what their Godfathers and Godmothers promised for them in Baptism, they may themselves, with their own mouth and consent, openly before the Church, ratify and confirm the same ; and also promise, that by the grace of God they will evermore endeavour themselves faithfully to observe such things, as they, by their own confession, have assented unto.

¶ *Then shall the Bishop say,*

DO ye here, in the presence of God, and of this congregation, renew the solemn promise and vow that was made in your name at your Baptism ; ratifying and confirming the same in your own persons, and acknowledging yourselves bound to believe, and to do, all those things, which your Godfathers and Godmothers then undertook for you?

¶ *And every one shall audibly answer,*

I do.

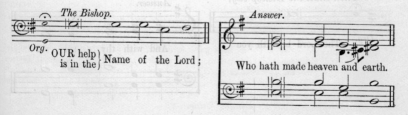

Org. OUR help} is in the } Name of the Lord ;   *Answer.* Who hath made heaven and earth.

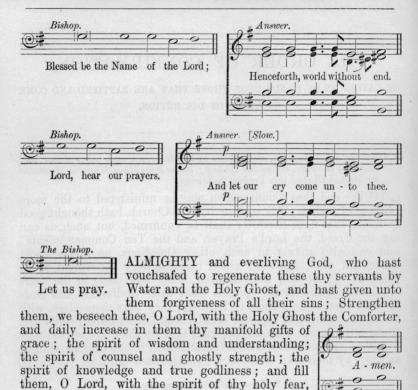

Bishop.

Blessed be the Name of the Lord;

Answer.

Henceforth, world without end.

Bishop.

Lord, hear our prayers.

Answer. [*Slow.*]

And let our cry come un - to thee.

The Bishop.

Let us pray.

ALMIGHTY and everliving God, who hast vouchsafed to regenerate these thy servants by Water and the Holy Ghost, and hast given unto them forgiveness of all their sins; Strengthen them, we beseech thee, O Lord, with the Holy Ghost the Comforter, and daily increase in them thy manifold gifts of grace; the spirit of wisdom and understanding; the spirit of counsel and ghostly strength; the spirit of knowledge and true godliness; and fill them, O Lord, with the spirit of thy holy fear, now and for ever.

A - men.

¶ *Then all of them in order kneeling before the Bishop, he shall lay his hand upon the head of every one severally, saying,*

DEFEND, O Lord, this thy Child [or *this thy Servant*] with thy heavenly grace, that *he* may continue thine for ever; and daily increase in thy Holy Spirit more and more, until *he* come unto thy everlasting kingdom. Amen.

¶ *Then shall the Bishop say,*

Org. The Lord be with you.

Answer.

And with thy spi - rit.

¶ *And (all kneeling down) the Bishop shall add,*

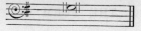

Let us pray.

OUR Father, which art in heaven,

Hallowed be thy Name. Thy kingdom come. Thy will be done in earth, As it is in heaven. Give us this day our daily bread. And forgive us our trespasses, As we forgive them that trespass against us. And lead us not into temptation; But deliver us from evil.

A - men.

And this Collect.

ALMIGHTY and everliving God, who makest us both to will and to do those things that be good and acceptable unto thy divine Majesty; We make our humble supplications unto thee for these thy servants, upon whom (after the example of thy holy Apostles) we have now laid our hands, to certify them (by this sign) of thy favour and gracious goodness toward them. Let thy fatherly hand, we beseech thee, ever be over them; let thy Holy Spirit ever be with them; and so lead them in the knowledge and obedience of thy Word, that in the end they may obtain everlasting life; through our Lord Jesus Christ, who with thee and the Holy Ghost liveth and reigneth, ever one God, world without end.

A - men.

O ALMIGHTY Lord, and everlasting God, vouchsafe, we beseech thee, to direct, sanctify, and govern, both our hearts and bodies, in the ways of thy laws, and in the works of thy commandments; that, through thy most mighty protection both here and ever, we may be preserved in body and soul; through our Lord and Saviour Jesus Christ. *Amen.*

¶ *Then the Bishop shall bless them, saying thus,*

THE blessing of God Almighty, the Father, the Son, and the Holy Ghost, be upon you, and remain with you for ever. *Amen.*

¶ *And there shall none be admitted to the Holy Communion, until such time as he be confirmed, or be ready and desirous to be confirmed.*

THE FORM OF

SOLEMNIZATION OF MATRIMONY.

¶ *First the Banns of all that are to be married together must be published in the Church three several Sundays, or Holy-days, in the time of Divine Service, immediately before the Sentences for the Offertory; the Curate saying after the accustomed manner,*

I PUBLISH the Banns of Marriage between *M.* of — and *N.* of —. If any of you know cause, or just impediment, why these two persons should not be joined together in holy Matrimony, ye are to declare it. This is the first [*second,* or *third*] time of asking.

¶ *And if the persons that are to be married dwell in divers Parishes, the Banns must be asked in both Parishes; and the Curate of the one Parish shall not solemnize Matrimony betwixt them, without a Certificate of the Banns being thrice asked, from the Curate of the other Parish.*

¶ *At the day and time appointed for solemnization of Matrimony, the persons to be married shall come into the body of the Church with their friends and neighbours: and there standing together, the Man on the right hand, and the Woman on the left, the Priest shall say,*

DEARLY beloved, we are gathered together here in the sight of God, and in the face of this congregation, to join together this Man and this Woman in holy Matrimony; which is an honourable estate, instituted of God in the time of man's innocency, signifying unto us the mystical union that is betwixt Christ and his Church: which holy estate Christ adorned and beautified with his presence, and first miracle that he wrought, in Cana of Galilee; and is commended of Saint Paul to be honourable among all men: and therefore is not by any to be enterprised, nor taken in hand, unadvisedly, lightly, or wantonly, to satisfy men's carnal lusts and appetites, like brute beasts that have no understanding; but reverently, discreetly, advisedly, soberly, and in the fear of God; duly considering the causes for which Matrimony was ordained.

First, It was ordained for the procreation of children, to be brought up in the fear and nurture of the Lord, and to the praise of his holy Name.

Secondly, It was ordained for a remedy against sin, and to avoid fornication; that such persons that have not the gift of continency might marry, and keep themselves undefiled members of Christ's body.

Thirdly, It was ordained for the mutual society, help, and comfort, that the one ought to have of the other, both in prosperity and adversity. Into which holy estate these two persons present come now to be joined. Therefore if any man can shew any just cause, why they may not lawfully be joined together, let him now speak, or else hereafter for ever hold his peace.

¶ *And also, speaking unto the persons that shall be married, he shall say,*

I REQUIRE and charge you both, as ye will answer at the dreadful day of judgement when the secrets of all hearts shall be disclosed, that if either of you know any impediment, why ye may not be lawfully joined together in Matrimony, ye do now confess it. For be ye well assured, that so many as are coupled together otherwise than God's Word doth allow are not joined together by God; neither is their Matrimony lawful.

¶ *At which day of Marriage, if any man do allege and declare any impediment, why they may not be coupled together in Matrimony, by God's Law, or the Laws of this Realm; and will be bound, and sufficient sureties with him, to the parties; or else put in a Caution (to the full value of such charges as the persons to be married do thereby sustain) to prove his allegation: then the solemnization must be deferred, until such time as the truth be tried.*

¶ *If no impediment be alleged, then shall the Curate say unto the Man,*

M. WILT thou have this Woman to thy wedded wife, to live together after God's ordinance in the holy estate of Matrimony? Wilt thou love her, comfort her, honour, and keep her in sickness and in health; and, forsaking all other, keep thee only unto her, so long as ye both shall live?

¶ *The Man shall answer,*

I will.

¶ *Then shall the Priest say unto the Woman,*

N. WILT thou have this Man to thy wedded husband, to live together after God's ordinance in the holy estate of Matrimony? Wilt thou obey him, and serve him, love, honour, and keep him in sickness and in health; and, forsaking all other, keep thee only unto him, so long as ye both shall live?

¶ *The Woman shall answer,*

I will.

¶ *Then shall the Minister say,*

Who giveth this Woman to be married to this Man?

¶ *Then shall they give their troth to each other in this manner. The Minister, receiving the Woman at her father's or friend's hands, shall cause the Man with his right hand to take the Woman by her right hand, and to say after him as followeth.*

I M. take thee N. to my wedded wife, to have and to hold from this day forward, for better for worse, for richer for poorer, in sickness and in health, to love and to cherish, till death us do part, according to God's holy ordinance ; and thereto I plight thee my troth.

¶ *Then shall they loose their hands; and the Woman, with her right hand taking the Man by his right hand, shall likewise say after the Minister,*

I N. take thee M. to my wedded husband, to have and to hold from this day forward, for better for worse, for richer for poorer, in sickness and in health, to love, cherish, and to obey, till death us do part, according to God's holy ordinance ; and thereto I give thee my troth.

¶ *Then shall they again loose their hands; and the Man shall give unto the Woman a Ring, laying the same upon the book with the accustomed duty to the Priest and Clerk. And the Priest, taking the Ring, shall deliver it unto the Man, to put it upon the fourth finger of the Woman's left hand. And the Man holding the Ring there, and taught by the Priest, shall say,*

WITH this Ring I thee wed, with my body I thee worship, and with all my worldly goods I thee endow : In the Name of the Father, and of the Son, and of the Holy Ghost. Amen.

¶ *Then the Man leaving the Ring upon the fourth finger of the Woman's left hand, they shall both kneel down ; and the Minister shall say,*

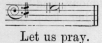

Let us pray.

O ETERNAL God, Creator and Preserver of all mankind, Giver of all spiritual grace, the Author of everlasting life ; Send thy blessing upon these thy servants, this man and this woman, whom we bless in thy Name ; that, as Isaac and Rebecca lived faithfully together, so these persons may surely perform and keep the vow and covenant betwixt them made, (whereof this Ring, given and received is a token and pledge,) and may ever remain in perfect love and peace together, and live according to thy laws ; through Jesus Christ our Lord.

A - men.

¶ *Then shall the Priest join their right hands together, and say,*

Those whom God hath joined together let no man put asunder.

¶ *Then shall the Minister speak unto the people.*

FORASMUCH as M. and N. have consented together in holy wedlock, and have witnessed the same before God and this company, and thereto have given and pledged their troth either to other, and have declared the same by giving and receiving of a Ring, and by joining of hands ; I pronounce that they be Man and Wife together, In the Name of the Father, and of the Son, and of the Holy Ghost. Amen.

¶ *And the Minister shall add this Blessing.*

GOD the Father, God the Son, God the Holy Ghost, bless, preserve, and keep you; the Lord mercifully with his favour look upon you; and so fill you with all spiritual benediction and grace, that ye may so live together in this life, that in the world to come ye may have life everlasting.

A - men.

¶ *Then the Minister or Clerks, going to the Lord's Table, shall say or sing this Psalm following.*

Beati omnes. Psalm cxxviii.

mf BLESSED are all théy that | fear the | Lord : ánd | walk | in his | ways.

2 For thou shalt eat the lábour | of thine | hands : O well is thée, and | happy | shalt thou | be.

3 Thy wife shall bé as the | fruitful | vine : upón the | walls | of thine | house.

4 Thy children líke the | olive- | -branches : róund | — a- | -bout thy | table.

5 Lo, thús shall the | man be | blessed : thát | fear- | -eth the | Lord.

6 The Lord from out of Síon shall | so | bless thee : that thou shalt see Jerusalem in prospérity | all thy | life | long.

2nd part. 7 Yea, that thou shalt sée thy | children's | children : ánd | peace up- | -on | Israel.

F. f Glory be to the Fáther, | and . to the | Son : ánd | to the | Holy | Ghost ;

F. As it was in the beginning * is nów, and | ever | shall be : wórld without | end. | A- | -men.

¶ *Or this Psalm.*

Deus misereatur. Psalm lxvii.

F. mf GOD be merciful únto | us and | bless us : and shew us the light of his countenance * ánd be | merciful | unto | us.

F. 2 That thy way may be knówn up- | -on | earth : thy sáving | health a- | -mong all | nations.

S

F.   3 Let the people práise | thee O | God : yeá, let | all the | people | praise thee.

4 O let the nations rejóice | and be | glad : for thou shalt judge the folk righteously * and góvern the | nations . up- | -on | earth.

F.   5 Let the people práise | thee O | God : yéa, let | all the | people | praise thee.

6 Then shall the éarth bring | forth her | increase : and God, even our own Gód, shall | give | us his | blessing.

2nd part.   7 Gód | shall | bless us : and all the énds of the | world shall | fear | him.

F.   *f*   Glory be to the Fáther, | and . to the | Son : ánd | to the | Holy | Ghost ;

F.   As it was in the beginning * is nów, and | ever | shall be : wórld without | end. | A- | -men.

¶ *The Psalm ended, and the Man and the Woman kneeling before the Lord's Table, the Priest standing at the Table, and turning his face towards them, shall say,*

Org.   Lord, have mercy upon us.

Answer.   *Minister [and People].*

Christ, have mercy upon us.   Lord, have mer - cy up - on . . us.

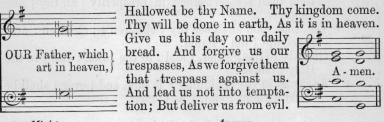

OUR Father, which art in heaven,   Hallowed be thy Name. Thy kingdom come. Thy will be done in earth, As it is in heaven. Give us this day our daily bread. And forgive us our trespasses, As we forgive them that trespass against us. And lead us not into temptation ; But deliver us from evil.

A - men.

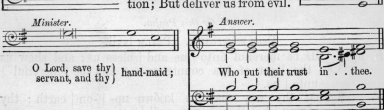

Minister.   *Answer.*

O Lord, save thy servant, and thy hand-maid ;   Who put their trust in . . thee.

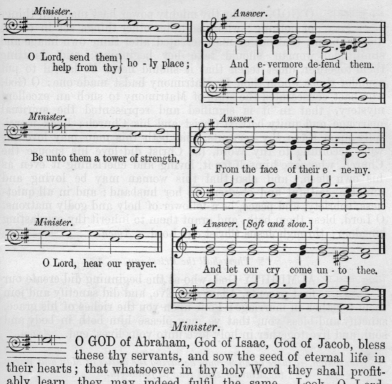

Minister.

O Lord, send them help from thy ho - ly place;

Answer.

And e - vermore de-fend them.

Minister.

Be unto them a tower of strength,

Answer.

From the face of their e - ne-my.

Minister.

O Lord, hear our prayer.

Answer. [Soft and slow.]

And let our cry come un - to thee.

Minister.

O GOD of Abraham, God of Isaac, God of Jacob, bless these thy servants, and sow the seed of eternal life in their hearts; that whatsoever in thy holy Word they shall profitably learn, they may indeed fulfil the same. Look, O Lord, mercifully upon them from heaven, and bless them. And as thou didst send thy blessing upon Abraham and Sarah, to their great comfort, so vouchsafe to send thy blessing upon these thy servants; that they obeying thy will, and alway being in safety under thy protection, may abide in thy love unto their lives' end; through Jesus Christ our Lord.

A - men.

¶ *This Prayer next following shall be omitted, where the Woman is past child-bearing.*

O MERCIFUL Lord, and heavenly Father, by whose gracious gift mankind is increased; We beseech thee, assist with thy blessing these two persons, that they may both be fruitful in procreation of children, and also live together so long in godly love and honesty, that they may see their children christianly and virtuously brought up, to thy praise and honour; through Jesus Christ our Lord.

A - men.

O GOD, who by thy mighty power hast made all things of nothing; who also (after other things set in order) didst appoint, that out of man (created after thine own image and similitude) woman should take her beginning; and, knitting them together, didst teach that it should never be lawful to put asunder those whom thou by Matrimony hadst made one: O God, who hast consecrated the state of Matrimony to such an excellent mystery, that in it is signified and represented the spiritual marriage and unity betwixt Christ and his Church; Look mercifully upon these thy servants, that both this man may love his wife, according to thy Word, (as Christ did love his spouse the Church, who gave himself for it, loving and cherishing it even as his own flesh,) and also that this woman may be loving and amiable, faithful and obedient to her husband; and in all quietness, sobriety, and peace, be a follower of holy and godly matrons. O Lord, bless them both, and grant them to inherit thy everlasting kingdom; through Jesus Christ our Lord. *Amen.*

¶ *Then shall the Priest say,*

ALMIGHTY God, who at the beginning did create our first parents, Adam and Eve, and did sanctify and join them together in marriage; Pour upon you the riches of his grace, sanctify and bless you, that ye may please him both in body and soul, and live together in holy love unto your lives' end. *Amen.*

¶ *After which, if there be no Sermon declaring the duties of Man and Wife, the Minister shall read as followeth.*

ALL ye that are married, or that intend to take the holy estate of Matrimony upon you, hear what the holy Scripture doth say as touching the duty of husbands towards their wives, and wives towards their husbands.

Saint Paul, in his Epistle to the Ephesians, the fifth chapter, doth give this commandment to all married men; Husbands, love your wives, even as Christ also loved the Church, and gave himself for it, that he might sanctify and cleanse it with the washing of water, by the Word; that he might present it to himself a glorious Church, not having spot, or wrinkle, or any such thing; but that it should be holy, and without blemish. So ought men to love their wives as their own bodies. He that loveth his wife loveth himself: for no man ever yet hated his own flesh, but nourisheth and cherisheth it, even as the Lord the Church: for we are members of his body, of his flesh, and of his bones. For this cause shall a man leave his father and mother, and shall be joined unto his wife; and they two shall be one flesh. This is a great mystery;

but I speak concerning Christ and the Church. Nevertheless, let every one of you in particular so love his wife, even as himself.

Likewise the same Saint Paul, writing to the Colossians, speaketh thus to all men that are married; Husbands, love your wives, and be not bitter against them.

Hear also what Saint Peter, the Apostle of Christ, who was himself a married man, saith unto them that are married, Ye husbands, dwell with your wives according to knowledge; giving honour unto the wife, as unto the weaker vessel, and as being heirs together of the grace of life, that your prayers be not hindered.

Hitherto ye have heard the duty of the husband toward the wife. Now likewise, ye wives, hear and learn your duties toward your husbands, even as it is plainly set forth in holy Scripture.

Saint Paul, in the aforenamed Epistle to the Ephesians, teacheth you thus; Wives, submit yourselves unto your own husbands, as unto the Lord. For the husband is the head of the wife, even as Christ is the head of the Church: and he is the Saviour of the body. Therefore as the Church is subject unto Christ, so let the wives be to their own husbands in everything. And again he saith, Let the wife see that she reverence her husband.

And in his Epistle to the Colossians, Saint Paul giveth you this short lesson; Wives, submit yourselves unto your own husbands, as it is fit in the Lord.

Saint Peter also doth instruct you very well, thus saying; Ye wives, be in subjection to your own husbands; that, if any obey not the Word, they also may without the Word be won by the conversation of the wives; while they behold your chaste conversation coupled with fear. Whose adorning, let it not be that outward adorning of plaiting the hair, and of wearing of gold, or of putting on of apparel; but let it be the hidden man of the heart, in that which is not corruptible; even the ornament of a meek and quiet spirit, which is in the sight of God of great price. For after this manner in the old time the holy women also, who trusted in God, adorned themselves, being in subjection unto their own husbands; even as Sarah obeyed Abraham, calling him lord; whose daughters ye are as long as ye do well, and are not afraid with any amazement.

¶ *It is convenient that the new-married persons should receive the holy Communion at the time of their Marriage, or at the first opportunity after their Marriage.*

THE ORDER FOR

THE VISITATION OF THE SICK.

¶ *When any person is sick, notice shall be given thereof to the Minister of the Parish ; who, coming into the sick person's house, shall say,*

PEACE be to this house, and to all that dwell in it.

¶ *When he cometh into the sick man's presence he shall say, kneeling down,*

REMEMBER not, Lord, our iniquities, nor the iniquities of our forefathers : Spare us, good Lord, spare thy people, whom thou hast redeemed with thy most precious blood, and be not angry with us for ever.

Answer. Spare us, good Lord.

¶ *Then the Minister shall say,*

Let us pray.

Lord, have mercy upon us.
Christ, have mercy upon us.
Lord, have mercy upon us.

OUR Father, which art in heaven, Hallowed be thy Name. Thy kingdom come. Thy will be done in earth, As it is in heaven. Give us this day our daily bread. And forgive us our trespasses, As we forgive them that trespass against us. And lead us not into temptation ; But deliver us from evil. Amen.

Minister. O Lord, save thy servant ;
Answer. Which putteth *his* trust in thee.
Minister. Send *him* help from thy holy place ;
Answer. And evermore mightily defend *him.*
Minister. Let the enemy have no advantage of *him ;*
Answer. Nor the wicked approach to hurt *him.*
Minister. Be unto *him,* O Lord, a strong tower,
Answer. From the face of *his* enemy.
Minister. O Lord, hear our prayers.
Answer. And let our cry come unto thee.

Minister.

O LORD, look down from heaven, behold, visit, and relieve this thy servant. Look upon *him* with the eyes of thy mercy, give *him* comfort and sure confidence in thee, defend *him* from the danger of the enemy, and keep *him* in perpetual peace and safety; through Jesus Christ our Lord. *Amen.*

HEAR us, Almighty and most merciful God and Saviour; extend thy accustomed goodness to this thy servant who is grieved with sickness. Sanctify, we beseech thee, this thy fatherly correction to *him*; that the sense of *his* weakness may add strength to *his* faith, and seriousness to *his* repentance: That, if it shall be thy good pleasure to restore *him* to *his* former health, *he* may lead the residue of *his* life in thy fear, and to thy glory: or else, give *him* grace so to take thy visitation, that, after this painful life ended, *he* may dwell with thee in life everlasting; through Jesus Christ our Lord. *Amen.*

¶ *Then shall the Minister exhort the sick person after this form, or other like.*

DEARLY beloved, know this, that Almighty God is the Lord of life and death, and of all things to them pertaining, as youth, strength, health, age, weakness, and sickness. Wherefore, whatsoever your sickness is, know you certainly that it is God's visitation. And for what cause soever this sickness is sent unto you; whether it be to try your patience for the example of others, and that your faith may be found in the day of the Lord laudable, glorious, and honourable, to the increase of glory and endless felicity; or else it be sent unto you to correct and amend in you whatsoever doth offend the eyes of your heavenly Father; know you certainly, that if you truly repent you of your sins, and bear your sickness patiently, trusting in God's mercy, for his dear Son Jesus Christ's sake, and render unto him humble thanks for his fatherly visitation, submitting yourself wholly unto his will, it shall turn to your profit, and help you forward in the right way that leadeth unto everlasting life.

¶ *If the person visited be very sick, then the Curate may end his exhortation in this place, or else proceed.*

TAKE therefore in good part the chastisement of the Lord: For (as Saint Paul saith in the twelfth Chapter to the Hebrews) whom the Lord loveth he chasteneth, and scourgeth every son whom he receiveth. If ye endure chastening, God dealeth with you as with sons; for what son is he whom the father chasteneth not?

But if ye be without chastisement, whereof all are partakers, then are ye bastards, and not sons. Furthermore, we have had fathers of our flesh, which corrected us, and we gave them reverence : shall we not much rather be in subjection unto the Father of spirits, and live? For they verily for a few days chastened us after their own pleasure ; but he for our profit, that we might be partakers of his holiness. These words, good *brother*, are written in holy Scripture for our comfort and instruction ; that we should patiently, and with thanksgiving, bear our heavenly Father's correction, whensoever by any manner of adversity it shall please his gracious goodness to visit us. And there should be no greater comfort to Christian persons, than to be made like unto Christ, by suffering patiently adversities, troubles, and sicknesses. For he himself went not up to joy, but first he suffered pain ; he entered not into his glory before he was crucified. So truly our way to eternal joy is to suffer here with Christ ; and our door to enter into eternal life is gladly to die with Christ ; that we may rise again from death, and dwell with him in everlasting life. Now therefore, taking your sickness, which is thus profitable for you, patiently, I exhort you, in the Name of God, to remember the profession which you made unto God in your Baptism. And forasmuch as after this life there is an account to be given unto the righteous Judge, by whom all must be judged, without respect of persons, I require you to examine yourself and your estate, both toward God and man ; so that, accusing and condemning yourself for your own faults, you may find mercy at our heavenly Father's hand for Christ's sake, and not be accused and condemned in that fearful judgement. Therefore I shall rehearse to you the Articles of our Faith, that you may know whether you do believe as a Christian man should or no.

¶ *Here the Minister shall rehearse the Articles of the Faith, saying thus,*

DOST thou believe in God the Father Almighty, Maker of heaven and earth ?

And in Jesus Christ his only begotten Son our Lord ? And that he was conceived by the Holy Ghost, born of the Virgin Mary ; that he suffered under Pontius Pilate, was crucified, dead, and buried ; that he went down into hell, and also did rise again the third day ; that he ascended into heaven, and sitteth at the right hand of God the Father Almighty ; and from thence shall come again at the end of the world, to judge the quick and the dead ?

And dost thou believe in the Holy Ghost ; the holy Catholick Church ; the Communion of Saints ; the Remission of sins ; the Resurrection of the flesh ; and everlasting life after death ?

¶ *The sick person shall answer,*

All this I stedfastly believe.

¶ *Then shall the Minister examine whether he repent him truly of his sins, and be in charity with all the world; exhorting him to forgive, from the bottom of his heart, all persons that have offended him; and if he hath offended any other, to ask them forgiveness; and where he hath done injury or wrong to any man, that he make amends to the uttermost of his power. And if he hath not before disposed of his goods, let him then be admonished to make his Will, and to declare his Debts, what he oweth, and what is owing unto him; for the better discharging of his conscience, and the quietness of his Executors. But men should often be put in remembrance to take order for the settling of their temporal estates, whilst they are in health.*

¶ *These words before rehearsed may be said before the Minister begin his Prayer, as he shall see cause.*

¶ *The Minister should not omit earnestly to move such sick persons as are of ability to be liberal to the poor.*

¶ *Here shall the sick person be moved to make a special Confession of his sins, if he feel his conscience troubled with any weighty matter. After which Confession, the Priest shall absolve him (if he humbly and heartily desire it) after this sort.*

OUR Lord Jesus Christ, who hath left power to his Church to absolve all sinners who truly repent and believe in him, of his great mercy forgive thee thine offences: And by his authority committed to me, I absolve thee from all thy sins, In the Name of the Father, and of the Son, and of the Holy Ghost. Amen.

¶ *And then the Priest shall say the Collect following.*

Let us pray.

O MOST merciful God, who, according to the multitude of thy mercies, dost so put away the sins of those who truly repent, that thou rememberest them no more; Open thine eye of mercy upon this thy servant, who most earnestly desireth pardon and forgiveness. Renew in *him*, most loving Father, whatsoever hath been decayed by the fraud and malice of the devil, or by *his* own carnal will and frailness; preserve and continue this sick member in the unity of the Church; consider *his* contrition, accept *his* tears, assuage *his* pain, as shall seem to thee most expedient for *him*. And forasmuch as *he* putteth *his* full trust only in thy mercy, impute not unto *him his* former sins, but strengthen *him* with thy blessed Spirit; and, when thou art pleased to take *him* hence, take *him* unto thy favour, through the merits of thy most dearly beloved Son Jesus Christ our Lord. *Amen.*

¶ Then shall the Minister say this Psalm.

In te, Domine, speravi, Psalm lxxi.

IN thee, O Lord, have I put my trust ; let me never be put to confusion : but rid me, and deliver me in thy righteousness ; incline thine ear unto me, and save me.

Be thou my strong hold, whereunto I may alway resort : thou hast promised to help me ; for thou art my house of defence, and my castle.

Deliver me, O my God, out of the hand of the ungodly : out of the hand of the unrighteous and cruel man.

For thou, O Lord God, art the thing that I long for : thou art my hope, even from my youth.

Through thee have I been holden up ever since I was born : thou art he that took me out of my mother's womb ; my praise shall alway be of thee.

I am become as it were a monster unto many : but my sure trust is in thee.

O let my mouth be filled with thy praise : that I may sing of thy glory and honour all the day long.

Cast me not away in the time of age : forsake me not when my strength faileth me.

For mine enemies speak against me, and they that lay wait for my soul take their counsel together, saying : God hath forsaken him, persecute him, and take him : for there is none to deliver him.

Go not far from me, O God : my God, haste thee to help me.

Let them be confounded and perish that are against my soul : let them be covered with shame and dishonour that seek to do me evil.

As for me, I will patiently abide alway : and will praise thee more and more.

My mouth shall daily speak of thy righteousness and salvation : for I know no end thereof.

I will go forth in the strength of the Lord God : and will make mention of thy righteousness only.

Thou, O God, hast taught me from my youth up until now : therefore will I tell of thy wondrous works.

Forsake me not, O God, in mine old age, when I am gray-headed : until I have shewed thy strength unto this generation, and thy power to all them that are yet for to come.

Thy righteousness, O God, is very high, and great things are they that thou hast done : O God, who is like unto thee ?

Glory be to the Father, and to the Son : and to the Holy Ghost ;

As it was in the beginning, is now, and ever shall be : world without end. Amen.

¶ Adding this.

O SAVIOUR of the world, who by thy Cross and precious Blood hast redeemed us, Save us, and help us, we humbly beseech thee, O Lord.

¶ Then shall the Minister say,

THE Almighty Lord, who is a most strong tower to all them that put their trust in him, to whom all things in heaven, in earth, and under the earth, do bow and obey, be now and evermore thy defence: and make thee know and feel, that there is none other Name under heaven given to man, in whom, and through whom, thou mayest receive health and salvation, but only the Name of our Lord Jesus Christ. Amen.

¶ And after that shall say,

UNTO God's gracious mercy and protection we commit thee. The Lord bless thee, and keep thee. The Lord make his face to shine upon thee, and be gracious unto thee. The Lord lift up his countenance upon thee, and give thee peace, both now and evermore. *Amen.*

A PRAYER FOR A SICK CHILD.

O ALMIGHTY God, and merciful Father, to whom alone belong the issues of life and death; Look down from heaven, we humbly beseech thee, with the eyes of mercy upon this child now lying upon the bed of sickness: Visit *him*, O Lord, with thy salvation; deliver *him* in thy good appointed time from *his* bodily pain, and save *his* soul for thy mercies' sake: That, if it shall be thy pleasure to prolong *his* days here on earth, *he* may live to thee, and be an instrument of thy glory, by serving thee faithfully, and doing good in *his* generation; or else receive *him* into those heavenly habitations, where the souls of them that sleep in the Lord Jesus enjoy perpetual rest and felicity. Grant this, O Lord, for thy mercies' sake, in the same thy Son our Lord Jesus Christ, who liveth and reigneth with thee and the Holy Ghost, ever one God, world without end. *Amen.*

A PRAYER FOR A SICK PERSON, WHEN THERE APPEARETH SMALL HOPE OF RECOVERY.

O FATHER of mercies, and God of all comfort, our only help in time of need; We fly unto thee for succour in behalf of this thy servant, here lying under thy hand in great weakness of body.

Look graciously upon *him*, O Lord; and the more the outward man decayeth, strengthen *him*, we beseech thee, so much the more continually with thy grace and Holy Spirit in the inner man. Give *him* unfeigned repentance for all the errors of *his* life past, and stedfast faith in thy Son Jesus; that *his* sins may be done away by thy mercy, and *his* pardon sealed in heaven, before *he* go hence, and be no more seen. We know, O Lord, that there is no word impossible with thee; and that, if thou wilt, thou canst even yet raise *him* up, and grant *him* a longer continuance amongst us: Yet, forasmuch as in all appearance the time of *his* dissolution draweth near, so fit and prepare *him*, we beseech thee, against the hour of death, that after *his* departure hence in peace, and in thy favour, *his* soul may be received into thine everlasting kingdom through the merits and mediation of Jesus Christ, thine only Son, our Lord and Saviour. *Amen.*

A COMMENDATORY PRAYER FOR A SICK PERSON AT THE POINT OF DEPARTURE.

O ALMIGHTY God, with whom do live the spirits of just men made perfect, after they are delivered from their earthly prisons; We humbly commend the soul of this thy servant, our dear *brother*, into thy hands, as into the hands of a faithful Creator, and most merciful Saviour; most humbly beseeching thee, that it may be precious in thy sight. Wash it, we pray thee, in the blood of that immaculate Lamb, that was slain to take away the sins of the world; that whatsoever defilements it may have contracted in the midst of this miserable and naughty world, through the lusts of the flesh, or the wiles of Satan, being purged and done away, it may be presented pure and without spot before thee. And teach us who survive, in this and other like daily spectacles of mortality, to see how frail and uncertain our own condition is; and so to number our days, that we may seriously apply our hearts to that holy and heavenly wisdom, whilst we live here, which may in the end bring us to life everlasting, through the merits of Jesus Christ thine only Son our Lord. *Amen.*

A PRAYER FOR PERSONS TROUBLED IN MIND OR IN CONSCIENCE.

O BLESSED Lord, the Father of mercies, and the God of all comforts; We beseech thee, look down in pity and compassion upon this thy afflicted servant. Thou writest bitter things against *him*, and makest *him* to possess *his* former iniquities; thy wrath lieth hard upon *him*, and *his* soul is full of trouble: But, O merciful

God, who hast written thy holy Word for our learning, that we, through patience and comfort of thy holy Scriptures, might have hope ; give *him* a right understanding of *himself*, and of thy threats and promises ; that *he* may neither cast away *his* confidence in thee, nor place it anywhere but in thee. Give *him* strength against all *his* temptations, and heal all *his* distempers. Break not the bruised reed, nor quench the smoking flax. Shut not up thy tender mercies in displeasure ; but make *him* to hear of joy and gladness, that the bones which thou hast broken may rejoice. Deliver *him* from fear of the enemy, and lift up the light of thy countenance upon *him*, and give *him* peace, through the merits and mediation of Jesus Christ our Lord. *Amen.*

THE COMMUNION OF THE SICK.

¶ *Forasmuch as all mortal men be subject to many sudden perils, diseases, and sicknesses, and ever uncertain what time they shall depart out of this life ; therefore, to the intent they may be always in a readiness to die, whensoever it shall please Almighty God to call them, the Curates shall diligently from time to time (but especially in the time of pestilence, or other infectious sickness) exhort their Parishioners to the often receiving of the holy Communion of the Body and Blood of our Saviour Christ, when it shall be publickly administered in the Church ; that so doing, they may, in case of sudden visitation, have the less cause to be disquieted for lack of the same. But if the sick person be not able to come to the Church, and yet is desirous to receive the Communion in his house ; then he must give timely notice to the Curate, signifying also how many there are to communicate with him, (which shall be three, or two at the least,) and having a convenient place in the sick man's house, with all things necessary so prepared, that the Curate may reverently minister, he shall there celebrate the holy Communion, beginning with the Collect, Epistle, and Gospel, here following.*

THE COLLECT.

ALMIGHTY, everliving God, Maker of mankind, who dost correct those whom thou dost love, and chastise every one whom thou dost receive ; We beseech thee to have mercy upon this thy servant visited with thine hand, and to grant that *he* may take *his* sickness patiently, and recover *his* bodily health, (if it be thy gracious will ;) and whensoever *his* soul shall depart from the body, it may be without spot presented unto thee ; through Jesus Christ our Lord. *Amen.*

THE EPISTLE. Hebr. xii. 5.

MY son, despise not thou the chastening of the Lord, nor faint when thou art rebuked of him. For whom the Lord loveth he chasteneth; and scourgeth every son whom he receiveth.

THE GOSPEL. St. John v. 24.

VERILY, verily I say unto you, He that heareth my word, and believeth on him that sent me, hath everlasting life, and shall not come into condemnation; but is passed from death unto life.

¶ *After which the Priest shall proceed according to the form before prescribed for the holy Communion, beginning at these words* [Ye that do truly, &c.]

¶ *At the time of the distribution of the holy Sacrament, the Priest shall first receive the Communion himself, and after minister unto them that are appointed to communicate with the sick, and last of all to the sick person.*

¶ *But if a man, either by reason of extremity of sickness, or for want of warning in due time to the Curate, or for lack of company to receive with him, or by any other just impediment, do not receive the Sacrament of Christ's Body and Blood, the Curate shall instruct him, that if he do truly repent him of his sins, and stedfastly believe that Jesus Christ hath suffered death upon the Cross for him, and shed his Blood for his redemption, earnestly remembering the benefits he hath thereby, and giving him hearty thanks therefore, he doth eat and drink the Body and Blood of our Saviour Christ profitably to his Soul's health, although he do not receive the Sacrament with his mouth.*

¶ *When the sick person is visited, and receiveth the holy Communion all at one time, then the Priest, for more expedition, shall cut off the form of the Visitation at the Psalm* [In thee, O Lord, have I put my trust, &c.] *and go straight to the Communion.*

¶ *In the time of the Plague, Sweat, or such other like contagious times of sickness or diseases, when none of the Parish or neighbours can be gotten to communicate with the sick in their houses, for fear of the infection, upon special request of the diseased, the Minister may only communicate with him.*

THE ORDER FOR
THE BURIAL OF THE DEAD.

¶ *Here is to be noted, that the Office ensuing is not to be used for any that die unbaptized, or excommunicate, or have laid violent hands upon themselves.*

¶ *The Priest and Clerks meeting the Corpse at the entrance of the Church-yard, and going before it, either into the Church, or towards the Grave, shall say, or sing,*

I AM the re-sur-rec-tion and the life, saith the Lord: he that be-lieveth in me, tho' he were dead, yet shall he live: and

---

* The Editor has chiefly followed Dyce's adaptation of Merbecke's notes to the form of words in our present Prayer Book. But in two passages where Dyce has followed Pickering's reprint, there are evidently mistakes in the setting of the Clef: in these passages Rimbault's edition has been followed.

THE BURIAL OF THE DEAD.

St. John xi. 25, 26.

who-so-e-ver liv-eth and be-liev-eth in me shall ne-ver die.

who-so-e-ver liv-eth and be-liev-eth in . . me shall ne-ver die.

I KNOW that my Re-deem-er liv-eth, and that He shall stand at the

I KNOW that my Re-deem-er liv-eth, and that He shall stand at the

lat-ter-day up-on the earth. And tho' af-ter my skin worms de-stroy this

lat-ter-day up-on the earth. And tho' af-ter my skin worms destroy this

bo-dy, yet in my flesh shall I see God: whom I shall

bo-dy, yet in my flesh shall I . . see God: whom I shall

Job xix. 25, 26, 27.

see for my-self, and mine eyes shall be-hold, and not a-no-ther.

dim. rall.

see for my-self, and mine eyes shall be-hold, and not a-no-ther.

WE brought no-thing in-to this world, and it is cer-tain we can

pp   *cres.*   *dim.*

WE brought no-thing in-to this world, and it is cer-tain we can

pp   *cres.*   *dim.*

car-ry no-thing out. The Lord gave, and the Lord hath

p   *f*   >   >   *pp*

car-ry no-thing out. The Lord gave, and the Lord hath

p   *f*   *pp*

1 *Tim.* vi. 7; *Job* i. 21.

ta-ken a-way; bless-ed be the Name of the Lord.

cres.   *f*

ta-ken a-way; bless-ed be the Name of the Lord.

cres.   *f*

T

¶ After they are come into the Church, shall be read one or both of these Psalms following.*

Dixi, custodiam. PSALM XXXIX.

p I SAID, I will take héed | to my | ways : that Í of- | -fend not | in my | tongue.

2 I will keep my mouth as it wére | with a | bridle : whíle the un- | -godly . is | in my | sight.

3 I held my tóngue, and | spake | nothing : I kept silence, yea, even from good words * bút it was | pain and | grief to | me.

4 My heart was hot within me * and while I was thus músing the | fire | kindled : and at the lást I | spake | with my | tongue ;

5 Lord, let me know mine end * and the númber | of my | days : that I may be certifíed how | long I | have to | live.

6 Behold, thou hast made my days as it wére a | span | long : and mine age is even as nothing in respect of thee * and verily every man líving is | alto- | -gether | vanity.

7 For man walketh in a vain shadow * and disquíeteth him- | -self in | vain : he heapeth up riches, and cánnot tell | who shall | gather | them.

8 And now, Lórd, what | is my | hope : trúly my | hope is | even . in | thee.

9 Deliver me from áll | mine of- | -fences : and make me nót a re- | -buke | unto . the | foolish.

10 I became dumb, and ópened | not my | mouth : fór | it was | thy | doing.

11 Take thy plágue a- | -way | from me : I am even consumed by méans | of thy | heavy | hand.

12 When thou with rebukes dost chasten man for sin * thou makest his beauty to consume away * like as it were a móth | fretting . a | garment : évery man | therefore | is but | vanity.

13 Hear my prayer, O Lord * and with thine éars con- | sider . my | calling : hóld not thy | peace | at my | tears.

14 For I′ am a | stranger . with | thee : and a sójourner, as | all my | fathers | were.

2nd part. 15 O spare me a little * that I′ may re- | -cover . my | strength : before I go hénce, and | be no | more | seen.

---

* These Psalms, set to a Plain Song Tone, will be found on p. 63 of the Appendix.

F. f   Glory be to the Fáther, | and . to the | Son : ánd | to the |
        Holy | Ghost ;

F.   As it was in the beginning * is nów, and | ever | shall be :
        wórld without | end. | A- | -men.

Domine, refugium.   PSALM XC.

p L ÓRD, thou hast | been our | refuge : from óne gener- |
     ation | to an- | ·other.

2 Before the mountains were brought forth * or ever the
     éarth and the | world were | made : thou art God from
     everlásting, and | world with- | -out | end.

3 Thou turnest mán | to de- | -struction : again thou sayest,
     Cóme a- | -gain ye | children . of | men.

4 For a thousand years in thý sight | are but . as | yester-
     day : seeing that is pást as a | watch | in the | night.

5 As soon as thou scatterest them * they are éven | as a |
     sleep : and fáde away | suddenly | like the | grass.

6 In the morning it is gréen, and | groweth | up : but in the
     evening it is cut dówn | dried | up and | withered.

7 For we consume awáy in | thy dis- | -pleasure : and are
     afráid at thy | wrathful | indig- | -nation.

8 Thou hast sét our mis- | -deeds be- | -fore thee : and our
     secret síns in the | light | of thy | countenance.

9 For when thou art angry áll our | days are | gone : we
     bring our years to an end * as it wére a | tale | that
     is | told.

10 The days of our age are three-score years and ten * and
     though men be so strong, that they cóme to | four-score |
     years : yet is their strength then but labour and sorrow *
     so soon pásseth it a- | -way and | we are | gone.

11 But who regardeth the pówer | of thy | wrath : for even
     thereafter as a man féareth | so is | thy dis- | -pleasure.

12 O téach us to | number . our | days : that we may applý
     our | hearts | unto | wisdom.

13 Turn thee again, O Lórd | at the | last : ánd be | gracious |
     unto . thy | servants.

14 O satisfy us with thy mércy, and | that | soon : so shall we
     rejoice and be glád all the | days | of our | life.

15 Comfort us again * now after the tíme that thou hast |
     plagued | us : and for the years whereín | we have |
     suffered . ad- | -versity.

16 Shéw thy | servants . thy | work : ánd their | children |
     thy | glory.

2nd part. 17 And the glorious Majesty of the Lord our Gód | be up- |
on us : prosper thou the work of our hands upon us *
O prósper | thou our | handy- | -work.

F. f Glory be to the Fáther, | and . to the | Son : ánd | to the |
Holy | Ghost ;

F. As it was in the beginning * is nów, and | ever | shall be :
wórld without | end. | A- | -men.

¶ *Then shall follow the Lesson taken out of the fifteenth Chapter of the former Epistle of Saint Paul to the Corinthians.*

1 Cor. xv. 20.

NOW is Christ risen from the dead, and become the first-fruits of
them that slept. For since by man came death, by man came
also the resurrection of the dead. For as in Adam all die, even so
in Christ shall all be made alive. But every man in his own order :
Christ the first-fruits ; afterward they that are Christ's, at his
coming. Then cometh the end, when he shall have delivered up
the kingdom to God, even the Father ; when he shall have put
down all rule, and all authority, and power. For he must reign,
till he hath put all enemies under his feet. The last enemy that
shall be destroyed is death. For he hath put all things under his
feet. But when he saith, all things are put under him, it is manifest
that he is excepted, which did put all things under him. And when
all things shall be subdued unto him, then shall the Son also himself be subject unto him that put all things under him, that God
may be all in all. Else what shall they do which are baptized for
the dead, if the dead rise not at all ? Why are they then baptized
for the dead ? and why stand we in jeopardy every hour ? I protest
by your rejoicing, which I have in Christ Jesus our Lord, I die
daily. If after the manner of men I have fought with beasts at
Ephesus, what advantageth it me, if the dead rise not ? Let us
eat and drink, for to-morrow we die. Be not deceived : evil
communications corrupt good manners. Awake to righteousness,
and sin not ; for some have not the knowledge of God. I speak this
to your shame. But some man will say, How are the dead raised
up ? and with what body do they come ? Thou fool, that which
thou sowest is not quickened, except it die. And that which thou
sowest, thou sowest not that body that shall be, but bare grain,
it may chance of wheat, or of some other grain : But God giveth it
a body, as it hath pleased him, and to every seed his own body.
All flesh is not the same flesh ; but there is one kind of flesh of
men, another flesh of beasts, another of fishes, and another of birds.
There are also celestial bodies, and bodies terrestrial ; but the glory
of the celestial is one, and the glory of the terrestrial is another.
There is one glory of the sun, and another glory of the moon, and

another glory of the stars; for one star differeth from another star in glory. So also is the resurrection of the dead: It is sown in corruption; it is raised in incorruption: It is sown in dishonour; it is raised in glory: It is sown in weakness; it is raised in power: It is sown a natural body; it is raised a spiritual body. There is a natural body, and there is a spiritual body. And so it is written, The first man Adam was made a living soul; the last Adam was made a quickening spirit. Howbeit, that was not first which is spiritual, but that which is natural; and afterward that which is spiritual. The first man is of the earth, earthy; the second man is the Lord from heaven. As is the earthy, such are they that are earthy: and as is the heavenly, such are they also that are heavenly. And as we have borne the image of the earthy, we shall also bear the image of the heavenly. Now this I say, brethren, that flesh and blood cannot inherit the kingdom of God; neither doth corruption inherit incorruption. Behold, I shew you a mystery: We shall not all sleep, but we shall all be changed, in a moment, in the twinkling of an eye, at the last trump, (for the trumpet shall sound,) and the dead shall be raised incorruptible, and we shall be changed. For this corruptible must put on incorruption, and this mortal must put on immortality. So when this corruptible shall have put on incorruption, and this mortal shall have put on immortality; then shall be brought to pass the saying that is written, Death is swallowed up in victory. O death, where is thy sting? O grave, where is thy victory? The sting of death is sin, and the strength of sin is the law. But thanks be to God, which giveth us the victory through our Lord Jesus Christ. Therefore, my beloved brethren, be ye stedfast, unmoveable, always abounding in the work of the Lord, forasmuch as ye know that your labour is not in vain in the Lord.

¶ *When they come to the Grave, while the Corpse is made ready to be laid into the earth, the Priest shall say, or the Priest and Clerks shall sing:*

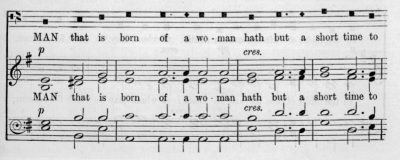

MAN that is born of a wo-man hath but a short time to

¶ *Then, while the earth shall be cast upon the body by some standing by, the Priest shall say,*

FORASMUCH as it hath pleased Almighty God of his great mercy to take unto himself the soul of our dear *brother* here departed, we therefore commit *his* body to the ground; earth to earth, ashes to ashes, dust to dust; in sure and certain hope of the Resurrection to eternal life, through our Lord Jesus Christ; who shall change our vile body, that it may be like unto his glorious body, according to the mighty working, whereby he is able to subdue all things to himself.

¶ *Then shall be said or sung,*

¶ *Then the Priest shall say,*

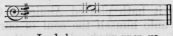

Lord, have mercy upon us.

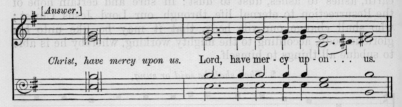

[*Answer.*]

Christ, have mercy upon us. Lord, have mer - cy up - on . . . us.

OUR Father, which art in heaven,

Hallowed be thy Name. Thy kingdom come. Thy will be done in earth, As it is in heaven. Give us this day our daily bread. And forgive us our trespasses, As we forgive them that trespass against us. And lead us not into temptation; But deliver us from evil.

A - men.

Priest.

ALMIGHTY God, with whom do live the spirits of them that depart hence in the Lord, and with whom the souls of the faithful, after they are delivered from the burden of the flesh, are in joy and felicity; We give thee hearty thanks, for that it hath pleased thee to deliver this our *brother* out of the miseries of this sinful world; beseeching thee, that it may please thee, of thy gracious goodness, shortly to accomplish the number of thine elect, and to hasten thy kingdom; that we, with all those that are departed in the true faith of thy holy Name, may have our perfect consummation and bliss, both in body and soul, in thy eternal and everlasting glory; through Jesus Christ our Lord.

A - men.

THE COLLECT.

O MERCIFUL God, the Father of our Lord Jesus Christ, who is the resurrection and the life; in whom whosoever believeth shall live, though he die; and whosoever liveth, and believeth in him, shall not die eternally; who also hath taught us (by his holy Apostle Saint Paul) not to be sorry, as men without hope, for them that sleep in him; We meekly beseech thee, O Father, to raise us from the death of sin unto the life of righteousness; that, when we shall depart this life, we may rest in him, as our hope is this our *brother* doth; and that, at the general Resurrection in the last day, we may be found acceptable in thy sight; and receive that blessing, which thy well-beloved Son shall then pronounce to all that love and fear thee, saying, Come, ye blessed children of my Father, receive the kingdom prepared for you from the beginning of the world: Grant this, we beseech thee, O merciful Father, through Jesus Christ, our Mediator and Redeemer. *Amen.*

THE grace of our Lord Jesus Christ, and the love of God, and the fellowship of the Holy Ghost, be with us all evermore. *Amen.*

THE BURIAL OF THE DEAD.

THE
THANKSGIVING OF WOMEN AFTER CHILD-BIRTH,

COMMONLY CALLED

THE CHURCHING OF WOMEN.

¶ *The Woman, at the usual time after her Delivery, shall come into the Church decently apparelled, and there shall kneel down in some convenient place, as hath been accustomed, or as the Ordinary shall direct: And then the Priest shall say unto her,*

FORASMUCH as it hath pleased Almighty God of his goodness to give you safe deliverance, and hath preserved you in the great danger of Child-birth; you shall therefore give hearty thanks unto God, and say,

¶ (*Then shall the Priest say the* cxvith *Psalm.*)

Dilexi quoniam.

mf I AM | well | pleased : that the Lord hath héard the | voice of | my | prayer ;

2 That he hath inclined his éar | unto | me : therefore will I call upon hím as | long | as I | live.

3 The snares of death cómpassed me | round a- | -bout : and the páins of | hell gat | hold up- | -on me.

4 I found trouble and heaviness * and I called upon the Náme | of the | Lord : O Lord, I beséech | thee de- | liver my | soul.

5 Gracious ís the | Lord and | righteous : yéa, our | God is | merci- | -ful.

6 The Lórd pre- | -serveth . the | simple : I was in mísery | and he | helped | me.

7 Turn again then unto thy rést | O my | soul : for the Lórd | hath re- | -warded | thee.

8 And why? thou hast delívered my | soul from | death : mine eyes from téars | and my | feet from | falling.

9 I will wálk be- | -fore the | Lord : ín the | land | of the | living.

10 I believed, and therefore will I speak * but I' was | sore | troubled : I said in my háste | All | men are | liars.

11 What reward shall I gíve | unto . the | Lord : for all the benefits that hé hath | done | unto | me ?

12 I will receive the cúp | of sal- | -vation : and cáll upon the | Name | of the | Lord.

13 I will pay my vows now in the présence of | all his | people : in the courts of the Lord's house * even in the midst of thee, O Jerúsalem. | Praise | — the | Lord.

F. ƒ Glory be to the Fáther, | and . to the | Son : ánd | to the | Holy | Ghost ;

F. As it was in the beginning * is nów, and | ever | shall be : wórld without | end. | A- | -men.

Or,

Nisi Dominus. PSALM cxxvii.

mƒ EXCEPT the Lórd | build the | house : their lábour | is but | lost that | build it.

2 Except the Lórd | keep the | city : the wátchman | waketh | but in | vain.

3 It is but lost labour that ye haste to rise up early * and so late take rest, and éat the | bread of | carefulness : for so he gíveth | his be- | -loved | sleep.

4 Lo, children and the frúit | of the | womb : are an heritage and gíft that | cometh | of the | Lord.

5 Like as the arrows in the hánd | of the | giant : even só | are the | young | children.

6 Happy is the man that hath his qúiver | full of | them : they shall not be ashamed when they spéak with their | enemies | in the | gate.

F. ƒ Glory be to the Fáther, | and . to the | Son : ánd | to the | Holy | Ghost ;

F. As it was in the beginning * is nów, and | ever | shall be : wórld without | end. | A- | -men.

¶ *Then the Priest shall say,*

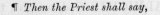

Let us pray.   Lord, have mercy upon us.

[*Answer.*]

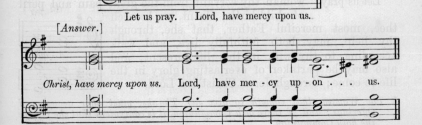

Christ, have mercy upon us.   Lord,   have mer - cy up - on . . . us.

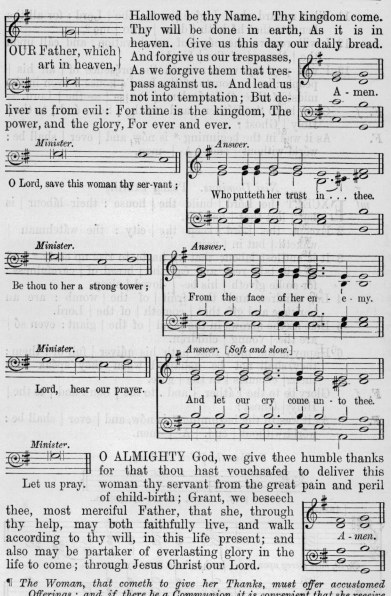

OUR Father, which art in heaven, Hallowed be thy Name. Thy kingdom come. Thy will be done in earth, As it is in heaven. Give us this day our daily bread. And forgive us our trespasses, As we forgive them that trespass against us. And lead us not into temptation; But deliver us from evil: For thine is the kingdom, The power, and the glory, For ever and ever.

A-men.

Minister.

O Lord, save this woman thy ser-vant;

Answer.

Who putteth her trust in . . . thee.

Minister.

Be thou to her a strong tower;

Answer.

From the face of her en-e-my.

Minister.

Lord, hear our prayer.

Answer. [Soft and slow.]

And let our cry come un-to thee.

Minister.

Let us pray.

O ALMIGHTY God, we give thee humble thanks for that thou hast vouchsafed to deliver this woman thy servant from the great pain and peril of child-birth; Grant, we beseech thee, most merciful Father, that she, through thy help, may both faithfully live, and walk according to thy will, in this life present; and also may be partaker of everlasting glory in the life to come; through Jesus Christ our Lord.

A-men.

¶ *The Woman, that cometh to give her Thanks, must offer accustomed Offerings; and, if there be a Communion, it is convenient that she receive the holy Communion.*

A COMMINATION,

OR DENOUNCING OF GOD'S ANGER AND JUDGEMENTS AGAINST SINNERS,

WITH CERTAIN PRAYERS, TO BE USED ON THE FIRST DAY OF LENT, AND AT OTHER TIMES, AS THE ORDINARY SHALL APPOINT.

¶ *After Morning Prayer, the Litany ended according to the accustomed manner, the Priest shall, in the Reading-Pew or Pulpit, say,*

BRETHREN, in the Primitive Church there was a godly discipline, that, at the beginning of Lent, such persons as stood convicted of notorious sin were put to open penance, and punished in this world, that their souls might be saved in the day of the Lord; and that others, admonished by their example, might be the more afraid to offend.

Instead whereof, (until the said discipline may be restored again, which is much to be wished,) it is thought good, that at this time (in the presence of you all) should be read the general sentences of God's cursing against impenitent sinners, gathered out of the seven and twentieth Chapter of Deuteronomy, and other places of Scripture; and that ye should answer to every Sentence, *Amen:* To the intent that, being admonished of the great indignation of God against sinners, ye may the rather be moved to earnest and true repentance; and may walk more warily in these dangerous days; fleeing from such vices, for which ye affirm with your own mouths the curse of God to be due.

 CURSED is the man that maketh any carved or molten image, to worship it.

¶ *And the people shall answer and say,*

A - men.

Minister.	Cursed is he that curseth his father or mother.
Answer.	*Amen.*
Minister.	Cursed is he that removeth his neighbour's land-mark.
Answer.	*Amen.*
Minister.	Cursed is he that maketh the blind to go out of his way.
Answer.	*Amen.*
Minister.	Cursed is he that perverteth the judgement of the stranger, the fatherless, and widow.
Answer.	*Amen.*
Minister.	Cursed is he that smiteth his neighbour secretly.
Answer.	*Amen.*
Minister.	Cursed is he that lieth with his neighbour's wife.
Answer.	*Amen.*
Minister.	Cursed is he that taketh reward to slay the innocent.
Answer.	*Amen.*
Minister.	Cursed is he that putteth his trust in man, and taketh man for his defence, and in his heart goeth from the Lord.
Answer.	*Amen.*
Minister.	Cursed are the unmerciful, fornicators, and adulterers, covetous persons, idolaters, slanderers, drunkards, and extortioners.
Answer.	*Amen.*

Minister.

NOW seeing that all they are accursed (as the prophet David beareth witness) who do err and go astray from the commandments of God; let us (remembering the dreadful judgement hanging over our heads, and always ready to fall upon us) return unto our Lord God, with all contrition and meekness of heart; bewailing and lamenting our sinful life, acknowledging and confessing our offences, and seeking to bring forth worthy fruits of penance. For now is the axe put unto the root of the trees, so that every tree that bringeth not forth good fruit is hewn down, and cast into the fire. It is a fearful thing to fall into the hands of the living God : he shall pour down rain upon the sinners, snares, fire and brimstone, storm and tempest; this shall be their portion to drink. For lo, the Lord is come out of his place to visit the wickedness of such as dwell upon the earth. But who may abide the day of his coming ? Who shall be able to endure when he appeareth ? His fan is in his hand, and he will purge his floor, and gather his wheat into the barn ; but he will burn the chaff with unquenchable fire. The day of the Lord cometh as a thief in the night: and when men shall say, Peace, and all things are safe, then shall sudden destruction come upon them, as sorrow cometh upon a woman travailing with child, and they shall not escape. Then shall appear the wrath of God in the day of vengeance, which obstinate sinners, through the stubbornness of their heart, have heaped unto themselves; which despised the goodness, patience, and long-sufferance of God, when he calleth them continually to repentance. Then shall they call upon me, (saith the Lord,) but I will not hear; they shall seek me early, but they shall not find me; and that, because they hated knowledge, and received not the fear of the Lord, but abhorred my counsel, and despised my correction. Then shall it be too late to knock when the door shall be shut; and too late to cry for mercy when it is the time of justice. O terrible voice of most just judgement, which shall be pronounced upon them, when it shall be said unto them, Go, ye cursed, into the fire everlasting, which is prepared for the devil and his angels. Therefore, brethren, take we heed betime, while the day of salvation lasteth; for the night cometh, when none can work. But let us, while we have the light, believe in the light, and walk as children of the light; that we be not cast into utter darkness, where is weeping and gnashing of teeth. Let us not abuse the goodness of God, who calleth us mercifully to amendment, and of his endless pity promiseth us forgiveness of that which is past, if with a perfect and true heart we return unto him. For though our sins be as red as scarlet, they shall be made white as snow; and though they be like purple, yet they shall be made white as wool. Turn ye (saith the Lord) from all your wickedness, and your sin shall not be your destruction: Cast away from you all your ungodliness that ye have done: Make you new hearts, and a new spirit: Wherefore will ye die, O ye house of Israel, seeing that I have no pleasure in the death of him that dieth, saith the Lord God? Turn ye then, and ye shall live. Although we have sinned, yet have we an Advocate with the Father, Jesus Christ the righteous; and he is the propitiation for our sins. For he was wounded for our offences, and smitten for our wickedness. Let us therefore return unto him, who is the merciful receiver of all true penitent sinners; assuring ourselves that he is ready to receive us, and most willing to pardon us, if we come unto him with faithful repentance: if we submit ourselves unto him, and from henceforth walk in his ways; if we will take his easy yoke, and light burden upon us, to follow him in lowliness, patience, and charity, and be ordered by the governance of his Holy Spirit; seeking always his glory, and serving him duly in our vocation with thanksgiving: This if we do, Christ will deliver us from the curse of the law, and from the extreme malediction which shall light upon them that shall be set on the left hand; and he will set us on his right hand, and give us the gracious benediction of his Father, commanding us to take possession of his glorious kingdom: Unto which he vouchsafe to bring us all, for his infinite mercy. Amen.

¶ *Then shall they all kneel upon their knees, and the Priest and Clerks kneeling (in the place where they are accustomed to say the Litany) shall say this Psalm.*

* *Miserere mei, Deus.* PSALM li.

p HAVE mercy upon me, O God * áfter thy | great | goodness : according to the multitude of thy mercies, dó a- | -way | mine of- | -fences.

2 Wash me thróughly | from my | wickedness : ánd | cleanse me | from my | sin.

3 For Í ac- | -knowledge . my | faults : ánd my | sin is | ever . be- | -fore me.

4 Against thee only have I sinned * and done this évil | in thy | sight : that thou mightest be justified in thy sáying, and | clear when | thou art | judged.

5 Behóld, I was | shapen . in | wickedness : and in sín hath my | mother . con- | -ceived | me.

6 But lo, thou requirest trúth in the | inward | parts : and shalt make me to únder- | -stand | wisdom | secretly.

7 Thou shalt purge me with hyssop * ánd I | shall be | clean : thou shalt wash me * ánd I | shall be | whiter . than | snow.

8 Thou shalt make me héar of | joy and | gladness : that the bones which thóu hast | broken | may re- | -joice.

9 Turn thy face awáy | from my | sins : and pút out | all | my mis- | -deeds.

10 Make me a cléan | heart O | God : ánd re- | -new a . right | spirit . with- | -in me.

11 Cast me not awáy | from thy | presence : and táke not thy | holy | Spirit | from me.

12 O give me the cómfort of thy | help a- | -gain : and stáblish me | with thy | free | Spirit.

2nd part 13 Then shall I teach thy wáys | unto . the | wicked : and sinners shall bé con- | -verted | unto | thee.

14 Deliver me from blood-guiltiness, O God * thou that art the Gód | of my | health : and my tóngue shall | sing | of thy | righteousness.

---

* This Psalm, adapted to the proper Tone, will be found on p. 68 of the Appendix.

15 Thou shalt ópen my | lips O | Lord : ánd my | mouth
shall | shew thy | praise.

16 For thou desirest no sacrifice * élse would I | give it |
thee : but thou delíghtest | not in | burnt- | -offerings.

17 The sacrifice of Gód is a | troubled | spirit : a broken and
contrite heart, O Gód, | shalt thou | not de- | -spise.

18 O be favourable and grácious | unto | Sion : búild thou
the | walls | of Je- | -rusalem.

19 Then shalt thou be pleased with the sacrifice of righteous-
ness * with the burnt-ófferings | and ob- | -lations :
then shall they óffer young | bullocks . up- | -on thine |
altar.

F. f   Glory be to the Fáther, | and . to the | Son : ánd | to the |
Holy | Ghost;

       Answer.

F.   As it was in the beginning * is nów, and | ever | shall be :
wórld without | end. | A- | -men.

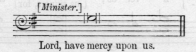

Lord, have mercy upon us.

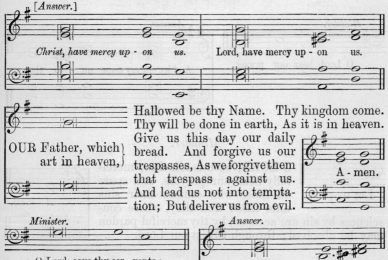

[Answer.]

Christ, have mercy up - on us.   Lord, have mercy up - on us.

OUR Father, which art in heaven,

Hallowed be thy Name. Thy kingdom come. Thy will be done in earth, As it is in heaven. Give us this day our daily bread. And forgive us our trespasses, As we forgive them that trespass against us. And lead us not into temptation; But deliver us from evil.

A - men.

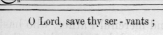

O Lord, save thy ser - vants ;

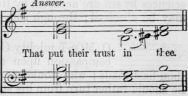

Minister.   *Answer.*

That their trust in thee.

u 2

Minister.

Send unto them help from a - bove,

Answer.

And evermore mightily de- fend them.

Minister.

Help us, O God our Sa - viour.

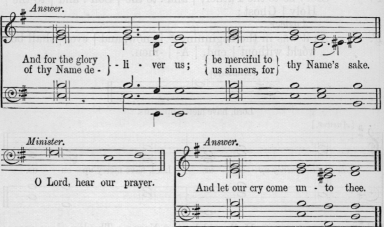

Answer.

And for the glory of thy Name de - } - li - ver us; { be merciful to us sinners, for } thy Name's sake.

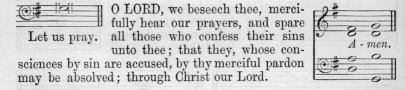

Minister.

O Lord, hear our prayer.

Answer.

And let our cry come un - to thee.

Minister.

Let us pray. O LORD, we beseech thee, mercifully hear our prayers, and spare all those who confess their sins unto thee; that they, whose consciences by sin are accused, by thy merciful pardon may be absolved; through Christ our Lord.

A - men.

O MOST mighty God, and merciful Father, who hast compassion upon all men, and hatest nothing that thou hast made; who wouldest not the death of a sinner, but that he should rather turn from his sin, and be saved; Mercifully forgive us our trespasses; receive and comfort us, who are grieved and wearied with the burden of our sins. Thy property is always to have mercy; to thee only it appertaineth to forgive sins. Spare us therefore, good Lord, spare thy people, whom thou hast redeemed; enter not into judgement with thy servants, who are vile earth, and miserable sinners; but so turn thine anger from us, who meekly acknowledge our vileness, and truly repent us of our faults, and so make haste to help us in this world, that we may ever live with thee in the world to come; through Jesus Christ our Lord.

A - men.

¶ *Then shall the people say this that followeth, after the Minister.* *

TURN thou us, }
O good Lord, }

and so shall we be turned. Be favourable, O Lord, Be favourable to thy people, Who turn to thee in weeping, fasting, and praying. For thou art a merciful God, Full of compassion, Long-suffering, and of great pity. Thou sparest when we deserve punishment, And in thy wrath thinkest upon mercy. Spare thy people, good Lord, spare them, And let not thine heritage be brought to confusion. Hear us, O Lord, for thy mercy is great, And after the multitude of thy mercies look upon us; Through the merits and mediation of thy blessed Son, Jesus Christ our Lord.

A - men.

¶ *Then the Minister alone shall say,*

THE Lord bless us, and keep us; the Lord lift up the light of his countenance upon us, and give us peace, now and for evermore.

A - men.

---

* A harmonized and inflected Form of this will be found on p. 77 of the Appendix.

us our trespasses: relieve and comfort us, who are grieved and wearied with the burden of our sins. Thy property is always to have mercy; to thee only it appertaineth to forgive sins. Spare us therefore, good Lord, spare thy people, whom thou hast redeemed; enter not into judgment with thy servants, who are vile earth, and miserable sinners; but so turn thine anger from us, who meekly acknowledge our vileness, and truly repent us of our faults, and so make haste to help us in this world, that we may ever live with thee in the world to come; through Jesus Christ our Lord.

¶ *Then shall the people say this that followeth, after the Minister.**

TURN thou us, O good Lord. and so shall we be turned. Be favourable, O Lord, Be favourable to thy people, Who turn to thee in weeping, fasting, and praying. For thou are a merciful God, Full of compassion, Long-suffering, and of great pity. Thou sparest when we deserve punishment, And in thy wrath thinkest upon mercy. Spare thy people, good Lord, spare them, And let not thine heritage be brought to confusion. Hear us, O Lord, for thy mercy is great, And after the multitude of thy mercies look upon us. Through the merits and meditation of thy blessed Son, Jesus Christ our Lord.

¶ *Then the Minister alone shall say.*

 THE Lord bless us, and keep us; the Lord lift up the light of his countenance upon us, and give us peace, now and for evermore.

* A harmonized and inflected Form of this will be found on p. 77 of the Appendix.

THE PSALMS OF DAVID.

THE PSALMS OF DAVID.

       MORNING PRAYER.

PSALM i.—*Beatus vir, qui non abiit.*

F. mf   **B**LESSED is the man that hath not walked in the counsel of the ungodly * nor stóod in the | way of | sinners : and hath not sát in the | seat | of the | scornful.

F.   2 But his delight is in the láw | of the | Lord : and in his law will he exercíse him- | -self | day and | night.

3 And he shall be like a tree planted bý the | water | side : that will bring fórth his | fruit in | due | season.

4 His léaf also | shall not | wither : and look, whatsoéver he | doeth | it shall | prosper.

5 As for the ungodly, it is nót | so with | them : but they are like the chaff * which the wind scattereth awáy from the | face | of the | earth.

6 Therefore the ungodly shall not be able to stánd | in the | judgement : neither the sinners in the cóngre- | gation | of the | righteous.

2nd part.   7 But the Lord knoweth the wáy | of the | righteous : and the wáy of the un- | -godly | shall | perish.

PSALM ii.—*Quare fremuerunt gentes ?*

f   **W**HY do the heathen so fúriously | rage to- | -gether : and why do the péople im- | -agine . a | vain | thing ?

2 The kings of the earth stand up * and the rúlers take | counsel . to- | -gether : against the Lórd, and a- | gainst | his A- | -nointed.

3 Let us bréak their | bonds a- | -sunder : and cást a- | -way their | .cords | from us.

4 He that dwelleth in héaven shall | laugh them . to | scorn : the Lórd shall | have them | in de- | -rision.

5 Then shall he speak unto thém | in his | wrath : and véx them | in his | sore dis- | -pleasure.

6 Yét have I | set my | King : upón my | holy | hill of | Sion.

7 I will preach the law * whereof the Lord hath sáid |
unto | me : Thou art my Son * this dáy have | I be- |
gotten | thee.

8 Desire of me * and I shall give thee the héathen for |
thine in- | -heritance : and the utmost párts of the |
earth for | thy pos- | -session.

9 Thou shalt brúise them with a | rod of | iron : and break
them in piéces | like a | potter's | vessel.

10 Be wise now thérefore | O ye | kings : be learned, yé
that are | judges | of the | earth.

11 Sérve the | Lord in | fear : and rejóice | unto | him with |
reverence.

12 Kiss the Son, lest he be angry, and so ye pérish from
the | right | way : if his wrath be kindled (yea, but a
little) * blessed are all théy that | put their | trust
in | him.

Psalm iii.—*Domine, quid multiplicati!*

mp   LORD, how are they incréased that | trouble | me : mány
are | they that | rise a- | -gainst me.

2 Many one there be that sáy | of my | soul : There is no
hélp | for him | in his | God.

3 But thou, O Lórd, art | my de- | -fender : thou art my
worship * and the lífter | up of | my | head.

4 I did call upon the Lórd | with my | voice : and he héard
me | out of . his | holy | hill.

5 I laid me down and slept * and róse | up a- | -gain : fór
the | Lord sus- | -tained | me.

6 I will not be afraid for ten thóusands | of the | people :
that have set themsélves a- | -gainst me | round a- | -bout.

f   7 Up, Lord, and hélp me | O my | God : for thou smitest
all mine enemies upon the cheek-bone * thou hast
bróken the | teeth of | the un- | -godly.

8 Salvation belóngeth | unto . the | Lord : and thy bléssing |
is up- | -on thy | people.

Psalm iv.—*Cum invocarem.*

mf   HEAR me when I call, O Gód | of my | righteousness :
thou hast set me at liberty when I was in trouble *
have mercy upon mé, and | hearken | unto . my | prayer.

2 O ye sons of men * how lóng will ye blas- | -pheme
mine | honour : and have such pleasure in vánity,
and | seek | after | leasing ?

3 Know this also * that the Lord hath chosen to himself the mán | that is | godly : when I cáll upon the | Lord | he will | hear me.

4 Stánd in | awe and | sin not : commune with your own heart * and ín your | chamber | and be | still.

5 Offer the sácri- | -fice of | righteousness : and pút your | trust | in the | Lord.

6 Thére be | many . that | say : Whó will | shew us | any | good?

7 Lórd | lift thou | up : the líght of thy | counte- | -nance up- | -on us.

8 Thou hast put gládness | in my | heart : since the time that their córn and | wine and | oil in- | -creased.

9 I will lay me down in péace, and | take my | rest : for it is thou, Lord, ónly that | makest . me | dwell in | safety.

Psalm v.—*Verba mea auribus.*

mf PONDER my | words O | Lord : cón- | -sider . my | medi- | tation.

2 O hearken thou unto the voice of my calling * my Kíng | and my | God : for unto thée | will I | make my | prayer.

3 My voice shalt thou héar be- | -times O | Lord : early in the morning will I direct my prayer unto thée | and will | look | up.

4 For thou art the God that hást no | pleasure . in | wickedness : neither shall ány | evil | dwell with | thee.

5 Such as be foolish shall not stánd | in thy | sight : for thou hátest all | them that | work | vanity.

6 Thou shalt destróy them that | speak | leasing : the Lord will abhor both the blóodthirsty | and de- | -ceitful | man.

7 But as for me, I will come into thine house * even upon the múltitude | of thy | mercy : and in thy fear will I wórship | toward . thy | holy | temple.

8 Lead me, O Lord, in thy righteousness * becáuse | of mine | enemies : make thy wáy | plain be- | -fore my | face.

9 For there is no fáithfulness | in his | mouth : their ínward | parts are | very | wickedness.

10 Their thróat is an | open | sepulchre : théy | flatter | with their | tongue.

11 Destroy thou them, O God * let them perish through their ówn im- | -agin- | -ations : cast them out in the multitude of their ungodliness * fór they | have re- | belled . a- | -gainst thee.

f 12 And let all them that put their trúst in | thee re- | -joice : they shall ever be giving of thanks because thou defendest them * they that love thy Náme | shall be | joyful . in | thee.

2nd part. 13 For thou, Lord, wilt give thy bléssing | unto . the | righteous : and with thy favourable kindness wilt thóu de- | -fend him | as . with a | shield.

Day 1.   EVENING PRAYER.

PSALM vi.—*Domine, ne in furore.*

F.mp O LORD, rebuke me nót in thine | indig- | -nation : neither chásten | me in | thy dis- | -pleasure.

F. 2 Have mercy upon me, O Lórd, for | I am | weak : O Lord, héal me | for my | bones are | vexed.

3 My soul álso is | sore | troubled : but, Lord, how lóng | wilt thou | punish | me ?

4 Turn thee, O Lórd, and de- | -liver . my | soul : O sáve me | for thy | mercy's | sake.

5 For in death nó man re- | -membereth | thee . : and who will gíve thee | thanks | in the | pit ?

6 I am weary of my groaning * every night wásh | I my | bed : and wáter my | couch | with my | tears.

7 My beauty is góne for | very | trouble : and worn awáy be- | -cause of | all mine | enemies.

8 Away from me, all yé that | work | vanity : for the Lord hath héard the | voice | of my | weeping.

9 The Lord hath héard | my pe- | -tition : the Lórd | will re- | -ceive my | prayer.

10 All mine enemies shall be confoúnded and | sore | vexed : they shall be turned báck, and | put to | shame | suddenly.

PSALM vii.—*Domine, Deus meus.*

mf O LORD my God, in thée have I | put my | trust : save me from all them that pérsecute me | and de- | -liver | me ;

2 Lest he devour my soul like a líon, and | tear it . in | pieces : whíle | there is | none to | help.

3 O Lord my God * if I have dóne | any . such | thing : or if there bé any | wickedness | in my | hands ;

4 If I have rewarded evil unto hím that dealt | friendly . with | me : yea, I have delivered him that withóut any | cause | is mine | enemy ;

5 Then let mine enemy pérsecute my | soul and | take me : yea, let him tread my life down upon the earth * and láy mine | honour | in the | dust.

6 Stand up, O Lord, in thy wrath, and lift up thyself * because of the indignátion | of mine | enemies : arise up for me in the júdgement | that thou | hast com- | manded.

7 And so shall the congregation of the péople | come a- | bout thee : for their sakes therefore líft | up thy- | -self a- | -gain.

8 The Lord shall judge the people * give séntence with | me O | Lord : according to my righteousness * and according to the ínnocency | that is | in | me.

9 O let the wickedness of the ungódly | come . to an | end : bút | guide | thou the | just.

10 Fór the | righteous | God : tríeth the | very | hearts and | reins.

f 11 My hélp | cometh . of | God : who preserveth thém | that are | true of | heart.

12 God is a righteous Júdge | strong and | patient : and Gód is pro- | -voked | every | day.

13 If a man will not túrn, he will | whet his | sword : he hath bént his | bow and | made it | ready.

14 He hath prepared for him the ínstru- | -ments of | death : he ordaineth his árrows a- | -gainst the | perse- | cutors.

15 Behold, he trávail- | -eth with | mischief : he hath conceived sórrow, and | brought | forth un- | -godli- ness.

16 He hath graven and dígged | up a | pit : and is fallen himself into the destrúction | that he | made for | other.

17 For his travail shall come upón his | own | head : and his wickedness shall fáll | on his | own | pate.

18 I will give thanks unto the Lord accórding | to his | right- eousness : and I will praise the Náme | of the | Lord most | High.

Psalm viii.—*Domine, Dominus noster.*

f   O LORD our Governour * how excellent is thy Náme in | all the | world : thou that hast sét thy | glory . a- | -bove the | heavens.

2 Out of the mouth of very babes and sucklings hast thou ordained strength * becáuse | of thine | enemies : that thou mightest stíll the | enemy | and . the a- | -venger.

3 For I will consider thy heavens * even the wórks | of thy | fingers : the moon and the stárs | which thou | hast or- | -dained.

4 What is man, that thóu art | mindful . of | him : and the són of man | that thou | visitest | him?

5 Thou madest him lówer | than the | angels : to crówn | him with | glory . and | worship.

6 Thou makest him to have dominion of the wórks | of thy | hands : and thou hast put all things ín sub- | jection | under . his | feet;

7 All | sheep and | oxen : yéa, and the | beasts | of the | field;

8 The fowls of the air, and the físhes | of the | sea : and whatsoever walketh throúgh the | paths | of the | seas.

2nd part.   9 Ó | Lord our | Governour : how excellent ís thy | Name in | all the | world!

Day 2.   MORNING PRAYER.

Psalm ix.—*Confitebor tibi.*

F. mf   I WILL give thanks unto thee, O Lord, wíth my | whole | heart : I will spéak of | all thy | marvellous | works.

F.   2 I will be glád and re- | -joice in | thee : yea, my songs will I máke of thy | Name O | thou most | Highest.

3 While mine énemies are | driven | back : they shall fáll and | perish | at thy | presence.

4 For thou hast maintained my ríght | and my | cause : thou art sét in the | throne that | judgest | right.

5 Thou hast rebuked the heathen * and destróyed | the un- | -godly : thou hast put oút their | name for | ever . and | ever.

6 O thou enemy, destructions are cóme to a per- | -petual | end : even as the cities which thou hast destroyed * théir me- | -morial . is | perished | with them.

7 But the Lórd shall en- | -dure for | ever : he hath álso
   pre- | -pared . his | seat for | judgement.

8 For he shall júdge the | world in | righteousness : and
   minister trúe | judgement | unto . the | people.

9 The Lord also will be a defénce | for . the op- | -pressed :
   even a réfuge in | due | time of | trouble.

10 And they that know thy Name will pút their | trust in |
    thee : for thou, Lord, hast néver | failed | them that |
    seek thee.

11 O praise the Lórd which | dwelleth . in | Sion : shéw
    the | people | of his | doings.

12 For when he maketh inquisition for blood, hé re- |
    membereth | them : and forgetteth nót the com- |
    plaint | of the | poor.

13 Have mercy upon me, O Lord * consider the trouble
    which I súffer of | them that | hate me : thou that
    liftest me úp | from the | gates of | death.

14 That I may shew all thy praises within the pórts of the |
    daughter . of | Sion : I' will re- | -joice in | thy sal- |
    vation.

15 The heathen are sunk down in the pít | that they |
    made : in the same net which they hid prívily | is
    their | foot | taken.

16 The Lord is knówn to | execute | judgement : the ungodly
    is trapped in the wórk | of his | own | hands.

17 The wicked shall be túrned | into | hell : and all the
    péople | that for- | -get | God.

18 For the poor shall not álway | be for- | -gotten : the
    patient abiding of the méek | shall not | perish . for | ever.

19 Up, Lord, and let not mán have the | upper | hand : let
    the héathen be | judged | in thy | sight.

20 Pút them in | fear O | Lord : that the heathen may knów
    them- | -selves to | be but | men.

Psalm x.—*Ut quid, Domine ?*

mp WHY standest thou so fár | off O | Lord : and hidest
       thy fáce in the | needful | time of | trouble ?

2 The ungodly for his own lust doth pérse- | -cute the |
   poor : let them be taken in the crafty wíliness | that
   they | have im- | -agined.

3 For the ungodly hath made boast of his ówn | heart's
   de- | -sire : and speaketh good of the cóvetous | whom |
   God ab- | -horreth.

4 The ungodly is so proud, that he cáreth | not for | God : neíther is | God in | all his | thoughts.

5 His wáys are | alway | grievous : thy judgements are far above out of his sight * and thérefore de- | -fieth . he | all his | enemies.

6 For he hath said in his heart * Tush, I shall néver be | cast | down : there shall no hárm | happen | unto | me.

7 His mouth is full of cúrsing, de- | -ceit and | fraud : under his tóngue is un- | -godli- | -ness and | vanity.

8 He sitteth lurking in the thievish córners | of the | streets : and privily in his lurking dens doth he murder the innocent * his éyes are | set a- | -gainst the | poor.

9 For he lieth waiting secretly * even as a lion lúrketh he | in his | den : thát | he may | ravish . the | poor.

10 Hé doth | ravish . the | poor : whén he | getteth . him | into . his | net.

11 He falleth dówn, and | humbleth . him- | -self : that the congregation of the poor may fáll into the | hands | of his | captains.

12 He hath said in his heart * Tush, Gód | hath for- | gotten : he hideth away his fáce, and | he will | never | see it.

13 Arise, O Lord God * and líft up | thine | hand : fór- | get | not the | poor.

14 Wherefore should the wícked blas- | -pheme | God : while he doth say in his heart * Túsh | thou God | carest . not | for it.

15 Súrely | thou hast | seen it : for thou behóldest un- | godli- | -ness and | wrong.

16 That thou mayest táke the matter | into . thine | hand : the poor committeth himself unto thee * for thóu art the | helper | of the | friendless.

17 Break thou the power of the ungódly | and ma- | licious : take away his ungódliness, and | thou shalt | find | none.

18 The Lord is Kíng for | ever . and | ever : and the héathen are | perished | out . of the | land.

19 Lord, thou hast heard the desíre | of the | poor : thou preparest their heart * and thine éar | hearkeneth | there- | -to ;

20 To help the fatherless and póor | unto . their | right : that the man of the éarth be no | more ex- | -alted . a- | gainst them.

Psalm xi.—*In Domino confido.*

mf IN the Lórd put | I my | trust : how say ye then to my
soul * that she should flée as a | bird | unto . the |
hill ?

2 For lo, the ungodly bend their bow * and make ready
their árrows with- | -in the | quiver : that they
may privily shoot at thém | which are | true of |
heart.

3 For the foundations wíll be | cast | down : and whát |
hath the | righteous | done ?

4 The Lord is ín his | holy | temple : the Lórd's | seat | is
in | heaven.

5 His éyes con- | -sider . the | poor : and his éyelids | try
the | children . of | men.

6 The Lórd al- | -loweth . the | righteous : but the un-
godly, and him that delighteth in wíckedness | doth
his | soul ab- | -hor.

7 Upon the ungodly he shall rain snares * fire and brím-
stone | storm and | tempest : thís shall | be their |
portion . to | drink.

8 For the righteous Lórd | loveth | righteousness : his
countenance will behóld the | thing | that is | just.

Day 2.   EVENING PRAYER.

Psalm xii.—*Salvum me fac.*

F. mf HELP me, Lord * for there is not óne | godly . man |
left : for the faithful are minished fróm a- | -mong
the | children . of | men.

F.   2 They talk of vanity évery one | with his | neighbour : they
do but flatter with their lips * and disสémble | in
their | double | heart.

3 The Lord shall root out áll de- | -ceitful | lips : and the
tóngue that | speaketh | proud | things ;

4 Which have said * With our tóngue will | we pre- | -vail :
we are they that ought to speak, whó is | lord | over | us?

5 Now for the comfortless troubles' sáke | of the | needy :
and because of the déep | sighing | of the | poor,

6 I will úp | saith the | Lord : and will help every one from
him that swelleth agáinst him | and will | set him . at |
rest.

7 The words of the Lórd are | pure | words : even as the silver * which from the earth is tried, and púrified | seven . times | in the | fire.

8 Thou shalt kéep | them O | Lord : thou shalt preserve him from thís | gener- | -ation . for | ever.

2nd part. 9 The ungodly wálk on | every | side : when they are exalted, the chíldren of | men are | put . to re- | buke.

PSALM xiii.—*Usque quo, Domine?*

mp HOW long wilt thou forgét me, O | Lord for | ever : how lóng wilt thou | hide thy | face | from me?

2 How long shall I seek counsel in my soul * and be so véxed | in my | heart : how long shall mine énemies | triumph | over | me?

3 Consider, and héar me, O | Lord my | God : lighten mine éyes, that I | sleep | not in | death.

4 Lest mine enemy say * I' have pre- | -vailed . a- | -gainst him : for if I be cast down * they that tróuble me | will re- | -joice | at it.

f 5 But my trúst is | in thy | mercy : and my heárt is | joyful . in | thy sal- | -vation.

6 I will sing of the Lord * because he hath déalt so | lovingly | with me : yea, I will praise the Náme | of the | Lord most | Highest.

PSALM xiv.—*Dixit insipiens.*

mf THE fool hath sáid | in his | heart : Thére | is | no | God.

2 They are corrupt, and become abóminable | in their | doings : there is none that dóeth | good | no not | one.

3 The Lord looked down from heaven upón the | children . of | men : to see if there were any that would under-stánd, and | seek | after | God.

4 But they are all gone out of the way * they are altogéther be- | -come a- | -bominable : there is none that dóeth | good | no not | one.

5 Their throat is an open sepulchre * with their tóngues have | they de- | -ceived : the póison of | asps is | under . their | lips.

6 Their mouth is fúll of | cursing . and | bitterness : their féet are | swift to | shed | blood.

Day 3.

2nd part.   7 Destruction and unhappiness is in their ways * and the way of péace have | they not | known : there is no féar of | God be- | -fore their | eyes.

8 Have they no knowledge, that they are áll such | workers . of | mischief : eating up my people as it were bréad, and | call . not up- | -on the | Lord?

9 There were they brought in great fear * éven where | no fear | was : for God is in the géner- | -ation | of the | righteous.

10 As for you * ye have made a mock at the counsel | of the | poor : because he pútteth his | trust | in the | Lord.

11 Who shall give salvation unto Israel out of Sion? * When the Lord turneth the captívity | of his | people : then shall Jacob rejóice, and | Israel | shall be | glad.

Day 3.   MORNING PRAYER.

Psalm xv.—*Domine, quis habitabit?*

mf LORD, who shall dwéll in thy | taber- | -nacle : or who shall rést up- | -on thy | holy | hill?

2 Even he that léadeth an | uncorrupt | life : and doeth the thing which is right * and spéaketh the | truth | from his | heart.

3 He that hath used no deceit in his tongue * nor done évil | to his | neighbour : ánd | hath not | slandered . his | neighbour.

4 He that setteth not by himself * but is lówly in his | own | eyes : and maketh múch of | them that | fear the | Lord.

5 He that sweareth unto his neighbour * and dísap- | pointeth . him | not : thóugh it | were . to his | own | hindrance.

6 He that hath not given his móney up- | -on | usury : nor táken re- | -ward a- | -gainst the | innocent.

2nd part.   7 Whóso | doeth . these | things : sháll | ne- | -ver | fall.

Psalm xvi.—*Conserva me, Domine.*

mf PRESÉRVE | me O | God : for in thée | have I | put my | trust.

2 O my soul, thou hast sáid | unto . the | Lord : Thou art my God * my góods are | nothing | unto | thee.

3 All my delight is upon the sáints that are | in the | earth : ánd upon | such as . ex- | -cel in | virtue.

4 But they that run áfter an- | -other god : sháll | have | great | trouble.

5 Their drink-offerings of blóod will | I not | offer : neither make méntion of their | names with- | -in my | lips.

6 The Lord himself is the portion of mine inhéritance and | of my | cup : thóu | shalt main- | -tain my | lot.

7 The lot is fallen unto mé in a | fair | ground : yéa, I | have a | goodly | heritage.

8 I will thank the Lórd for | giving . me | warning : my reins also chásten me | in the | night- | -season.

9 I have set Gód | always . be- | -fore me : for he is on my right hánd | therefore . I | shall not | fall.

10 Wherefore my heart was glád, and my | glory . re- | joiced : my flésh | also . shall | rest in | hope.

11 For why * thou shalt not léave my | soul in | hell : neither shalt thou suffer thy Hóly | One to | see cor- | -ruption.

12 Thou shalt shew me the path of life * in thy presence ís the | fulness . of | joy : and at thy right hánd there is | pleasure . for | ever- | -more.

Psalm xvii.—*Exaudi, Domine.*

mp   HEAR the right, O Lord * consíder | my com- | -plaint : and hearken unto my prayer * that góeth not | out of | feigned | lips.

2 Let my sentence come fórth | from thy | presence : and let thine eyes look upón the | thing | that is | equal.

3 Thou hast proved and visited mine heart in the night-season * thou hast tried me, and shalt fínd no | wickedness | in me :: for I am utterly purposed thát my | mouth shall | not of- | -fend.

4 Because of men's works that are done against the wórds | of thy | lips : I have kept me fróm the | ways of | the de- | -stroyer.

5 O hold thou up my góings | in thy | paths : thát my | footsteps | slip | not.

6 I have called upon thee, O Gód, for | thou shalt | hear me : incline thine ear to mé, and | hearken | unto . my | words.

mf 7 Shew thy marvellous loving-kindness * thou that art the Saviour of them which pút their | trust in | thee : from súch as re- | -sist thy | right | hand.

8 Keep me as the ápple | of an | eye : hide me únder the | shadow | of thy | wings,

9 From the ungódly that | trouble | me : mine enemies compass me round abóut to | take a- | -way my | soul.

10 They are enclósed in their | own | fat : and their móuth | speaketh | proud | things.

11 They lie waiting in our wáy on | every | side : turning their éyes | down | to the | ground ;

12 Like as a lion that is gréedy | of his | prey : and as it were a lion's whélp | lurking . in | secret | places.

13 Up, Lord, disappóint him, and | cast him | down : deliver my soul from the ungódly, which | is a | sword of | thine ;

14 From the men of thy hand, O Lord * from the men I say, and fróm the | evil | world : which have their portion in this life * whose bellies thou fíllest | with thy | hid | treasure.

15 They have chíldren at | their de- | -sire : and leave the rést of their | substance | for their | babes.

16 But as for me * I will behóld thy | presence . in | righteousness : and when I awake up after thy likeness * I' shall be | satis- | -fied | with it.

Day 3. **EVENING PRAYER.**

Psalm xviii.—*Diligam te, Domine.*

F. f I WILL love thee, O Lord my strength * the Lord is my stony róck and | my de- | -fence : my Saviour, my God, and my might, in whom I will trust * my buckler, the horn also of mý sal- | -vation | and my | refuge.

F. 2 I will call upon the Lord, which is wórthy | to be | praised : so shall I' be | safe | from mine | enemies.

p 3 The sorrows of déath | compassed | me : and the overflowings of ungódliness | made | me a- | -fraid.

4 The pains of héll | came a- | -bout me : the snáres of | death | over- | -took me.

5 In my trouble I will cáll up- | -on the | Lord : ánd com- | plain | unto . my | God.

6 So shall he hear my voice oút of his | holy | temple : and my complaint shall come before him * it shall énter | even | into . his | ears.

mf 7 The éarth | trembled . and | quaked : the very foundations
also of the hills shook * and were remóved, be- | -cause |
he was | wroth.

8 There went a smóke out | in his | presence : and a
consuming fire out of his mouth * só that | coals
were | kindled | at it.

9 He bowed the heavens álso, and | came | down : ánd it
was | dark | under . his | feet.

10 He rode upon the chérubims | and did | fly : he came
flying upón the | wings | of the | wind.

11 He made dárkness his | secret | place : his pavilion
round about him with dark water * and thíck | clouds
to | cover | him.

12 At the brightness of his présence his | clouds re- |
moved : háil- | -stones and | coals of | fire.

f 13 The Lord also thundered out of heaven * and the
Híghest | gave his | thunder : háil- | -stones and |
coals of | fire.

14 He sent out his árrows, and | scattered | them : he
cast forth líghtnings | and des- | -troyed | them.

2nd part. 15 The springs of waters were seen, and the foundations of
the round world were discovered * át thy | chiding .
O | Lord : at the blásting of the | breath of | thy dis- |
pleasure.

mf 16 He shall send dówn from on | high to | fetch me : and
shall táke me | out of | many | waters.

17 He shall deliver me from my strongest enemy * ánd
from | them which | hate me : fór they | are too |
mighty . for | me.

18 They prevented me in the dáy | of my | trouble : bút
the | Lord was | my up- | -holder.

19 He brought me forth also ínto a | place of | liberty : he
brought me forth * even because he hád a | favour |
unto | me.

20 The Lord shall reward me áfter my | righteous | dealing :
according to the cleanness of my hánds | shall he |
recompense | me.

21 Because I have kept the wáys | of the | Lord : and
have not forsaken my Gód | as the | wicked |
doth.

22 For I have an éye unto | all his | laws : and will not cást
out | his com- | -mandments | from me.

23 I was also úncor- | -rupt be- | -fore him : ánd es- |
chewed . mine | own | wickedness.

24 Therefore shall the Lord reward me áfter my | righteous | dealing : and according unto the cléanness of my | hands | in his | eyesight.

25 With the hóly thou | shalt be | holy : and with a pérfect man | thou | shalt be | perfect.

26 With the cléan thou | shalt be | clean : and with the fróward | thou shalt | learn | frowardness.

27 For thou shalt save the péople that are | in ad- | versity : and shalt bring dówn the | high looks | of the | proud.

28 Thou álso shalt | light my | candle : the Lord my God shall máke my | darkness | to be | light.

29 For in thee I shall discómfit an | host of | men : and with the help of my Gód I shall | leap | over . the | wall.

f 30 The way of God is an únde- | -filed | way : the word of the Lord also is tried in the fire * he is the defender of all thém that | put their | trust in | him.

31 For who is Gód | but the | Lord : or whó hath any | strength ex- | -cept our | God ?

32 It is God that gírdeth me with | strength of | war : ánd | maketh . my | way | perfect.

33 He máketh my | feet like | harts' feet : ánd | setteth . me | up on | high.

34 He téacheth mine | hands to | fight : and mine arms shall bréak | even a | bow of | steel.

35 Thou hast given me the défence of | thy sal- | -vation : thy right hand also shall hold me up * and thy lóving cor- | -rection . shall | make me | great.

36 Thou shalt make room enough únder me | for to | go : thát my | footsteps | shall not | slide.

37 I will follow upon mine énemies and | over- | -take them : neither will I turn agáin till I | have des- | -troyed | them.

38 I will smite them * that they shall nót be | able . to | stand : bút | fall | under . my | feet.

39 Thou hast girded me with stréngth | unto . the | battle : thou shalt throw dówn mine | enemies | under | me.

40 Thou hast made mine enemies also to túrn their | backs up- | -on me : and I′ shall de- | -stroy | them that | hate me.

41 They shall cry * but thére shall be | none to | help them : yea, even unto the Lord shall they crý | but he | shall not | hear them.

42 I will beat them as small as the dúst be- | -fore the | wind : I will cast them óut as the | clay | in the | streets.

43 Thou shalt deliver me from the strívings | of the | people : and thou shalt máke me the | head | of the | heathen.

44 A péople whom I | have not | known : shắll | serve | — | me.

45 As soon as they héar of me, they | shall o- | -bey me : but the stránge children | shall dis- | -semble | with me.

46 The stránge | children . shall | fail : ánd be a- | -fraid | out of . their | prisons.

47 The Lord liveth * and blessed bé my | strong | helper : and praised bé the | God of | my sal- | -vation.

48 Even the God that séeth that I | be a- | -venged : and subdúeth the | people | unto | me.

49 It is he that delivereth me from my cruel enemies * and setteth me úp a- | -bove mine | adversaries : thou shalt ríd me | from the | wicked | man.

50 For this cause will I give thanks unto thee, O Lórd, a- | -mong the | Gentiles : and síng | praises | unto . thy | Name.

51 Great prosperity gíveth he | unto . his | king : and sheweth loving-kindness unto David his Anointed * and únto his | seed for | ever- | -more.

Day 4.   MORNING PRAYER.

Psalm xix.—*Cœli enarrant.*

THE heavens decláre the | glory . of | God : and the fírmament | sheweth . his | handy- | -work.

2 One dáy | telleth . an- | -other : and one níght | certi- | fieth . an- | -other.

3 There is neíther | speech nor | language : bút their | voices . are | heard a- | -mong them.

4 Their sound is gone óut into | all | lands : and their wórds into the | ends | of the | world.

5 In them hath he set a tábernacle | for the | sun : which cometh forth as a bridegroom out of his chamber * and rejóiceth as a | giant . to | run his | course.

6 It goeth forth from the uttermost part of the heaven * and runneth about unto the énd of | it a- | -gain : and there is nothing híd | from the | heat there- | of.

7 The law of the Lord is an undefiled láw, con- | -verting . the | soul : the testimony of the Lord is sure * and gíveth | wisdom | unto . the | simple.

8 The statutes of the Lord are ríght, and re- | -joice the | heart : the commandment of the Lord is pure * and gíveth | light | unto . the | eyes.

2nd part. 9 The fear of the Lord is cléan, and en- | -dureth . for | ever : the judgements of the Lord are trúe, and | righteous | alto- | -gether.

10 More to be desired are they than gold * yéa, than | much fine | gold : sweeter álso than | honey | and the | honeycomb.

11 Moreover, by thém is thy | servant | taught : and in kéeping of them | there is | great re- | -ward.

mp 12 Who can téll how | oft . he of- | -fendeth : O cleanse thou mé | from my | secret | faults.

13 Keep thy servant also from presumptuous sins * lest they get the domínion | over | me : so shall I be undefiled, and ínnocent | from the | great of- | -fence.

14 Let the words of my mouth * and the meditátion | of my | heart : be álway ac- | -ceptable | in thy | sight,

15 O' | — | Lord : mý | strength and | my re- | -deemer.

Psalm xx.—*Exaudiat te Dominus.*

mf THE Lord hear thee ín the | day of | trouble : the Náme of the | God of | Jacob . de- | -fend thee ;

2 Send thee hélp | from the | sanctuary : ánd | strengthen . thee | out of | Sion ;

3 Remémber | all thy | offerings : ánd ac- | -cept thy | burnt | sacrifice ;

4 Gránt thee thy | heart's de- | -sire : ánd ful- | -fil | all thy | mind.

5 We will rejoice in . thy salvation * and triumph in the Náme of the | Lord our | God : the Lórd per- | -form all | thy pe- | -titions.

6 Now know I that the Lord helpeth his Anointed * and will hear him fróm his | holy | heaven : even with the whólesome | strength of | his right | hand.

Y

7 Some put their trust in cháriots and | some in | horses :
but we will remember the Náme | of the | Lord our |
God.

8 Théy are brought | down and | fallen : but wé are | risen .
and | stand | upright.

2nd part. 9 Save, Lord, and héar us, O | King of | heaven : whén we |
call up- | -on | thee.

Psalm xxi.—*Domine, in virtute tua.*

mf THE King shall rejóice in thy | strength O | Lord : ex-
ceeding glád shall he | be of | thy sal- | -vation.

2 Thou hast gíven him his | heart's de- | -sire : and hast
not deníed him the re- | -quest | of his | lips.

3 For thou shalt prevent him wíth the | blessings . of |
goodness : and shalt set a crówn of pure | gold up- | -on
his | head.

4 He asked life of thee * and thou gávest him a | long | life :
éven for | ever | and | ever.

5 His honour is gréat in | thy sal- | -vation : glory and
great wórship | shalt thou | lay up- | -on him.

6 For thou shalt give him éver- | -lasting . fe- | -licity :
and make him glád with the | joy | of thy | counte-
nance.

7 And why * because the King putteth his trúst | in the |
Lord : and in the mercy of the Most Híghest | he
shall | not mis- | -carry.

8 All thine énemies shall | feel thy | hand : thy right hánd
shall | find out | them that | hate thee.

9 Thou shalt make them like a fiery oven in tíme | of thy |
wrath : the Lord shall destroy them in his displeasure *
ánd the | fire | shall con- | -sume them.

10 Their fruit shalt thou róot | out . of the | earth : and
their séed from a- | -mong the | children . of |
men.

11 For they inténded | mischief . a- | -gainst thee : and
imagined such a device as they áre not | able | to
per- | -form.

12 Therefore shalt thou pút | them to | flight : and the
strings of thy bow shalt thou make réady a- | -gainst
the | face of | them.

2nd part. 13 Be thou exalted, Lórd, in thine | own | strength : só will
we | sing and | praise thy | power.

Day 4. EVENING PRAYER.

Psalm xxii.—*Deus, Deus meus.*

F. p MY God, my God, look upon me * why hast thou for- | saken | me : and art so far from my health * and from the | words of | my com- | -plaint?

F. 2 O my God, I cry in the day-time * but thou | hearest | not : and in the night-season | also . I | take no | rest.

3 And thou con- | -tinuest | holy : O' | — thou | worship . of | Israel.

4 Our fathers | hoped . in | thee : they trusted in thee, and thou | didst de- | -liver | them.

5 They called upon thee | and were | holpen : they put their trust in thee | and were | not con- | -founded.

6 But as for me, I am a worm, and | no | man : a very scorn of men, and the | outcast | of the | people.

7 All they that see me * laugh | me to | scorn : they shoot out their lips, and | shake their | heads | saying,

8 He trusted in God, that he would de- | -liver | him : let him deliver him | if he | will | have him.

9 But thou art he that took me out of my | mother's | womb : thou wast my hope, when I hanged yet up- | -on my | mother's | breasts.

10 I have been left unto thee ever since | I was | born : thou art my God, even | from my | mother's | womb.

11 O go not from me * for trouble is | hard at | hand : and | there is | none to | help me.

12 Many oxen are | come a- | -bout me : fat bulls of Basan close me | in on | every | side.

13 They gape upon me | with their | mouths : as it were a ramping | and a | roaring | lion.

14 I am poured out like water * and all my bones are | out of | joint : my heart also in the midst of my body is | even . like | melting | wax.

15 My strength is dried up like a potsherd * and my tongue cleaveth | to my | gums : and thou shalt bring me | into . the | dust of | death.

16 For many dogs are | come a- | -bout me : and the counsel of the wicked | layeth | siege a- | -gainst me.

17 They pierced my hands and my feet * I may tell | all my | bones : they stand | staring . and | looking . up- | -on me.

18 They part my | garments . a- | -mong them : and cast | lots up- | -on my | vesture.

19 But be not thou fár from | me O | Lord : thou art my súccour | haste | thee to | help me.

20 Deliver my sóul | from the | sword : my darling fróm the | power | of the | dog.

21 Save me fróm the | lion's | mouth : thou hast heard me also from amóng the | horns | of the | unicorns.

mf 22 I will declare thy Náme | unto my | brethren : in the midst of the cóngre- | -gation | will I | praise thee.

f 23 O praise the Lórd | ye that | fear him : magnify him, all ye of the seed of Jacob * and féar him | all ye | seed of | Israel.

24 For he hath not despised nor abhorred the low estáte | of the | poor : he hath not hid his face from him * but when he cálled | unto | him he | heard him.

25 My praise is of thee in the gréat | congre- | -gation : my vows will I perfórm in the | sight of | them that | fear him.

26 The poor shall éat | and be | satisfied : they that seek after the Lord shall praise him * yóur | heart shall | live for | ever.

27 All the ends of the world shall remember themselves * and be túrned | unto . the | Lord : and all the kíndreds of the | nations . shall | worship . be- | -fore him.

28 For the kíngdom | is the | Lord's : and he is the Góver- | nour a- | -mong the | people.

29 All súch as be | fat up- . -on | earth : háve | eaten | and | worshipped.

30 All they that go down into the dúst shall | kneel be- | -fore him : and nó man hath | quickened . his | own | soul.

31 Mý | seed shall | serve him : they shall be counted unto the Lórd | for a | gener- | -ation.

32 They shall come * and the héavens shall de- | -clare his | righteousness : unto a people that shall be bórn | whom the | Lord hath | made.

Psalm xxiii.—*Dominus regit me.*

mp THE Lórd | is my | Shepherd : thérefore | can I | lack | nothing.

2 He shall féed me in a | green | pasture : and lead me fórth be- | -side the | waters . of | comfort.

3 Hé shall con- | -vert my | soul : and bring me forth in the paths of rígteousness | for his | Name's | sake.

4 Yea, though I walk through the valley of the shadow of death * I' will | fear no | evil : for thou art with me * thy ród and thy | staff | comfort | me.

5 Thou shalt prepare a table before me * against thém that | trouble | me : thou hast anointed my head with oíl, and my | cup | shall be | full.

6 But thy loving-kindness and mercy * shall follow me all the dáys | of my | life : and I will dwell in the hóuse | of the | Lord for | ever.

Day 5.   MORNING PRAYER.

Psalm xxiv.—*Domini est terra.*

F. *f*   THE earth is the Lord's * and áll that | therein | is : the compass of the wórld, and | they that | dwell there- | -in.

F.   2 For he hath foúnded it up- | -on the | seas : and prepáred | it up- | -on the | floods.

3 Who shall ascend into the híll | of the | Lord : or who shall rise úp | in his | holy | place ?

4 Even he that hath clean hánds and a | pure | heart : and that hath not lift up his mind unto vanity * nor swórn | to de- | -ceive his | neighbour.

5 He shall receive the bléssing | from the | Lord : and righteousness fróm the | God of | his sal- | -vation.

6 This is the generátion of | them that | seek him : even of thém that | seek thy | face O | Jacob.

7 Lift up your heads, O ye gates * and be ye lift up, ye éver- | -lasting | doors : and the Kíng of | glory | shall come | in.

8 Whó is the | King of | glory : it is the Lord strong and mighty * éven the | Lord | mighty . in | battle.

9 Lift up your heads, O ye gates * and be ye lift up, ye éver- | lasting | doors : and the Kíng of | glory | shall come | in.

10 Whó is the | King of | glory : even the Lord of hósts | he . is the | King of | glory.

Psalm xxv.—*Ad te, Domine, levavi.*

mp   UNTO thee, O Lord, will I lift up my soul * my God, I have pút my | trust in | thee : O let me not be con-founded * neither let mine énemies | triumph | over | me.

2 For all they that hope in thée shall | not . be a- |
    shamed : but such as transgress without a cáuse | shall
    be | put . to con- | -fusion.
3 Shéw me thy | ways O | Lord : ánd | teach | me thy |
    paths.
4 Lead me fórth in thy | truth and | learn me : for thou art
    the God of my salvation * in thee hath been my hópe |
    all the | day | long.
5 Call to remembrance, O Lórd, thy | tender | mercies : and
    thy loving-kindnesses * whích | have been | ever . of |
    old.
6 O remember not the sins and offénces | of my | youth :
    but according to thy mercy think thou upon mé, O |
    Lord | for thy | goodness.
7 Gracious and ríghteous | is the | Lord : therefore will he
    téach | sinners | in the | way.
8 Them that are méek shall he | guide in | | judgement : and
    such as are géntle | them . shall he | learn his | way.
9 All the paths of the Lórd are | mercy . and | truth :
    unto such as kéep his | covenant | and his | testi-
    monies.
10 For thy Náme's | sake O | Lord : be merciful únto my |
    sin for | it is | great.
11 What man is hé that | feareth . the | Lord : him shall he
    téach in the | way that | he shall | choose.
12 His sóul shall | dwell at | ease : and his séed | shall in- |
    herit . the | land.
13 The secret of the Lord is amóng | them that | fear him :
    and hé will | shew | them his | covenant.
14 Mine eyes are ever lóoking | unto . the | Lord : for he
    shall plúck my | feet | out . of the | net.
15 Turn thee unto mé, and have | mercy . up- | -on me : for
    I′ am | desolate | and in | misery.
16 The sorrows of my héart | are en- | -larged : O bríng
    thou | me | out of . my | troubles.
17 Look upon my advérsi- | -ty and | misery : ánd for- |
    give me | all my | sin.
18 Consider mine énemies how | many . they | are : and
    they beár a | tyrannous | hate a- | -gainst me.
19 O keep my sóul, and de- | -liver | me : let me not be
    confounded * for I′ have | put my | trust in | thee.
20 Let perfectness and righteous déaling | wait up- | -on
    me : fór my | hope hath | been in | thee.
2nd part. 21 Deliver I′srael | O | God : oút of | all | his | troubles.

PSALM xxvi.—*Judica me, Domine.*

mp BE thou my Judge, O Lord * for I' have | walked | innocently : my trust hath been also in the Lórd | therefore | shall I . not | fall.

2 Exámine me, O | Lord and | prove me : try oút my | reins | and my | heart.

3 For thy loving-kindness is éver be- | -fore mine | eyes : and I' will | walk | in thy | truth.

4 I have not dwélt with | vain | persons : neither will I have féllowship | with | the de- | -ceitful.

5 I have hated the congregátion | of the | wicked : and wíll not | sit a- | -mong . the un- | -godly.

6 I will wash my hands in ínnocency | O | Lord : and só will I | go | to thine | aítar ;

7 That I may shew the vóice of | thanks- | -giving : and téll of | all thy | wondrous | works.

8 Lord, I have loved the habitátion | of thy | house : and the pláce | where thine | honour | dwelleth.

9 O shut not up my sóul | with the | sinners : nor my lífe | , with the | blood- | -thirsty ;

10 Ín whose | hands is | wickedness : and their ríght | hand is | full of | gifts.

11 But as for me * I' will | walk | innocently : O deliver me, ánd be | merciful | unto | me.

12 My fóot | standeth | right : I will praíse the Lórd | in the | congre- | -gations.

Day 5.   **EVENING PRAYER.**

PSALM xxvii.—*Dominus illuminatio.*

F. mf THE Lord is my light and my salvation * whóm then | shall I | fear : the Lord is the strength of my life * of whóm then | shall I | be a- | -fraid ?

F. 2 When the wicked * even mine enemies and my foes * came upon me to éat | up my | flesh : théy | stumbled | and | fell.

3 Though an host of men were laid against me * yet shall not my heárt | be a- | -fraid : and though there rose up war against me * yét will I | put my | trust in | him.

4 One thing have I desired of the Lórd, which I | will re- |
quire : even that I may dwell in the house of the Lord
all the days of my life * to behold the fair beauty of
the Lórd | and to | visit . his | temple.

5 For in the time of trouble he shall híde me in his | taber- |
nacle : yea, in the secret place of his dwelling shall he
hide me * and set me úp up- | -on a | rock of | stone.

6 And now shall he líft | up mine | head : abóve mine |
enemies | round a- | -bout me.

7 Therefore will I offer in his dwelling an oblátion with |
great | gladness : I will síng and speak | praises | unto .
the | Lord.

mp 8 Hearken unto my voice, O Lord * when I crý | unto |
thee : have mércy up- | -on me | and | hear me.

9 My heart hath talked of thee * Séek | ye my | face :
Thý | face Lord | will I | seek.

10 O hide not thóu thy | face | from me : nor cast thy sér-
vant a- | -way | in dis- | -pleasure.

11 Thóu hast | been my | succour : leave me not, neither for-
sáke me, O | God of | my sal- | -vation.

12 When my fáther and my | mother . for- | -sake me : the
Lórd | taketh | me | up.

13 Téach me thy | way O | Lord : and lead me in the right
wáy be- | -cause of | mine | enemies.

14 Deliver me not over into the wíll | of mine | adversaries :
for there are false witnesses risen up against me, ánd |
such as | speak | wrong.

15 I should útterly | have | fainted : but that I believe verily to
see the goodness of the Lórd in the | land | of the | living.

16 O tárry thou the | Lord's | leisure : be strong, and he shall
comfort thine heart * and pút thou thy | trust | in the |
Lord.

PSALM xxviii.—*Ad te, Domine.*

mp UNTO thee will I crý, O | Lord my | strength : think no
scorn of me * lest, if thou make as though thou
hearest not * I become like thém that go | down |
into . the | pit.

2 Hear the voice of my humble petitions * when I crý |
unto | thee : when I hold up my hands towards the
mércy-seat | of thy | holy | temple.

3 O pluck me not away * neither destroy me with the ungódly
and | wicked | doers : which speak friendly to their
neighbours * but imágine | mischief | in their | hearts.

4 Reward them accórding | to their | deeds : and according
to the wíckedness | of their | own in- | -ventions.

5 Recompense them after the wórk | of their | hands : páy
them | that they | have de- | -served.

6 For they regard not in their mind the works of the
Lord * nor the operátion | of his | hands : therefore
shall he break them dówn, and | not | build them | up.

mf 7 Práised | be the | Lord : for he hath heard the vóice | of
my | humble . pe- | -titions.

8 The Lord is my strength and my shield * my heart hath
trusted in hím, and | I am | helped : therefore my heart
danceth for joy * and ín my | song | will I | praise
him.

9 The Lórd | is my | strength : and he is the whólesome
de- | -fence of | his A- | -nointed.

10 O save thy people * and give thy blessing únto | thine
in- | -heritance : féed them, and | set them | up for |
ever.

Psalm xxix.—*Afferte Domino.*

BRING unto the Lord, O ye mighty * bring young ráms |
unto . the | Lord : ascribe unto the Lórd | worship |
and | strength.

2 Give the Lord the honour dúe | unto . his | Name :
wórship the | Lord with | holy | worship.

3 It is the Lórd that com- | -mandeth . the | waters : it is
the glórious | God that | maketh . the | thunder.

4 It is the Lord that ruleth the sea * the voice of the Lord
is míghty in | oper- | -ation : the voice of the Lórd | is
a | glorious | voice.

5 The voice of the Lórd | breaketh . the | cedar-trees : yeá,
the Lord | breaketh . the | cedars . of | Libanus.

6 He maketh them also to skíp | like a | calf : Libanus also,
and Sírion | like a | young | unicorn.

7 The voice of the Lord divideth the flames of fire * the
voice of the Lórd | shaketh . the | wilderness : yea, the
Lord sháketh the | wilder- | -ness of | Cades.

8 The voice of the Lord maketh the hinds to bring forth
young * and discóvereth the | thick | bushes : in his
temple doth évery man | speak | of his | honour.

9 The Lord sítteth a- | -bove the | water-flood : and the
Lórd re- | -maineth . a | King for | ever.

10 The Lord shall give stréngth | unto . his | people : the
Lord shall gíve his | people . the | blessing . of | peace.

DAY 6.   MORNING PRAYER.

PSALM XXX.—*Exaltabo te, Domine.*

F.mf 1 I WILL magnify thee, O Lord * for thóu hast | set me | up : and not made my fóes to | triumph | over | me.

F. 2 O Lord my God, I críed | unto | thee : ánd | thou hast | healed | me.

3 Thou, Lord, hast brought my sóul | out of | hell : thou hast kept my life from thém that go | down | to the | pit.

4 Sing praises unto the Lórd, O ye | saints of | his : and give thanks unto him * fór a re- | -membrance | of his | holiness.

5 For his wrath endureth but the twinkling of an eye * and ín his | pleasure . is | life : heaviness may endure for a night * but jóy | cometh | in the | morning.

6 And in my prosperity I said * I shall néver | be re- | -moved : thou, Lord, of thy góodness hast | made my | hill so | strong.

p 7 Thou didst túrn thy | face | from me : ánd | I | was | troubled.

8 Then cried I únto | thee O | Lord : and gát me | to my | Lord right | humbly.

9 What profit ís there | in my | blood : whén I go | down | to the | pit ?

10 Shall the dust give thánks | unto | thee : ór shall | it de- | clare thy | truth ?

11 Hear, O Lórd, and have | mercy . up- | -on me : Lórd, be | thou | my | helper.

mf 12 Thou hast turned my héaviness | into | joy : thou hast put off my sáckcloth, and | girded | me with | gladness.

2nd part. 13 Therefore shall every good man sing of thy práise with- | out | ceasing : O my God, I will give thánks | unto | thee for | ever.

PSALM XXXI.—*In te, Domine, speravi.*

mf 1 IN thee, O Lórd, have I | put my | trust : let me never be put to confúsion, de- | -liver . me | in thy | righteous-ness.

2 Bow dówn thine | ear to | me : make háste | to de- | liver | me.

3 And be thou my strong rock, and hóuse | of de- | -fence : thát | thou . mayest | save | me.

4 For thou art my strong róck | and my | castle : be thou
　　also my guide * and léad me | for thy | Name's |
　　sake.

5 Draw me out of the net that they have láid | privily | for
　　me : fór | thou | art my | strength.

6 Into thy hánds I com- | -mend my | spirit : for thou hast
　　redeemed me * O' | Lord thou | God of | truth.

7 I have hated them that hóld of super- | -stitious | vani-
　　ties : and my trúst hath | been | in the | Lord.

8 I will be glad, and rejóice | in thy | mercy : for thou hast
　　considered my trouble * and hast knówn my | soul | in
　　ad- | -versities.

*2nd
part.* 9 Thou hast not shut me up into the hánd | of the |
　　enemy : but hast set my féet | in a | large | room.

p 10 Have mercy upon me, O Lórd, for | I am . in | trouble :
　　and mine eye is consumed for very heaviness * yéa,
　　my | soul | and my | body.

11 For my life is wáxen | old with | heaviness : ánd my |
　　years | with | mourning.

12 My strength faileth me, becáuse of | mine in- | -iquity :
　　ánd my | bones | are con- | -sumed.

13 I became a reproof among all mine enemies * but
　　espécially a- | -mong my | neighbours : and they of
　　mine acquaintance were afraid of me * and they that
　　did see me withóut con- | -veyed . them- | -selves | from
　　me.

14 I am clean forgotten, as a déad man | out of | mind : I
　　am becóme | like a | broken | vessel.

15 For I have heard the blásphemy | of the | multitude : and
　　fear is on every side * while they conspire together
　　against me * and take their cóunsel to | take a- | -way
　　my | life.

16 But my hope hath béen in | thee O | Lord : I have sáid |
　　Thou art | my | God.

17 My time is in thy hand * deliver me from the hánd | of
　　mine | enemies : ánd from | them that | persecute | me.

18 Shew thy servant the líght | of thy | countenance : and
　　sáve me | for thy | mercy's | sake.

19 Let me not be confounded, O Lord * for I' have | called .
　　up- | -on thee : let the ungodly be put to confusion *
　　and be pút to | silence | in the | grave.

*2nd
part.* 20 Let the lying líps be | put to | silence : which cruelly,
　　disdainfully, and despítefully | speak a- | -gainst the |
　　righteous.

f 21 O how plentiful is thy goodness * which thou hast laid úp for | them that | fear thee : and that thou hast prepared for them that put their trust in thee * éven be- | -fore the | sons of | men !

22 Thou shalt hide them privily by thine own presence * from the provóking of | all | men : thou shalt keep them secretly in thy tábernacle | from the | strife of | tongues.

23 Thánks be | to the | Lord : for he hath shewed me marvellous great kíndness | in a | strong | city.

24 And whén I made | haste I | said : I am cast óut of the | sight | of thine | eyes.

25 Nevertheless, thou heardest the vóice | of my | prayer : whén I | cried | unto | thee.

26 O love the Lórd, all | ye his | saints : for the Lord preserveth them that are faithful * and plénteously re- | -wardeth . the | proud | doer.

2nd part. 27 Be strong, and hé shall es- | -tablish . your | heart : all ye that pút your | trust | in the | Lord.

Day 6. EVENING PRAYER.

Psalm xxxii.—*Beati, quorum.*

F. mp BLESSED is he whose unrighteousness | is for- | -given : ánd whose | sin | is | covered.

F. 2 Blessed is the man unto whom the Lórd im- | -puteth . no | sin : and ín whose | spirit . there | is no | guile.

3 For whíle I | held my | tongue : my bones consumed awáy | through my | daily . com- | -plaining.

4 For thy hand is heavy upón me | day and | night : and my móisture is | like the | drought in | summer.

5 I will acknowledge my sín | unto | thee : and mine unríghteousness | have I | not | hid.

6 I said, I will confess my síns | unto . the | Lord : and so thou forgávest the | wickedness | of my | sin.

7 For this shall every one that is godly make his prayer unto thee * in a tíme when thou | mayest . be | found : but in the great wáter-floods | they shall | not come | nigh him.

8 Thou art a place to hide me in * thou shalt presérve | me from | trouble : thou shalt compass me abóut with | songs | of de- | -liverance.

9 I will inform thee, and teach thee in the wáy wherein |
thou shalt | go : and I' will | guide thee | with mine |
eye.

10 Be ye not like to horse and mule * which háve no |
under- | -standing : whose mouths must be held with
bit and brídle | lest they | fall up- | -on thee.

11 Great plagues remáin | for . the un- | -godly : but whoso
putteth his trust in the Lord * mercy embráceth | him
on | every | side.

12 Be glad, O ye righteous * and rejóice | in the | Lord :
and be joyful, all yé | that are | true of | heart.

Psalm xxxiii.—*Exultate, justi.*

mf   REJOICE in the Lórd | O ye | righteous : for it becometh
wéll the | just | to be | thankful.

2 Práise the | Lord with | harp : sing praises unto him with
the lute * and ínstru- | -ment of | ten | strings.

3 Sing unto the Lórd a | new | song : sing praises lustily
unto hím | with a | good | courage.

4 For the wórd of the | Lord is | true : ánd | all his | works
are | faithful.

5 He loveth ríghteous- | -ness and | judgement : the earth
is fúll of the | goodness | of the | Lord.

6 By the word of the Lórd were the | heavens | made :
and all the hosts of them bý the | breath | of his |
mouth.

7 He gathereth the waters of the sea together * as it wére
up- | -on an | heap : and layeth úp the | deep as | in
a | treasure-house.

8 Let all the éarth | fear the | Lord : stand in awe of him *
all yé that | dwell | in the | world.

9 For he spáke, and | it was | done : he commánded | and
it | stood | fast.

10 The Lord bringeth the cóunsel of the | heathen . to |
nought : and maketh the devices of the people to be of
none effect * and cásteth | out the | counsels . of |
princes.

11 The counsel of the Lórd shall en- | -dure for | ever : and
the thoughts of his heart from géner- | -ation . to |
gener- | -ation.

12 Blessed are the people whose Gód is the | Lord Je- |
hovah : and blessed are the folk that he hath chosen to
hím to | be | his in- | -heritance.

13 The Lord looked down from heaven * and behéld all the |
children . of | men : from the habitation of his dwelling *
he considereth all thém that | dwell | on the | earth.

14 He fashioneth áll the | hearts of | them : and únder- |
standeth | all their | works.

15 There is no king that can be saved by the múltitude | of
an | host : neither is any mighty mán de- | -livered .
by | much | strength.

16 A horse is counted but a váin thing to | save a | man :
neither shall he deliver ány man | by his | great |
strength.

17 Behold, the eye of the Lord is upón | them that | fear him :
and upon them that pút their | trust | in his | mercy.

18 To delíver their | soul from | death : and to féed them |
in the | time of | dearth.

19 Our soul hath patiently tárried | for the | Lord : for hé is
our | help | and our | shield.

20 For our héart shall re- | -joice in | him : because we have
hóped | in his | holy | Name.

2nd
part. 21 Let thy merciful kindness, O Lórd | be up- | -on us : like
as wé do | put our | trust in | thee.

Psalm xxxiv.—*Benedicam Domino.*

mf   I WILL alway give thánks | unto . the | Lord : his práise
shall | ever . be | in my | mouth.

2 My soul shall make her bóast | in the | Lord : the humble
shall héar there- | -of | and be | glad.

3 O práise the | Lord with | me : and let us mágni- | -fy
his | Name to- | -gether.

4 I sought the Lórd | and he | heard me : yea, he delívered
me | out of | all my | fear.

5 They had an eye unto hím | and were | lightened : ánd
their | faces . were | not a- | -shamed.

6 Lo, the poor crieth, and the Lórd | heareth | him : yea,
and sáveth him | out of | all his | troubles.

7 The angel of the Lord tarrieth róund about | them that |
fear him : ánd | — de- | -livereth | them.

8 O taste and see how grácious the | Lord | is : blessed ís
the | man that | trusteth . in | him.

9 O fear the Lord, yé that | are his | saints : for théy that |
fear him | lack | nothing.

10 The lions do láck and | suffer | hunger : but they who seek
the Lord, shall want no mánner of | thing | that is | good.

11 Come, ye children, and héarken | unto | me : I will téach
    you the | fear | of the | Lord.

12 What man is hé that | lusteth . to | live : ánd would |
    fain | see good | days ?

13 Kéep thy | tongue from | evil : and thy líps | that they |
    speak no | guile.

14 Eschew évil and | do | good : séek | peace | and en- |
    sue it.

15 The eyes of the Lórd are | over . the | righteous : and his
    éars are | open | unto . their | prayers.

16 The countenance of the Lord is against thém that | do |
    evil : to root out the remémbrance | of them | from
    the | earth.

17 The righteous cry, and the Lórd | heareth | them : and
    delívereth them | out of | all their | troubles.

18 The Lord is nigh unto them that áre of a | contrite |
    heart : and will sáve such as | be . of an | humble |
    spirit.

19 Great are the tróubles | of the | righteous : but the Lórd
    de- | -livereth . him | out of | all.

20 He kéepeth | all his | bones : só that not | one of | them
    is | broken.

21 But misfortune shall sláy | the un- | -godly : and they
    that háte the | righteous | shall be | desolate.

22 The Lord delivereth the sóuls | of his | servants : and all
    they that put their trúst in | him shall | not be |
    destitute.

Day 7.   MORNING PRAYER.

Psalm xxxv.—*Judica, Domine.*

mf PLEAD thou my cause, O Lord, with thém that | strive
    with | me : and fight thou against thém that | fight
    a- | -gainst | me.

2 Lay hand upón the | shield and | buckler : ánd | stand |
    up to | help me.

3 Bring forth the spear * and stop the way against thém
    that | persecute | me : say unto my sóul | I am | thy
    sal- | -vation.

4 Let them be confounded, and put to shame * that séek |
    after . my | soul : let them be turned back and brought
    to confusion * thát im- | -agine | mischief | for me.

5 Let them be as the dúst be- | -fore the | wind : and the ángel of the | Lord | scattering | them.

6 Let their wáy be | dark and | slippery : and let the ángel of the | Lord | persecute | them.

7 For they have privily laid their net to destróy me with- | out a | cause : yea, even without a cause have they máde a | pit | for my | soul.

8 Let a sudden destruction come upon him unawares * and his net, that he hath laid prívily | catch him- | self : that he may fáll | into . his | own | mischief.

9 And my soul, be jóyful | in the | Lord : ít shall re- | joice in | his sal- | -vation.

10 All my bones shall say, Lord, who is like unto thee * who deliverest the poor from him that is tóo | strong for | him : yea, the poor, and him that is in mísery, from | him that | spoileth | him ?

p 11 False wítnesses did | rise | up : they laid to my chárge | things | that I | knew not.

12 They rewárded me | evil . for | good : to the gréat dis- | comfort | of my | soul.

13 Nevertheless, when they were sick, I put on sackcloth * and húmbled my | soul with | fasting : and my prayer shall túrn | into . mine | own | bosom.

14 I behaved myself as though it had been my friénd | or my | brother : I went heavily * as óne that | mourneth | for his | mother.

15 But in mine adversity they rejoiced * and gáthered them- | -selves to- | -gether : yea, the very abjects came together against me unawares * making móuths at | me and | ceased | not.

16 With the flátterers were | busy | mockers : who gnáshed up- | -on me | with their | teeth.

17 Lord, how lóng wilt thou | look up- . -on | this : O deliver my soul from the calamities which they bring on me * ánd my | darling | from the | lions.

18 So will I give thee thanks in the gréat | congre- | -gation : I will práise | thee a- | -mong much | people.

19 O let not them that are mine enemies triumph óver | me un- | -godly : neither let them wink with their éyes that | hate . me with- | -out a | cause.

20 And why * their cómmuning is | not for | peace : but they imagine deceitful words against thém that are | quiet | in the | land.

21 They gaped upon me wíth their | mouths and | said :
Fie on thee, fie on thée, we | saw it | with our |
eyes.

22 Thís thou hast | seen O | Lord : hold not thy tongue
then * gó not | far from | me O | Lord.

mf 23 Awake, and stand úp to | judge my | quarrel : avenge thou
my cáuse, my | God | and my | Lord.

24 Judge me, O Lord my God, accórding | to thy | righteous-
ness : and lét them not | triumph | over | me.

25 Let them not say in their hearts * There, thére | so .
would we | have it : neither let them sáy | We . have
de- | -voured | him.

26 Let them be put to confusion and shame together * that
rejóice | at my | trouble : let them be clothed with
rebuke and dishónour, that | boast them- | -selves a- |
gainst me.

27 Let them be glad and rejoice, that fávour my | righteous |
dealing : yea, let them say alway * Blessed be the
Lord, who hath pleasure ín the pros- | -perity | of his |
servant.

28 And as for my tongue, it shall be tálking | of thy |
righteousness : and of thy práise | all the | day | long.

PSALM XXXVI.—*Dixit injustus.*

mp   MY heart sheweth me the wíckedness | of . the un- |
godly : that there is no féar of | God be- | -fore his |
eyes.

2 For he flattereth himsélf in his | own | sight : until his
abóminable | sin be | found | out.

3 The words of his mouth are unríghteous and | full . of
de- | -ceit : he hath left off to behave himself wísely |
and to | do | good.

4 He imagineth mischief upon his bed * and hath set
himsélf in | no good | way : neither doth he abhór |
any . thing | that is | evil.

f 5 Thy mercy, O Lord, rácheth | unto . the | heavens : ánd
thy | faithfulness | unto . the | clouds.

6 Thy righteousness standeth líke the | strong | mountains :
thy júdgements are | like the | great | deep.

7 Thou, Lord, shalt save both man and beast * how
excellent ís thy | mercy . O | God : and the chíldren of
men shall put their trust * únder the | shadow | of
thy | wings.

z

8 They shall be satisfied with the plénteousness | of thy |
house : and thou shalt give them drink of thy
pléasures, as | out | of the | river.

9 For with thée is the | well of | life : and in thy líght |
shall we | see | light.

10 O continue forth thy loving-kindness únto | them that |
know thee : and thy righteousness unto thém | that
are | true of | heart.

11 O let not the foot of príde | come a- | -gainst me : and
let not the hánd of the un- | -godly | cast me | down.

12 There are they fallen, áll that | work | wickedness : they
are cast dówn, and shall | not be | able . to | stand.

Day 7.   EVENING PRAYER.

Psalm xxxvii.—*Noli æmulari.*

F. mf   **F**RET not thyself becáuse of | the un- | -godly : neither be
thou énvious a- | -gainst the | evil- | -doers.

F.   2 For they shall soon be cut dówn | like the | grass : and
be wíthered | even . as the | green | herb.

3 Put thou thy trust in the Lórd, and be | doing | good :
dwell in the lánd, and | verily . thou | shalt be | fed.

4 Delíght thou | in the | Lord : and he shall gíve | thee thy |
heart's de- | -sire.

5 Commit thy way unto the Lord * and pút thy | trust in |
him : ánd | he shall | bring it . to | pass.

6 He shall make thy righteousness as cléar | as the | light :
and thy júst | dealing | as the | noon-day.

7 Hold thee still in the Lord * and abide pátient- | -ly
up- | -on him : but grieve not thyself at him whose way
doth prosper * against the man that dóeth | after |
evil | counsels.

8 Leave off from wráth, and let | go dis- | -pleasure : fret
not thyself * élse shalt thou be | moved . to | do | evil.

9 Wicked doers sháll be | rooted | out : and they that
patiently abide the Lórd | those . shall in- | -herit .
the | land.

10 Yet a little while * and the ungódly shall be | clean |
gone : thou shalt look after his pláce, and | he shall |
be a- | -way.

11 But the meek-spirited sháll pos- | -sess the | earth : and
shall be refréshed in the | multi- | -tude of | peace.

12 The ungodly seeketh cóunsel a- | -gainst the | just : and
gnásheth up- | -on him | with his | teeth.

13 The Lord shall láugh | him to | scorn : for he hath
séen | that his | day is | coming.

14 The ungodly have drawn out the swórd, and have | bent
their | bow : to cast down the poor and needy * and to
slay such as áre of a | right | conver- | -sation.

15 Their sword shall go thróugh their | own | heart : ánd
their | bow | shall be | broken.

16 A small thing thát the | righteous | hath : is better than
gréat | riches . of | the un- | -godly.

17 For the arms of the ungódly | shall be | broken : ánd the |
Lord up- | -holdeth . the | righteous.

18 The Lord knoweth the dáys | of the | godly : and their
inhéritance | shall en- | -dure for | ever.

19 They shall not be confóunded in the | perilous | time :
and in the days of déarth | they shall | have e- | -nough.

20 As for the ungodly they shall perish * and the enemies of
the Lord shall consúme as the | fat of | lambs : yea,
even as the smóke shall | they con- | -sume a- | -way.

21 The ungodly borroweth, and páyeth | not a- | -gain : but
the ríghteous is | merci- | -ful and | liberal.

22 Such as are blessed of Gód shall pos- | -sess the | land :
and they that are cúrsed of him | shall be | rooted | out.

23 The Lord órdereth a | good man's | going : and maketh
his wáy ac- | -ceptable | to him- | -self.

24 Though he fall * he shall nót be | cast a- | -way : for the
Lórd up- | -holdeth . him | with his | hand.

25 I have been yóung, and | now am | old : and yet saw I
never the righteous forsaken * nór his | seed | begging .
their | bread.

26 The righteous is ever mérci- | -ful and | lendeth : ánd
his | seed | is | blessed.

27 Flee from evil * and do the thíng | that is | good : ánd |
dwell for | ever- | -more.

28 For the Lord loveth the thíng | that is | right : he
forsaketh nót his that be gódly, but | they are . pre- |
served . for | ever.

29 The unríghteous | shall be | punished : as for the seed of
the ungódly | it . shall be | rooted | out.

30 The righteous sháll in- | -herit . the | land : ánd | dwell
there- | -in for | ever.

31 The mouth of the righteous is éxer- | -cised . in | wisdom :
and his tóngue | will be | talking of | judgement.

z 2

32 The law of his Gód is | in his | heart : ánd his | goings |
　　shall not | slide.

33 The ungódly | seeth . the | righteous : ánd | seeketh .
　　oc- | -casion . to | slay him.

34 The Lord will not léave him | in his | hand : nór con- |
　　demn him | when . he is | judged.

35 Hope thou in the Lord, and keep his way * and he shall
　　promote thee that thóu shalt pos- | -sess the | land :
　　when the ungódly shall | perish | thou shalt | see it.

36 I myself have seen the ungódly in | great | power : and
　　floúrishing | like a | green | bay-tree.

37 I went by, and ló | he was | gone : I sought him, but his
　　pláce could | no- | -where be | found.

38 Keep innocency * and take heed unto the thíng | that
　　is | right : for that shall bríng a man | peace | at the |
　　last.

39 As for the transgressors, théy shall | perish . to- |
　　gether : and the end of the ungodly is * they shall
　　be róoted | out | at the | last.

40 But the salvation of the righteous cómeth | of the | Lord :
　　who is also their stréngth | in the | time of | trouble.

2nd
part.
41 And the Lord shall stánd by | them and | save them : he
　　shall deliver them from the ungodly * and shall save
　　them, becáuse they | put their | trust in | him.

Day 8.　　　　MORNING PRAYER.

Psalm xxxviii.—*Domine, ne in furore.*

p　PUT me not to rebuke, O Lórd | in thine | anger : neither
　　chásten me | in thy | heavy . dis- | -pleasure.

2 For thine árrows stick | fast in | me : ánd thy | hand |
　　presseth . me | sore.

3 There is no health in my flesh * becáuse of | thy dis- |
　　pleasure : neither is there any rest in my bónes, by |
　　reason | of my | sin.

4 For my wickednesses are góne | over . my | head : and
　　are like a sore búrden, too | heavy . for | me to | bear.

5 My wounds stínk and | are cor- | -rupt : throúgh | my |
　　foolish- | -ness.

6 I am brought into so gréat | trouble . and | misery : that
　　I go móurning | all the | day | long.

7 For my loins are fílled with a | sore dis- | -ease : and there is nó | whole part | in my | body.

8 I am féeble and | sore | smitten : I have roared for the véry dis- | -quietness | of my | heart.

9 Lord, thou knowest áll | my de- | -sire : and my gróaning | is not | hid from | thee.

10 My heart panteth, my stréngth hath | failed | me : and the síght of mine | eyes is | gone | from me.

11 My lovers and my neighbours did stand lóoking up- | -on my | trouble : and my kínsmen | stood a- | -far | off.

12 They also that sought after my lífe laid | snares for | me : and they that went about to do me evil talked of wickedness * and imagined decéit | all the | day | long.

13 As for me, I was like a déaf | man and | heard not : and as one that is dúmb, who | doth not | open . his | mouth.

14 I became even as a mán that | heareth | not : and in whóse | mouth are | no re- | -proofs.

15 For in thee, O Lórd, have I | put my | trust : thou shalt ánswer for | me O | Lord my | God.

16 I have required that they, even mine enemies * should not tríumph | over | me : for when my foot slipped * théy re- | -joiced | greatly . a- | -gainst me.

17 And I truly am sét | in the | plague : and my héaviness is | ever | in my | sight.

18 For I' will con- | -fess my | wickedness : ánd be | sorry | for my | sin.

19 But mine enemies líve | and are | mighty : and they that hate me wróngfully | are | many . in | number.

20 They also that reward evil for góod | are a- | -gainst me : because I fóllow the | thing that | good | is.

21 Forsake me nót, O | Lord my | God : bé not | thou | far | from me.

22 Háste | thee to | help me : O Lórd | God of | my sal- | -vation.

Psalm xxxix.—*Dixi, custodiam.*

p   **I** SAID, I will take héed | to my | ways : that I' of- | -fend not | in my | tongue.

2 I will keep my mouth as it wére | with a | bridle : whíle the un- | -godly . is | in my | sight.

3 I held my tóngue and | spake | nothing : I kept silence, yea, even from good words * bút it was | pain and | grief to | me.

4 My heart was hot within me * and while I was thus
     músing the | fire | kindled : and at the lást I | spake |
     with my | tongue ;

5 Lord, let me know mine end * and the númber | of my |
     days : that I may be certiffed how | long I | have to |
     live.

6 Behold, thou hast made my days as it wére a | span |
     long : and mine age is even as nothing in respect of
     thee * and verily, every man lfving is | alto- | -gether |
     vanity.

7 For man walketh in a vain shadow * and disquíeteth
     him- | -self in | vain : he heapeth up riches, and cán-
     not tell | who shall | gather | them.

8 And now, Lórd, what | is my | hope : trúly my | hope is |
     even . in | thee.

9 Deliver me from áll | mine of- | -fences : and make me
     nót a re- | -buke | unto . the | foolish.

10 I became dumb, and ópened | not my | mouth : fór | it
     was | thy | doing.

11 Take thy plágue a- | -way | from me : I am even consum-
     ed by the méans | of thy | heavy | hand.

12 When thou with rebukes dost chasten man for sin *
     thou makest his beauty to consume away * like as it
     were a móth | fretting . a | garment : évery man |
     therefore | is but | vanity.

13 Hear my prayer, O Lord * and with thine éars con- |
     sider . my | calling : hóld not thy | peace | at my |
     tears.

14 For I' am a | stranger . with | thee : and a sójourner, as |
     all my | fathers | were.

2nd part. 15 O spare me a little * that I' may re- | -cover . my |
     strength : before I go hénce, and | be no | more | seen.

Psalm xl.—*Expectans expectavi.*

mf I WAITED pátiently | for the | Lord : and he inclined
     únto | me and | heard my | calling.

2 He brought me also out of the horrible pit * óut of the |
     mire and | clay : and set my feet upon the róck, and |
     ordered | my | goings.

3 And he hath put a new sóng | in my | mouth : even a
     thánks- | -giving | unto . our | God.

4 Mány shall | see it . and | fear : and shall pút their |
     trust | in the | Lord.

5 Blessed is the man that hath set his hópe | in the |
Lord : and turned not unto the proud * and to súch as |
go a- | -bout with | lies.

6 O Lord my God, great are the wondrous works which thou
hast done * like as be also thy thóughts which | are to |
us-ward : and yet there is no man that órdereth |
them | unto | thee.

7 If I should decláre them and | speak of | them : they
should be more than I' am | able | to ex- | -press.

8 Sacrifice and meat-óffering thou | wouldest | not : bút
mine | ears | hast thou | opened.

9 Burnt-offerings and sacrifice for sin * hast thóu | not
re- | -quired : thén | said I | Lo I | come.

10 In the volume of the book it is written of me * that I
should fulfil thy wíll | O my | God : I am content to do
it * yea, thy láw | is with- | -in my | heart.

11 I have declared thy righteousness in the gréat | congre- |
gation : lo, I will not refrain my líps, O | Lord and |
that thou | knowest.

12 I have not hid thy ríghteousness with- | -in my | heart : my
talk hath been of thy trúth | and of | thy sal- | -vation.

2nd
part. 13 I have not kept back thy lóving | mercy . and | truth :
fróm the | great | congre- | -gation.

mp 14 Withdraw not thou thy mércy from | me O | Lord : let thy
loving-kindness and thy trúth | al- | -way pre- | -serve me.

15 For innumerable troubles are come about me * my sins
have taken such hold upon me * that I am not áble to |
look | up : yea, they are more in number than the
hairs of my head * ánd my | heart hath | failed | me.

16 O Lord, let it be thy pléasure to de- | -liver | me : máke |
haste O | Lord to | help me.

17 Let them be ashamed and confounded together * that
seek after my sóul | to de- | -stroy it : let them be
driven backward * and pút to re- | -buke that | wish
me | evil.

18 Let them be desolate, ánd re- | -warded . with | shame :
that say unto me, Fíe up- | -on thee | fie up- | -on thee.

19 Let all those that seek thee be jóyful and | glad in | thee :
and let such as love thy salvation say álway The |
Lord | be | praised.

20 As for mé, I am | poor and | needy : bút the | Lord |
careth | for me.

21 Thou art my hélper | and re- | -deemer : make nó long |
tarrying | O my | God.

Day 8.　　　　EVENING PRAYER.

Psalm xli.—*Beatus qui intelligit.*

F.mp　B LESSED is he that considereth the | poor and | needy :
　　　　the Lord shall deliver him | in the | time of | trouble.

F.　　2 The Lord preserve him, and keep him alive * that he
　　　　may be blessed up- | -on | earth : and deliver not thou
　　　　him into the | will | of his | enemies.

　　　3 The Lord comfort him, when he lieth sick up- | -on his |
　　　　bed : make thou all his | bed | in his | sickness.

　　　4 I said, Lord, be merciful | unto | me : heal my soul, for |
　　　　I have | sinned . a- | -gainst thee.

　　　5 Mine enemies speak | evil | of me : When shall he die |
　　　　and his | name | perish ?

　　　6 And if he come to see me, he | speaketh | vanity : and his
　　　　heart conceiveth falsehood within himself * and when
　　　　he cometh | forth he | telleth | it.

　　　7 All mine enemies whisper to- | -gether . a- | -gainst me :
　　　　even against me do | they im- | -agine . this | evil.

　　　8 Let the sentence of guiltiness pro- | -ceed a- | -gainst him :
　　　　and now that he lieth | let him . rise | up no | more.

　　　9 Yea, even mine own familiar friend | whom I | trusted :
　　　　who did also eat of my bread, hath | laid great | wait
　　　　for | me.

　　　10 But be thou merciful unto | me O | Lord : raise thou me
　　　　up again | and I | shall re- | -ward them.

　　　11 By this I know thou | favourest | me : that mine enemy |
　　　　doth not | triumph . a- | -gainst me.

　　　12 And when I am in my health * thou up- | -holdest | me :
　　　　and shalt set me be- | -fore thy | face for | ever.

2nd　13 Blessed be the Lord | God of | Israel : world without |
part.　　end. | A- | -men.

Psalm xlii.—*Quemadmodum.*

mf　L IKE as the hart de- | -sireth . the | waterbrooks : so
　　　　longeth my soul | after | thee O | God.

　　　2 My soul is athirst for God * yea, even for the | living |
　　　　God : when shall I come to appear be- | -fore the |
　　　　presence . of | God ?

　　　3 My tears have been my meat | day and | night : while
　　　　they daily say unto me | Where is | now thy | God ?

　　　4 Now when I think thereupon * I pour out my heart | by
　　　　my- | -self : for I went with the multitude * and
　　　　brought them forth | into . the | house of | God ;

5 In the voice of práise and | thanks- | -giving : amóng |
    such as | keep | holyday.

6 Why art thou so full of héaviness | O my | soul : and why
    art thou só dis- | -quiet- | -ed with- | -in me ?

7 Pút thy | trust in | God : for I will yet give him thánks
    for the | help | of his | countenance.

8 My God, my sóul is | vexed . with- | -in me : therefore
    will I remember thee concerning the land of Jordan *
    ánd the | little | hill of | Hermon.

9 One deep calleth another * because of the nóise | of the |
    water-pipes : all thy waves and stórms are | gone |
    over | me.

10 The Lord hath granted his loving-kíndness | in the | day-
    time : and in the night-season did I sing of him * and
    made my prayer únto the | God | of my | life.

11 I will say unto the God of my strength * Whý hast thou
    for- | -gotten | me : why go I thus heavily * whíle
    the | ene- . -my op- | -presseth | me ?

12 My bones are smitten asúnder | as . with a | sword : while
    mine enemies that troúble me | cast me | in the | teeth;

13 Namely, while they say dáily | unto | me : Whére | —
    is | now thy | God ?

14 Why art thou so véxed | O my | soul : and why art thou
    só dis- | -quiet- | -ed with- | -in me ?

15 O pút thy | trust in | God : for I will yet thank him *
    which is the hélp of my | countenance | and my | God.

Psalm xliii.—*Judica me, Deus.*

mf   GIVE sentence with me, O God * and defend my cause
    agáinst the un- | -godly | people : O deliver me fróm
    the de- | -ceitful . and | wicked | man.

2 For thou art the God of my strength * whý hast thou |
    put me | from thee : and why go I so heavily * whíle
    the | ene- . -my op- | -presseth | me ?

3 O send out thy light and thy trúth, that | they may |
    lead me : and bring me unto thy hóly | hill and | to
    thy | dwelling.

4 And that I may go unto the altar of God * even unto the
    Gód of my | joy and | gladness : and upon the harp will
    I give thanks unto thée, O | God | my | God.

5 Why art thou so héavy | O my | soul : and why art thou
    só dis- | -quiet- | -ed with- | -in me ?

6 O pút thy | trust in | God : for I will yet give him thanks *
    which is the hélp of my | countenance | and my | God.

Day 9.   MORNING PRAYER.

PSALM xliv.—*Deus, auribus.*

mf WE have heard with our ears, O Gód, our | fathers . have | told us : what thou hast dóne | in their | time of | old ;

2 How thou hast driven out the heathen with thy hand * and plánted | them | in : how thou hast destróyed the | nations . and | cast them | out.

3 For they gat not the land in possession * thróugh their | own | sword : neither was it their ówn | arm that | helped | them ;

4 But thy right hand and thine arm * and the líght | of thy | countenance : because thou hádst a | favour | unto | them.

5 Thóu art my | King O | God : sénd | help | unto | Jacob.

6 Through thee will we óver- | -throw our | enemies : and in thy Name will we tread them únder that | rise | up a- | -gainst us.

7 For I will not trúst | in my | bow : it is nót my | sword | that shall | help me ;

8 But it is thou that sávest us | from our | enemies : and púttest them | to con- | -fusion . that | hate us.

9 We make our boast of Gód | all day | long : ánd will | praise thy | Name for | ever.

p 10 But now thou art far off * and púttest us | to con- | fusion : and góest not | forth | with our | armies.

11 Thou makest us to turn our bácks up- | -on our | enemies : so that théy which | hate us | spoil our | goods.

12 Thou lettest us be éaten | up like | sheep : and hast scáttered | us a- | -mong the | heathen.

13 Thou séllest thy | people . for | nought : ánd | takest . no | money | for them.

14 Thou makest us to be rebúked | of our | neighbours : to be laughed to scorn * and had in derision of thém | that are | round a- | -bout us.

15 Thou makest us to be a bý-word a- | -mong the | heathen : and that the péople | shake their | heads | at us.

16 My confúsion is | daily . be- | -fore me : and the sháme of my | face hath | covered | me.

17 For the voice of the slánderer | and blas- | -phemer : fór the | enemy | and a- | -venger.

18 And though all this be come upon us * yét do we | not
   for- | -get thee : nor behåve ourselves | frowardly | in
   thy | covenant.

19 Our heárt is not | turned | back : neíther our | steps
   gone | out of . thy | way ;

20 No, not when thou hast smitten us ínto the | place of |
   dragons : and cóvered us | with the | shadow . of | death.

21 If we have forgotten the Name of our God * and holden
   up our hánds to any | strange | god : shall not God
   search it out * for he knoweth the véry | secrets | of
   the | heart.

22 For thy sake also are we kílled | all the . day | long : and
   are counted as shéep ap- | -pointed | to be | slain.

mf 23 Up, Lórd, why | sleepest | thou : awake, and bé not |
   absent . from | us for | ever.

24 Wherefore hídest | thou thy | face : and forgéttest our |
   mise- | -ry and | trouble ?

25 For our soul is brought lów, even | unto . the | dust : our
   bélly | cleaveth | unto . the | ground.

26 Aríse | and | help us : and delíver us | for thy | mercy's |
   sake.

Psalm xlv.—*Eructavit cor meum.*

mf   M Y heart is indíting of a | good | matter : I speak of the
   things which I' have | made | unto . the | King.

2 My tóngue | is the | pen : óf | — a | ready | writer.

3 Thou art fairer thán the | children . of | men : full of
   grace are thy lips * because Gód hath | blessed | thee
   for | ever.

4 Gird thee with thy sword upon thy thígh, O | thou most |
   Mighty : accórding to thy | worship | and re- | -nown.

5 Good lúck have thou | with thine | honour : ride on,
   because of the word of truth * of meekness and right-
   eousness * and thy right hánd shall | teach thee |
   terrible | things.

6 Thy arrows are very sharp * and the people shall be
   subdúed | unto | thee : even in the mídst a- | -mong
   the | King's | enemies.

7 Thy seat, O Gód, en- | -dureth . for | ever : the sceptre of
   thy kíngdom | is a | right | sceptre.

8 Thou hast loved ríghteousness and | hated . in- | -iquity :
   wherefore God, even thy God * hath anointed thee with
   the óil of | gladness . a- | -bove thy | fellows.

9 All thy garments smell of mýrrh | aloes . and | cassia : out of the ivory palaces * wherebý | they have | made thee | glad.

10 Kings' daughters were among thy hónour- | -able | women : upon thy right hand did stand the queen in a vesture of gold * wróught a- | -bout with | divers | colours.

11 Hearken, O daughter, and consíder, in- | -cline thine | ear : forget also thine own péople | and thy | father's | house.

12 So shall the King have pléasure | in thy | beauty : for he is thy Lord Gód, and | worship | thou | him.

13 And the daughter of Tyre shall be thére | with a | gift : like as the rich also among the people * shall máke their | suppli- | -cation . be- | -fore thee.

14 The King's daughter is all glóri- | -ous with- | -in : her clóthing | is of | wrought | gold.

15 She shall be brought unto the Kíng in | raiment . of | needlework : the virgins that be her fellows shall bear her company * and sháll be | brought | unto | thee.

16 With joy and gládness shall | they be | brought : and shall énter | into . the | King's | palace.

17 Instead of thy fáthers thou | shalt have | children : whom thou máyest make | princes . in | all | lands.

18 I will remember thy Name from one generátion | to an- | other : therefore shall the people give thanks unto thée | world with- | -out | end.

PSALM xlvi.—*Deus noster refugium.*

f GÓD is our | hope and | strength : a véry | present | help in | trouble.

2 Therefore will we not fear, thóugh the | earth be | moved : and though the hills be carried ínto the | midst | of the | sea.

3 Though the waters theréof | rage and | swell : and though the mountains sháke at the | tempest | of the | same.

4 The rivers of the flood thereof, shall make glád the | city . of | God : the holy place of the tábernacle | of the | most | Highest.

5 God is in the midst of her * therefore shall she nót | be re- | -moved : Gód shall | help her . and | that right | early.

6 The heathen make much adó, and the | kingdoms . are | moved : but God hath shewed his vóice, and the | earth shall | melt a- | -way.

^{2nd}
^{part.}
7 The Lórd of | hosts is | with us : the Gód of | Jacob | is our | refuge.

8 O come hither, and behold the wórks | of the | Lord : what destruction hé hath | brought up- | -on the | earth.

9 He maketh wars to céase in | all the | world : he breaketh the bow, and knappeth the spear in sunder * and búrneth the | chariots | in the | fire.

10 Be still then, and knów that | I am | God : I will be exalted among the heathen * and I' will be ex- | alted | in the | earth.

11 The Lórd of | hosts is | with us : the Gód of | Jacob | is our | refuge.

DAY 9. EVENING PRAYER.

PSALM xlvii.—*Omnes gentes, plaudite.*

F. *f*
O CLAP your hands togéther | all ye | people : O sing unto Gód | with the | voice of | melody.

F.
2 For the Lord is hígh, and | to be | feared : he is the great Kíng up- | -on | all the | earth.

3 He shall subdue the péople | under | us : ánd the | nations | under . our | feet.

4 He shall choose óut an | heritage | for us : even the wórship of | Jacob | whom he | loved.

5 God is gone úp with a | merry | noise : and the Lórd with the | sound | of the | trump.

6 O sing praises, sing práises | unto . our | God : O sing práises, sing | praises | unto . our | King.

7 For God is the Kíng of | all the | earth : síng ye | praises . with | under- | -standing.

8 God réigneth | over . the | heathen : God sítteth up- | -on his | holy | seat.

^{2nd}
^{part.}
9 The princes of the people * are joined unto the péople of the | God of | Abraham : for God, which is very high exalted * doth defend the éarth, as it | were | with a | shield.

Psalm xlviii.—*Magnus Dominus.*

f GREAT is the Lord, and híghly | to be | praised : in the city of our God * éven up- | -on his | holy | hill.

2 The hill of Sion is a fair place * and the jóy of the | whole | earth : upon the north side lieth the city of the great King * God is well known in her pálaces | as a | sure | refuge.

3 For lo, the kíngs | of the | earth : are gáthered and | gone | by to- | -gether.

4 They márvelled to | see such | things : they were astónished, and | sudden- . -ly | cast | down.

5 Fear came thére upon | them and | sorrow : as upón a | woman | in her | travail.

6 Thou shalt break the shíps | of the | sea : throúgh | — the | east- | -wind.

7 Like as we have heard * so have we seen in the city of the Lord of hosts * in the cíty | of our | God : Gód up- | -holdeth . the | same for | ever.

8 We wait for thy lóving- | -kindness . O | God : ín the | midst of | thy | temple.

9 O God, according to thy Name * so is thy praise únto the | world's | end : thy ríght | hand is | full of | righteousness.

10 Let the mount Sion rejoice * and the dáughter of | Judah . be | glad : bé- | -cause of | thy | judgements.

11 Walk about Sion, and gó | round a- | -bout her : ánd | tell the | towers there- | -of.

12 Mark well her bulwarks, sét | up her | houses : that ye may téll | them that | come | after.

2nd part. 13 For this God is our Gód for | ever . and | ever : he shall bé our | guide | unto | death.

Psalm xlix.—*Audite hæc, omnes.*

f O HEAR ye thís | all ye | people : ponder it with your ears * all yé that | dwell | in the | world;

2 High and lów | rich and | poor : óne | with | an- | -other.

mf 3 My móuth shall | speak of | wisdom : and my héart shall | muse of | under- | -standing.

4 I will incline mine éar | to the | parable : and shéw my dark | speech up- | -on the | harp.

5 Wherefore should I féar in the | days of | wickedness :
and when the wickedness of my heels cómpasseth |
me | round a- | -bout ?

6 There be some that put their trúst | in their | goods :
and boast themsélves in the | multitude | of their |
riches.

7 But no man máy de- | -liver . his | brother : nor make
agréement | unto | God | for him.

8 For it cost móre to re- | -deem their | souls : so that he
must lét | that a- | -lone for | ever ;

9 Yea, thóugh he | live | long : ánd | see | not the | grave.

10 For he seeth that wise men also díe and | perish . to- |
gether : as well as the ignorant and fóolish, and | leave
their | riches . for | other.

11 And yet they think that their houses sháll con- | -tinue .
for | ever : and that their dwelling-places shall endure
from one generation to another * and call the lánds |
after . their | own | names.

12 Nevertheless, mán will not a- | -bide in | honour : seeing
he may be compared unto the beasts that pérish |
this . is the | way of | them.

13 Thís | is their | foolishness : and théir pos- | -terity |
praise their | saying.

14 They lie in the hell like sheep * death gnaweth upon
them * and the righteous shall have domination óver
them | in the | morning : their beauty shall consúme in
the | sepulchre | out of . their | dwelling.

15 But God hath delivered my sóul from the | place of | hell :
fór | he | shall re- | -ceive me.

16 Be not thou afraid * thóugh one be | made | rich : or if
the glóry of his | house | be in- | -creased ;

17 For he shall carry nothing awáy with him | when he |
dieth : neither sháll his | pomp | follow | him.

18 For while he lived * he counted himsélf an | happy |
man : and so long as thou doest well unto thyself *
mén will | speak | good of | thee.

19 He shall follow the generátion | of his | fathers : ánd
shall | never | see | light.

20 Man being in honour hath nó | under- | -standing : but is
compáred | unto . the | beasts that | perish.

Day 10.   MORNING PRAYER.

Psalm 1.—*Deus deorum.*

F. *f*   THE Lord, even the most míghty | God hath | spoken :
          and called the world, from the rising up of the sun *
          únto the | going | down there- | -of.

F.   2 Out of Síon hath | God ap· | -peared : ín | per- | -fect |
          beauty.

       3 Our God shall cóme, and shall | not keep | silence : there
          shall go before him a consuming fire * and a mighty
          tempest sháll be | stirred . up | round a- | -bout
          him.

       4 He shall call the héaven | from a- | -bove : and the éarth,
          that | he may | judge his | people.

       5 Gather my saints togéther | unto | me : those that have
          made a cóve- | -nant with | me with | sacrifice.

       6 And the héavens shall de- | -clare his | righteousness :
          fór | God is | judge him- | -self.

       7 Hear, O my péople, and | I will | speak : I myself will
          testify against thee, O Israel * for I am Gód | even |
          thy | God.

       8 I will not reprove thee because of thy sacrifices * or fór
          thy | burnt- | -offerings : becáuse they | were not |
          alway . be- | -fore me.

       9 I will take no búllock | out of . thine | house : nór | he-
          goat | out of . thy | folds.

      10 For all the béasts of the | forest . are | mine : and so are
          the cáttle up- | -on a | thousand | hills.

      11 I know all the fówls up- | -on the | mountains : and the
          wild béasts of the | field are | in my | sight.

      12 If I be hungry, I' will | not tell | thee : for the whole
          world is míne, and | all that | is there- | -in.

      13 Thinkest thou that I' will | eat bulls' | flesh : ánd | drink
          the | blood of | goats ?

      14 Offer unto Gód | thanks- | -giving : and pay thy vóws |
          unto . the | most | Highest.

2nd 15 And call upon mé in the | time of | trouble : so will I
part.   héar thee, and | thou shalt | praise | me.

      16 But unto the ungódly | said | God : Why dost thou preach
          my laws * and tákest my | covenant | in thy | mouth ;

      17 Whereas thou hátest to | be re- | -formed : ánd hast |
          cast my | words be- | -hind thee ?

18 When thou sawest a thief * thou conséntedst | unto | him : and hast béen par- | -taker | with . the a- | dulterers.

19 Thou hast lét thy | mouth speak | wickedness : and with thy tóngue thou hast | set | forth de- | -ceit.

20 Thou satest, and spákest a- | -gainst thy | brother : yea, and hast slándered thine | own | mother's | son.

21 These things hast thou done, and I held my tongue * and thou thoughtest wickedly that I am even súch a one | as thy- | -self : but I will reprove thee * and set befóre thee the | things that | thou hast | done.

22 O consider this, yé that for- | -get | God : lest I pluck you away * and there be nóne | to de- | -liver | you.

23 Whoso offereth me thanks and práise, he | honoureth | me : and to him that ordereth his conversation ríght will I | shew the . sal- | -vation . of | God.

Psalm li.—*Miserere mei, Deus.*

p HAVE mercy upon me, O God * áfter thy | great | good-ness : according to the multitude of thy mercies, dó a- | -way | mine of- | -fences.

2 Wash me throúghly | from my | wickedness : ánd | cleanse me | from my | sin.

3 For I ac- | -knowledge . my | faults : ánd my | sin is | ever . be- | -fore me.

4 Against thee only have I sinned * and done this évil | in thy | sight : that thou mightest be justified in thy sáying, and | clear when | thou art | judged.

5 Behóld, I was | shapen . in | wickedness : and in sín hath my | mother . con- | -ceived | me.

6 But lo, thou requirest trúth in the | inward | parts : and shalt make me to únder- | -stand | wisdom | secretly.

7 Thou shalt purge me with hyssop * ánd I | shall be | clean : thou shalt wash me * ánd I | shall be | whiter . than | snow.

8 Thou shalt make me héar of | joy and | gladness : that the bones which thóu hast | broken | may re- | -joice.

9 Turn thy fáce | from my | sins : and pút out | all | my mis- | -deeds.

10 Make me a cléan | heart O | God : ánd re- | -new a . right | spirit . with- | -in me.

11 Cast me not awáy | from thy | presence : and táke not thy | holy | Spirit | from me.

AA

12 O give me the cómfort of thy | help a- | -gain : and stáblish me | with thy | free | Spirit.

2nd part. 13 Then shall I teach thy wáys | unto . the | wicked : and sinners shall bé con- | -verted | unto | thee.

14 Deliver me from blood-guiltiness, O God * thou that art the Gód | of my | health : and my tóngue shall | sing | of thy | righteousness.

15 Thou shalt ópen my | lips O | Lord : ánd my | mouth shall | shew thy | praise.

16 For thou desirest no sacrifice * élse would I | give it | thee : but thou delíghtest | not in | burnt- | -offerings.

17 The sacrifice of Gód is a | troubled | spirit : a broken and contrite heart, O Gód | shalt thou | not de- | -spise.

18 O be favourable and grácious | unto | Sion : buíld thou the | walls | of Je- | -rusalem.

19 Then shalt thou be pleased with the sacrifice of righteousness * with the burnt-ófferings | and ob- | -lations : then shall they óffer young | bullocks . up- | -on thine | altar.

Psalm lii.—*Quid gloriaris ?*

mf WHY bóastest thou thy- | -self thou | tyrant : thát | thou canst | do | mischief ;

2 Whereás the | goodness . of | God : én- | -dureth | yet | daily ?

3 Thy tóngue im- | -agineth | wickedness : and with lies thou cúttest | like a | sharp | razor.

4 Thou hast loved unríghteousness | more than | goodness : and to tálk of | lies | more than | righteousness.

5 Thou hast loved to speak all wórds that | may do | hurt : O' | — thou | false | tongue.

6 Therefore shall God destróy | thee for | ever : he shall take thee, and pluck thee out of thy dwelling * and root thee óut of the | land | of the | living.

7 The righteous also shall sée | this and | fear : ánd shall | laugh | him to | scorn.

8 Lo, this is the man that took not Gód | for his | strength : but trusted unto the multitude of his riches * and stréngthened him- | -self | in his | wickedness.

9 As for me, I am like a green olive trée in the | house of | God : my trust is in the tender mércy of | God for | ever . and | ever.

10 I will always give thanks unto thee for thát | thou hast | done : and I will hope in thy Name, fór thy | saints | like it | well.

Day 10.   EVENING PRAYER.

Psalm liii.—*Dixit insipiens.*

F. mp   THE foolish body hath sáid | in his | heart : Thére | is | no | God.

F.   2 Corrupt are they * and become abóminable | in their | wickedness : thére is | none that | doeth | good.

3 God looked down from heaven upón the | children . of | men : to see if there were any that would understánd, and | seek | after | God.

4 But they are all gone out of the way * they are alto-géther be- | -come a- | -bominable : there is also none that dóeth | good | no not | one.

5 Are not they without understánding that | work | wicked-ness : eating up my people as if they would eat bread * they háve not | called . up- | -on | God.

6 They were afráid where | no fear | was : for God hath broken the bones of him that besieged thee * thou hast put them to confusion * because Gód | hath de- | spised | them.

f   7 Oh, that the salvation were given unto Ísrael | out of | Sion : Oh, that the Lord would delíver his | people | out of . cap- | -tivity !

8 Thén should | Jacob . re- | -joice : and Ísrael | should be | right | glad.

Psalm liv.—*Deus, in nomine.*

mp   SAVE me, O Gód, for thy | Name's | sake : ánd a- | venge me | in thy | strength.

2 Héar my | prayer O | God : and hearken únto the | words | of my | mouth.

2nd part   3 For strangers are rísen | up a- | -gainst me : and tyrants, which have not God before their éyes | seek | after . my | soul.

4 Behold, Gód | is my | helper : the Lord is with thém | that up- | -hold my | soul.

5 He shall reward évil | unto . mine | enemies : destróy thou | them | in thy | truth.

6 An offering of a free heart will I give thee * and práise thy | Name O | Lord : bé- | -cause it | is so | com-fortable.

7 For he hath delivered me óut of | all my | trouble : and mine eye hath séen his de- | -sire up- | -on mine | enemies.

AA 2

Psalm lv.—*Exaudi, Deus.*

p HÉAR my | prayer O | God : and híde not thy- | -self
from | my pe- | -tition.

2 Take héed unto | me and | hear me : how I moúrn in
my | prayer | and am | vexed.

3 The enemy crieth so * and the ungodly cómeth | on so |
fast : for they are minded to do me some mischief * so
malíciously | are they | set a- | -gainst me.

4 My heart is disquíet- | -ed with- | -in me : and the féar
of | death is | fallen . up- | -on me.

5 Fearfulness and trémbling are | come up- | -on me : and
an horrible dréad hath | over- | -whelmed | me.

6 And I said, O that I had wíngs | like a | dove : for then
would I flée a- | -way and | be at | rest.

7 Lo, then would I gét me a- | -way far | off : ánd re- |
main | in the | wilderness.

8 I would make háste | to es- | -cape : becáuse of the |
stormy | wind and | tempest.

9 Destroy their tongues, O Lórd | and di- | -vide them : for
I have spied unríghteousness and | strife | in the | city.

10 Day and night they go about withín the | walls there- |
of : mischief also and sórrow are | in the | midst of | it.

11 Wíckedness | is there- | -in : deceit and guíle | go not |
out of . their | streets.

12 For it is not an open enemy that hath dóne me | this
dis- | -honour : fór | then I | could have | borne it.

13 Neither was it mine adversary * that did mágnify him- |
self a- | -gainst me : for then, peradventure, I' would
have | hid my- | -self | from him.

14 But it was even thóu | my com- | -panion : my guíde, and
mine | own fa- | -miliar | friend.

15 We tóok sweet | counsel . to- | -gether : and wálked in
the | house of | God as | friends.

16 Let death come hastily upon them * and let them go
down quíck | into | hell : for wickedness is ín their |
dwellings | and a- | -mong them.

mf 17 As for mé, I will | call up- . -on | God : ánd the | Lord |
shall | save me.

18 In the evening and morning * and at noonday will I práy,
and | that | instantly : ánd | he shall | hear my | voice.

19 It is he that hath delivered my soul in peace * from the
báttle that | was a- | -gainst me : fór | there were |
many | with me.

20 Yea, even God that endureth for ever * shall héar me, and | bring them | down : for they wíll not | turn nor | fear | God.

21 He laid his hands upon such as bé at | peace with | him : ánd he | brake | his | covenant.

22 The words of his mouth were softer than butter * having wár | in his | heart : his words were smoother than oil * and yét | be they | very | swords.

23 O cast thy burden upon the Lord * and hé shall | nourish | thee : and shall not súffer the | righteous . to | fall for | ever.

24 And | as for | them : thou, O God, shalt bring them ínto the | pit | of de- | -struction.

2nd part. 25 The blood-thirsty and deceitful men * shall not live óut | half their | days : nevertheless, my trúst shall | be in | thee O | Lord.

Day 11.   MORNING PRAYER.

PSALM lvi.—*Miserere mei, Deus.*

mp BE merciful unto me, O God * for man goeth abóut | to de- | -vour me : he is dáily | fighting . and | troubling | me.

2 Mine enemies are daily in hánd to | swallow . me | up : for they be many that fíght against | me O | thou most | Highest.

3 Nevertheless, thóugh I am | sometime . a- | -fraid : yét put | I my | trust in | thee.

4 I will praise God, becáuse | of his | word : I have put my trust in God * and will not féar what | flesh can | do . unto | me.

5 They dáily mis- | -take my | words : all that they imágine | is to | do me | evil.

6 They hold all togéther and | keep them- . -selves | close : and mark my steps * whén they lay | wait | for my | soul.

7 Shall they escápe | for their | wickedness : thou, O Gód, in thy dis- | -pleasure . shalt | cast them | down.

8 Thou tellest my flittings * put my téars | into . thy | bottle : are not thése things | noted | in thy | book?

9 Whensoever I call upon thee * then shall mine énemies
be | put to | flight : this I knów, for | God is | on my |
side.

10 In God's wórd will | I re- | -joice : in the Lórd's word |
will I | comfort | me.

11 Yea, in Gód have I | put my | trust : I will not be afráid
what | man can | do . unto | me.

12 Unto thee, O Gód, will I | pay my | vows : unto thée |
will I | give | thanks.

2nd part. 13 For thou hast delivered my soul from déath and my |
feet from | falling : that I may walk before Gód in the |
light | of the | living.

PSALM lvii.—*Miserere mei, Deus.*

mp   Be merciful unto me, O God * be merciful unto me, for
my sóul | trusteth . in | thee : and under the shadow
of thy wings shall be my refuge * untíl this | tyranny .
be | over- | -past.

2 I will cáll unto the | most high | God : even unto the God
that shall perform the cáuse | which I | have in | hand.

3 Hé shall | send from | heaven : and save me from the
reproof of hím | that would | eat me | up.

4 God shall send fórth his | mercy . and | truth : my sóul |
is a- | -mong | lions.

5 And I lie even among the children of mén that are | set
on | fire : whose teeth are spears and arrows * ánd
their | tongue a | sharp | sword.

6 Set up thyself, O Gód, a- | -bove the | heavens : and thy
glóry a- | -bove | all the | earth.

7 They have laid a net for my feet * and préssed | down
my | soul : they have digged a pit before me * and are
fallen ínto the | midst of | it them- | -selves.

8 My heart is fixed, O Gód, my | heart is | fixed : Í will |
sing and | give | praise.

mf   9 Awake up, my glory * awáke | lute and | harp : I mysélf |
will a- | -wake right | early.

10 I will give thanks unto thee, O Lórd, a- | -mong the |
people : and I will síng unto | thee a- | -mong the |
nations.

11 For the greatness of thy mercy réacheth | unto . the |
heavens : ánd thy | truth | unto . the | clouds.

12 Set up thyself, O Gód, a- | -bove the | heavens : and thy
glóry a- | -bove | all the | earth.

Psalm lviii.—*Si vere utique.*

mf ARE your minds set upon righteousness * O´ ye | congre- | -gation : and do ye judge the thing that is ríght |
O ye | sons of | men ?

2 Yea, ye imagine mischief in your héart up- | -on the |
earth : ánd your | hands | deal with | wickedness.

3 The ungodly are froward * even fróm their | mother's |
womb : as soon as they are born * they gó a- | -stray
and | speak | lies.

4 They are as venomous as the póison | of a | serpent : even
like the déaf | adder . that | stoppeth . her | ears ;

5 Which refuseth to hear the vóice | of the | charmer :
chárm he | never | so | wisely.

6 Break their teeth, O God, in their mouths * smite the
jaw-bónes of the | lions . O | Lord : let them fall away
like water that runneth apace * and when they shoot
their árrows | let them . be | rooted | out.

7 Let them consume away like a snail * and be like the
untimely frúit | of a | woman : ánd | let them . not |
see the | sun.

8 Or ever your póts be made | hot with | thorns : so let
indignation vex him * éven as a | thing | that is |
raw.

9 The righteous shall rejóice when he | seeth . the |
vengeance : he shall wash his footsteps ín the | blood
of | the un- | -godly.

10 So that a man shall say, Verily there is a rewárd | for
the | righteous : doubtless, there ís a | God that |
judgeth . the | earth.

Day 11.   EVENING PRAYER

Psalm lix.—*Eripe me de inimicis.*

F. mp DELIVER me from mine énemies | O | God : defend me
from thém that | rise | up a- | -gainst me.

F.   2 O deliver me fróm the | wicked | doers : and sáve me |
from the | blood-thirsty | men.

3 For lo, they lie wáiting | for my | soul : the mighty men
are gathered against me * without any offénce or |
fault of | me O | Lord.

4 They run and prepare themsélves with- | -out my | fault :
arise thou thérefore to | help me | and be- | -hold.

5 Stand up, O Lord God of hosts, thou God of Israel * to
vísit | all the | heathen : and be not merciful unto
them that offénd | of ma- | -licious | wickedness.

6 They go to and frô | in the | evening : they grin like a
dog, and rún a- | -bout | through the | city.

7 Behold, they speak with their mouth * and swôrds are |
in their | lips : fôr | who | doth | hear ?

8 But thou, O Lord, shalt háve them | in de- | -rision : and
thou shalt láugh | all the | heathen . to | scorn.

9 My strength will I ascríbe | unto | thee : for thôu art
the | God | of my | refuge.

10 God shéweth me his | goodness | plenteously : and God
shall let me sée my de- | -sire up- | -on mine |
enemies.

11 Slay them not, lést my | people . for- | -get it : but
scatter them abroad among the people * and put them
dówn, O | Lord | our de- | -fence.

12 For the sin of their mouth, and for the words of their
lips * they shall be táken | in their | pride : and why *
their préaching | is of | cursing . and | lies.

13 Consume them in thy wrath * consúme them that | they
may | perish : and know that it is God that ruleth in
Jacob * and únto the | ends | of the | world.

14 And in the évening they | will re- | -turn : grin like a
dôg, and will | go a- | -bout the | city.

15 They will rún here and | there for | meat : and grúdge |
if they | be not | satisfied.

16 As for me, I will sing of thy power * and will praise thy
mercy betímes | in the | morning : for thou hast been
my defence and refuge * ín the | day | of my | trouble.

2nd part. 17 Unto thee, O my stréngth | will I | sing : for thou, O God,
art my réfuge | and my | ·merciful | God.

Psalm lx.—*Deus, repulisti nos.*

mp O GOD, thou hast cast us out * and scáttered | us a- |
broad : thou hast also been displeased * O túrn thee |
unto | us a- | -gain.

2 Thou hast moved the lánd, and di- | -vided | it : heal the
sóres there- | -of | for it | shaketh.

3 Thou hast shewed thy péople | heavy | things : thou hast
gíven us a | drink of | deadly | wine.

4 Thou hast given a tóken for | such as | fear thee : that
they may tríumph be- | -cause | of the | truth.

5 Therefore were thý be- | -loved . de- | -livered : hélp me
with | thy right | hand and | hear me.

6 God hath spoken in his holiness * I will rejóice, and di- |
vide | Sichem : and méte | out the | valley . of |
Succoth.

7 Gilead is míne, and Ma- | -nasses . is | mine : Ephraim
also is the strength of my héad | Judah | is my | law-
giver ;

8 Moab is my wash-pot * over Edom will I cást | out my |
shoe : Philístia | be thou | glad of | me.

9 Who will lead me ínto the | strong | city : whó will |
bring me | into | Edom ?

10 Hast not thou cást us | out O | God : wilt not thou, O
Gód, go | out | with our | hosts ?

11 O be thóu our | help in | trouble : for váin | is the | help
of | man.

12 Through Gód will we | do great | acts : for it is hé that
shall | tread | down our | enemies.

Psalm lxi.—*Exaudi, Deus.*

mf HÉAR my | crying . O | God : gíve | ear | unto . my |
prayer.

2 From the ends of the éarth will I | call up- . -on | thee :
whén my | heart | is in | heaviness.

3 O set me up upon the róck that is | higher . than | I : for
thou hast been my hope * and a strong tówer for | me
a- | -gainst the | enemy.

4 I will dwell in thy táber- | -nacle . for | ever : and my
trust shall be únder the | covering | of thy | wings.

5 For thou, O Lord, hast héard | my de- | -sires : and hast
given an heritage únto | those that | fear thy | Name.

6 Thou shalt grant the Kíng a | long | life : that his years
may endúre throughout | all | gener- | -ations.

7 He shall dwéll before | God for | ever : O prepare thy
loving mercy and fáithfulness | that they | may pre- |
serve him.

8 So will I alway sing práise | unto . thy | Name : that Í
may | daily . per- | -form my | vows.

Day 12.   MORNING PRAYER.

Psalm lxii.—*Nonne Deo?*

mf MY soul truly wáiteth | still up- . -on | God : for of hím | cometh | my sal- | -vation.

2 He verily is my stréngth and | my sal- | -vation : he is my defence, só that I | shall not | greatly | fall.

3 How long will ye imagine mischief agáinst | every | man : ye shall be slain all the sort of you * yea, as a tottering wall shall ye bé, and | like a | broken | hedge.

4 Their device is only how to put him out whom Gód | will ex- | -alt : their delight is in lies * they give good words with their móuth, but | curse | with their | heart.

5 Nevertheless, my soul * wáit thou | still up- . -on | God : fór my | hope | is in | him.

6 He truly is my stréngth and | my sal- | -vation : he is my deféence | so that . I | shall not | fall.

7 In God is my héalth | and my | glory : the rock of my might * ánd in | God | is my | trust.

8 O put your trust in hím | alway . ye | people : pour out your hearts befóre him, for | God | is our | hope.

9 As for the children of mén | they are . but | vanity : the children of men are deceitful upon the weights * they are altogether líghter than | vani- | -ty it- | -self.

10 O trust not in wrong and robbery * give not yoursélves | unto | vanity : if riches increase, sét | not your | heart up- | -on them.

11 God spake once, and twice I have álso | heard the | same : that pówer be- | -longeth | unto | God ;

12 And that thóu | Lord art | merciful : for thou rewardest every mán ac- | -cording | to his | work.

Psalm lxiii.—*Deus, Deus meus.*

mf O GÓD, thou art | my | God : éarly | will I | seek | thee.

2 My soul thirsteth for thee * my flesh also lóngeth | after | thee : in a barren and dry lánd | where no | water | is.

3 Thus have I lóoked for | thee in | holiness : that I míght be- | -hold thy | power . and | glory.

4 For thy loving-kindness is better thán the | life it- | -self : mý | lips | shall | praise thee.

5 As long as I live will I mágnify thee | on this | manner :
  and lift úp my | hands in | thy | Name.

6 My soul shall be satisfied * even as it wére with |
  marrow . and | fatness : when my mouth práiseth | thee
  with | joyful | lips.

7 Have I not remembered thée | in my | bed : and thóught
  upon | thee when | I was | waking ?

8 Becáuse thou hast | been my | helper : therefore under
  the shádow of thy | wings will | I re- | -joice.

9 My sóul | hangeth . up- | -on thee : thy right hánd | hath
  up- | -holden | me.

10 These also that seek the húrt | of my | soul : théy shall |
   go | under . the | earth.

11 Let them fall upon the édge | of the | sword : that théy
   may | be a | portion . for | foxes.

12 But the King shall rejoice in God * all they also that
   swear by hím shall | be com- | -mended : for the mouth
   of thém that speak | lies | shall be | stopped.

Psalm lxiv.—*Exaudi, Deus.*

mp HEAR my voice, O Gód | in my | prayer : preserve my
      lífe from | fear | of the | enemy.

2 Hide me from the gathering togéther | of the | froward :
  and from the ínsur- | -rection . of | wicked | doers ;

3 Who have whet their tóngue | like a | sword : and shoot
  out their árrows | even | bitter | words :

4 That they may privily shoot at hím | that is | perfect :
  suddenly dó they | hit him | and | fear not.

5 They encóurage them- | -selves in | mischief : and com-
  mune among themselves, how they may lay snares *
  and sáy that | no | man shall | see them.

6 They imagine wíckedness and | practise | it : that they
  keep secret among themselves * every man ín the |
  deep | of his | heart.

7 But God shall suddenly shoot at thém with a | swift |
  arrow : thát | they | shall be | wounded.

8 Yea, their own tóngues shall | make them | fall : insomuch
  that whoso séeth them shall | laugh | them to | scorn.

9 And all men that see it shall say, Thís hath | God |
  done : for they shall percéive that | it is | his | work.

10 The righteous shall rejoice in the Lord * and pút his |
   trust in | him : and all they that are trúe of | heart |
   shall be | glad.

Day 12.   EVENING PRAYER.

Psalm lxv.—*Te decet hymnus.*

F.mf   THOU, O Gód, art | praised . in | Sion : and unto thee
           shall the vów be per- | -formed | in Je- | -rusalem.

F.   2 Thóu that | hearest . the | prayer : únto | thee shall |
        all flesh | come.

    3 My misdéeds pre- | -vail a- | -gainst me : O′ be thou |
        merciful | unto . our | sins.

    4 Blessed is the man, whom thou choosest, and recéivest |
        unto | thee : he shall dwell in thy court * and shall be
        satisfied with the pleasures of thy house * éven | of
        thy | holy | temple.

    5 Thou shalt shew us wonderful things in thy righteous-
        ness * O Gód of | our sal- | -vation : thou that art the
        hope of all the ends of the earth * and of them that
        remáin | in the | broad | sea.

    6 Who in his stréngth setteth | fast the | mountains : ánd
        is | girded . a- | -bout with | power.

    7 Who stilleth the ráging | of the | sea : and the noise of
        his wáves, and the | madness | of the | people.

    8 They also that dwell in the uttermost parts of the earth *
        shall be afráid | at thy | tokens : thou that makest the
        outgoings of the mórning and | evening . to | praise |
        thee.

    9 Thou visitest the eárth and | blessest | it : thóu |
        makest . it | very | plenteous.

  10 The river of Gód is | full of | water : thou preparest
        their corn * for só thou pro- | -videst | for the |
        earth.

  11 Thou waterest her furrows * thou sendest rain into the
        líttle | valleys . there- | -of : thou makest it soft with
        the drops of ráin, and | blessest . the | increase |
        of it.

  12 Thou crownest the yéar | with thy | goodness : ánd thy |
        clouds | drop | fatness.

  13 They shall drop upon the dwéllings | of the | wilder-
        ness : and the little hílls shall re- | -joice on | every |
        side.

  14 The fólds shall be | full of | sheep : the valleys also shall
        stand so thick with córn that | they shall | laugh and |
        sing.

Psalm lxvi.—*Jubilate Deo.*

f O BE joyful in Gód | all ye | lands : sing praises unto the honour of his Name * máke his | praise | to be | glorious.

2 Say unto God, O how wonderful art thóu | in thy | works : through the greatness of thy power * shall thine enemies be fóund | liars | unto | thee.

3 For all the wórld shall | worship | thee : síng of | thee and | praise thy | Name.

4 O come hither, and behóld the | works of | God : how wonderful he is in his dóing | towards . the | children . of | men.

5 He turned the séa into | dry | land : so that they went through the water on foot * thére did | we re- | -joice there- | -of.

6 He ruleth with his power for ever * his éyes be- | -hold the | people : and such as will not believe, shall not be áble | to ex- | -alt them- | -selves.

7 O práise our | God ye | people : and make the vóice of his | praise | to be | heard ;

8 Who hóldeth our | soul in | life : and súffereth | not our | feet to | slip.

9 For thou, O Gód, hast | proved | us : thou also hast tríed us | like as | silver . is | tried.

10 Thou bróughtest us | into . the | snare : and láidest | trouble . up- | -on our | loins.

11 Thou sufferedst men to ríde | over . our | heads : we went through fire and water * and thou broughtest us óut | into . a | wealthy | place.

12 I will go into thine hóuse with | burnt- | -offerings : ánd will pay thee my vows * which I promised with my lips, and spake with my móuth | when I | was in | trouble.

13 I will offer unto thee fat burnt-sacrifices * wíth the | incense . of | rams : I′ will | offer | bullocks . and | goats.

14 O come hither, and hearken * all yé that | fear | God : and I will tell you what hé hath | done | for my | soul.

15 I called unto hím | with my | mouth : and gáve him | praises | with my | tongue.

16 If I incline unto wíckedness | with mine | heart : thé | Lord | will not | hear me.

17 Bút | God hath | heard me : and consídered the | voice | of my | prayer.

18 Praised be God, who hath nót cast | out my | prayer : nór | turned . his | mercy | from me.

Psalm lxvii.—*Deus misereatur.*

mf GOD be merciful únto | us and | bless us : and shew us
the light of his countenance * ánd be | merciful |
unto | us ;

2 That thy way may be knówn up- | -on | earth : thy
sáving | health a- | -mong all | nations.

F. 3 Let the people práise | thee O | God : yéa, let | all the |
people | praise thee.

4 O let the nations rejóice | and be | glad : for thou shalt
judge the folk righteously * and góvern the | nations .
up- | -on | earth.

F. 5 Let the people práise | thee O | God : lét | all the |
people | praise thee.

6 Then shall the éarth bring | forth her | increase : and
God, even our own Gód, shall | give | us his | blessing.

2nd part. 7 Gód | shall | bless us : and all the énds of the | world
shall | fear | him.

Day 13. MORNING PRAYER.

Psalm lxviii.—*Exurgat Deus.*

F. f LET God arise, and let his éne- | -mies be | scattered : let
them álso that | hate him | flee be- | -fore him.

F. 2 Like as the smoke vanisheth * so shalt thou dríve | them
a- | -way : and like as wax melteth at the fire * so let
the ungodly pérish | at the | presence . of | God.

3 But let the righteous be glád and re- | -joice be- . -fore |
God : lét them | also . be | merry . and | joyful.

4 O sing unto God, and sing práises | unto . his | Name :
magnify him that rideth upon the heavens as it were
upon an horse * praise him in his Name JA'H | and
re- | -joice be- | -fore him.

5 He is a Father of the fatherless * and defendeth the
cáuse | of the | widows : even Gód in his | holy |
habit- | -ation.

6 He is the God that maketh men to be of óne mind in an
house * and bringeth the prísoners | out of . cap- |
tivity : but letteth the runagátes con- | -tinue | in |
scarceness.

7 O God, when thou wentest fórth be- | -fore the | people :
whén thou | wentest | through the | wilderness,

8 The earth shook, and the heavens dropped át the |
   presence . of | God : even as Sinai also was moved at
   the presence of Gód, who | is the | God of | Israel.

9 Thou, O God, sentest a gracious ráin upon | thine in- |
   heritance : and refréshedst | it when | it was | weary.

10 Thy congregátion shall | dwell there- | -in : for thou, O
   God, hast of thy góodness pre- | -pared | for the |
   poor.

11 The Lórd | gave the | word : gréat was the | company |
   of the | preachers.

12 Kings with their armies did flée, and | were dis- |
   comfited : and théy of the | household . di- | -vided .
   the | spoil.

13 Though ye have lien among the pots * yet shall ye be as
   the wíngs | of a | dove : that is covered with silver
   wíngs | and her | feathers . like | gold.

14 When the Almighty scattered kíngs | for their | sake :
   thén were they as | white as | snow in | Salmon.

15 As the hill of Basan, só is | God's | hill : even an hígh
   hill | as the | hill of | Basan.

16 Why hop ye so ye high hills * this is God's hill, in the
   which it pléaseth | him to | dwell : yea, the Lórd will
   a- | -bide in | it for | ever.

17 The chariots of God are twenty thousand * éven |
   thousands . of | angels : and the Lord is among them *
   as ín the | holy | place of | Sinai.

18 Thou art gone up on high * thou hast led captivity
   captive, and recéived | gifts for | men : yea, even for
   thine enemies * that the Lórd | God might | dwell a- |
   mong them.

19 Praised bé the | Lord | daily : even the God who helpeth
   us, and póureth his | bene- | -fits up- | -on us.

20 He is our God * even the Gód of whom | cometh . sal- |
   vation : God is the Lórd, by | whom . we es- | -cape |
   death.

21 God shall wound the héad | of his | enemies : and the
   hairy scalp of such a one as góeth on | still | in his |
   wickedness.

22 The Lord hath said * I will bring my people agáin, as I |
   did from | Basan : mine own will I bring again * as I
   did sometime fróm the | deep | of the | sea.

2nd part. 23 That thy foot may be dipped in the blóod | of thine |
   enemies : and that the tongue of thy dógs may be | red |
   through the | same.

24 It is well seen, O Gód | how thou | goest : how thou, my
God and Kíng | goest | in the | sanctuary.

25 The singers go before * the mínstrels | follow | after : in
the midst are the dámsels | playing | with the |
timbrels.

26 Give thanks, O Israel, unto God the Lórd in the | congre- |
gations : fróm the | ground | of the | heart.

27 There is little Benjamin their ruler * and the prínces of |
Judah . their | counsel : the princes of Zabúlon | and
the | princes . of | Nephthali.

28 Thy God hath sént forth | strength for | thee : stablish the
thing, O Gód, that | thou hast | wrought in | us,

29 For thy temple's sáke | at Je- | -rusalem : so shall kíngs
bring | presents | unto | thee.

30 When the company of the spear-men, and multitude of
the mighty * are scattered abroad among the beasts of
the people * so that they húmbly bring | pieces . of |
silver : and when he hath scattered the péople | that
de- | -light in | war;

31 Then shall the princes cóme | out of | Egypt : the
Morians' land shall soon stretch óut her | hands | unto |
God.

ff 32 Sing unto God, O ye kíngdoms | of the | earth : O' sing |
praises | unto . the | Lord;

33 Who sitteth in the heavens over áll | from . the be- |
ginning : lo, he doth send out his voice * yéa, and |
that a | mighty | voice.

34 Ascribe ye the power to Gód | over | Israel : his wórship
and | strength is | in the | clouds.

35 O God, wonderful art thóu in thy | holy | places : even
the God of Israel * he will give strength and power
unto his péople | blessed | be | God.

Day 13.   EVENING PRAYER.

PSALM lxix.—*Salvum me fac.*

F. mp SÁVE | me O | God : for the waters are come ín | even |
unto . my | soul.

F.   2 I stick fast in the deep mire * whére no | ground | is : I
am come into deep waters * só that the | floods run |
over | me.

3 I am weary of crying; my | throat is | dry : my sight faileth me for waiting so | long up- | -on my | God.

4 They that hate me without a cause, are more than the hairs | of my | head : they that are mine enemies, and would de- | -stroy me | guiltless . are | mighty.

5 I paid them the things that I | never | took : God, thou knowest my simpleness * and my faults | are not | hid from | thee.

6 Let not them that trust in thee, O Lord God of hosts * be ashamed for | my | cause : let not those that seek thee * be confounded through me, O | Lord | God of | Israel.

7 And why * for thy sake have I | suffered . re- | -proof : shame hath | covered | my | face.

8 I am become a stranger | unto . my | brethren : even an alien | unto . my | mother's | children.

9 For the zeal of thine house hath even | eaten | me : and the rebukes of them that rebuked | thee are | fallen . up- | -on me.

10 I wept, and chastened my- | -self with | fasting : and that was | turned . to | my re- | -proof.

11 I put on | sackcloth | also : and they | jested . up- | -on | me.

12 They that sit in the gate | speak a- | -gainst me : and the | drunkards . make | songs up- | -on me.

13 But, Lord, I make my prayer | unto | thee : in | an ac- | ceptable | time.

14 Hear me, O God, in the multitude | of thy | mercy : even in the | truth of | thy sal- | -vation.

15 Take me out of the mire | that I | sink not : O let me be delivered from them that hate me * and | out . of the | deep | waters.

16 Let not the water-flood drown me * neither let the deep | swallow . me | up : and let not the pit | shut her | mouth up- | -on me.

17 Hear me, O Lord, for thy loving- | -kindness . is | comfortable : turn thee unto me according to the | multitude | of thy | mercies.

18 And hide not thy face from thy servant for | I am . in | trouble : O | haste | thee and | hear me.

19 Draw nigh unto my | soul and | save it : O deliver me, be- | -cause of | mine | enemies.

20 Thou hast known my reproof, my sháme, and | my dis- | -honour : mine ádversaries are | all in | thy | sight.

21 Thy rebuke hath broken my heart * I′ am | full of | heaviness : I looked for some to have pity on me, but there was no man * neither fóund I | any . to | comfort | me.

22 They gáve me | gall to | eat : and when I was thirsty they gáve me | vine- | -gar to | drink.

23 Let their table be made a snare to táke them- | -selves with- | -al : and let the things that should have been for their wealth * be unto thém | an oc- | -casion . of | falling.

24 Let their eyes be blínded | that they | see not : and éver | bow thou | down their | backs.

25 Pour out thine índig- | -nation . up- | -on them : and let thy wráthful dis- | -pleasure . take | hold of | them.

26 Let their hábit- | -ation . be | void : and nó man to | dwell | in their | tents.

27 For they persecute hím whom | thou hast | smitten : and they talk how they may véx | them whom | thou hast | wounded.

28 Let them fall from one wíckedness | to an- | -other : ánd | not come | into . thy | righteousness.

29 Let them be wiped out of the bóok | of the | living : and nót be | written . a- | -mong the | righteous.

30 As for me, when I am póor | and in | heaviness : thy hélp, O | God shall | lift me | up.

f 31 I will praise the name of Gód | with a | song : and mágni- | -fy it . with | thanks- | -giving.

32 This álso shall | please the | Lord : better than a búllock | that hath | horns and | hoofs.

33 The humble shall consider thís | and be | glad : seek ye after Gód | and your | soul shall | live.

34 For the Lórd | heareth . the | poor : ánd de- | -spiseth | not his | prisoners.

35 Let héaven and | earth | praise him : the séa, and | all that | moveth . there- | -in.

36 For God will save Sion * and buíld the | cities . of | Judah : that men may dwell thére, and | have it | in pos- | -session.

2nd part. 37 The posterity also of his servants sháll in- | -herit | it : and they that lóve his | Name shall | dwell there- | in.

PSALM lxx.—*Deus in adjutorium.*

p HASTE thee, O Gód, to de- | -liver | me : make háste to | help | me O | Lord.

2 Let them be ashamed and confounded, that séek | after . my | soul : let them be turned backward * and pút to con- | -fusion . that | wish me | evil.

3 Let them for their reward be sóon | brought to | shame : that crý | over . me | There | there.

4 But let all those that seek thee be jóyful and | glad in | thee : and let all such as delight in thy salvation say álway, The | Lord | be | praised.

5 As for me, I am póor | and in | misery : háste thee | unto | me O | God.

6 Thou art my hélper and | my re- | -deemer : O Lórd | make no | long | tarrying.

Day 14.   MORNING PRAYER.

PSALM lxxi.—*In te, Domine, speravi.*

mp IN thee, O Lord, have I put my trust * let me never be pút | to con- | -fusion : but rid me, and deliver me in thy righteousness * incline thine éar | unto | me and | save me.

2 Be thou my stronghold * whereuntó I may | alway . re- | sort : thou hast promised to help me * for thou art my hóuse of de- | -fence | and my | castle.

3 Deliver me, O my God, out of the hánd of | the un- | godly : out of the hánd of the un- | -righteous . and | cruel | man.

4 For thou, O Lord God, art the thíng | that I | long for : thou art my hópe | even | from my | youth.

5 Through thee have I been holden up ever sínce | I was | born : thou art he that took me out of my mother's womb * my práise | shall be | always . of | thee.

6 I am become as it were a mónster | unto | many : but my súre | trust | is in | thee.

7 O let my mouth be fílled | with thy | praise : that I may sing of thy glory and hónour | all the | day | long.

8 Cast me not awáy in the | time of | age : forsake me not whén my | strength | faileth | me.

9 For mine enemies speak against me * and they that lay
wait for my soul take their cóunsel to- | -gether | say-
ing : God hath forsaken him * persecute him and take
him * for there is nóne | to de- | -liver | him.

10 Go not fár from | me O | God : my Gód | haste | thee to |
help me.

11 Let them be confounded and perish that áre a- | -gainst
my | soul : let them be covered with shame and dis-
hónour that | seek to | do me | evil.

12 As for me, I will pátiently a- | -bide | alway : ánd will |
praise thee | more and | more.

f 13 My mouth shall daily speak of thy ríghteousness | and
sal- | -vation : fór I | know no | end there- | -of.

14 I will go forth in the stréngth of the | Lord | God : and
will make méntion | of thy | righteousness | only.

mf 15 Thou, O God, hast taught me from my yoúth up | until |
now : therefore will I téll | of thy | wondrous | works.

16 Forsake me not, O God, in mine old age * whén I am |
gray- | -headed : until I have shewed thy strength unto
this generation * and thy power to all thém that are |
yet | for to | come.

17 Thy righteousness, O Gód, is | very | high : and great
things are they that thou hast done * O Gód | who is |
like . unto | thee ?

18 O what great troubles and adversities hast thou shewed
me * and yet didst thou túrn | and re- | -fresh me :
yea, and broughtest me from the déep | of the | earth
a- | -gain.

19 Thou hast bróught me to | great | honour : and cóm-
forted | me on | every | side.

20 Therefore will I praise thee and thy faithfulness, O God *
playing upon an ínstru- | -ment of | musick : unto thee
will I sing upon the harp * O' thou| Holy|One of | Israel.

21 My lips will be fain when I síng | unto | thee : and so
will my sóul | whom thou | hast de- | -livered.

22 My tongue also shall talk of thy ríghteousness | all the .
day | long : for they are confounded and brought unto
sháme that | seek to | do me | evil.

Psalm lxxii.—*Deus, judicium.*

f GIVE the Kíng thy | judgements . O | God : and thy
ríghteousness | unto . the | King's | son.

2 Then shall he judge thy people accórding | unto | right :
ánd de- | -fend | the | poor.

3 The mountains álso shall | bring | peace : and the little
hílls | righteousness | unto . the | people.

4 He shall keep the símple folk | by their | right : defend
the children of the póor, and | punish . the | wrong |
doer.

5 They shall fear thee, as long as the sún and | moon en- |
dureth : from óne gener- | -ation | to an- | -other.

6 He shall come down like the ráin into a | fleece of | wool :
éven as the | drops that | water . the | earth.

7 In his tíme shall the | righteous | flourish : yea, and
abundance of péace, so | long . as the | moon en- |
dureth.

8 His dominion shall be also from the óne sea | to the |
other : and from the flóod | unto . the | world's | end.

9 They that dwell in the wílderness shall | kneel be- | -fore
him : his éne- | -mies shall | lick the | dust.

10 The kings of Tharsis and of the ísles shall | give |
presents : the kings of Arábia and | Saba | shall bring |
gifts.

11 All kings shall fáll | down be- | -fore him : áll | nations .
shall | do him | service.

12 For he shall deliver the póor | when he | crieth : the
needy álso, and | him that | hath no | helper.

13 He shall be favourable tó the | simple . and | needy : and
shall presérve the | souls | of the | poor.

14 He shall deliver their sóuls from | falsehood . and |
wrong : and déar shall their | blood be | in his |
sight.

15 He shall live * and unto him shall be given of the góld |
of A- | -rabia : prayer shall be made ever unto hím,
and | daily . shall | he be | praised.

16 There shall be an heap of corn in the earth * hígh up- |
on the | hills : his fruit shall shake like Libanus * and
shall be green in the cíty, like | grass up- | -on the |
earth.

17 His Name shall endure for ever * his Name shall remain
under the sún a- | -mong the . pos- | -terities : which
shall be blessed through hím, and | all the | heathen .
shall | praise him.

18 Blessed be the Lord God * éven the | God of | Israel :
which ónly | doeth | wondrous | things ;

2nd part. 19 And blessed be the Name of his Májes- | -ty for | ever :
and all the earth shall be filled with his Májesty. |
Amen | A- | -men.

DAY 14. EVENING PRAYER.

PSALM lxxiii.—*Quam bonus Israel!*

F. mp TRULY God is lóving | unto | Israel : even unto súch as | are . of a | clean | heart.

F. 2 Nevertheless, my féet were | almost | gone : mý | treadings . had | well-nigh | slipt.

3 And why * I was gríeved | at the | wicked : I do also sée the un- | -godly . in | such pros- | -perity.

4 For they are ín no | peril . of | death : bút are | lusty | and | strong.

5 They come in no misfórtune like | other | folk : neither áre they | plagued . like | other | men.

6 And this is the cause that they áre so | holden . with | pride : ánd | over- | -whelmed . with | cruelty.

7 Their éyes | swell with | fatness : and they dó | even | what they | lust.

8 They corrupt other * and spéak of | wicked | blasphemy : their talking ís a- | -gainst the | most | High.

9 For they stretch forth their móuth | unto . the | heaven : and their tóngue | goeth | through the | world.

10 Therefore fall the péople | unto | them : and theróut suck | they no | small ad- | -vantage.

11 Tush, say they * hów should | God per- | -ceive it : is there knówledge | in the | most | High?

12 Lo, these are the ungodly, these prosper in the world * and these have ríches | in pos- | -session : and I said, Then have I cleansed my heart in váin, and | washed . mine | hands in | innocency.

13 All the day lóng have | I been | punished : ánd | chastened | every | morning.

14 Yea, and I had almost sáid | even . as | they : but lo, then I should have condemned the géner- | -ation | of thy | children.

15 Then thought I to únder- | -stand | this : bút it | was too | hard for | me,

16 Until I went into the sánctu- | -ary . of | God : then understóod I the | end of | these | men ;

17 Namely, how thou dost sét them in | slippery | places : and castest them dówn | and de- | -stroyest | them.

18 Oh, how súddenly do | they con- | -sume : pérish, and | come . to a | fearful | end

19 Yea, even like as a dréam | when . one a- | -waketh : so shalt thou make their ímage to | vanish | out . of the | city.

20 Thús my | heart was | grieved : and it wént | even | through my | reins.

^{2nd} 21 So fóolish was | I and | ignorant : éven as it | were a |
^{part.} beast be- | -fore thee.

mf 22 Nevertheléss, I am | alway . by | thee : for thou hast hólden me | by my | right | hand.

23 Thou shalt guíde me | with thy | counsel : and after thát re- | -ceive | me with | glory.

24 Whóm have I in | heaven . but | thee : and there is none upon earth that I desíre in com- | -pari- | -son of | thee.

25 My flésh and my | heart | faileth : but God is the strength of my héart | and my | portion . for | ever.

26 For lo, they that forsáke | thee shall | perish : thou hast destroyed all them that commít | forni- | -cation . a- | gainst thee.

27 But it is good for me to hold me fast by God * to put my trúst in the | Lord | God : and to speak of all thy works in the gátes | of the | daughter . of | Sion.

PSALM lxxiv.—*Ut quid, Deus ?*

mf O GOD, wherefore art thou ábsent from | us so | long : why is thy wrath so hot agáinst the | sheep of | thy | pasture ?

2 O think upón thy | congre- | -gation : whom thou hast púrchased | and re- | -deemed . of | old.

3 Think upon the tríbe of | thine in- | -heritance : and Mount Síon, where- | -in | thou hast | dwelt.

4 Lift up thy feet * that thou mayest utterly destróy | every | enemy : which hath dóne | evil | in thy | sanctuary.

5 Thine adversaries roar in the mídst of thy | congre- | gations : and sét | up their | banners . for | tokens.

6 He that hewed timber afore óut of the | thick | trees : was known to bríng it | to an | excellent | work.

mp 7 But now they break down all the cárved | work there- | of : wíth | axes | and | hammers.

8 They have set fire upón thy | holy | places : and have defiled the dwelling-place of thy Náme | even | unto . the | ground.

9 Yea, they said in their hearts * Let us make hávock of them | alto- | -gether : thus have they burnt up all the hóuses of | God | in the | land.

10 We see not our tokens * there is not óne | prophet | more : no, not one is there among us * that únder- | standeth | any | more.

mf 11 O God, how long shall the adversary dó | this dis- | honour : how long shall the énemy blas- | -pheme thy | Name for | ever?

12 Why withdráwest | thou thy | hand : why pluckest thou not thy right hand out of thy bósom | to con- | -sume the | enemy?

13 For Gód is my | King of | old : the help that is done upon éarth he | doeth | it him- | -self.

14 Thou didst divide the séa | through thy | power : thou brakest the héads of the | dragons | in the | waters.

15 Thou smotest the heads of Levía- | -than in | pieces : and gavest him to be méat for the | people | in the | wilderness.

16 Thou broughtest out fountains and waters óut of the | hard | rocks : thóu | driedst . up | mighty | waters.

17 The day is thíne, and the | night is | thine : thou hast prepáred the | light | and the | sun.

18 Thou hast set all the bórders | of the | earth : thóu hast | made | summer . and | winter.

19 Remember this, O Lord * how the énemy | hath re- | buked : and how the foolish péople | hath blas- | phemed . thy | Name.

20 O deliver not the soul of thy turtle-dove * unto the múltitude | of the | enemies : and forget not the con- gregátion | of the | poor for | ever.

21 Lóok up- | -on the | covenant : for all the earth is full of dárkness and | cruel | habit- | -ations.

22 O let not the simple gó a- | -way a- | -shamed : but let the poor and néedy give | praise | unto . thy | Name.

23 Arise, O God, maintáin thine | own | cause : remember how the foolish mán blas- | -phemeth | thee | daily.

24 Forget not the vóice | of thine | enemies : the pre- sumption of them that hate thee, incréaseth | ever | more and | more.

Day 15.   MORNING PRAYER.

Psalm lxxv.—*Confitebimur tibi.*

F. mf UNTO thee, O Gód, do | we give | thanks : yéa, unto | thee do | we give | thanks.

F.   2 Thy náme also | is so | nigh : and thát do thy | wondrous | works de- | -clare.

3 When I recéive the | congre- | -gation : I shall júdge ac- | cording | unto | right.

4 The earth is weak * and all the inhábit- | -ers there- | -of : I' bear | up the | pillars | of it.

5 I said unto the fools, Déal | not so | madly : and to the ungódly | Set not | up your | horn.

6 Set not úp your | horn on | high : and spéak not | with a | stiff | neck.

7 For promotion cometh neither from the éast nor | from the | west : nór | yet | from the | south.

8 And whý ? | God . is the | Judge : he putteth down óne, and | setteth | up an- | -other.

9 For in the hand of the Lord there is a cúp, and the | wine is | red : it is full mixed * and he póureth | out | of the | same.

10 As for the | dregs there- | -of : all the ungodly of the éarth shall | drink . them and | suck them | out.

f 11 But I will tálk of the | God of | Jacob : ánd | praise | him for | ever.

12 All the horns of the ungodly álso | will I | break : and the hórns of the | righteous . shall | be ex- | -alted.

Psalm lxxvi.—*Notus in Judæa.*

mf IN Jéwry is | God | known : hís | Name is | great in | Israel.

2 At Salem ís his | taber- | -nacle : ánd his | dwelling | in | Sion.

3 There brake he the árrows | of the | bow : the shíeld, the | sword | and the | battle.

4 Thou art of móre | honour . and | might : thán the | hills | of the | robbers.

5 The proud are robbed, théy have | slept their | sleep : and all the men whose hánds were | mighty . have | found | nothing.

6 At thy rébuke, O | God of | Jacob : bóth the | chariot . and | horse are | fallen.

7 Thou, even thóu, art | to be | feared : and who may stánd in thy | sight when | thou art | angry.

8 Thou didst cause thy júdgement to be | heard from | heaven : the éarth | trembled | and was | still.

9 When Gód a- | -rose to | judgement : and to hélp | all the | meek up- . -on | earth.

10 The fierceness of man shall túrn | to thy | praise : and the fiérceness of | them shalt | thou re- | -frain.

11 Promise unto the Lord your God * and keep it, all yé that are | round a- | -bout him : bring presents unto hím that | ought | to be | feared.

12 He shall refráin the | spirit . of | princes : and is wonderful amóng the | kings | of the | earth.

Psalm lxxvii.—*Voce mea ad Dominum.*

mp I WILL cry unto Gód | with my | voice : even unto God will I cry with my voice * and hé shall | hearken | unto | me.

2 In the time of my tróuble I | sought the | Lord : my sore ran, and ceased not in the night-season * mý | soul re- | fused | comfort.

3 When I am in heaviness * Í will | think up- . -on | God : when my héart is | vexed . I | will com- | -plain.

4 Thou hóldest mine | eyes | waking : I am so féeble | that I | cannot | speak.

5 I have consídered the | days of | old : ánd the | years | that are | past.

6 I cáll to re- | -membrance . my | song : and in the night I commune with mine own héart, and | search | out my | spirits.

7 Will the Lord absént him- | -self for | ever : and will he | be no | more en- | -treated ?

8 Is his mercy cléan | gone for | ever : and is his promise come utterly tó an | end for | ever- | -more ?

9 Hath God forgótten | to be | gracious : and will he shut up his lóving- | -kindness | in dis- | -pleasure ?

10 And I said, It ís mine | own in- | -firmity : but I will remember the years of the right hánd | of the | most | Highest.

f 11 I will remember the wórks | of the | Lord : and call to mínd thy | wonders . of | old | time.

12 I will think álso of | all thy | works : and my tálking shall | be of | thy | doings.

13 Thy wáy, O | God is | holy : who is so gréat a | God as | our | God ?

14 Thou art the Gód that | doeth | wonders : and hast declåred thy | power . a- | -mong the | people.

15 Thou hast míghtily de- | -livered . thy | people : éven the | sons of | Jacob . and | Joseph.

16 The waters saw thee, O God * the waters såw thee, and | were a- | -fraid : the dépths | also | were | troubled.

17 The clouds poured out wåter the | air | thundered : ánd thine | arrows | went a- | -broad.

18 The voice of thy thunder was héard | round a- | -bout : the lightnings shone upon the ground * the éarth was | moved . and | shook with- | -al.

19 Thy way is in the sea * and thy påths in the | great | waters : ánd thy | footsteps | are not | known.

20 Thou léddest thy | people . like | sheep : bý the | hand of | Moses . and | Aaron.

EVENING PRAYER.

Psalm lxxviii.—*Attendite, popule.*

F. mf HEAR my låw | O my | people : incline your éars unto the | words | of my | mouth.

F. 2 I will open my móuth | in a | parable : I will declåre hard | senten- | -ces of | old ;

3 Whích we have | heard and | known : and súch | as our | fathers . have | told us ;

4 That we should not hide them * from the children of the géner- | -ations . to | come : but to shew the honour of the Lord * his mighty and wónderful | works that | he hath | done.

5 He made a covenant with Jacob * and gave Ísra- | -el a | law : which he commanded óur fore- | -fathers . to | teach their | children ;

6 That their postéri- | -ty might | know it : and the chíldren | which were | yet un- | -born ;

7 To the intént that when | they came | up : théy might | shew their | children . the | same ;

8 That they might pút their | trust in | God : and not to forget the works of Gód, but to | keep | his com- | mandments ;

9 And not to be as their forefathers * a faithless and
stúbborn | gener- | -ation : a generation that set not
their heart aright * and whose spirit cléaveth not |
stedfastly | unto | God ;

10 Líke as the | children . of | Ephraim : who being
harnessed and carrying bows * turned themselves
báck | in the | day of | battle.

11 They kept not the cóve- | -nant of | God : and wóuld
not | walk | in his | law ;

12 But forgát what | he had | done : and the wonderful
wórks that | he had | shewed | for them.

f 13 Marvellous things did he in the sight of our forefathers *
ín the | land of | Egypt : éven | in the | field of | Zoan.

14 He divided the séa, and let | them go | through : he made
the wáters to | stand | on an | heap.

15 In the day-time also he léd them | with a | cloud : and
all the níght through | with a | light of | fire.

16 He clave the hard rócks | in the | wilderness : and gave
them drink thereof * as it had béen | out . of the |
great | depth.

17 He brought waters oút of the | stony | rock : so that it
gúshed | out | like the | rivers.

p 18 Yet for all this they sínned | more a- | -gainst him : and
provóked the most | Highest | in the | wilderness.

19 They tempted Gód | in their | hearts : and requíred |
meat | for their | lust.

20 They spake against Gód | also | saying : Shall God
prepáre a | table | in the | wilderness ?

21 He smote the stony rock indeed * that the water gushed
out, and the stréams | flowed . with- | -al : but can he
give bread also * or províde | flesh | for his | people ?

mf 22 When the Lord heard thís | he was | wroth : so the fire
was kindled in Jacob * and there came up héavy dis- |
pleasure . a- | -gainst | Israel ;

23 Because they belíeved | not in | God : and pút not their |
trust | in his | help.

24 So he commánded the | clouds a- | -bove : ánd | opened .
the | doors of | heaven.

25 He rained down manna also upón them | for to | eat :
ánd | gave them | food from | heaven.

26 So mán did eat | angels' | food : fór he | sent them |
meat e- | -nough.

27 He caused the east wind to blów | under | heaven : and
through his pówer he brought | in the | south-west | wind.

28 He rained flesh upón them as | thick as | dust : and
feathered fowls, líke as the | sand | of the | sea.

29 He let it fáll a- | -mong their | tents : even róund a- |
bout their | habit- | -ation.

30 So they did eat, and were well filled * for he gáve them
their | own de- | -sire : they were nót disap- | -pointed |
of their | lust.

mp 31 But while the meat was yet in their mouths * the
heavy wrath of God came upon them, and sléw the |
wealthiest | of them : yea, and smote down the chósen |
men that | were in | Israel.

32 But for all thís they | sinned . yet | more : and belíeved |
not his | wondrous | works.

33 Therefore their dáys did he con- | -sume in | vanity : ánd
their | years | in | trouble.

34 When he sléw | them they | sought him : and turned
them early * ánd en- | -quired | after | God.

35 And they remembered that Gód | was their | strength :
and that the hígh | God was | their Re- | -deemer.

36 Nevertheless, they did but flátter him | with their |
mouth : and dissémbled | with him | in their | tongue.

37 For their héart was not | whole with | him : neither con-
tínued they | stedfast | in his | covenant.

38 But he was so merciful * that he forgáve | their mis- |
deeds : ánd de- | -stroyed | them | not.

39 Yea, many a time túrned he his | wrath a- | -way : and
would not suffer his whóle dis- | -pleasure | to a- | -rise.

40 For he considered thát they | were but | flesh : and that
they were even a wind that passeth awáy, and |
cometh | not a- | -gain.

41 Many a time did they provóke him | in the | wilderness :
ánd | grieved . him | in the | desert.

42 They turned báck, and | tempted | God : and móved the |
Holy | One in | Israel.

43 They thóught not | of his | hand : and of the day when
he delivered them fróm the | hand | of the | enemy ;

44 How he had wróught his | miracles . in | Egypt : and his
wónders | in the | field of | Zoan.

45 He turned their wáters | into | blood : so that they míght
not | drink | of the | rivers.

46 He sent lice among them * ánd de- | -voured . them | up :
ánd | frogs | to de- | -stroy them.

47 He gave their frúit | unto . the | caterpillar : ánd their |
labour | unto . the | grasshopper.

48 He destróyed their | vines with | hailstones : and their
múlberry- | -trees | with the | frost.

49 He smote their cáttle | also . with | hailstones : ánd
their | flocks with | hot | thunderbolts.

50 He cast upon them the furiousness of his wrath * ánger,
dis- | -pleasure . and | trouble : and sént | evil | angels .
a- | -mong them.

51 He made a way to his indignation * and spáred not
their | soul from | death : but gáve their life | over | to
the | pestilence ;

52 And smóte all the | first-born . in | Egypt : the most
principal and míghtiest | in the | dwellings . of | Ham.

mf 53 But as for his own people * he léd them | forth like |
sheep : and carried them ín the | wilderness | like a |
flock.

54 He brought them out safely * thát they | should not |
fear : and overwhélmed their | enemies | with the | sea.

55 And brought them within the bórders | of his | sanc-
tuary : even to his mountain, which he púrchased |
with his | right | hand.

56 He cast out the héathen | also . be- | -fore them : caused
their land to be divided among them for an heritage *
and made the tribes of I'srael to | dwell in | their |
tents.

mp 57 So they tempted and displéased the | most high | God :
ánd | kept | not his | testimonies ;

58 But turned their backs, and fell awáy | like their | fore-
fathers : starting asíde | like a | broken | bow.

59 For they grieved him wíth their | hill- | -altars : and
provoked him tó dis- | -pleasure | with their | images.

60 When God heard thís | he was | wroth : and tóok | sore
dis- | -pleasure . at | Israel.

61 So that he forsook the tában- | -nacle . in | Silo : even the
tént that he had | pitched . a- | -mong | men.

62 He delivered their pówer | into . cap- | -tivity : and their
béauty | into . the | enemy's | hand.

63 He gave his people óver also | unto . the | sword : ánd
was | wroth with | his in- | -heritance.

64 The fire consúmed their | young | men : and their
máidens | were not | given . to | marriage.

2nd part. 65 Their priests were sláin | with the | sword : and there
were no wídows to | make | lamen- | -tation.

ff 66 So the Lord awaked as óne | out of | sleep : and líke a |
giant . re- | -freshed . with | wine.

67 He smote his enemies ín the | hinder | parts : and pút
them | to a . per- | -petual | shame.

68 He refused the táber- | -nacle . of | Joseph : and chóse |
not the | tribe of | Ephraim ;

69 But chóse the | tribe of | Judah : even the híll of | Sion |
which he | loved.

70 And there he buílt his | temple . on | high : and laid the
foundation of it * like the gróund which | he hath |
made con- | -tinually.

71 He chose Dávid | also . his | servant : and tóok him a- |
way | from the | sheepfolds.

72 As he was following the éwes great with | young ones .
he | took him : that he might feed Jacob his péople,
and | Israel | his in- | -heritance.

73 So he fed them with a fáithful and | true | heart : and
ruled them prúdent- | -ly with | all his | power.

Day 16.   MORNING PRAYER.

Psalm lxxix.—*Deus, venerunt.*

p O GOD, the heathen are cóme into | thine in- | -herit-
ance : thy holy temple have they defiled * and made
Jerúsa- | -lem an | heap of | stones.

2 The dead bodies of thy servants * have they given to be
meat unto the fówls | of the | air : and the flesh of thy
sáints unto the | beasts | of the | land.

3 Their blood have they shed like water on every síde | of
Je- | -rusalem : and there was nó | man to | bury |
them.

We are become an open sháme | to our | enemies : a
very scorn and derision unto thém | that are | round
a- | -bout us.

mf 5 Lord, how lóng wilt | thou be | angry : shall thy
.   jéalousy | burn like | fire for | ever ?

6 Pour out thine indignation upon the héathen that | have
not | known thee : and upon the kingdoms that háve
not | called . up- | -on thy | Name.

7 For théy have de- | -voured | Jacob : ánd | laid | waste
his | dwelling-place.

p 8 O remember not our old sins * but have mercy upón us,
and | that | soon : fór we are | come to | great | misery.

9 Help us, O God of our salvation * for the glóry | of thy |
   Name : O deliver us * and be merciful unto our síns |
   for thy | Name's | sake.

10 Whérefore do the | heathen | say : Whére | — is | now
   their | God ?

11 O let the vengeance of thy servants' blóod | that is |
   shed : be openly shewed upón the | heathen | in our |
   sight.

12 O let the sorrowful sighing of the prísoners | come be- |
   fore thee : according to the greatness of thy power *
   preserve thou thóse that | are ap- |-pointed . to | die.

mf 13 And for the blasphemy wherewith our neighbours háve
   blas- | -phemed | thee : reward thou them, O Lórd |
   sevenfold | into . their | bosom.

f 14 So we that are thy people and sheep of thy pasture *
   shall gíve thee | thanks for | ever : and will alway be
   shewing forth thy praise * from géner- | -ation . to |
   gener- | -ation.

Psalm lxxx.—*Qui regis Israel.*

mf HEAR, O thou Shepherd of Israel * thou that leadest
   Jóseph | like a ⌈ sheep : shew thyself also * thóu
   that | sittest . up- | -on the | cherubims.

2 Before Ephraim, Bénjamin | and Ma- | -nasses : stir úp
   thy | strength and | come and | help us.

3 Túrn us a- | -gain O | God : shew the light of thy
   cóuntenance | and we | shall be | whole.

4 O Lórd | God of | hosts : how long wilt thou be ángry |
   with thy | people . that | prayeth ?

5 Thou feedest them wíth the | bread of | tears : and givest
   them plénteous- | -ness of | tears to | drink.

6 Thou hast made us a very strífe | unto . our | neigh-
   bours : and our énemies | laugh | us to | scorn.

2nd 7 Turn us agáin, thou | God of | hosts : shew the light of
part. thy cóuntenance | and we | shall be | whole.

8 Thou hast brought a víne | out of | Egypt : thou hast
   cast óut the | heathen . and | planted | it.

9 Thou mádest | room for | it : and when it had táken |
   root it | filled . the | land.

10 The hills were covered wíth the | shadow | of it : and the
   boughs thereóf were | like the | goodly | cedar-trees.

11 She stretched out her bránches | unto . the | sea : ánd
   her | boughs | unto . the | river.

p 12 Why hast thou then bróken | down her | hedge : that all
théy that go | by pluck | off her | grapes ?

13 The wild boar out of the wóod doth | root it | up : and the
wild béasts | of the | field de- | -vour it.

14 Turn thee again, thou God of hósts, look | down from |
heaven : behóld, and | visit | this | vine ;

15 And the place of the vineyard that thy ríght | hand
hath | planted : and the branch that thou mádest so |
strong | for thy- | -self.

16 It is burnt with fíre and | cut | down : and they shall
perish át the re- | -buke | of thy | countenance.

17 Let thy hand be upon the mán of thy | right | hand : and
upon the son of man * whom thou madest so stróng |
for thine | own | self.

18 And so will not wé go | back from | thee : O let us live *
and wé shall | call up- | -on thy | Name.

mf 19 Turn us again, O Lórd | God of | hosts : shew the light of
thy cóuntenance | and we | shall be | whole.

Psalm lxxxi.—*Exultate Deo.*

f   SING we merrily únto | God our | strength : make a
cheerful nóise | unto . the | God of | Jacob.

2 Take the psálm, bring | hither . the | tabret : the mérry |
harp | with the | lute.

3 Blow up the trúmpet in the | new | moon : even in the
time appointed * ánd up- | -on our | solemn | feast-day.

4 For this was máde a | statute . for | Israel : and a láw |
of the | God of | Jacob.

2nd part.   5 This he ordained in Jóseph | for a | testimony : when he
came out of the land of Egypt * ánd had | heard a |
strange | language.

6 I eased his shóulder | from the | burden : and his hánds
were de- | -livered . from | making . the | pots.

7 Thou calledst upon me in troubles * and I' de- | -livered |
thee : and heard thee what tíme as the | storm | fell
up- | -on thee.

8 Í | proved . thee | also : át the | waters | of | strife.

9 Hear, O my people * and I will assúre | thee O | Israel :
íf thou wilt | hearken | unto | me.

10 There shall no strange gód | be in | thee : neither shalt
thou wórship | any | other | god.

11 I am the Lord thy God * who brought thee óut of the | land
of | Egypt : open thy móuth | wide and | I shall | fill it.

CC

mf 12 But my people would not | hear my | voice : and Ísrael |
would | not o- | -bey me,

13 So I gave them up unto their ówn | hearts' | lusts : and
let them fóllow their | own im- | -agin- | -ations.

mf 14 O that my people would have héarkened | unto | me : for
if Ísrael had | walked | in my | ways,

15 I should sóon have put | down their | enemies : and
túrned my | hand a- | -gainst their | adversaries.

16 The haters of the Lord shóuld have been | found | liars :
but théir time | should have . en- | -dured . for | ever.

17 He should have fed them álso with the | finest | wheat-
flour : and with honey out of the stony róck should | I
have | satisfied | thee.

Day 16. EVENING PRAYER.

PSALM lxxxii.—*Deus stetit.*

F. mf **G**OD standeth in the cóngre- | -gation . of | princes : hé is
a | Judge a- | -mong | gods.

F. 2 How lóng will ye | give wrong | judgement : and accépt
the | persons | of . the un- | -godly ?

3 Defénd the | poor and | fatherless : see that such as are
in néed and ne- | -cessity | have | right.

4 Delíver the | outcast . and | poor : save them fróm the |
hand of | the un- | -godly.

5 They will not be learned nor understand * but wálk on |
still in | darkness : all the foundátions of the | earth
are | out of | course.

6 I have sáid | Ye are | gods : and ye are all the chíldren |
of the | most | Highest.

7 Bút ye shall | die like | men : ánd | fall like | one . of
the | princes.

8 Arise, O God, and júdge | thou the | earth : for thou shalt
táke all | heathen . to | thine in- | -heritance.

PSALM lxxxiii.—*Deus, quis similis ?*

mf **H**OLD not thy tongue, O God * kéep | not still | silence :
refráin | not thy- | -self O | God.

2 For lo, thine énemies | make a | murmuring : and they
that háte thee have | lift | up their | head.

3 They have imagined cráftily a- | -gainst thy | people : and taken cóunsel a- | -gainst thy | secret | ones.

4 They have said, Come, and let us root them out * that they bé no | more a | people : and that the name of Israel may bé no | more | in re- | -membrance.

5 For they have cast their heads togéther with | one con- | -sent : and áre con- | -feder- | -ate a- | -gainst thee.

6 The tabernacles of the Édomites | and the | Ismaelites : thé | Moab- | -ites and | Hagarens ;

7 Gébal and | Ammon . and | Amalek : the Philistines, with | them that | dwell at | Tyre.

8 Assur álso is | joined | with them : ánd have | holpen . the | children . of | Lot.

9 But do thou to thém as | unto . the | Madianites : unto Sisera, and unto Jábin | at the | brook of | Kison ;

10 Who pérished | at | Endor : and becáme as the | dung | of the | earth.

11 Make them and their prínces like | Oreb . and | Zeb : yea, make all their princes líke as | Zeba | and Sal- | mana ;

12 Who say, Let us táke | to our- | -selves : the hoúses of | God | in pos- | -session.

13 O my God, make them líke | unto . a | wheel : and ás the | stubble . be- | -fore the | wind ;

14 Like as the fire that búrneth | up the | wood : and as the fláme | that con- | -sumeth . the | mountains.

15 Persecute them even só | with thy | tempest : and máke them a- | -fraid | with thy | storm.

16 Make their fáces a- | -shamed . O | Lord : thát | they may | seek thy | Name.

17 Let them be confounded and véxed ever | more and | more : lét them be | put to | shame and | perish.

f 18 And they shall know that thou, whose Náme | is Je- | hovah : art only the most Híghest | over | all the | earth.

Psalm lxxxiv.—*Quam dilecta !*

mf O HOW ámiable | are they | dwellings : thóu | Lord | of | hosts !

2 My soul hath a desire and longing * to enter into the cóurts | of the | Lord : my heart and my flesh rejóice | in the | living | God.

cc 2

3 Yea, the sparrow hath found her an house * and the swallow a nest, where shé may | lay her | young : even thy altars, O Lord of hósts, my | King | and my | God.

4 Blessed are they that dwéll | in thy | house : théy will be | alway | praising | thee.

5 Blessed is the man whose stréngth | is in | thee : ín whose | heart | are thy | ways.

6 Who going through the vale of misery úse it | for a | well : ánd the | pools are | filled . with | water.

2nd part. 7 They will gó from | strength to | strength : and unto the God of gods appeareth évery | one of | them in | Sion.

8 O Lord God of hósts | hear my | prayer : héarken | O | God of | Jacob.

9 Behold, O Gód | our de- | -fender : and look upón the | face of | thine A- | -nointed.

10 For one dáy | in thy | courts : ís | better | than a | thousand.

11 I had rather be a door-keeper in the hóuse | of my | God : than to dwéll in the | tents | of un- | -godliness.

12 For the Lord God is a líght | and de- | -fence : the Lord will give grace and worship * and no good thing shall he withhold from thém that | live a | godly | life.

13 O Lórd | God of | hosts : blessed is the mán that | putteth . his | trust in | thee.

Psalm lxxxv.—*Benedixisti, Domine.*

mp LORD, thou art become grácious | unto . thy | land : thou hast turned awáy the cap- | -tivi- | -ty of | Jacob.

2 Thou hast forgiven the offénce | of thy | people : ánd | covered | all their | sins.

3 Thou hast taken awáy all | thy dis- | -pleasure : and turned thysélf from thy | wrathful | indig- | -nation.

4 Turn us thén, O | God our | Saviour : and lét thine | anger | cease | from us.

5 Wilt thou be displéased at | us for | ever : and wilt thou stretch out thy wrath from óne gener- | -ation | to an- | other ?

6 Wilt thou not turn agáin, and | quicken | us : that thy péople | may re- | -joice in | thee ?

2nd part. 7 Shéw us thy | mercy . O | Lord : ánd | grant us | thy sal- | -vation.

8 I will hearken what the Lord God will sáy con- | -cern-
ing | me : for he shall speak peace unto his people and
to his saints * thát they | turn | not a- | -gain.

9 For his salvation is nígh | them that | fear him : that
glóry may | dwell | in our | land.

10 Mercy and trúth are | met to- | -gether : ríghteousness
and | peace have | kissed . each | other.

11 Truth shall floúrish | out . of the | earth : and ríghteous-
ness hath | looked | down from | heaven.

12 Yea, the Lord shall shéw | loving- | -kindness : ánd our |
land shall | give her | increase.

13 Ríghteousness shall | go be- | -fore him : and he shall
diréct his | going | in the | way.

Day 17.   MORNING PRAYER.

Psalm lxxxvi.—*Inclina, Domine.*

np   BOW down thine éar, O | Lord and | hear me : for Í am |
poor | and in | misery.

2 Preserve thou my sóul, for | I am | holy : my God, save
thy sérvant that | putteth . his | trust in | thee.

3 Be merciful únto | me O | Lord : for Í will | call | daily
up- | -on thee.

4 Comfort the sóul | of thy | servant : for unto thee, O
Lórd, do I | lift | up my | soul.

5 For thou, Lórd, art | good and | gracious : and of great
mercy unto áll | them that | call up- | -on thee.

6 Give ear, Lórd | unto . my | prayer : and ponder the
vóice | of my | humble . de- | -sires.

7 In the time of my trouble Í will | call up- . -on | thee :
fór | thou | hearest | me.

8 Among the gods there is none líke unto | thee O | Lord :
there is not óne that can | do as | thou | doest.

9 All nations whom thou hast made * shall come and
wórship | thee O | Lord : ánd shall | glori- | -fy thy |
Name.

10 For thou art great, and dóest | wondrous | things :
thóu | — art | God a- | -lone.

11 Teach me thy way, O Lord * and I will wálk | in thy |
truth : O knit my heart unto thée, that | I may | fear
thy | Name.

12 I will thank thee, O Lord my Gód, with | all my | heart :
and will práise thy | Name for | ever- | -more.

13 For gréat is thy | mercy | toward me : and thou hast
delivered my sóul | from the | nethermost | hell.

14 O God, the próud are | risen . a- | -gainst me : and the
congregations of naughty men have sought after my
soul * and have nót set | thee be- | -fore their | eyes.

15 But thou, O Lord God, art fúll of com- | -passion . and |
mercy : long-súffering | plenteous . in | goodness . and |
truth.

16 O turn thee then unto mé, and have | mercy . up- | -on
me : give thy strength unto thy servant * and hélp
the | son | of thine | handmaid.

2nd part. 17 Shew some token upon me for good * that they who hate
me may sée it and | be a- | -shamed : because thou,
Lord, hast hólpen | me and | comforted | me.

Psalm lxxxvii.—*Fundamenta ejus.*

mp HER foundations are upón the | holy | hills : the Lord
loveth the gates of Sion, móre than | all the | dwel-
lings . of | Jacob.

2 Very excellent thíngs are | spoken . of | thee : thóu |
city | of | God.

3 I will thínk upon | Rahab . and | Babylon : wíth | them
that | know | me.

4 Behóld ye the | Philistines | also : and they of Tyre with
the Morians * ló | there | was he | born.

5 And of Sion it shall be reported that hé was | born in |
her : ánd the most | High shall | stablish | her.

6 The Lord shall rehearse it when he wríteth | up the |
people : thát | he was | born | there.

2nd part. 7 The singers also and trúmpeters shall | he re- |
hearse : Áll my fresh | springs shall | be in | thee.

Psalm lxxxviii.—*Domine Deus.*

mp O LORD God of my salvation * I have críed day and |
night be- | -fore thee : O let my prayer enter into thy
presence * inclíne thine | ear | unto . my | calling.

2 For my sóul is | full of | trouble : and my lífe draweth |
nigh | unto | hell.

3 I am counted as one of them that go dówn | into . the |
pit : and I have been éven as a | man that | hath no |
strength.

4 Free among the dead * like unto them that are wounded
and lie | in the | grave : who are out of remembrance *
and are cut a- | -way | from thy | hand.

5 Thou hast láid me in the | lowest | pit : in a pláce of |
darkness . and | in the | deep.

6 Thine indignation lieth | hard up- | -on me : and thou
hast véxed | me with | all thy | storms.

7 Thou hast put away mine acquáintance | far | from me :
and máde me to | be ab- | -horred | of them.

8 I' am so | fast in | prison : thát I | cannot | get | forth.

9 My sight fáileth for | very | trouble : Lord, I have called
daily upon thee * I have stretched fórth my | hands |
unto | thee.

10 Dost thou shew wónders a- | -mong the | dead : or shall
the déad rise | up a- | -gain and | praise thee ?

11 Shall thy loving-kindness be shéwed | in the | grave : ór
thy | faithfulness | in de- | -struction ?

12 Shall thy wondrous works be knówn | in the | dark : and
thy righteousness in the lánd where | all things | are
for- | -gotten ?

13 Unto thée have I | cried O | Lord : and early shall my |
prayer | come be- | -fore thee.

14 Lord, why abhórrest | thou my | soul : and hídest | thou
thy | face | from me ?

15 I am in misery * and like unto him that is át the |
point to | die : even from my youth up, thy terrors
have I súffered | with a | troubled | mind.

16 Thy wrathful displeasure góeth | over | me : and the féar
of | thee | hath un- | -done me.

17 They came round abóut me | daily . like | water : and
cómpassed me to- | -gether . on | every | side.

18 My lovers and friends hast thou pút a- | -way | from me :
and híd mine ac- | -quaintance | out of . my | sight.

Day 17. EVENING PRAYER.

Psalm lxxxix.—*Misericordias Domini.*

F. mf MY song shall be alway of the loving-kíndness | of the |
Lord : with my mouth will I ever be shewing thy
truth * from óne gener- | -ation | to an- | -other.

F. 2 For I have said, Mercy shall be sét | up for | ever : thy
trúth shalt thou | stablish | in the | heavens.

3 I have made a cóvenant | with my | chosen : I have swórn | unto | David . my | servant ;

4 Thy séed will I | stablish . for | ever : and set up thy throne from óne gener- | -ation | to an- | -other.

5 O Lord, the very heavens shall práise thy | wondrous | works : and thy truth in the cóngre- | -gation | of the | saints.

6 For who is hé a- | -mong the | clouds : that sháll be com- | -pared | unto . the | Lord ?

7 And what is hé a- | -mong the | gods : that sháll be | like | unto . the | Lord ?

8 God is very greatly to be feared in the cóuncil | of the | saints : and to be had in reverence of all thém | that are | round a- | -bout him.

9 O Lord God of Hosts * whó is | like . unto | thee : thy truth, most mighty Lórd | is on | every | side.

10 Thou rulest the ráging | of the | sea : thou stillest the wáves there- | -of when | they a- | -rise.

11 Thou hast subdued Egypt * ánd de- | -stroyed | it : thou hast scattered thine enemies abróad | with thy | mighty | arm.

12 The heavens are thine, the éarth | also . is | thine : thou hast laid the foundation of the round wórld, and | all that | therein | is.

13 Thou hast made the nórth | and the | south : Tabor and Hermon sháll re- | -joice | in thy | Name.

14 Thou hást a | mighty | arm : strong is thy hánd, and | high is | thy right | hand.

15 Righteousness and equity are the habitátion | of thy | seat : mercy and trúth shall | go be- | -fore thy | face.

16 Blessed is the people, O Lord * that cán re- | -joice in | thee : they shall wálk in the | light | of thy | countenance.

17 Their delight shall be dáily | in thy | Name : and in thy ríghteousness | shall they | make their | boast.

18 For thou art the glóry | of their | strength : and in thy loving-kindness thóu shalt | lift | up our | horns.

19 For the Lórd is | our de- | -fence : the Hóly One of | Israel | is our | King.

20 Thou spakest sometime in visions únto thy | saints and | saidst : I have laid help upon one that is mighty * I have exálted one | chosen | out . of the | people.

21 I have fóund | David . my | servant : with my holy óil have | I a- | -nointed | him.

22 My hánd shall | hold him | fast : ánd my | arm shall | strengthen | him.

23 The enemy shall not be áble to | do him | violence : the són of | wickedness | shall not | hurt him.

24 I will smite down his fóes be- | -fore his | face : ánd | plague | them that | hate him.

25 My truth also and my mércy | shall be | with him : and in my Náme shall his | horn | be ex- | -alted.

26 I will set his dominion álso | in the | sea : ánd his | right hand | in the | floods.

27 He shall call me, Thóu | art my | Father : my Gód | and my | strong sal- | -vation.

28 And I will máke | him my | firstborn : hígher than the | kings | of the | earth.

29 My mercy will I kéep for him for | ever- | -more : and my cóvenant shall | stand | fast | with him.

30 His seed also will I máke to en- | -dure for | ever : and his thróne | as the | days of | heaven.

mf 31 But if his chíldren for- | -sake my | law : ánd | walk not | in my | judgements;

32 If they break my statutes * and kéep not | my com- | mandments : I will visit their offences with the ród | and their | sin with | scourges.

33 Nevertheless, my loving-kindness will I not útterly | take | from him : nór | suffer . my | truth to | fail.

34 My covenant will I not break * nor alter the thing that is góne | out of . my | lips : I have sworn once by my holiness * that I' | will not | fail | David.

35 His séed shall en- | -dure for | ever : and his séat is | like . as the | sun be- | -fore me.

36 He shall stand fast for evermóre | as the | moon : and ás the | faithful | witness . in | heaven.

p 37 But thou has abhorred and forsáken | thine A- | -nointed : ánd | art dis- | -pleased | at him.

38 Thou hast broken the cóvenant | of thy | servant : and cást his | crown | to the | ground.

39 Thou hast overthrówn | all his | hedges : ánd | broken | down his | strongholds.

40 All théy that go | by | spoil him : and he is becóme a re- | -proach | to his | neighbours.

41 Thou hast set up the right hánd | of his | enemies : and máde all his | adversaries | to re- | -joice.

42 Thou hast taken away the édge | of his | sword : and givest him nót | victory | in the | battle.

43 Thóu hast put | out his | glory : and cást his | throne |
down . to the | ground.

44 The days of his yóuth | hast thou | shortened : ánd |
covered . him | with dis- | -honour.

45 Lord, how long wilt thou híde thy- | -self for | ever : and
shall thy | wrath | burn like | fire ?

46 O remember how short my | time | is : wherefore hast
thou máde | all | men for | nought ?

47 What man is he that líveth and shall | not see | death :
and shall he deliver his sóul | from the | hand of | hell ?

48 Lord, where are thy óld | loving- | -kindnesses : which
thou swárest unto | David | in thy | truth ?

49 Remember, Lord, the rebúke that thy | servants | have :
and how I do bear in my bósom the re- | -bukes of |
many | people ;

50 Wherewith thine enemies have blasphemed thee * and
slandered the fóotsteps of | thine A- | -nointed : Praised
be the Lord for evermóre. | A- . -men and | A- | -men.

Day 18.   MORNING PRAYER.

PSALM XC.—*Domine, refugium.*

p LÓRD, thou hast | been our | refuge : from óne gener- |
ation | to an- | -other.

2 Before the mountains were brought forth * or ever the
éarth and the | world were | made : thou art God from
everlásting, and | world with- | -out | end.

3 Thou turnest mán | to de- | -struction : again thou sayest,
Cóme a- | -gain ye | children . of | men.

4 For a thousand years in thý sight | are but . as | yester-
day : seeing that is pást as a | watch | in the | night.

5 As soon as thou scatterest them * they are éven | as a |
sleep : and fáde away | suddenly | like the | grass.

6 In the morning it is gréen and | groweth | up : but in the
evening it is cut dówn | dried | up and | withered.

7 For we consume awáy in | thy dis- | -pleasure : and are
afráid at thy | wrathful | indig- | -nation.

8 Thou hast sét our mis- | -deeds be- | -fore thee : and our
secret síns in the | light | of thy | countenance.

9 For when thou art angry, áll our | days are | gone : we
bring our years to an end * as it wére a | tale | that
is | told.

10 The days of our age are three-score years and ten * and
     though men be so strong that they cóme to | four-
     score | years : yet is their strength then but labour and
     sorrow * so soon pásseth it a- | -way and | we are |
     gone.

11 But who regardeth the pówer | of thy | wrath : for even
     thereafter as a man féareth | so is | thy dis- | -pleasure.

12 So téach us to | number . our | days : that we may applý
     our | hearts | unto | wisdom.

13 Turn thee again, O Lórd | at the | last : ánd be |
     gracious | unto . thy | servants.

14 O satisfy us with thy mércy, and | that | soon : so shall
     we rejoice and be glád all the | days | of our | life.

15 Comfort us again * now after the tíme that thou hast |
     plagued | us : and for the years whereín | we have |
     suffered . ad- | -versity.

16 Shéw thy | servants . thy | work : ánd their | children |
     thy | glory.

2nd part.   17 And the glorious Majesty of the Lord our Gód | be up- |
     on us : prosper thou the work of our hands upon us *
     O prósper | thou our | handy- | -work.

Psalm xci.— *Qui habitat.*

mf   WHOSO dwelleth under the defénce of the | most |
       High : shall abíde under the | shadow . of | the Al- |
       mighty.

2 I will say unto the Lord * Thou art my hópe | and my |
     stronghold : my Gód, in | him | will I | trust.

3 For he shall deliver thee from the snáre | of the |
     hunter : ánd | from the | noisome | pestilence.

4 He shall defend thee under his wings * and thou shalt be
     sáfe | under . his | feathers : his faithfulness and trúth
     shall | be thy | shield and | buckler.

5 Thou shalt not be afráid for any | terror . by | night :
     nór for the | arrow . that | flieth . by | day ;

6 For the péstilence that | walketh . in | darkness : nor for
     the síckness that de- | -stroyeth | in the | noonday.

7 A thousand shall fall beside thee * and ten thóusand at |
     thy right | hand : bút it shall | not come | nigh | thee.

8 Yea, with thine éyes shalt | thou be- | -hold : and sée the
     re- | -ward of | the un- | -godly.

9 For thou, Lórd | art my | hope : thou hast set thine
     hóuse of de- | -fence | very | high.

10 There shall no evil háppen | unto | thee : neither shall
    ány | plague come | nigh thy | dwelling.

11 For he shall give his angels chárge | over | thee : to
    kéep | thee in | all thy | ways.

12 They shall béar thee | in their | hands : that thou húrt
    not thy | foot a- | -gainst a | stone.

13 Thou shalt go upón the | lion and | adder : the young
    lion and the dragon shált thou | tread | under . thy |
    feet.

14 Because he hath set his love upon me * therefore will
    I′ de- | -liver | him : I will set him up * becáuse | he
    hath | known my | Name.

15 He shall call upon mé, and | I will | hear him : yea, I am
    with him in trouble * I will delíver him, and | bring |
    him to | honour.

16 With long lífe will I | satisfy | him : ánd | shew him | my
    sal- | -vation.

Psalm xcii.—Bonum est confiteri.

f   IT is a good thing to give thánks | unto . the | Lord : and
    to sing praises únto thy | Name | O most | Highest ;

2 To tell of thy loving-kindness éarly | in the | morning :
    and of thy trúth | in the | night- | -season ;

3 Upon an instrument of ten strings * ánd up- | -on the |
    lute : upon a loud ínstrument | and up- | -on the |
    harp.

4 For thou, Lord, hast made me glád | through thy |
    works : and I will rejoice in giving praise, for the
    óper- | -ations | of thy | hands.

5 O Lord, how glórious | are thy | works : thý | thoughts
    are | very | deep.

6 An unwise man doth not wéll con- | -sider | this : and a
    fóol | doth not | under- | -stand it.

7 When the ungodly are green as the grass * and when all
    the workers of wícked- | -ness do | flourish : then shall
    they be destroyed for ever * but thou, Lord, árt the
    most | Highest . for | ever- | -more.

8 For lo, thine enemies, O Lord * lo, thine éne- | -mies
    shall | perish : and all the workers of wícked- | -ness
    shall | be de- | -stroyed.

9 But mine horn shall be exalted like the hórn | of
    an | unicorn : for I′ am a- | -nointed . with | fresh |
    oil.

10 Mine eye also shall see his lúst | of mine | enemies : and mine ear shall hear his desire of the wícked that a- | rise | up a- | -gainst me.

11 The righteous shall flóurish | like a | palm-tree : and shall spread abróad | like a | cedar . in | Libanus.

12 Such as are planted in the hóuse | of the | Lord : shall flourish in the córts of the | house of | our | God.

13 They also shall bring forth more frúit | in their | age : and sháll be | fat and | well- | -liking.

14 That they may shew how true the Lórd my | strength | is : and that there is nó un- | -righteous- | -ness in | him.

EVENING PRAYER.

Psalm xciii.—*Dominus regnavit.*

F. f THE Lord is King * and hath put on glóri- | -ous ap- | parel : the Lord hath put on his appárel and | girded . him- | -self with | strength.

F. 2 He hath máde the round | world so | sure : thát it | cannot | be | moved.

3 Ever since the world began hath thy séat | been pre- | pared : thóu | art from | ever- | -lasting.

4 The floods are risen, O Lord * the flóods have lift | up their | voice : thé | floods lift | up their | waves.

5 The waves of the sea are míghty and | rage | horribly : but yet the Lórd, who | dwelleth . on | high is | mightier.

6 Thy testimonies, O Lórd, are | very | sure : hóliness be- | cometh . thine | house for | ever.

Psalm xciv.—*Deus ultionum.*

mf O LORD Gód, to whom | vengeance . be- | -longeth : thou God, to whom véngeance be- | -longeth | shew thy- | self.

2 Arise, thou Júdge | of the | world : and reward the próud | after | their de- | -serving.

3 Lord, how lóng | shall . the un- | -godly : how lóng | shall . the un- | -godly | triumph ?

4 How long shall all wicked doers spéak | so dis- | dainfully : ánd | make such | proud | boasting ?

5 They smite dówn thy | people . O | Lord : ánd | trouble | thine | heritage.

6 They murder the wídow | and the | stranger : and pút the | father- | -less to | death.

2nd part. 7 And yet they say, Tush, the Lórd | shall not | see : neither sháll the | God of | Jacob . re- | -gard it.

8 Take heed, ye unwíse a- | -mong the | people : O ye fóols | when . will ye | under- | -stand ?

9 He that planted the éar, shall | he not | hear : or he that máde the | eye shall | he not | see ?

10 Or he that núrtur- | -eth the | heathen : it is he that teacheth man knówledge | shall not | he | punish ?

11 The Lord knóweth the | thoughts of | man : thát | they | are but | vain.

12 Blessed is the man whom thou chástenest | O | Lord : ánd | teachest . him | in thy | law ;

13 That thou mayest give him patience in tíme | of ad- | versity : until the pit be dígged | up for | the un- | godly.

14 For the Lórd will not | fail his | people : neither wíll he for- | -sake | his in- | -heritance ;

15 Until righteousness túrn again | unto | judgement : all such as are trúe in | heart shall | follow | it.

16 Who will rise up with mé a- | -gainst the | wicked : or who will take my párt a- | -gainst the | evil- | -doers ?

17 If the Lórd had not | helped | me : it had not failed but my sóul | had been | put to | silence.

18 But when I sáid My | foot hath | slipt : thy mércy, O | Lord | held me | up.

19 In the multitude of the sorrows that I hád | in my | heart : thy cómforts | have re- | -freshed . my | soul.

20 Wilt thou have anything to dó with the | stool of | wickedness : which imágineth | mischief | as a | law ?

21 They gather them together against the sóul | of the | righteous : ánd con- | -demn the | innocent | blood.

22 But the Lórd | is my | refuge : and my Gód is the | strength | of my | confidence.

23 He shall recompense them their wickedness * and destroy them ín their | own | malice : yea, the Lórd our | God | shall de- | -stroy them.

Day 19.   MORNING PRAYER.

Psalm xcv.—*Venite, exultemus Domino.*

F. *f* O COME, let us síng | unto . the | Lord : let us heartily
rejóice in the | strength of | our sal- | -vation.

F.   2 Let us come before his présence with | thanks- | -giving :
and shéw ourselves | glad in | him with | psalms.

3 For the Lórd is a | great | God : and a gréat | King a- |
bove all | gods.

4 In his hand are all the córners | of the | earth : and the
stréngth of the | hills is | his | also.

2nd   5 The séa is his | and he | made it : and his hánds pre- |
part.   pared . the | dry | land.

mf   6 O come, let us wórship and | fall | down : and knéel be- |
fore the | Lord our | Maker.

7 For hé is the | Lord our | God : and we are the people of
his pasture * ánd the | sheep of | his | hand.

8 To-day if ye will hear his voice * hárden | not your |
hearts : as in the provocation * and as in the dáy of
tempt- | -ation | in the | wilderness ;

9 When your fáthers | tempted | me : próved | me and |
saw my | works.

10 Forty years long was I grieved with thís gener- | -ation
and | said : It is a people that do err in their hearts *
fór they | have not | known my | ways ;

11 Unto whom I swáre | in my | wrath : that they shóuld
not | enter | into . my | rest.

Psalm xcvi.—*Cantate Domino.*

f O SING unto the Lórd a | new | song : sing unto the
Lórd | all the | whole | earth.

2 Sing unto the Lórd and | praise his | Name : be telling of
hís sal- | -vation . from | day to | day.

3 Declare his hónour | unto . the | heathen : and his
wónders | unto | all | people.

4 For the Lord is great * and cannot wórthi- | -ly be |
praised : he is móre to be | feared . than | all | gods.

5 As for all the gods of the héathen | they are . but |
idols : but it ís the | Lord that | made the | heavens.

6 Glory and wórship | are be- | -fore him : pówer and |
honour . are | in his | sanctuary.

7 Ascribe unto the Lord * O ye kíndreds | of the | people :
ascribe unto the Lórd | worship | and | power.

8 Ascribe unto the Lord the honour due | unto . his |
Name : bring présents, and | come | into . his | courts.

9 O worship the Lórd in the | beauty . of | holiness : let the
whole éarth | stand in | awe of | him.

10 Tell it out among the héathen that the | Lord is | King :
and that it is he who hath made the round world so
fast * that it cannot be moved * and how that hé
shall | judge the | people | righteously.

11 Let the heavens rejóice, and let the | earth be | glad :
let the sea make a nóise, and | all that | therein | is.

12 Let the field be jóyful and | all that . is | in it : then shall
all the trees of the wóod re- | -joice be- | -fore the | Lord.

2nd 13 For he cometh, for he cómeth to | judge the | earth : and
part. with righteousness to judge the wórld, and the | people |
with his | truth.

Psalm xcvii.—*Dominus regnavit.*

f THE Lord is King * the éarth may be | glad there- | of :
yea, the multitude of the ísles | may be | glad there- | -of.

2 Clouds and dárkness are | round a- | -bout him : right-
eousness and judgement are the hábit- | -ation | of
his | seat.

3 There shall gó a | fire be- | -fore him : and burn úp his |
ene- . -mies on | every | side.

4 His lightnings gave shíne | unto . the | world : the
éarth | saw it . and | was a- | -fraid.

5 The hills melted like wax * at the présence | of the |
Lord : at the presence of the Lórd | of the | whole | earth.

6 The héavens have de- | -clared . his | righteousness : and
áll the | people . have | seen his | glory.

7 Confounded be all they that worship carved images * and
that delíght in | vain | gods : wórship | him | all ye | gods.

8 Sion héard of it | and re- | -joiced : and the daughters of
Judah were glad * becáuse of thy | judgements | O | Lord.

9 For thou, Lord, art higher than áll that are | in the |
earth : thou art exálted | far a- | -bove all | gods.

10 O ye that love the Lord * see that ye hate the thíng |
which is | evil : the Lord preserveth the souls of his
saints * he shall deliver them fróm the | hand of |
the un- | -godly.

11 There is sprung up a líght | for the | righteous : and
joyful gládness for | such as | are true- | -hearted.

12 Rejóice in the | Lord ye | righteous : and give thanks *
fór a re- | -membrance | of his | holiness.

Day 19.   EVENING PRAYER.

Psalm xcviii.—*Cantate Domino.*

F. f   O SING unto the Lórd a | new | song : for hé hath | done | marvellous | things.

F.   2 With his own right hand * and wíth his | holy | arm : háth he | gotten . him- | -self the | victory.

3 The Lord declàred | his sal- | -vation : his righteousness hath he openly shéwed in the | sight | of the | heathen.

4 He hath remembered his mercy and truth towárd the | house of | Israel : and all the ends of the world have séen the sal- | -vation | of our | God.

5 Shew yourselves joyful unto the Lórd | all ye | lands : síng, re- | -joice and | give | thanks.

6 Praise the Lórd up- | -on the | harp : sing to the hárp with a | psalm of | thanks- | -giving.

7 With trúmpets | also and | shawms : O shew yourselves jóyful be- | -fore the | Lord the | King.

8 Let the sea make a noise * and áll that | therein | is : the round wórld, and | they that | dwell there- | -in.

9 Let the floods clap their hands * and let the hills be joyful togéther be- | -fore the | Lord : fór he is | come to | judge the | earth.

10 With righteousness sháll he | judge the | world : ánd the | people | with | equity.

Psalm xcix.—*Dominus regnavit.*

f   THE Lord is King * be the people néver | so im- | patient : he sitteth between the cherubims * be the éarth | never | so un- | -quiet.

2 The Lórd is | great in | Sion : ánd | high a- | -bove all | people.

3 They shall give thánks | unto . thy | Name : which is gréat | wonder- | -ful and | holy.

4 The king's power loveth judgement * thóu hast pre- | pared | equity : thou hast executed júdgement and | righteous- | -ness in | Jacob.

5 O mágnify the | Lord our | God : and fall down before his fóotstool | for | he is | holy.

6 Moses and Aaron among his priests * and Samuel among such as cáll up- | -on his | Name : these called upón the | Lord | and he | heard them.

7 He spake unto them óut of the | cloudy | pillar : for they kept his testimonies * ánd the | law | that he | gave them.

8 Thou héardest them, O | Lord our | God : thou forgavest them, O God * and púnish- | -edst their | own in- | ventions.

2nd part. 9 O magnify the Lord our God * and worship him upón his | holy | hill : fór the | Lord our | God is | holy.

PSALM c.—*Jubilate Deo.*

f O BE joyful in the Lórd | all ye | lands : serve the Lord with gladness * and come befóre his | presence | with a | song.

2 Be ye sure that the Lórd | he is | God : it is he that hath made us and not we ourselves * we are his people, ánd the | sheep of | his | pasture.

3 O go your way into his gates with thanksgiving * and ínto his | courts with | praise : be thankful unto hím, and | speak good | of his | Name.

mf 4 For the Lord is gracious * his mércy is | ever- | -lasting : and his truth endureth from géner- | -ation . to | gener- | -ation.

PSALM ci.—*Misericordiam et judicium.*

mf M Y sóng shall be of | mercy . and | judgement : unto thée, O | Lord | will I | sing.

2 O lét me have | under- | -standing : ín the | way of | godli- | -ness.

3 When wilt thou cóme | unto | me : I will walk in my hóuse | with a | perfect | heart.

4 I will take no wicked thing in hand * I hate the síns | of un- | -faithfulness : there shall nó such | cleave | unto | me.

5 A froward héart shall de- | -part from | me : I wíll not | know a | wicked | person.

6 Whoso privily slánder- | -eth his | neighbour : hím | — will | I de- | -stroy.

7 Whoso hath also a proud lóok and | high | stomach : I' | will not | suffer | him.

8 Mine eyes look upon such as are fáithful | in the | land : thát | they may | dwell with | me.

9 Whoso léadeth a | godly | life : hé | — shall | be my | servant.

10 There shall no deceitful person dwéll | in my | house : he that telleth lies sháll not | tarry | in my | sight.

2nd part. 11 I shall soon destroy all the ungódly that are | in the | land : that I may root out all wicked doers fróm the | city | of the | Lord.

Day 20.   MORNING PRAYER.

PSALM cii.—*Domine, exaudi.*

F.mp HÉAR my | prayer O | Lord : and let my crýing | come | unto | thee.

F. 2 Hide not thy face from me in the tíme | of my | trouble : incline thine ear unto me when I call * O héar | me and | that right | soon.

3 For my days are consúmed a- | -way like | smoke : and my bones are burnt úp | as it | were a | firebrand.

4 My heart is smitten dówn, and | withered . like | grass : so that I' for- | -get to | eat my | bread.

5 For the vóice | of my | groaning : my bones will scárce | cleave | to my | flesh.

6 I am become like a pélican | in the | wilderness : and like an ówl | that is | in the | desert.

7 I have watched * and am éven as it | were a | sparrow : that sítteth a- | -lone up- | -on the | house-top.

8 Mine enemies revíle me | all the . day | long : and they that are mad upón me are | sworn to- | -gether . a- | gainst me.

9 For I have eaten áshes | as it . were | bread : ánd | mingled . my | drink with | weeping ;

10 And that because of thine índig- | -nation and | wrath : for thou hast táken me | up and | cast me | down.

11 My days are góne | like a | shadow : and I' am | withered | like | grass.

12 But thou, O Lórd, shalt en- | -dure for | ever : and thy remembrance throughóut | all | gener- | -ations.

13 Thou shalt arise, and have mércy up- | -on | Sion : for it is time that thou have mercy upón her | yea the | time is | come.

14 And why * thy servants think up- | -on her | stones : and
it pitieth them to | see her | in the | dust.

15 The heathen shall fear thy | Name O | Lord : and all the
kings | of the | earth thy | Majesty ;

16 When the Lord shall | build up | Sion : and when his |
glory | shall ap- | -pear ;

17 When he turneth him unto the prayer of the | poor |
destitute : and de- | -spiseth . not | their de- | -sire.

18 This shall be written for those that | come | after : and
the people which shall be | born shall | praise the |
Lord.

19 For he hath looked down | from his | sanctuary : out of
the heaven did the | Lord be- | -hold the | earth ;

20 That he might hear the mournings of such as are | in
cap- | -tivity : and deliver the children ap- | -pointed |
unto | death ;

21 That they may declare the Name of the | Lord in | Sion :
and his | worship | at Je- | -rusalem ;

22 When the people are | gathered . to- | -gether : and the
kingdoms | also . to | serve the | Lord.

23 He brought down my strength | in my | journey : and |
shortened | my | days.

24 But I said * O my God, take me not away in the midst |
of mine | age : as for thy years, they endure through-
out | all | gener- | -ations.

mf 25 Thou, Lord, in the beginning * hast laid the foundation |
of the | earth : and the heavens are the | work of |
thy | hands.

26 They shall perish, but thou | shalt en- | -dure : they all
shall wax | old as | doth a | garment ;

27 And as a vesture shalt thou change them * and they |
shall be | changed : but thou art the same, and thy |
years | shall not | fail.

28 The children of thy servants | shall con- | -tinue : and
their seed shall stand | fast | in thy | sight.

PSALM ciii.—*Benedic, anima mea.*

f PRAISE the Lord | O my | soul : and all that is within
me | praise his | holy | Name.

2 Praise the Lord | O my | soul : and for- | -get not | all
his | benefits ;

3 Who forgiveth | all thy | sin : and healeth | all | thine
in- | -firmities ;

4 Who saveth thy lífe | from de- | -struction : and crowneth
thée with | mercy . and | loving- | -kindness ;

5 Who satisfieth thy móuth with | good | things : making
thee yoúng and | lusty | as an | eagle.

6 The Lord executeth ríghteous- | -ness and | judgement :
for all thém that | are op- | -pressed . with | wrong.

7 He shéwed his wáys | unto | Moses : his wórks | unto .
the | children . of | Israel.

8 The Lord is fúll of com- | -passion . and | mercy : long-
súffering | and of | great | goodness.

9 He wíll not | alway . be | chiding : neither kéepeth | he
his | anger . for | ever.

10 He hath not déalt with us | after . our | sins : nor
rewárded us ac- | -cording | to our | wickednesses.

11 For look how high the heaven is in compárison | of the |
earth : so great is his mercy álso | toward | them that |
fear him.

12 Look how wide also the éast is | from the | west : so fár
hath he | set our | sins | from us.

13 Yea, like as a father pítieth his | own | children : even
so is the Lord mérciful | unto | them that | fear him.

14 For he knoweth wheréof | we are | made : he remémber-
eth | that we | are but | dust.

mp 15 The days of mán are | but as | grass : for he flourisheth
ás a | flower | of the | field.

16 For as soon as the wind goeth óver it | it is | gone : and
the place theréof shall | know it | no | more.

mf 17 But the merciful goodness of the Lord * endureth for ever
and éver upon | them that | fear him : and his ríght-
eousness up- | -on | children's | children ;

18 Even upon súch as | keep his | covenant : and thínk
upon | his com- | -mandments . to | do them.

f 19 The Lord hath prepáred his | seat in | heaven : and his
kíngdom | ruleth | over | all.

20 O praise the Lord, ye angels of his * yé that ex- | -cel
in | strength : ye that fulfil his commandment * and
hearken únto the | voice | of his | words.

21 O praise the Lórd, all | ye his | hosts : ye sérvants of |
his that | do his | pleasure.

22 O speak good of the Lord, all ye works of his * in all
pláces of | his do- | -minion : práise thou the | Lord |
O my | soul.

Day 20. EVENING PRAYER.

Psalm civ.—*Benedic, anima mea.*

F. f **P**RAISE the Lórd | O my | soul : O Lord my God, thou art become exceeding glorious * thou art clóthed with | majes- | -ty and | honour.

F. 2 Thou deckest thyself with light as it wére | with a | garment : and spreadest óut the | heavens | like a | curtain.

3 Who layeth the beams of his chámbers | in the | waters : and maketh the clouds his chariot * and walketh upón the | wings | of the | wind.

4 He máketh his | angels | spirits : and his mínis- | -ters a | flaming | fire.

5 He laid the foundátions | of the | earth : that it néver should | move at | any | time.

6 Thou coveredst it with the deep, líke as | with a | garment : the wáters | stand | in the | hills.

7 At thý re- | -buke they | flee : at the vóice of thy | thunder . they | are a- | -fraid.

8 They go up as high as the hills * and dówn to the | valleys . be- | -neath : even unto the pláce which | thou . hast ap- | -pointed | for them.

9 Thou hast set them their bóunds which they | shall not | pass : neither túrn a- | -gain to | cover . the | earth.

10 He sendeth the spríngs | into . the | rivers : whích | run a- | -mong the | hills.

11 All beasts of the fiéld | drink there- | -of : ánd the wild | asses | quench their | thirst.

12 Beside them shall the fowls of the aír have their | habit- | -ation : ánd | sing a- | -mong the | branches.

13 He watereth the hílls | from a- | -bove : the earth is fílled with the | fruit | of thy | works.

14 He bringeth forth grás | for the | cattle : and green hérb | for the | service . of | men ;

15 That he may bring food out of the earth * and wine that maketh glád the | heart of | man : and oil to make him a cheerful countenance * and bréad to | strengthen | man's | heart.

16 The trees of the Lord álso are | full of | sap : even the cedars of Líban- | -us which | he hath | planted ;

17 Wherein the bírds | make their | nests : and the fir-trees áre a | dwelling | for the | stork.

18 The high hills are a refuge fór the | wild | goats : and so
are the stóny | rocks | for the | conies.

19 He appointed the móon for | certain | seasons : and the
sún | knoweth . his | going | down.

20 Thou makest darkness * thát it | may be | night : where-
in all the béasts | of the | forest . do | move.

21 The lions róaring | after . their | prey : dó | seek their |
meat from | God.

22 The sun ariseth * and they gét them a- | -way to- |
gether : and láy them | down | in their | dens.

2nd part. 23 Man goeth forth to his wórk, and | to his | labour : ún- |
til the | even- | -ing.

ff 24 O Lord, how mánifold | are thy | works : in wisdom hast
thou made them all * the éarth is | full | of thy |
riches.

25 So is the gréat and | wide sea | also : wherein are things
creeping innumerable * bóth | small and | great |
beasts.

f 26 There go the ships * and thére is | that Le- | -viathan :
whom thou hast máde to | take his | pastime .
there- | -in.

27 These wáit | all up- . -on | thee : that thou mayest gíve
them | meat in | due | season.

28 When thou givest it thém they | gather | it : and when
thou openest thy hánd | they are | filled . with | good.

mp 29 When thou hidest thy fáce | they are | troubled : when
thou takest away their breath they die * and are
túrned a- | -gain | to their | dust.

mf 30 When thou lettest thy breath go fórth they | shall be |
made : and thou shalt renéw the | face | of the | earth.

f 31 The glorious Majesty of the Lórd shall en- | -dure for |
ever : the Lórd shall re- | -joice | in his | works.

32 The earth shall trémble at the | look of | him : if he do
but toúch the | hills | they shall | smoke.

33 I will sing unto the Lórd as | long as . I | live : I will
praise my Gód | while I | have my | being.

34 And só shall my | words | please him : my jóy shall | be |
in the | Lord.

35 As for sinners, they shall be consumed out of the earth *
and the ungódly shall | come . to an | end : praise thou
the Lord, O my sóul | praise | — the | Lord.

Day 21.   MORNING PRAYER.

Psalm cv.—*Confitemini Domino.*

F. mf   O GIVE thanks unto the Lord * and call up- | -on his | Name : tell the people what | things | he hath | done.

F.   2 O let your songs be of | him and | praise him : and let your talking be of | all his | wondrous | works.

3 Rejoice in his | holy | Name : let the heart of them re- | joice that | seek the | Lord.

4 Seek the Lord | and his | strength : seek his | face | ever- | -more.

5 Remember the marvellous works that | he hath | done : his wonders, and the | judgements | of his | mouth.

6 O ye seed of Abra- | -ham his | servant : ye | children . of | Jacob . his | chosen.

7 He is the | Lord our | God : his judgements | are in | all the | world.

8 He hath been alway mindful of his cove- | -nant and | promise : that he made to a | thousand | gener- | ations ;

9 Even the covenant that he made with | Abra- | -ham : and the oath that he | sware | unto | Isaac ;

10 And appointed the same unto Jacob | for a | law : and to Israel for an | ever- | -lasting | testament ;

11 Saying, Unto thee will I give the | land of | Canaan : the | lot of | your in- | -heritance ;

12 When there were yet but a | few of | them : and they | strangers | in the | land ;

13 What time as they went from one nation | to an- | other : from one kingdom | to an- | -other | people ;

14 He suffered no man to | do them | wrong : but reproved even | kings for | their | sakes ;

15 Touch not | mine A- | -nointed : and | do my | prophets . no | harm.

16 Moreover, he called for a dearth up- | -on the | land : and destroyed | all the . pro- | -vision . of | bread.

17 But he had sent a | man be- | -fore them : even Joseph, who was sold to | be a | bond- | -servant ;

18 Whose feet they hurt | in the | stocks : the iron | entered | into . his | soul ;

19 Until the time came that his | cause was | known : the word | of the | Lord | tried him.

20 The king sént, and de- | -livered | him : the prince of the
people | let him | go | free.

21 He made him lórd also | of his | house : ánd | ruler .
of | all his | substance ;

22 That he might inform his prínces | after . his | will :
ánd | teach his | senators | wisdom.

23 Israel also cáme | into | Egypt : and Jacob was a
stránger | in the | land of | Ham.

24 And he incréased his | people . ex- | -ceedingly : and
máde them | stronger | than their | enemies ;

25 Whose heart turned só that they | hated . his | people :
and déalt un- | -truly | with his | servants.

26 Thén sent he | Moses . his | servant : ánd | Aaron .
whom | he had | chosen.

27 And these shéwed his | tokens . a- | -mong them : and
wónders | in the | land of | Ham.

28 He sent dárkness, and | it was | dark : and they were nót
o- | -bedient | unto . his | word.

29 He turned their wáters | into | blood : ánd | slew | their |
fish.

30 Their lánd | brought forth | frogs : yea, éven | in their |
kings' | chambers.

31 He spake the word * and there cáme all | manner . of |
flies : ánd | lice in | all their | quarters.

32 He gave them háil- | -stones for | rain : and flámes of |
fire | in their | land.

33 He smote their vínes | also . and | fig-trees : and destroyed
the trées | that were | in their | coasts.

34 He spake the word, and the grasshoppers came * and
cáter- | -pillars . in- | -numerable : and did eat up all
the grass in their land * and devóured the | fruit | of
their | ground.

35 He smote all the fírst-born | in their | land : éven the |
chief of | all their | strength.

36 He brought them forth álso with | silver . and | gold : there
was not óne feeble | person . a- | -mong their | tribes.

37 Egypt was gládd at | their de- | -parting : fór they | were
a- | -fraid of | them.

38 He spread out a clóud to | be a | covering : and fire to give
líght | in the | night- | -season.

39 At their desíre he | brought | quails : and he fílled them |
with the | bread of | heaven.

40 He opened the rock of stone * and the wáters | flowed |
out : so that rivers rán | in the | dry | places.

41 For why, he remémbered his | holy | promise : ánd |
    Abra- | -ham his | servant.

42 And he brought fórth his | people . with | joy : ánd his |
    chosen | with | gladness ;

43 And gave them the lánds | of the | heathen : and they
    took the lábours of the | people | in pos- | -session ;

44 That théy might | keep his | statutes : ánd ob- | -serve |
    his | laws.

Day 21.   EVENING PRAYER.

Psalm cvi.—*Confitemini Domino.*

F. mf   O GIVE thanks unto the Lórd, for | he is | gracious : ánd
      his | mercy . en- | -dureth . for | ever.

F.   2 Who can express the noble ácts | of the | Lord : ór | shew
    forth | all his | praise ?

3 Blessed are théy that | alway . keep | judgement : ánd |
    do | righteous- | -ness.

4 Remember me, O Lord * according to the favour that
    thou béarest | unto . thy | people : O vísit | me with |
    thy sal- | -vation ;

5 That I may see the felícity | of thy | chosen : and rejoice
    in the gladness of thy people * ánd give | thanks with |
    thine in- | -heritance.

6 We have sínned | with our | fathers : we have dóne
    a- | -miss and | dealt | wickedly.

7 Our fathers regarded not thy wonders in Egypt * neither
    kept they thy great góodness | in re- | -membrance :
    but were disobedient at the sea * éven | at the | Red |
    sea.

8 Nevertheless, he helped them fór his | Name's | sake : that
    he might máke his | power | to be | known.

9 He rebuked the Red sea also * ánd it was | dried | up : so
    he led them thróugh the | deep as | through a | wilder-
    ness.

10 And he saved them from the ádver- | -sary's | hand : and
    delivered them fróm the | hand | of the | enemy.

11 As for those that troubled them * the waters óver- |
    whelmed | them : there wás not | one of | them | left.

12 Then belíeved | they his | words : and sáng | praise |
    unto | him.

13 But within a whíle they for- | -gat his | works : ánd
    would | not a- | -bide his | counsel.

14 But lust came upón them | in the | wilderness : and they
témpted | God | in the | desert.

15 And he gáve them | their de- | -sire : and sent léanness
with- | -al | into . their | soul.

16 They angered Moses álso | in the | tents : and Aáron,
the | saint | of the | Lord.

17 So the earth ópened, and | swallowed . up | Dathan : and
covered the cóngre- | -gation | of A- | -biram.

18 And the fire was kíndled | in their | company : the
fláme | burnt up | the un- | -godly.

19 They máde a | calf in | Horeb : ánd | worshipped . the |
molten | image.

20 Thús they | turned . their | glory : into the similitude óf
a | calf that | eateth | hay.

21 And they forgát | God their | Saviour : who had dóne so |
great | things in | Egypt ;

22 Wondrous wórks in the | land of | Ham : and fearful
thíngs | by the | Red | Sea.

23 So he said, he would have destroyed them * had not
Moses his chosen stood befóre him | in the | gap : to
turn away his wrathful indignátion | lest he | should
de- | -stroy them.

24 Yea, they thought scórn of that | pleasant | land : and
gáve no | credence | unto . his | word ;

25 But múrmured | in their | tents : and hearkened not únto
the | voice | of the | Lord.

26 Then lift he úp his | hand a- | -gainst them : to óver- |
throw them | in the | wilderness ;

27 To cast out their séed a- | -mong the | nations : ánd to |
scatter . them | in the | lands.

28 They joined themsélves unto | Baal- | -peor : and áte
the | offerings | of the | dead.

29 Thus they provoked him to anger wíth their | own in- |
ventions : ánd the | plague was | great a- | -mong them.

30 Thén stood up | Phinees . and | prayed : ánd | so the |
plague | ceased.

31 And that was coúnted unto | him for | righteousness :
among áll pos- | -teri- . -ties for | ever- | -more.

32 They angered him also át the | waters . of | strife : so
that he púnished | Moses . for | their | sakes ;

33 Becáuse they pro- | -voked . his | spirit : so that he spáke
unad- | -visedly | with his | lips.

34 Neither destróyed | they the | heathen : ás the | Lord
com- | -manded | them ;

35 But were míngled a- | -mong the | heathen : ánd | learned | their | works.

36 Insomuch that they worshipped their idols * which túrned to their | own de- | -cay : yea, they offered their sóns and their | daughters | unto | devils ;

37 And shed innocent blood * even the blood of their sóns and | of their | daughters : whom they offered unto the idols of Canaan * and the lánd | was de- | -filed . with | blood.

38 Thus they were stained wíth their | own | works : and went a whóring | with their | own in- | -ventions.

39 Therefore was the wrath of the Lord kíndled a- | -gainst his | people : insomúch that he ab- | -horred . his | own in- | -heritance.

40 And he gave them over into the hánd | of the | heathen : and they that háted them were | lords | over | them.

41 Their énemies op- | -pressed | them : ánd | had them | in sub- | -jection.

42 Many a tíme did he de- | -liver | them : but they rebelled against him with their own inventions * and were bróught | down | in their | wickedness.

43 Nevertheless, when he sáw | their ad- | -versity : hé | heard | their com- | -plaint.

44 He thought upon his covenant, and pitied them * according unto the múltitude | of his | mercies : yea, he made all those that led them awáy | captive . to | pity | them.

45 Deliver us, O Lord our God * and gather us fróm a- | mong the | heathen : that we may give thanks unto thy holy Name * and máke our | boast | of thy | praise.

46 Blessed be the Lord God of Israel from everlásting, and | world with- . -out | end : and let áll the | people | say A- | -men.

Day 22.   MORNING PRAYER.

Psalm cvii.—*Confitemini Domino.*

F. mf **O** GIVE thanks unto the Lórd, for | he is | gracious : ánd his | mercy . en- | -dureth . for | ever.

F.   2 Let them give thanks whom the Lórd | hath re- | deemed : and delivered fróm the | hand | of the | enemy ;

3 And gathered them out of the lands * from the éast and | from the | west : fróm the | north and | from the | south.

4 They went astray in the wílderness | out . of the | way :
  ánd | found no | city . to | dwell in ;

5 Húngry | and | thirsty : théir | soul | fainted | in them.

6 So they cried unto the Lórd | in their | trouble : and he
  delívered them | from | their dis- | -tress.

2nd
part.
7 He led them fórth by the | right | way : that they might
  gó to the | city | where they | dwelt.

7.
8 O that men would therefore praise the Lórd | for his |
  goodness : and declare the wonders that he dóeth | for
  the | children . of | men !

9 For he satisfíeth the | empty | soul : and fílleth the |
  hungry | soul with | goodness.

10 Such as sit in darkness * and ín the | shadow . of |
  death : being fast boúnd in | mise- | -ry and | iron ;

11 Because they rebelled against the wórds | of the | Lord :
  and lightly regarded the cóunsel | of the | most | Highest ;

12 He also brought dówn their | heart through | heaviness :
  they fell dówn, and | there was | none to | help them.

13 So when they cried unto the Lórd | in their | trouble : he
  delívered them | out of | their dis- | -tress.

2nd
part.
14 For he brought them out of darkness * and óut of the |
  shadow . of | death : ánd | brake their | bonds in | sunder.

7.
15 O that men would therefore praise the Lórd | for his |
  goodness : and declare the wonders that he dóeth | for
  the | children . of | men !

16 For he hath bróken the | gates of | brass : and smítten
  the | bars of | iron . in | sunder.

17 Foolish men are plágued for | their of- | -fence : ánd be- |
  cause of | their | wickedness.

18 Their soul abhórred all | manner . of | meat : and they
  were éven | hard at | death's | door.

19 So when they cried unto the Lórd | in their | trouble : he
  delívered them | out of | their dis- | -tress.

20 He sent his wórd, and | healed | them : and théy were |
  saved . from | their de- | -struction.

7.
21 O that men would therefore praise the Lórd | for his |
  goodness : and declare the wonders that he dóeth | for
  the | children . of | men !

22 That they would offer unto him the sácrifice of | thanks- |
  giving : and téll | out his | works with | gladness !

23 They that go dówn to the | sea in | ships : and óccupy
  their | business . in | great | waters ;

24 These men see the wórks | of the | Lord : ánd his |
  wonders | in the | deep.

25 For at his word the stórmy | wind a- | -riseth : which lífteth | up the | waves there- | -of.

26 They are carried up to the heaven * and dówn again | to the | deep : their soul melteth awáy be- | -cause | of the | trouble.

27 They reel to and fro * and stagger líke a | drunken | man : ánd are | at their | wits' | end.

28 So when they cry unto the Lórd | in their | trouble : he delívereth them | out of | their dis- | -tress.

29 For he máketh the | storm to | cease : só that the | waves there- | -of are | still.

30 Then are they glad, becáuse they | are at | rest : and so he bringeth them unto the háven | where they | would | be.

F. 31 O that men would therefore praise the Lórd | for his | goodness : and declare the wonders that he dóeth | for the | children . of | men !

. 32 That they would exalt him also in the congregátion | of the | people : and práise him in the | seat | of the | elders !

33 Who turneth the flóods | into . a | wilderness : ánd | drieth | up the | water-springs.

34 A fruitful lánd | maketh . he | barren : for the wíckedness of | them that | dwell there- | -in.

35 Again, he maketh the wílderness a | standing | water : and wáter-springs | of a | dry | ground.

36 And thére he | setteth . the | hungry : that théy may | build . them a | city . to | dwell in ;

37 That they may sow their lánd, and | plant | vineyards : tó | yield them | fruits of | increase.

38 He blesseth them * so that they múlti- | -ply ex- | ceedingly : and suffereth nót their | cattle | to de- | crease.

39 And again * when they are mínished and | brought | low : through oppréssion, through | any | plague or | trouble ;

40 Though he suffer them to be évil in- | -treated . through | tyrants : and let them wander óut of the | way | in the | wilderness ;

41 Yet helpeth he the póor | out of | misery : and maketh him hóuseholds | like a | flock of | sheep.

42 The righteous will consider thís | and re- | -joice : and the móuth of all | wickedness | shall be | stopped.

2nd part. 43 Whoso is wíse will | ponder . these | things : and they shall understánd the loving- | -kindness | of the | Lord.

Day 22.   EVENING PRAYER.

Psalm cviii.—*Paratum cor meum.*

mf   O GOD, my heart is reády, my | heart is | ready : I will sing and give praise with the bést | member | that I | have.

'.   2 Awáke, thou | lute and | harp : I mysélf | will a- | -wake right | early.

3 I will give thanks unto thee, O Lórd, a- | -mong the | people : I will sing práises unto | thee a- | -mong the | nations.

4 For thy mercy is gréater | than the | heavens : and thy trúth | reacheth | unto . the | clouds.

5 Set up thyself, O Gód, a- | -bove the | heavens : and thy glóry a- | -bove | all the | earth.

6 That thy belóved may | be de- | -livered : let thy right hand sáve | them and | hear thou | me.

7 God hath spóken | in his | holiness : I will rejoice therefore, and divide Sichem * and méte | out the | valley . of | Succoth.

8 Gilead is míne, and Ma- | -nasses . is | mine : Ephraim also ís the | strength | of my | head.

2nd part.   9 Judah is my law-giver * Móab | is my | wash-pot : over Edom will I cast out my shoe * upón Phi- | -listia | will I | triumph.

10 Who will lead me ínto the | strong | city : and whó will | bring me | into | Edom?

11 Hast not thou forsáken | us O | God : and wilt not thou, O Gód, go | forth | with our | hosts?

12 O hélp us a- | -gainst the | enemy : for váin | is the | help of | man.

13 Through Gód we shall | do great | acts : and it is hé that shall | tread | down our | enemies.

Psalm cix.—*Deus laudum.*

mp   HOLD not thy tongue, O Gód | of my | praise : for the mouth of the ungodly * yea, the moúth of the de- | -ceitful . is | opened . up- | -on me.

2 And they have spoken agáinst me with | false | tongues : they compassed me about also with words of hatred * and fóught against | me with- | -out a | cause.

3 For the love that I had unto them * lo, they take nów my | contrary | part : bút I | give my- . -self | unto | prayer.

4 Thus have they rewárded me | evil . for | good : ánd | hatred . for | my good | will.

5 Set thou an ungodly man to be rúler | over | him : and let Satan stánd | at his | right | hand.

6 When sentence is given upon him * lét him | be con- | demned : and let his práyer be | turned | into | sin.

7 Lét his | days be | few : and lét an- | -other | take his | office.

8 Lét his | children . be | fatherless : ánd | — his | wife a | widow.

9 Let his children be vágabonds, and | beg their | bread : let them seek it álso | out of | desolate | places.

10 Let the extortioner consúme | all that . he | hath : and lét the | stranger | spoil his | labour.

11 Let there be nó man to | pity | him : nor to have compássion up- | -on his | fatherless | children.

12 Let his postérity | be de- | -stroyed : and in the next generation lét his | name be | clean put | out.

13 Let the wickedness of his fathers be had in remembrance * in the síght | of the | Lord : and let not the sín of his | mother . be | done a- | -way.

14 Let them alway bé be- | -fore the | Lord : that he may root out the memórial of | them from | off the | earth ;

15 And that, because his mínd was | not to . do | good : but persecuted the poor helpless man * that he might slay hím that was | vexed | at the | heart.

16 His delight was in cursing * and it shall háppen | unto | him : he loved not blessing * thérefore shall | it be | far from | him.

17 He clothed himself with cursing * líke as | with a | raiment : and it shall come into his bowels like water * ánd like | oil | into . his | bones.

18 Let it be unto him as the clóke that he | hath up- | -on him : and as the girdle that hé is | alway | girded . with- | -al.

19 Let it thus happen from the Lórd | unto . mine | enemies : and to thóse that speak | evil . a- | -gainst my | soul.

20 But deal thou with me, O Lord God * accórding | unto . thy | Name : fór | sweet | is thy | mercy.

21 O deliver me * for I' am | helpless . and | poor : ánd my | heart is | wounded . with- | -in me.

22 I go hence like the shádow | that de- | -parteth : and am dríven a- | -way | as the | grasshopper.

23 My knées are | weak through | fasting : my flésh is
　　dried | up for | want of | fatness.

24 I became also a repróach | unto | them : they that lóoked
　　up- | -on me | shaked . their | heads.

25 Hélp me, O | Lord my | God : O sáve me, ac- | -cording |
　　to thy | mercy ;

26 And they shall know * how that thís is | thy | hand : ánd
　　that | thou | Lord hast | done it.

27 Though they cúrse, yet | bless | thou : and let them be
　　confounded that rise up against me * bút | let thy |
　　servant . re- | -joice.

28 Let mine ádversaries be | clothed . with | shame : and
　　let them cover themselves with their ówn con- | -fusion .
　　as | with a | cloke.

29 As for me * I will give great thanks unto the Lórd | with
　　my | mouth : and práise | him a- | -mong the | multi-
　　tude ;

30 For he shall stand at the right hánd | of the | poor : to
　　save his sóul | from un- | -righteous | judges.

Day 23.　　　　MORNING PRAYER.

Psalm cx.—*Dixit Dominus.*

mf　THE Lord sáid unto | my | Lord : Sit thou on my right
　　　hand * until I máke thine | ene- | -mies thy | foot-
　　　stool.

2 The Lord shall send the rod of thy pówer | out of | Sion :
　　be thou ruler * éven in the | midst a- | -mong thine |
　　enemies.

3 In the day of thy power shall the people offer thee free-
　　will-offerings * wíth an | holy | worship : the dew of
　　thy birth is óf the | womb | of the | morning.

4 The Lord swáre, and will | not re- | -pent : Thou art a
　　Priest for ever * áfter the | order | of Mel- | -chisedech.

5 The Lórd upon | thy right | hand : shall wound even
　　kíngs in the | day | of his | wrath.

6 He shall judge among the heathen * he shall fill the
　　pláces with the | dead | bodies : and smite in sunder
　　the héads | over | divers | countries.

2nd part.　7 He shall drink of the bróok | in the | way : therefore sháll
　　he | lift | up his | head.

Psalm cxi.—*Confitebor tibi.*

mf I WILL give thanks unto the Lórd with my | whole | heart : secretly among the fáithful, and | in the | congre- | -gation.

2 The wórks of the | Lord are | great : sought out of all thém | that have | pleasure . there- | -in.

3 His work is worthy to be práised, and | had in | honour : and his ríghteous- | -ness en- | -dureth . for | ever.

4 The merciful and gracious Lord hath so dóne his | marvellous | works : that they oúght to be | had | in re- | -membrance.

5 He hath given méat unto | them that | fear him : he shall éver be | mindful | of his | covenant.

6 He hath shewed his people the pówer | of his | works : that he may gíve them the | heritage | of the | heathen.

7 The works of his hands are vérity | and | judgement : áll | his com- | -mandments . are | true.

8 They stand fást for | ever . and | ever : ánd are | done in | truth and | equity.

9 He sent redémption | unto . his | people : he hath commanded his covenant for ever * hóly and | reverend | is his | Name.

10 The fear of the Lórd is the be- | -ginning . of | wisdom : a good understanding have all they that do thereafter * the práise of | it en- | -dureth . for | ever.

Psalm cxii.—*Beatus vir.*

mf B LESSED is the mán that | feareth . the | Lord : he hath gréat de- | -light in | his com- | -mandments.

2 His seed shall be míghty up- | -on | earth : the generátion of the | faithful | shall be | blessed.

3 Riches and plenteousness shall bé | in his | house : and his ríghteous- | -ness en- | -dureth . for | ever.

4 Unto the godly there ariseth up líght | in the | darkness : hé is | merciful | loving . and | righteous.

5 A good man is mérci- | -ful and | lendeth : and will guíde his | words | with dis- | -cretion.

6 For hé shall | never . be | moved : and the righteous shall be hád in | ever- | -lasting . re- | -membrance.

7 He will not be afráid of any | evil | tidings : for his heart standeth fást, and be- | -lieveth | in the | Lord.

8 His heart is estáblished, and | will not | shrink : until he sée his de- | -sire up- | -on his | enemies.

9 He hath dispersed abroad * and gíven | to the | poor :
and his righteousness remaineth for ever * his hórn
shall | be ex- | -alted . with | honour.

10 The ungodly shall sée it, and | it shall | grieve him : he
shall gnash with his teeth, and consume away * the
desíre of the un- | -godly | shall | perish.

PSALM cxiii.—*Laudate, pueri.*

f   PRÁISE the | Lord ye | servants : O práise the | Name |
of the | Lord.

2 Blessed be the Náme | of the | Lord : from thís time |
forth for | ever- | -more.

3 The Lórd's | Name is | praised : from the rising up of the
sun, unto the góing | down | of the | same.

4 The Lord is hígh a- | -bove all | heathen : ánd his |
glory . a- | -bove the | heavens.

5 Who is like unto the Lord our God * that háth his |
dwelling . so | high : and yet humbleth himself to
behold the thíngs that | are in | heaven and | earth ?

6 He taketh up the símple | out . of the | dust : and lífteth
the | poor | out . of the | mire ;

7 That he may sét him | with the | princes : even wíth
the | princes | of his | people.

8 He maketh the barren wóman to | keep | house : and to
bé a | joyful | mother . of | children.

Day 23.   EVENING PRAYER.

PSALM cxiv.—*In exitu Israel.*

F. mf   WHEN Israel cáme | out of | Egypt : and the house of
Jacob fróm a- | -mong the | strange | people.

F.   2 Júdah | was his | sanctuary : ánd | Israel | his do- |
minion.

3 The séa saw | that and | fled : Jór- | -dan was | driven |
back.

4 The móuntains | skipped . like | rams : and the líttle |
hills like | young | sheep.

5 What aileth thee, O thou séa | that thou | fleddest : and
thou Jórdan, that | thou wast | driven | back ?

6 Ye mountains, thát ye | skipped . like | rams : and ye
líttle | hills like | young | sheep ?

7 Tremble thou earth, at the présence | of the | Lord : at the présence | of the | God of | Jacob ;

8 Who turned the hard róck into a | standing | water : and the flínt-stone | into . a | springing | well.

Psalm cxv.—*Non nobis, Domine.*

mf NOT unto us, O Lord, not unto us ✻ but unto thy Náme | give the | praise : for thy loving mércy, and | for thy | truth's | sake.

2 Wherefore shall the | heathen | say : Whére | — is | now their | God ?

3 As for óur God | he is . in | heaven : he hath dóne whatso- | -ever | pleased | him.

4 Their ídols are | silver . and | gold : éven the | work of | men's | hands.

5 Théy have | mouths and | speak not : éyes | have | they and | see not.

6 Théy have | ears and | hear not : nóses | have | they and | smell not.

7 They have hands and handle not ✻ féet have | they and | walk not : neíther | speak they | through their | throat.

8 They that make them are líke | unto | them : and so are all súch as | put their | trust in | them.

9 But thou house of Israel ✻ trúst thou | in the | Lord : hé is their | succour | and de- | -fence.

10 Ye house of Aaron ✻ put your trúst | in the | Lord : hé is their | helper | and de- | -fender.

11 Ye that fear the Lord ✻ put your trúst | in the | Lord : hé is their | helper | and de- | -fender.

12 The Lord hath been mindful of ús, and | he shall | bless us : even he shall bless the house of Israel ✻ hé shall | bless the | house of | Aaron.

13 He shall bless thém that | fear the | Lord : bóth | small | and | great.

14 The Lord shall incréase you | more and | more : yóu | and | your | children.

.5 Ye are the bléssed | of the | Lord : whó | made | heaven and | earth.

16 All the whole héavens | are the | Lord's : the earth hath he gíven | to the | children . of | men.

17 The dead práise not | thee O | Lord : neither all théy that go | down | into | silence.

18 But wé will | praise the | Lord : from this time forth for evermóre. | Praise | — the | Lord.

Day 24. MORNING PRAYER.

Psalm cxvi.—*Dilexi, quoniam.*

mf I AM | well | pleased : that the Lord hath héard the | voice of | my | prayer ;

2 That he hath inclined his éar | unto | me : therefore will I call upon hím as | long | as I | live.

3 The snares of death cómpassed me | round a- | -bout : and the páins of | hell gat | hold up- | -on me.

4 I shall find trouble and heaviness * and I will call upon the Náme | of the | Lord : O Lord, I beséech | thee de- | liver my | soul.

5 Gracious ís the | Lord and | righteous : yéa, our | God is | merci- | -ful.

6 The Lórd pre- | -serveth . the | simple : I was in mísery | and he | helped | me.

7 Turn again then unto thy rést | O my | soul : for the Lórd | hath re- | -warded | thee. .

8 And why? thou hast delívered my | soul from | death : mine eyes from téars | and my | feet from | falling.

9 I will wálk be- | -fore the | Lord : ín the | land | of the | living.

10 I believed, and therefore will I speak * but Í was | sore | troubled : I said in my háste | All | men are | liars.

11 What reward shall I gíve | unto . the | Lord : for all the benefits that hé hath | done | unto | me ?

12 I will receive the cúp | of sal- | -vation : and cáll upon the | Name | of the | Lord.

13 I will pay my vows now in the présence of | all his | people : right dear in the sight of the Lórd is the | death | of his | saints.

14 Behold, O Lord, hów that | I am . thy | servant : I am thy servant and the son of thine handmaid * thóu hast | broken . my | bonds in | sunder.

15 I will offer to thee the sácrifice of | thanks- | -giving : and will call upón the | Name | of the | Lord.

16 I will pay my vows unto the Lord * in the síght of | all his | people : in the courts of the Lord's house * even in the midst of thee, O Jerúsalem. | Praise | — the | Lord.

Psalm cxvii.—*Laudate Dominum.*

f O PRAISE the Lórd | all ye | heathen : práise | — him | all ye | nations.

2 For his merciful kindness is ever more and móre | towards | us : and the truth of the Lord endureth for éver. | Praise | — the | Lord.

Psalm cxviii.—*Confitemini Domino.*

f O GIVE thanks unto the Lórd, for | he is | gracious : becáuse his | mercy . en- | -dureth . for | ever.

2 Let Israel now conféss that | he is | gracious : and thát his | mercy . en- | -dureth . for | ever.

3 Let the house of Aáron | now con- | -fess : thát his | mercy . en- | -dureth . for | ever.

4 Yea, let them now that féar the | Lord con- | -fess : thát his | mercy . en- | -dureth . for | ever.

mf 5 I called upón the | Lord in | trouble : and the Lórd | heard | me at | large.

6 The Lórd is | on my | side : I will not féar what | man . doeth | unto | me.

7 The Lord taketh my párt with | them that | help me : therefore shall I sée my de- | -sire up- | -on mine | enemies.

8 It is better to trúst | in the | Lord : than to pút any | confi- | -dence in | man.

9 It is better to trúst | in the | Lord : than to pút any | confi- | -dence in | princes.

10 All nations cómpassed me | round a- | -bout : but in the Náme of the | Lord will | I de- | -stroy them.

11 They kept me in on every side * they kept me in, I sáy, on | every | side : but in the Náme of the | Lord will | I de- | -stroy them.

12 They came about me like bees * and are extinct even as the fíre a- | -mong the | thorns : for in the Náme of the | Lord I | will de- | -stroy them.

13 Thou hast thrust sore at mé, that | I might | fall : bút the | Lord | was my | help.

14 The Lord is my stréngth | and my | song : and ís be- | come | my sal- | -vation.

15 The voice of joy and health is in the dwéllings | of the | righteous : the right hand of the Lórd bringeth | mighty | things to | pass.

16 The right hand of the Lórd | hath . the pre- | -eminence :
the right hand of the Lórd bringeth | mighty | things
to | pass.

17 I shall not | die but | live : and decláre the | works | of
the | Lord.

18 The Lord hath chástened and cor- | -rected | me : but he
, hath not gíven me | over | unto | death.

19 Ópen me the | gates of | righteousness : that I may go
into them * ánd give | thanks | unto . the | Lord.

20 This is the gáte | of the | Lord : the ríghteous shall |
enter | into | it.

21 I will thánk thee, for | thou hast | heard me : and árt
be- | -come | my sal- | -vation.

22 The same stóne which the | builders . re- | -fused : is
becóme the | head-stone | in the | corner.

23 Thís is the | Lord's | doing : ánd it is | marvellous | in
our | eyes.

24 This is the dáy which the | Lord hath | made : we will
rejóice | and be | glad in | it.

25 Hélp me | now O | Lord : O Lórd | send us | now pros- |
perity.

26 Blessed be he that cometh in the Náme | of the | Lord :
we have wished you good luck * ye that áre of the |
house | of the | Lord.

27 God is the Lórd, who hath | shewed . us | light : bind the
sacrifice with cords * yea, even únto the | horns | of
the | altar.

28 Thou art my Gód, and | I will | thank thee : thóu art
my | God and | I will | praise thee.

2nd 29 O give thanks unto the Lórd, for | he is | gracious : ánd
part.   his | mercy . en- | -dureth . for | ever.

Day 24.   EVENING PRAYER.

Psalm cxix.—*Beati immaculati.*

F.*mf*   BLESSED are those that are undefíled | in the | way :
and wálk in the | law | of the | Lord.

F.   2 Blessed are théy that | keep his | testimonies : and séek
him | with their | whole | heart.

3 For théy who | do no | wickedness : wálk | — in | his | ways.

4 Thóu | hast | charged : that we shall díligently | keep |
thy com- | -mandments.

5 O that my ways were máde | so di- | -rect : thát | I might |
keep thy | statutes !

6 So shall I nót | be con- | -founded : while I have respéct
unto | all | thy com- | -mandments.

7 I will thank thee wíth an un- | -feigned | heart : when I
shall have léarned the | judgements | of thy | right-
, eousness.

8 Í will | keep thy | ceremonies : Ó for- | -sake me | not |
utterly.

In quo corriget ?

WHEREWITHAL shall a yoúng man | cleanse his | way :
even by rúling him- | -self | after . thy | word.

10 With my whole héart | have I | sought thee : O let me not
go wróng | out of | thy com- | -mandments.

11 Thy words have I híd with- | -in my | heart : thát I |
should not | sin a- | -gainst thee.

12 Bléssed art | thou O | Lord : O′ | teach | me thy | statutes.

13 With my líps have | I been | telling : of áll the | judge-
ments | of thy | mouth.

14 I have had as great delight in the wáy | of thy | testi-
monies : ás in | all | manner . of | riches.

15 I will tálk of | thy com- | -mandments : and háve re- |
spect | unto . thy | ways.

16 My delight shall bé | in thy | statutes : and Í will | not
for- | -get thy | word.

Retribue servo tuo.

O DO wéll | unto . thy | servant : that Í may | live and |
, keep thy | word.

18 Ópen | thou mine | eyes : that I may sée the wondrous |
things | of thy | law.

19 I am a stránger up- | -on | earth : O híde not | thy
com- | -mandments | from me.

20 My soul breaketh out for the véry | fervent . de- | sire :
that it háth | alway | unto . thy | judgements.

21 Thóu hast re- | -buked . the | proud : and cursed are théy
that do | err from | thy com- | -mandments.

22 O turn from me sháme | and re- | -buke : fór | I have |
kept thy | testimonies.

23 Princes also did sít and | speak a- | -gainst me : but thy
sérvant is | occupied | in thy | statutes.

24 For thy téstimonies are | my de- | -light : ánd | — |
my | counsellors.

Adhæsit pavimento.

MY soul cléaveth | to the | dust : O quicken thou mé, ac- | -cording | to thy | word.

26 I have acknowledged my wáys, and thou | heardest | me : O' | teach | me thy | statutes.

27 Make me to understand the wáy of | thy com- | -mandments : and so shall I tálk | of thy | wondrous | works.

28 My soul melteth awáy for | very | heaviness : comfort thou mé ac- | -cording | unto . thy | word.

29 Take from mé the | way of | lying : and cause thou me to máke | much | of thy | law.

30 I have chósen the | way of | truth : and thy júdgements | have I | laid be- | -fore me.

31 I have stúck | unto . thy | testimonies : Ó | Lord con- | found me | not.

32 I will run the wáy of | thy com- | -mandments : whén thou hast | set my | heart at | liberty.

———

Day 25.　　　　MORNING PRAYER.

Legem pone.

mf TEACH me, O Lord, the wáy | of thy | statutes : and I' shall | keep it | unto . the | end.

34 Give me understanding, and I' shall | keep thy | law : yea, I shall kéep it | with my | whole | heart.

35 Make me to go in the páth of | thy com- | -mandments : fór there- | -in is | my de- | -sire.

36 Incline my heárt | unto . thy | testimonies : ánd | not to | covetous- | -ness.

37 O turn away mine eyes * lést they be- | -hold | vanity : and quícken thou | me in | thy | way.

38 O stablish thy wórd | in thy | servant : thát | I may | fear | thee.

39 Take away the rebúke that | I am . a- | -fraid of : fór thy | judgements | are | good.

40 Behold, my delíght is in | thy com- | -mandments : O' | quicken . me | in thy | righteousness.

Et veniat super me.

L ET thy loving mercy come also únto | me O | Lord : even thy salvátion, ac- | -cording | unto . thy | word.

42 So shall I make answer únto | my blas- | -phemers : fór my | trust is | in thy | word.

43 O take not the word of thy truth útterly | out of . my | mouth : fór my | hope is | in thy | judgements.

44 So shall I álway | keep thy | law : yéa, for | ever | and | ever.

45 And I' will | walk at | liberty : fór I | seek | thy com- | mandments.

46 I will speak of thy testimonies also * éven be- | -fore | kings : ánd | will not | be a- | -shamed.

47 And my delight shall bé in | thy com- | -mandments : whích | I | have | loved.

48 My hands also will I lift up unto thy commándments, which | I have | loved : and my stúdy shall | be in | thy | statutes.

Memor esto servi tui.

O THINK upon thy servant, ás con- | -cerning . thy | word : wherein thou hast cáused | me to | put my | trust.

50 The same is my cómfort | in my | trouble : fór thy | word hath | quickened | me.

51 The proud have had me excéedingly | in de- | -rision : yet háve I not | shrinked | from thy | law.

52 For I remembered thine everlásting | judgements . O | Lord : ánd | — re- | -ceived | comfort.

53 I am hórri- | -bly a- | -fraid : for the ungódly | that for- | sake thy | law.

54 Thy státutes have | been my | songs : ín the | house | of my | pilgrimage.

55 I have thought upon thy Name, O Lórd, in the | night- | season : ánd have | kept | thy | law.

56 Thís | I | had : becáuse I | kept | thy com- | -mandments.

Portio mea, Domine.

T HÓU art my | portion O | Lord : I have prómised to | keep | thy | law.

58 I made my humble petition in thy presence * wíth my | whole | heart : O be merciful unto mé, ac- | -cording | to thy | word.

59 I called mine own wáys | to re- | -membrance : and
túrned my | feet | unto . thy | testimonies.

60 I made haste, and prolónged | not the | time : tó | keep |
thy com- | -mandments.

61 The congregations of the ungódly have | robbed | me :
but I' have | not for- | -gotten . thy | law.

62 At midnight I will rise to give thánks | unto | thee :
becáuse | of thy | righteous | judgements.

63 I am a companion of áll | them that | fear thee : ánd |
keep | thy com- | -mandments.

64 The earth, O Lord, is fúll | of thy | mercy : O' | teach |
me thy | statutes.

Bonitatem fecísti.

O LORD, thou hast dealt gráciously | with thy | servant :
ác- | -cording | unto . thy | word.

66 O learn me trúe under- | -standing . and | knowledge :
for I' have be- | -lieved | thy com- | -mandments.

67 Before I was tróubled, I | went | wrong : but nów | have
I | kept thy | word.

68 Thóu art | good and | gracious : O' | teach | me thy |
statutes.

69 The proud have imágined a | lie a- | -gainst me : but I
will keep thy commándments | with my | whole | heart.

70 Their heárt is as | fat as | brawn : but my delíght hath |
been in | thy | law.

71 It is good for me that I' have | been in | trouble : thát |
I may | learn thy | statutes.

72 The law of thy mouth is déarer | unto | me : thán |
thousands . of | gold and | silver.

EVENING PRAYER.

Manus tuæ fecerunt me.

F. mf THY hands have máde me and | fashioned | me : O give
me understanding * that I' may | learn | thy com- |
mandments.

F. 74 They that fear thee will be glád | when they | see me :
because I have pút my | trust | in thy | word.

75 I know, O Lórd, that thy | judgements . are | right : and
that thou of very fáithfulness hast | caused . me | to
be | troubled.

76 O let thy merciful kíndness | be my | comfort : accórding
to thy | word | unto . thy | servant.

77 O let thy loving mercies come unto mé, that | I may |
live : fór thy | law is | my de- | -light.

78 Let the proud be confounded * for they go wickedly
abóut | to de- | -stroy me : but I will be óccu- | -pied
in | thy com- | -mandments.

79 Let such as fear thee * ánd have | known thy | testi-
monies : bé | turned | unto | me.

80 O let my heart be sóund | in thy | statutes : thát I | be |
not a- | -shamed.

Defecit anima mea.

MY soul hath lónged for | thy sal- | -vation : and I have
a good hópe be- | -cause of | thy | word.

82 Mine eyes long sóre | for thy | word : saying, O whén |
wilt thou | comfort | me?

83 For I am become like a bóttle | in the | smoke : yét do I |
not for- | -get thy | statutes.

84 How many are the dáys | of thy | servant : when wilt
thou be avénged of | them that | persecute | me?

85 The proud have dígged | pits for | me : whích | are not |
after . thy | law.

86 Áll thy com- | -mandments . are | true : they persecute
me fálsely | O be | thou my | help.

87 They had almost made an end of mé up- | -on | earth :
but I' for- | -sook not | thy com- | -mandments.

88 O quicken me áfter thy | loving- | -kindness : and so
shall I kéep the | testimonies | of thy | mouth.

In æternum, Domine.

O LÓRD | thy | word : én- | -dureth . for | ever in |
heaven.

90 Thy truth also remaineth from one generátion | to an- |
other : thou hast laid the foundátion of the | earth
and | it a- | -bideth.

91 They continue this day accórding | to thine | ordinance :
fór | all things | serve | thee.

92 If my delight had nót been | in thy | law : Í should
have | perished | in my | trouble.

93 I will never forgét | thy com- | -mandments : for with
thém | thou hast | quickened | me.

94 Í am | thine O | save me : for Í have | sought | thy
     com- | -mandments.

95 The ungodly laid wáit for me | to de- | -stroy me : but Í
     will con- | -sider | thy | testimonies.

96 I see that áll things | come . to an | end : but thy
     commándment | is ex- | -ceeding | broad.

Quomodo dilexi!

L ORD, what lóve have I | unto . thy | law : all the day
     lóng | is my | study | in it.

98 Thou through thy commandments * hast made me
     wíser | than mine | enemies : fór | they are | ever |
     with me.

99 I have more understánding | than my | teachers : fór
     thy | testimonies | are my | study.

100 I am wíser | than the | aged : becáuse I | keep | thy
     com- | -mandments.

101 I have refrained my feet from évery | evil | way : thát | I
     may | keep thy | word.

102 I have not shrúnk | from thy | judgements : fór | thou |
     teachest | me.

103 O how sweet are thy wórds | unto . my | throat : yea,
     swéeter than | honey | unto . my | mouth.

104 Through thy commandments I gét | under- | -standing :
     thérefore I | hate all | evil | ways.

Day 26.   MORNING PRAYER.

Lucerna pedibus meis.

mf T HY word is a lántern | unto . my | feet : ánd a | light |
     unto . my | paths.

106 I have swórn, and am | stedfastly | purposed : tó | keep
     thy | righteous | judgements.

107 I am tróubled a- | -bove | measure : quicken me, O Lórd,
     ac- | -cording | to thy | word.

108 Let the free-will-offerings of my mouth pléase | thee O |
     Lord : ánd | teach | me thy | judgements.

109 My soul is álway | in my | hand : yét do I | not for- | -get
     thy | law.

110 The ungodly have láid a | snare for | me : but yet I
swérved | not from | thy com- | -mandments.
111 Thy testimonies have I claimed as mine hérit- | -age for |
ever : and why? they are the véry | joy | of my | heart.
112 I have applied my heart to fulfíl thy | statutes | alway :
éven | un- | -to the | end.

Iniquos odio habui.

I HATE them that imágine | evil | things : bút thy | law | do
I | love.
114 Thou art mý de- | -fence and | shield : ánd my | trust is |
in thy | word.
115 Awáy from | me ye | wicked : I will kéep the com- |
mandments | of my | God.
116 O stablish me according to thy wórd, that | I may | live :
and let me not be dísap- | -pointed | of my | hope.
117 Hold thou me úp, and I | shall be | safe : yea, my delíght
shall be | ever | in thy | statutes.
118 Thou hast trodden down all them that depárt | from thy |
statutes : for théy im- | -agine | but de- | -ceit.
119 Thou puttest away all the ungódly of the | earth like |
dross : thérefore I | love | thy | testimonies.
120 My flesh trémbleth for | fear of | thee : and Í am a- |
fraid of | thy | judgements.

Feci judicium.

I DEAL with the thíng that is | lawful . and | right : O give
me not óver | unto | mine op- | -pressors.
122 Make thou thy servant to delíght in | that which . is |
good : that the próud | do me | no | wrong.
123 Mine eyes are wasted away with lóoking | for thy | health :
and fór the | word | of thy | righteousness.
124 O deal with thy servant according únto thy | loving |
mercy : ánd | teach | me thy | statutes.
125 I am thy servant, O gránt me | under- | -standing : thát |
I may | know thy | testimonies.
126 It is time for thee, Lórd, to lay | to thine | hand : fór
they | have de- | -stroyed . thy | law.
127 For I lóve | thy com- | -mandments : abóve | gold and |
precious | stone.
128 Therefore hold I stráight all | thy com- | -mandments :
and all false wáys I | utter- | -ly ab- | -hor.

Mirabilia.

THY téstimonies | are | wonderful : thérefore | doth my | soul | keep them.

130 When thy wórd | goeth | forth : it giveth light and únder- | -standing | unto . the | simple.

131 I opened my móuth, and drew | in my | breath : for my delíght | was in | thy com- | -mandments.

132 O look thou upon me * and be mérciful | unto | me : as thou usest to dó unto | those that | love thy | Name.

133 Order my stéps | in thy | word : and so shall no wickedness háve do- | -minion | over | me.

134 O deliver me from the wróngful | dealings . of | men : and só shall I | keep | thy com- | -mandments.

135 Shew the light of thy cóuntenance up- | -on thy | servant : ánd | teach | me thy | statutes.

136 Mine éyes gush | out with | water : becáuse men | keep | not thy | law.

Justus es, Domine.

RÍGHTEOUS art | thou O | Lord : ánd | true | is thy | judgement.

138 The testimonies that thóu | hast com- | manded : áre ex- | -ceeding | righteous . and | true.

139 My zeal hath éven con- | -sumed | me : because mine énemies | have for- | -gotten . thy | words.

140 Thy word is tríed | to the | uttermost : ánd thy | servant | loveth | it.

141 I am small, and of nó | repu- | -tation : yet do I nót for- | get | thy com- | -mandments.

142 Thy righteousness is an éver- | -lasting | righteousness : ánd thy | law | is the | truth.

143 Trouble and heaviness have táken | hold up- | -on me : yet is mý de- | -light in | thy com- | -mandments.

144 The righteousness of thy téstimonies is | ever- | -lasting : O gránt me under- | -standing . and | I shall | live.

Day 26. EVENING PRAYER.

Clamavi in toto corde meo.

mf I CÁLL with my | whole | heart : hear me, O Lórd | I will | keep thy | statutes.

146 Yea, even unto thée | do I | call : hélp me, and | I shall | keep thy | testimonies.

147 Early in the morning do I crý | unto | thee : for ín thy |
  word | is my | trust.
148 Mine eyes prevént the | night- | -watches : that I míght
  be | occupied | in thy | words.
149 Hear my voice, O Lord * according únto thy | loving- |
  kindness : quícken me, ac- | -cording . as | thou art |
  wont.
150 They draw nigh that of málice | persecutᵒ | me : ánd
  are | far | from thy | law.
151 Be thou nígh at | hand O | Lord : for áll | thy com- |
  mandments . are | true.
152 As concerning thy testimonies * Í have | known long |
  since : that thóu hast | grounded | them for | ever.

Vide humilitatem.

O CONSIDER mine adversity * ánd de- | -liver | me : for
  I' do | not for- | -get thy | law.
154 Avenge thou my cáuse, and de- | -liver | me : quícken me,
  ac- | -cording | to thy | word.
155 Health is fár from | the un- | -godly : for théy re- |
  gard | not thy | statutes.
156 Gréat is thy | mercy . O | Lord : quícken | me as | thou
  art | wont.
157 Many there are that troúble me, and | persecute | me :
  yet do I' not | swerve | from thy | testimonies.
158 It grieveth me whén I | see the . trans- | -gressors :
  becáuse they | keep | not thy | law.
159 Consider, O Lord, how I lóve | thy com- | -mandments :
  O quicken me, accórding | to thy | loving- | -kindness.
160 Thy word is trúe from | ever- | -lasting : all the judge-
  ments of thy righteousness * én- | -dure for | ever- | -more.

Principes persecuti sunt.

PRINCES have persecuted mé with- | -out a | cause : but
  my heart stándeth in | awe | of thy | word.
162 I am as glád | of thy | word : as óne that | findeth |
  great | spoils.
163 As for lies, I háte | and ab- | -hor them : bút thy | law |
  do I | love.
164 Seven times a dáy do I | praise | thee : becáuse | of thy |
  righteous | judgements.
165 Gréat is the peace that théy have who | love thy | law :
  ánd they are | not of- | -fended | at it.

166 Lord, I have lóoked for thy | saving | health : and dóne |
     after | thy com- | -mandments.
167 My sóul hath | kept thy | testimonies : ánd | loved | them
     ex- | -ceedingly.
168 I have képt thy com- | -mandments . and | testimonies :
     for áll my | ways | are be- | -fore thee.

Appropinquet deprecatio.

L ET my complaint cóme before | thee O | Lord : give me
     understánding, ac- | -cording | to thy | word.
170 Let my supplicátion | come be- | -fore thee : delíver me,
     ac- | -cording | to thy | word.
171 My lips shall spéak | of thy | praise : when thóu hast |
     taught | me thy | statutes.
172 Yea, my tongue shall síng | of thy | word : for áll | thy
     com- | -mandments . are | righteous.
173 Lét thine | hand | help me : for I' have | chosen | thy
     com- | -mandments.
174 I have longed for thy sáving | health O | Lord : and ín
     thy | law is | my de- | -light.
175 O let my soul líve, and | it shall | praise thee : ánd thy |
     judgements | shall | help me.
176 I have gone astray like a shéep | that is | lost : O seek
     thy servant * for I do nót for- | -get | thy com- |
     mandments.

Day 27.   MORNING PRAYER.

Psalm cxx.—*Ad Dominum.*

mp   W HEN I was in trouble I cálled up- | -on the | Lord :
     ánd | — he | heard | me.
2 Deliver my soul, O Lórd, from | lying | lips : ánd | from .
     a de- | -ceitful | tongue.
3 What reward shall be given or done unto thée, thou |
     false | tongue : even mighty and sharp árrows, with |
     hot | burning | coals.
4 Woe is me, that I am constráined to | dwell with |
     Mesech : and to have my habitátion a- | -mong the |
     tents of | Kedar.
5 My soul hath lóng | dwelt a- . -mong | them : thát are |
     enemies | unto | peace.
6 I labour for peace * but when I spéak unto | them
     there- | -of : théy | make them | ready . to | battle.

FF

PSALM cxxi.—*Levavi oculos.*

mf I WILL lift up mine éyes | unto . the | hills : frôm | whence | cometh . my | help.

2 My help cometh éven | from the | Lord : whô hath | made | heaven and | earth.

3 He will not suffer thy fôot | to be | moved : and hé that | keepeth . thee | will not | sleep.

4 Behold, hé that | keepeth | Israel : shâll | neither | slumber . nor | sleep.

5 The Lord himsélf | is thy | keeper : the Lord is thy deféncé up- | -on thy | right | hand ;

6 So that the sun shall not bûrn | thee by | day : neîther the | moon | by | night.

7 The Lord shall presérve thee from | all | evil : yea, it is even hé | that shall | keep thy | soul.

8 The Lord shall preserve thy going out * ând thy | coming | in : from thîs time | forth for | ever- | -more.

PSALM cxxii.—*Lætatus sum.*

mf I WAS glad when they sâid | unto | me : We will gô into the | house | of the | Lord.

2 Our feet shall stând | in thy | gates : Ô | — Je- | rusa- | -lem.

3 Jerusalem is buîlt | as a | city : that îs at | unity | in it- | self.

4 For thither the tribes go up * even the trîbes | of the | Lord : to testify unto Israel * to give thânks unto the | Name | of the | Lord.

5 For thére is the | seat of | judgement : even the séat | of the | house of | David.

6 O pray for the péace | of Je- | -rusalem : théy shall | prosper . that | love | thee.

7 Péace be with- | -in thy | walls : and plénteous- | -ness with- | -in thy | palaces.

8 For my bréthren and com- | -panions' | sakes : Í will | wish | thee pros- | -perity.

2nd part. 9 Yea, because of the hóuse of the | Lord our | God : Í will | seek to | do thee | good.

PSALM cxxiii.—*Ad te levavi oculos meos.*

mp UNTO thée lift I | up mine | eyes : O thôu that | dwellest | in the | heavens.

2 Behold, even as the eyes of servants look unto the hand of their masters * and as the eyes of a maiden unto the hánd | of her | mistress : even so our eyes wait upon the Lord our God * untíl | he have | mercy . up- | -on us.

3 Have mercy upon us, O Lórd, have | mercy . up- | -on us : for wé are | utter- | -ly de- | -spised.

4 Our soul is filled with the scornful repróof | of the | wealthy : and wíth the de- | -spitefulness | of the | proud.

Psalm cxxiv.—*Nisi quia Dominus.*

mp IF the Lord himself had not been on our side * nów may | Israel | say : If the Lord himself had not been on our síde, when | men rose | up a- | -gainst us ;

2 They had swállowed | us up | quick : when they were so wráthful- | -ly dis- | -pleased | at us.

3 Yea, the wáters had | drowned | us : and the stréam had | gone | over . our | soul.

4 The déep waters | of the | proud : had góne | even | over . our | soul.

mf 5 But práised | be the | Lord : who hath not given us over fór a | prey | unto . their | teeth.

6 Our soul is escaped * even as a bird out of the snáre | of the | fowler : the snare is bróken | and we | are de- | -livered.

2nd part. 7 Our help standeth in the Náme | of the | Lord : whó hath | made | heaven and | earth.

Psalm cxxv.—*Qui confidunt.*

mf THEY that put their trust in the Lord shall be éven as the | mount | Sion : which may not be remóved, but | standeth | fast for | ever.

2 The hills stánd a- | -bout Je- | -rusalem : even so standeth the Lord round about his people * from thís time | forth for | ever- | -more.

3 For the rod of the ungodly cometh not into the lót | of the | righteous : lest the righteous pút their | hand | unto | wickedness.

4 Dó | well O | Lord : unto thóse that are | good and | true of | heart.

2nd part. 5 As for such as turn báck unto their | own | wickedness : the Lord shall lead them forth with the evil doers * but péace shall | be up- | -on | Israel.

Day 27. EVENING PRAYER.

Psalm cxxvi.—*In convertendo.*

F. mf WHEN the Lord turned again the captívi- | -ty of | Sion :
then were we líke | unto | them that | dream.

F. 2 Then was our móuth | filled . with | laughter : ánd our |
tongue | with | joy.

3 Then sáid they a- | -mong the | heathen : The Lórd
hath | done great | things for | them.

4 Yea, the Lord hath done great thíngs for | us al- |
ready : whére- | -of | we re- | -joice.

5 Turn our captívity | O | Lord : ás the | rivers | in the |
south.

6 Théy that | sow in | tears : sháll | reap | in | joy.

2nd part. 7 He that now goeth on his way weeping * and béareth |
forth good | seed : shall doubtless come again with jóy,
and | bring his | sheaves | with him.

Psalm cxxvii.—*Nisi Dominus.*

mf EXCEPT the Lórd | build the | house : their lábour | is
but | lost that | build it.

2 Except the Lórd | keep the | city : the wátchman |
waketh | but in | vain.

3 It is but lost labour that ye haste to rise up early * and
so late take rest, and éat the | bread of | carefulness :
for so he gíveth | his be- | -loved | sleep.

4 Lo, children and the frúit | of the | womb : are an
heritage and gíft that | cometh | of the | Lord.

5 Like as the arrows in the hánd | of the | giant : even só |
are the | young | children.

6 Happy is the man that hath his quíver | full of | them :
they shall not be ashamed when they spéak with
their | enemies | in the | gate.

Psalm cxxviii.—*Beati omnes.*

mf BLESSED are all théy that | fear the | Lord : ánd |
walk | in his | ways.

2 For thou shalt eat the lábours | of thine | hands : O well
is thée, and | happy | shalt thou | be.

3 Thy wife shall bé as the | fruitful | vine : upón the |
walls | of thine | house.

4 Thy children líke the | olive- | -branches : róund | —
a- | -bout thy | table.

5 Lo, thús shall the | man be | blessed : thát | fear- | -eth
the | Lord.

6 The Lord from out of Síon shall | so | bless thee : that thou
shalt see Jerusalem in prospérity | all thy | life | long.

2nd
part.
7 Yea, that thou shalt sée thy | children's | children : ánd |
peace up- | -on | Israel.

Psalm cxxix.—*Sæpe expugnaverunt.*

mp
MANY a time have they fought against me fróm my |
youth | up : máy | Israel | now | say.

2 Yea, many a time have they vexed me fróm my | youth |
up : bút they have | not pre- | -vailed . a- | -gainst me.

3 The plowers plówed up- | -on my | back : ánd | made |
long | furrows.

4 Bút the | righteous | Lord : hath hewn the snáres of the
un- | -godly | in | pieces.

5 Let them be confóunded and | turned | backward : as
many as háve | evil | will at | Sion.

6 Let them be even as the grass grówing up- | -on the |
house-tops : which withereth afóre | it be | plucked | up.

7 Whereof the mower fílleth | not his | hand : neither he
that bíndeth | up the | sheaves his | bosom.

8 So that they who go by * say not so much as, The Lórd |
prosper | you : we wish you good lúck in the | Name | of
the | Lord.

Psalm cxxx.—*De profundis.*

p
OUT of the deep have I called únto | thee O | Lord :
Lórd | hear | my | voice.

2 O let thine éars con- | -sider | well : thé | voice of | my
com- | -plaint.

3 If thou, Lord, wilt be extreme to márk what is | done a- |
miss : O Lórd | who | may a- | -bide it ?

4 Fór there is | mercy . with | thee : thérefore | shalt | thou
be | feared.

5 I look for the Lord; my sóul doth | wait for | him : ín
his | word | is my | trust.

6 My soul fléeth | unto . the | Lord : before the morning
watch, I sáy, be- | -fore the | morning | watch.

7 O Israel, trust in the Lord * for with the Lórd | there is |
mercy : ánd with | him is | plenteous . re- | -demption.

8 And hé shall re- | -deem | Israel : fróm | all | his | sins.

PSALM CXXXI.—*Domine, non est.*

p LÓRD, I am | not high- | -minded : Í have | no | proud |
     looks.

2 I do not exercise mysélf in | great | matters : whích | are
     too | high for | me.

3 But I refrain my soul, and keep it low * like as a child
     that is wéaned | from his | mother : yea, my soul is
     éven | as a | weaned | child.

4 O Israel, trúst | in the | Lord : from thís time | forth for |
     ever- | -more.

Day 28.   MORNING PRAYER.

PSALM CXXXII.—*Memento, Domine.*

mf LÓRD, re- | -member | David : ánd | all | his |
     trouble ;

2 How he swáre | unto . the | Lord : and vowed a vow únto
     the Al- | -mighty | God of | Jacob ;

3 I will not come within the tábernacle | of mine | house :
     nór | climb up | into . my | bed ;

4 I will not suffer mine eyes to sléep, nor mine | eyelids .
     to | slumber : neither the temples of my héad to |
     take | any | rest ;

5 Until I find out a place for the témple | of the | Lord : an
     habitation fór the | mighty | God of | Jacob.

6 Lo, we héard of the | same at | Ephrata : ánd | found it |
     in the | wood.

7 We will gó into his | taber- | -nacle : and fall lów on
     our | knees be- | -fore his | footstool.

8 Arise, O Lórd | into . thy | resting-place : thóu, and the |
     ark | of thy | strength.

9 Let thy príests be | clothed . with | righteousness : and
     lét thy | saints | sing with | joyfulness.

10 For thy sérvant | David's | sake : turn not awáy the |
     presence . of | thine A- | -nointed.

11 The Lord hath made a faithful óath | unto | David : ánd
     he | shall not | shrink | from it.

12 Of the frúit | of thy | body : sháll I | set up- | -on thy |
     seat.

13 If thy children will keep my covenant * and my testi-
monies that | I shall | learn them : their children also
shall sit upon thy | seat for | ever- | -more.

14 For the Lord hath chosen Sion to be an habitátion | for
him- | -self : he hath | longed | for | her.

15 This shall be my | rest for | ever : here will I dwell * for
I | have . a de- | -light there- | -in.

16 I will bless her | victuals . with | increase : and will
sátis- | -fy her | poor with | bread.

17 I will deck her | priests with | health : and her saints |
shall re- | -joice and | sing.

18 There shall I make the horn of | David . to | flourish :
I have ordáined a | lantern . for | mine A- | -nointed.

2nd part. 19 As for his enemies * I shall clothe | them with | shame |
but upon himself | shall his | crown | flourish.

Psalm cxxxiii.—*Ecce, quam bonum!*

mf BEHOLD, how good and joyful a | thing it | is : bréthren,
to | dwell to- | -gether . in | unity !

2 It is like the precious ointment upon the head * that ran
down | unto . the | beard : even unto Aaron's beard *
and went down to the | skirts | of his | clothing.

3 Like as the | dew of | Hermon : which fell up- | -on the |
hill of | Sion.

4 For there the Lord | promised . his | blessing : and |
life for | ever- | -more.

Psalm cxxxiv.—*Ecce nunc.*

mf BEHOLD, now | praise the | Lord : all ye | servants | of
the | Lord ;

2 Ye that by night stand in the house | of the | Lord : even
in the courts of the | house of | our | God.

3 Lift up your hands | in the | sanctuary : and | praise |
— the | Lord.

4 The Lord that made | heaven . and | earth : give thee |
blessing | out of | Sion.

Psalm cxxxv.—*Laudate Nomen.*

f O PRAISE the Lord * laud ye the Náme | of the | Lord :
praise it, O' ye | servants | of the | Lord ;

2 Ye that stand in the house | of the | Lord : in the courts
of the | house of | our | God.

3 O praise the Lórd, for the | Lord is | gracious : O sing praises únto his | Name for | it is | lovely.

4 For why? the Lord hath chosen Jácob | unto . him- | self : and Ísrael | for his | own pos- | -session.

5 For I knów that the | Lord is | great : and that our Lórd | is a- | -bove all | gods.

6 Whatsoever the Lord pleased * that did he in héaven | and in | earth : and in the séa | and in | all deep | places.

7 He bringeth forth the clouds from the énds | of the | world : and sendeth forth lightnings with the rain * brínging the | winds | out of . his | treasures.

8 He smóte the | first-born . of | Egypt : bóth of | man | and | beast.

9 He hath sent tokens and wonders into the midst of thee, O' thou | land of | Egypt : upón | Pharaoh . and | all his | servants.

10 He smóte | divers | nations : ánd | slew | mighty | kings :

11 Sehon, king of the Amorites * and Óg, the | king of | Basan : ánd | all the | kingdoms . of | Canaan.

12 And gave their lánd to | be an | heritage : even an heritage únto | Isra- | -el his | people.

13 Thy Name, O Lórd, en- | -dureth . for | ever : so doth thy memorial, O Lord * from óne gener- | -ation | to an- | -other.

14 For the Lórd will a- | -venge his | people : ánd be | gracious | unto . his | servants.

15 As for the images of the heathen * théy are but | silver . and | gold : thé | work of | men's | hands.

16 Théy have | mouths and | speak not : éyes | have they | but they | see not.

17 They have éars, and | yet they | hear not : neither is there ány | breath | in their | mouths.

18 They that make them are líke | unto | them : and so are all théy that | put their | trust in | them.

19 Praise the Lórd, ye | house of | Israel : práise the | Lord ye | house of | Aaron.

20 Praise the Lórd, ye | house of | Levi : ye that féar the | Lord | praise the | Lord.

2nd part. 21 Praised be the Lórd | out of | Sion : whó | dwelleth | at Je- | -rusalem.

Day 28.   EVENING PRAYER.

Psalm cxxxvi.—*Confitemini.*

f   O GIVE thanks unto the Lórd, for | he is | gracious : ánd his | mercy . en- | -dureth . for | ever.*

2 O give thanks unto the Gód of | all | gods : fór his | mercy . en- | -dureth . for | ever.

3 O thank the Lórd of | all | lords : fór his | mercy . en- | dureth . for | ever.

4 Who ónly | doeth . great | wonders : fór his | mercy . en- dureth . for | ever.

5 Who by his excellent wísdom | made the | heavens : fór his | mercy . en- | -dureth . for | ever.

6 Who laid out the éarth a- | -bove the | waters : fór his | mercy . en- | -dureth . for | ever.

7 Who hath máde | great | lights : fór his | mercy . en- | dureth . for | ever.

8 The sún to | rule the | day : fór his | mercy . en- | -dureth . for | ever.

9 The moon and the stárs to | govern . the | night : fór his | mercy . en- | -dureth . for | ever.

10 Who smote E'gypt | with their | first-born : fór his | mercy . en- | -dureth . for | ever.

11 And brought out I'srael | from a- | -mong them : fór his | mercy . en- | -dureth . for | ever.

12 With a mighty hánd, and | stretched-out | arm : fór his | mercy . en- | -dureth . for | ever.

13 Who divided the Red Séa in | two | parts : fór his | mercy . en- | -dureth . for | ever ;

14 And made Israel to gó through the | midst of | it : fór his | mercy . en- | -dureth . for | ever.

15 But as for Pharaoh and his host * he overthréw them in the | Red | Sea : fór his | mercy . en- | -dureth . for | ever.

16 Who led his péople | through the | wilderness : fór his | mercy . en- | -dureth . for | ever.

17 Who smóte | great | kings : fór his | mercy . en- | dureth . for | ever.

18 Yea, and sléw | mighty | kings : fór his | mercy . en- | dureth . for | ever ;

* The second part of each verse to be sung *full.*

19 Sehon, kíng | of the | Amorites : fór his | mercy . en- |
 dureth . for | ever ;

20 And Óg, the | king of | Basan : fór his | mercy . en- |
 dureth . for | ever ;

21 And gave away their lánd | for an | heritage : fór his |
 mercy . en- | -dureth . for | ever.

22 Even for an heritage unto I'sra- | -el his | servant : fór
 his | mercy . en- | -dureth . for | ever.

23 Who remembered us | whén we | were in | trouble ; fór
 his | mercy . en- | -dureth . for | ever.

24 And hath delívered us | from our | enemies : fór his |
 mercy . en- | -dureth . for | ever.

25 Who giveth fóod to | all | flesh : fór his | mercy . en- |
 dureth . for | ever.

26 O give thánks unto the | God of | heaven : fór his |
 mercy . en- | -dureth . for | ever.

2nd part. 27 O give thánks unto the | Lord of | lords : fór his | mercy .
 en- | -dureth . for | ever.

Psalm cxxxvii.—*Super flumina.*

p BY the waters of Babylon we sát | down and | wept :
 whén we re- | -membered | thee O | Sion.

2 As for our hárps, we | hanged . them | up : upón the |
 trees that | are there- | -in.

3 For they that led us away captive * required of us then a
 song and mélody | in our | heaviness : Síng us | one .
 of the | songs of | Sion.

4 How shall we síng the | Lord's | song : ín | — a |
 strange | land ?

5 If I forget thée | O Je- | -rusalem : lét my right | hand
 for- | -get her | cunning.

6 If I do not remember thee * let my tongue cleave to the
 róof | of my | mouth : yea, if I prefér not Je- |
 rusalem | in my | mirth.

7 Remember the children of Edom, O Lord * in the dáy |
 of Je- | -rusalem : how they said, Down with it, dówn
 with it | even | to the | ground.

8 O daughter of Bábylon | wasted . with | misery : yea,
 happy shall he be that rewardeth thée, as | thou hast |
 served | us.

2nd part. 9 Blessed shall he bé that | taketh . thy | children : and
 thróweth | them a- | -gainst the | stones.

Psalm cxxxviii.—*Confitebor tibi.*

mf I WILL give thanks unto thee, O Lórd, with my | whole | heart : even before the gods will I síng | praise | unto | thee.

2 I will worship toward thy holy temple, and praise thy Name * because of thy lóving- | -kindness . and | truth : for thou hast magnified thy Náme, and thy | Word a- | -bove | all things.

3 When I called upon thée, thou | heardest | me : and endúedst my | soul with | much | strength.

4 All the kings of the earth shall práise | thee O | Lord : for they have héard the | words | of thy | mouth.

5 Yea, they shall sing in the wáys | of the | Lord : that gréat is the | glory | of the | Lord.

6 For though the Lord be high * yet hath he respéct | unto . the | lowly : as for the proud, he behóldeth | them a- | far | off.

7 Though I walk in the midst of trouble * yét shalt | thou re- | -fresh me : thou shalt stretch forth thy hand upon the furiousness of mine enemies * ánd thy | right | hand shall | save me.

8 The Lord shall make good his loving-kíndness | toward | me : yea, thy mercy, O Lord, endureth for ever * despise not then the wórks | of thine | own | hands.

Day 29. MORNING PRAYER.

Psalm cxxxix.—*Domine, probasti.*

mf O LORD, thou hast séarched me | out and | known me : thou knowest my down-sitting and mine uprising * thou understándest my | thoughts | long be- | -fore.

2 Thou art about my páth, and a- | -bout my | bed : ánd | spiest . out | all my | ways.

3 For lo, there is not a wórd | in my | tongue : but thou, O Lórd | knowest it | alto- | -gether.

4 Thou hast fashioned me behínd | and be- | -fore : ánd | laid thine | hand up- | -on me.

5 Such knowledge is too wónderful and | excellent | for me : I cánnot at- | -tain | unto | it.

6 Whither shall I gó then | from thy | Spirit : or whíther shall I | go then | from thy | presence?

7 If I climb up into héaven | thou art | there : if I go down to héll | thou art | there | also.

8 If I take the wíngs | of the | morning : and remain in the úttermost | parts | of the | sea ;

9 Even there álso shall | thy hand | lead me : ánd | thy right | hand shall | hold me.

10 If I say, Peradventure the dárkness shall | cover | me : thén shall my | night be | turned . to | day.

11 Yea, the darkness is no darkness with thee * but the night is as cléar | as the | day : the darkness and líght to | thee are | both a- | -like.

12 Fór my | reins are | thine : thou hast cóvered me | in my | mother's | womb.

13 I will give thanks unto thee * for I am fearfully and wónder- | -fully | made : marvellous are thy works * and thát my | soul | knoweth . right | well.

14 My bónes are not | hid from | thee : though I be made secretly * and fáshioned be- | -neath | in the | earth.

15 Thine eyes did see my súbstance, yet | being . im- | perfect : and in thy bóok were | all my | members | written ;

16 Which dáy by | day were | fashioned : when as yét | there was | none of | them.

17 How dear are thy counsels únto | me O | God : O how gréat | is the | sum of | them !

18 If I tell them * they are more in númber | than the | sand : when I wake úp | I am | present . with | thee.

19 Wilt thou not sláy the | wicked . O | God : depart from mé, ye | blood- | -thirsty | men.

20 For they speak unríghteous- | -ly a- | -gainst thee : and thine énemies | take thy | Name in | vain.

21 Do not I hate them, O Lórd, that | hate | thee : and am not I grieved with thóse that | rise | up a- | -gainst thee ?

22 Yea, I háte | them right | sore : éven as | though they | were mine | enemies.

23 Try me, O God, and seek the gróund | of my | heart : próve me | and ex- | -amine . my | thoughts.

24 Look well if there be any wáy of | wickedness | in me : and léad me in the | way | ever- | -lasting.

Psalm cxl.—*Eripe me, Domine.*

mp DELIVER me, O Lórd, from the | evil | man : and
presérve me | from the | wicked | man.

2 Who imagine míschief | in their | hearts : and stir up
strífe | all the | day | long.

3 They have sharpened their tóngues | like a | serpent :
ádder's | poison . is | under . their | lips.

4 Keep me, O Lord, from the hánds of | the un- | -godly :
preserve me from the wicked men * who are púrposed
to | over- | -throw my | goings.

5 The proud have laid a snare for me * and spread a nét a- |
broad with | cords : yéa, and set | traps | in my | way.

6 I said unto the Lord, Thóu | art my | God : hear the
vóice | of my | prayers O | Lord.

7 O Lord God, thou stréngth | of my | health : thou hast
covered my héad | in the | day of | battle.

8 Let not the ungodly háve his de- | -sire O | Lord : let not
his mischievous imagination prósper | lest they | be
too | proud.

9 Let the mischief of their own lips fall upón the | head
of | them : thát | compass | me a- | -bout.

10 Let hot burning cóals | fall up- | -on them : let them be
cast into the fire, and into the pit * that they néver |
rise | up a- | -gain.

11 A man full of words shall not prósper up- | -on the |
earth : evil shall húnt the wicked | person . to | over- |
throw him.

12 Sure I am that the Lórd will a- | -venge the | poor : and
maintáin the | cause | of the | helpless.

2nd
part. 13 The righteous also shall give thánks | unto . thy |
Name : and the júst shall con- | -tinue | in thy | sight.

Psalm cxli.—*Domine, clamavi.*

mp LORD, I call upon thee * háste thee | unto | me : and
consider my vóice when I | cry | unto | thee.

2 Let my prayer be set forth in thy síght | as the |
incense : and let the lifting up of my hánds | be an |
evening | sacrifice.

3 Set a watch, O Lórd, be- | -fore my | mouth : and kéep
the | door | of my | lips.

4 O let not mine heart be inclined to ány | evil | thing : let
me not be occupied in ungodly works with the men that
work wickedness * lest I éat of such | things as |
please | them.

5 Let the righteous ráther | smite me | friendly : ánd | —
re- | -prove | me.

6 But let not their precious bálms | break my | head : yea,
I will práy | yet a- | -gainst their | wickedness.

7 Let their judges be overthrówn in | stony | places : that
they may héar my | words for | they are | sweet.

8 Our bones lie scáttered be- | -fore the | pit : like as
when one breaketh and héweth | wood up- | -on the |
earth.

9 But mine eyes look unto thée, O | Lord | God : in thee is
my trúst, O | cast not | out my | soul.

10 Keep me from the snare that théy have | laid for | me :
and from the tráps | of the | wicked | doers.

2nd part. 11 Let the ungodly fall into their ówn | nets to- | -gether :
ánd let | me | ever . es- | -cape them.

Day 29.	EVENING PRAYER.

Psalm cxlii.—*Voce mea ad Dominum.*

F. mp **I** CRIED unto the Lórd | with my | voice : yea, even unto
the Lórd did I | make my | suppli- | -cation.

F. 2 I poured out mý com- | -plaints be- | -fore him : ánd |
shewed . him | of my | trouble.

3 When my spirit was in héaviness thou | knewest . my |
path : in the way wherein I walked have they prívily |
laid a | snare for | me.

4 I looked also upón my | right | hand : and sáw there was |
no man | that would | know me.

5 I had no pláce to | flee | unto : and nó man | cared | for
my | soul.

6 I cried unto thée, O | Lord and | said : Thou art
my hope * and my portion ín the | land | of the |
living.

7 Consíder | my com- | -plaint : for I′ am | brought | very |
low.

8 O delíver me | from my | persecutors : fór they | are
too | strong for | me.

2nd part 9 Bring my soul out of prison * that I may give thánks |
unto . thy | Name : which thing if thou wilt grant
me * then shall the ríghteous re- | -sort | unto . my |
company.

Psalm cxliii.—*Domine, exaudi.*

mp HEAR my prayer, O Lord * and consíder | my de- | sire : hearken unto mé for thy | truth and | righteous- ness' | sake.

2 And enter not into júdgement | with thy | servant : for in thy síght shall | no man | living . be | justified.

3 For the enemy hath persecuted my soul * he hath smitten my lífe | down . to the | ground : he hath laid me in the darkness * as the mén that | have been | long | dead.

4 Therefore is my spírit | vexed . with- | -in me : ánd my | heart with- | -in me . is | desolate.

5 Yet do I remember the time past * I múse upon | all thy | works : yea, I exercise mysélf in the | works | of thy | hands.

6 I stretch forth my hánds | unto | thee : my soul gaspeth unto thée | as a | thirsty | land.

7 Hear me, O Lord, and that soon * for my spírit | waxeth | faint : hide not thy face from me * lest I be like unto thém that go | down | into . the | pit.

8 O let me hear thy loving-kindness betimes in the morning * for in thée | is my | trust : shew thou me the way that I should walk in * for I lift úp my | soul | unto | thee.

9 Deliver me, O Lórd | from mine | enemies : for I flée | unto | thee to | hide me.

10 Teach me to do the thing that pleaseth thee * for thóu | art my | God : let thy loving Spirit lead me fórth | into . the | land of | righteousness.

11 Quicken me, O Lórd, for thy | Name's | sake : and for thy righteousness' sake bríng my | soul | out of | trouble.

12 And of thy góodness | slay mine | enemies : and destroy all them that vex my sóul, for | I am | thy | servant.

———

Day 30. MORNING PRAYER.

Psalm cxliv.—*Benedictus Dominus.*

mf BLESSED bé the | Lord my | strength : who teacheth my hands to wár | and my | fingers . to | fight ;

2 My hope and my fortress, my castle and deliverer * my defénder in | whom I | trust : who subdueth my péople | that is | under | me.

3 Lord, what is man * that thou hast such respéct | unto | him : or the son of man * thát thou | so re- | -gardest | him ?

4 Man is líke a | thing of | nought : his time pásseth a- | way | like a | shadow.

5 Bow thy heavens, O Lórd, and | come | down : touch the | mountains . and | they shall | smoke.

6 Cast fórth thy | lightning . and | tear them : shoot óut thine | arrows | and con- | -sume them.

7 Send down thine hánd | from a- | -bove : deliver me, and take me out of the great waters * fróm the | hand of | strange | children ;

8 Whose móuth | talketh . of | vanity : and their right hánd is a | right | hand of | wickedness.

9 I will sing a new sóng unto | thee O | God : and sing praises unto thée upon a | ten- | -stringed | lute.

10 Thou hast given víctóry | unto | kings : and hast delivered David thy servant fróm the | peril | of the | sword.

11 Save me, and deliver me from the hánd of | strange | children : whose mouth talketh of vanity * and their right hánd is a | right | hand . of in- | -iquity.

12 That our sons may grow úp as the | young | plants : and that our daughters may be as the pólished | corners | of the | temple.

13 That our garners may be full and plenteous with áll | manner . of | store : that our sheep may bring forth thousands * and tén | thousands | in our | streets.

14 That our oxen may be strong to labour * that thére be | no de- | -cay : no leading into captivity * and nó com- | -plaining | in our | streets.

2nd part. 15 Happy are the people that áre in | such a | case : yea, blessed are the people who háve the | Lord | for their | God.

Psalm cxlv.—*Exaltabo te, Deus.*

mf I WILL magnify thée, O | God my | King : and I will práise thy | Name for | ever . and | ever.

2 Every day will I give thánks | unto | thee : and práise thy | Name for | ever . and | ever.

3 Great is the Lord, and marvellous * wórthy | to be | praised : there ís no | end | of his | greatness.

4 One generation shall praise thy wórks | unto . an- | other : ánd de- | -clare | thy | power.

5 As for me, I will be tálking | of thy | worship : thy glóry,
   thy | praise and | wondrous | works ;

6 So that men shall speak of the míght of thy | mar-
   vellous | acts : and I will álso | tell | of thy | great-
   ness.

7 The memorial of thine abundant kíndness | shall be |
   shewed : and mén shall | sing | of thy | righteousness.

8 The Lórd is | gracious . and | merciful : long-súffering |
   and of | great | goodness.

9 The Lord is loving únto | every | man : and his mércy
   is | over | all his | works.

10 All thy works práise | thee O | Lord : and thy sáints
   give | thanks | unto | thee.

11 They shew the glóry | of thy | kingdom : ánd | talk | of
   thy | power ;

12 That thy power, thy glory, and míghtiness | of thy |
   kingdom : míght be | known | unto | men.

13 Thy kingdom is an éver- | -lasting | kingdom : and thy
   domínion en- | -dureth . through- | -out all | ages.

14 The Lord uphóldeth all | such as | fall : and lifteth úp
   all | those | that are | down.

15 The eyes of all wáit upon | thee O | Lord : and thou
   gívest them their | meat in | due | season.

16 Thou ópenest | thine | hand : and fíllest | all things |
   living . with | plenteousness.

17 The Lord is ríghteous in | all his | ways : ánd | holy .
   in | all his | works.

18 The Lord is nigh unto all thém that | call up- | -on him :
   yea, áll such as | call up- | -on him | faithfully.

19 He will fulfil the desíre of | them that | fear him : he also
   will héar their | cry | and will | help them.

20 The Lord presérveth all | them that | love him : but
   scáttereth a- | -broad | all . the un- | -godly.

2nd 21 My mouth shall speak the práise | of the | Lord : and let
part.   all flesh give thanks unto his hóly | Name for | ever .
   and | ever.

Psalm cxlvi.—*Lauda, anima mea.*

mf PRAISE the Lord, O my soul * while I líve will I | praise
   the | Lord : yea, as long as I have any being * I will
   síng | praises | unto . my | God.

2 O put not your trust in princes * nor in ány | child of |
   man : fór there is | no | help in | them.

3 For when the breath of man goeth forth * he shall túrn again | to his | earth : and thén | all his | thoughts | perish.

4 Blessed is he that hath the God of Jácob | for his | help : and whose hópe is | in the | Lord his | God ;

5 Who made heaven and earth * the sea, and áll that | therein | is : whó | keepeth . his | promise . for | ever ;

6 Who helpeth them to ríght that | suffer | wrong : whó | feed- | -eth the | hungry.

7 The Lord looseth mén | out of | prison : the Lórd giveth | sight | to the | blind.

8 The Lord helpeth thém | that are | fallen : the Lórd | careth | for the | righteous.

9 The Lord careth for the strangers * he defendeth the fáther- | -less and | widow : as for the way of the ungódly, he | turneth . it | upside | down.

10 The Lord thy God, O Sion, shall be Kíng for | ever- | more : ánd throughout | all | gener- | -ations.

Day 30. EVENING PRAYER.

Psalm cxlvii.—*Laudate Dominum.*

F. f **O** PRAISE the Lord * for it is a good thing to sing práises | unto . our | God : yea, a joyful and pleasant thíng it | is to | be | thankful.

F. 2 The Lord doth buíld | up Je- | -rusalem : and gather togéther the | out- | -casts of | Israel.

3 He healeth thóse that are | broken . in | heart : and gíveth | medicine . to | heal their | sickness.

4 He telleth the númber | of the | stars : and cálleth them | all | by their | names.

5 Great is our Lord * and gréat | is his | power : yéa, and his | wisdom | is | infinite.

6 The Lórd setteth | up the | meek : and bringeth the ungódly | down | to the | ground.

7 O sing unto the Lórd with | thanks- | -giving : sing praises upón the | harp | unto . our | God.

8 Who covereth the heaven with clouds * and prepareth ráin | for the | earth : and maketh the grass to grow upon the mountains * and hérb | for the | use of | men.

9 Who giveth fódder | unto . the | cattle : and feedeth the yóung | ravens . that | call up- | -on him.

10 He hath no pleasure in the stréngth | of an | horse :
neither delíghteth | he in | any . man's | legs.

11 But the Lord's delíght is in | them that | fear him : and
pút their | trust | in his | mercy.

12 Praise the Lórd | O Je- | -rusalem : práise thy | God |
O | Sion.

13 For he hath made fast the bárs | of thy | gates : ánd
hath | blessed . thy | children . with- | -in thee.

14 He maketh péace | in thy | borders : and fílleth thee |
with the | flour of | wheat.

15 He sendeth forth his commándment up- | -on | earth :
and his wórd | runneth | very | swiftly.

16 He gíveth | snow like | wool : and scáttereth the | hoar- |
frost like | ashes.

17 He casteth fórth his | ice like | morsels : who is áble | to
a- | -bide his | frost ?

18 He sendeth out his wórd, and | melteth | them : he
bloweth with his wínd | and the | waters | flow.

19 He sheweth his wórd | unto | Jacob : his statutes and
órdinances | unto | Isra- | -el.

20 He hath not dealt só with | any | nation : neither have
the héathen | knowledge | of his | laws.

Psalm cxlviii.—*Laudate Dominum.*

f O PRÁISE the | Lord of | heaven : práise | — him | in
the | height.

2 Praise him, áll ye | angels . of | his : práise | — him | all
his | host.

3 Práise him | sun and | moon : práise him | all ye | stars
and | light.

4 Práise him | all ye | heavens : and ye wáters that | are
a- | -bove the | heavens.

5 Let them praise the Náme | of the | Lord : for he spake
the word, and they were made * he commánded | and
they | were cre- | -ated.

6 He hath made them fást for | ever . and | ever : he hath
given them a láw | which shall | not be | broken.

7 Praise the Lórd up- | -on | earth : yé | dragons . and |
all | deeps ;

8 Fire and háil | snow and | vapours : wínd and | storm
ful- | -filling . his | word ;

9 Moúntains and | all | hills : frúitful | trees and | all |
cedars ;

10 Beasts and | all | cattle : wórms | — and | feathered | fowls;

11 Kings of the éarth and | all | people : princes and áll | judges | of the | world ;

12 Young men and maidens, old men and children * praise the Náme | of the | Lord : for his Name only is excellent * and his práise a- | -bove | heaven and | earth.

2nd part. 13 He shall exalt the horn of his people * áll his | saints shall | praise him : even the children of Israel * éven the | people . that | serveth | him.

Psalm cxlix.—*Cantate Domino.*

f   O SING unto the Lórd a | new | song : let the cóngre- | gation . of | saints | praise him.

2 Let Israel rejóice in | him that | made him : and let the children of Síon be | joyful | in their | King.

3 Let them praise his Náme | in the | dance : let them sing praises únto | him with | tabret . and | harp.

4 For the Lord hath pléasure | in his | people : ánd | helpeth . the | meek- | -hearted.

5 Let the sáints be | joyful . with | glory : lét them re- | joice | in their | beds.

6 Let the praises of Gód be | in their | mouth : and a twó-edged | sword | in their | hands ;

7 To be avénged | of the | heathen : ánd | to re- | -buke the | people ;

8 To bínd their | kings in | chains : ánd their | nobles . with | links of | iron.

2nd part. 9 That they may be avenged of thém | as it . is | written : Súch | honour . have | all his | saints.

Psalm cl.—*Laudate Dominum.*

ff   O PRAISE Gód | in his | holiness : práise him in the | firmament | of his | power.

2 Práise him in his | noble | acts : praise him accórding | to his | excellent | greatness.

3 Praise him in the sóund | of the | trumpet : práise him up- | -on the | lute and | harp.

4 Práise him in the | cymbals and | dances : práise him up- | -on the | strings and | pipe.

5 Praise him upon the wéll- | -tuned | cymbals : práise him up- | -on the | loud | cymbals.

F.   6 Let évery thing | that hath | breath : práise | — — | — the | Lord.

PROPER PSALMS

ON CERTAIN DAYS.

CHRISTMAS DAY.

MORNING PRAYER.

PSALM xix.—*Cœli enarrant.*

ᵛ. f   **1** THE heavens decláre the | glory . of | God : and the
firmament | sheweth . his | handy- | -work.

ᵛ.   **2** One dáy | telleth . an- | -other : and one níght | certi- |
fieth . an- | -other.

3 There is neíther | speech nor | language : bút their |
voices . are | heard a- | -mong them.

4 Their sound is gone óut into | all | lands : and their
wórds into the | ends | of the | world.

5 In them hath he set a tábernacle | for the | sun : which
cometh forth as a bridegroom out of his chamber * and
rejóiceth as a | giant . to | run his | course.

6 It goeth forth from the uttermost part of the heaven *
and runneth about unto the énd of | it a- | -gain : and
there is nothing híd | from the | heat there- | -of.

7 The law of the Lord is an undefiled láw, con- | -verting .
the | soul : the testimony of the Lord is sure * and
gíveth | wisdom | unto . the | simple.

8 The statutes of the Lord are ríght, and re- | -joice the |
heart : the commandment of the Lord is pure * and
gíveth | light | unto . the | eyes.

*2nd
part.*   **9** The fear of the Lord is cléan and en- | -dureth . for |
ever : the judgements of the Lord are trúe, and |
righteous | alto- | -gether.

10 More to be desired are they than gold * yéa, than |
much fine | gold : sweeter álso than | honey | and the |
honeycomb.

11 Moreover, by thém is thy | servant | taught : and in
kéeping of them | there is | great re- | -ward.

mp **12** Who can téll how | oft . he of- | -fendeth : O cleanse thou
mé | from my | secret | faults.

13 Keep thy servant also from presumptuous sins * lest
they get the domínion | over | me : so shall I be
undefiled, and ínnocent | from the | great of- | -fence.

14 Let the words of my mouth * and the meditátion | of
my | heart : be álway ac- | -ceptable | in thy | sight,

15 O' | — | Lord : mý | strength and | my re- | -deemer.

PSALM xlv.—*Eructavit cor meum.*

mf MY heart is indíting of a | good | matter : I speak of the
things which I' have | made | unto . the | King.

2 My tóngue | is the | pen : óf | — a | ready | writer.

3 Thou art fairer thán the | children . of | men : full of
grace are thy lips * because Gód hath | blessed | thee
for | ever.

4 Gird thee with thy sword upon thy thígh, O | thou most |
Mighty : accórding to thy | worship | and re- | -nown.

5 Good lúck have thou | with thine | honour : ride on,
because of the word of truth * of meekness and
righteousness * and thy right hánd shall | teach thee |
terrible | things.

6 Thy arrows are very sharp * and the people shall be
: subdúed | unto | thee : even in the mídst a- | -mong
the | King's | enemies.

7 Thy seat, O Gód, en- | -dureth . for | ever : the sceptre of
thy kíngdom | is a | right | sceptre.

8 Thou hast loved ríghteousness and | hated . in- | -iquity :
wherefore God, even thy God * hath anointed thee
with the óil of | gladness . a- | -bove thy | fellows.

9 All thy garments smell of mýrrh | aloes . and | cassia :
out of the ivory palaces * wherebý | they have | made
thee | glad.

10 Kings' daughters were among thy hónour- | -able |
women : upon thy right hand did stand the queen in a
vesture of gold * wróught a- | -bout with | divers |
colours.

11 Hearken, O daughter, and consíder, in- | -cline thine |
ear : forget also thine own péople | and thy | father's |
house.

12 So shall the King have pléasure | in thy | beauty : for he
is thy Lord Gód, and | worship | thou | him.

13 And the daughter of Tyre shall be thére | with a | gift :
like as the rich also among the people * shall máke
their | suppli- | -cation . be- | -fore thee.

14 The King's daughter is all glóri- | -ous with- | -in : her
    clóthing | is of | wrought | gold.

15 She shall be brought unto the Kíng in | raiment . of |
    needlework : the virgins that be her fellows shall
    bear her company * and shall be | brought | unto |
    thee.

16 With joy and gládness shall | they be | brought : and
    shall énter | into . the | King's | palace.

17 Instead of thy fáthers thou | shalt have | children : whom
    thou máyest make | princes . in | all | lands.

18 I will remember thy Name from one generátion | to an- |
    other : therefore shall the people give thanks unto
    thée | world with- | -out | end.

PSALM lxxxv.—*Benedixisti, Domine.*

mp LORD, thou art become grácious | unto . thy | land : thou
    hast turned awáy the cap- | -tivi- | -ty of | Jacob.

2 Thou hast forgiven the offénce | of thy | people : ánd |
    covered | all their | sins.

3 Thou hast taken awáy all | thy dis- | -pleasure : and
    turned thysélf from thy | wrathful | indig- | -nation.

4 Turn us thén, O | God our | Saviour : and lét thine |
    anger | cease | from us.

5 Wilt thou be displéased at | us for | ever : and wilt thou
    stretch out thy wrath from óne gener- | -ation | to
    an- | -other?

6 Wilt thou not turn agáin, and | quicken | us : that thy
    péople | may re- | -joice in | thee?

2nd part. 7 Shéw us thy | mercy . O | Lord : ánd | grant us | thy
    sal- | -vation.

8 I will hearken what the Lord God will sáy con- | -cern-
    ing | me : for he shall speak peace unto his people and
    to his saints * thát they | turn | not a- | -gain.

9 For his salvation is nígh | them that | fear him : that
    glóry may | dwell | in our | land.

10 Mercy and trúth are | met to- | -gether : ríghteousness
    and | peace have | kissed . each | other.

11 Truth shall floúrish | out . of the | earth : and ríght-
    eousness hath | looked | down from | heaven.

12 Yea, the Lord shall shéw | loving- | -kindness : ánd our |
    land shall | give her | increase.

13 Ríghteousness shall | go be- | -fore him : and he shall
    diréct his | going | in the | way.

EVENING PRAYER.

PSALM lxxxix.—*Misericordias Domini.*

F. mf MY song shall be alway of the loving-kíndness | of the | Lord : with my mouth will I ever be shewing thy truth * from óne gener- | -ation | to an- | -other.

F. 2 For I have said, Mercy shall be sét | up for | ever : thy trúth shalt thou | stablish | in the | heavens.

3 I have made a cóvenant | with my | chosen : I have swórn | unto | David . my | servant;

4 Thy séed will I | stablish . for | ever : and set up thy throne from óne gener- | -ation | to an- | -other.

5 O Lord, the very heavens shall práise thy | wondrous | works : and thy truth in the cóngre- | -gation | of the | saints.

6 For who is hé a- | -mong the | clouds : that sháll be com- | -pared | unto . the | Lord ?

7 And what is hé a- | -mong the | gods : that sháll be | like | unto . the | Lord ?

8 God is very greatly to be feared in the cóuncil | of the | saints : and to be had in reverence of all thém | that are | round a- | -bout him.

9 O Lord God of hosts * whó is | like . unto | thee : thy truth, most mighty Lórd | is on | every | side.

10 Thou rulest the ráging | of the | sea : thou stillest the wáves there- | -of when | they a- | -rise.

11 Thou hast subdued Egypt * ánd de- | -stroyed | it : thou hast scattered thine enemies abróad | with thy | mighty | arm.

12 The heavens are thine, the éarth | also . is | thine : thou hast laid the foundation of the round wórld, and | all that | therein | is.

13 Thou hast made the nórth | and the | south : Tabor and Hermon sháll re- | -joice | in thy | Name.

14 Thou hást a | mighty | arm : strong is thy hánd, and | high is | thy right | hand.

15 Righteousness and equity are the habitátion | of thy | seat : mercy and trúth shall | go be- | -fore thy | face.

16 Blessed is the people, O Lord * that cán re- | -joice in | thee : they shall wálk in the | light | of thy | countenance.

17 Their delight shall be dáily | in thy | Name : and in thy ríghteousness | shall they | make their | boast.

18 For thou art the glóry | of their | strength : and in thy loving-kindness thóu shalt | lift | up our | horns.

19 For the Lórd is | our de- | -fence : the Hóly One of | Israel | is our | King.

20 Thou spakest sometime in visions únto thy | saints and | saidst : I have laid help upon one that is mighty * I have exálted one | chosen | out . of the | people.

21 I have fóund | David . my | servant : with my holy óil have | I a- | -nointed | him.

22 My hánd shall | hold him | fast : ánd my | arm shall | strengthen | him.

23 The enemy shall not be áble to | do him | violence : the són of | wickedness | shall not | hurt him.

24 I will smite down his fóes be- | -fore his | face : ánd | plague | them that | hate him.

25 My truth also and my mércy | shall be | with him : and in my Náme shall his | horn | be ex- | -alted.

26 I will set his dominion álso | in the | sea : ánd his | right hand | in the | floods.

27 He shall call me, Thóu | art my | Father : my Gód | and my | strong sal- | -vation.

28 And I will máke | him my | first-born : hígher than the | kings | of the | earth.

29 My mercy will I kéep for him for | ever- | -more : and my cóvenant shall | stand | fast | with him.

30 His seed also will I máke to en- | -dure for | ever : and his thróne | as the | days of | heaven.

mf 31 But if his chíldren for- | -sake my | law : ánd | walk not | in my | judgements ;

32 If they break my statutes * and kéep not | my com- | mandments : I will visit their offences with the ród | and their | sin with | scourges.

33 Nevertheless, my loving-kindness will I not útterly | take | from him : nór | suffer . my | truth to | fail.

34 My covenant will I not break * nor alter the thing that is góne | out of . my | lips : I have sworn once by my holiness * that I' | will not | fail | David.

35 His séed shall en- | -dure for | ever : and his séat is | like . as the | sun be- | -fore me.

36 He shall stand fast for evermóre | as the | moon : and ás the | faithful | witness . in | heaven.

p 37 But thou hast abhorred and forsáken | thine A- | nointed : ánd | art dis- | -pleased | at him.

38 Thou hast broken the cóvenant | of thy | servant : and
cást his | crown | to the | ground.

39 Thou hast overthrówn | all his | hedges : ánd | broken |
down his | strongholds.

40 All théy that go | by | spoil him : and he is becóme a
re- | -proach | to his | neighbours.

41 Thou hast set up the right hánd | of his | enemies : and
máde all his | adversaries | to re- | -joice.

42 Thou hast taken away the édge | of his | sword : and
givest him nót | victory | in the | battle.

43 Thóu hast put | out his | glory : and cást his | throne |
down . to the | ground.

44 The days of his yóuth | hast thou | shortened : ánd |
covered . him | with dis- | -honour.

45 Lord, how long wilt thou híde thy- | -self for | ever : and
sháll thy | wrath | burn like | fire ?

46 O remember how shórt my | time | is : wherefore hast
thou máde | all | men for | nought ?

47 What man is he that líveth and shall | not see | death :
and shall he deliver his sóul | from the | hand of |
hell ?

48 Lord, where are thy óld | loving- | -kindnesses : which
thou swárest unto | David | in thy | truth ?

49 Remember, Lord, the rebúke that thy | servants | have :
and how I do bear in my bósom the re- | -bukes of |
many | people ;

50 Wherewith thine enemies have blasphemed thee * and
slandered the fóotsteps of | thine A- | -nointed : Praised
be the Lord for evermóre. | A- . -men and | A- | -men.

PSALM CX.—*Dixit Dominus.*

mf THE Lord sáid unto | my | Lord : Sit thou on my
right hand * until I máke thine | ene- | -mies thy |
footstool.

2 The Lord shall send the rod of thy pówer | out of | Sion :
be thou ruler * éven in the | midst a- | -mong thine |
enemies.

3 In the day of thy power shall the people offer thee free-
will-offerings * wíth an | holy | worship : the dew of
thy birth is óf the | womb | of the | morning.

4 The Lord swáre, and will | not re- | -pent : Thou art a
Priest for ever * áfter the | order | of Mel- | -chise-
dech.

5 The Lórd upon | thy right | hand : shall wound even
kíngs in the | day· | of his | wrath.

6 He shall judge among the heathen * he shall fill the
pláces with the | dead | bodies : and smite in sunder
the héads | over | divers | countries.

2nd part. 7 He shall drink of the bróok | in the | way : therefore
sháll he ⌊ lift | up his | head.

PSALM cxxxii.—Memento, Domine.

mf LÓRD, re- | -member | David : ánd | all | his |
trouble ;

2 How he swáre | unto . the | Lord : and vowed a vow
únto the Al- | -mighty | God of | Jacob ;

3 I will not come within the tábernacle | of mine | house :
nór | climb up | into . my | bed ;

4 I will not suffer mine eyes to sléep, nor mine | eyelids .
to | slumber : neither the temples of my héad to |
take | any | rest ;

5 Until I find out a place for the témple | of the | Lord :
an habitation fór the | mighty | God of | Jacob.

6 Lo, we héard of the | same at | Ephrata : ánd | found it |
in the | wood.

7 We will gó into his | taber- | -nacle : and fall lów on
our | knees be- | -fore his | footstool.

8 Arise, O Lórd | into . thy | resting-place : thóu, and the |
ark | of thy | strength.

9 Let thy príests be | clothed . with | righteousness : and
lét thy | saints | sing with | joyfulness.

10 For thy sérvant | David's | sake : turn not awáy the |
presence . of | thine A- | -nointed.

11 The Lord hath made a faithful óath | unto | David : ánd
he | shall not | shrink | from it.

12 Of the frúit | of thy | body : sháll I | set up- | -on thy |
seat.

13 If thy children will keep my covenant * and my tésti-
monies that | I shall | learn them : their children also
shall sit upón thy | seat for | ever- | -more.

14 For the Lord hath chosen Sion to be an habitátion | for
him- | -self : hé hath | longed | for | her.

15 This shall bé my | rest for | ever : here will I dwell * fór
I | have . a de- | -light there- | -in.

16 I will bléss her | victuals . with | increase : and will
sátis- | -fy her | poor with | bread.

17 I will déck her | priests with | health : and her sáints |
shall re- | -joice and | sing.

18 There shall I make the hórn of | David . to | flourish : I
have ordáined a | lantern . for | mine A- | -nointed.

2nd part. 19 As for his enemies * I shall clóthe | them with | shame :
but upon himsélf | shall his | crown | flourish.

ASH WEDNESDAY.

MORNING PRAYER.

Psalm vi.—*Domine, ne in furore.*

F. mp   O LORD, rebuke me nót in thine | indig- | -nation :
neither chásten | me in | thy dis- | -pleasure.

F.   2 Have mercy upon me, O Lórd, for | I am | weak : O Lord,
héal me | for my | bones are | vexed.

3 My soul álso is | sore | troubled : but, Lord, how lóng |
wilt thou | punish | me ?

4 Turn thee, O Lórd, and de- | -liver . my | soul : O sáve
me | for thy | mercy's | sake.

5 For in death nó man re- | -membereth | thee : and who
will gíve thee | thanks | in the | pit ?

6 I am weary of my groaning * every night wásh | I my |
bed : and wáter my | couch | with my | tears.

7 My beauty is góne for | very | trouble : and worn awáy
be- | -cause of | all mine | enemies.

8 Away from me, all yé that | work | vanity : for the Lord
hath héard the | voice | of my | weeping.

9 The Lord hath héard | my pe- | -tition : the Lórd | will
re- | -ceive my | prayer.

10 All mine enemies shall be confóunded and | sore | vexed :
they shall be turned báck, and | put to | shame |
suddenly.

Psalm xxxii.—*Beati, quorum.*

mp   B LESSED is he whose unríghteousness | is for- | -given :
ánd whose | sin | is | covered.

2 Blessed is the man unto whom the Lórd im- | -puteth .
no | sin : and ín whose | spirit . there | is no |
guile.

3 For whíle I | held my | tongue : my bones consumed
  awáy | through my | daily . com- | -plaining.

4 For thy hand is heavy upón me | day and | night : and
  my móisture is | like the | drought in | summer.

5 I will acknowledge my sín | unto | thee : and mine
  unríghteousness | have I | not | hid.

6 I said, I will confess my síns | unto . the | Lord : and so
  thou forgávest the | wickedness | of my | sin.

7 For this shall every one that is godly make his prayer
  unto thee * in a tíme when thou | mayest . be | found :
  but in the great wáter-floods | they shall | not come |
  nigh him.

8 Thou art a place to hide me in * thou shalt presérve | me
  from | trouble : thou shalt compass me abóut with |
  songs | of de- | -liverance.

9 I will inform thee, and teach thee in the wáy wherein |
  thou shalt | go : and I′ will | guide thee | with mine |
  eye.

10 Be ye not like to horse and mule * which háve no |
   under- | -standing : whose mouths must be held with
   bit and brídle | lest they | fall up- | -on thee.

11 Great plagues remáin | for . the un- | -godly : but whoso
   putteth his trust in the Lord * mercy embráceth | him
   on | every | side.

12 Be glad, O ye righteous * and rejóice | in the | Lord :
   and be joyful, all yé | that are | true of | heart.

Psalm xxxviii.—*Domine, ne in furore.*

p PUT me not to rebuke, O Lórd | in thine | anger : neither
      chásten me | in thy | heavy . dis- | -pleasure.

2 For thine árrows stick | fast in | me : ánd thy | hand |
  presseth . me | sore.

3 There is no health in my flesh * becáuse of | thy dis- |
  pleasure : neither is there any rest in my bónes, by |
  reason | of my | sin.

4 For my wickednesses are góne | over . my | head : and
  are like a sore búrden, too | heavy . for | me to | bear.

5 My wounds stínk and | are cor- | -rupt : thróugh | my |
  foolish- | -ness.

6 I am brought into so gréat | trouble . and | misery : that
  I go móurning | all the | day | long.

7 For my loins are fílled with a | sore dis- | -ease : and
  there is nó | whole part | in my | body.

8 I am féeble and | sore | smitten : I have roared for the
véry dis- | -quietness | of my | heart.

9 Lord, thou knowest áll | my de- | -sire : and my gróaning |
is not | hid from | thee.

10 My heart panteth, my stréngth hath | failed | me : and
the síght of mine | eyes is | gone | from me.

11 My lovers and my neighbours did stand lóoking up- | -on
my | trouble : and my kínsmen | stood a- | -far | off.

12 They also that sought after my lífe laid | snares for | me :
and they that went about to do me evil talked of
wickedness * and imagined decéit | all the | day | long.

13 As for me, I was like a déaf | man and | heard not : and
as one that is dúmb, who | doth not | open . his |
mouth.

14 I became even as a mán that | heareth | not : and in
whóse | mouth are | no re- | -proofs.

15 For in thee, O Lórd, have I | put my | trust : thou shalt
ánswer for | me O | Lord my | God.

16 I have required that they, even mine enemies * should
not tríumph | over | me : for when my foot slipped *
théy re- | -joiced | greatly . a- | -gainst me.

17 And I truly am sét | in the | plague : and my héaviness
is | ever | in my | sight.

18 For I' will con- | -fess my | wickedness : ánd be | sorry |
fór my | sin.

19 But mine enemies líve | and are | mighty : and they that
hate me wróngfully | are | many . in | number.

20 They also that reward evil for góod | are a- | -gainst me :
because I fóllow the | thing that | good | is.

21 Forsake me nót, O | Lord my | God : bé not | thou | far |
from me.

22 Háste | thee to | help me : O Lórd | God of | my sal- |
vation.

EVENING PRAYER.

Psalm cii.—*Domine, exaudi.*

F. *mp* HÉAR my | prayer O | Lord : and let my crýing | come |
unto | thee.

F. 2 Hide not thy face from me in the tíme | of my | trouble :
incline thine ear unto me when I call * O héar | me
and | that right | soon.

3 For my days are consúmed a- | -way like | smoke : and
my bones are burnt úp | as it | were a | firebrand.

4 My heart is smitten dówn and | withered . like | grass :
so that I' for- | -get to | eat my | bread.

5 For the vóice | of my | groaning : my bones will scárce |
cleave | to my | flesh.

6 I am become like a pélican | in the | wilderness : and like
an ówl | that is | in the | desert.

7 I have watched * and am éven as it | were a | sparrow :
that sítteth a- | -lone up- | -on the | house-top.

8 Mine enemies revíle me | all the . day | long : and they
that are mad upón me are | sworn to- | -gether . a- |
gainst me.

9 For I have eaten áshes | as it . were | bread : ánd |
mingled . my | drink with | weeping ;

10 And that because of thine índig- | -nation and | wrath :
for thou hast táken me | up and | cast me | down.

11 My days are góne | like a | shadow : and I' am |
withered | like | grass.

12 But thou, O Lórd, shalt en- | -dure for | ever : and thy
remembrance throughóut | all | gener- | -ations.

13 Thou shalt arise, and have mércy up- | -on | Sion : for it
is time that thou have mercy upón her | yea the | time
is | come.

14 And why * thy servants thínk up- | -on her | stones : and
it pitieth thém to | see her | in the | dust.

15 The heathen shall féar thy | Name O | Lord : and all the
kíngs | of the | earth thy | Majesty ;

16 When the Lórd shall | build up | Sion : and whén his |
glory | shall ap- | -pear ;

17 When he turneth him unto the práyer of the | poor |
destitute : ánd de- | -spiseth . not | their de- | -sire.

18 This shall be written for thóse that | come | after : and
the people which sháll be | born shall | praise the |
Lord.

19 For he hath looked dówn | from his | sanctuary : out of
the héaven did the | Lord be- | -hold the | earth ;

20 That he might hear the mournings of súch as are | in
cap- | -tivity : and deliver the chíldren ap- | -pointed |
unto | death ;

21 That they may declare the Náme of the | Lord in | Sion :
ánd his | worship | at Je- | -rusalem ;

22 When the péople are | gathered . to- | -gether : and the
kíngdoms | also . to | serve the | Lord.

23 He brought down my stréngth | in my | journey : ánd | shortened | my | days.

24 But I said * O my God, take me not away in the mídst | of mine | age : as for thy years, they endure through- óut | all | gener- | -ations.

mf 25 Thou, Lord, in the beginning * hast laid the foundátion | of the | earth : and the héavens are the | work of | thy | hands.

26 They shall perish, but thóu | shalt en- | -dure : they áll shall wax | old as | doth a | garment ;

27 And as a vesture shalt thou change them * ánd they | shall be | changed : but thou art the same, ánd thy | years | shall not | fail.

28 The children of thy sérvants | shall con- | -tinue : and their séed shall stand | fast | in thy | sight.

Psalm cxxx.—*De profundis.*

p OUT of the deep have I called únto | thee O | Lord : Lórd | hear | my | voice.

2 O let thine éars con- | -sider | well : thé | voice of | my com- | -plaint.

3 If thou, Lord, wilt be extreme to márk what is | done a- | -miss : O Lórd | who | may a- | -bide it ?

4 Fór there is | mercy . with | thee : thérefore | shalt | thou be | feared.

5 I look for the Lord; my sóul doth | wait for | him : ín his | word | is my | trust.

6 My soul fléeth | unto . the | Lord : before the morning watch, I sáy, be- | -fore the | morning | watch.

7 O Israel, trust in the Lord * for with the Lórd | there is | mercy : ánd with | him is | plenteous . re- | -demption.

8 And hé shall re- | -deem | Israel : fróm | all | his | sins.

Psalm cxliii.—*Domine, exaudi.*

mp HEAR my prayer, O Lord * and consíder | my de- | sire : hearken unto mé for thy | truth and | righteousness' | sake.

2 And enter not into júdgement | with thy | servant : for in thy síght shall | no man | living . be | justified.

3 For the enemy hath persecuted my soul * he hath smitten my lífe | down . to the | ground : he hath laid me in the darkness * as the mén that | have been | long | dead.

4 Therefore is my spírit | vexed . with- | -in me : ánd my | heart with- | -in me . is | desolate.

5 Yet do I remember the time past * I múse upon | all thy | works : yea, I exercise mysélf in the | works | of thy | hands.

6 I stretch forth my hánds | unto | thee : my soul gaspeth unto theé | as a | thirsty | land.

7 Hear me, O Lord, and that soon * for my spírit | waxeth | faint : hide not thy face from me * lest I be like unto thém that go | down | into . the | pit.

8 O let me hear thy loving-kindness betimes in the morning * for in theé | is my | trust : shew thou me the way that I should walk in * for I lift úp my | soul | unto | thee.

9 Deliver me, O Lórd | from mine | enemies : for I fleé | unto | thee to | hide me.

10 Teach me to do the thing that pleaseth thee * for thóu | art my | God : let thy loving Spirit lead me fórth | into . the | land of | righteousness.

11 Quicken me, O Lórd, for thy | Name's | sake : and for thy righteousness' sake, bríng my | soul | out of | trouble.

12 And of thy góodness | slay mine | enemies : and destroy all them that vex my sóul, for | I am | thy | servant.

GOOD FRIDAY.

MORNING PRAYER.

Psalm xxii.—*Deus, Deus meus.*

F. *p* MY God, my God, look upon me * whý hast thou for- | saken | me : and art so far from my health * and fróm the | words of | my com- | -plaint?

F. 2 O my God, I cry in the day-time * bút thou | hearest | not : and in the níght-season | also . I | take no | rest.

3 And thóu con- | -tinuest | holy : O' | — thou | worship . of | Israel.

4 Our fáthers | hoped . in | thee : they trusted in theé, and thou | didst de- | -liver | them.

HH

5 They called upon thée | and were | holpen : they put their
    trust in thée | and were | not con- | -founded.

6 But as for me, I am a wórm, and | no | man : a very
    scorn of mén, and the | outcast | of the | people.

7 All they that see me * láugh | me to | scorn : they shoot
    out their líps, and | shake their | heads | saying,

8 He trusted in God, that hé would de- | -liver | him :
    let him delíver him | if he | will | have him.

9 But thou art he that took me óut of my | mother's |
    womb : thou wast my hope, when I hanged yét up- | -on
    my | mother's | breasts.

10 I have been left unto thee ever sínce | I was | born :
    thou art my God, éven | from my | mother's |
    womb.

11 O go not from me * for troúble is | hard at | hand : ánd |
    there is | none to | help me.

12 Many óxen are | come a- | -bout me : fat bulls of Basan
    clóse me | in on | every | side.

13 They gape upón me | with their | mouths : as it were a
    rámping | and a | roaring | lion.

14 I am poured out like water * and all my bónes are | out
    of | joint : my heart also in the midst of my bódy is |
    even . like | melting | wax.

15 My strength is dried up like a potsherd * and my tongue
    cléaveth | to my | gums : and thou shalt bríng me |
    into . the | dust of | death.

16 For many dógs are | come a- | -bout me : and the counsel
    of the wícked | layeth | siege a- | -gainst me.

17 They pierced my hands and my feet * I may téll | all
    my | bones : they stánd | staring . and | looking . up- |
    on me.

18 They párt my | garments . a- | -mong them : and cást |
    lots up- | -on my | vesture.

19 But be not thou fár from | me O | Lord : thou art my
    súccour | haste | thee to | help me.

20 Deliver my sóul | from the | sword : my darling fróm
    the | power | of the | dog.

21 Save me fróm the | lion's | mouth : thou hast heard me
    also from amóng the | horns | of the | unicorns.

mf 22 I will declare thy Náme | unto my | brethren : in the
    midst of the cóngre- | -gation | will I | praise thee.

f 23 O praise the Lórd | ye that | fear him : magnify him all
    ye of the seed of Jacob * and féar him | all ye | seed
    of | Israel ;

24 For he hath not despised nor abhorred the low estáte |
    of the | poor : he hath not hid his face from him * but
    when he cálled | unto | him he | heard him.

25 My praise is of thee in the gréat | congre- | -gation : my
    vows will I perfórm in the | sight of | them that | fear
    him.

26 The poor shall éat | and be | satisfied : they that seek
    after the Lord shall praise him * yóur | heart shall |
    live for | ever.

27 All the ends of the world shall remember themselves *
    and be túrned | unto . the | Lord : and all the kíndreds
    of the | nations . shall | worship . be- | -fore him.

28 For the kíngdom | is the | Lord's : and he is the Góver- |
    nour a- | -mong the | people.

29 All súch as be | fat up- . -on | earth : háve | eaten | and |
    worshipped.

30 All they that go down into the dúst shall | kneel be- |
    fore him : and nó man hath | quickened . his | own | soul.

31 Mý | seed shall | serve him : they shall be counted unto
    the Lórd | for a | gener- | -ation.

32 They shall come * and the héavens shall de- | -clare his |
    righteousness : unto a people that shall be bórn |
    whom the | Lord hath | made.

Psalm xl.—*Expectans expectavi.*

mf I WAITED pátiently | for the | Lord : and he inclined
    únto | me and | heard my | calling.

2 He brought me also out of the horrible pit * óut of the |
    mire and | clay : and set my feet upon the róck, and |
    ordered | my | goings.

3 And he hath put a new sóng | in my | mouth : even a
    thánks- | -giving | unto . our | God.

4 Mány shall | see it . and | fear : and shall pút their . |
    trust | in the | Lord.

5 Blessed is the man that hath set his hópe | in the |
    Lord : and turned not unto the proud * and to súch
    as | go a- | -bout with | lies.

6 O Lord my God, great are the wondrous works which
    thou hast done * like as be also thy thóughts which |
    are to | us-ward : and yet there is no man that
    órdereth | them | unto | thee.

7 If I should decláre them, and | speak of | them : they
    should be more than I' am | able | to ex- | -press.

8 Sacrifice and meat-óffering thou | wouldest | not : bút mine | ears | hast thou | opened.

9 Burnt-offerings and sacrifice for sin * hast thóu | not re- | -quired : thén | said I | Lo I | come,

10 In the volume of the book it is written of me * that I should fulfil thy wíll | O my | God : I am content to do it * yea, thy láw | is with- | -in my | heart.

11 I have declared thy righteousness in the gréat | congre- | gation : lo, I will not refrain my líps, O | Lord and | that thou | knowest.

12 I have not hid thy ríghteousness with- | -in my | heart : my talk hath been of thy trúth | and of | thy sal- | -va- tion.

2nd part. 13 I have not kept back thy lóving | mercy . and | truth : fróm the | great | congre- | -gation.

mp 14 Withdraw not thou thy mércy from | me O | Lord : let thy loving-kindness and thy trúth | al- | -way pre- | serve me.

15 For innumerable troubles are come about me * my sins have taken such hold upon me * that I am not áble to | look | up : yea, they are more in number than the hairs of my head * ánd my | heart hath | failed | me.

16 O Lord, let it be thy pléasure to de- | -liver | me : máke | haste O | Lord to | help me.

17 Let them be ashamed and confounded together * that seek after my sóul | to de- | -stroy it : let them be driven backward * and pút to re- | buke that | wish me | evil.

18 Let them be desolate, ánd re- | -warded . with | shame : that say unto me, Fíe up- | -on thee | fie up- | -on thee.

19 Let all those that seek thee be jóyful and | glad in | thee : and let such as love thy salvation say álway The | Lord | be | praised.

20 As for mé, I am | poor and | needy : bút the | Lord | careth | for me.

21 Thou art my hélper | and re- | -deemer : make nó long | tarrying | O my | God.

Psalm liv.—*Deus, in nomine.*

mp SAVE me, O Gód, for thy | Name's | sake : ánd a- | venge me | in thy | strength.

2 Héar my | prayer O | God : and hearken únto the | words | of my | mouth.

2nd part.

3 For strangers are rísen | up a- | -gainst me : and tyrants, which have not God before their éyes | seek | after . my | soul.

4 Behold, Gód | is my | helper : the Lord is with thém | that up- | -hold my | soul.

5 He shall reward évil | unto . mine | enemies : destróy thou | them | in thy | truth.

6 An offering of a free heart will I give thee * and práise thy | Name O | Lord : bé- | -cause it | is so | comfortable.

7 For he hath delivered me óut of | all my | trouble : and mine eye hath séen his de- | -sire up- | -on mine | enemies.

EVENING PRAYER.

PSALM lxix.—*Salvum me fac.*

F. mp SÁVE | me O | God : for the waters are come ín | even | unto . my | soul.

F. 2 I stick fast in the deep mire * whére no | ground | is : I am come into deep waters * só that the | floods run | over | me.

3 I am weary of crýing; my | throat is | dry : my sight faileth me for wáiting so | long up- | -on my | God.

4 They that hate me without a cause are more than the háirs | of my | head : they that are mine enemies, and wóuld de- | -stroy me | guiltless . are | mighty.

5 I paid them the thíngs that I | never | took : God, thou knowest my simpleness * and my fáults | are not | hid from | thee.

6 Let not them that trust in thee, O Lord God of hosts * be ashámed for | my | cause : let not those that seek thee * be confounded through mé, O | Lord | God of | Israel.

7 And why * for thy sáke have I | suffered . re- | -proof : sháme hath | covered | my | face.

8 I am become a stránger | unto . my | brethren : even an álien | unto . my | mother's | children.

9 For the zeal of thine house hath éven | eaten | me : and the rebukes of them that rebúked | thee are | fallen . up- | -on me.

10 I wept, and chástened mý- | -self with | fasting : and
that was | turned . to | my re- | -proof.

11 I pút on | sackcloth | also : ánd they | jested . up- | -on |
me.

12 They that sit in the gáte | speak a- | -gainst me : ánd
the | drunkards . make | songs up- | -on me.

13 But, Lord, I make my práyer | unto | thee : ín | an ac- |
ceptable | time.

14 Hear me, O God, in the múltitude | of thy | mercy : even
ín the | truth of | thy sal- | -vation.

15 Take me out of the míre | that I | sink not : O let me be
delivered from them that hate me * ánd | out . of the |
deep | waters.

16 Let not the water-flood drown me * neither let the déep |
swallow . me | up : and let not the pít | shut her |
mouth up- | -on me.

17 Hear me, O Lord, for thy lóving- | -kindness . is |
comfortable : turn thee unto me, accórding to the |
multitude | of thy | mercies.

18 And hide not thy face from thy sérvant, for | I am . in |
trouble : O' | haste | thee and | hear me.

19 Draw nígh unto my | soul and | save it : O delíver me,
be- | -cause of | mine | enemies.

20 Thou hast known my reproof, my sháme and | my dis- |
honour : mine ádversaries are | all in | thy | sight.

21 Thy rebuke hath broken my heart * I' am | full of |
heaviness : I looked for some to have pity on me, but
there was no man * neither fóund I | any . to |
comfort | me.

22 They gáve me | gall to | eat : and when I was thirsty
they gáve me | vine- | -gar to | drink.

23 Let their table be made a snare to táke them- | -selves
with- | -al : and let the things that should have been
for their wealth * be unto thém | an oc- | -casion . of |
falling.

24 Let their eyes be blínded | that they | see not : and
éver | bow thou | down their | backs.

25 Pour out thine índig- | -nation . up- | -on them : and let
thy wráthful dis- | -pleasure . take | hold of | them.

26 Let their hábit- | -ation . be | void : and nó man to |
dwell | in their | tents.

27 For they persecute hím whom | thou hast | smitten : and
they talk how they may véx | them whom | thou hast |
wounded.

28 Let them fall from one wickedness | to an- | -other : and | not come | into . thy | righteousness.

29 Let them be wiped out of the book | of the | living : and not be | written . a- | -mong the | righteous.

30 As for me, when I am poor | and in | heaviness : thy help, O | God shall | lift me | up.

f 31 I will praise the Name of God | with a | song : and magni- | -fy it . with | thanks- | -giving.

32 This also shall | please the | Lord : better than a bullock | that hath | horns and | hoofs.

33 The humble shall consider this | and be | glad : seek ye after God | and your | soul shall | live.

34 For the Lord | heareth . the | poor : and de- | -spiseth | not his | prisoners.

35 Let heaven and | earth | praise him : the sea, and | all that | moveth . there- | -in.

36 For God will save Sion * and build the | cities . of | Judah : that men may dwell there, and | have it | in pos- | -session.

2nd part. 37 The posterity also of his servants shall in- | -herit | it : and they that love his | Name shall | dwell there- | -in.

PSALM lxxxviii.—*Domine Deus.*

mp O LORD God of my salvation * I have cried day and | night be- | -fore thee : O let my prayer enter into thy presence * incline thine | ear | unto . my | calling.

2 For my soul is | full of | trouble : and my life draweth | nigh | unto | hell.

3 I am counted as one of them that go down | into . the | pit : and I have been even as a | man that | hath no | strength.

4 Free among the dead * like unto them that are wounded and lie | in the | grave : who are out of remembrance * and are cut a- | -way | from thy | hand.

5 Thou hast laid me in the | lowest | pit : in a place of | darkness . and | in the | deep.

6 Thine indignation lieth | hard up- | -on me : and thou hast vexed | me with | all thy | storms.

7 Thou hast put away mine acquaintance | far | from me : and made me to | be ab- | -horred | of them.

8 I am so | fast in | prison : that I | cannot | get | forth.

9 My sight fáileth for | very | trouble : Lord, I have called daily upon thee * I have stretched fórth my | hands | unto | thee.

10 Dost thou shew wónders a- | -mong the | dead : or shall the déad rise | up a- | -gain and | praise thee ?

11 Shall thy loving-kindness be shéwed | in the | grave : ór thy | faithfulness | in de- | -struction ?

12 Shall thy wondrous works be knówn | in the | dark : and thy righteousness in the lánd where | all things | are for- | -gotten ?

13 Unto thée have I | cried . O | Lord : and early sháll my | prayer | come be- | -fore thee.

14 Lord, why abhórrest | thou my | soul : and hídest | thou thy | face | from me ?

15 I am in misery * and like unto him that is át the | point to | die : even from my youth up, thy terrors have I súffered | with a | troubled | mind.

16 Thy wrathful displeasure góeth | over | me : and the féar of | thee | hath un- | -done me.

17 They came round abóut me | daily . like | water : and cómpassed me to- | -gether . on | every | side.

18 My lovers and friends hast thou pút a- | -way | from me : and híd mine ac- | -quaintance | out of . my | sight.

EASTER DAY.

MORNING PRAYER.

¶ *At Morning Prayer, instead of the Psalm, O come, let us sing, &c., these Anthems shall be sung or said.*

F. *f* CHRIST our passover is sácri- | -ficed . for | us : thére-fore | let us | keep the | feast.

F. 2 Not with the old leaven, nor with the léaven of | malice . and | wickedness : but with the unleavened bréad of sin- | -ceri- | -ty and | truth. 1 *Cor.* v. 7.

3 CHRIST being raised from the déad | dieth . no | more : death hath no móre do- | -minion | over | him.

p 4 For in that he died, he díed unto | sin | once : (*f*) but in that he líveth, he | liveth | unto | God.

5 Likewise reckon ye also yourselves to be déad indeed |
unto | sin : but alive unto Gód through | Jesus | Christ
our | Lord.   *Rom.* vi. 9.

6 Christ is rísen | from the | dead : and become the fírst- |
fruits of | them that | slept.

7 For sínce by | man came | death : by man came also the
résur- | -rection | of the | dead.

p 8 For as in A'dam | all | die : even so in Chríst (*f*) shall | all
be | made a- | -live.   1 *Cor.* xv. 20.

F. f   Glory be to the Fáther | and . to the | Son : ánd | to the |
Holy | Ghost ;

F.   As it was in the beginning * is nów, and | ever | shall be :
wórld without | end. | A- | -men.

Psalm ii.—*Quare fremuerunt gentes ?*

f WHY do the heathen so fúriously | rage to- | -gether :
and why do the péople im- | -agine . a | vain | thing?

2 The kings of the earth stand up * and the rúlers take |
counsel . to- | -gether : against the Lórd, and a- |
gainst | his A- | -nointed.

3 Let us bréak their | bonds a- | -sunder : and cást a- |
way their | cords | from us.

4 He that dwelleth in héaven shall | laugh them . to |
scorn : the Lórd shall | have them | in de- | -rision.

5 Then shall he speak unto thém | in his | wrath : and véx
them | in his | sore dis- | -pleasure.

6 Yét have I | set my | King : upón my | holy | hill of |
Sion.

7 I will preach the law * whereof the Lord hath sáid |
unto | me : Thou art my Son * this dáy have | I be- |
gotten | thee.

8 Desire of me * and I shall give thee the héathen for |
thine in- | -heritance : and the utmost párts of the |
earth for | thy pos- | -session.

9 Thou shalt brúise them with a | rod of | iron : and break
them in píeces | like a | potter's | vessel.

10 Be wise now thérefore | O ye | kings : be learned, yé that
are | judges | of the | earth.

11 Sérve the | Lord in | fear : and rejóice | unto | him with |
reverence.

12 Kiss the Son lest he be angry, and so ye pérish from the |
right | way : if his wrath be kindled, (yea, but a little,) *
blessed are all théy that | put their | trust in | him.

Psalm lvii.—*Miserere mei, Deus.*

mp BE merciful unto me, O God * be merciful unto me, for my soul | trusteth . in | thee : and under the shadow of thy wings shall be my refuge * until this | tyranny . be | over- | -past.

2 I will call unto the | most high | God : even unto the God that shall perform the cause | which I | have in | hand.

3 He shall | send from | heaven : and save me from the reproof of him | that would | eat me | up.

4 God shall send forth his | mercy . and | truth : my soul | is a- | -mong | lions.

5 And I lie even among the children of men that are | set on | fire : whose teeth are spears and arrows * and their | tongue a | sharp | sword.

6 Set up thyself, O God, a- | -bove the | heavens : and thy glory a- | -bove | all the | earth.

7 They have laid a net for my feet * and pressed | down my | soul : they have digged a pit before me * and are fallen into the | midst of | it them- | -selves.

8 My heart is fixed, O God, my | heart is | fixed : I will | sing and | give | praise.

mf 9 Awake up, my glory * awake | lute and | harp : I myself | will a- | -wake right | early.

10 I will give thanks unto thee, O Lord, a- | -mong the | people : and I will sing unto | thee a- | -mong the | nations.

11 For the greatness of thy mercy reacheth | unto . the | heavens : and thy | truth | unto . the | clouds.

12 Set up thyself, O God, a- | -bove the | heavens : and thy glory a- | -bove | all the | earth.

Psalm cxi.—*Confitebor tibi.*

mf I WILL give thanks unto the Lord with my | whole | heart : secretly among the faithful, and | in the | congre- | -gation.

2 The works of the | Lord are | great : sought out of all them | that have | pleasure . there- | -in.

3 His work is worthy to be praised, and | had in | honour : and his righteous- | -ness en- | -dureth . for | ever.

4 The merciful and gracious Lord hath so done his | marvellous | works : that they ought to be | had | in re- | membrance.

5 He hath given méat unto | them that | fear him : he shall
   éver be | mindful | of his | covenant.

6 He hath shewed his people the pówer | of his | works :
   that he may gíve them the | heritage | of the | heathen.

7 The works of his hands are vérity | and | judgement :
   áll | his com- | -mandments . are | true.

8 They stand fást for | ever . and | ever : ánd are | done
   in | truth and | equity.

9 He sent redémption | unto . his | people : he hath com-
   manded his covenant for ever * hóly and | reverend |
   is his | Name.

10 The fear of the Lórd is the be- | -ginning . of | wisdom :
   a good understanding have all they that do thereafter *
   the práise of | it en- | -dureth . for | ever.

EVENING PRAYER.

Psalm cxiii.—*Laudate, pueri.*

F. f PRÁISE the | Lord ye | servants : O práise the | Name |
     of the | Lord.

F. 2 Blessed be the Náme | of the | Lord : from thís time |
    forth for | ever- | -more.

3 The Lórd's | Name is | praised : from the rising up of
   the sun, unto the góing | down | of the | same.

4 The Lord is hígh a- | -bove all | heathen : ánd his |
   glory . a- | -bove the | heavens.

5 Who is like unto the Lord our God * that háth his |
   dwelling . so | high : and yet humbleth himself to
   behold the thíngs that | are in | heaven and | earth ?

6 He taketh up the símple | out . of the | dust : and
   lífteth the | poor | out . of the | mire ;

7 That he may sét him | with the | princes : even wíth
   the | princes | of his | people.

8 He maketh the barren wóman to | keep | house : and to
   bé a | joyful | mother . of | children.

Psalm cxiv.—*In exitu Israel.*

mf WHEN Israel cáme | out of | Egypt : and the house of
     Jacob fróm a- | -mong the | strange | people,

  2 Júdah | was his | sanctuary : ánd | Israel | his do- |
   minion.

3 The séa saw | that and | fled : Jór- | -dan was | driven | back.

4 The móuntains | skipped like | rams : and the líttle | hills like | young | sheep.

5 What aileth thee, O thou séa | that thou | fleddest : and thou Jórdan, that | thou wast | driven | back?

6 Ye mountains, thát ye | skipped . like | rams : and ye líttle | hills like | young | sheep?

7 Tremble thou earth, at the présence | of the | Lord : at the présence | of the | God of | Jacob ;

8 Who turned the hard róck into a | standing | water : and the flínt-stone | into . a | springing | well.

PSALM cxviii.—*Confitemini Domino.*

f   O GIVE thanks unto the Lórd, for | he is | gracious : becáuse his | mercy . en- | -dureth . for | ever.

2 Let Israel now conféss that | he is | gracious : and thát his | mercy . en- | -dureth . for | ever.

3 Let the house of Aáron | now con- | -fess : thát his | mercy . en- | -dureth . for | ever.

4 Yea, let them now that féar the | Lord con- | -fess : thát his | mercy . en- | -dureth . for | ever.

mf   5 I called upón the | Lord in | trouble : and the Lórd | heard | me at | large.

6 The Lórd is | on my | side : I will not féar what | man . doeth | unto | me.

7 The Lord taketh my párt with | them that | help me : therefore shall I sée my de- | -sire up- | -on mine | enemies.

8 It is better to trúst | in the | Lord : than to pút any | confi- | -dence in | man.

9 It is better to trúst | in the | Lord : than to pút any | confi- | -dence in | princes.

10 All nations cómpassed me | round a- | -bout : but in the Náme of the | Lord will | I de- | -stroy them.

11 They kept me in on every side * they kept me in, I sáy, on | every | side : but in the Náme of the | Lord will | I de- | -stroy them.

12 They came about me like bees * and are extinct even as the fíre a- | -mong the | thorns : for in the Náme of the | Lord I | will de- | -stroy them.

13 Thou hast thrust sore at mé, that | I might | fall : bút the | Lord | was my | help.

14 The Lord is my stréngth | and my | song : and ís be- | come | my sal- | -vation.

15 The voice of joy and health is in the dwéllings | of the | righteous : the right hand of the Lórd bringeth | mighty | things to | pass.

16 The right hand of the Lórd | hath . the pre- | -eminence : the right hand of the Lórd bringeth | mighty | things to | pass.

17 I sháll not | die but | live : and decláre the | works | of the | Lord.

18 The Lord hath chástened and cor- | -rected | me : but he hath not gíven me | over | unto | death.

19 Ópen me the | gates of | righteousness : that I may go into them * ánd give | thanks | unto . the | Lord.

20 This is the gáte | of the | Lord : the ríghteous shall | enter | into | it.

21 I will thánk thee, for | thou hast | heard me : and árt be- | -come | my sal- | -vation.

22 The same stóne which the | builders . re- | -fused : is becóme the | head-stone | in the | corner.

23 Thís is the | Lord's | doing : ánd it is | marvellous | in our | eyes.

24 This is the dáy which the | Lord hath | made : we will rejóice | and be | glad in | it.

25 Hélp me | now O | Lord : O Lórd | send us | now pros- | perity.

26 Blessed be he that cometh in the Náme | of the | Lord : we have wished you good luck * ye that áre of the | house | of the | Lord.

27 God is the Lórd who hath | shewed . us | light : bind the sacrifice with cords * yea, even únto the | horns | of the | altar.

28 Thou art my Gód, and | I will | thank thee : thóu art my | God and | I will | praise thee.

2nd part. 29 O give thanks unto the Lórd, for | he is | gracious : ánd his | mercy . en- | -dureth . for | ever.

ASCENSION DAY.

MORNING PRAYER.

PSALM viii.—*Domine, Dominus noster.*

F. ƒ **O** LORD our Governour * how excellent is thy Náme in | all the | world : thou that hast sét thy | glory . a- | bove the | heavens.

F. 2 Out of the mouth of very babes and sucklings hast thou ordained strength * becáuse | of thine | enemies : that thou mightest stíll the | enemy | and . the a- | -venger.

3 For I will consider thy heavens * even the wórks | of thy | fingers : the moon and the stárs | which thou | hast or- | -dained.

4 What is man, that thóu art | mindful . of | him : and the són of man | that thou | visitest | him ?

5 Thou madest him lówer | than the | angels : to crówn | him with | glory . and | worship.

6 Thou makest him to have dominion of the wórks | of thy | hands : and thou hast put all things ín sub- | jection | under . his | feet ;

7 Áll | sheep and | oxen : yéa, and the | beasts | of the | field ;

8 The fowls of the air, and the físhes | of the | sea : and whatsoever walketh thróugh the | paths | of the | seas.

2nd part. 9 Ó | Lord our | Governour : how excellent ís thy | Name in | all the | world !

PSALM xv.—*Domine, quis habitabit ?*

mƒ **L** ORD, who shall dwéll in thy | taber- | -nacle : or who shall rést up- | -on thy | holy | hill ?

2 Even he that léadeth an | uncorrupt | life : and doeth the thing which is right * and spéaketh the | truth | from his | heart.

3 He that hath used no deceit in his tongue * nor done évil | to his | neighbour : ánd | hath not | slandered . his | neighbour.

4 He that setteth not by himself * but is lówly in his | own | eyes : and maketh múch of | them that | fear the | Lord.

5 He that sweareth unto his neighbour * and disap- |
pointeth . him | not : though it | were . to his | own |
hindrance.

6 He that hath not given his móney up- | -on | usury : nor
táken re- | -ward a- | -gainst the | innocent.

2nd part. 7 Whóso | doeth . these | things : shall | ne- | -ver | fall.

PSALM xxi.—*Domine, in virtute tua.*

mf THE King shall rejóice in thy | strength O | Lord :
exceeding glád shall he | be of | thy sal- | -vation.

2 Thou hast gíven him his | heart's de- | -sire : and hast
not deníed him the re- | -quest | of his | lips.

3 For thou shalt prevent him wíth the | blessings . of |
goodness : and shalt set a crówn of pure | gold up- |
on his | head.

4 He asked life of thee * and thou gávest him a | long |
life : éven for | ever | and | ever.

5 His honour is gréat in | thy sal- | -vation : glory and
great wórship | shalt thou | lay up- | -on him.

6 For thou shalt give him éver- | -lasting . fe- | -licity : and
make him glád with the | joy | of thy | counten-
ance.

7 And why * because the King putteth his trúst | in the |
Lord : and in the mercy of the Most Híghest | he
shall | not mis- | -carry.

8 All thine énemies shall | feel thy | hand : thy right hánd
shall | find out | them that | hate thee.

9 Thou shalt make them like a fiery oven in tíme | of thy |
wrath : the Lord shall destroy them in his displeasure *
ánd the | fire | shall con- | -sume them.

10 Their fruit shalt thou róot | out . of the | earth : and their
séed from a- | -mong the | children . of | men.

11 For they inténded | mischief . a- | -gainst thee : and
imagined such a device as they áre not | able | to
per- | -form.

12 Therefore shalt thou pút | them to | flight : and the
strings of thy bow shalt thou make réady a- | -gainst
the | face of | them.

2nd part. 13 Be thou exalted, Lórd, in thine | own | strength : só will
we | sing and | praise thy | power.

———

EVENING PRAYER.

Psalm xxiv.—*Domini est terra.*

F. *f* THE earth is the Lord's * and áll that | therein | is :
the compass of the wórld, and | they that | dwell
there- | -in.

F. 2 For he hath fóunded it up- | -on the | seas : and
prepáred | it up- | -on the | floods.

3 Who shall ascend into the híll | of the | Lord : or who
shall rise úp | in his | holy | place ?

4 Even he that hath clean hánds and a | pure | heart : and
that hath not lift up his mind unto vanity * nor
swórn | to de- | -ceive his | neighbour.

5 He shall receive the bléssing | from the | Lord : and
righteousness fróm the | God of | his sal- | -vation.

6 This is the generátion of | them that | seek him : even of
thém that | seek thy | face O | Jacob.

7 Lift up your heads, O ye gates * and be ye lift up, ye éver- |
lasting | doors : and the Kíng of | glory | shall come |
in.

8 Whó is the | King of | glory : it is the Lord strong and
mighty * éven the | Lord | mighty . in | battle.

9 Lift up your heads, O ye gates * and be ye lift up, ye
éver- | -lasting | doors : and the Kíng of | glory | shall
come | in.

10 Whó is the | King of | glory : even the Lord of hósts |
he . is the | King of | glory.

Psalm xlvii.—*Omnes gentes, plaudite.*

f O CLAP your hands togéther | all ye | people : O sing
unto Gód | with the | voice of | melody.

2 For the Lord is hígh, and | to be | feared : he is the great
Kíng up- | -on | all the | earth.

3 He shall subdue the péople | under | us : ánd the |
nations | under . our | feet.

4 He shall choose óut an | heritage | for us : even the
wórship of | Jacob | whom he | loved.

5 God is gone úp with a | merry | noise : and the Lórd
with the | sound | of the | trump.

6 O sing praises, sing práises | unto . our | God : O sing
práises, sing | praises | unto . our | King.

7 For God is the Kíng of | all the | earth : síng ye | praises . with | under- | -standing.

8 God réigneth | over . the | heathen : God sítteth up- | on his | holy | seat.

2nd part. 9 The princes of the people * are joined unto the péople of the | God of | Abraham : for God, which is very high exalted * doth defend the éarth as it | were | with a | shield.

PSALM cviii.—Paratum cor meum.

mf O GOD, my heart is réady, my | heart is | ready : I will sing and give praise with the bést | member | that I | have.

2 Awáke, thou | lute and | harp : I mysélf | will a- | -wake right | early.

3 I will give thanks unto thee, O Lórd, a- | -mong the | people : I will sing práises unto | thee a- | -mong the | nations.

4 For thy mercy is gréater | than the | heavens : and thy trúth | reacheth | unto . the | clouds.

5 Set up thyself, O Gód, a- | -bove the | heavens : and thy glóry a- | -bove | all the | earth.

6 That thy belóved may | be de- | -livered : let thy right hand sáve | them and | hear thou | me.

7 God hath spóken | in his | holiness : I will rejoice therefore, and divide Sichem * and méte | out the | valley . of | Succoth.

8 Gilead is míne, and Ma- | -nasses . is | mine : Ephraim also ís the | strength | of my | head.

2nd part. 9 Judah is my law-giver * Móab | is my | washpot : over Edom will I cast out my shoe * upón Phi- | -listia | will I | triumph.

10 Who will lead me ínto the | strong | city : and whó will | bring me | into | Edom ?

11 Hast not thou forsáken | us O | God : and wilt not thou, O Gód, go | forth | with our | hosts ?

12 O hélp us a- | -gainst the | enemy : for váin | is the | help of | man.

13 Through Gód we shall | do great | acts : and it is hé that shall | tread | down our | enemies.

WHITSUNDAY.

MORNING PRAYER.

Psalm xlviii.—*Magnus Dominus.*

F. *f* GREAT is the Lord, and híghly | to be | praised : in the city of our God * éven up- | -on his | holy | hill.

F. 2 The hill of Sion is a fair place * and the jóy of the | whole | earth : upon the north-side lieth the city of the great King * God is well known in her pálaces | as a | sure | refuge.

3 For lo, the kíngs | of the | earth : are gáthered and / gone | by to- | -gether.

4 They márvelled to | see such | things : they were astónished, and | suddenly | cast | down.

5 Fear came thére upon | them and | sorrow : as upón a | woman | in her | travail.

6 Thou shalt breạk the shíps | of the | sea : throúgh |— the | east- | -wind.

7 Like as we have heard * so have we seen in the city of the Lord of hosts * in the cíty | of our | God : Gód up- | -holdeth . the | same for | ever.

8 We wait for thy lóving- | -kindness . O | God : ín the | midst of | thy | temple.

9 O God, according to thy Name * so is thy praise únto the | world's | end : thy ríght | hand is | full of | righteousness.

10 Let the mount Sion rejoice * and the dáughter of | Judah . be | glad : bé- | -cause of | thy | judgements.

11 Walk about Sion, and gó | round a- | -bout her : ánd | tell the | towers there- | -of.

12 Mark well her bulwarks, sét | up her | houses : that ye may téll | them that | come | after.

2nd part. 13 For this God is our Gód for | ever . and | ever : he shall bé our | guide | unto | death.

Psalm lxviii.—*Exurgat Deus.*

f LET God arise, and let his éne- | -mies be | scattered : let them álso that | hate him | flee be- | -fore him.

2 Like as the smoke vanisheth * so shalt thou dríve | them a- | -way : and like as wax melteth at the fire * so let the ungodly pérish | at the | presence . of | God.

3 But let the righteous be glád and re- | -joice be- . -fore |
God : lét them | also . be | merry . and | joyful.

4 O sing unto God, and sing práises | unto . his | Name :
magnify him that rideth upon the heavens as it were
upon an horse * praise him in his Name JA'H | and
re- | -joice be- | -fore him.

5 He is a Father of the fatherless * and defendeth the
cáuse | of the | widows : even Gód in his | holy |
habit- | -ation.

6 He is the God that maketh men to be of one mind in an
house * and bringeth the prísoners | out of . cap- | -tivity :
but letteth the runagátes con- | -tinue | in | scarceness.

7 O God, when thou wentest fórth be- | -fore the | people :
whén thou | wentest | through the | wilderness.

8 The earth shook, and the heavens dropped át the |
presence . of | God : even as Sinai also was moved at
the presence of Gód, who | is the | God of | Israel.

9 Thou, O God, sentest a gracious ráin upon | thine in- |
heritance : and refréshedst | it when | it was | weary.

10 Thy congregátion shall | dwell there- | -in : for thou, O
God, hast of thy góodness pre- | -pared | for the | poor.

11 The Lórd | gave the | word : gréat was the | company | of
the | preachers.

12 Kings with their armies did flée, and | were dis- | -comfited :
and théy of the | household . di- | -vided . the | spoil.

13 Though ye have lien among the pots * yet shall ye be as
the wíngs | of a | dove : that is covered with silver
wíngs | and her | feathers . like | gold.

14 When the Almighty scattered kíngs | for their | sake :
thén were they as | white as | snow in | Salmon.

15 As the hill of Basan, só is | God's | hill : even an hígh
hill | as the | hill of | Basan.

16 Why hop ye so, ye high hills * this is God's hill, in the
which it pléaseth | him to | dwell : yea, the Lórd will
a- | -bide in | it for | ever.

17 The chariots of God are twenty thousand * éven |
thousands . of | angels : and the Lord is among them *
as ín the | holy | place of | Sinai.

18 Thou art gone .up on high * thou hast led captivity
captive, and recéived | gifts for | men : yea, even for
thine enemies * that the Lórd | God might | dwell a- |
mong them.

19 Praised bé the | Lord | daily : even the God who helpeth
us, and póureth his | bene- | -fits up- | -on us.

20 He is our God * even the Gód of whom | cometh . sal- | vation : God is the Lórd, by | whom . we es- | -cape | death.

21 God shall wound the héad | of his | enemies : and the hairy scalp of such a one as góeth on | still | in his | wickedness.

22 The Lord hath said * I will bring my people agáin as I | did from | Basan : mine own will I bring again * as I did sometime fróm the | deep | of the | sea.

2nd part. 23 That thy foot may be dipped in the blóod | of thine | enemies : and that the tongue of thy dógs may be | red | through the | same.

24 It is well seen, O Gód | how thou | goest : how thou, my God and Kíng | goest | in the | sanctuary.

25 The singers go before * the mínstrels | follow | after : in the midst are the dámsels | playing | with the | timbrels.

26 Give thanks, O Israel, unto God the Lórd in the | congre- | -gations : fróm the | ground | of the | heart.

27 There is little Benjamin their ruler * and the prínces of | Judah . their | counsel : the princes of Zabúlon | and the | princes . of | Nephthali.

28 Thy God hath sént forth | strength for | thee : stablish the thing, O Gód, that | thou hast | wrought in | us.

29 For thy temple's sáke | at Je- | -rusalem : so shall kíngs bring | presents | unto | thee.

30 When the company of the spear-men, and multitude of the mighty * are scattered abroad among the beasts of the people * so that they húmbly bring | pieces . of | silver : and when he hath scattered the péople | that de- | -light in | war;

31 Then shall the princes cóme | out of | Egypt : the Morians' land shàll soon stretch óut her | hands | unto | God.

ff 32 Sing unto God, O ye kíngdoms | of the | earth : O′ sing | praises | unto . the | Lord;

33 Who sitteth in the heavens over áll | from . the be- | ginning : lo, he doth send out his voice * yéa, and | that a | mighty | voice.

34 Ascribe ye the power to Gód | over | Israel : his wórship and | strength is | in the | clouds.

35 O God, wonderful art thóu in thy | holy | places : even the God of Israel * he will give strength and power unto his péople | blessed | be | God.

EVENING PRAYER.

Psalm civ.—*Benedic, anima mea.*

ᵍ. *f* PRAISE the Lórd | O my | soul : O Lord my God, thou
art become exceeding glorious * thou art clóthed with |
majes- | -ty and | honour.

ᵍ. 2 Thou deckest thyself with light as it wére | with a |
garment : and spreadest óut the | heavens | like a |
curtain.

3 Who layeth the beams of his chámbers | in the | waters :
and maketh the clouds his chariot * and walketh upón
the | wings | of the | wind.

4 He máketh his | angels | spirits : and his mínis- | -ters
a | flaming | fire.

5 He laid the foundátions | of the | earth : that it néver
should | move at | any | time.

6 Thou coveredst it with the deep, líke as | with a |
garment : the wáters | stand | in the | hills.

7 At thý re- | -buke they | flee : at the vóice of thy | thunder .
they | are a- | -fraid.

8 They go up as high as the hills * and dówn to the |
valleys . be- | -neath : even unto the pláce which |
thou . hast ap- | -pointed | for them.

9 Thou hast set them their bóunds which they | shall
not | pass : neither túrn a- | -gain to | cover . the |
earth.

10 He sendeth the spríngs | into . the | rivers : whích | run
a- | -mong the | hills.

11 All beasts of the fiéld | drink there- | -of : ánd the wild |
asses | quench their | thirst.

12 Beside them shall the fowls of the áir have their | habit- |
ation : ánd | sing a- | -mong the | branches.

13 He watereth the hílls | from a- | -bove : the earth is fílled
with the | fruit | of thy | works.

14 He bringeth forth gráss | for the | cattle : and green
hérb | for the | service . of | men ;

15 That he may bring food out of the earth * and wine that
maketh glád the | heart of | man : and oil to make him
a cheerful countenance * and bréad to | strengthen |
man's | heart.

16 The trees of the Lord álso are | full of | sap : even the
cedars of Líban- | -us which | he hath | planted ;

17 Wherein the bírds | make their | nests : and the fir-trees áre a | dwelling | for the | stork.

18 The high hills are a refuge fór the | wild | goats : and so are the stóny | rocks | for the | conies.

19 He appointed the móon for | certain | seasons : and the sún | knoweth . his | going | down.

20 Thou makest darkness * thát it | may be | night : wherein all the béasts | of the | forest . do | move.

21 The lions róaring | after . their | prey : dó | seek their | meat from | God.

22 The sun ariseth * and they gét them a- | -way to- | gether : and láy them | down | in their | dens.

2nd part. 23 Man goeth forth to his wórk, and | to his | labour : ún- | til the | even- | -ing.

ff 24 O Lord, how mánifold | are thy | works : in wisdom hast thou made them all * the éarth is | full | of thy | riches.

25 So is the gréat and | wide sea | also : wherein are things creeping innumerable * bóth | small and | great | beasts.

f 26 There go the ships * and thére is | that Le- | -viathan : whom thou hast máde to | take his | pastime . there- | in.

27 These wáit | all up- . -on | thee : that thou mayest gíve them | meat in | due | season.

28 When thou givest it thém they | gather | it : and when thou openest thy hánd | they are | filled . with | good.

mp 29 When thou hidest thy fáce | they are | troubled : when thou takest away their breath they die * and are túrned a- | -gain | to their | dust.

mf 30 When thou lettest thy breath go fórth they | shall be | made : and thou shalt renéw the | face | of the | earth.

f 31 The glorious Majesty of the Lórd shall en- | -dure for | ever : the Lórd shall re- | -joice | in his | works.

32 The earth shall trémble at the | look of | him : if he do but toúch the | hills | they shall | smoke.

33 I will sing unto the Lórd as | long as . I | live : I will praise my Gód | while I | have my | being.

34 And só shall my | words | please him : my jóy shall | be | in the | Lord.

35 As for sinners, they shall be consumed out of the earth * and the ungódly shall | come . to an | end : praise thou the Lord, O my sóul | praise | — the | Lord.

PSALM CXLV.—*Exaltabo te, Deus.*

mf   I WILL magnify thée, O | God my | King : and I will práise thy | Name for | ever . and | ever.

2 Every day will I give thánks | unto | thee : and práise thy | Name for | ever . and | ever.

3 Great is the Lord, and marvellous ✻ wórthy | to be | praised : there ís no | end | of his | greatness.

4 One generation shall praise thy wórks | unto . an- | other : ánd de- | -clare | thy | power.

5 As for me, I will be tálking | of thy | worship : thy glóry, thy | praise and | wondrous | works ;

6 So that men shall speak of the míght of thy | marvel- lous | acts : and I will álso | tell | of thy | greatness.

7 The memorial of thine abundant kíndness | shall be | shewed : and mén shall | sing | of thy | righteousness.

8 The Lórd is | gracious . and | merciful : long-súffering | and of | great | goodness.

9 The Lord is loving únto | every | man : and his mércy is | over | all his | works.

10 All thy works práise | thee O | Lord : and thy sáints give | thanks | unto | thee.

11 They shew the glóry | of thy | kingdom : ánd | talk | of thy | power ;

12 That thy power, thy glory, and míghtiness | of thy | king- dom : míght be | known | unto | men.

13 Thy kingdom is an éver- | -lasting | kingdom : and thy domínion en- | -dureth . through- | -out all | ages.

14 The Lord uphóldeth all | such as | fall : and lifteth úp all | those | that are | down.

15 The eyes of all wáit upon | thee O | Lord : and thou gívest them their | meat in | due | season.

16 Thou ópenest | thine | hand : and fíllest | all things | living . with | plenteousness.

17 The Lord is ríghteous in | all his | ways : ánd | holy . in | all his | works.

18 The Lord is nigh unto all thém that | call up- | -on him : yea, áll such as | call up- | -on him | faithfully.

19 He will fulfil the desíre of | them that | fear him : he also will héar their | cry | and will | help them.

20 The Lord presérveth all | them that | love him : but scáttereth a- | -broad | all . the un- | -godly.

2nd part. 21 My mouth shall speak the práise | of the | Lord : and let all flesh give thanks unto his hóly | Name for | ever . and | ever.

FORMS OF PRAYER TO BE USED AT SEA.

¶ *The Morning and Evening Service to be used daily at Sea shall be the same which is appointed in the Book of Common Prayer.*

¶ *These two following Prayers are to be also used in her Majesty's Navy every day.*

O ETERNAL Lord God, who alone spreadest out the heavens, and rulest the raging of the sea; who hast compassed the waters with bounds until day and night come to an end; Be pleased to receive into thy Almighty and most gracious protection the persons of us thy servants, and the Fleet in which we serve. Preserve us from the dangers of the sea, and from the violence of the enemy; that we may be a safeguard unto our most gracious Sovereign Lady, Queen *VICTORIA,* and her Dominions, and a security for such as pass on the seas upon their lawful occasions; that the inhabitants of our Island may in peace and quietness serve thee our God; and that we may return in safety to enjoy the blessings of the land, with the fruits of our labours, and with a thankful remembrance of thy mercies to praise and glorify thy holy Name; through Jesus Christ our Lord. *A - men.*

THE COLLECT.

PREVENT us, O Lord, in all our doings, with thy most gracious favour, and further us with thy continual help; that in all our works begun, continued, and ended in thee, we may glorify thy holy Name, and finally by thy mercy obtain everlasting life; through Jesus Christ our Lord. *Amen.*

¶ *Prayers to be used in Storms at Sea.*

O MOST powerful and glorious Lord God, at whose command the winds blow, and lift up the waves of the sea, and who stillest the rage thereof; We thy creatures, but miserable sinners, do in this our great distress cry unto thee for help: Save, Lord, or else we perish. We confess, when we have been safe, and seen all things quiet about us, we have forgot thee our God, and refused to hearken to the still voice of thy word, and to obey thy commandments: But now we see, how terrible thou art in all thy works of wonder ; the great God to be feared above all : And therefore we adore thy Divine Majesty, acknowledging thy power, and imploring thy goodness. Help, Lord, and save us for thy mercy's sake in Jesus Christ thy Son, our Lord. *Amen.*

Or this.

O MOST glorious and gracious Lord God, who dwellest in heaven, but beholdest all things below ; Look down we beseech thee, and hear us, calling out of the depth of misery, and out of the jaws of this death, which is ready now to swallow us up : Save, Lord, or else we perish. The living, the living, shall praise thee. O send thy word of command to rebuke the raging winds, and the roaring sea ; that we, being delivered from this distress, may live to serve thee, and to glorify thy Name all the days of our life. Hear, Lord, and save us, for the infinite merits of our blessed Saviour, thy Son, our Lord Jesus Christ. *Amen.*

¶ *The Prayer to be said before a Fight at Sea against any Enemy.*

O MOST powerful and glorious Lord God, the Lord of hosts, that rulest and commandest all things ; Thou sittest in the throne judging right, and therefore we make our address to thy Divine Majesty in this our necessity, that thou wouldest take the cause into thine own hand, and judge between us and our enemies. Stir up thy strength, O Lord, and come and help us ; for thou givest not alway the battle to the strong, but canst save by many or by few. O let not our sins now cry against us for vengeance ; but hear us thy poor servants begging mercy, and imploring thy help, and that thou wouldest be a defence unto us against the face of the enemy. Make it appear that thou art our Saviour and mighty Deliverer, through Jesus Christ our Lord. *Amen.*

¶ *Short Prayers for single persons, that cannot meet to join in Prayer with others, by reason of the Fight, or Storm.*

GENERAL PRAYERS.

LORD, be merciful to us sinners, and save us for thy mercy's sake.

Thou art the great God, that hast made and rulest all things : O deliver us for thy Name's sake.

Thou art the great God to be feared above all : O save us, that we may praise thee.

SPECIAL PRAYERS WITH RESPECT TO THE ENEMY.

THOU, O Lord, art just and powerful : O defend our cause against the face of the enemy.

O God, thou art a strong tower of defence to all that flee unto thee : O save us from the violence of the enemy.

O Lord of hosts, fight for us, that we may glorify thee.

O suffer us not to sink under the weight of our sins, or the violence of the enemy.

O Lord, arise, help us, and deliver us for thy Name's sake.

SHORT PRAYERS IN RESPECT OF A STORM.

THOU, O Lord, that stillest the raging of the sea, hear, hear us, and save us, that we perish not.

O blessed Saviour, that didst save thy disciples ready to perish in a storm, hear us, and save us, we beseech thee.

Lord, have mercy upon us.

Christ, have mercy upon us.

Lord, have mercy upon us.

O Lord, hear us.

O Christ, hear us.

God the Father, God the Son, God the Holy Ghost, have mercy upon us, save us now and evermore. Amen.

OUR Father, which art in heaven, Hallowed be thy Name. Thy kingdom come. Thy will be done in earth, As it is in heaven. Give us this day our daily bread. And forgive us our trespasses, As we forgive them that trespass against us. And lead us not into temptation; But deliver us from evil: For thine is the kingdom, The power, and the glory, For ever and ever. Amen.

¶ *When there shall be imminent danger, as many as can be spared from necessary service in the Ship shall be called together, and make an humble Confession of their sin to God : In which every one ought seriously to reflect upon those particular sins of which his conscience shall accuse him; saying as followeth,*

THE CONFESSION.

ALMIGHTY God, Father of our Lord Jesus Christ, Maker of all things, Judge of all men ; We acknowledge and bewail our manifold sins and wickedness, Which we, from time to time, most grievously have committed, By thought, word, and deed, Against thy Divine Majesty, Provoking most justly thy wrath and indignation against us. We do earnestly repent, And are heartily sorry for these our misdoings; The remembrance of them is grievous unto us; The burden of them is intolerable. Have mercy upon us, Have mercy upon us, most merciful Father; For thy Son our Lord Jesus Christ's sake, Forgive us all that is past; And grant that we may ever hereafter Serve and please thee In newness of life, To the honour and glory of thy Name; Through Jesus Christ our Lord. Amen.

¶ *Then shall the Priest, if there be any in the Ship, pronounce this Absolution.*

ALMIGHTY God, our heavenly Father, who of his great mercy hath promised forgiveness of sins to all them that with hearty repentance and true faith turn unto him; Have mercy upon you; pardon and deliver you from all your sins; confirm and strengthen you in all goodness, and bring you to everlasting life; through Jesus Christ our Lord. *Amen.*

THANKSGIVING AFTER A STORM.

Jubilate Deo. Psalm lxvi.

f O BE joyful in Gód | all ye | lands : sing praises unto the honour of his Name * máke his | praise | to be | glorious.

2 Say unto God, O how wonderful art thóu | in thy | works : through the greatness of thy power * shall thine enemies be fóund | liars | unto | thee.

3 For all the wórld shall | worship | thee : síng of | thee and | praise thy | Name.

4 O come hither, and behóld the | works of | God : how wonderful he is in his dóing | toward . the | children . of | men.

5 He turned the séa into | dry | land : so that they went through the water on foot * thére did | we re- | -joice there- | -of.

6 He ruleth with his power for ever * his éyes be- | -hold the | people : and such as will not believe, shall not be áble | to ex- | -alt them- | -selves.

7 O práise our | God ye | people : and make the vóice of his | praise | to be | heard ;

8 Who hóldeth our | soul in | life : and súffereth | not our | feet to | slip.

9 For thou, O Gód, hast | proved | us : thou also hast tríed us | like as | silver . is | tried.

10 Thou bróughtest us | into . the | snare : and láidest | trouble . up- | -on our | loins.

11 Thou sufferedst men to ríde | over . our | heads : we went through fire and water * and thou broughtest us óut | into . a | wealthy | place.

12 I will go into thine hóuse with | burnt- | -offerings : and will pay thee my vows * which I promised with my lips, and spake with my móuth | when I | was in | trouble.

13 I will offer unto thee fat burnt-sacrifices * wíth the | incense . of | rams : I' will | offer | bullocks . and | goats.

14 O come hither, and hearken * all yé that | fear | God : and I will tell you what hé hath | done | for my | soul.

15 I called unto hím | with my | mouth : and gáve him | praises | with my | tongue.

16 If I incline unto wíckedness | with mine | heart : thé | Lord | will not | hear me.

17 Bút | God hath | heard me : and consídered the | voice | of my | prayer.

18 Praised be God, who hath nót cast | out my | prayer : nór | turned . his | mercy | from me.

F. f   Glory be to the Fáther, | and . to the | Son : ánd | to the | Holy | Ghost ;

F.   As it was in the beginning * is nów, and | ever | shall be : wórld without | end. | A- | -men.

Confitemini Domino. PSALM cvii.

mf O GIVE thanks unto the Lórd, for | he is | gracious : ánd his | mercy . en- | -dureth . for | ever.

2 Let them give thanks whom the Lórd | hath re- | -deemed : and delivered fróm the | hand | of the | enemy ;

3 And gathered them out of the lands * from the éast, and | from the | west : fróm the | north and | from the | south.

4 They went astray in the wílderness | out . of the | way : ánd | found no | city . to | dwell in ;

5 Húngry | and | thirsty : théir | soul | fainted | in them.

6 So they cried unto the Lórd | in their | trouble : and he delívered them | from | their dis- | -tress.

2nd part. 7 He led them fórth by the | right | way : that they might gó to the | city | where they | dwelt.

F. 8 O that men would therefore praise the Lórd | for his | goodness : and declare the wonders that he dóeth | for the | children . of | men !

9 For he satisfíeth the | empty | soul : and fílleth the | hungry | soul with | goodness.

10 Such as sit in darkness * and ín the | shadow . of | death : being fast bóund in | mise- | -ry and | iron ;

11 Because they rebelled against the wórds | of the | Lord : and lightly regarded the cóunsel | of the | most | Highest ;

12 He also brought dówn their | heart through | heaviness : they fell dówn, and | there was | none to | help them.

13 So when they cried unto the Lórd | in their | trouble : he delívered them | out of | their dis- | -tress.

2nd part. 14 For he brought them out of darkness * and óut of the | shadow . of | death : ánd | brake their | bonds in | sunder.

F. 15 O that men would therefore praise the Lórd | for his | goodness : and declare the wonders that he dóeth | for the | children . of | men !

16 For he hath bróken the | gates of | brass : and smítten the | bars of | iron . in | sunder.

17 Foolish men are plágued for | their of- | -fence : ánd be- | cause of | their | wickedness.

18 Their soul abhórred all | manner . of | meat : and they were éven | hard at | death's | door.

19 So when they cried unto the Lórd | in their | trouble : he delívered them | out of | their dis- | -tress.

20 He sent his wórd, and | healed | them : and théy were | saved . from | their de- | -struction.

F. 21 O that men would therefore praise the Lórd | for his | goodness : and declare the wonders that he dóeth | for the | children . of | men !

22 That they would offer unto him the sácrifice of | thanks- | giving : and téll | out his | works with | gladness !

23 They that go dówn to the | sea in | ships : and óccupy their | business . in | great | waters ;

24 These men see the wórks | of the | Lord : ánd his | wonders | in the | deep.

25 For at his word the stórmy | wind a- | -riseth : which lífteth | up the | waves there- | -of.

26 They are carried up to the heaven * and dówn again | to the | deep : their soul melteth awáy be- | -cause | of the | trouble.

27 They reel to and fro * and stagger líke a | drunken | man : ánd are | at their | wits' | end.

28 So when they cry unto the Lórd | in their | trouble : he delívereth them | out of | their dis- | -tress.

29 For he máketh the | storm to | cease : só that the | waves there- | -of are | still.

30 Then are they glad, becáuse they | are at | rest : and so he bringeth them unto the háven | where they | would | be.

F.   31 O that men would therefore praise the Lórd | for his | goodness : and declare the wonders that he dóeth | for the | children . of | men !

32 That they would exalt him also in the congregátion | of the | people : and práise him in the | seat | of the | elders !

33 Who turneth the flóods | into . a | wilderness : ánd | drieth | up the | water-springs.

34 A fruitful lánd | maketh . he | barren : for the wíckedness of | them that | dwell there- | -in.

35 Again, he maketh the wílderness a | standing | water : and wáter-springs | of a | dry | ground.

36 And thére he | setteth . the | hungry : that théy may | build . them a | city . to | dwell in ;

37 That they may sow their lánd, and | plant | vineyards : tó | yield them | fruits of | increase.

38 He blesseth them * so that they múlti- | -ply ex- | -ceedingly : and suffereth nót their | cattle | to de- | crease.

39 And again * when they are mínished and | brought | low : through oppréssion, through | any | plague or | trouble ;

40 Though he suffer them to be évil in- | -treated . through | tryants : and let them wander óut of the | way | in the | wilderness ;

41 Yet helpeth he the póor | out of | misery : and maketh him hóuseholds | like a | flock of | sheep.

42 The righteous will consider thís | and re- | -joice : and the móuth of all | wickedness | shall be | stopped.

2nd part.   43 Whoso is wíse will | ponder . these | things : and they shall understánd the loving- | -kindness | of the | Lord.

F. ƒ   Glory be to the Fáther, | and . to the | Son : ánd | to the | Hcly | Ghost ;

F.   As it was in the beginning * is nów, and | ever | shall be : wórld without | end. | A- | -men.

COLLECTS OF THANKSGIVING.

O MOST blessed and glorious Lord God, who art of infinite goodness and mercy; We thy poor creatures, whom thou hast made and preserved, holding our souls in life, and now rescuing us out of the jaws of death, humbly present ourselves again before thy Divine Majesty, to offer a sacrifice of praise and thanksgiving, for that thou heardest us when we called in our trouble, and didst not cast out our prayer, which we made before thee in our great distress: Even when we gave all for lost, our ship, our goods, our lives, then didst thou mercifully look upon us, and wonderfully command a deliverance; for which we, now being in safety, do give all praise and glory to thy holy Name; through Jesus Christ our Lord.

A - men.

Or this :

O MOST mighty and gracious good God, thy mercy is over all thy works, but in special manner hath been extended toward us, whom thou hast so powerfully and wonderfully defended. Thou hast shewed us terrible things, and wonders in the deep, that we might see how powerful and gracious a God thou art; how able and ready to help them that trust in thee. Thou hast shewed us how both winds and seas obey thy command; that we may learn, even from them, hereafter to obey thy voice, and to do thy will. We therefore bless and glorify thy Name, for this thy mercy in saving us, when we were ready to perish. And, we beseech thee, make us as truly sensible now of thy mercy, as we were then of the danger: And give us hearts always ready to express our thankfulness, not only by words, but also by our lives, in being more obedient to thy holy commandments. Continue, we beseech thee, this thy goodness to us; that we, whom thou hast saved, may serve thee in holiness and righteousness all the days of our life; through Jesus Christ our Lord and Saviour. *Amen.*

A HYMN OF PRAISE AND THANKSGIVING AFTER A DANGEROUS TEMPEST.

O COME, let us give thanks unto the Lórd, for | he is | gracious : ánd his | mercy . en- | -dureth . for | ever.
2 Great is the Lord, and greatly to be praised * let the redéemed of the | Lord say | so : whom he hath delivered from the mérciless | rage | of the | sea.

3 The Lord is gracious and fúll | of com- | -passion : slow to ánger, | and of | great | mercy.

4 He hath not dealt with us accórding | to our | sins : neither rewarded ús ac- | -cording . to | our in- | iquities.

5 But as the heaven is hígh a- | -bove the | earth : so great hath béen his | mer- | -cy to- | -wards us.

6 Wé found | trouble . and | heaviness : wé were | even . at | death's | door.

7 The waters of the sea had wéll-nigh | covered | us : the proud waters hád well-nigh | gone | over . our | soul.

8 Thé | sea | roared : and the stormy wind lífted | up the | waves there- | -of.

9 We were carried up as it were to heaven, and then dówn again | into the | deep : our soul melted within ús, be- | cause | of | trouble ;

10 Then cried we únto | thee O | Lord : and thou didst delíver us | out of | our dis- | -tress.

11 Blessed be thy Name, who didst not despise the práyer | of thy | servants : but didst hear our crý | and hast | saved | us.

12 Thou didst sénd forth | thy com- | -mandment : and the windy storm ceased, ánd was | turned | into . a | calm.

13 O let us therefore praise the Lórd | for his | goodness : and declare the wonders that he hath done, and still dóeth | for the | children . of | men.

14 Práised be the | Lord | daily : even the Lord that helpeth us, and póureth his | bene- | -fits up- | -on us.

15 He is our God, even the Gód of whom | cometh . sal- | vation : God is the Lord by whóm we | have es- | caped | death.

16 Thou, Lord, hast made us glad through the operátion | of thy | hands : and wé will | triumph | in thy | praise.

17 Bléssed be the | Lord | God : even the Lord God, whó only | doeth | wondrous | things ;

18 And blessed be the Name of his Májes- | -ty for | ever : and let every one of us sáy, | Amen | A- | -men.

F. f   Glory be to the Fáther, | and . to the | Son : ánd | to the | Holy | Ghost ;

F.   As it was in the beginning * is nów, and | ever | shall be : wórld without | end. | A- | -men.

2 *Cor.* xiii.

THE grace of our Lord Jesus Christ, and the love of God, and the fellowship of the Holy Ghost, be with us all evermore.

A - men.

AFTER VICTORY OR DELIVERANCE FROM AN ENEMY.

A Psalm or Hymn of Praise and Thanksgiving after Victory.

IF the Lord had not been on our side, nów | may we | say : if the Lord himself had not been on our síde, when | men rose | up a- | -gainst us ;

2 They had swállowed | us up | quick : when they were so wráthful- | -ly dis- | -pleased | at us.

3 Yea, the waters had drowned us * and the stréam had gone | over . our | soul : the deep waters of the próud had | gone | over . our | soul.

4 But práised | be the | Lord : who hath not given us óver as a | prey | unto | them.

5 The Lórd | hath | wrought : a míghty sal- | -va- | -tion for | us.

6 We gat not this by our own sword * neither was it our own árm that | saved | us : but thy right hand, and thine arm, and the light of thy countenance * because thou hádst a | favour | unto | us.

7 The Lord háth ap- | -peared | for us : the Lord hath covered our heads, and made ús to stand | in the | day of | battle.

8 The Lord háth ap- | -peared | for us : the Lord hath overthrown our enemies * and dashed in pieces thóse that | rose . up a- | -gainst | us.

9 Therefore not unto us, O Lórd, not | unto | us : but únto thy | Name be | given . the | glory.

10 The Lord háth done | great things | for us : the Lord hath done great things for us, fór | which | we re- | -joice.

11 Our help standeth in the Náme | of the | Lord : whó hath | made | heaven . and | earth.

12 Blessed be the Náme | of the | Lord : from thís time | forth for | ever- | -more.

F. f　Glory be to the Fáther, | and . to the | Son : ánd | to the | Holy | Ghost ;

F.　As it was in the beginning * is nów, and | ever | shall be : wórld without | end. | A- | -men.

¶ *After this Hymn may be sung the* Te Deum.

¶ *Then this Collect.*

O ALMIGHTY God, the Sovereign Commander of all the world, in whose hand is power and might which none is able to withstand; We bless and magnify thy great and glorious Name for this happy Victory, the whole glory whereof we do ascribe to thee, who art the only giver of Victory. And, we beseech thee, give us grace to improve this great mercy to thy glory, the advancement of thy Gospel, the honour of our Sovereign, and, as much as in us lieth, to the good of all mankind. And, we beseech thee, give us such a sense of this great mercy, as may engage us to a true thankfulness, such as may appear in our lives by an humble, holy, and obedient walking before thee all our days, through Jesus Christ our Lord; to whom with thee and the Holy Spirit, as for all thy mercies, so in particular for this Victory and Deliverance, be all glory and honour, world without end.

A - men.

2 *Cor.* xiii.

THE grace of our Lord Jesus Christ, and the love of God, and the fellowship of the Holy Ghost, be with us all evermore. *Amen.*

AT THE BURIAL OF THEIR DEAD AT SEA.

¶ *The Office in the Common Prayer-book may be used; only instead of these words* [We therefore commit *his* body to the ground, earth to earth, *&c.*] *say,*

WE therefore commit *his* body to the deep, to be turned into corruption, looking for the resurrection of the body, (when the Sea shall give up her dead,) and the life of the world to come, through our Lord Jesus Christ; who at his coming shall change our vile body, that it may be like his glorious body, according to the mighty working, whereby he is able to subdue all things to himself.

THE FORM AND MANNER OF

MAKING, ORDAINING, AND CONSECRATING

OF

BISHOPS, PRIESTS, AND DEACONS,

ACCORDING TO THE ORDER OF

The Church of England.

THE PREFACE.

*I*T *is evident unto all men diligently reading the holy Scripture and ancient Authors, that from the Apostles' time there have been these Orders of Ministers in Christ's Church; Bishops, Priests, and Deacons. Which Offices were evermore had in such reverend Estimation, that no man might presume to execute any of them, except he were first called, tried, examined, and known to have such qualities as are requisite for the same; and also by publick Prayer, with Imposition of Hands, were approved and admitted thereunto by lawful Authority. And therefore, to the intent that these Orders may be continued, and reverently used and esteemed, in the Church of England; no man shall be accounted or taken to be a lawful Bishop, Priest, or Deacon in the Church of England, or suffered to execute any of the said Functions, except he be called, tried, examined, and admitted thereunto, according to the Form hereafter following, or hath had formerly Episcopal Consecration, or Ordination.*

And none shall be admitted a Deacon, except he be Twenty-three years of age, unless he have a Faculty. And every man which is to be admitted a Priest shall be full Four-and-twenty years old. And every man which is to be ordained or consecrated Bishop shall be fully Thirty years of age.

And the Bishop, knowing either by himself, or by sufficient testimony, any Person to be a man of virtuous conversation, and without crime; and, after examination and trial, finding him learned in the Latin Tongue, and sufficiently instructed in holy Scripture, may at the times appointed in the Canon, or else, on urgent occasion, upon some other Sunday or Holy-day, in the face of the Church, admit him a Deacon, in such manner and form as hereafter followeth.

THE FORM AND MANNER OF

MAKING OF DEACONS.

¶ *When the day appointed by the Bishop is come, after Morning Prayer is ended, there shall be a Sermon or Exhortation, declaring the Duty and Office of such as come to be admitted Deacons; how necessary that Order is in the Church of Christ, and also, how the people ought to esteem them in their Office.*

¶ *First, the Archdeacon, or his Deputy, shall present unto the Bishop (sitting in his chair near to the holy Table) such as desire to be ordained Deacons, (each of them being decently habited,) saying these words,*

REVEREND Father in God, I present unto you these persons present, to be admitted Deacons.

The Bishop.

TAKE heed that the persons, whom ye present unto us, be apt and meet, for their learning and godly conversation, to exercise their Ministry duly to the honour of God, and the edifying of his Church.

¶ *The Archdeacon shall answer,*

I HAVE enquired of them, and also examined them, and think them so to be.

¶ *Then the Bishop shall say unto the people:*

BRETHREN, if there be any of you who knoweth any Impediment, or notable Crime, in any of these persons presented to be ordered Deacons, for the which he ought not to be admitted to that Office, let him come forth in the Name of God, and shew what the Crime or Impediment is.

¶ *And if any great Crime or Impediment be objected, the Bishop shall surcease from Ordering that person, until such time as the party accused shall be found clear of that Crime.*

¶ *Then the Bishop (commending such as shall be found meet to be Ordered to the Prayers of the Congregation) shall, with the Clergy and people present, sing or say the Litany, with the Prayers as followeth.*

[*For the* Litany, *see the Order for Morning Prayer.*]

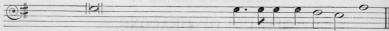

That it may please thee to bless these thy servants, now to be admitted to the Order of Deacons, [*or Priests,*] and to pour thy grace upon them; that they may duly execute their Office, to the edifying of thy Church, and the

glo-ry of thy ho-ly Name;

We beseech thee to hear us, good Lord.

¶ *Then shall be sung or said the Service for the Communion, with the Collect, Epistle, and Gospel, as followeth.*

THE COLLECT.

ALMIGHTY God, who by thy Divine Providence hast appointed divers Orders of Ministers in thy Church, and didst inspire thine Apostles to choose into the Order of Deacons the first Martyr Saint Stephen, with others; Mercifully behold these thy servants now called to the like Office and Administration; replenish them so with the truth of thy Doctrine, and adorn them with innocency of life, that, both by word and good example, they may faithfully serve thee in this Office, to the glory of thy Name, and the edification of thy Church; through the merits of our Saviour Jesus Christ, who liveth and reigneth with thee and the Holy Ghost, now and for ever.

A - men.

THE EPISTLE. 1 Tim. iii. 8.

LIKEWISE must the Deacons be grave, not double tongued, not given to much wine, not greedy of filthy lucre, holding the mystery of the faith in a pure conscience. And let these also first be proved; then let them use the Office of a Deacon, being found blameless. Even so must their wives be grave, not slanderers, sober, faithful in all things. Let the Deacons be the husbands of one wife, ruling their children and their own houses well. For they that have used the Office of a Deacon well purchase to themselves a good degree, and great boldness in the faith which is in Christ Jesus.

¶ *Or else this, out of the sixth of the Acts of the Apostles.*

ACTS vi. 2.

THEN the twelve called the multitude of the disciples unto them, and said, It is not reason that we should leave the Word of God, and serve tables. Wherefore, brethren, look ye out among you seven men of honest report, full of the Holy Ghost and wisdom, whom we may appoint over this business. But we will give ourselves continually to prayer, and to the ministry of the Word. And the saying pleased the whole multitude. And they chose Stephen, a man full of faith, and of the Holy Ghost, and Philip, and Prochorus, and Nicanor, and Timon, and Parmenas, and Nicolas a proselyte of Antioch; whom they set before the Apostles; and, when they had prayed, they laid their hands on them. And the Word of God increased, and the number of the disciples multiplied in Jerusalem greatly, and a great company of the Priests were obedient to the faith.

¶ *And before the Gospel, the Bishop, sitting in his chair, shall examine every one of them that are to be Ordered, in the presence of the people, after this manner following.*

DO you trust that you are inwardly moved by the Holy Ghost to take upon you this Office and Ministration, to serve God for the promoting of his glory, and the edifying of his people?
Answer. I trust so.

The Bishop.

DO you think that you are truly called, according to the will of our Lord Jesus Christ, and the due Order of this Realm, to the Ministry of the Church?
Answer. I think so.

The Bishop.

DO you unfeignedly believe all the Canonical Scriptures of the Old and New Testament?
Answer. I do believe them.

The Bishop.

WILL you diligently read the same unto the people assembled in the Church where you shall be appointed to serve?
Answer. I will.

The Bishop.

IT appertaineth to the Office of a Deacon, in the Church where he shall be appointed to serve, to assist the Priest in Divine Service, and specially when he ministereth the holy Communion, and to help him in the distribution thereof, and to read holy Scriptures and Homilies in the Church; and to instruct the youth in the Catechism; in the absence of the Priest to baptize infants, and to preach, if he be admitted thereto by the Bishop. And furthermore, it is his Office, where provision is so made, to search for the sick, poor, and impotent people of the Parish, to intimate their estates, names, and places where they dwell, unto the Curate, that by his exhortation they may be relieved with the alms of the Parishioners, or others. Will you do this gladly and willingly?

Answer. I will so do, by the help of God.

The Bishop.

WILL you apply all your diligence to frame and fashion your own lives, and the lives of your families, according to the Doctrine of Christ; and to make both yourselves and them, as much as in you lieth, wholesome examples of the flock of Christ?

Answer. I will so do, the Lord being my helper.

The Bishop.

WILL you reverently obey your Ordinary, and other chief Ministers of the Church, and them to whom the charge and government over you is committed, following with a glad mind and will their godly admonitions?

Answer. I will endeavour myself, the Lord being my helper.

¶ *Then the Bishop laying his Hands severally upon the Head of every one of them, humbly kneeling before him, shall say,*

TAKE thou Authority to execute the Office of a Deacon in the Church of God committed unto thee; In the Name of the Father, and of the Son, and of the Holy Ghost. Amen.

¶ *Then shall the Bishop deliver to every one of them the New Testament, saying,*

TAKE thou Authority to read the Gospel in the Church of God, and to preach the same, if thou be thereto licensed by the Bishop himself.

¶ *Then one of them, appointed by the Bishop, shall read*

THE GOSPEL. St. Luke xii. 35.

LET your loins be girded about, and your lights burning; and ye yourselves like unto men that wait for their Lord, when he will return from the wedding that, when he cometh and knocketh, they may open unto him immediately. Blessed are those servants, whom the Lord when he cometh shall find watching. Verily I say unto you, that he shall gird himself, and make them to sit down to meat, and will come forth and serve them. And if he shall come in the second watch, or come in the third watch, and find them so, blessed are those servants.

¶ *Then shall the Bishop proceed in the Communion, and all that are Ordered shall tarry, and receive the holy Communion the same day with the Bishop.*

¶ *The Communion ended, after the last Collect, and immediately before the Benediction, shall be said these Collects following.*

ALMIGHTY God, giver of all good things, who of thy great goodness hast vouchsafed to accept and take these thy servants unto the Office of Deacons in thy Church; Make them, we beseech thee, O Lord, to be modest, humble, and constant in their Ministration, to have a ready will to observe all spiritual Discipline; that they having always the testimony of a good conscience, and continuing ever stable and strong in thy Son Christ, may so well behave themselves in this inferior Office, that they may be found worthy to be called unto the higher Ministries in thy Church; through the same thy Son our Saviour Jesus Christ, to whom be glory and honour world without end. *A - men.*

PREVENT us, O Lord, in all our doings with thy most gracious favour, and further us with thy continual help; that in all our works begun, continued, and ended in thee, we may glorify thy holy Name, and finally by thy mercy obtain everlasting life; through Jesus Christ our Lord. *Amen.*

THE peace of God, which passeth all understanding, keep your hearts and minds in the knowledge and love of God, and of his Son Jesus Christ our Lord: And the Blessing of God Almighty, the Father, the Son, and the Holy Ghost, be amongst you, and remain with you always. *Amen.*

[*For Sevenfold* Amen, *see after the Benediction in the Order for the Administration of the Holy Communion.*]

¶ *And here it must be declared unto the Deacon, that he must continue in that Office of a Deacon the space of a whole year (except for reasonable causes it shall otherwise seem good unto the Bishop) to the intent he may be perfect, and well expert in the things appertaining to the Ecclesiastical Administration. In executing whereof if he be found faithful and diligent, he may be admitted by his Diocesan to the Order of Priesthood, at the times appointed in the Canon; or else, on urgent occasion, upon some other Sunday, or Holy-day, in the face of the Church, in such manner and form as hereafter followeth.*

THE FORM AND MANNER OF

ORDERING OF PRIESTS.

¶ *When the day appointed by the Bishop is come, after Morning Prayer is ended, there shall be a Sermon or Exhortation, declaring the Duty and Office of such as come to be admitted Priests; how necessary that Order is in the Church of Christ, and also how the people ought to esteem them in their Office.*

¶ *First, the Archdeacon, or, in his absence, one appointed in his stead, shall present unto the Bishop (sitting in his chair near to the holy Table) all them that shall receive the Order of Priesthood that day (each of them being decently habited) and say,*

REVEREND Father in God, I present unto you these persons present, to be admitted to the Order of Priesthood.

The Bishop.

TAKE heed that the persons, whom ye present unto us, be apt and meet, for their learning and godly conversation, to exercise their Ministry duly, to the honour of God, and the edifying of his Church.

¶ *The Archdeacon shall answer,*

I HAVE enquired of them, and also examined them, and think them so to be.

¶ *Then the Bishop shall say unto the people;*

GOOD people, these are they whom we purpose, God willing, to receive this day unto the holy Office of Priesthood: For after due examination we find not to the contrary, but that they be lawfully called to their Function and Ministry, and that they be persons meet for the same. But yet if there be any of you, who knoweth any Impediment, or notable Crime, in any of them, for the which he ought not to be received into this holy Ministry, let him come forth in the Name of God, and shew what the Crime or Impediment is.

¶ *And if any great Crime or Impediment be objected, the Bishop shall surcease from Ordering that person, until such time as the party accused shall be found clear of that Crime.*

¶ *Then the Bishop (commending such as shall be found meet to be Ordered to the Prayers of the Congregation) shall, with the Clergy and people present, sing or say the Litany, with the Prayers, as is before appointed in the Form of Ordering Deacons ; save only, that, in the proper Suffrage there added, the word [Deacons] shall be omitted, and the word [Priests] inserted instead of it.*

¶ *Then shall be sung or said the Service for the Communion, with the Collect, Epistle, and Gospel, as followeth.*

THE COLLECT.

ALMIGHTY God, giver of all good things, who by thy Holy Spirit hast appointed divers Orders of Ministers in the Church ; Mercifully behold these thy servants now called to the Office of Priesthood ; and replenish them so with the truth of thy doctrine, and adorn them with innocency of life, that, both by word and good example, they may faithfully serve thee in this Office, to the glory of thy Name, and the edification of thy Church ; through the merits of our Saviour Jesus Christ, who liveth and reigneth with thee and the Holy Ghost, world without end.

A - men.

THE EPISTLE. Ephes. iv. 7.

UNTO every one of us is given grace, according to the measure of the gift of Christ. Wherefore he saith, When he ascended up on high, he led captivity captive, and gave gifts unto men. (Now that he ascended, what is it but that he also descended first into the lower parts of the earth? He that descended, is the same also that ascended up far above all heavens, that he might fill all things.) And he gave some Apostles, and some Prophets, and some Evangelists, and some Pastors and Teachers ; for the perfecting of the Saints, for the work of the Ministry, for the edifying of the Body of Christ ; till we all come in the unity of the faith, and of the knowledge of the Son of God, unto a perfect man, unto the measure of the stature of the fulness of Christ.

¶ *After this shall be read for the Gospel part of the ninth Chapter of Saint Matthew, as followeth.*

St. Matthew ix. 36.

WHEN Jesus saw the multitudes, he was moved with compassion on them, because they fainted, and were scattered abroad as sheep having no shepherd. Then saith he unto his disciples, The harvest truly is plenteous, but the labourers are few. Pray ye therefore the Lord of the harvest, that he will send forth labourers into his harvest.

¶ *Or else this that followeth, out of the tenth Chapter of Saint* John.

ST. JOHN x. 1.

VERILY, verily I say unto you, He that entereth not by the door into the sheepfold, but climbeth up some other way, the same is a thief and a robber. But he that entereth in by the door is the Shepherd of the sheep. To him the porter openeth, and the sheep hear his voice ; and he calleth his own sheep by name, and leadeth them out. And when he putteth forth his own sheep he goeth before them, and the sheep follow him; for they know his voice. And a stranger will they not follow, but will flee from him ; for they know not the voice of strangers. This parable spake Jesus unto them, but they understood not what things they were which he spake unto them. Then said Jesus unto them again, Verily, verily I say unto you, I am the door of the sheep. All that ever came before me are thieves and robbers ; but the sheep did not hear them. I am the door; by me if any man enter in, he shall be saved, and shall go in and out, and find pasture. The thief cometh not but for to steal, and to kill, and to destroy : I am come that they might have life, and that they might have it more abundantly. I am the good Shepherd : the good Shepherd giveth his life for the sheep. But he that is an hireling, and not the Shepherd, whose own the sheep are not, seeth the wolf coming, and leaveth the sheep, and fleeth ; and the wolf catcheth them, and scattereth the sheep. The hireling fleeth, because he is an hireling, and careth not for the sheep. I am the good Shepherd, and know my sheep, and am known of mine. As the Father knoweth me, even so know I the Father ; and I lay down my life for the sheep. And other sheep I have, which are not of this fold : them also I must bring, and they shall hear my voice ; and there shall be one fold, and one Shepherd.

¶ *Then the Bishop, sitting in his chair, shall say unto them as hereafter followeth.*

YOU have heard, Brethren, as well in your private examination, as in the exhortation which was now made to you, and in the holy Lessons taken out of the Gospel, and the writings of the Apostles, of what dignity, and of how great importance this Office is, whereunto ye are called. And now again we exhort you, in the Name of our Lord Jesus Christ, that you have in remembrance, into how high a Dignity, and to how weighty an Office and Charge ye are called : that is to say, to be Messengers, Watchmen, and Stewards of the Lord ; to teach, and to premonish, to feed and provide for the Lord's family ; to seek for Christ's sheep that are dispersed abroad, and for his children who are in the midst of this naughty world, that they may be saved through Christ for ever.

Have always therefore printed in your remembrance, how great a treasure is committed to your charge. For they are the sheep of Christ, which he bought with his death, and for whom he shed his blood. The Church and Congregation whom you must serve, is his Spouse, and his Body. And if it shall happen the same Church, or any Member thereof, to take any hurt or hindrance by reason of your negligence, ye know the greatness of the fault, and also the horrible punishment that will ensue. Wherefore consider with yourselves the end of your Ministry towards the children of God, towards the Spouse and Body of Christ; and see that you never cease your labour, your care and diligence, until you have done all that lieth in you, according to your bounden duty, to bring all such as are or shall be committed to your charge, unto that agreement in the faith and knowledge of God, and to that ripeness and perfectness of age in Christ, that there be no place left among you, either for error in religion, or for viciousness in life.

Forasmuch then as your Office is both of so great excellency, and of so great difficulty, ye see with how great care and study ye ought to apply yourselves, as well that ye may shew yourselves dutiful and thankful unto that Lord, who hath placed you in so high a Dignity; as also to beware, that neither you yourselves offend, nor be occasion that others offend. Howbeit, ye cannot have a mind and will thereto of yourselves; for that will and ability is given of God alone: therefore ye ought, and have need, to pray earnestly for his Holy Spirit. And seeing that you cannot by any other means compass the doing of so weighty a work, pertaining to the salvation of man, but with doctrine and exhortation taken out of the holy Scriptures, and with a life agreeable to the same; consider how studious ye ought to be in reading and learning the Scriptures, and in framing the manners both of yourselves, and of them that specially pertain unto you, according to the rule of the same Scriptures: and for this selfsame cause, how ye ought to forsake and set aside (as much as you may) all worldly cares and studies.

We have good hope that you have well weighed and pondered these things with yourselves long before this time; and that you have clearly determined, by God's grace, to give yourselves wholly to this Office, whereunto it hath pleased God to call you: so that, as much as lieth in you, you will apply yourselves wholly to this one thing, and draw all your cares and studies this way; and that you will continually pray to God the Father, by the Mediation of our only Saviour Jesus Christ, for the heavenly assistance of the

Holy Ghost; that, by daily reading and weighing of the Scriptures, ye may wax riper and stronger in your Ministry; and that ye may so endeavour yourselves, from time to time, to sanctify the lives of you and yours, and to fashion them after the Rule and Doctrine of Christ, that ye may be wholesome and godly examples and patterns for the people to follow.

And now, that this present Congregation of Christ here assembled may also understand your minds and wills in these things, and that this your promise may the more move you to do your duties, ye shall answer plainly to these things, which we, in the Name of God, and of his Church, shall demand of you touching the same.

DO you think in your heart, that you be truly called, according to the will of our Lord Jesus Christ, and the order of this Church of *England*, to the Order and Ministry of Priesthood?

Answer. I think it.

The Bishop.

ARE you persuaded that the holy Scriptures contain sufficiently all Doctrine required of necessity for eternal salvation through faith in Jesus Christ? and are you determined, out of the said Scriptures to instruct the people committed to your charge, and to teach nothing, as required of necessity to eternal salvation, but that which you shall be persuaded may be concluded and proved by the Scripture?

Answer. I am so persuaded, and have so determined by God's grace.

The Bishop.

WILL you then give your faithful diligence always so to minister the Doctrine and Sacraments, and the Discipline of Christ, as the Lord hath commanded, and as this Church and Realm hath received the same, according to the Commandments of God; so that you may teach the people committed to your Cure and Charge with all diligence to keep and observe the same?

Answer. I will so do, by the help of the Lord.

The Bishop.

WILL you be ready, with all faithful diligence, to banish and drive away all erroneous and strange doctrines contrary to God's word; and to use both publick and private monitions and exhortations, as well to the sick as to the whole, within your Cures, as need shall require, and occasion shall be given?

Answer. I will, the Lord being my helper.

The Bishop.

WILL you be diligent in Prayers, and in reading of the holy Scriptures, and in such studies as help to the knowledge of the same, laying aside the study of the world and the flesh ?

Answer. I will endeavour myself so to do, the Lord being my helper.

The Bishop.

WILL you be diligent to frame and fashion your own selves, and your families, according to the Doctrine of Christ ; and to make both yourselves and them, as much as in you lieth, wholesome examples and patterns to the flock of Christ ?

Answer. I will apply myself thereto, the Lord being my helper.

The Bishop.

WILL you maintain and set forwards, as much as lieth in you, quietness, peace, and love, among all Christian people, and especially among them that are or shall be committed to your charge ?

Answer. I will so do, the Lord being my helper.

The Bishop.

WILL you reverently obey your Ordinary, and other chief Ministers, unto whom is committed the charge and government over you ; following with a glad mind and will their godly admonitions, and submitting yourselves to their godly judgements ?

Answer. I will so do, the Lord being my helper.

¶ *Then shall the Bishop, standing up, say,*

ALMIGHTY God, who hath given you this will to do all these things ; Grant also unto you strength and power to perform the same ; that he may accomplish his work which he hath begun in you ; through Jesus Christ our Lord.

A - men.

¶ *After this, the Congregation shall be desired, secretly in their Prayers, to make their humble supplications to God for all these things : for the which Prayers there shall be silence kept for a space.*

¶ *After which shall be sung or said by the Bishop (the persons to be Ordained Priests all kneeling) Veni, Creator Spiritus; the Bishop beginning, and the Priests, and others that are present, answering by verses, as followeth.*

[*Voices in Unison.*]

COME, Holy Ghost, our souls inspire,
And lighten with celestial fire.
Thou the anointing Spirit art,
Who dost thy seven-fold gifts impart.

Thy blessed Unction from above,
Is comfort, life, and fire of love.
Enable with perpetual light
The dulness of our blinded sight.

Anoint and cheer our soiled face
With the abundance of thy grace.
Keep far our foes, give peace at home:
Where thou art guide, no ill can come.

Teach us to know the Father, Son,
And thee, of both, to be but One.
That, through the ages all along,
This may be our endless song;

Praise . . . to Thy . . e - ter - nal me - rit,

Fa - ther, Son, and Ho - ly Spi - rit. [A - men.]

Or this:

A - men.

COME, Holy Ghost, eternal God,
    Proceeding from above,
Both from the Father and the Son,
    The God of peace and love;

Visit our minds, into our hearts
    Thy heavenly grace inspire;
That truth and godliness we may
    Pursue with full desire.

Thou art the very Comforter
   In grief and all distress;
The heav'nly gift of God most high,
   No tongue can it express;

The fountain and the living spring
   Of joy celestial;
The fire so bright, the love so sweet,
   The Unction spiritual.

Thou in thy gifts art manifold,
   By them Christ's Church doth stand:
In faithful hearts thou writ'st thy law,
   The finger of God's hand.

According to thy promise, Lord,
   Thou givest speech with grace;
That through thy help, God's praises may
   Resound in every place.

O Holy Ghost, into our minds
   Send down thy heav'nly light;
Kindle our hearts with fervent zeal,
   To serve God day and night.

Our weakness strengthen and confirm,
   (For, Lord, thou know'st us frail;)
That neither devil, world, nor flesh,
   Against us may prevail.

Put back our enemy far from us,
   And help us to obtain
Peace in our hearts with God and man,
   (The best, the truest gain;)

And grant that thou being, O Lord,
   Our leader and our guide,
We may escape the snares of sin,
   And never from thee slide.

Such measures of thy powerful grace
   Grant, Lord, to us, we pray;
That thou may'st be our Comforter
   At the last dreadful day.

Of strife and of dissention
Dissolve, O Lord, the bands,
And knit the knots of peace and love
Throughout all Christian lands.

Grant us the grace that we may know
The Father of all might,
That we of his beloved Son
May gain the blissful sight;

And that we may with perfect faith
Ever acknowledge thee,
The Spirit of Father, and of Son,
One God in Persons Three.

To God the Father laud and praise,
And to his blessed Son,
And to the Holy Spirit of grace,
Co-equal Three in One.

And pray we, that our only Lord
Would please his Spirit to send
On all that shall profess his Name,
From hence to the world's end. Amen.

¶ *That done, the Bishop shall pray in this wise, and say,*

Let us pray.

ALMIGHTY God, and heavenly Father, who, of thine infinite love and goodness towards us, hast given to us thy only and most dearly beloved Son Jesus Christ, to be our Redeemer, and the Author of everlasting life; who, after he had made perfect our redemption by his death, and was ascended into heaven, sent abroad into the world his Apostles, Prophets, Evangelists, Doctors, and Pastors; by whose labour and ministry he gathered together a great flock in all the parts of the world, to set forth the eternal praise of thy holy Name: For these so great benefits of thy eternal goodness, and for that thou hast vouchsafed to call these thy servants here present to the same Office and Ministry appointed for the salvation of mankind, we render unto thee most hearty thanks, we praise and worship thee; and we humbly beseech thee, by the same thy blessed Son, to grant unto all, which either here or elsewhere call upon thy holy Name, that we may continue to shew ourselves thankful unto thee for these and all other thy benefits; and that we may daily increase and go forwards in the knowledge and faith of thee and thy Son, by the Holy Spirit. So that as well by these thy Ministers, as by them over whom they shall be appointed thy Ministers, thy holy Name may be for ever glorified, and thy blessed kingdom enlarged; through the same thy Son Jesus Christ our Lord, who liveth and reigneth with thee in the unity of the same Holy Spirit, world without end.

A - men.

¶ *When this Prayer is done, the Bishop with the Priests present shall lay their hands severally upon the head of every one that receiveth the Order of Priesthood; the Receivers humbly kneeling upon their knees, and the Bishop saying,*

RECEIVE the Holy Ghost for the Office and Work of a Priest in the Church of God, now committed unto thee by the Imposition of our hands. Whose sins thou dost forgive, they are forgiven; and whose sins thou dost retain, they are retained. And be thou a faithful Dispenser of the Word of God, and of his holy Sacraments; In the Name of the Father, and of the Son, and of the Holy Ghost. Amen.

¶ *Then the Bishop shall deliver to every one of them kneeling, the Bible into his hand, saying,*

TAKE thou Authority to preach the Word of God, and to minister the holy Sacraments in the Congregation, where thou shalt be lawfully appointed thereunto.

¶ *When this is done, the* Nicene *Creed shall be sung or said; and the Bishop shall after that go on in the Service of the Communion, which all they that receive Orders shall take together, and remain in the same place where Hands were laid upon them, until such time as they have received the Communion.*

¶ *The Communion being done, after the last Collect, and immediately before the Benediction, shall be said these Collects.*

MOST merciful Father, we beseech thee to send upon these thy servants thy heavenly blessing; that they may be clothed with righteousness, and that thy Word spoken by their mouths may have such success, that it may never be spoken in vain. Grant also, that we may have grace to hear and receive what they shall deliver out of thy most holy Word, or agreeable to the same, as the means of our salvation; that in all our words and deeds we may seek thy glory, and the increase of thy kingdom; through Jesus Christ our Lord.

A - men.

PREVENT us, O Lord, in all our doings, with thy most gracious favour, and further us with thy continual help; that in all our works begun, continued, and ended in thee, we may glorify thy holy Name, and finally by thy mercy obtain everlasting life; through Jesus Christ our Lord. *Amen.*

THE peace of God, which passeth all understanding, keep your hearts and minds in the knowledge and love of God, and of his Son Jesus Christ our Lord; And the blessing of God Almighty, the Father, the Son, and the Holy Ghost, be amongst you, and remain with you always. *Amen.*

[*For Sevenfold* Amen, *see after the Benediction in the Order for the Administration of the Holy Communion.*]

¶ *And if on the same day the Order of Deacons be given to some, and the Order of Priesthood to others; the Deacons shall be first presented, and then the Priests; and it shall suffice that the Litany be once said for both. The Collects shall both be used; first, that for Deacons, then that for Priests. The Epistle shall be* Ephes. iv. 7—13, *as before in this Office. Immediately after which, they that are to be made Deacons shall be examined, and Ordained, as is above prescribed. Then one of them having read the Gospel (which shall be either out of* St. Matth. ix. 36—38, *as before in this Office; or else* St. Luke xii. 35—38, *as before in the Form for the Ordering of Deacons,) they that are to be made Priests shall likewise be examined, and Ordained, as is in this Office before appointed.*

Jesus Christ our Lord.

through Jesus Christ our Lord. Amen.

THE FORM OF ORDAINING OR CONSECRATING

OF AN

ARCHBISHOP OR BISHOP;

Which is always to be performed upon some Sunday or Holy-day.

¶ *When all things are duly prepared in the Church, and set in order, after
Morning Prayer is ended, the Archbishop (or some other Bishop appointed)
shall begin the Communion Service; in which this shall be*

THE COLLECT.

ALMIGHTY God, who by thy Son Jesus Christ didst
give to thy holy Apostles many excellent gifts, and
didst charge them to feed thy flock; Give grace, we beseech
thee, to all Bishops, the Pastors of thy Church,
that they may diligently preach thy Word, and
duly administer the godly Discipline thereof; and
grant to the people, that they may obediently follow
the same; that all may receive the crown of
everlasting glory; through Jesus Christ our Lord.

A - men.

¶ *And another Bishop shall read*

THE EPISTLE. 1 Tɪᴍ. iii. 1.

THIS is a true saying, If a man desire the Office of a Bishop, he
desireth a good work. A Bishop then must be blameless, the
husband of one wife, vigilant, sober, of good behaviour, given to
hospitality, apt to teach; not given to wine, no striker, not greedy
of filthy lucre, but patient, not a brawler, not covetous; one that
ruleth well his own house, having his children in subjection with
all gravity; (For if a man know not how to rule his own house,
how shall he take care of the Church of God?) Not a novice, lest
being lifted up with pride he fall into the condemnation of the
devil. Moreover, he must have a good report of them which are
without; lest he fall into reproach, and the snare of the devil.

Or this.

FOR THE EPISTLE. Acts xx. 17.

FROM Miletus Paul sent to Ephesus, and called the elders of the Church. And when they were come to him, he said unto them, Ye know, from the first day that I came into Asia, after what manner I have been with you at all seasons, serving the Lord with all humility of mind, and with many tears and temptations which befel me by the lying in wait of the Jews : And how I kept back nothing that was profitable unto you, but have shewed you, and have taught you publickly, and from house to house, testifying both to the Jews, and also to the Greeks, repentance toward God, and faith toward our Lord Jesus Christ. And now behold, I go bound in the spirit unto Jerusalem, not knowing the things that shall befal me there ; save that the Holy Ghost witnesseth in every city, saying, That bonds and afflictions abide me. But none of these things move me, neither count I my life dear unto myself, so that I might finish my course with joy, and the ministry which I have received of the Lord Jesus, to testify the Gospel of the grace of God. And now behold, I know that ye all, among whom I have gone preaching the kingdom of God, shall see my face no more. Wherefore I take you to record this day, that I am pure from the blood of all men. For I have not shunned to declare unto you all the counsel of God. Take heed therefore unto yourselves, and to all the flock over the which the Holy Ghost hath made you Overseers, to feed the Church of God, which he hath purchased with his own blood. For I know this, that after my departing shall grievous wolves enter in among you, not sparing the flock. Also of your own selves shall men arise speaking perverse things, to draw away disciples after them. Therefore watch, and remember, that by the space of three years, I ceased not to warn every one night and day with tears. And now, brethren, I commend you to God, and to the word of his grace, which is able to build you up, and to give you an inheritance among all them which are sanctified. I have coveted no man's silver, or gold, or apparel ; yea, ye yourselves know, that these hands have ministered unto my necessities, and to them that were with me. I have shewed you all things, how that so labouring ye ought to support the weak ; and to remember the words of the Lord Jesus, how he said, It is more blessed to give than to receive.

¶ Then another Bishop shall read

THE GOSPEL. St. John xxi. 15.

JESUS saith to Simon Peter, Simon, son of Jonas, lovest thou me more than these? He saith unto him, Yea, Lord, thou knowest that I love thee. He saith unto him, Feed my lambs. He saith to him again the second time, Simon, son of Jonas, lovest thou me? He saith unto him, Yea, Lord, thou knowest that I love thee. He saith unto him, Feed my sheep. He saith unto him the third time, Simon, son of Jonas, lovest thou me? Peter was grieved because he said unto him the third time, Lovest thou me? And he said unto him, Lord, thou knowest all things; thou knowest that I love thee. Jesus saith unto him, Feed my sheep.

Or else this.

St. John xx. 19.

THE same day at evening, being the first day of the week, when the doors were shut where the disciples were assembled for fear of the Jews, came Jesus, and stood in the midst, and saith unto them, Peace be unto you. And when he had so said, he shewed unto them his hands and his side. Then were the disciples glad, when they saw the Lord. Then saith Jesus to them again, Peace be unto you: as my Father hath sent me, even so send I you. And when he had said this, he breathed on them, and saith unto them, Receive ye the Holy Ghost. Whosoever sins ye remit, they are remitted unto them; and whosoever sins ye retain, they are retained.

Or this.

St. Matth. xxviii. 18.

JESUS came and spake unto them, saying, All power is given unto me in heaven and in earth. Go ye therefore and teach all nations, baptizing them In the Name of the Father, and of the Son, and of the Holy Ghost; teaching them to observe all things whatsoever I have commanded you: and lo, I am with you alway, even unto the end of the world.

¶ After the Gospel, and the Nicene *Creed, and the Sermon are ended, the Elected Bishop (vested with his Rochet) shall be presented by two Bishops unto the Archbishop of that province (or to some other Bishop appointed by lawful commission) the Archbishop sitting in his chair near the holy Table, and the Bishops that present him saying,*

MOST Reverend Father in God, we present unto you this godly and well-learned man to be Ordained and Consecrated Bishop.

¶ *Then shall the Archbishop demand the Queen's Mandate for the Consecration, and cause it to be read. And then shall also be ministered unto them the Oath of due Obedience to the Archbishop, as followeth.*

THE OATH OF DUE OBEDIENCE TO THE ARCHBISHOP.

IN the Name of God. Amen. I *N.* chosen Bishop of the Church and See of *N.* do profess and promise all due reverence and obedience to the Archbishop and to the Metropolitical Church of *N.* and to their Successors : So help me God, through Jesus Christ.

¶ *This Oath shall not be made at the Consecration of an Archbishop.*

¶ *Then the Archbishop shall move the Congregation present to pray, saying thus to them :*

BRETHREN, it is written in the Gospel of Saint Luke, That our Saviour Christ continued the whole night in prayer, before he did choose and send forth his twelve Apostles. It is written also in the Acts of the Apostles, That the Disciples who were at Antioch did fast and pray, before they laid hands on Paul and Barnabas, and sent them forth. Let us therefore, following the example of our Saviour Christ, and his Apostles, first fall to prayer, before we admit, and send forth this person presented unto us, to the work whereunto we trust the Holy Ghost hath called him.

¶ *And then shall be said the Litany, as before in the Form of Ordering Deacons, save only, that after this place,* That it may please thee to illuminate all Bishops, *&c., the proper Suffrage there following shall be omitted, and this inserted instead of it ;*

[*For the* Litany, *see the Order for Morning Prayer.*]

That it may please thee to bless this our Brother elected, and to send thy grace upon him, that he may duly execute the Office whereunto he is called, to the edifying of thy Church, and to the honour, praise and glo - ry of thy Name ;

Answer. *We beseech thee to hear us, good Lord.*

¶ *Then shall be said this Prayer following.*

ALMIGHTY God, giver of all good things, who by thy Holy Spirit hast appointed divers Orders of Ministers in thy Church ; Mercifully behold this thy servant now called to the Work and Ministry of a Bishop ; and replenish him so with the truth of thy doctrine, and adorn him with innocency of life, that, both by word and deed, he may faithfully serve thee in this Office, to the glory of thy Name, and the edifying and well-governing of thy Church; through the merits of our Saviour Jesus Christ, who liveth and reigneth with thee and the Holy Ghost, world without end.

A - men.

¶ *Then the Archbishop, sitting in his chair, shall say to him that is to be Consecrated,*

BROTHER, forasmuch as the Holy Scripture and the ancient Canons command, that we should not be hasty in laying on hands, and admitting any person to Government in the Church of Christ, which he hath purchased with no less price than the effusion of his own blood; before I admit you to this Administration, I will examine you in certain Articles, to the end that the Congregation present may have a trial, and bear witness, how you be minded to behave yourself in the Church of God.

ARE you persuaded that you be truly called to this Ministration, according to the will of our Lord Jesus Christ, and the order of this Realm?

Answer. I am so persuaded.

The Archbishop.

ARE you persuaded that the holy Scriptures contain sufficiently all Doctrine required of necessity for eternal salvation through faith in Jesus Christ? And are you determined out of the same holy Scriptures to instruct the people committed to your charge; and to teach or maintain nothing as required of necessity to eternal salvation, but that which you shall be persuaded may be concluded and proved by the same?

Answer. I am so persuaded, and determined, by God's grace.

The Archbishop.

WILL you then faithfully exercise yourself in the same holy Scriptures, and call upon God by prayer, for the true understanding of the same; so as you may be able by them to teach and exhort with wholesome Doctrine, and to withstand and convince the gainsayers?

Answer. I will so do, by the help of God.

The Archbishop.

ARE you ready, with all faithful diligence, to banish and drive away all erroneous and strange doctrine contrary to God's Word; and both privately and openly to call upon and encourage others to the same?

Answer. I am ready, the Lord being my helper.

The Archbishop.

WILL you deny all ungodliness and worldly lusts, and live soberly, righteously, and godly, in this present world; that you may shew yourself in all things an example of good works unto others, that the adversary may be ashamed, having nothing to say against you?

Answer. I will so do, the Lord being my helper.

The Archbishop.

WILL you maintain and set forward, as much as shall lie in you, quietness, love, and peace among all men; and such as be unquiet, disobedient, and criminous, within your Diocese, correct and punish, according to such authority as you have by God's Word, and as to you shall be committed by the Ordinance of this Realm?

Answer. I will so do, by the help of God.

The Archbishop.

WILL you be faithful in ordaining, sending, or laying hands upon others?

Answer. I will so be, by the help of God.

The Archbishop.

WILL you shew yourself gentle, and be merciful for Christ's sake to poor and needy people, and to all strangers destitute of help?

Answer. I will so shew myself, by God's help.

¶ *Then the Archbishop, standing up, shall say,*

ALMIGHTY God, our heavenly Father, who hath given you a good will to do all these things, Grant also unto you strength and power to perform the same; that, he accomplishing in you the good work which he hath begun, you may be found perfect and irreprehensible at the latter day; through Jesus Christ our Lord.

A - men.

¶ *Then shall the Bishop elect put on the rest of the Episcopal habit; and kneeling down,* Veni, Creator Spiritus, *shall be sung or said over him, the Archbishop beginning, and the Bishops, with others that are present, answering by verses, as followeth.*

COME, Holy Ghost, our souls inspire,
 And lighten with celestial fire.
Thou the anointing Spirit art,
Who dost thy seven-fold gifts impart.

Thy blessed Unction from above,
Is comfort, life, and fire of love.
Enable with perpetual light
The dulness of our blinded sight.

Anoint and cheer our soiled face
With the abundance of thy grace.
Keep far our foes, give peace at home:
Where thou art guide, no ill can come.

Teach us to know the Father, Son,
And thee, of both, to be but One.
That, through the ages all along,
This may be our endless song ;
 Praise to thy eternal merit,
 Father, Son, and Holy Spirit.

Or this :

COME, Holy Ghost, eternal God,
 Proceeding from above, &c.

As before in the Form for Ordering Priests.

¶ *That ended, the Archbishop shall say,*

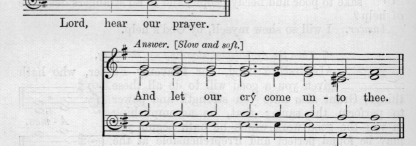

Lord, hear our prayer.

Answer. [Slow and soft.]

And let our cry come un-to thee.

Let us pray.

ALMIGHTY God, and most merciful Father, who of thine infinite goodness hast given thine only and dearly beloved Son Jesus Christ, to be our Redeemer, and the Author of everlasting life; who, after that he had made perfect our Redemption by his death, and was ascended into heaven, poured down his gifts abundantly upon men, making some Apostles, some Prophets, some Evangelists, some Pastors and Doctors, to the edifying and making perfect his Church; Grant, we beseech thee, to this thy servant such grace, that he may evermore be ready to spread abroad thy Gospel, the glad tidings of reconciliation with thee; and use the authority given him, not to destruction, but to salvation; not to hurt, but to help: so that as a wise and faithful servant, giving to thy family their portion in due season, he may at last be received into everlasting joy; through Jesus Christ our Lord, who, with thee and the Holy Ghost liveth and reigneth, one God, world without end.

A - men.

¶ *Then the Archbishop and Bishops present shall lay their hands upon the head of the elected Bishop kneeling before them upon his knees, the Archbishop saying,*

RECEIVE the Holy Ghost, for the Office and Work of a Bishop in the Church of God, now committed unto thee by the Imposition of our hands; In the Name of the Father, and of the Son, and of the Holy Ghost. Amen. And remember that thou stir up the grace of God which is given thee by this Imposition of our hands: for God hath not given us the spirit of fear, but of power, and love, and soberness.

¶ *Then the Archbishop shall deliver him the Bible, saying,*

GIVE heed unto reading, exhortation, and doctrine. Think upon the things contained in this Book. Be diligent in them, that the increase coming thereby may be manifest unto all men. Take heed unto thyself, and to doctrine, and be diligent in doing them: for by so doing thou shalt both save thyself and them that hear thee. Be to the flock of Christ a shepherd, not a wolf; feed them, devour them not. Hold up the weak, heal the sick, bind up the broken, bring again the outcasts, seek the lost. Be so merciful, that you be not too remiss; so minister discipline, that you forget not mercy: that when the chief Shepherd shall appear you may receive the never-fading crown of glory; through Jesus Christ our Lord.

¶ *Then the Archbishop shall proceed in the Communion Service : with whom the new Consecrated Bishop (with others) shall also communicate.*

¶ *And for the last Collect, immediately before the Benediction, shall be said these Prayers.*

MOST merciful Father, we beseech thee to send down upon this thy servant thy heavenly blessing ; and so endue him with thy Holy Spirit, that he, preaching thy Word, may not only be earnest to reprove, beseech, and rebuke with all patience and doctrine ; but also may be to such as believe a wholesome example, in word, in conversation, in love, in faith, in chastity, and in purity; that, faithfully fulfilling his course, at the latter day he may receive the crown of righteousness laid up by the Lord the righteous Judge, who liveth and reigneth one God with the Father and the Holy Ghost, world without end.

A - men.

PREVENT us, O Lord, in all our doings, with thy most gracious favour, and further us with thy continual help ; that in all our works begun, continued, and ended in thee, we may glorify thy holy Name, and finally by thy mercy obtain everlasting life ; through Jesus Christ our Lord. *Amen.*

THE peace of God, which passeth all understanding, keep your hearts and minds in the knowledge and love of God, and of his Son Jesus Christ our Lord : And the blessing of God Almighty, the Father, the Son, and the Holy Ghost, be amongst you, and remain with you always. *Amen.*

[*For Sevenfold* Amen, *see after the Benediction in the Order for the Administration of the Holy Communion.*]

A FORM OF PRAYER WITH THANKSGIVING

TO ALMIGHTY GOD;

To be used in all Churches and Chapels within this Realm, every Year,
upon the Twentieth Day of *June;* being the Day on which Her
Majesty began Her happy Reign.

¶ *The Service shall be the same with the usual Office for Holy-days in all
things; except where it is in this Office otherwise appointed.*

¶ *If this Day shall happen to be* Sunday, *this whole Office shall be used, as it
followeth, entirely.*

¶ *Morning Prayer shall begin with these Sentences.*

I EXHORT that first of all, Supplications, Prayers, Intercessions,
and giving of Thanks, be made for all men ; for Kings, and for
all that are in Authority ; that we may lead a quiet and peaceable
life, in all godliness and honesty : For this is good and acceptable
unto God our Saviour. 1 *Tim.* ii. 1, 2, 3.

If we say that we have no sin, we deceive ourselves, and the
truth is not in us ; but, if we confess our sins, he is faithful and
just to forgive us our sins, and to cleanse us from all unrighteousness. 1 *St. John* i. 8, 9.

¶ *Instead of* Venite, exultemus, *the Hymn following shall be said or sung; one
Verse by the Priest, and another by the Clerk and people.*

F.   *f* O' | LORD our | Governour : how excellent is thy | Name
      in | all the | world ! *Psalm* viii. 1.

F.   2 Lord, what is man * that thou hast such respect | unto |
      him : or the son of man * that thou | so re- | -gardest |
      him ? *Psalm* cxliv. 3.

    3 The merciful and gracious Lord hath so done his |
      marvellous | works : that they ought to be | had | in
      re- | -membrance. *Psalm* cxi. 4.

    4 O that men would therefore praise the Lord | for his |
      goodness : and declare the wonders that he doeth | for
      the | children . of | men ! *Psalm* cvii. 8.

mf 5 Behold, O God our de- | -fender : and look upon the | face
      of | thine A- | -nointed. *Psalm* lxxxiv. 9.

    6 O hold thou up her goings | in thy | paths : that her |
      footsteps | slip | not. *Psalm* xvii. 5.

7 Grant the Quéen a | long | life : and make her glád with the | joy | of thy | countenance. *Psalms* lxi. 6 and xxi. 6.

8 Let her dwéll before | thee for | ever : O prepare thy loving mercy and fáithfulness | that they | may pre- | serve her. *Psalm* lxi. 7.

9 In her tíme let the | righteous | flourish : and let péace | be in | all our | borders. *Psalms* lxxii. 7, and cxlvii. 14.

10 As for her enemies * clóthe | them with | shame : but upon hersélf | let her | crown | flourish. *Psalm* cxxxii. 19.

f 11 Blessed be the Lord God * éven the | God of | Israel : which ónly | doeth | wondrous | things. *Psalm* lxxii. 18.

12 And blessed be the Name of his Májes- | -ty for | ever : and all the earth shall be filled with his Májesty. | Amen, | A- | -men. *Psalm* lxxii. 19.

F. f   Glory be to the Fáther, | and . to the | Son : ánd | to the | Holy | Ghost ;

F.   As it was in the beginning * is nów, and | ever | shall be : wórld without | end. | A- | -men.

Proper Psalms, xx., xxi., ci.

PSALM XX.—*Exaudiat te Dominus.*

mf THE Lord hear thee ín the | day of | trouble : the Náme of the | God of | Jacob . de- | -fend thee ;

2 Send thee hélp | from the | sanctuary : ánd | strengthen . thee | out of | Sion ;

3 Remémber | all thy | offerings : ánd ac- | -cept thy | burnt | sacrifice ;

4 Gránt thee thy | heart's de- | -sire : ánd ful- | -fil | all thy | mind.

5 We will rejoice in thy salvation * and triumph in the Náme of the | Lord our | God : the Lórd per- | -form all | thy pe- | -titions.

6 Now know I that the Lord helpeth his Anointed * and will hear him fróm his | holy | heaven : even with the whólesome | strength of | his right | hand.

7 Some put their trust in cháriots and | some in | horses : but we will remember the Náme | of the | Lord our | God.

8 Théy are brought | down and | fallen : but wé are | risen . and | stand | upright.

2nd
part.
9 Save, Lord, and héar us, O | King of | heaven : whén we | call up- | -on | thee.

PSALM xxi.—*Domine, in virtute tua.*

mf THE King shall rejóice in thy | strength O | Lord : exceeding glád shall he | be of | thy sal- | -vation.

2 Thou hast gíven him his | heart's de- | -sire : and hast not deníed him the re- | -quest | of his | lips.

3 For thou shalt prevent him wíth the | blessings . of | goodness : and shalt set a crówn of pure | gold up- | -on his | head.

4 He asked life of thee * and thou gávest him a | long | life : éven for | ever | and | ever.

5 His honour is gréat in | thy sal- | -vation : glory and great wórship'| shalt thou | lay up- | -on him.

6 For thou shalt give him éver- | -lasting . fe- | -licity : and make him glád with the | joy | of thy | countenance.

7 And why * because the King putteth his trúst | in the | Lord : and in the mercy of the most Híghest | he shall | not mis- | -carry.

8 All thine énemies shall | feel thy | hand : thy right hánd shall | find out | them that | hate thee.

9 Thou shalt make them like a fiery oven in tíme | of thy | wrath : the Lord shall destroy them in his displeasure * ánd the | fire | shall con- | -sume them.

10 Their fruit shalt thou róot | out . of the | earth : and their séed from a- | -mong the | children . of | men.

11 For they inténded | mischief . a- | -gainst thee : and imagined such a device as they áre not | able | to per- | form.

12 Therefore shalt thou pút | them to | flight : and the strings of thy bow shalt thou make réady a- | -gainst the | face of | them.

2nd part. 13 Be thou exalted, Lórd, in thine | own | strength : só will we | sing and | praise thy | power.

PSALM ci.—*Misericordiam et judicium.*

mf MY sóng shall be of | mercy . and | judgement : unto thée, O | Lord | will I | sing.

2 O lét me have | under- | -standing : ín the | way of | godli- | -ness.

3 When wilt thou cóme | unto | me : I will walk in my hóuse | with a | perfect | heart.

4 I will take no wicked thing in hand * I hate the síns | of un- | -faithfulness : there shall nó such | cleave | unto | me.

5 A froward héart shall de- | -part from | me : I will not | know a | wicked | person.

6 Whoso privily slánder- | -eth his | neighbour : hím | — will | I de- | -stroy.

7 Whoso hath also a proud lóok and | high | stomach : I' | will not | suffer | him.

8 Mine eyes look upon such as are fáithful | in the | land : thát | they may | dwell with | me.

9 Whoso léadeth a | godly | life : hé | — shall | be my | servant.

10 There shall no deceitful person dwéll | in my | house : he that telleth lies, sháll not | tarry | in my | sight.

2nd part. 11 I shall soon destroy all the ungódly that are | in the | land : that I may root out all wicked doers fróm the | city | of the | Lord.

Proper Lessons.

The First, Josh. i. to the end of the 9th Verse.

Te Deum.

The Second, Rom. xiii.

Jubilate Deo.

¶ *The Suffrages next after the Creed shall stand thus.*

Priest.

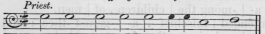

O Lord, shew thy mer - cy up-on us.

And grant us thy sal - va - tion.

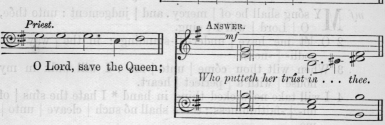

Priest.

O Lord, save the Queen;

Who putteth her trúst in . . . thee.

THE TWENTIETH OF JUNE.

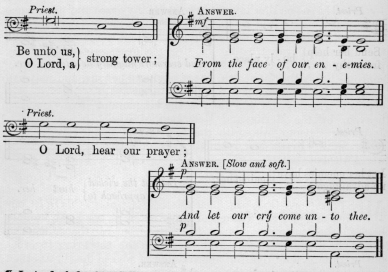

Priest.

Be unto us,
O Lord, a } strong tower;

Answer.

From the face of our en - e-mies.

Priest.

O Lord, hear our prayer;

Answer. [*Slow and soft.*]

And let our cry come un - to thee.

¶ *Instead of the first Collect at Morning Prayer shall be used this following Collect of Thanksgiving for Her Majesty's Accession to the Throne.*

ALMIGHTY God, who rulest over all the kingdoms of the World, and disposest of them according to thy good pleasure; We yield thee unfeigned thanks, for that thou wast pleased, as on this day, to place thy Servant our Sovereign Lady, Queen *VICTORIA* upon the Throne of this Realm. Let thy wisdom be her guide, and let thine arm strengthen her; let justice, truth, and holiness, let peace and love, and all those virtues that adorn the Christian Profession, flourish in her days; direct all her counsels and endeavours to thy glory, and the welfare of her people; and give us grace to obey her cheerfully and willingly for conscience sake; that neither our sinful passions, nor our private interests, may disappoint her cares for the publick good; let her always possess the hearts of her people, that they may never be wanting in honour to her person, and dutiful submission to her Authority; let her Reign be long and prosperous, and crown her with immortality in the life to come; through Jesus Christ our Lord.

A - men.

¶ *In the end of the Litany (which shall always be used upon this Day) after the Collect* [We humbly beseech thee, O Father, &c.] *shall the following Prayer, for the Queen and Royal Family, be used.*

O LORD our God, who upholdest and governest all things in heaven and earth; receive our humble prayers, with our hearty thanksgivings, for our Sovereign Lady

VICTORIA, as on this day, set over us by thy grace and providence to be our Queen; and so together with her bless *Albert Edward* Prince of *Wales*, the Princess of *Wales*, and all the Royal Family; that they all, ever trusting in thy goodness, protected by thy power, and crowned with thy gracious and endless favour, may continue before thee in health, peace, joy, and honour, and may live long and happy lives upon earth, and after death obtain everlasting life and glory in the kingdom of heaven, by the Merits and Mediation of Christ Jesus our Saviour, who with the Father and the Holy Spirit, liveth and reigneth ever one God, world without end.

A - men.

¶ *Then shall follow this Collect, for God's protection of the Queen against all her enemies.*

MOST gracious God, who hast set thy servant *VICTORIA* our Queen upon the Throne of her Ancestors, we most humbly beseech thee to protect her on the same from all the dangers to which she may be exposed; Hide her from the gathering together of the froward, and from the insurrection of wicked doers; Do thou weaken the hands, blast the designs, and defeat the enterprizes of all her enemies, that no secret conspiracies, nor open violences, may disquiet her Reign; but that, being safely kept under the shadow of thy wing, and supported by thy power, she may triumph over all opposition; that so the world may acknowledge thee to be her defender and mighty deliverer in all difficulties and adversities; through Jesus Christ our Lord. *Amen.*

¶ *Then the Prayer for the High Court of Parliament (if sitting).*

¶ *In the Communion Service, immediately before the reading of the Epistle, instead of the Collect for the Queen, and that of the Day, shall be used this Prayer for the Queen, as supreme Governour of this Church.*

BLESSED Lord, who hast called Christian Princes to the defence of thy Faith, and hast made it their duty to promote the spiritual welfare, together with the temporal interest of their people; We acknowledge with humble and thankful hearts thy great goodness to us, in setting thy Servant our most gracious Queen over this Church and Nation; Give her, we beseech thee, all those heavenly graces that are requisite for so high a trust; Let the work of thee her God prosper in her hands; Let her eyes behold the success of her designs for the service of thy true Religion established amongst us; And make her a blessed instrument of protecting and advancing thy Truth, wherever it is persecuted and oppressed; Let Hypocrisy and Profaneness, Superstition and Idolatry, fly before her face; Let not Heresies and false Doctrines disturb the peace of the

Church, nor Schisms and causeless Divisions weaken it; But grant us to be of one heart and one mind in serving thee our God, and obeying her according to thy will: And that these blessings may be continued to after-ages, let there never be one wanting in her house to succeed her in the government of this United Kingdom, that our posterity may see her children's children, and peace upon Israel. So we that are thy people, and sheep of thy pasture, shall give thee thanks for ever, and will always be shewing forth thy praise from generation to generation.

A - men.

THE EPISTLE. 1 St. Peter ii. 11.

DEARLY beloved, I beseech you as strangers and pilgrims, abstain from fleshly lusts, which war against the soul; having your conversation honest among the Gentiles: that, whereas they speak against you as evildoers, they may, by your good works which they shall behold, glorify God in the day of visitation. Submit yourselves to every ordinance of man for the Lord's sake; whether it be to the King, as supreme; or unto governours, as unto them that are sent by him for the punishment of evildoers, and for the praise of them that do well. For so is the will of God, that with well-doing ye may put to silence the ignorance of foolish men: as free, and not using your liberty for a cloke of maliciousness, but as the servants of God. Honour all men. Love the brotherhood. Fear God. Honour the King.

THE GOSPEL. St. Matth. xxii. 16.

AND they sent out unto him their disciples, with the Herodians, saying, Master, we know that thou art true, and teachest the way of God in truth, neither carest thou for any man: for thou regardest not the person of men. Tell us therefore, What thinkest thou? Is it lawful to give tribute unto Cæsar, or not? But Jesus perceived their wickedness, and said, Why tempt ye me, ye hypocrites? shew me the tribute-money. And they brought unto him a penny. And he saith unto them, Whose is this image and superscription? They say unto him, Cæsar's. Then saith he unto them, Render therefore unto Cæsar the things which are Cæsar's; and unto God the things that are God's. When they had heard these words, they marvelled, and left him, and went their way.

¶ *After the* Nicene *Creed shall follow the Sermon.*

¶ *In the Offertory shall this Sentence be read:*

LET your light so shine before men, that they may see your good works, and glorify your Father which is in heaven. *St. Matth.* v. 16.

¶ *After the Prayer* [For the whole state of Christ's Church, *&c.*] *these Collects following shall be used.*

A PRAYER FOR UNITY.

O GOD the Father of our Lord Jesus Christ, our only Saviour, the Prince of Peace; Give us grace seriously to lay to heart the great dangers we are in by our unhappy divisions. Take away all hatred and prejudice, and whatsoever else may hinder us from godly Union and Concord : that, as there is but one Body, and one Spirit, and one Hope of our Calling, one Lord, one Faith, one Baptism, one God and Father of us all, so we may henceforth be all of one heart, and of one soul, united in one holy bond of Truth and Peace, of Faith and Charity, and may with one mind and one mouth glorify thee; through Jesus Christ our Lord.

A - men.

GRANT, O Lord, we beseech thee, that the course of this world may be so peaceably ordered by thy governance, that thy Church may joyfully serve thee in all godly quietness, through Jesus Christ our Lord. *Amen.*

GRANT, we beseech thee, Almighty God, that the words, which we have heard this day with our outward ears, may through thy grace be so grafted inwardly in our hearts, that they may bring forth in us the fruit of good living, to the honour and praise of thy Name ; through Jesus Christ our Lord. *Amen.*

ALMIGHTY God, the fountain of all wisdom, who knowest our necessities before we ask, and our ignorance in asking ; We beseech thee to have compassion upon our infirmities ; and those things, which for our unworthiness we dare not, and for our blindness we cannot ask, vouchsafe to give us for the worthiness of thy Son Jesus Christ our Lord. *Amen.*

THE peace of God which passeth all understanding, keep your hearts and minds in the knowledge and love of God, and of his Son Jesus Christ our Lord : And the blessing of God Almighty, the Father, the Son, and the Holy Ghost, be amongst you, and remain with you always. *Amen.*

" VICTORIA R.

" OUR Will and Pleasure is, That these Four Forms of Prayer and Service,
" made for the Fifth of November, the Thirtieth of January, the Twenty-
" ninth of May, and the Twentieth of June, be forthwith printed and published,
" and annexed to the Book of Common Prayer and Liturgy of the United
" Church of England and Ireland, to be used yearly on the said Days, in all
" Cathedral and Collegiate Churches and Chapels ; in all Chapels of Colleges
" and Halls within our Universities of Oxford, Cambridge, and Dublin, and of
" Our Colleges of Eton and Winchester, and in all Parish-Churches and
" Chapels within those parts of Our United Kingdom called England and
" Ireland.

" Given at Our Court at Kensington, the Twenty-first Day of June, 1837,
" in the First Year of Our Reign.

" By Her Majesty's Command,

" J. RUSSELL."

" VICTORIA R.

" WHEREAS, by Our Royal Warrant of the Twenty-first Day of June One
" thousand eight hundred and thirty-seven, in the First year of Our
" Reign, We commanded that certain Forms of Prayer and Service made for
" the Fifth of November, the Thirtieth of January. and the Twenty-ninth of
" May should be forthwith printed and published and annexed to the Book of
' Common Prayer and Liturgy of the United Church of England and Ireland,
" to be used yearly on the said Days in all Cathedral and Collegiate Churches
" and Chapels, in all Chapels of Colleges and Halls within Our Universities of
" Oxford, Cambridge, and Dublin, and of Our Colleges of Eton and Winchester,
" and in all Parish-Churches and Chapels within those Parts of our United
" Kingdom called England and Ireland :

" And whereas, in the last Session of Parliament, Addresses were presented
" to Us by both Houses of Parliament, praying Us to take into Our Considera-
" tion Our Proclamation in relation to the said Forms of Prayer and Service
" made for the Fifth Day of November, the Thirtieth Day of January, and
" the Twenty-ninth Day of May, with a view to their Discontinuance :

" And whereas We have taken into Our Consideration the Subject of the said
" Addresses ; and, after due Deliberation, We have resolved that the Use of the
" said Forms of Prayer and service shall be discontinued :

" Now, therefore, Our Will and Pleasure is, that so much of Our said Royal
" Warrant of the Twenty-first Day of June One thousand eight hundred and
" thirty-seven, in the First Year of Our Reign, as is hereinbefore recited, be
" revoked, and that the Use of the said Forms of Prayer and Service made for
" the Fifth of November, the Thirtieth of January, and the Twenty-ninth of
" May be henceforth discontinued in all Cathedral and Collegiate Churches and
" Chapels, in all Chapels of Colleges and Halls within Our Universities of
" Oxford, Cambridge, and Dublin, and of our Colleges of Eton and Winchester,
" and in all Parish-Churches and Chapels within the Parts of our United
" Kingdom called England and Ireland, and that the said Forms of Prayer
" and Service be not henceforth printed and published with or annexed to the
" Book of Common Prayer and Liturgy of the United Church of England and
" Ireland.

" Given at Our Court at Saint James's, the Seventeenth Day of January, 1859,
" in the Twenty-second Year of Our Reign.

" By Her Majesty's Command,

" S. H. WALPOLE."

ARTICLES

AGREED UPON BY

THE ARCHBISHOPS AND BISHOPS OF BOTH PROVINCES,
AND THE WHOLE CLERGY,

In the Convocation holden at *London* in the Year 1562, for the avoiding of Diversities of Opinions, and for the establishing of Consent touching true Religion : Reprinted by His Majesty's Commandment, with His Royal Declaration prefixed thereunto.

HIS MAJESTY'S DECLARATION.

BEING by God's Ordinance, according to Our just Title, *Defender of the Faith, and Supreme Governour of the Church, within these our Dominions,* We hold it most agreeable to this Our Kingly Office, and Our own religious Zeal, to conserve and maintain the Church committed to Our Charge, in the Unity of true Religion, and in the Bond of Peace; and not to suffer unnecessary Disputations, Altercations, or Questions to be raised, which may nourish Faction both in the Church and Commonwealth. We have therefore, upon mature Deliberation, and with the Advice of so many of Our Bishops as might conveniently be called together, thought fit to make this Declaration following :

That the Articles of the Church of *England* (which have been allowed and authorized heretofore, and which Our Clergy generally have subscribed unto) do contain the true Doctrine of the Church of *England* agreeable to God's Word : which We do therefore ratify and confirm, requiring all Our loving Subjects to continue in the uniform profession thereof, and prohibiting the least difference from the said Articles ; which to that End We command to be new printed, and this Our Declaration to be published therewith.

That We are Supreme Governour of the Church of *England* : And that if any difference arise about the external Policy, concerning the *Injunctions, Canons,* and other *Constitutions* whatsoever thereto belonging, the Clergy in their Convocation is to order and settle them, having first obtained leave under Our Broad Seal so to do : and We approving their said Ordinances and Constitutions ; providing that none be made contrary to the Laws and Customs of the Land.

That out of our Princely Care that the Churchmen may do the Work which is proper unto them, the Bishops and Clergy, from time to time in Convocation, upon their humble Desire, shall have Licence under Our Broad Seal to deliberate of, and to do all such Things, as, being made plain by them, and assented unto by Us, shall concern the settled Continuance of the Doctrine and Discipline of the Church of *England* now established ; from which We will not endure any varying or departing in the least Degree.

That for the present, though some differences have been ill raised, yet We take comfort in this, that all Clergymen within Our Realm have always most willingly subscribed to the Articles established ; which is an argument to Us, that they all agree in the true, usual, literal meaning of the said Articles ;

and that even in those curious points, in which the present differences lie, men of all sorts take the Articles of the Church of *England* to be for them; which is an argument again, that none of them intend any desertion of the Articles established.

That therefore in these both curious and unhappy differences, which have for so many hundred years, in different times and places, exercised the Church of Christ, We will, that all further curious search be laid aside, and these disputes shut up in God's promises, as they be generally set forth to us in the holy Scriptures, and the general meaning of the Articles of the Church of *England* according to them. And that no man hereafter shall either print, or preach, to draw the Article aside any way, but shall submit to it in the plain and full meaning thereof: and shall not put his own sense or comment to be the meaning of the Article, but shall take it in the literal and grammatical sense.

That if any publick Reader in either of Our Universities, or any Head or Master of a College, or any other person respectively in either of them, shall affix any new sense to any Article, or shall publickly read, determine, or hold any publick Disputation, or suffer any such to be held either way, in either the Universities or Colleges respectively; or, if any Divine in the Universities shall preach or print any thing either way, other than is already established in Convocation with Our Royal Assent; he, or they the Offenders, shall be liable to Our displeasure, and the Church's censure in Our Commission Ecclesiastical, as well as any other: And We will see there shall be due Execution upon them.

ARTICLES OF RELIGION.

I. *Of Faith in the Holy Trinity.*

THERE is but one living and true God, everlasting, without body, parts, or passions; of infinite power, wisdom, and goodness; the Maker, and Preserver of all things both visible and invisible. And in unity of this Godhead there be three Persons, of one substance, power, and eternity; the Father, the Son, and the Holy Ghost.

II. *Of the Word or Son of God, which was made very Man.*

THE Son, which is the Word of the Father, begotten from everlasting of the Father, the very and eternal God, and of one substance with the Father, took Man's nature in the womb of the blessed Virgin, of her substance: so that two whole and perfect Natures, that is to say, the Godhead and Manhood, were joined together in one Person, never to be divided, whereof is one Christ, very God, and very Man; who truly suffered, was crucified, dead and buried, to reconcile his Father to us, and to be a sacrifice, not only for original guilt, but also for all actual sins of men.

III. *Of the going down of Christ into Hell.*

AS Christ died for us, and was buried, so also is it to be believed, that he went down into Hell.

IV. *Of the Resurrection of Christ.*

CHRIST did truly rise again from death, and took again his body, with flesh, bones, and all things appertaining to the perfection of man's nature; wherewith he ascended into Heaven, and there sitteth, until he return to judge all Men at the last day.

V. *Of the Holy Ghost.*

THE Holy Ghost, proceeding from the Father and the Son, is of one substance, majesty, and glory, with the Father and the Son, very and eternal God.

VI. *Of the Sufficiency of the holy Scriptures for Salvation.*

HOLY Scripture containeth all things necessary to salvation : so that whatsoever is not read therein, nor may be proved thereby, is not to be required of any man, that it should be believed as an article of the Faith, or be thought requisite or necessary to salvation. In the name of the holy Scripture we do understand those Canonical Books of the Old and New Testament, of whose authority was never any doubt in the Church.

Of the Names and Number of the Canonical Books.

GENESIS,
Exodus,
Leviticus,
Numbers,
Deuteronomy,
Joshua,
Judges,
Ruth,
The First Book of Samuel,
The Second Book of Samuel,
The First Book of Kings,
The Second Book of Kings,

The First Book of Chronicles,
The Second Book of Chronicles,
The First Book of Esdras,
The Second Book of Esdras,
The Book of Esther,
The Book of Job,
The Psalms,
The Proverbs,
Ecclesiastes, or Preacher,
Cantica, or Songs of Solomon,
Four Prophets the greater,
Twelve Prophets the less.

And the other Books (as *Hierome* saith) the Church doth read for example of life and instruction of manners; but yet doth it not apply them to establish any doctrine; such are these following :

The Third Book of Esdras,
The Fourth Book of Esdras,
The Book of Tobias,
The Book of Judith,
The rest of the Book of Esther,
The Book of Wisdom,
Jesus the Son of Sirach,

Baruch the Prophet,
The Song of the Three Children,
The Story of Susanna,
Of Bel and the Dragon,
The Prayer of Manasses,
The First Book of Maccabees,
The Second Book of Maccabees.

All the Books of the New Testament, as they are commonly received, we do receive, and account them Canonical.

VII. *Of the Old Testament.*

THE Old Testament is not contrary to the New: for both in the Old and New Testament everlasting life is offered to Mankind by Christ, who is the only Mediator between God and Man, being both God and Man. Wherefore they are not to be heard, which feign that the old Fathers did look only for transitory promises. Although the Law given from God by Moses, as touching Ceremonies and Rites, do not bind Christian men, nor the Civil precepts thereof ought of necessity to be received in any commonwealth; yet notwithstanding, no Christian man whatsoever is free from the obedience of the Commandments which are called Moral.

VIII. *Of the Three Creeds.*

THE Three Creeds, *Nicene* Creed, *Athanasius's* Creed, and that which is commonly called the *Apostles'* Creed, ought thoroughly to be received and believed: for they may be proved by most certain warrants of holy Scripture.

IX. *Of Original or Birth-sin.*

ORIGINAL Sin standeth not in the following of *Adam,* (as the *Pelagians* do vainly talk;) but it is the fault and corruption of the Nature of every man, that naturally is engendered of the offspring of *Adam;* whereby man is very far gone from original righteousness, and is of his own nature inclined to evil, so that the flesh lusteth always contrary to the spirit; and therefore in every person born into this world, it deserveth God's wrath and damnation. And this infection of nature doth remain, yea in them that are regenerated; whereby the lust of the flesh, called in the Greek, Φρόνημα σαρκὸς, which some do expound the wisdom, some sensuality, some the affection, some the desire, of the flesh, is not subject to the Law of God. And although there is no condemnation for them that believe and are baptized, yet the Apostle doth confess, that concupiscence and lust hath of itself the nature of sin.

X. *Of Free-Will.*

THE condition of Man after the fall of *Adam* is such, that he cannot turn and prepare himself, by his own natural strength and good works, to faith, and calling upon God: Wherefore we have no power to do good works pleasant and acceptable to God, without the grace of God by Christ preventing us, that we may have a good will, and working with us, when we have that good will.

XI. *Of the Justification of Man.*

WE are accounted righteous before God, only for the merit of our Lord and Saviour Jesus Christ by Faith, and not for our own works or deservings: Wherefore, that we are justified by Faith only is a most wholesome doctrine, and very full of comfort, as more largely is expressed in the Homily of Justification.

XII. *Of Good Works.*

ALBEIT that Good Works, which are the fruits of Faith, and follow after Justification, cannot put away our sins, and endure the severity of God's Judgement; yet are they pleasing and acceptable to God in Christ, and do spring out necessarily of a true and lively faith; insomuch that by them a lively Faith may be as evidently known as a tree discerned by the fruit.

XIII. *Of Works before Justification.*

WORKS done before the grace of Christ, and the Inspiration of his Spirit, are not pleasant to God, forasmuch as they spring not of faith in Jesus Christ, neither do they make men meet to receive grace, or (as the School-authors say) deserve grace of congruity: yea rather, for that they are not done as God hath willed and commanded them to be done, we doubt not but they have the nature of sin.

XIV. *Of Works of Supererogation.*

VOLUNTARY Works besides, over and above, God's Commandments, which they call Works of Supererogation, cannot be taught without arrogancy and impiety: for by them men do declare, that they do not only render unto God as much as they are bound to do, but that they do more for his sake, than of bounden duty is required: whereas Christ saith plainly, When ye have done all that are commanded to you, say, We are unprofitable servants.

XV. *Of Christ alone without Sin.*

CHRIST in the truth of our nature was made like unto us in all things, sin only except, from which he was clearly void, both in his flesh, and in his spirit. He came to be the Lamb without spot, who, by sacrifice of himself once made, should take away the sins of the world, and sin, as Saint *John* saith, was not in him. But all we, the rest, although baptized, and born again in Christ, yet offend in many things; and if we say we have no sin, we deceive ourselves, and the truth is not in us.

XVI. *Of Sin after Baptism.*

NOT every deadly sin willingly committed after Baptism is sin against the Holy Ghost, and unpardonable. Wherefore the grant of repentance is not to be denied to such as fall into sin after Baptism. After we have received the Holy Ghost, we may depart from grace given, and fall into sin, and by the grace of God we may arise again, and amend our lives. And therefore they are to be condemned, which say, they can no more sin as long as they live here, or deny the place of forgiveness to such as truly repent.

XVII. *Of Predestination and Election.*

PREDESTINATION to Life is the everlasting purpose of God, whereby (before the foundations of the world were laid) he hath constantly decreed by his counsel secret to us, to deliver from curse and damnation those whom he hath chosen in Christ out of mankind, and to bring them by Christ to everlasting salvation, as vessels made to honour. Wherefore, they which be endued with so excellent a benefit of God be called according to God's purpose by his Spirit working in due season: they through grace obey the calling: they be justified freely: they be made sons of God by adoption: they be made like the image of his only begotten Son Jesus Christ: they walk religiously in good works, and at length, by God's mercy, they attain to everlasting felicity.

As the godly consideration of Predestination, and our Election in Christ, is full of sweet, pleasant, and unspeakable comfort to godly persons, and such as feel in themselves the working of the Spirit of Christ, mortifying the works of the flesh, and their earthly members, and drawing up their mind to high and heavenly things, as well because it doth greatly establish and confirm their faith of eternal Salvation to be enjoyed through Christ, as because it doth fervently kindle their love towards God: So, for curious and carnal persons, lacking the Spirit of Christ, to have continually before their eyes the sentence of God's Predestination, is a most dangerous downfall, whereby the Devil doth thrust them either into desperation, or into wretchlessness of most unclean living, no less perilous than desperation.

Furthermore, we must receive God's promises in such wise, as they be generally set forth to us in holy Scripture: and, in our doings, that Will of God is to be followed, which we have expressly declared unto us in the Word of God.

XVIII.   *Of obtaining eternal Salvation only by the Name of Christ.*

THEY also are to be had accursed that presume to say, That every man shall be saved by the Law or Sect which he professeth, so that he be diligent to frame his life according to that Law, and the light of Nature.   For holy Scripture doth set out unto us only the Name of Jesus Christ, whereby men must be saved.

XIX.   *Of the Church.*

THE visible Church of Christ is a congregation of faithful men, in the which the pure Word of God is preached, and the Sacraments be duly ministered according to Christ's ordinance in all those things that of necessity are requisite to the same.

As the Church of *Jerusalem, Alexandria,* and *Antioch,* have erred; so also the Church of *Rome* hath erred, not only in their living and manner of Ceremonies, but also in matters of Faith.

XX.   *Of the Authority of the Church.*

THE Church hath power to decree Rites or Ceremonies, and authority in Controversies of Faith : And yet it is not lawful for the Church to ordain any thing that is contrary to God's Word written, neither may it so expound one place of Scripture, that it be repugnant to another.   Wherefore, although the Church be a witness and a keeper of holy Writ, yet, as it ought not to decree any thing against the same, so besides the same ought it not to enforce any thing to be believed for necessity of Salvation.

XXI.   *Of the Authority of General Councils.*

GENERAL Councils may not be gathered together without the commandment and will of Princes.   And when they be gathered together, (forasmuch as they be an assembly of men, whereof all be not governed with the Spirit and Word of God,) they may err, and sometimes have erred, even in things pertaining unto God.   Wherefore things ordained by them as necessary to salvation have neither strength nor authority, unless it may be declared that they be taken out of holy Scripture.

XXII.   *Of Purgatory.*

THE Romish Doctrine concerning Purgatory, Pardons, Worshipping and Adoration, as well of Images as of Reliques, and also invocation of Saints, is a fond thing vainly invented, and grounded upon no warranty of Scripture, but rather repugnant to the Word of God.

XXIII. *Of Ministering in the Congregation.*

IT is not lawful for any man to take upon him the office of publick preaching, or ministering the Sacraments in the Congregation, before he be lawfully called, and sent to execute the same. And those we ought to judge lawfully called and sent, which be chosen and called to this work by men who have publick authority given unto them in the Congregation, to call and send Ministers into the Lord's vineyard.

XXIV. *Of speaking in the Congregation in such a tongue as the people understandeth.*

IT is a thing plainly repugnant to the Word of God, and the custom of the Primitive Church, to have publick Prayer in the Church, or to minister the Sacraments in a tongue not understanded of the people.

XXV. *Of the Sacraments.*

SACRAMENTS ordained of Christ be not only badges or tokens of Christian men's profession, but rather they be certain sure witnesses, and effectual signs of grace, and God's good will towards us, by the which he doth work invisibly in us, and doth not only quicken, but also strengthen and confirm our Faith in him.

There are two Sacraments ordained of Christ our Lord in the Gospel, that is to say, Baptism, and the Supper of the Lord.

Those five commonly called Sacraments, that is to say, Confirmation, Penance, Orders, Matrimony, and extreme Unction, are not to be counted for Sacraments of the Gospel, being such as have grown partly of the corrupt following of the Apostles, partly are states of life allowed in the Scriptures ; but yet have not like nature of Sacraments with Baptism, and the Lord's Supper, for that they have not any visible sign or ceremony ordained of God.

The Sacraments were not ordained of Christ to be gazed upon, or to be carried about, but that we should duly use them. And in such only as worthily receive the same they have a wholesome effect or operation : but they that receive them unworthily purchase to themselves damnation, as Saint *Paul* saith.

XXVI. *Of the Unworthiness of the Ministers, which hinders not the effect of the Sacrament.*

ALTHOUGH in the visible Church the evil be ever mingled with the good, and sometimes the evil have chief authority in the Ministration of the Word and Sacraments, yet forasmuch as they do not the same in their own name, but in Christ's, and do minister by his commission and authority, we may use their Ministry, both in hearing the Word of God, and in receiving of the Sacraments. Neither is the effect of Christ's ordinance taken away by their wickedness, nor the grace of God's gifts diminished from such as by faith and rightly do receive the Sacraments ministered unto them; which be effectual, because of Christ's institution and promise, although they be ministered by evil men.

Nevertheless, it appertaineth to the discipline of the Church, that enquiry be made of evil Ministers, and that they be accused by those that have knowledge of their offences; and finally being found guilty, by just judgement be deposed.

XXVII. *Of Baptism.*

BAPTISM is not only a sign of profession, and mark of difference, whereby Christian men are discerned from others that be not christened, but it is also a sign of Regeneration or new Birth, whereby, as by an instrument, they that receive Baptism rightly are grafted into the Church; the promises of the forgiveness of sin, and of our adoption to be the sons of God by the Holy Ghost, are visibly signed and sealed; Faith is confirmed, and Grace increased by virtue of prayer unto God. The Baptism of young Children is in any wise to be retained in the Church, as most agreeable with the institution of Christ.

XXVIII. *Of the Lord's Supper.*

THE Supper of the Lord is not only a sign of the love that Christians ought to have among themselves one to another; but rather it is a Sacrament of our Redemption by Christ's death: insomuch that to such as rightly, worthily, and with faith, receive the same, the Bread which we break is a partaking of the Body of Christ; and likewise the Cup of Blessing is a partaking of the Blood of Christ.

Transubstantiation (or the change of the substance of Bread and Wine) in the Supper of the Lord, cannot be proved by holy Writ; but it is repugnant to the plain words of Scripture, overthroweth the nature of a Sacrament, and hath given occasion to many superstitions.

The Body of Christ is given, taken, and eaten, in the Supper, only after an heavenly and spiritual manner. And the mean whereby the Body of Christ is received and eaten in the Supper is Faith.

The Sacrament of the Lord's Supper was not by Christ's ordinance reserved, carried about, lifted up, or worshipped.

XXIX. *Of the Wicked which eat not the Body of Christ in the use of the Lord's Supper.*

THE Wicked, and such as be void of a lively faith, although they do carnally and visibly press with their teeth (as Saint *Augustine* saith) the Sacrament of the Body and Blood of Christ, yet in no wise are they partakers of Christ : but rather, to their condemnation, do eat and drink the sign or Sacrament of so great a thing.

XXX. *Of both kinds.*

THE Cup of the Lord is not to be denied to the Lay-people : for both the parts of the Lord's Sacrament, by Christ's ordinance and commandment, ought to be ministered to all Christian men alike.

XXXI. *Of the one Oblation of Christ finished upon the Cross.*

THE Offering of Christ once made is that perfect redemption, propitiation, and satisfaction, for all the sins of the whole world, both original and actual ; and there is none other satisfaction for sin, but that alone. Wherefore the sacrifices of Masses, in the which it was commonly said, that the Priest did offer Christ for the quick and the dead, to have remission of pain or guilt, were blasphemous fables, and dangerous deceits.

XXXII. *Of the Marriage of Priests.*

BISHOPS, Priests, and Deacons, are not commanded by God's Law, either to vow the estate of single life, or to abstain from marriage : therefore it is lawful also for them, as for all other Christian men, to marry at their own discretion, as they shall judge the same to serve better to godliness.

XXXIII. *Of excommunicate Persons, how they are to be avoided.*

THAT person which by open denunciation of the Church is rightly cut off from the unity of the Church, and excommunicated, ought to be taken of the whole multitude of the faithful, as an Heathen and Publican, until he be openly reconciled by penance, and received into the Church by a Judge that hath authority thereunto.

XXXIV. *Of the Traditions of the Church.*

IT is not necessary that Traditions and Ceremonies be in all places one, or utterly like ; for at all times they have been divers, and may be changed according to the diversities of countries.

times, and men's manners, so that nothing be ordained against God's Word. Whosoever through his private judgement, willingly and purposely, doth openly break the traditions and ceremonies of the Church, which be not repugnant to the Word of God, and be ordained and approved by common authority, ought to be rebuked openly, (that others may fear to do the like,) as he that offendeth against the common order of the Church, and hurteth the authority of the Magistrate, and woundeth the consciences of the weak brethren.

Every particular or national Church hath authority to ordain, change, and abolish, ceremonies or rites of the Church ordained only by man's authority, so that all things be done to edifying.

XXXV. *Of the Homilies.*

THE second Book of Homilies, the several titles whereof we have joined under this Article, doth contain a godly and whole-some Doctrine, and necessary for these times, as doth the former Book of Homilies, which were set forth in the time of *Edward* the Sixth; and therefore we judge them to be read in Churches by the Ministers, diligently and distinctly, that they may be understanded of the people.

Of the Names of the Homilies.

1 *OF the right Use of the Church.*
   2 *Against peril of Idolatry.*
3 *Of repairing and keeping clean of Churches.*
4 *Of good Works : first of Fasting.*
5 *Against Gluttony and Drunkenness.*
6 *Against Excess of Apparel.*
7 *Of Prayer.*
8 *Of the Place and Time of Prayer.*
9 *That Common Prayers and Sacraments ought to be ministered in a known tongue.*
10 *Of the reverend estimation of God's Word.*

11 *Of Alms-doing.*
12 *Of the Nativity of Christ.*
13 *Of the Passion of Christ.*
14 *Of the Resurrection of Christ.*
15 *Of the worthy receiving of the Sacrament of the Body and Blood of Christ.*
16 *Of the Gifts of the Holy Ghost.*
17 *For the Rogation-days.*
18 *Of the State of Matrimony.*
19 *Of Repentance.*
20 *Against Idleness.*
21 *Against Rebellion.*

XXXVI. *Of Consecration of Bishops and Ministers.*

THE Book of Consecration of Archbishops and Bishops, and Ordering of Priests and Deacons, lately set forth in the time of *Edward* the Sixth, and confirmed at the same time by authority of Parliament, doth contain all things necessary to such Consecration and Ordering : neither hath it any thing, that of itself is super-stitious and ungodly. And therefore whosoever are consecrated or ordered according to the Rites of that Book, since the second year of the fore-named King *Edward* unto this time, or hereafter shall be consecrated or ordered according to the same Rites; we decree all such to be rightly, orderly, and lawfully consecrated and ordered.

XXXVII. *Of the Civil Magistrates.*

THE Queen's Majesty hath the chief power in this Realm of *England,* and other her Dominions, unto whom the chief Government of all Estates of this Realm, whether they be Ecclesiastical or Civil, in all causes doth appertain, and is not, nor ought to be, subject to any foreign Jurisdiction.

Where we attribute to the Queen's Majesty the chief government, by which Titles we understand the minds of some slanderous folks to be offended; we give not to our Princes the ministering either of God's Word, or of the Sacraments, the which thing the Injunctions also lately set forth by *Elizabeth* our Queen do most plainly testify; but that only prerogative, which we see to have been given always to all godly Princes in holy Scriptures by God himself; that is, that they should rule all estates and degrees committed to their charge by God, whether they be Ecclesiastical or Temporal, and restrain with the civil sword the stubborn and evildoers.

The Bishop of *Rome* hath no jurisdiction in this Realm of *England.*

The Laws of the Realm may punish Christian men with death, for heinous and grievous offences.

It is lawful for Christian men, at the commandment of the Magistrate, to wear weapons, and serve in the wars.

XXXVIII. *Of Christian men's Goods, which are not common.*

THE Riches and Goods of Christians are not common, as touching the right, title, and possession of the same, as certain Anabaptists do falsely boast. Notwithstanding, every man ought, of such things as he possesseth, liberally to give alms to the poor, according to his ability.

XXXIX. *Of a Christian man's Oath.*

AS we confess that vain and rash Swearing is forbidden Christian men by our Lord Jesus Christ, and *James* his Apostle, so we judge, that Christian Religion doth not prohibit, but that a man may swear when the Magistrate requireth, in a cause of faith and charity, so it be done according to the Prophet's teaching, in justice, judgement, and truth.

THE RATIFICATION.

*T*HIS *Book of Articles before rehearsed, is again approved, and allowed to be holden and executed within the Realm, by the assent and consent of our Sovereign Lady* ELIZABETH, *by the grace of God, of England, France, and Ireland, Queen, Defender of the Faith, &c. Which Articles were deliberately read, and confirmed again by the subscription of the hands of the Archbishop and Bishops of the Upper-house, and by the subscription of the whole Clergy of the Nether-house in their Convocation, in the Year of our Lord* 1571.

A TABLE OF THE ARTICLES.

A TABLE

OF

KINDRED AND AFFINITY,

WHEREIN WHOSOEVER ARE RELATED ARE FORBIDDEN IN
SCRIPTURE AND OUR LAWS TO MARRY TOGETHER.

A Man may not marry his	*A Woman may not marry with her*
1 GRANDMOTHER,	1 GRANDFATHER,
2 Grandfather's Wife,	2 Grandmother's Husband,
3 Wife's Grandmother.	3 Husband's Grandfather.
4 Father's Sister,	4 Father's Brother,
5 Mother's Sister,	5 Mother's Brother,
6 Father's Brother's Wife.	6 Father's Sister's Husband.
7 Mother's Brother's Wife,	7 Mother's Sister's Husband,
8 Wife's Father's Sister,	8 Husband's Father's Brother,
9 Wife's Mother's Sister.	9 Husband's Mother's Brother.
10 Mother,	10 Father,
11 Step-Mother,	11 Step-Father,
12 Wife's Mother.	12 Husband's Father.
13 Daughter,	13 Son,
14 Wife's Daughter,	14 Husband's Son,
15 Son's Wife.	15 Daughter's Husband.
16 Sister,	16 Brother,
17 Wife's Sister,	17 Husband's Brother,
18 Brother's Wife.	18 Sister's Husband.
19 Son's Daughter,	19 Son's Son,
20 Daughter's Daughter,	20 Daughter's Son,
21 Son's Son's Wife.	21 Son's Daughter's Husband.
22 Daughter's Son's Wife,	22 Daughter's Daughter's Husband,
23 Wife's Son's Daughter,	23 Husband's Son's Son,
24 Wife's Daughter's Daughter.	24 Husband's Daughter's Son.
25 Brother's Daughter,	25 Brother's Son,
26 Sister's Daughter,	26 Sister's Son,
27 Brother's Son's Wife.	27 Brother's Daughter's Husband.
28 Sister's Son's Wife,	28 Sister's Daughter's Husband
29 Wife's Brother's Daughter,	29 Husband's Brother's Son,
30 Wife's Sister's Daughter.	30 Husband's Sister's Son.

THE END.

APPENDIX.

Tallis's Festal Responses.

¶ *At the beginning of Morning Prayer the Minister shall read with a loud voice some one or more of these Sentences of the Scriptures that follow. And then he shall say that which is written after the said Sentences.*

When the wicked man, &c.

Minister.

Dearly beloved brethren, . . . saying after me ;

¶ *A general Confession to be said of the whole Congregation after the Minister, all kneeling.*

Almighty and most merciful Father, . . . Thy holy Name.   A - men.

¶ *The Absolution, or Remission of sins, to be pronounced by the Priest alone, standing ; the people still kneeling.*

Almighty God, . . . through Jesus Christ our Lord.   A - men.

¶ *Then the Minister shall kneel, and say the Lord's Prayer; the people also kneeling, and repeating it with him.*

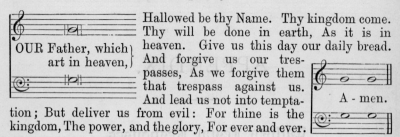

OUR Father, which art in heaven, Hallowed be thy Name. Thy kingdom come. Thy will be done in earth, As it is in heaven. Give us this day our daily bread. And forgive us our trespasses, As we forgive them that trespass against us. And lead us not into temptation; But deliver us from evil: For thine is the kingdom, The power, and the glory, For ever and ever. A - men.

¶ *Then likewise he shall say,*

Org. O Lord, open Thou our lips.   [or this:]   Org. O Lord, open Thou our lips.

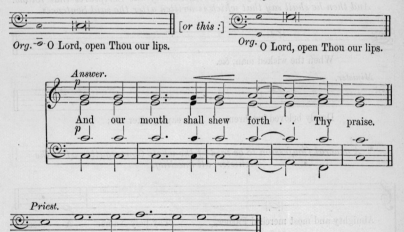

Answer.

And our mouth shall shew forth . . Thy praise.

Priest.

O God, make speed to save us.

Answer.

O Lord, make haste to help us.

¶ *Here, all standing up, the Priest shall say,*

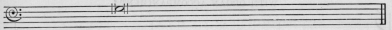

Glory be to the Father, and to the Son, and to the Holy Ghost;

Answer.

As . . . it was in the be - gin- ning, is now,

Org.

and e - ver shall be: world with - out . . . end. A - men.

Org.

Priest. *Answer.*

Praise ye the Lord.

The Lord's Name be prais - ed.

Org.

The Apostles' Creed.

WITH ORGAN ACCOMPANIMENT.*

I BELIEVE in God the Father Almighty, Maker of heaven and earth :

mf

And in Jesus Christ His only Son our Lord, Who was conceived by the Holy Ghost,

Born of the Virgin Mary, Suffered under Pontius Pilate, Was crucified,

dim. *p*

rall. *a tempo.* *f*

dead, and bur - ied, He descended into hell ; { The third day He rose again from the dead, }

rall. *a tempo.* *f*

* See Novello's Music Primers, No. 27, on Organ Accompaniment.

He ascended into heaven, { And sitteth on the right hand of God the Father Almighty; }

From thence He shall come to judge the quick and the dead. } I believe in the Holy Ghost;

The Holy Catholick Church; } The Communion of Saints; The Forgiveness of sins;

rall.

The Resurrection of the body, And the life everlasting. A - men.

rall. A - men.

oo **2**

¶ *And after that, the Prayers following, all devoutly kneeling; the Minister
first pronouncing with a loud voice,*

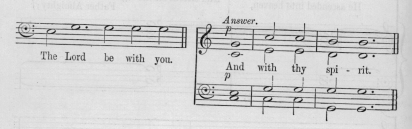

The Lord   be   with   you.

Answer.

And   with   thy   spi - rit.

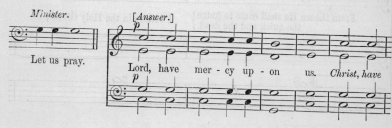

Minister.

Let us pray.

[*Answer.*]

Lord, have   mer - cy up - on   us.   Christ, have

mer - cy up - on   us.   Lord, have mer - cy up - on   us.

¶ *Then the Minister, Clerks, and people, shall say the Lord's Prayer
with a loud voice.*

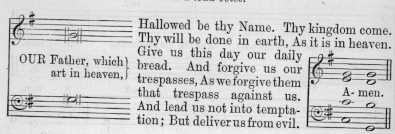

OUR Father, which art in heaven,

Hallowed be thy Name. Thy kingdom come.
Thy will be done in earth, As it is in heaven.
Give us this day our daily bread. And forgive us our
trespasses, As we forgive them
that trespass against us.
And lead us not into temptation; But deliver us from evil.

A- men.

¶ *Then the Priest standing up shall say,*

O Lord, shew Thy mer - cy up - on us.

Answer.

And grant us Thy sal - va - - tion.

Org.

Priest.

O Lord, save the Queen.

Answer.

And mer - ci - ful - ly hear us when we call up - on Thee.

Org.

Priest.

En - due Thy Min - is - ters with righ - teous - ness.

Answer.

And make Thy cho - sen peo - ple joy - ful.

Org.

Priest.

O Lord, save Thy peo - ple.

Answer.

And bless Thine in - he - ri - tance.

Org.

Give peace in our time, O Lord.

Be - cause there is none o - ther that fight-eth for us, but on - ly Thou, O God.

O God, make clean our hearts with - in us.

And take not Thy Ho - ly Spi-rit from us.

No. 1.   No. 2.   No. 3.

A - men.   A - men.   A - men.

[These three Amens should be sung in the above order at the end of every succeeding Prayer. It is necessary, however, to sing the Amen No. 2 after the last Prayer.]

The Ambrosian Te Deum.*

AFTER MERBECKE.

* In singing this Te Deum, no accent should be made on the first note of each bar, and the rhythm should not be rigidly observed. It will thus in time be found to assume the form of a free chant-service. It may be divided into portions to be sung in harmony or in unison at the will of the choirmaster.

Christ. Thou art the e - ver-last-ing Son of the Fa-ther. When Thou tookest up -

Voices in unison.   *Slower.*

- on Thee to de - li - ver man, Thou didst not abhor the Vir-gin's womb. When

Thou hadst o - vercome the sharp-ness of death, Thou didst o-pen the Kingdom of
cres.

Heav'n to all be - liev-ers. Thou sit-test at the right hand of God, in the
a tempo.

Glo-ry of the Fa-ther. We be-lieve that Thou shalt come to be our Judge. We

Slower. p

Glo-ry of the Fa-ther. We be-lieve that Thou shalt come to be our Judge. We

p

there-fore pray Thee, help Thy servants: whom Thou hast re-deem- ed with Thy

pp

there-fore pray Thee, help Thy servants: whom Thou hast re-deem- ed with Thy

pp

pre-cious blood. Make them to be num-ber'd with Thy Saints in glo- ry e - ver -

cres. tempo.

pre-cious blood. Make them to be number'd with Thy Saints in glo - ry e - ver -

cres.

- last-ing. O Lord, save Thy people : and bless Thine he-ri-tage. Go-vern them and

cres. mf

pp

- last-ing. O Lord, save Thy people : and bless Thine he-ri-tage. Go vern them and

pp *cres.* mf

lift them up for e - ver. Day by day we mag-ni - fy Thee; And we

lift them up for e - ver. Day by day we mag-ni - fy Thee; And we

worship Thy Name, e- ver world without end. Vouchsafe, O Lord, to keep us this day

a little slower.

worship Thy Name, e-ver world without end. Vouchsafe, O Lord, to keep us this day

with-out sin. O Lord, have mer-cy up - on us, have mer-cy up-on

cres.

with- out sin. O Lord, have mer-cy up - on us, have mer-cy up-on

cres.

us. O Lord, let Thy mer - cy light-en up - on us, as our trust is in

us. O Lord, let Thy mer - cy light-en up - on us, as our trust is in

Thee. O Lord, in Thee have I trust-ed: let me ne-ver be con-found- ed.

Slow. *p* *rall.*

Thee. O Lord, in Thee have I trust - ed: let me ne-ver be con - founded.

ff *p* *rall.*

The Athanasian Creed.

WITH ORGAN ACCOMPANIMENT.

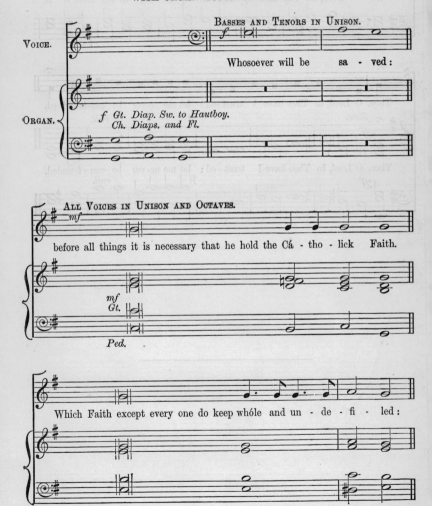

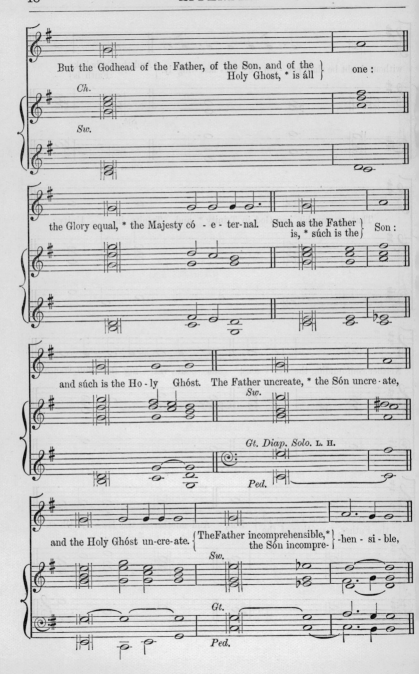

and the Holy Ghóst in-comprehen-si-ble. ⎰The Father eternal,*⎱ -ter - nal,
⎱ the Són e-⎰

Ch. both hands.

senza Ped.

and the Holy Ghóst e - ter-nal. And yet they are not thrée e - ter - nals,
Ch. mf

Left hand ff
(Gt. & Full Sw.)

Ped. ff

but óne e - ternal. ⎰As also there are not three incom-⎱ - a - ted :
⎱ prehensibles,* nor thrée uncre-⎰

Gt.

Ch. both hands.

mf

senza Ped.

but one uncreated, and óne in-comprehen-si-ble. ⎰So likewise the Fa-⎱ -might-y,
⎰ther is Almighty,*⎰
⎱ the Són Al-⎰

Full Sw.   cres.

Ch.

And yet not thrée Lords, but óne Lord, { For like as we are com- } veri - ty
{ pelled by the Chrístian }

to acknowledge every } Gód and Lord ; { So are we forbidden } - li -gion
Person by himself to be } { by the Cátholick Re- }

to say, There be three Gods,* or thrée Lords. The Father is máde of none,

neither created, nór be-gotten. The Son is of the Fáther a - lone :

PP 2

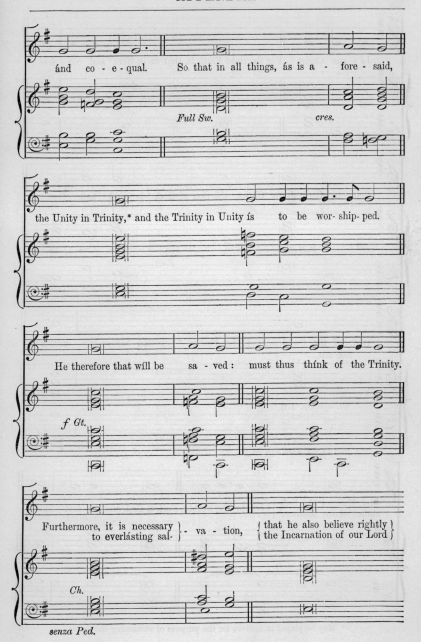

ánd co - e - qual. So that in all things, ás is a - fore - said,

Full Sw. *cres.*

the Unity in Trinity,* and the Trinity in Unity ís to be wor- ship- ped.

He therefore that wíll be sa - ved : must thus thínk of the Trinity.

f Gt.

Furthermore, it is necessary } - va - tion, { that he also believe rightly }
to everlásting sal- } { the Incarnation of our Lord }

Ch.

senza Ped.

Jé - sus Christ.   For the right Faith is, that we be-líeve and con - fess :

that our Lord Jesus Christ, the Son of God, * is Gód   and   Man ;

Full Sw.

God, of the Substance of the Father, * begotten befóre the   worlds :

Sw. R.H.

Gt. soft Op. L.H.*

Ped to Sw. with soft 16-*ft.*

and Man, of the Sub-
stance of his Mother,* } bórn in the world ; Perfect God, and pér- fect   Man :

* May be played in octaves for the purpose of sustaining the voices.

but by ú - ni-ty of Per-son. For as the reasonable soul and flesh is óne man :

so God and Man is óne Christ ;   Who suffered for oúr sal - va - tion,

Sw. p

Ped.

descended into hell,* rose again the third dáy   from the dead.

Full Sw. cres. . . . .

He ascended into heaven,* He sitteth on }
the right hand of the Father, Gód Al- }   - might - y,

Gt. mf

from whence He shall come to judge the quick and the dead.

dim.

At whose coming all men shall rise agáin with their bo - dies,

Sw. mf

and shall give } own works. { And they that have done } - last - ing,
account for their } { good shall go into lífe ever- }

senza Ped.

and they that have } - lást - ing fire. This is the Cátholick Faith:
done evil into ever- }

R.H. *Full Sw.*

Ch.

L.H. *Gt.*

senza Ped.

Ped.

Tallis's Litany.

Priest.

O God the Father, of Heaven: have mercy upon us, mis - er - a - ble sin - ners.

Answer.

O God the Fa - ther, of Heaven: have mer - cy up - on us, mis - er - a - ble sin - - ners.

Priest.

O God the Son,
Redeemer of the } world: have mercy upon us, mis - er - a - ble sin - ners.

Answer.

O God the Son, Re - deem-er of the world: have mer - cy up - on us, mis - er - a - ble sin - ners.

Priest.

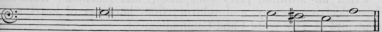

Remember not, Lord, our offences, nor
the offences of our forefathers; neither take
Thou vengeance of our sins : spare us, good
Lord, spare Thy people, whom Thou hast
redeemed with Thy most precious blood,
and be not angry } with us for ever,

Answer.

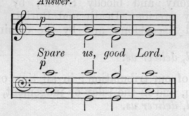

Spare us, good Lord.

Priest.

From all evil and mischief; from sin,
from the crafts and assaults of the devil : } -last - ing dam -na - tion,
from Thy wrath, and from ever - -

Answer.

Good Lord, de - li - ver us.

From all blindness of heart; from pride, vain-glory, and
hypocrisy; from envy, hatred, and malice, and | all uncharitable-
ness,
Good Lord, deliver us.

From fornication and all other deadly sin; and from all the
deceits of the world, the flesh, | and the devil,
Good Lord, deliver us.

From lightning and tempest; from plague, pestilence, and
famine; from battle and murder, and from | sudden death,
Good Lord, deliver us.

From all sedition, privy conspiracy, and rebellion; from all false doctrine, heresy, and schism; from hardness of heart, and contempt of Thy Word | and Commandment,
Good Lord, deliver us.

By the mystery of Thy holy Incarnation; by Thy holy Nativity and Circumcision; by Thy Baptism, Fasting, | and Temptation,
Good Lord, deliver us.

By Thine Agony and bloody Sweat; by Thy Cross and Passion; by Thy precious Death and Burial; by Thy glorious Resurrection and Ascension; and by the coming of the | Holy Ghost,
Good Lord, deliver us.

pp In all time of our tribulation; in all time of our wealth; in the hour of death, and in the | day of judgement,
pp Good Lord, deliver us.

Priest.

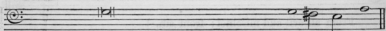

We sinners do beseech Thee to hear us, O Lord
God; and that it may please Thee to rule and ⎬ in the right way.
govern Thy holy Church universal

Answer.

We   be - seech Thee to   hear   us, good Lord.

That it may please Thee to keep and strengthen in the true worshipping of Thee, in righteousness and holiness of life, Thy Servant *VICTORIA*, our most gracious | Queen and Governour;
We beseech Thee to hear us, good Lord.

That it may please Thee to rule her heart in Thy faith, fear, and love, and that she may evermore have affiance in Thee, and ever seek Thy ho- | -nour and glory;
We beseech Thee to hear us, good Lord.

That it may please Thee to be her defender and keeper, giving her the victory over | all her enemies ;
We beseech Thee to hear us, good Lord.

That it may please Thee to bless and preserve *Albert Edward,* Prince of *Wales,* the Princess of *Wales,* and all the | Royal Family ;
We beseech Thee to hear us, good Lord.

That it may please Thee to illuminate all Bishops, Priests, and Deacons, with true knowledge and understanding of Thy Word ; and that both by their preaching and living they may set it forth, and shew | it accordingly ;
We beseech Thee to hear us, good Lord.

[*The Proper Suffrage in the Ordination Services follows here.*]

That it may please Thee to endue the Lords of the Council, and all the Nobility, with grace, wisdom, and | understanding ;
We beseech Thee to hear us, good Lord.

That it may please Thee to bless and keep the Magistrates, giving them grace to execute justice, and to | maintain truth ;
We beseech Thee to hear us, good Lord.

That it may please Thee to bless and keep | all Thy people ;
We beseech Thee to hear us, good Lord.

That it may please Thee to give to all nations unity, | peace, and concord ;
We beseech Thee to hear us, good Lord.

That it may please Thee to give us an heart to love and dread Thee, and diligently to live after | Thy commandments ;
We beseech Thee to hear us, good Lord.

That it may please Thee to give to all Thy people increase of grace to hear meekly Thy Word, and to receive it with pure affection, and to bring forth the fruits | of the Spirit ;
We beseech Thee to hear us, good Lord.

That it may please Thee to bring into the way of truth all such as have erred, and | are deceived ;
We beseech Thee to hear us, good Lord.

That it may please Thee to strengthen such as do stand ; and to comfort and help the weak-hearted ; and to raise up them that fall ; and finally to beat down Satan un- | -der our feet ;
We beseech Thee to hear us, good Lord.

That it may please Thee to succour, help, and comfort, all that are in danger, necessity, and | tribulation ;
We beseech Thee to hear us, good Lord.

That it may please Thee to preserve all that travel by land or by water, all women labouring of child, all sick persons and young children ; and to shew thy pity upon all | prisoners and captives ;
  We beseech Thee to hear us, good Lord.

That it may please Thee to defend, and provide for, the fatherless children, and widows, and all that are desolate | and oppressed ;
  We beseech Thee to hear us, good Lord.

That it may please Thee to have mercy | upon all men ;
  We beseech Thee to hear us, good Lord.

That it may please Thee to forgive our enemies, persecutors, and slanderers, and to | turn their hearts ;
  We beseech Thee to hear us, good Lord.

That it may please Thee to give and preserve to our use the kindly fruits of the earth, so as in due time we | may enjoy them ;
  We beseech Thee to hear us, good Lord.

That it may please Thee to give us true repentance, to forgive us all our sins, negligences, and ignorances ; and to endue us with the grace of Thy Holy Spirit to amend our lives according to Thy | holy Word ;
  We beseech Thee to hear us, good Lord.

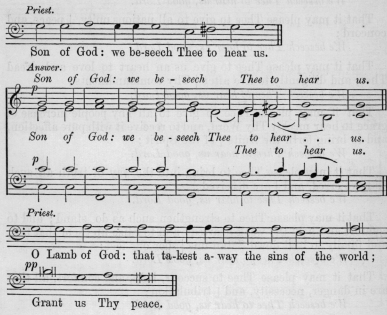

Priest.

Son of God: we be-seech Thee to hear us.

Answer.

Son of God: we be-seech Thee to hear us.

Son of God: we be-seech Thee to hear . . . us.
Thee to hear us.

Priest.

O Lamb of God: that ta-kest a-way the sins of the world ;

Grant us Thy peace.

Priest and People.

Our Father, ... from evil.

A - men.

Priest.

O Lord, deal not with us after our sins.

Answer.

Nei - ther re - ward us af - ter our in - i - qui - ties.

Priest.

Let us pray. O God, merciful Father, . . . through Jesus Christ our Lord.

Answer.

O Lord, a - rise, help us, and de - li - ver us for Thy Name's sake.

Priest.

O God, we have heard, . . . be - fore them.

Answer.

O Lord, a - rise, help us, and de - li - ver us for Thine ho - nour.

Priest.

Glory be to the Father, and to the Son : and to the Holy Ghost ;

Answer.

As . . it was in the be - gin - ning, is now,

Org.

and ev - er shall be : world with - out end. A - men.

Org.

Priest.

From our enemies defend us, O Christ.

Answer.

Gra - cious - ly look up - on our af - flic - tions.

Priest.

Pitifully behold the sorrows of our hearts.

Answer.

Mer - ci - ful - ly for - give the sins of Thy . . peo - ple.

Priest.

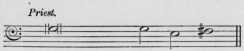

Favourably with mercy hear our prayers.

Answer.

O Son of Da - vid, have mer - cy up - on us.

Org.

Priest.

Both now and ever vouchsafe to hear us, O Christ.

Answer.

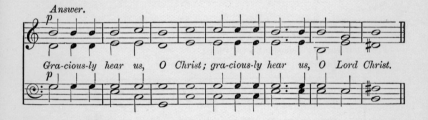

Gra-cious-ly hear us, O Christ; gra-cious-ly hear us, O Lord Christ.

Priest.

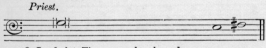

O Lord, let Thy mercy be shewed up - on us.

Answer.

As we do put our trust in Thee.

Org.

Priest.

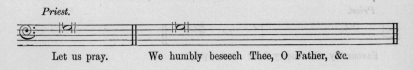

Let us pray.　　We humbly beseech Thee, O Father, &c.

No. 1.　　**No. 2.***　　**No. 3.**

A - men.　　A - men.　　A - men.

* *End with* Amen No. 2.

Holy Communion.

The Offertory.

¶ *After which done, the Priest shall say,*

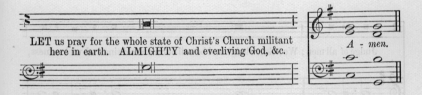

LET us pray for the whole state of Christ's Church militant here in earth. ALMIGHTY and everliving God, &c.

A - men.

The Exhortation.

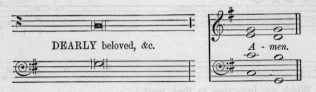

DEARLY beloved, &c.

A - men.

¶ *Then shall the Priest say to them that come to receive the Holy Communion,*

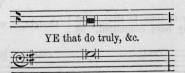

YE that do truly, &c.

The Confession

WITH INFLECTIONS AND HARMONIZED.

¶ Then shall this general Confession be made, all humbly kneeling upon their knees.

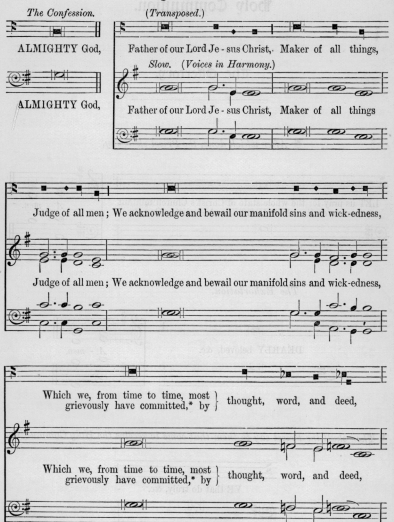

The Confession.   *(Transposed.)*

ALMIGHTY God,   Father of our Lord Je - sus Christ,   Maker of all things,

Slow. (Voices in Harmony.)

ALMIGHTY God,   Father of our Lord Je - sus Christ,   Maker of all things

Judge of all men ; We acknowledge and bewail our manifold sins and wick-edness,

Judge of all men ; We acknowledge and bewail our manifold sins and wick-edness,

Which we, from time to time, most ⎬ thought, word, and deed,
grievously have committed,* by ⎭

Which we, from time to time, most ⎬ thought, word, and deed,
grievously have committed,* by ⎭

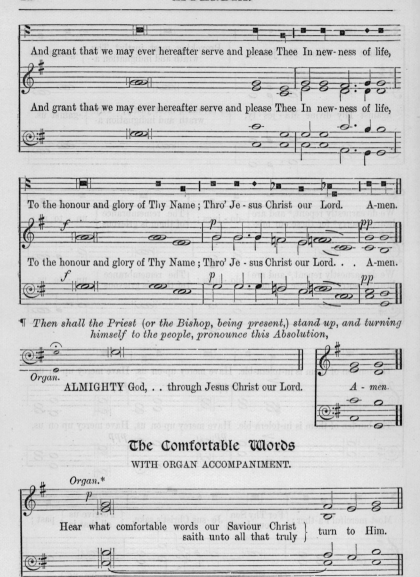

And grant that we may ever hereafter serve and please Thee In new-ness of life,

And grant that we may ever hereafter serve and please Thee In new-ness of life,

To the honour and glory of Thy Name; Thro' Je-sus Christ our Lord. A-men.

To the honour and glory of Thy Name; Thro' Je-sus Christ our Lord. . . A-men.

¶ *Then shall the Priest (or the Bishop, being present,) stand up, and turning himself to the people, pronounce this Absolution,*

Organ.

ALMIGHTY God, . . through Jesus Christ our Lord. A - men.

The Comfortable Words

WITH ORGAN ACCOMPANIMENT.

*Organ.**

Hear what comfortable words our Saviour Christ saith unto all that truly } turn to Him.

* NOTE.—A soft combination of Stops on the Swell Organ should be used for the following accompaniments, and as a general rule the *Manual* only should be used, not the Pedal Organ. The Organist must, of course, be prepared to transpose the Organ Part to suit any pitch previously selected by the Minister.

Come unto Me, all that travail and are hea - vy la - den, and I will re - fresh you.

So God loved the world, that He gave His only be - gotten Son,

to the end that all that believe in Him should not pe - rish, but have ever - last - ing life.

Hear also what Saint Paul saith, This is a true say - ing, and worthy of all men to

be re - ceiv - ed, That Christ Jesus came into the world to save sin - ners.

Hear also what Saint John saith. If any man sin, we have an Advocate with the Fa - ther, Jesus Christ the righteous; and He is the propiti - ation for our sins.

Sursum Corda.

Lift .... up your hearts.

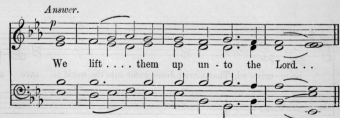

We lift .... them up un - to the Lord. ..

Priest.

Let us give . . . thanks un - to our . . Lord God.

Answer.

It is meet and right so to do. . . .

¶ *Then shall the Priest turn to the Lord's Table, and say,*

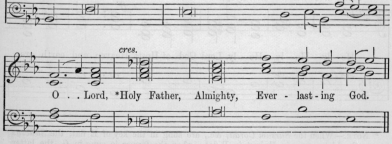

It is very meet, right, and our bound - en du - ty,

that we should at all times, and in all places, give thanks un - to Thee,

cres.

O . . Lord, *Holy Father, Almighty, Ever - last - ing God.

* These words [*Holy Father*] must be omitted on *Trinity Sunday.*

¶ *Here shall follow the Proper Preface, according to the time, if there be any specially appointed; or else immediately shall follow,*

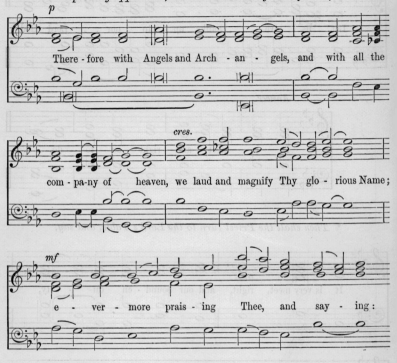

p

Therefore with Angels and Arch - an - gels, and with all the

cres.

com - pa-ny of heaven, we laud and magnify Thy glo - rious Name;

mf

e - ver - more prais - ing Thee, and say - ing:

Sanctus.

Organ copy, transposed.

Voices in Unison (not Harmony).*

pp   *ff*

Ho - ly, Ho - ly, Ho - ly, Lord God of Hosts, Heaven and earth are

* NOTE.—When the *Sursum Corda*, &c., are sung in the key of E flat, the *Sanctus* should be sung in Unison in B flat: when the former is sung in G, the latter should be in G also.

full of Thy Glo - ry : Glo - ry be to Thee, O Lord most High. *A - men.*

or this : (*see Note,* p. 48).

Voices in Harmony (or Unison).

Ho - ly, Ho - ly, Ho - ly, Lord God of Hosts, Heaven and earth are

full of Thy Glo - ry : Glo - ry be to Thee, O Lord most High. *A - men.*

Proper Prefaces.

Upon CHRISTMAS DAY, *and seven days after.*

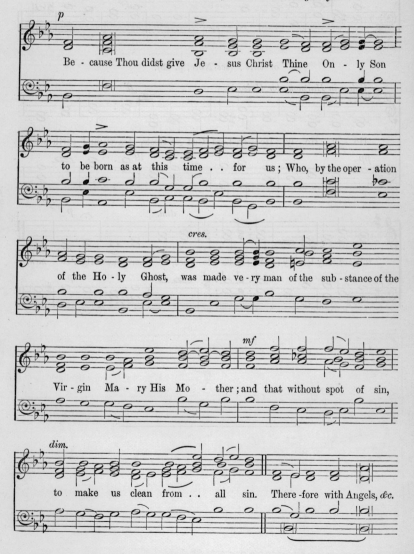

Be - cause Thou didst give Je - sus Christ Thine On - ly Son to be born as at this time . . for us ; Who, by the oper - ation of the Ho - ly Ghost, was made ve - ry man of the sub - stance of the Vir - gin Ma - ry His Mo - ther ; and that without spot of sin, to make us clean from . . all sin. There - fore with Angels, &c.

Upon EASTER DAY, *and seven days after.*

But chiefly are we bound to praise Thee for the glorious Resur - rection of Thy Son Je - sus Christ our Lord: for He is the ve - ry Pas - chal Lamb, which was offer - ed for us, and hath ta - ken a- way the sin . . of . . the . . world: . . Who by His death hath de - stroy - ed death, and by . . His rising to life again hath restored to

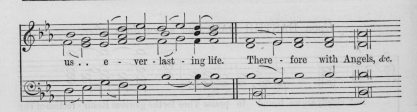

us .. e - ver - last - ing life.   There - fore with Angels, *&c.*

Upon ASCENSION DAY, *and seven days after.*

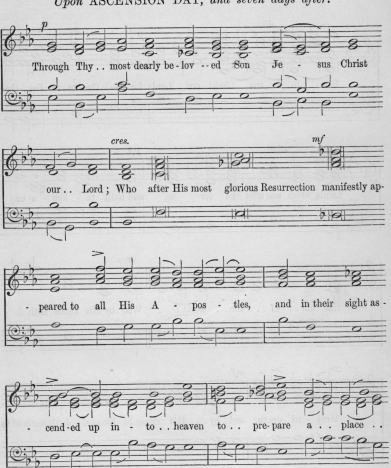

Through Thy .. most dearly be - lov - - ed Son   Je - sus Christ

our .. Lord ; Who   after His most   glorious Resurrection manifestly ap-

- peared to   all His   A - pos - tles,   and in their   sight as -

- cend - ed up in - to .. heaven to .. pre - pare   a .. place ..

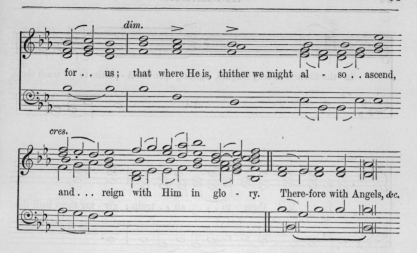

for . . us; that where He is, thither we might al - so . . ascend,

and . . . reign with Him in glo - ry. There-fore with Angels, &c.

Upon WHITSUNDAY, and six days after.

Through Je - sus . . Christ . . . our . . Lord; ac - cording to Whose

most true pro - mise, the Holy Ghost came down as at this time from

Heaven with a sud - den great sound, as it had been a . . migh - ty wind,

RR 2

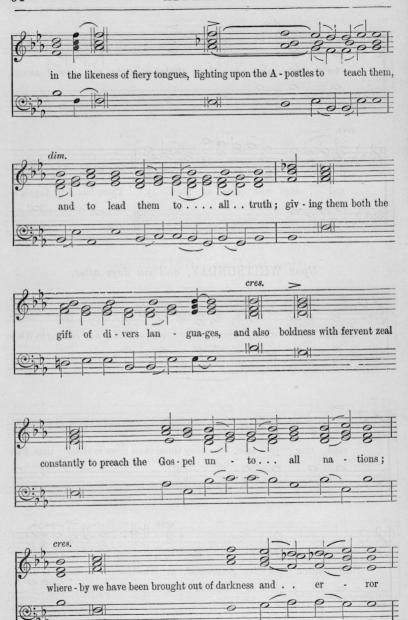

in the likeness of fiery tongues, lighting upon the A - postles to teach them,

dim.

and to lead them to . . . . all . . truth ; giv - ing them both the

cres.

gift of di - vers lan - gua-ges, and also boldness with fervent zeal

constantly to preach the Gos - pel un - to . . . all na - tions ;

cres.

where - by we have been brought out of darkness and . . er - ror

in - to the clear light and true knowledge of Thee, . . and of Thy . .

Son . . Je - sus Christ. There - fore with Angels, &c.

Upon the Feast of TRINITY only.

Who art one God, one Lord; not one

on - ly Per - son, but three Per - sons in one

Sub - stance. For that which we believe of the glory of the Fa - ther,

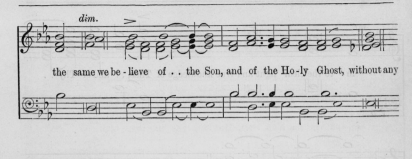

the same we be - lieve of . . the Son, and of the Ho - ly Ghost, without any

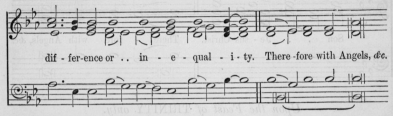

dif - fer-ence or . . in - e - qual - i - ty. There - fore with Angels, &c.

Benedictus.

(AFTER MERBECKE.)

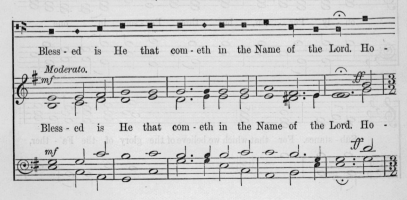

Bless - ed is He that com - eth in the Name of the Lord. Ho -

Bless - ed is He that com - eth in the Name of the Lord. Ho -

- san-na in the highest.

Allegro.

- san - na in the high - est, Ho - san - na in the high - est.

Tempo primo.

mf

Bless - ed is He that com - eth in the Name of the Lord. Ho -

mf

Allegro.

- san - na in the high - est, Ho - san - na in the high - est, the

ff

high - - est, Ho - san - na in the high - - est.

ff

Agnus Dei.

(AFTER MERBECKE.)

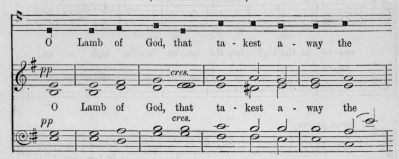

O Lamb of God, that ta - kest a - way the

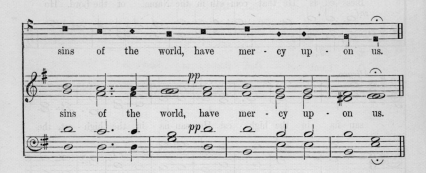

sins of the world, have mer - cy up - on us.

A short Interlude on the Organ.

O Lamb of God, that ta - kest a - way the

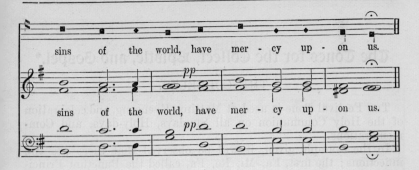

sins of the world, have mer - cy up - on us.

sins of the world, have mer - cy up - on us.

A short Interlude on the Organ.

O Lamb of God, that ta - kest a way the

O Lamb of God, that ta - kest a - way the

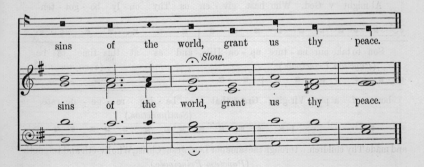

sins of the world, grant us thy peace.

sins of the world, grant us thy peace.

The Tones for the Collect, Epistle, and Gospel.*

THE COLLECTS.

The Festival Tone is used at Mattins, Evensong, and celebration of the Holy Communion on all Sundays, Holy-days, and Commemorations.

In the example given, it will be observed that there are two inflections; the first, Fa, Mi, Re, Fa, called the Punctum Principale; the second, Fa, Mi, called the Semipunctum. Care must be taken that the Collect itself, or the body of the Collect, be distinguished from the conclusion. The Collect generally consists of two, three, or more members; but whatever number of members there may be, the Punctum and Semipunctum are only used *once* each in the same Collect, and *once* in the conclusion of the Collect.

At the end of the first member or clause the Punctum is placed; the Semipunctum closes the second member, which frequently begins with the word "Grant," or "Grant, we beseech Thee." If the Collect concludes with "Through Jesus Christ our Lord," *e.g.*, Collect for Ash Wednesday,† or with, "Who livest and reignest" (without "Through Jesus Christ"), *e.g.*, first Sunday in Lent,‡ the Semipunctum is omitted, and the Punctum only is used.

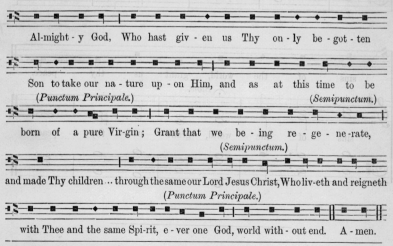

Al-might-y God, Who hast giv-en us Thy on-ly be-got-ten

Son to take our na-ture up-on Him, and as at this time to be
(Punctum Principale.)   *(Semipunctum.)*

born of a pure Vir-gin; Grant that we be-ing re-ge-ne-rate,
                                    (Semipunctum.)

and made Thy children ... through the same our Lord Jesus Christ, Who liv-eth and reigneth
(Punctum Principale.)

with Thee and the same Spi-rit, e-ver one God, world with-out end. A-men.

* By the kind permission of the Rev. Henry Aston Walker, M.A., these Rules are quoted from his Manual for the Holy Communion (Novello).

† *Conclusion of Collect for Ash Wednesday, an example of the Semipunctum being omitted.*

(*Punctum Principale.*)

Through Je - sus Christ our Lord,   A - men.

‡ *Conclusion of Collect for 1st Sunday in Lent, shewing the Semipunctum omitted.*

(*Punctum Principale.*)

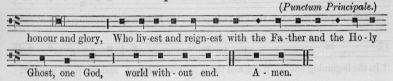

honour and glory,   Who liv-est and reign-est with the Fa -ther and the Ho - ly

Ghost, one God,   world with - out end.   A - men.

The Ferial Tone is used on Simples and Ferias, and at Burials, and has no inflections : the Collect is sung on one note throughout, *e.g.*, Fa. However, there is an inflection allowed on Ferias when many prayers have been said, *e.g.*, at the last prayer of Mattins, Evensong, and the Litany. It is on the penultimate syllable from Fa to Re.

THE EPISTLE.

The Epistle is sung on one note, *e.g.*, Fa.* There is an inflection, when an interrogation occurs, *e.g.*, Epistle for Christmas Day.

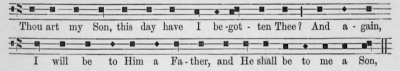

Thou art my Son, this day have I be -got - ten Thee? And a - gain,

I will be to Him a Fa - ther, and He shall be to me a Son,

The fourth syllable before a period is much prolonged, *e.g.*—

And let all the an - gels of God wor -ship Him.

And an inflection on the fourth syllable, or nearest important to that from the end, *e.g.*—

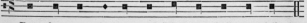

But thou art the same, and Thy years shall not fail.

---

* In the Manual from which these Rules are quoted the Clef for the Epistle and Gospel is given as C.

THE GOSPEL.

The Gospel admits of an inflection from the dominant to a third
below, *e.g.*, Fa to Re, on the fourth* syllable from a period.† Also
before an interrogation, as in the Epistle, and on the fifth syllable
from the end,‡ as *e.g.*, in the Gospel for Christmas Day.

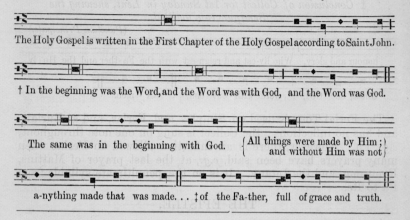

The Holy Gospel is written in the First Chapter of the Holy Gospel according to Saint John.

† In the beginning was the Word, and the Word was with God,   and the Word was God.

The same was in the beginning with God.   { All things were made by Him ; }
                                          {   and without Him was not }

a-nything made that was made. . . ‡ of the Fa-ther, full of grace and truth.

---

* This rule cannot always be rigidly kept; when not, the inflection should be made on the
most important word or syllable of a word nearest the fourth.

At the Burial of the Dead.

Dixi, custodiam.—Psalm xxxix.

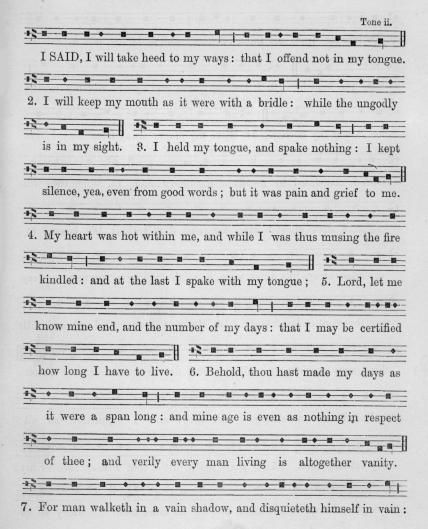

Tone ii.

I SAID, I will take heed to my ways: that I offend not in my tongue.

2. I will keep my mouth as it were with a bridle: while the ungodly

is in my sight. 3. I held my tongue, and spake nothing: I kept

silence, yea, even from good words; but it was pain and grief to me.

4. My heart was hot within me, and while I was thus musing the fire

kindled: and at the last I spake with my tongue; 5. Lord, let me

know mine end, and the number of my days: that I may be certified

how long I have to live. 6. Behold, thou hast made my days as

it were a span long: and mine age is even as nothing in respect

of thee; and verily every man living is altogether vanity.

7. For man walketh in a vain shadow, and disquieteth himself in vain:

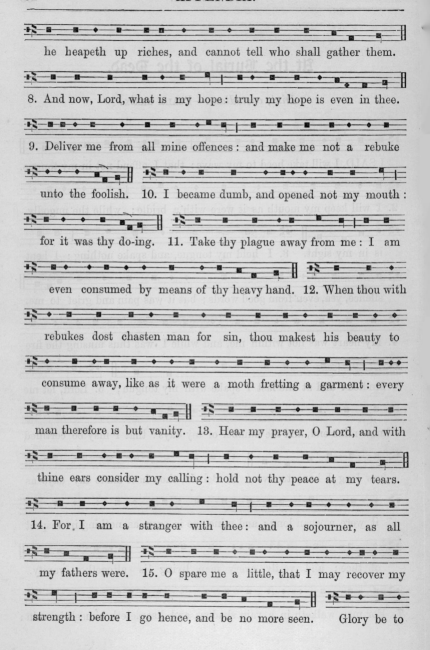

he heapeth up riches, and cannot tell who shall gather them.

8. And now, Lord, what is my hope: truly my hope is even in thee.

9. Deliver me from all mine offences: and make me not a rebuke

unto the foolish. 10. I became dumb, and opened not my mouth:

for it was thy do-ing. 11. Take thy plague away from me: I am

even consumed by means of thy heavy hand. 12. When thou with

rebukes dost chasten man for sin, thou makest his beauty to

consume away, like as it were a moth fretting a garment: every

man therefore is but vanity. 13. Hear my prayer, O Lord, and with

thine ears consider my calling: hold not thy peace at my tears.

14. For I am a stranger with thee: and a sojourner, as all

my fathers were. 15. O spare me a little, that I may recover my

strength: before I go hence, and be no more seen. Glory be to

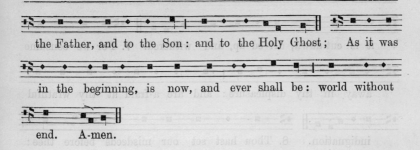

the Father, and to the Son : and to the Holy Ghost ;   As it was

in the beginning, is now, and ever shall be : world without

end.   A-men.

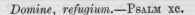

Domine, refugium.—PSALM XC.

Tone ii.

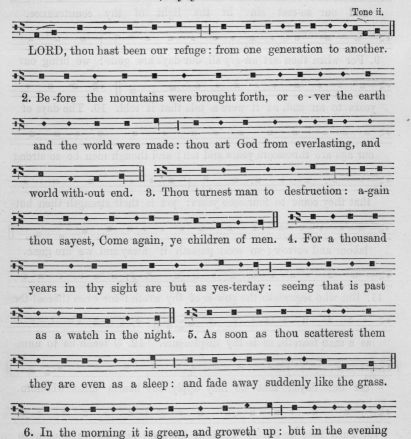

LORD, thou hast been our refuge : from one generation to another.

2. Be -fore the mountains were brought forth, or e - ver the earth

and the world were made : thou art God from everlasting, and

world with-out end.   3. Thou turnest man to destruction : a-gain

thou sayest, Come again, ye children of men.   4. For a thousand

years in thy sight are but as yes-terday : seeing that is past

as a watch in the night.   5. As soon as thou scatterest them

they are even as a sleep : and fade away suddenly like the grass.

6. In the morning it is green, and groweth up : but in the evening

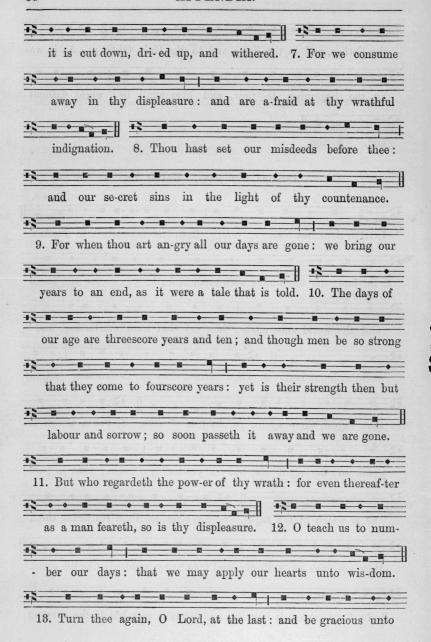

it is cut down, dri- ed up, and withered. 7. For we consume

away in thy displeasure : and are a-fraid at thy wrathful

indignation. 8. Thou hast set our misdeeds before thee :

and our se-cret sins in the light of thy countenance.

9. For when thou art an-gry all our days are gone : we bring our

years to an end, as it were a tale that is told. 10. The days of

our age are threescore years and ten; and though men be so strong

that they come to fourscore years : yet is their strength then but

labour and sorrow; so soon passeth it away and we are gone.

11. But who regardeth the pow-er of thy wrath : for even thereaf-ter

as a man feareth, so is thy displeasure. 12. O teach us to num-

- ber our days : that we may apply our hearts unto wis-dom.

13. Turn thee again, O Lord, at the last : and be gracious unto

thy servants. 14. O satis-fy us with thy mercy, and that soon :

so shall we rejoice and be glad all the days of our life.

15. Comfort us again now after the time that thou hast plagued

us : and for the years wherein we have suffered adversi-ty.

16. Shew thy servants thy work : and their children thy glo-ry.

17. And the glorious Majesty of the Lord our God be upon us : prosper

thou the work of our hands upon us, O prosper thou our handywork.

Glory be to the Fa-ther, and to the Son : and to the Ho-ly Ghost ;

As it was in the beginning, is now, and ever shall be : world

without end. A-men.

Miserere mei, Deus.*

Psalm li.

(From the COMMINATION SERVICE.)

¶ *Then shall they all kneel upon their knees, and the Priest and Clerks kneeling (in the place where they are accustomed to say the Litany) shall say this Psalm,*

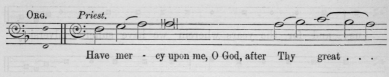

Have mer - cy upon me, O God, after Thy great . . .

good - ness; according to the multitude of Thy mercies, do a - way mine

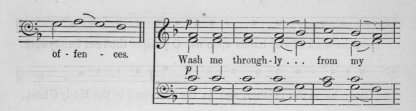

of - fen - ces. Wash me through-ly . . . from my

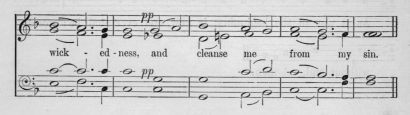

wick - ed - ness, and cleanse me from my sin.

For . . . I ac - know - ledge my . . faults : and my sin is . .

* This setting was expressly written by Sir John Stainer for use in St. Paul's Cathedral at the Special Service in Holy Week.

e - ver be - fore me,

Against Thee only have I sinned, and done this

cres.

e - vil in Thy . . sight; That Thou mightest be justified in Thy saying, and

dim.

clear when . . Thou art . . judg - - ed.

Priest.

Be - hold, I was sha - pen in wick - edness, and in sin hath my

mo - ther con - ceiv - ed me.

But lo, Thou re - qui - rest . .

truth in the in - ward parts, and shalt make me to

un - der - stand wis - dom . . se - - cret - ly.

Priest.

Thou shalt purge me with hyssop, and I shall be . . clean:

Thou shalt wash me, and I shall be whi - ter than snow.

Thou shalt make me hear of . . joy and glad -

- ness, that the bones which Thou hast bro - ken may re - joice.

may . . . re - joice.

Priest.

Turn Thy face a - way from my . . sins, and put out

all **my** . . misdeeds.

Make me a clean heart, O . . . .

cres.

God, and re-new .. a right spi-rit with-in .. me.

Priest.

Cast me not a-way from Thy pre-sence, and take not Thy Ho-ly ..

Spi-rit .. from me.

O give me the com-fort ..

of .. Thy .. help .. a-gain, and sta-blish

me with .. Thy .. free .. Spi - - rit.

Priest.

Then shall I teach Thy ways un-to the wick-ed, and sinners shall be

Priest.
The sa - crifice of God is a . . troub - led . . spi - rit;

a broken and contrite heart, O . . . God, shalt Thou not . , des-pise

O be favourable and gra - cious un - to . . Si - - - on: build Thou the . . walls of Je - ru - sa - lem.

Priest.
Then shalt . . . { Thou be pleased with the sacrifice of / righteousness, with the burnt-offer- } -ings . . . and ob - la - tions : { then shall they offer / young bullocks } up - on Thine al - tar.

Glo - ry . . . be to the
Glo - ry . . . be . . . to the Fa - ther,
Glo - ry . . . be . . . to the Fa - ther, and to . . . the . .

* An easy setting of the Gloria Patri, which may be substituted for this, will be found on page 76.

-gin- ning, is now, and .. e - ver shall be -

now, is now, and e - ver shall be:

e - ver, now, and e - ver shall be:

As it was in the be - gin- ning, is now, and e - ver shall be:

1st Choir.

TREBLE.

ALTO.
world with- out end.

TENOR.

BASS.

2nd Choir.

TREBLE.

ALTO.
A - men, A - - - - - -

TENOR.

BASS.

world with - out end, world with - out